T0281828

LAKȞÓTA

THE CIVILIZATION OF THE AMERICAN INDIAN SERIES

RANI-HENRIK ANDERSSON
AND DAVID C. POSTHUMUS

LAKȞÓTA

AN INDIGENOUS HISTORY

UNIVERSITY OF OKLAHOMA PRESS : NORMAN

*Published through the Recovering Languages and Literacies of the
Americas initiative, supported by the Andrew W. Mellon Foundation*

RECOVERING
LANGUAGES & LITERACIES
OF THE AMERICAS

Lakȟóta: An Indigenous History is published as part of the Recovering Languages and Literacies of the Americas initiative. Recovering Languages and Literacies of the Americas is generously supported by the Andrew W. Mellon Foundation.

Library of Congress Cataloging-in-Publication Data

Names: Andersson, Rani-Henrik, author. | Posthumus, David C., author.
Title: Lakȟóta : an indigenous history / Rani-Henrik Andersson and David C. Posthumus.
Other titles: Civilization of the American Indian series ; v. 281.
Description: Norman : University of Oklahoma Press, [2022] | Series: The civilization of the
   American Indian series ; volume 281 | Includes bibliographical references and index. | Sum-
   mary: "An updated comprehensive history of the Lakotas, decentralizing war and politics
   and focusing on cultural understanding. Major historical events are viewed through Lakota
   sources, such as winter counts, oral histories, letters, and speeches."—Provided by publisher.
Identifiers: LCCN 2022015089 | ISBN 978-0-8061-9075-4 (hardcover)
Subjects: LCSH: Lakota Indians—History. | BISAC: HISTORY / Indigenous Peoples of
   the Americas | LANGUAGE ARTS & DISCIPLINES / Translating & Interpreting
Classification: LCC E99.T34 A624 2022 | DDC 978.004/975244—dc23/eng/20220527
LC record available at https://lccn.loc.gov/2022015089

Lakȟóta: An Indigenous History is Volume 281 in The Civilization of the American Indian
Series.

To the Lakȟóta people

CONTENTS

Part III

ILLUSTRATIONS

Figures

PREFACE

Spring 2020

The road was blocked. Masked men and women stood by a barricade, stopping vehicles trying to drive through the Cheyenne River Sioux Reservation. The masked men and women politely asked drivers to turn back. Some did so without hesitation, others were furious. Who were these masked people and what right did they have to stop people from traveling on a public road? They were Lakȟóta, members of the Cheyenne River Sioux Tribe, and their actions, like their masks, were intended to protect their land, traditions, and relatives. They were there to shield their people from a devastating pandemic, the novel coronavirus Covid-19, that was wreaking havoc around the globe in the spring of 2020. The Lakȟóta knew that their reservation could not provide medical care to all if the virus spread freely across their lands. South Dakota governor Kristi Noem attempted to negotiate with the tribal president, but when this failed, she threatened to call for the police, the National Guard, and even President Donald J. Trump to disperse the Lakȟóta roadblocks. The Lakȟóta refused, adamant in their determination to keep their people safe. Despite their efforts, by the fall of 2020 the pandemic made its way to Lakȟóta country. Covid-19 did not care about borders, whether reservation or national.

Only four years earlier, in 2016, the Lakȟóta of Standing Rock Reservation had faced an onslaught by police and the National Guard when an outside force threatened Lakȟóta lands. But this one was man-made. The Dakota Access Pipeline, a massive oil pipeline construction project, threatened the waters of the Missouri River and thus was a direct hazard to Lakȟóta communities situated downstream. Any oil spill would have dire consequences. The Lakȟóta saw no other alternative than to raise their voices. Led by several women, they established the Íŋyaŋ Wakȟáŋaǧapi Othí (Sacred Stone Camp), and people started pouring in to show support. There were Lakȟóta, Cheyenne, Haida, and other Indigenous people from around the world joined them in solidarity. Mní wičhóni (water is life) became the rallying cry of the water protectors. They were committed to nonviolence, but violence was brought in by outside forces. Still the Lakȟóta stood firm in protecting their relatives and their homelands—Lakȟóta Tȟamákȟočhe.

The Lakȟóta are perhaps the best-known Native American people, due largely to their resilience in fighting outside forces and colonialism. They are the people of Sitting Bull, Red Cloud, and Crazy Horse, but they are also a modern people of #NoDAPL and the twenty-first century. These two examples highlight the Lakȟóta determination to guard the Lakȟóta way of life. Despite more than two hundred years of colonial pressure, they are still here, continuing the fight their ancestors fought. We begin this book with the Lakȟóta origins but intend to reaffirm that the Lakȟóta people are still here in the twenty-first century and Lakȟóta culture is alive and well.

Our Approach and Sources

Much has been written about the Lakȟóta. Not only have they been the focus of scholarly works by historians, anthropologists, and linguists, but they have also been prominent in popular film and literature, and they have inspired a certain romanticism associated with the "Wild West" and a back-to-the-land ethos. Much of the scholarly work has been written by nonnative outsiders and that is also true of this book. What makes this book different is that we have tried to turn the narrative focus away from the white Euro-Americans and toward the Lakȟóta. We do not want to retell the story of Euro-American imperialism, warfare, and conquest from the perspective of those who initiated and carried out those actions and policies, but the story as lived by the Lakȟóta. It is fair to ask how we have done that. There is no comprehensive book that investigates Lakȟóta history, culture, and society giving priority to Lakȟóta voices. In Lakȟóta culture "listening" is a virtue and a sign of respect and maturity, and we have tried to listen. We have listened to contemporary Lakȟóta people, and, through Lakȟóta accounts, stories, and oral histories (wičhóoyake), to the voices from the past. By observing a wide historical, cultural, social, and religious context, we let the Lakȟóta of the past speak, and we do our best to "listen" and "have ears."[1]

As we explore continuity and change in Lakȟóta culture and society, we have attempted to let core Lakȟóta values, symbols, and themes direct the narrative. These key cultural values and themes—Lakȟól wičȟóȟ'aŋ (Lakȟóta traditions, customs, culture), kinship, relationship, generosity, bravery, pluralism, diversity of viewpoint, adaptability, innovation—have structured the Lakȟóta experience in its encounter with modernity, providing a distinctive lens through which the world is viewed, interpreted, and understood.

We approach major historical events through sources left by the Lakȟóta. We use winter counts, oral traditions and histories, letters written by Lakȟóta, their speeches during treaty commissions, in addition to accounts included in the annual reports and letters sent by Indian agents. These all help to reveal themes that have gone unnoticed or have usually been interpreted from a Euro-American perspective. We believe our approach creates a narrative that highlights Lakȟóta agency and belonging, in both the past and the present.

When we look at the Battle of the Little Bighorn, we do not dwell on George Armstrong Custer or his men of the Seventh Cavalry. We want to tell the story of fifteen-year-old Black Elk who put a revolver against the head of one of Custer's soldiers and pulled the trigger. What did he think about counting his first coup on a white man, and how did he see the unfolding battle around him? Similarly, we do not tell the usual story of the 1889 Crook Commission, which sought to reduce Lakȟóta reservations, as a tale where Crook emerges as the hero who coerced the Lakȟóta into signing the controversial agreement. Instead, we tell the story of American Horse, who first gave a long speech against the agreement, then was the first to sign it. Why did he do that? What do his actions tell us about Lakȟóta culture, and what did it mean for the future inauguration of the Ghost Dance among the Lakȟóta? We are not rehashing the usual version of the story of the Fort Laramie Treaty of 1851 as one where the United States imposed an agenda on the Lakȟóta. The Lakȟóta, too, had an agenda, and they organized their various thiyóšpaye (lodge groups) to execute that agenda. These are the historical events we want to bring into focus. Correspondingly, we want to tell the story of Lakȟóta religious and cultural revitalization in the twentieth and twenty-first centuries from the standpoint of those who experienced it firsthand. We want to understand the changing roles of women in the context of the twentieth-century reservation, and what contemporary Lakȟóta think when after years of language suppression in boarding schools, they witness current efforts to revitalize their language. How does the Lakȟóta artist Arthur Amiotte understand the role of religion and kinship in contemporary Lakȟóta culture and society? We will tell the story of the #NoDAPL protest as it was experienced by those who in 2016–17 were protecting their sacred waters against oil pipelines and corporate interests and see themselves in that role to this day.

The different chapters of this book use diverse sources as their key material. For example, Lakȟóta waníyetu iyáwapi (winter counts) are a valuable primary source for understanding what was important to various Lakȟóta groups throughout the eighteenth and nineteenth centuries. Winter counts were calendars kept by several Plains tribes that consisted of pictographs on hides, cloth, or paper commemorating the most significant or memorable event for each year. One pictograph represented each year, and they were called waníyetu (winter) because each covered the period from the first snowfall of one year to the first snowfall of the next. Winter counts were kept by designated keepers who used the pictographs as mnemonic devices tied to detailed oral histories associated with each year or winter, represented visually by the pictograph. In the wintertime, often the entire tribe or smaller social groups would gather to hear the history of their people told by the winter count keeper.[2]

Our approach allows us to create a narrative heavily influenced by the winter counts and other Lakȟóta sources, with Euro-American sources, for example, government documents and reports, used to support Lakȟóta sources, not vice versa. Beginning in the 1880s there is an increasing number of extant letters written by Lakȟóta, many of them in Lakȟóta or Dakȟóta. We have translated several of these letters ourselves where no translations already exist. We understand that most historical Lakȟóta accounts were written down through an interpreter and may have been misunderstood or mistranslated at the time. They are nevertheless the best sources available. The twentieth century in contrast shows an increasing quantity of material produced by Lakȟóta themselves. Everything from official records to informal oral history collections, newspapers, websites, and even social media platforms are valuable for contemporary stories. Finally, to be informed about the most recent developments in Lakȟóta country we have done our best to listen. We have worked with Lakȟóta communities since 2000 and have established longstanding connections with many Lakȟóta. These made it possible for us to send out a questionnaire to our Lakȟóta friends asking them to contribute to this book by sharing their family stories and personal histories. We had intended to follow-up with personal visits for additional commentary and storytelling, but the Covid-19 pandemic in 2020 prevented us from doing so. Still, these contributions, whether through Zoom or email, are invaluable, and we want to express our sincere thanks to all our Lakȟóta friends. Not all individuals wanted their names published, and out of respect for those who did not we do not cite them directly or mention their names in the endnotes. Regardless, all accounts by contemporary Lakȟóta have been published with their permission. Their involvement made this book much better, and we hope we have listened well.

For writing the Lakȟóta language we use the most current orthography, which was developed first by Indiana University's American Indian Studies Research Institute (AISRI) and expanded upon by the Lakȟóta Language Consortium (LLC). Translating old Lakȟóta texts has been a challenging yet rewarding task. The process is tedious as the language and writing systems have changed since the late nineteenth century, making transcription difficult. Yet we are confident that the time spent on this process has been worthwhile. When quoting from historical sources we have made silent grammatical corrections and, for the sake of consistency, changed Lakȟóta words into modern orthography.

Translations, Pronunciation, and Glossary

Recently there has been a growing debate about the use of native names for native people in research literature and this is an important question. There are always issues of translation with Lakȟóta names that have specific meanings that are not always conveyed accurately when translated into English. Why use Man Afraid of His Horses when his name is Tȟašúŋke Kȟokípȟapi, which should really be translated as Man Whose Horses They Are Afraid Of? More important is the question of identities. Before the reservation era, until the late 1890s, the Lakȟóta, of course, used Lakȟóta names. By the twentieth century they were forced to drop them and use English names, but today many increasingly prefer Lakȟóta names. It would be ideal to use Lakȟóta names throughout the book, but these could be confusing to readers more familiar with Sitting Bull than Tȟatȟáŋka Íyotake. Therefore, to make the book more reader friendly to English-speaking audiences, we use English, but provide Lakȟóta names in parentheses when the person is first mentioned. To ensure names are correct, we used various sources, including US Census Records. These contain Indian censuses, which at that time were done annually. The 1890s censuses are exceptionally rich sources because they often provide both Lakȟóta and English names. Some names have been hard to identify, as the handwritten census can be difficult to read in the best of circumstances. To avoid misspellings and mistranslations, we have compared

the census documents to other known sources to accurately provide individuals'
names. If the name is still unclear, we discuss the form in the notes.

Another important consideration is placenames. Obviously the Lakȟóta
named rivers and mountains in their own language, and these places have specific
meanings that are reflected in the Lakȟóta names. For that reason, whenever
possible, Lakȟóta names for locations, rivers, mountains, and other geograph-
ical features are given in parentheses. For Lakȟóta band and tribe names we
use modern Lakȟóta orthography throughout. For example, instead of writing
Hunkpapa, we use Húŋkpapȟa, and instead of Sans Arc, we use Itázipčho. For
tribal names, as well as other nouns, we do not use plural "s" to make Lakȟóta
words seem more English. For example, we say oyáte instead of oyátes to avoid
twisting Lakȟóta terms into an inauthentic form.

For certain terms we use the Lakȟóta language first but provide an English
translation in parentheses, for example, waníyetu (winter); however, for Lakȟóta
personal and place names we use English but provide Lakȟóta names in parentheses. We also provide Lakȟóta names for other tribes in parentheses at first
mention, as for example, Pawnee (Sčíli). Obviously, all tribes had their own
names for themselves, but here we reflect Lakȟóta perceptions of these tribes.

Finally, a guide to pronunciation follows this preface, and a glossary of terms
is provided at the back of the book.

Organization

Indeed, being a good relative, observing the proper kinship protocols, and protecting Lakȟóta lands and Lakȟól wičhóȟ'aŋ (the Lakȟóta way of life) are major
themes running throughout the entire work. This book is arranged in three parts,
chronological at first and then both chronological and thematic as appropriate.
The first few chapters, part 1, present the fundamentals of historical Lakȟóta
culture and systems of belief. We describe the way of life and the importance
of wótakuye (kinship). Until the early eighteenth century, the Lakȟóta were
living east of the Missouri River as part of the Dakȟóta people, only gradually
emerging as a distinct Plains people in the latter part of the century. While we
briefly touch upon the earlier period, our narrative in part 2 focuses on Lakȟóta
history in the nineteenth century. Beginning with the reservation period around
1880, the narrative in part 3 becomes more thematic, and the chronology runs
parallel within themes. As noted earlier, we include comments from Lakȟóta
people whom we invited to tell in their own words what it means to them to be
Lakȟóta in the twentieth and twenty-first centuries.

Acknowledgments

Working on this book has been a wonderful, almost lifelong, process for both of us. Seeing it published is very gratifying. Granted, writing this on two continents and over the last two years in the middle of a pandemic may not have been ideal, but like the rest of the world, we did our best to cope. This book was made possible only by the contributions of many people and institutions that shared their time, knowledge, and, sometimes, funds to support us.

Our greatest gratitude goes to Professor Raymond J. DeMallie. There are not enough words to describe his influence on our work, but also on us as scholars and human beings. We are happy that he was able to see an early version of the manuscript before he sadly passed away in the spring of 2021. Professor Douglas R. Parks as our Lakȟóta language teacher deserves a special mention here. We miss both gentlemen. Professor Mark Van de Logt deserves our warmest gratitude for extensively reading, commenting, and improving the final version of the manuscript. We also want to thank our two anonymous readers for thoughtful comments and suggestions to improve the text. Susan Walters Schmid did a wonderful job copyediting the manuscript. Alessandra Jacobi Tamulevich has been very supportive of our work, and we thank her for her patience and understanding. We also express thanks to Nicky Belle, Phillip J. Deloria, Francis E. Flavin, and Justin R. Gage for their contributions. Extended special thanks go to Arthur Amiotte, Jace Cuny DeCory, and Robert Brave Heart (Čhaŋté Tʼíŋza) Senior.

Many of the people and organizations mentioned below would be entitled to a paragraph or two for their generosity and input, but a list in alphabetical order will have to suffice for now.

We extend our thanks to the American Indian Studies Research Institute, Indiana University, Basil Brave Heart (Čhaŋté Tʼíŋza), Buffalo Bill Center of the West, Boyd Cothran, Christina Burke, Cindy Giago, Erin Greb, Corey Yellow Boy, Daisy Njoku, Dennis Christafferson, Department of Cultures University of Helsinki, Ernie and Sonja LaPointe, Eugene and Phyllis Young, Floris Pté Sáŋ Huŋká, Freda Goodsell Mesteth, Gemma Lockhart, Gerri LeBeau, Jeremy Johnston, Joshua Reid, Kingsley Bray, LaDonna Brave Bull Allard (Tamakawastewin, Good Earth Woman), Lula Red Cloud, Mack Frost, Mark Fritch, Markku Henriksson, Matthew Reitzel, Rachel Lovelace-Portal, Pekka Hämäläinen, Rainer Smedman, Richard and Ethleen Two Dogs and the American Horse family, Richard Myers, Rose Speirs, Sebastian Braun, Shannon Kring, the Helsinki

Collegium for Advanced Studies, Tipiziwin Tolman, Tokata Iron Eyes, Waste Win Young, Wilmer Mesteth. Finally, our families, Saara Kekki, Aarni, and Kaisla Andersson, and Emily, Ella, and Will Posthumus. Saara deserves special thanks for reading, editing, and fixing our text. To many others, especially our Lakȟóta friends, who allowed us to share in their daily lives and ceremonies and just "listen," we are forever grateful.

LAKȞÓTA ORTHOGRAPHY PRONUNCIATION GUIDE

Following are the phonetic symbols used throughout the text that have special significance:

A, a   a, oral a (pronounced like the 'a' in *father*)

Á, á   stressed a, stressed oral a

Aŋ, aŋ   nasal a, nasalized a (pronounced like the 'o' in *donkey*)

Áŋ, áŋ   stressed nasal a, stressed nasalized a

Č, č   c-wedge (pronounced like the 'ch' in *stitch*)

Čh, čh   aspirated c-wedge, soft-aspirated c-wedge (pronounced like the 'ch' in *chair*)

Č', č'   c-wedge glottal, c-wedge glottal stop

E, e   e, oral e (pronounced like the 'e' in *bed*)

É, é   stressed e, stressed oral e

Ǧ, ǧ   g-wedge (pronounced like the German Ma*ch*en)

Ȟ, ȟ   h-wedge (pronounced like the German a*ch*)

Ȟ', ȟ'   h-wedge glottal, h-wedge glottal stop

I, i   i, oral i (pronounced like the 'i' in *pit*)

Í, í   stressed i, stressed oral i

Iŋ, iŋ   nasal i, nasalized i (pronounced like the 'i' in *tint*)

Íŋ, íŋ   stressed nasal i, stressed nasalized i

K, k   k, unaspirated k (pronounced like the 'k' in *skid*)

Kh, kh   aspirated k, soft-aspirated k (pronounced like the 'k' in *kite*)

Kȟ, kȟ   hard-aspirated k, guttural k (no English equivalent)

K', k'   k glottal, k glottal stop

O, o   o, oral o (pronounced like the 'o' in *potent*)

Ó, ó   stressed o, stressed oral o

P, p   p, unaspirated p (pronounced like the 'p' in *spit*)

Ph, ph   aspirated p, soft-aspirated p (pronounced like the 'p' in *pit*)

Pȟ, pȟ   hard-aspirated p, guttural p (no English equivalent)

P', p'   p glottal, p glottal stop

S', s'   s glottal, s glottal stop

Š, š   s-wedge (pronounced like the 'sh' in *shout*)

Š', š'   s-wedge glottal, s-wedge glottal stop

T, t   t, unaspirated t (pronounced like the 't' in *start*)

Th, th   aspirated t, soft-aspirated t (pronounced like the 't' in *tool*)

Tȟ, tȟ   hard-aspirated t, guttural t (no English equivalent)

T', t'   t glottal, t glottal stop

U, u   u, oral u (pronounced like the 'oo' in *hook*)

Ú, ú   stressed u, stressed oral u

Uŋ, uŋ   nasal u, nasalized u (pronounced like the 'oo' in *moon*)

Úŋ, úŋ   stressed nasal u, stressed nasalized u

Ž, ž   z-wedge (pronounced like the 's' in *treasure*)

HINÁPȞAPI
(EMERGENCE)

Eháŋni (long time ago), Pté Oyáte (Buffalo People) dwelled under the earth, so it is said. Wazí was their chief, and he was married to a woman, Káŋka, who was a seer. Wazí and Káŋka had a daughter named Ité, who was the most beautiful of all women. Ité was married to Tȟaté, the wind. Ité gave birth to four sons all at once, the sons of the wind, who would establish the four directions and hence all time and space. By marrying the wind, Ité established a link between the Pté Oyáte and Wakȟáŋ Tȟáŋka, the great spirits of the universe.

Iktómi (Spider) the trickster, deceiver, and nourisher of discontent, was the son of Wakȟáŋpi (the sacred / gods), the creator of language, and namer of all things. He enjoyed sowing trouble and causing people shame so he could laugh at them in their misery. Iktómi schemed to trick Ité so he could ridicule her. The trickster began to weave his web, telling her she was as beautiful as Haŋwí, the moon, the wife of Wí, the sun, chief of the great spirits. He told her that Wí had noticed her beauty and spoken of it.

Wí invited Ité to sit at the feast of the spirits. Iktómi tricked Haŋwí into arriving at the feast late and arranged for Ité to sit next to Wí. Then Haŋwí came and saw the other woman sitting in her place. Embarrassed, she covered her head with her robe.

After the feast, Škáŋ, the great spirit of movement, investigated the matter. Škáŋ learned that Iktómi was at the center of everyone's stories, the spider in the center of the web.

Škáŋ began to dole out judgments and punishments based on what had happened. Ité was separated from her husband and four sons. For her vanity, she was banished to the world's surface, where she would live forever without friends. She would keep half of her beautiful face, but the other side was transformed into a horrid sight that would strike fear into the hearts of those who saw it, causing them to go mad. From then on, Ité would be known as Anúŋg Ité, the Double Woman or Double Face. Wazí and Káŋka were also banished to the earth's surface, where they would live alone until they could redeem themselves.

Iktómi, that deceitful spider, laughed as Škáŋ proclaimed his judgments. But then it was Iktómi's turn to be held in judgment. Škáŋ told him that because he laughed when others were shamed or suffered and because he had threatened the harmony of the great spirits, he too would be banished to the earth's surface and would remain there forever without friends. But Iktómi only laughed, saying that if the humans and spirits detested him, then he would just befriend the birds and animals and would continue his quest to make fools of humankind. And that is exactly what Iktómi has done ever since.[1]

But when Iktómi played his pranks on the animals, they were not shamed, so he longed to play his tricks on humankind. At that time the only humans on the earth were the banished Wazí, Káŋka, and their daughter Anúŋg Ité, the Double Woman. Iktómi and Double Woman decided they could lure the people to the earth's surface by letting them taste meat and see clothes and tipis made of skins, because then they would want such things. Iktómi made a deal with the wolves: in exchange for their help he would bother them no more.

The wolves made a legendary drive for game and brought many moose, deer, and bears to Double Woman's tipi, who dried the flesh and tanned the hides and cooked the meat and made beautiful robes out of the hides. She prepared a pack of beautiful clothing and delicious foods and Iktómi gave this to a wolf. He instructed him to go to the cave entrance that opens down through the world. The wolf did as he was told and eventually encountered a strong young man named Tȟokáhe. The wolf gave him the pack of fine things and told him to show it to his people and let them taste the food and touch the soft hides, that this pack would make him a great leader.

Tȟokáhe's people tried the food and clothes and liked them. Tȟokáhe chose three brave young men and they went to meet the wolf when the moon was full. The wolf led them up through the cave to the earth's surface and took them to Anúŋg Ité's lodge. She and Iktómi, invited Tȟokáhe and his companions to a feast. Iktómi told them that he and the woman were both very old, but because they ate the meat and soup, they remained young.

Iktómi gave the young men presents to bring back to their people. He told the wolf to lead them back to their people, but then to wait by the cave's mouth and guide any others who wished to come to the earth's surface and lead them far from food and water. When Tȟokáhe and the three young men returned to their people they showed them the gifts Iktómi had given them. They told them that there was plenty of game on the earth's surface and that the people there were beautiful and appeared young even when they were very old.

Seven men, along with their wives and children, left the Pté Oyáte camp within the earth and headed for the cave leading to the earth's surface. The wolf met them and guided them through the cave all day, until nighttime fell, and the people had been led to a strange desolate place. The children cried for food and drink. Then Iktómi appeared and laughed at them in their misery, and Tȟokáhe was shamed. The Double Woman next appeared, to comfort them, but when they saw her horrid face, they fled from her in terror.

In the morning Tȟokáhe and his people did not know where to go or what to do. They were hungry and thirsty. Then Wazí and Káŋka appeared and gave them food and drink. The old man and old woman taught them how to hunt game, care for the meat and hides, and how to make clothing, tipis, and live on the earth's surface. They are the ancient ancestors of the Lakȟóta; their children are the Lakȟóta.[2] This story is central to appreciating the Lakȟóta as a people—how they understand their place in and relationship to both the visible and the invisible Wakȟáŋ (sacred) world. It is also at the center of Lakȟól wičhóȟ'aŋ (the Lakȟóta way of life).

PART ONE

1

PTÉ OYÁTE
THE BUFFALO PEOPLE

Ptesáŋwiŋ and the Gift of the Sacred Pipe

Long before humans were born, different powers, spirits, and creatures fought for dominion over the world. Once the four winds (tȟatúye tópa) were born, each with their own task, the directions and most important powers of the world were set. At that time, humans lived underground together with the buffalo in a state of chaos. According to some versions of the story, the people and the buffalo emerged from beneath the earth together. That is why the people were called Pté Oyáte (the Buffalo People).[1]

The people emerged onto the earth's surface, and henceforward were known as wakȟáŋ akáŋtula, freely translated into English as "things on top." According to Lakȟóta mythology, a contest took place in those early times. Animals raced around the sacred Ȟesápa or Pahá Sápa (Black Hills) to decide who was the most powerful. The bison seemed to be clearly in the lead. Just as the end of the race was near, a magpie rose to its wings from the bison's shoulders and crossed the finish line first. Because the magpie, like the human being, is one of the two-legged creatures (hunúŋpa) of the earth, it meant that human beings also got credit for the victory. As a result, humans received the right to use animals for sustenance.[2]

In the beginning, there was disharmony between humans, animals, and nonhuman elements. Then the sacred Ptesáŋwiŋ or Wóȟpe (White Buffalo

Woman) came to resolve the conflict and to establish a relationship between humans and nonhumans. That deeply symbolic story is central to the Lakȟóta belief system.

> Early one morning, many winters ago, two Lakȟóta were out hunting with their bows and arrows. As they were standing on a hill looking for game, they saw in the distance something coming towards them in a very strange and wonderful manner. When this mysterious thing came nearer to them, they saw that it was a very beautiful woman, dressed in white buckskin, and bearing a bundle on her back. Now this woman was so good to look at that one of the Lakȟóta had bad intentions and told his friend of his desire, but this good man said that he must not have such thoughts, for surely this is a wakȟáŋ woman. . . . As the young man approached the mysterious woman, they were both covered by a great cloud, and soon when it lifted, the sacred woman was standing there, and at her feet was the man with the bad thoughts who was now nothing but bones, and terrible snakes were eating him.
>
> "Behold what you see!" the strange woman said to the good man. "I am coming to your people and wish to talk with your chief Heȟlóǧeča Nážiŋ [Standing Hollow Horn]. I wish to tell you something of great importance!"[3]

Once back in camp the young man told his chief what had happened. The chief, Standing Hollow Horn, had several tipis taken down and put together into a thiyóthipi (council lodge). The people were excited, wondering where this mysterious woman came from and what it was that she wished to say. Suddenly she entered the lodge, walked around sunwise, and stood in front of Standing Hollow Horn. Then she took a bundle from her back and, holding it with both hands, said: "Behold this and always love it! It is líla wakȟáŋ [very sacred], and you must treat it as such. No impure man should ever be allowed to see it, for within this bundle there is a sacred pipe. With this you will, during the winters to come, send your voices to Wakȟáŋ Tȟáŋka, your Father and Grandfather." IThen she took from the bundle a pipe and a small round stone, which she placed upon the ground. Holding the pipe up with its stem to the heavens, she said:

> With this sacred pipe you will walk upon the Earth; for the Earth is your Grandmother and Mother, and She is sacred. Every step that is taken upon Her should be as a prayer. The bowl of this pipe is of red stone; it is the Earth. Carved in the stone and facing the center is this buffalo calf who

represents all the four-leggeds who live upon your Mother. The stem of the pipe is of wood, and this represents all that grows upon the Earth. And these twelve feathers which hang here where the stem fits into the bowl are from Waŋblí Gleška, the Spotted Eagle, and they represent the eagle and all the wingeds of the air. All these peoples and all the things of the universe are joined to you who smoke the pipe—and all send their voices to Wakȟáŋ Tȟáŋka, the Great Spirit. . . . With this pipe you will be bound to all your relatives: your Grandfather and Father, your Grandmother and Mother. This round rock, which is made of the same red stone as the bowl of the pipe, your Father Wakȟáŋ Tȟáŋka has also given to you. It is the Earth, your Grandmother and Mother, and it is where you will live and increase. This Earth which He has given to you is red, and the two-leggeds who live upon the Earth are red; and the Great Spirit has also given to you a red day and a red road. All of this is sacred and so do not forget! Every dawn as it comes is a holy event, and every day is holy, for the light comes from your Father Wakȟáŋ Tȟáŋka; and also you must always remember that the two-leggeds and all the other peoples who stand upon this earth are sacred and should be treated as such. These seven circles which you see on the stone have much meaning, for they represent the seven rites in which the pipe will be used. From above Wakȟáŋ Tȟáŋka has given to you this sacred pipe, so that through it you may have knowledge.[4]

The woman told them about the sacred ceremonies. She told the Lakȟóta how to walk the sacred red road and lead a good life. When she departed, she turned into a young red and brown buffalo calf. Then this calf walked farther, lay down, and rolled, looking back at the people, and when she got up, she was a white buffalo. The white buffalo walked farther and rolled on the ground, becoming a black buffalo. The black buffalo walked even farther away, stopped, and after bowing to each of the universe's four quarters, disappeared over the hill. Before leaving the people, she transformed into a white buffalo again and said: "Behold this pipe! Always remember how sacred it is, and treat it as such, for it will take you to the end. . . . and at the end I shall return."[5]

There are multiple versions of the story, but the main idea remains: When the sacred woman gave the pipe to the people, she created a connection between the buffalo and the human and between the human and Wakȟáŋ Tȟáŋka, the Great Mystery or spirits. White Buffalo Woman is a link or intermediary between Wakȟáŋ Tȟáŋka and the Lakȟóta. The woman calls the Lakȟóta her relatives, saying that she was their sister and at the same time she was one with them. When she brought the Lakȟóta the sacred buffalo calf pipe (ptehíŋčala čhaŋnúŋpa), she gave them the foundation of their culture and religious ceremonies. The pipe symbolizes the universe, and the fire in the bowl is the universe's symbolic center, serving as a direct link to Wakȟáŋ Tȟáŋka through prayer. In her great generosity, White Buffalo Woman gave the Lakȟóta sacred ceremonies to ensure that the buffalo would fill the earth and the Lakȟóta nation would thrive.

The Structure of Lakȟóta Oyáte

Lakȟóta or Sioux society in the nineteenth century was adaptable. Several divisions constitute what is called in English the Sioux Nation, and the Lakȟóta are the western division of the Sioux people. According to most accounts, the name Sioux is a French corruption of the Ojibwe word Nadowessiwak, "little snakes." Traditionally scholars divided the Sioux into the Lakȟóta, Dakȟóta, and Nakȟóta nations or divisions. Modern analysis, largely based on anthropological and linguistic research, argues that the people whose self-designation is Nakȟóta are not Sioux, but the closely related Assiniboine and Stoney people, living farther north in Montana and Canada. The Lakȟóta or Teton are the western branch with seven tribes, Oglála (Oglala), Sičháŋǧu (Brulé), Húŋkpapȟa (Hunkpapa), Mnikȟówožu (Minneconjou), Oóhenuŋpa (Two Kettle), Sihásapa (Blackfeet), and Itázipčho (Sans Arc). The last five, the Saóne, separated into distinctive social units over time. The eastern Dakȟóta or Isáŋyathi (Santee) are divided into the Sisíthuŋwaŋ (Sisseton), Bdewákȟaŋthuŋwaŋ (Mdewakanton), Waȟpéthuŋwaŋ (Wahpeton), and Waȟpékhute (Wahpekute), and the western Dakȟóta comprised the Iháŋkthuŋwaŋ (Yankton) and Iháŋktȟuŋwaŋna (Yanktonai) people.

Dividing the larger groups based on linguistic details is appropriate. The Sioux did not have centralized leadership or an organized political structure. The main unifying element for these independent groups was common culture, history, and, most importantly, language, though each division spoke a dialect of that language. In fact, their own name, whether spelled Lakȟóta, Dakȟóta, or Nakȟóta, means "allies," not "people" as sometimes suggested.[6] For the Lakȟóta, all people speaking the same language were referred to as lakȟólkičhiyapi (allies) and were wólakȟota (related). Together they made up the čhaŋgléška wakȟáŋ (sacred hoop), which represents the unity of the people. All non-Lakȟóta Native Americans were seen as outside the Lakȟóta sacred hoop and were related to as tȟókakičhiyapi (enemies). The whites were not originally included in the same category as Indians, and thus were not related to as enemies. Instead, they were called wašíču, a term that initially referred to special guardian spirits, often related to war. Perhaps this reflected the guns and other mysterious technologies used by the whites.[7]

The Lakȟóta are also known by the name Teton, deriving from the Lakȟóta word thítȟuŋwaŋ (possibly meaning "dwellers on the plains"). The Lakȟóta refer to their seven original tribes as Očhéthi Šakówiŋ or Seven Council Fires. Sometimes this term also refers to the origins of the entire Sioux Nation, not just the Lakȟóta. While there is no historical evidence that a unit of seven tribes existed as a political entity, the Seven Council Fires is a powerful unifying symbol of identity for the Lakȟóta and Dakȟóta people. Even though the seven Lakȟóta tribes have remained the same, the number of bands belonging to these larger units has changed considerably over time. Therefore, to neatly categorize Lakȟóta society is impossible; historians have often failed to appreciate both the complexity and the flexibility of this structure. Many written descriptions are snapshots in time that fail to capture the ever-changing number and composition of oyáte and thiyóšpaye. The terminology makes things even more problematic. What is a nation, what is a tribe, what is a band, and what should be called a sub-band? These are all English terms used by outsiders to try to understand a foreign culture. In the Lakȟóta language, the word most used to describe all these levels of societal structures is oyáte, people. There is, for example, Lakȟóta oyáte, but also Húŋkpapȟa oyáte, and any group of people down to the smallest family unit could be referred to as oyáte, but most often it is used as a synonym for the English word "band." In research literature, the considerable variation in nomenclature perhaps reflects a need to categorize Lakȟóta society in terms familiar to Euro-Americans rather than any relevance for the Lakȟóta people historically.[8]

The most significant societal unit for the Lakȟóta was the thiyóšpaye, the extended family or lodge group. The thiyóšpaye was formed around an itȟáŋčhaŋ (leader or chief) and ranged from 100 to 150 people. The smallest unit for the Lakȟóta was the thiwáhe (immediate or nuclear family). The thiyóšpaye and thiwáhe are gateways to kinship networks, which are at the core of Lakȟóta society. Nineteenth-century Lakȟóta society may be conceptualized as a great circle composed of many thiyóšpaye varying in size, each led by a chief appointed by a council of elder decision-makers. Thiyóšpaye were designated by a prominent member's name—often a nickname—or by some noteworthy event associated with the group. Each thiyóšpaye had its own identity, dialect, and corporate economic activity. All the members of a thiyóšpaye were related to one another, either through descent or marriage. Usually, a group of brothers and male cousins with their families formed the core. Individuals identified themselves first with their thiyóšpaye. Political and economic authority focused on men, but the nexus of kin focused on women, who owned and maintained the tipis.[9] The bonds that united the members of a thiyóšpaye were based on the shared buffalo economy, blood, residence, choice, and common identity. These were relationships of diffuse, enduring solidarity defined in terms of a shared code of conduct and behavior.[10]

Understanding Lakȟóta societal structures and the flexibility of those structures is key to understanding Lakȟóta interaction with the wašíču. Tracing the changing names and numbers of various Lakȟóta tribes and thiyóšpaye through time is, however, difficult. Early European traders and travelers gave varying, often unreliable estimates of these groups. Based on the narratives of early travelers such as Pierre-Esprit Radisson, Joseph Nicollet, Jonathan Carver, and Pierre-Antoine Tabeau it is safe to say that the basic tribal structure and the subdivision into smaller units has been a Sioux and Lakȟóta custom since at least the seventeenth century. While Radisson's journeys took him mostly through Isáŋyathi country in the 1640s, he too reports several divisions among the Sioux. More detailed information about the Sioux in general emerges when Carver, traveling in the 1770s, reported eleven, and Tabeau, traveling in 1803–4, reported five bands or tribes for the entire Sioux Nation. Gradually, more specific information about the Lakȟóta was recorded through the writings of Meriwether Lewis, William Clark, Joseph Nicollet, and Edwin Denig. Lewis and Clark listed five bands belonging to the Sičháŋǧu in 1804–1805, and Nicollet reported six bands almost forty years later. Lakȟóta tribes living north of the Oglála and Sičháŋǧu receive practically no attention in the writings of these early travelers. Perhaps the most useful description of Lakȟóta life in the first part of the nineteenth century is provided by Denig, who lived among the Lakȟóta in the early 1830s.[11]

A rare Lakȟóta source for understanding the early nineteenth-century Oglála tribal structure is a winter count ledger book kept by the family of American Horse (Wašíču Tȟašúŋka).[12] This ledger details seven Oglála bands in 1825: Walúta Wápaha (Red Banner), Tȟašnáȟeča Yúta (Ground Squirrel Eaters), Itéšiča (Bad Face), Khiyúksa (Break One's Own), Kuhíŋyaŋ (Sacred Stone Returning), Thiyóčhesli (Defecates in Lodge), and Pȟayábya (Pushed to Head). Each consisted of several thiyóšpaye. Among the Walúta Wápaha, the Húŋkpathila were the oldest group, comprising three distinct thiyóšpaye, but perhaps the most prominent of all the Oglála groups at the time were the Khiyúksa. According to the historian Kingsley Bray, the Khiyúksa "seniority in tribal history was reflected in social, political, and ceremonial eminence." Over the years some of these groups split into new social units, or merged, but many oyáte like the Khiyúksa or Pȟayábya remained central in the Oglála camp circle throughout the nineteenth century and are still prominent today.[13]

The detailed description of the Oglála tribal circle in 1825 in the American Horse ledger gives a glimpse of how the entire Lakȟóta nation may have been structured early in the nineteenth century. While we do not have such a detailed description from other Lakȟóta oyáte, it is possible to piece together enough information to say that, at least by the 1820s, similar structures were already in place among the other Lakȟóta oyáte. In fact, the American Horse ledger records similar structures for at least the Mnikȟówožu and Itázipčho.[14] Based on other winter counts and observations by whites it is possible to follow the development and changes among the Húŋkpapȟa even for the early 1800s. Húŋkpapȟa bands and thiyóšpaye in the early nineteenth century provide an excellent example of how leadership within and between Lakȟóta oyáte changed over time. In the late eighteenth century, the Húŋkpapȟa were struggling, which caused many families to move to live with the Oglála, but as the Húŋkpapȟa gradually gained prestige, they saw people from other Lakȟóta oyáte join their camp circle. Marriages, kinship, and political opinions drove these allegiances and changes. This constant change and mixing among people also affected ceremonies and other societal structures. For instance, the Húŋkpapȟa originally did not have a Čhaŋté T'íŋza (Strong Heart) warrior society at all. They adopted it from the Oglála, and by the 1830s it had become one of the most powerful and vocal societies advocating insulation of the Húŋkpapȟa from American influence. Through expanding kinship networks, ceremonies traveled from one oyáte to another. It was common, for example, for the Sihásapa and Húŋkpapȟa to hold Sun Dances together, which was a powerful unifying mechanism for them. In fact, these groups sometimes camped and hunted together for extended periods of time.[15] These changes and modifications were completely normal in Lakȟóta society, but it was difficult for white observers to understand this interrelatedness, and their attempts to categorize the Lakȟóta people often failed. During the latter part of the nineteenth century and into the reservation period, these misunderstandings were obvious and affected government policies that impacted the Lakȟóta.

As increasing numbers of whites encroached on Lakȟóta lands, the Lakȟóta chose not to remain mere onlookers to events affecting their lives. As a people, the Lakȟóta changed; they adapted and embraced the newcomers but indigenized elements of their culture according to their own needs, and they fought the wašíču whenever they threatened the Lakȟóta way of life.

The Making of Lakȟóta Tȟamákȟočhe

Looking west from the east bank of the mighty Missouri River (Mníšoše), one cannot help wondering at how different the landscape is on the other side. The Missouri, like any great river, has been a thoroughfare, a vein for trade and intercourse that has connected people, but it has also been a divider. On the east side, the land is fertile and for the past century and a half it has facilitated large-scale agriculture. Three hundred years ago the land provided sustenance to many tribes, including the portion of the Sioux Nation that eventually became the Lakȟóta people. At first glance, the lands west of the river do not seem so appealing: the soil is hard, dry, and rocky. Rivers and buttes fragment the endless landscape. It was certainly not good for farming three hundred years ago, but that was not what the Lakȟóta were looking for; they were not, nor would they become, farmers. There was other bounty to be found on those lands beyond the river: buffalo. Once the Lakȟóta reached the Missouri River, they kept looking westward, always in pursuit of the buffalo. Perhaps this is the true birth of the Pté Oyáte—the Buffalo People. By establishing themselves as a dominant power along the Missouri River, the Lakȟóta were establishing themselves as a people of the Plains.

Since at least the sixteenth century, the Lakȟóta with their close relatives the Dakȟóta, Iháŋktȟuŋwaŋ (Yankton), and Iháŋktȟuŋwaŋna (Yanktonai) had been living in the area that roughly encompasses present-day Minnesota and Wisconsin, gradually making their way to the grasslands and rolling prairies that lie between the Mississippi and Missouri Rivers. They had been exposed to the colonial struggles between competing European powers and the neighboring Native American tribes. They had learned to navigate between war and peace; their representatives had traveled to Montreal since the mid-seventeenth century to seek favorable trading with the French, they had allowed the British to establish trading posts in the heart of their country, and they had fought both their European trading partners and their native neighbors.[16]

By the early 1700s, living space east of the Mississippi River was getting scarce. Increasing numbers of people, white and Indian, were moving west. While we do not know exactly when the Lakȟóta started to truly separate from the rest of the Sioux people, by the mid-eighteenth century many had moved closer to the Missouri River. By 1736 most of the Sioux lived west of the Mississippi, and by 1750, western Sioux groups were hunting on the prairies east of the Missouri River but had not yet crossed it.[17] Since at least 1700, according to French fur trader Pierre-Charles Le Sueur, the Western Sioux oyáte (band) had been living "only by the hunt" in typical nomadic hunter-gatherer fashion. During the eighteenth century, the Missouri River became a major trading route and the Sioux, both Lakȟóta and Iháŋktȟuŋwaŋna, wanted a share of the trade and were quick to establish a system that required fees from the traders traveling upriver. Early traders such as Jean-Baptiste Truteau and Pierre-Antoine Tabeau noted that the Lakȟóta forced them to abandon their trade goods or pay to continue trading up the Missouri.[18]

The Lakȟóta were quick to adapt to the changing circumstances. Trade led them to ally at times with the French, at times with the British, and later with the Americans. From the mid-eighteenth century onward, the Lakȟóta experienced the consequences of the power struggles between colonial Europeans who were expanding their influence into the interior of North America. The Lakȟóta had their own agenda, as they always had, and trade, warfare, and conquest remained integral aspects of Lakȟóta life, but in the colonial context these took on new forms. Kinship and other core Lakȟóta values provided the foundation for Lakȟóta adaptation to emergent circumstances. It is important to realize that while trade was significant, the Lakȟóta were not looking to accumulate individual wealth per se; it was all about the prosperity of the Lakȟóta as a people. They did not operate under the same premises as Euro-American traders who were looking for maximal individual gain and the accumulation of wealth, as has been suggested by some scholars. One of the key virtues for a Lakȟóta was–and still is–generosity. One made a name for oneself by giving, often recklessly. As Lakȟóta territory expanded westward through warfare and trade, wealth was redistributed with the common good as the goal.[19]

The exact year the Lakȟóta crossed the Missouri is not known, but it does not really matter. They arrived on the Plains on the other side in small, independent groups. According to Lakȟóta legends, "the people made winter camps at Blé Wakȟáŋ (Sacred Lake), but then some wandered so far in the summertime that they did not return to the winter camp, which was made in the place of the pines. These people made their winter camp where the leaves fall in the winter and some made it upon the tinte [thíŋta] or plains." Lakȟóta winter counts also describe a division of the people around the mid-eighteenth century. The Oglála winter count keeper Makȟúla (Breast, also known as Left Heron), a famous storyteller, states that "a division of the tribes" took place so that there were

Santee (Isáŋyathi) and Teton (Lakȟóta) groups, and the Tetons further divided later in either 1769 or 1785. Although the period is not exact, Lakȟóta stories confirm that the move beyond the Missouri happened gradually, each group separating so that they eventually became the "seven council fires that would not be extinguished."[20]

The Oglála (Oglala) and Sičháŋǧu (Brulé) moved first; the remaining five oyáte, known in the nineteenth century as the Saóne, gradually followed them.[21] Throughout their westward expansion, the Lakȟóta pushed aside the Kiowa (Wítapahatu), Arikara (Pȟaláni), and Crow (Kȟaŋǧí Wičháša / Psáloka) tribes, facilitated by diseases that took their toll on the Plains Indian village populations and by the numerical strength of the Lakȟóta people. By the mid-eighteenth century, the Lakȟóta started to acquire guns and horses from the eastern and southern frontiers. They quickly established themselves as the major power on the Plains west of the Missouri River, expanding their domain to the Black Hills and beyond. Alongside the Cheyenne (Šahíyela) and Arapaho (Maȟpíya Tȟó), the Lakȟóta became the rulers of the North-Central Plains. By 1825, the Lakȟóta occupied an area stretching from the Missouri River to the Black Hills and from the Platte River (Pȟaŋkéska Wakpá) to the Yellowstone River (Heȟáka Wakpá). The Oglála and Sičháŋǧu lived in the southern parts and the Saóne occupied the northern parts.[22]

In a recent study, historian Pekka Hämäläinen, in analyzing the value of rivers in Lakȟóta expansion, argues that the Lakȟóta were more riverine people than plains people. The many rivers running through the Northern Plains are the arteries of life and certainly aided the Lakȟóta in their westward push. River bottoms provided critical shelter, firewood, water, and game for food. However, unlike typical riverine peoples, fish never played an important role in the Lakȟóta diet, nor did they hold an important position in their belief system. The Lakȟóta historically viewed tribes that ate fish with contempt and only resorted to eating fish in times of scarcity. Hämäläinen's claim notwithstanding, use of and partial dependency on rivers and river bottoms does not render the Lakȟóta, or any nomadic plains people, riverine people.[23]

Hunting buffalo became the Lakȟóta's primary means of support. The acquisition of horses allowed them to hunt more efficiently, which immediately resulted in a higher living standard and an increase in population. Diseases of European origin wreaked havoc among all the Plains tribes but, because the Lakȟóta lived in small groups constantly on the move, they were more flexible in responding to infectious diseases than the more sedentary tribes living in larger, densely populated permanent villages. While other Plains tribes struggled, the Lakȟóta prospered. Their population growth was rapid: in 1804 the Americans esti-mated that there were approximately 8,000 Sioux, about 3,000 of whom were Lakȟóta, but in 1850 the approximate number was already 24,000 Sioux, of which 13,000–14,000 were Lakȟóta. However, early estimates of the Lakȟóta population are necessarily unreliable as white observers really had no way of measuring their exact numbers.[24]

At the time, measuring their numbers held no real significance for the Lakȟóta. They knew they were numerous, their tribes and thiyóšpaye were independent, and they were rapidly becoming the most powerful people on the Northern Plains. They had found a new homeland, Lakȟóta tȟamákȟočhe.

"He Carried Home with Him a Pine Tree"

Lakȟóta eighteenth-century winter counts describe numerous battles with tra-ditional enemies, but they also depict trade with their neighbors and the whites. Relationships with whites were peaceful as the winter counts mostly refer to peaceful parleys or trading. Before the 1750s, Lakȟóta winter counts seldom mention white men at all, but as trade became more significant for the Lakȟóta, winter counts increasingly reflect this interaction. The 1791 winter count of the Oglála No Ears (Núŋǧe Waníče) recalls that "Wówapi waŋ makȟó kawíŋȟ yuhá hiyáya yápi" (They went around carrying flags), which may refer to a military expedition or an English trading party that traveled along the Missouri. In Iron Crow's (Kȟaŋǧi Máza) winter count the year 1797 was marked by "Čhápa číkʼa hí waníyetu" (Coming of Little Beaver). Little Beaver was the Lakȟóta name given to St. Louis-based trader Régis Loisel, who built a trading post at Cedar Island around 1802. Many 1804–5 winter counts recognized a significant meeting. Iron Crow noted that "Wówapi óta oyáte okížu" (The people came together with many flags), and American Horse describes a big meeting at the Missouri River.[25] The winter counts refer to a meeting with Meriwether Lewis and William Clark at the mouth of Bad River (Wakpášiča) in September 1804. During the meeting, the Lakȟóta displayed Spanish flags they had received earlier, and the Americans displayed their own. The Lakȟóta noted their meeting with the expedition, but so did Lewis and Clark, who described the Sioux as "the vilest miscreants of the savage race." The Lakȟóta were the only tribe with whom they nearly had a serious engagement during their two-year trek across the continent. Still, they also describe them as "stout, bold looking people," a sentiment echoed by other white travelers.[26]

The presence and influence of the wašíču had unforeseen consequences that were at times acutely felt and were articulated in winter counts. Several describe terrible epidemics ravaging neighboring tribes and the Lakȟóta. Battiste Good's (Waphóštaŋ) winter count notes that the year 1779–80 was a winter when "small-pox used them up." The No Ears winter count for the year 1782 simply states "nawíčhašli" (measles). The first encounter with this terrible disease occurred as early as the 1730s. According to Battiste Good, up to fifty people died of a disease that was illustrated in the pictograph as a human figure dotted with red spots and signs of internal pain.[27]

The nineteenth century's first two decades saw the Lakȟóta transforming into a nomadic Plains Indian tribe, always on the move, ready to adapt, flexible, and prepared to assert their power over other tribes. The great herds of buffalo drew the Lakȟóta to the Plains and made their economy flourish. To be able to hunt the buffalo freely and more efficiently, they needed to expand. Warfare, already an essential part of Lakȟóta life, took on an economic role and needs to be understood within an economic and political framework. Although warfare was very individualistic, success in war was the most important route to prestige and status for a Lakȟóta man. While intertribal warfare may seem disorganized at first glance, Lakȟóta expansion and rise to dominance on the Northern Plains was complicated. By the late eighteenth and early nineteenth centuries the Lakȟóta were exercising expansive policies that parallel some imperialist practices. Although the Lakȟóta did not have a larger, Manifest Destiny-like ideology for expansion as the Americans did, nor a concept of a specific "Lakȟóta America," parallel to British or Spanish America as suggested by a recent study, many Lakȟóta looked at other tribes as inferior and considered them natural enemies.[28] They were opportunistic and knew their growing power. As a testimony to the Lakȟóta expansionist way of thinking, Oglála chief Black Hawk (Čhetáŋ Sápa) said in 1854, "we whipped these nations [Kiowa and Crow] out of the way, and in this we did what the white men do when they want the land of the Indians."[29] The Lakȟóta were not living in isolation nor were they unaware of what was going on around them. They knew the whites were hungry for land, and some Lakȟóta used that as an argument to justify their own expansion.

Thus, we can see Lakȟóta warfare's dual nature of individualism within wider political and economic implications. The accumulation of horses and access to hunting grounds and trading routes were key aspects of war. Gaining new land for hunting and horse pasturing generated aggressive "politics of expansion" that led to a type of domino effect, when tribes took turns forcing weaker neighbors out of their way. As early as 1717–18, Battiste Good recorded in his winter count that horses were stolen from the Pawnee (Sčíli) and Assiniboine. The following few years recorded several incidents of horse raiding, demonstrating the growing significance of horses and setting the scene for cycles of intertribal warfare that lasted until the reservation period.[30]

Lakȟóta expansion has sometimes been attributed to their "warlike nature" and to the buffalo economy. To reduce Lakȟóta warfare to a sport for war honors is far too simplistic. Although intertribal warfare often was about demonstrating bravery, it was very real and very violent. While touching a living enemy was honorable and an integral part of the Plains Indian coup system, warriors aimed to cause maximum destruction. Lakȟóta aggression against the Pawnee was so severe that the Pawnee faced the possibility of extinction. According to Pawnee sources, the Lakȟóta were attempting to "wipe them out." The writings of Jean-Baptiste Truteau provide evidence of this attitude also in relation to the Arikara.[31] Lakȟóta expansion was also noted in their winter counts. American Horse's winter count states that in the year 1775–76 the Oglála Standing Buffalo (Tȟatȟáŋka Nážiŋ) entered the Black Hills and brought back with him a piece of wood that was unfamiliar to the Lakȟóta. "He carried home with him a pine tree of a species he had never seen before," notes No Ears in his calendar. This may be one of the earliest Lakȟóta references to the Black Hills, although it is likely that they had at least visited the area earlier.[32] In any case, just a few years later the Lakȟóta were patrolling the Black Hills and had found the place that soon became the center of their universe, a sacred place of origin, Ȟesápa or Wagmúŋka ógnaka ičháŋte, the "heart of everything that is."[33]

Ȟesápa and the surrounding geological formation known as the khiíŋyaŋka očháŋku (racetrack) do resemble a heart when viewed from above. The entire area is understood by many Lakȟóta today as a hóčhoka (sacred circle or semicircle) where the opening is to the southeast and at the center is a place called Pȟešlá (Mount Baldy), where the Welcoming Back All Life in Peace ceremony is performed. Other ceremonial locations are found throughout the hills and especially during the summer solstice a round of ceremonies, like the Welcoming Back the Thunders, take place in this sacred hoop. Thus, when entering Ȟesápa one enters a sacred space that is a circle within a circle. It is a hóčhoka within a hóčhoka and it connects the spirits with the human world.[34]

The Ȟesápa became so central to the Lakȟóta that the stories of Lakȟóta origins in the wooded areas east of the Missouri and subsequent migrations were, if not replaced, at least integrated into the story of Iktómi and the Pté

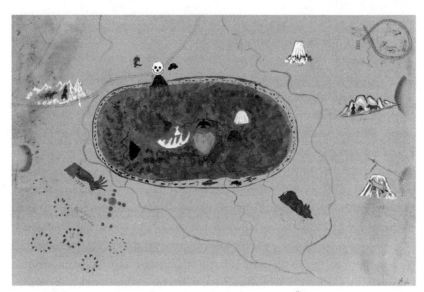

The "Dragonfly map" of the Black Hills by an unknown Lakȟóta artist circa 1940. The map shows the Black Hills area as a ceremonial complex, including the "racetrack" that surrounds it, the center, and several sacred sites around the area, such as Matȟó Pahá (Bear Butte) and Matȟó Thípila (Devil's Tower). Courtesy of Deadwood History, Inc., City of Deadwood, Don Clowser Collection, Deadwood, South Dakota.

Oyáte. Thus, Lakȟóta stories take the Lakȟóta to the Black Hills and explain Lakȟóta origins and their relationship with the universe. These stories connect the Lakȟóta to the land, the environment surrounding them, and to the sacred, wakȟáŋ. Any study of the Lakȟóta must start with the concept of wakȟáŋ. This requires a completely different mindset than the Euro-American, or Judeo-Christian, perception of God and the sacred. The Lakȟóta differentiated between the everyday world and the nonhuman, sacred world, but both worlds belonged to the same experienced universe. For the Lakȟóta there was traditionally no single God. Instead, the foundation for Lakȟóta belief is a general, animistic spiritual force or energy that manifests itself in nature in the visible and invisible worlds. This all-encompassing spirit force is known as Wakȟáŋ Tȟáŋka, sometimes translated as Great Spirit or Great Mystery. However, neither of these English terms fully captures the essence of wakȟáŋ or Wakȟáŋ Tȟáŋka. While Wakȟáŋ Tȟáŋka can be considered as a godlike or divine being or energy, it is more complex. On a fundamental level, wakȟáŋ is everything: anything that is mysterious or causes awe can be considered wakȟáŋ, be it a shooting star or a newborn baby. Above all these things is Wakȟáŋ Tȟáŋka, which encompasses everything wakȟáŋ, all the wakȟáŋ energy or force in the universe. Wakȟáŋ also reflects kinship networks, composed of human-human relationships, human-nonhuman relationships, and human-sacred relationships. Understanding these kinship relationships is another key to understanding Lakȟóta society, indeed all indigenous societies. This opens a door to their worldviews and to appreciating their agency in the past and the present, and this concept will be central to the discussion in the next chapter.

2

WAKȞÁŊ KIŊ
THE SACRED

Mitákuye Oyás'iŋ

All Lakȟóta—indeed all Sioux people—share core cultural assumptions that we examine here. That the Sioux were originally one people who shared a common culture, language, social organization, and history is supported by native oral traditions and historical documents. Around 1900, Ringing Shield (Waháčhaŋka Hotȟúŋ), an elderly Oglála holy man, explained, "The Lakȟóta all lived together a long time ago. . . . That was before there were any Oglála. All were Lakȟóta."[1] According to No Flesh (Čhoníčha Waníče), also Oglála, "Before the Seven Council Fires the Sioux Indians all made their winter camp together. Before then, in ancient times, there was a head chief of all the Sioux."[2] To be Lakȟóta meant to share certain kinship concepts as well as religious ideas and an understanding of the great mysteries that formed and animated the universe.

Kinship is foundational to Lakȟóta culture. For the Lakȟóta, all lifeforms are related, and the universe is experienced as being alive and characterized by its unity. According to Nicholas Black Elk (Heȟáka Sápa) an eminent Oglála holy man, "The Great Spirit made the Two-Legged to live like relatives with the Four-Legged and the Wings of the Air and all things that live and are green."[3] This fundamental unity or relatedness is expressed in the Lakȟóta axiom mitákuye oyás'iŋ (all my relatives, we are all related), which refers not only to relationships between human beings, but also to relationships with other species, places, objects, and indeed extends to a cosmic level to include spirits and the entire universe.[4]

Among the Lakȟóta, there was, and continues to be, a clear distinction between body and soul, although they are interrelated. The body was the great differentiator in the animist worldview of the traditional Lakȟóta, distinguishing one species or tribe from another. It was conceptualized as transient, capable of transformation in certain contexts, and likened to clothing. The word tȟaŋčháŋ refers to the body, while há refers to the skin, hide, bark, or outer casing or shell of anything. Há can also be translated as clothes or clothing, indicating the unstable and unpredictable nature of outward appearances in Lakȟóta culture. To paraphrase Gene Thin Elk, a Sičháŋǧu Lakȟóta elder and educator, Lakȟóta are not humans on a soul journey. Rather, they are naǧípi (souls) making a journey through the material world.[5]

The soul or spirit was—and still is—the basis for the Lakȟóta relational world-view, the common element that unites beings of different species. The soul is conceptualized as three or four distinct elements, depending on source. The niyá (life, breath) is the animating soul of the body, giving life to an organism and allowing for its proper biological functioning. The naǧí is the spirit or ghost, the "true soul" closest to the Western notion of soul or spirit. It is the charac-teristic, enduring essence of a person, yet mobile and capricious. It retains the idiosyncrasies and personality of its worldly, human host. The naǧí "is much like a mirror image of the person's form, at once ephemeral when seen, transparent, and capable of easy transition to and from the spirit world," notes Oglála artist Arthur Amiotte."[6]

The Lakȟóta concept of šičúŋ—the third aspect of the soul—is multifaceted. It is essentially the emitted or imparted potency of a wakȟáŋ being or spirit. Each person is given a šičúŋ at birth from the stars, but additional šičúŋ can be acquired throughout the life cycle through the vision quest and dreams. The given šičúŋ is likened to a guardian spirit. Oglála holy man Finger explains that "It remains with the body during life, to guard it from danger and help it in a wakȟáŋ manner." The šičúŋ guards against evil spirits and guides the naǧí to the land of the spirits when the person dies.[7] Another aspect of the soul is the naǧíla, which refers to nonhuman spirit or the divine spirit imminent in all beings, but this term is problematic; it is poorly documented in the literature and apparently little is known about it today.[8]

Lakȟóta author Luther Standing Bear (Matȟó Nážiŋ) sums up traditional Lakȟóta culture's animist relational worldview when he writes, "From Wakȟáŋ

Tȟáŋka there came a great unifying life force that flowed in and through all things—the flowers of the plains, blowing winds, rocks, trees, birds, animals—and was the same force that had been breathed into the first man. Thus, all things were kindred and brought together by the same Great Mystery. Kinship with all creatures of the earth, sky, and water was a real and active principle."[9]

This relational worldview effectively dissolves the boundary between what Westerners call nature and culture. According to Standing Bear, "We did not think of the great open plains, the beautiful rolling hills, and winding streams with tangled growth, as 'wild.' Only to the white man was nature a 'wilderness' and only to him was the land 'infested' with 'wild' animals and 'savage' people. To us it was tame."[10] Indeed, there is no word in the Lakȟóta language for nature as it is understood in the Euro-American sense—as a passive, impersonal, abstract domain of objects distinct and separate from human culture or society. Rather than objectivizing nature, the Lakȟóta participated in nature as full partner.[11]

The Lakȟóta considered themselves to be related to all other lifeforms and to the earth from which they came. Thus, they incorporated the entire universe into the sacred hoop of kinship. Not only was there no sharp distinction between nature and culture or society, but there was also no division between natural and supernatural, another Western assumption that is untenable according to Lakȟóta thought.[12] These foundational assumptions are the point of departure for any in-depth understanding of Lakȟóta traditions and ceremonial life but also of Lakȟóta political decisions. Understanding Lakȟóta agency in past actions, such as behavior toward whites, also requires knowledge of the role of the sacred and kinship.

Wakȟáŋ

The central intangible symbol of nineteenth-century Lakȟóta spirituality, the great animating force of the universe, and the common denominator of its oneness was wakȟáŋ—nonhuman power or energy often glossed as "medicine." Wakȟáŋ is commonly translated as sacred or holy, but early attempts at translation by Christian missionaries often obfuscate this concept, which might better be understood as mysterious, incomprehensible, or simply power or powerful. Wakȟáŋ is the force that integrates the Lakȟóta cosmos, underlying and flowing through all things in both the seen and unseen realms, and manifesting in various ways.[13]

Wakȟáŋ is deeply intertwined with the Lakȟóta animist, relational worldview. At the most fundamental level, it is the sacred, animating energy or power that imbues and unifies all things.[14] Pioneering anthropologist Alice Fletcher writes, "The earth, the four winds, the sun, moon and stars, the stones, the water, the various animals, are all exponents of a mysterious life and power encompassing the Indian and filling him with vague apprehension and desire to propitiate and induce to friendly relations. . . . The claim of relationship is used to strengthen the appeal, since the tie of kindred among the Indians is one which cannot be ignored or disregarded."[15] The words of Lakȟóta elders who lived the traditional buffalo-hunting lifestyle in the nineteenth century provide a deeper, more nuanced understanding of wakȟáŋ.

Good Seat (Tȟóyaŋke Wašté-wiŋ) was an Oglála from the White Clay district of Pine Ridge Reservation (Wazí Aháŋhaŋ Oyáŋke) born circa 1827. Around the turn of the twentieth century, she explained that wakȟáŋ was "anything that was hard to understand."[16] George Sword (Míwakȟaŋ) was an influential Oglála holy man and leader from the Wakpamni district of Pine Ridge born circa 1847. According to Sword, "The Lakȟóta understands what [wakȟáŋ] means from the things that are considered wakȟáŋ; yet sometimes its meaning must be explained to him. It is something that is hard to understand . . . anything may be wakȟáŋ if a wakȟáŋ spirit goes into it. . . . Every object in the world has a spirit and that spirit is wakȟáŋ. . . . Wakȟáŋ comes from the wakȟáŋ beings."[17]

Because of the incomprehensible nature of the wakȟáŋ, and because it often manifests itself in powerful ways that may be good or bad for humans, the wakȟáŋ was honored and revered, treated with respect, and even feared. It was generally considered to be extremely wókȟokiphe (dangerous), something that humans should not meddle with unless they are cautious and have experience with such things. The late Albert White Hat Sr., a Rosebud Lakȟóta educator and linguist, discusses the inherent dangerousness and ambivalence of wakȟáŋ things: "Every ritual we have is Wókȟokiphe. . . . The reason they say every creation is Wókȟokiphe is that everyone has a good side and an evil side. Every creation has good and bad in it, and in working with them, we might use the wrong energy. It's Wókȟokiphe because of who we are and our own good and bad sides."[18]

For Sword, Good Seat, and others of their generation, the essence of wakȟáŋ was its incomprehensibility, the fact that things, persons, or actions classified as wakȟáŋ were mysterious and powerful, defying human comprehension. Speaking of the Wakȟáŋ Tȟáŋka, the totality of all the wakȟáŋ power in the universe, Sword said "It is called Wakȟáŋ because no man can understand it."[19] The unifying force wakȟáŋ, conceived of as mysterious, sacred power or energy, was foundational to Lakȟóta thought, but it was articulated in terms of kinship, the dominant interpretive principle of Lakȟóta culture.

Wakȟáŋ Tȟáŋka

Wakȟáŋ Tȟáŋka, frequently glossed as "Great Spirit" or "Great Mystery," is perhaps the most misunderstood concept in the literature on Lakȟóta ceremonial traditions. This is largely due to syncretic confusion introduced by missionaries in early bible translations, in which they used traditional Sioux theological terms to express Christian theological ideas that were frequently incompatible with the Sioux words and concepts. This mismatch led to concept creep and a communication and enculturation disruption between generations of Lakȟóta speakers in the early twentieth century. According to Sword, "The young Oglála do not understand a formal talk by an old Lakȟóta, because the white people have changed the Lakȟóta language, and the young people speak it as the white people have written it."[20] Sword explains, "The younger Oglála mean the God of the Christians when they say Wakȟáŋ Tȟáŋka. When a shaman says Wakȟáŋ Tȟáŋka, he means the same as Wakȟáŋ Kiŋ as used in former times. This means all the Wakȟáŋ [spirits] and the Wakȟáŋpila [things like a spirit or exhibiting similar mysterious qualities], both of mankind and of other things, for the old Oglála believed that these were all the same as one."[21]

When speaking of Wakȟáŋ Tȟáŋka, the eminent Standing Rock Sioux author Vine Deloria Jr. wrote, "Only later, when Christian missionaries attempted to link Sioux traditions to their own religious systems, did this mysterious presence begin to take on human forms and demand a groveling, flattering kind of worship."[22] In a later posthumously published work Deloria discussed a more faithful or unadulterated traditional understanding of the concept that might be characterized as an animist, relational perspective: "Sioux people understood that Wakȟáŋ Tȟáŋka . . . is in everything, so that there was no doubt that humans shared certain elements with all other creatures."[23] One can argue that early missionary translations misconstrued Lakȟóta religious concepts that were originally grounded in that animist, relational worldview, forcefully altering them to fit a more Western or Eurocentric worldview, a naturalist worldview wherein a firm distinction was made between nature and culture and natural and supernatural. Both distinctions were foreign to traditional Lakȟóta culture and thought.

Rather than a personalized monotheistic deity like the Christian god, the traditional understanding of Wakȟáŋ Tȟáŋka was much more amorphous.

It was the impersonal totality of all that is mysterious in the universe; all the mysterious power or energy that connects all things, making them related, and is manifested in things, landscapes, persons, and actions that are considered incomprehensible, powerful, dangerous, sacred, or holy. Wakȟáŋ Tȟáŋka was never born and so will never die. Wakȟáŋ Tȟáŋka created the universe and everything in it, while also being embodied in the universe. Wakȟáŋ Tȟáŋka was the power that controls all things. According to the Oglála chief Little Wound (Tȟaópi Čík'ala), "The Wakȟáŋ Tȟáŋka are those which made everything. They are Wakȟáŋpi. Wakȟáŋpi are all things that are above mankind. . . . They control everything that mankind does. Mankind should please them in all things. If mankind does not please them, they will do harm to them."[24]

Since Lakȟóta spirituality is inherently idiosyncratic, experiential, and vision-based, it is natural that different Lakȟóta people conceptualized Wakȟáŋ Tȟáŋka in different ways. Around the turn of the twentieth century many Lakȟóta from Pine Ridge understood the complexity of Wakȟáŋ Tȟáŋka using a sixteen-part classification, which they referred to as Tóbtob Kiŋ (the four-times-four). Four is a sacred number in Lakȟóta culture,[25] and the four-times-four includes the most significant spirits in the Lakȟóta pantheon, including, Wí (Sun, the chief of the spirits), Haŋwí (Moon), Škáŋ or Táku Škaŋškáŋ (That Which Moves or Sky), Tȟaté (Wind), Tȟatúye Tópa or Tób Kiŋ (The Four Winds), Yumní (Whirlwind), Makȟá (Earth), Ptesáŋwiŋ/Wóȟpe (White Buffalo Woman or the Beautiful Woman), Íŋyaŋ (Rock), Wakíŋyaŋ (Thunder Being), Tȟatȟáŋka (Buffalo Bull), and Hunúŋpa (Grizzly Bear; literally, 'two-legged,' the ceremonial name for the Grizzly Bear spirit), along with the four sacred elements that comprise the Lakȟóta cosmos: Naǧí (Human Spirit), Niyá (Human Life), Naǧíla (Nonhuman Spirit), and Šičúŋ(pi) (Guardian Spirit[s]). According to Sword, "These are the names of the good Gods as they are known to the people." Some of these spirits have physical properties while others do not, some are visible while others are invisible, and still others are visible or invisible as they so choose. Each spirit has the power to do wakȟáŋ or miraculous things and is above humankind in terms of a hierarchy of power and knowledge. Collectively these sixteen spiritual entities govern the universe.[26]

While every individual had access to the sacred in Lakȟóta culture, a form of "democratized shamanism" according to Arthur Amiotte, it was religious practitioners who had the most experience with the various spirits that peopled the Lakȟóta religious landscape. Religious practitioners, known by many names and specializing in various functions, attempted to wield and control the power of Wakȟáŋ Tȟáŋka, often speaking for and representing the universe's nonhuman entities.[27]

Wičháša Wakȟáŋ: Holy Men

Wičháša wakȟáŋ (holy men) and medicine men or pȟežúta wičháša (herbalists) were those who specialized in the wakȟáŋ. Historically, Lakȟóta religious leaders were part-time practitioners. They utilized helper spirits, mediated between worlds, and were believed to leave their bodies and enter trance states in ritual contexts. In nineteenth-century Lakȟóta ceremonial practice, a holy man might have spirit helpers that were seen as subservient, owned by the practitioner, who referred to them using possessive forms. A spirit served its human master much like a faithful dog would, the two parties sharing a kinship relationship defined in terms of kȟolátakuya (friendship).[28] Likewise, as Ella Deloria explains about the related Dakȟóta, "[The] attitude towards the medium or source of his power was, as nearly as I can tell, something like a master's towards a faithful servant—one of affectionate dependence. I have heard of a holy man, for example, speaking sharply to his medium for overdoing a thing; much as you might scold a dog you love for barking too hard and frightening someone who is not used to him."[29]

Like Lakȟóta spirituality, traditional Lakȟóta healing practice was inherently individualistic and idiosyncratic, but also fluid and undogmatic. It was often based on visions and revelatory experiences, and hence open to innovation and practical adaptation. That said, however, there were and continue to be specialized types of practitioners who used specific medicines and techniques, conducted specific ceremonies, and were affiliated with specific illnesses, treatments, and spirits.[30]

Two significant and intersecting levels of practitioner classification are those who work via spirit guardian or nonhuman power source and those who operate based on ability, method, practice, and technique. The classification of Lakȟóta healers is complicated, defying simplistic and neat categorization. Beginning with the earliest sources on Sioux spirituality a distinction has been made between three types of practitioners: (1) holy men or prophets, (2) conjurors, and (3) herbalists or doctors. Within each of these categories there is great variation, innovation, and numerous subcategories, and the categories are cumulative, permeable, often overlapping with indistinct boundaries, and not mutually exclusive.[31] The first distinction to be made is between wičháša wakȟáŋ (holy men) and medicine men, who were really pȟežúta wičháša (herbalists).

Holy men or prophets were those old, wise men who had accumulated many spirit guardians, abilities, powers, and ceremonial knowledge throughout their lives. They obtained or attained visions of the most powerful spirits, often the celestial or sky deities, such as the Sun, Wind, and Sky. Holy men underwent rigorous and lengthy training with other more experienced and established holy men. Through the master-apprentice model it took years to learn the ways of the holy men and how to perform the Lakȟóta rituals. Holy men also had to perform initiation rites, such as the wakȟáŋ wačhípi (mystery dance) and the wiwáŋyaŋg wačhípi (Sun Dance). In addition, they were the repositories of sacred knowledge, including social customs, philosophy, myth, ritual, songs, and techniques.[32]

Holy men typically had multiple successful vision haŋbléčheyapi (fasts) and had to dance a particularly trying form of the Sun Dance as a prerequisite to becoming a holy man. According to three Oglála sources, "If one wishes to become a shaman of the highest order, he should dance the Sun Dance suspended from the pole so that his feet will not touch the ground."[33] Communicating with the spirits and interpreting their wills for the people was a major responsibility of Lakȟóta holy men. They were also tasked with directing the major collective ceremonies, and they alone could alter or prohibit a given ceremony. Holy men were the only ones who could be masters in the master-apprentice model and were frequently the leaders of dream societies that brought together people—men and women—who had experienced similar visions.[34]

Through the proper rituals, prayers, and songs Lakȟóta holy men could infuse a person or inanimate object with tȟúŋ (endowed mystical power or quality; power to do miraculous things; essence; potency; potentiality) or tȟuŋwáŋ (potency), rendering them powerful. Common objects infused with tȟúŋ or tȟuŋwáŋ included weapons, charms, and ceremonial paints. The most important category of objects was personal ceremonial or "medicine" bags or bundles, usually owned and carried by men in battle or by religious specialists, and variously referred to as šičúŋ, wašíčuŋ, or wóphiye. Each holy man typically had his own ceremonial bundle or implement containing the šičúŋ (spiritual essence, potency) or tȟúŋ of his spirit guardian, which was prayed over, invoked, and utilized in his wakȟáŋ doings.[35] As George Sword, Bad Wound (Oóšiča Hokšíla), No Flesh, and Thomas Tyon explained, "A shaman must always have his wašíčuŋ and must always use it in a ceremony. It is a God. . . . The wašíčuŋ is like the God whose power it has. . . . A shaman has his songs and his formulae. He has a song and formula for each God."[36] According to Sword, "When the holy man treats the sick, he performs a ceremony and invokes his ceremonial bag and the familiar (šičúŋ) in it does what he asks it to do."[37]

Holy men were often diviners or prophets, and hence they were the prognosticators of the Lakȟóta people. Those who could foretell the future were held in high esteem, and the preeminent holy men were often those who started out in life as great warriors but were changed by portentous visions. They gained power through vision fasting and sacrifice. Holy men diagnosed sickness to discern its cause and nature, identify who was most qualified to cure it, and prescribe and proscribe courses of treatment.[38] Some holy men had the ability to divine the future, locate lost objects or people, control and manipulate the weather, and call animals closer to camp in times of famine and scarcity. Some extremely powerful holy men could transform their physical appearance, ward off evil influences, and provide magical protection to their patients and clients. It is unlikely that a single holy man could have obtained, acquired, or mastered all the abilities and techniques, but certainly some exceptional individuals mastered and practiced many of them.[39]

According to Sword:

> Wičháša wakȟáŋ (holy man, or shaman) is made by other shamans by ceremony and teaching that which a shaman should know. . . . A shaman governs all the ceremonies of the Lakȟóta, so he must know them. He must know iyé wakȟáŋ (holy language, or the language of the shamans), and haŋblóglaka (spirit language). . . . The oldest or wisest shamans are the most respected. A shaman should conduct the larger ceremonies, but anyone may perform the smaller. . . . There are many diseases that only a shaman can cure. He does this with his wašíčuŋ [sacred bundle] and not with medicines.[40]

The distinguishing features of Lakȟóta holy men are clearer when compared with those of the pȟežúta wičháša.

Pȟežúta wičháša (herbalists, literally, "medicine man") may be conceived of as the medical doctors, physicians, or pharmacists of Lakȟóta society. They differed from holy men in several key ways. Typically, medicine men or herbalists did not utilize ceremonial bundles in their practice; rather, they utilized medicine bundles that contained herbs and various pharmacopeia used in their treatment of mainly physical ailments. They did not usually possess bundles with the most potent spirit powers or prepare and consecrate sacred bundles for others. Unlike holy men, medicine men usually did not direct large collective ceremonies, nor act as intermediaries between humans and nonhumans. They were not usually the leaders of the dream societies or at the top of the religious hierarchy in Lakȟóta society, nor did they train apprentices.[41]

Medicine men were individuals with knowledge of plants and herbs and their medicinal use and value. This knowledge could be shared by a spirit in a vision, but could also be learned, inherited, or purchased from other practitioners. As No Flesh explains, "The medicine men learn their medicines from the spirits in a vision. The spirits tell them what to use and how to use it. Their medicines are nearly always herbs (watȟó) or roots (ȟutkȟáŋ). Therefore, all their medicines are called grass roots (pȟežúta)."[42] Hence, in Lakȟóta, this practitioner category is called pȟežúta wičháša (literally, grass roots [medicine] man).

Sources of power are an important distinction between holy men and medicine men. A holy man treated the sick and performed his wakȟáŋ wičhóȟʼaŋ (ceremonies) using his wašíčuŋ (ceremonial bundle), which was the šíčuŋ of a wičháša wakȟáŋ (holy man). A medicine man, on the other hand, treated the sick and performed his doctoring rites using his ožúha pȟežúta (medicine bag), which, along with the medicines and medical implements and paraphernalia contained therein, was the šíčúŋ of a medicine man or pȟežúta wičháša (herbalist). While there was and is a spiritual element in all Lakȟóta healing practice, medicine men were not considered the great spiritual leaders of the Lakȟóta.[43] According to Standing Bear, "A medicine-man was simply a healer—curing, or trying to cure, such few diseases and ailments as beset his people in the body, having nothing to do with their spiritual suffering. A medicine-man was no holier than other men, no closer to Wakȟáŋ Tȟáŋka and no more honored than a brave or a scout."[44]

The treatment methods of medicine men tended to be more physiological, more empirical or practical, than those utilized by holy men to treat more psychological or spiritual ailments. As Sword explains, "When the medicine man treats the sick, his medicines must be swallowed or smoked or steamed."[45] Although the medicines they used were often revealed in a dream or trance state, the medicine man's practice was based largely on accumulated, systematic knowledge of the natural world, physiology, and trial and error akin to contemporary conceptions of Western biomedicine.

Some medicine men had and utilized only one medicine, while for others it was many. Because there were many types of medicines, there were numerous types or subcategories of medicine men, each associated with the specific sicknesses they treated and the medicines they used. According to Tyon, William Garnett,

Thunder Bear (Matȟó Wakíŋyaŋ), Sword, and John Blunt Horn (Hé Wótoka), "If one wants to become a medicine man he seeks a vision, and if he sees the right thing it will instruct him what he must do. It will also instruct him what medicine he must use. Then when he has related his vision to the wise men [holy men], they will tell him what he must do. When they have instructed him, he will belong to a cult in medicine [dream society]."[46] Typically, the training process of a medicine man was shorter and much less rigorous than that of a holy man.

Waphíya wičháša, commonly glossed in English as conjuror or healer, are the third type of Lakȟóta religious practitioner and they reflect characteristics and methods of both medicine men and holy men. They tended to use both scientific-empirical methods and spiritual-nonempirical methods in their practice, and treated physical or physiological ailments as well as psychological, psychosomatic, or spiritual sickness.[47]

Conjurors primarily treated victims of waȟmúŋǧa (sorcery), often using some form of the yaǧópa/yapȟá technique, a technique that extracted sickness either by blowing or sucking it out using the mouth, a bone tube, or some other hollow object. Once the illness was located in the body and extracted, it was presented to the patient in the form of a physical object, such as a worm, bug, feather, fingernail, toenail, phlegm, or blood. According to Ella Deloria:

> When a person is ill and nobody seems to know why, someone says, "Perhaps someone has thrown a projectile of poison into him." And sometimes it is said to be an animal, a mole usually, who has done this. Then a skilled doctor comes in and draws the offending piece, usually a tufted bit of something said to be very potent, from the patient. The object is said to be sucked out, from anywhere it is lodged, by the mere touch of the doctor's lips on the body, and a quick intake of breath.[48]

Conjurors were also known for producing powerful charms and potions. At the request of their patients and clientele—and for a handsome price—conjurors concocted powerful and alluring wiíčhuwa (love medicines), often made from an extracted hair of the target or a sample of menstrual flow; good-luck charms for success in gambling, games, and hunting; or deadly poisons. According to Sword, a wakȟáŋ škáŋ wičháša (evil conjuror who causes sickness) "makes charms and philters and he may make very deadly potions. He is in league with the great evil one. He can do mysterious things to anyone, either present or far away. The things he does or makes are not medicines. He makes charms to win games or to kill enemies, or to win the love of men and women."[49]

Many varieties of conjurors existed in Lakȟóta society, known by the method or technique used and their nonhuman power source. Those who dreamt of Toad, Bear, Bird, Fish, Heyókȟa (Contrary), and Double Woman were particularly associated with the conjuror category, as well as the mysterious and menacing Hohú Yuhá (Bone Keepers) discussed by Tyon. Apparently, dreaming of certain things, mainly terrestrial creatures or animals that roamed the earth, compelled an individual to become a conjuror. As Tyon explains, "The dreams they have of animals are what cause them to believe they are doctors."[50]

The training of a waphíya wičháša was more rigorous than that of a medicine man, but less extreme than that of a holy man. Conjurors typically mastered various herbalist techniques and went on to accumulate multiple abilities, methods, powers, and spirit guardians through additional vision quests and apprenticeships with other reputable conjurors or holy men. Usually, conjurors were not experts on Lakȟóta mythology, philosophy, and sacred lore; did not have extensive or comprehensive ritual knowledge; and did not direct major ceremonies. In nearly every respect, the waphíya wičháša occupied an intermediate space between the medicine man and the holy man. A key feature distinguishing conjurors from the other practitioner categories is that they often treated their patients and manufactured their charms and potions in darkness and secrecy, sometimes for malevolent purposes.[51]

Wíŋyaŋ Wakȟáŋ: Holy Women

Religion and medicine were largely male concerns. Typically, men were the religious leaders and doctors, the seekers of visions, the intermediaries who controlled relations between humans and nonhumans, and the directors of the major religious ceremonies. Women had little involvement in these matters, although they were essential participants in ceremonies. For instance, most ceremonies included female singers called wičháglata who sang the high harmonies along with the male singers and dressed in their finest regalia for ritual performances. Some women became healers and spiritual leaders after menopause, but they did not typically direct ceremonies before that life change.[52] Standing Bear characterized his grandmother as a medicine woman, writing that "She prepared all food for the sick and looked after them; she kept the bags of herbs and made the teas which she gave us to drink, and when we children got hurt she bound our wounds or bruises and dried our childish tears."[53]

In traditional Lakȟóta culture and thought a woman's major sacred or mysterious power revolved around her ability to create and sustain life through conception, childbirth, and child rearing. Male sacred power was thought of as active, while female sacred power was passive. This passive or receptive power, like all wakȟáŋ power, was conceptualized as potentially dangerous, but also as conflicting with the aggressive or active power characteristic of men. For these reasons, various abstinence taboos existed, and the religious lives of men and women were distinct. The female power to create life, give birth, and nurse was tied to menstruation. According to Ella Deloria, menstrual blood gave a woman a temporary wakȟáŋ power that was not polluting but rather at odds with male power. A woman's menstrual power clashed with male spiritual power. For this reason, women had to be secluded in išnáthi (menstrual lodges) and avoid men during their periods and were especially not permitted to attend any type of ceremony.[54] Deloria writes, "Medicine is rendered impotent by the presence of a woman who is menstruating. So they are very careful to stay away from sickness if they have their flow. A woman who knows herself to be in that state and yet goes to see the sick is said to be cruel."[55]

Women did not typically go on formal vision quests, at least not in the same capacity as men. Nevertheless, some women had visions that gave them power and knowledge to use herbs to cure bodily ailments, to act as midwives, or to make charms to protect pregnant women and growing children. Visions might also give women specific powers to masterfully execute quill or beadwork designs, specifically visions of Double Woman, the mythical character who first taught Lakȟóta women to dye quills and do quillwork. Like men, women who had visions of religious significance could band together into dream societies, such as the Double Woman dreamers and Women's Medicine society.[56]

Standing Bear explained how Double Woman dreamers might also use their knowledge and power to become healers: "According to legend, a woman once had a vision in which she saw the Laughing Woman, or Double Woman, as she was also known. The Laughing Woman gave her laugh with its magic power to the Dreamer so that she might use it in curing the sick and ailing. Thenceforth the Laugh Dreamer became a medicine-woman, curing many people with the magic laugh."[57] Like all wakȟáŋ power, Double Woman's power was a double-edged sword, potentially dangerous and antisocial. Some Double Woman dreamers were promiscuous, using their powers to seduce men, which was considered dishonorable and unbefitting a proper Lakȟóta woman.

According to Black Elk, "Every man can cry for a vision, or 'lament'; and in the old days we all—men and women—'lamented' all the time. . . . Our women also 'lament,' after first purifying themselves in the Inípi [sweat lodge]; they are helped by other women, but they do not go up on a very high and lonely mountain. They go up on a hill in a valley, for they are women and need protection."[58] Standing Bear corroborates that women had sweat lodges and purified themselves in the same way men did.[59] However, typically men and women sweat separately.

Standing Bear described a wíŋyaŋ wakȟáŋ "holy woman," a woman who was reverenced and honored by the people for her special powers and abilities and considered a great benefactor of her tribe. When she went to cure, she carried with her a doll made of buffalo hide and filled with buffalo wool (haŋpóšpu hokšíčala). She had her own medicine song, she could bring the rain and ward away evil, cure the sick, and prophesize events. She was the "only woman allowed to make and decorate war shields for the warriors. It was she who in a dream was given the game Tȟahúka čhaŋgléška [hoop game], and the knowledge of dyeing porcupine quills and sewing them into designs," recalled Standing Bear, continuing, "with her magic power she could hurt us if she willed, and we had no defense, for her power was invisible. This was called ȟmúŋǧa [to bewitch someone or something]."[60] Standing Bear had seen a medicine-woman play with a medicine-man, each throwing invisible missiles at the other and each trying to ward off the blows. He could not see what went through the air, but the injured one had great pain, and suffered until relieved by his or her own powers.[61]

Today many Lakȟóta women seek visions in the traditional manner for guidance, medicine, and to become herbalists, and some also participate in the Sun Dance. Mrs. George White Bull and Mrs. Mary Fast Horse were two female Lakȟóta herbalists from Pine Ridge who practiced in the 1950s and 1960s. Mrs. White Bull treated people for arthritic conditions, among other ailments, using medicines consisting of dried roots, flowers, and leaves. Mrs. Fast Horse was well versed in the gathering of various medicines and their healing properties. She had been given the power by medicine men to gather and use pȟežúta pȟá (bitter medicine), made from the dried leaves and flowers of golden prairie clover, and sometimes mixed with ičáȟpe hú ("rubs against root" or purple coneflower) to treat a variety of ailments, particularly kidney, liver, and venereal diseases.[62]

Wačhékiya: Prayer and Sacred Ceremonies

Prayer was the basis of all Lakȟóta ceremonies, the established method by which humans related to nonhumans and typically associated with the čhaŋnúŋpa (pipe), the preeminent means of prayer given to the people by White Buffalo Woman along with instructions on its use. The Lakȟóta word for prayer is wačhékiya, a complex concept that means both "to call on someone for aid" and "to address someone using a kin term." The stem of wačhékiya is čhékiya "to beg; to cry, weep, or wail to someone or something." Prayer was conceptualized and interpreted in terms of kinship. It was an invocation of relationship, often accompanied by cries, tears, and sacrifices of objects, or physical suffering.[63] Through wačhékiya, nonhumans or spirits "could be counted on to answer with due respect, honor, and dignity as a man to his relative."[64]

Wačhékiya refers more specifically to smoking or offering the pipe ceremonially. When the pipe is ritually filled in this context, pinches of tobacco are offered to each of the four directions and to the above and below; hence the entire universe is symbolized, present and ready to participate. According to Charging Thunder (Wakíŋyaŋ Wathákpe), a chief at Standing Rock (Íŋyaŋ Woslál He) in the early 1900s, "When we hold the pipe toward the sky, we are offering it to Wakȟáŋ Tȟáŋka. We offer it to the earth because that is our home and we are thankful to be here; we offer it to the east, south, west, and north because those are the homes of the four winds; a storm may come from any direction, therefore we wish to make peace with the winds that bring the storms."[65]

When smoked or offered in the proper ceremonial fashion, the supplicant's prayers, thoughts, and desires travel upward to the spirits in the exhaled smoke. The thúŋ (spiritual essence) of White Buffalo Woman herself is said to be present in the pipe smoke. As Sword explained, "The spirit is soothed by smoking the pipe. . . . The spirit of the God [White Buffalo Woman] is in the smoke of any pipe if the pipe is smoked in the proper manner." The preparation of the smoking material and the filling of the pipe are important parts of the pipe offering ceremony and may be accompanied by prayer and songs. The ceremonial pipe should be lit with a phetáǧa (live coal), not an open flame, and must be smoked until all the contents are consumed. "When a pipe is smoked in this manner, the spirit that is in the smoke goes with it into the mouth and body and then it comes out and goes upward. When this spirit is in the body, it soothes the spirit of the smoker. When it goes upward, it soothes the God. So the God and the spirit are as friends. . . . The Lakȟóta should smoke the pipe first when considering any matter of importance. . . . The first rite in any ceremony of the Lakȟóta should be to smoke the pipe."[66] Thus, while offering the pipe was a ritual, it was also an essential preliminary to all other rituals.

Along with the gift of the sacred pipe, White Buffalo Woman taught the people the original sacred ceremonies. Depending on the source, this might be four, five, or seven distinct rituals. There were individual or personal rituals and collective ceremonies, some of which were compound rituals consisting of several lesser rites. The pipe ceremony and sweat lodge were common preliminary ceremonies. Many rituals were performed to please or placate the spirits and to secure their favor through prayer, offerings, and sacrifice.[67]

Little Wound, American Horse, and Lone Star (Wičháȟpi Waŋžíla) explained, "The Oglála do ceremonies because this pleases the Gods. Some ceremonies please some of the Gods and other ceremonies please other Gods. A shaman has authority over all ceremonies. A shaman should conduct all the greater ceremonies. . . . A simple ceremony may affect only the one who does it. . . . Some ceremonies affect all the people. In such ceremonies all the people have a part to do. If the people do not do their part in such ceremonies, the Gods will be angry."[68]

The idiosyncratic, antidogmatic nature of traditional Lakȟóta religion leads to different interpretations and classifications of ritual. An important factor in ritual variation is that visions received by religious leaders could necessitate changes in existing ceremonies or the creation of new ones. In 1896, Little Wound, chief of the Khiyáksa band, described the different ceremonies:

> They have dances for war and for peace; for victory and defeat; for chase and for ripe fruits; for enjoyment and for mourning; for going away and for returning; for warriors and for all the people; for the societies and for individuals; for men and for women; for widows and for maidens; for shamans. . . . The sacred dances are the Dance for the Dead, the Scalp Dance, the Holy Dance, and the Sun Dance. . . . Each dance has its songs. . . . The music of the songs is different for each dance.[69]

In 1896, when Sword described the Lakȟóta foundational ceremonies, he explained that each ceremony had to be carefully performed exactly as it was taught or else it would be inefficacious and could cause great harm or misfortune. According to Sword, "The ceremonies of the Lakȟóta are the ceremonies of the people, the ceremonies of the warriors, and the ceremonies of the shamans."[70] He describes the ritual elements common in Lakȟóta ceremonial practice: "There are some ceremonies that must be understood before one can understand other ceremonies. These are soothing the spirit, strengthening the ghost, pleasing the God, and learning the will of the God."[71] Soothing the spirit refers to the pipe ceremony, strengthening the ghost is the sweat lodge, pleasing the God refers to wazílya or incensing with sweetgrass or sage, and learning the will of the God refers to the vision quest or vision fast. Little Wound, Sword, and others of their generation clearly had a similar understanding of ritual, yet it was less structured and more idiosyncratic than it is today.

Ella Deloria provides the most complex and detailed classification of Lakȟóta ritual to date. She hypothesized that all the Sioux groups shared common ceremonies but that each performed them in distinctive ways. "The original ceremonies (according to the legend of the Oglála) are three in number; but others also were strongly in existence for longer periods than anyone could say."[72] She lists more than twenty separate rituals, generally distinguishing among four sometimes overlapping categories: (1) general ceremonies, (2) esoteric ceremonies, (3) individual ceremonies, and (4) other ceremonies, local and temporal.[73]

Seven Foundational Ceremonies

Oglála holy man and Catholic catechist Nicholas Black Elk described the coming of White Buffalo Woman, the gift of the sacred pipe, the pipe ceremony or offering, and chronicled the "seven" communal rituals central to Oglála religious practice as (1) wanáǧi yuhápi (keeping of the soul or ghost keeping), (2) inípi (rite of purification or sweat lodge), (3) haŋbléčheyapi (crying for a vision or vision quest), (4) wiwáŋyaŋg wačhípi (Sun Dance), (5) huŋkápi (making of relatives), (6) išnáthi awíčhalowaŋpi (preparing a girl for womanhood or the buffalo sing), and (7) tȟápa waŋkáyeyapi (throwing of the ball).[74]

Aside from the pipe offering ceremony, the most basic Lakȟóta ceremony is the iníkaǧapi (sweat lodge, freely translated as "life renewal"), a purification ceremony. Like offering the pipe, the sweat lodge is a ritual itself and a preliminary to and conclusion of all other ceremonies. It is held in a low, dome-shaped lodge, typically constructed of willows and covered with hides or, more recently, blankets and tarps. Nearby a firepit is dug in which rocks are heated until they are glowing red hot, and then ritually transported to a pit dug in the center of the lodge. The participants sit around the lodge periphery, and when all the rocks are in the pit, the door is closed, and the ritual begins. Incense of sage, sweetgrass, or cedar is sprinkled on the rocks and then water is poured from a dipper onto the heated stones. Steam rises thickly as the intense heat and pitch dark surround the participants. There are typically four rounds in which prayers are said, songs are sung, and the pipe is passed and smoked communally. After each round the door is opened, letting in cool, fresh air.[75]

The vision fast or haŋbléčheyapi (vision quest) was a ritual means to learn one's destiny or path in life and to learn the will of the spirits in relation to the person or their community. It was essential for success in any endeavor. Typically, a young man would seek a vision around the time of puberty, when his voice changed. After the preliminary sweat bath, a holy man, the vision seeker's mentor, would lead him to a lonely hilltop away from human habitation where he would fast for as long as four days and four nights. He made himself pitiable before the spirits, crying and praying with a filled and sealed pipe for aid and guidance. Spirits might appear, in human or animal form, taking him on a journey in the spirit, and offering him knowledge or power for war or curing. After the vision experience, the seeker returned to camp and underwent another sweat bath, during which he would relate his vision to the holy man who sponsored his vision quest, who would help him interpret its meaning. The true meaning of the vision might not be apparent for many years, becoming clearer only through contemplation; any powers originating with the vision remained dormant until they were activated, usually through a public ritual performance.[76]

The wiwáŋyaŋg wačhípi (Sun Dance) was the most important collective calendrical ritual. It was typically held at the peak of summer, when the bands would come together, and it publicly celebrated tribal unity. The high point was reached in a dance held around the čháŋwakȟáŋ (sacred tree). In the Sun Dance, the dancer was attached to the sacred tree with a rawhide thong looped around a stick inserted through pairs of slits in the chest or back. The goal was to dance and pull against the thong until the skin tore and the dancer was released. No food or drink was allowed; the pain and suffering helped the dancer reach another world. Self-mortification convinced the spirits of the dancer's sincerity and pitifulness. Originally a warrior's ceremony to obtain power over enemies, it also functioned as a prayer for abundance and increase of both the people and the buffalo. The Sun Dance was a preeminent compound ritual, with many lesser rites performed in association with it, such as naming and ear-piercing ceremonies, as well as more secular or social events such as feasting, dancing, and courtship.[77]

The huŋká (hunka) was a ritual adoption ceremony. During the dance, wands decorated with eagle feathers or the skin of a mallard duck were swung over the heads of participants who became ritually related to one another through the performance. Originally the huŋká was an intertribal adoption ceremony, as most Plains tribes had some version of it, but it was also used intratribally to forge relationships and honor families. The huŋká relationship was said to be even stronger and more enduring than blood relationships and this is true even today. The huŋká ceremony regained importance in the late twentieth century, and for many it is a way to help relatives in need.[78]

The tȟatȟáŋka lowáŋpi (buffalo sing), sometimes referred to as the išnáthi awíčhalowaŋpi (preparing a girl for womanhood), was the women's puberty or

"Sun Dance Ceremony" by Walter Bone Shirt (Hohú Ógle) also known as Never Misses, Sičháŋǧu (Brulé), circa 1890, Plate 2. The image portrays a man in full regalia blowing a whistle during a Sun Dance ceremony. Offerings are hanging from the sacred tree. Courtesy of Walter Bone Shirt Ledger, Archives and Special Collections, Maureen and Mike Mansfield Library, the University of Montana–Missoula.

coming-of-age ceremony. Typically, the buffalo sing was performed by a buffalo dreamer. The ceremony taught girls the virtues of Lakȟóta womanhood, including modesty, generosity, and industriousness. During the ritual, the young woman's hair was braided in the proper fashion of adult women, the part was painted with sacred red paint, and an eagle plume attached. The girl was also taught the proper way for a woman to sit, with her knees together, legs beneath her, and feet out to one side.[79]

The wanáǧi yuhápi (spirit-keeping ceremony) was performed upon the death of a relative, often a child, and was a means of delaying the departure of the wanáǧi (spirit) to the spirit world. A ghost dreamer typically officiated, cutting a lock of the deceased's hair and attaching it to a wooden effigy representing the deceased, which was dressed in the appropriate clothing and wrapped in a special ghost bundle. The bundle was then treated as if it were alive, as if it was the deceased relative. A family member vowed to be the ghost keeper and was tasked with feeding, smudging, and ritually caring for the bundle daily. Typically, this was done for a year concluding with a large feast and giveaway to honor the deceased. At the climax of the ritual, the holy man would unwrap the bundle in dramatic fashion, releasing the spirit to travel to the spirit world.[80]

Tȟápa waŋkáyeyapi (throwing of the ball) is a lesser-known ceremony and a bit of a mystery because it is not well documented in the literature or oral traditions. There is speculation that Black Elk included this as the seventh major ceremony because the number seven reflected the influence of Roman Catholicism on his thinking. There is also speculation that he included the throwing of the ball rather than yuwípi, a much more common ceremony, because the overtly occult or spiritualist elements of yuwípi would have been viewed negatively by the Jesuit missionaries at Pine Ridge at the time. In any case, the throwing of the ball apparently originated as a puberty ceremony or sacred competition in which a girl tossed a ball to the four directions. The quest for the ball was likened to the quest for Wakȟáŋ Tȟáŋka (spiritual enlightenment), and those who caught the ball were said to receive blessings.[81]

While there were many other ceremonies integral to Lakȟóta ceremonial life, including many related to the ritual (re)enactment of visions and to dream societies, one important ritual that deserves mention is yuwípi. Yuwípi (wrapped up) is a conjuring ceremony that developed from older ritual forms but was especially adaptable to the reservation setting. In the yuwípi ceremony a holy man is wrapped in a hide, quilt, or blanket and bound head to foot. Once he is wrapped and bound, the lights are extinguished, and sacred songs are sung to the accompaniment of the drum. The practitioner calls on his helper spirits, and when they arrive, their presence is announced by mysterious blue sparks and the shaking of gourd rattles, apparently animated by the spirits themselves. The holy man communicates with the spirits, discovering the location of enemies, bison, lost objects, or people. Sometimes the spirits predict the future or explain how to cure certain illnesses. At the ceremony's conclusion the lights are rekindled, and the practitioner sits calmly in the center of the ritual space, the blanket and ropes used to bind him folded at his side, the belief being that the spirits freed him. Lowáŋpi (sings) is a similar ritual in which the practitioner is not bound; both rituals are held in the dark, usually at night, for the purposes of healing the sick, finding lost objects, or foretelling the future. On Lakȟóta reservations today, yuwípi, along with the sweat lodge, is the most common life-crisis ritual, while the Sun Dance is the most common calendrical ritual. Over the past century or so, Lakȟóta beliefs and rituals have been under tremendous pressure and have changed dramatically, but this should not be interpreted as an end of traditional Lakȟóta religion and culture. Change, adaptability, and renewal are foundational to the Lakȟóta belief system, and all forms of ritual are intertwined with kinship (wótakuye)—the critical underpinning of Lakȟóta society and culture.[82]

3

WÓTAKUYE

KINSHIP AND SOCIAL ORGANIZATION

"A Scheme of Life That Worked": The Sacred Hoop of Kinship

Wótakuye (kinship) presented the Lakȟóta with the most important obligations in social life. It was the basis of sociopolitical unity and the mechanism by which the people lived together harmoniously with decency and order. Ella Deloria characterized the Dakȟóta, and by extension the Lakȟóta, kinship system as "a scheme of life that worked."[1] "Kinship was the all-important matter. Its demands and dictates for all phases of social life were relentless and exact; but, on the other hand, its privileges and honorings and rewarding prestige were not only tolerable but downright pleasant and desirable for all who conformed."[2] Further, "the ultimate aim of Dakȟóta life, stripped of accessories, was quite simple: One must obey kinship rules; one must be a good relative. No Dakȟóta who has participated in that life will dispute that."[3] Dakȟóta and Lakȟóta kinship is based upon feeling and acting, attitudes and behavior, not just upon biology or genealogical connections and marriage. It embraces all significant social interaction.[4]

Kinship transcended biological relatedness, providing a mechanism for incorporating everyone into the network of relatives. Through kinship the Sioux people were held together in a great network of relationship that extended beyond tribal boundaries outward to the rest of the universe. This all-inclusive sacred hoop of relationship is expressed by the Lakȟóta axiom mitákuye oyás'iŋ (all my relatives, we are all related). Luther Standing Bear writes, "Kinship with all creatures of the earth, sky, and water was a real and active principle." Through kinship the Lakȟóta maintained civility, good manners, and a sense of responsibility toward all individuals, human and nonhuman. In any Lakȟóta camp any individual could easily make a connection to a relative, even if the visit was only temporary. Typically, at least one blood relative could be identified, no matter how distant, and through that relative an entire network of relatives by marriage became available. In Lakȟóta society everyone shared relations by marriage with his or her own blood relatives.[5]

In traditional Lakȟóta society kin terms structured all social interaction, and order was maintained in daily life through the kinship system. Kin terms were signals for culturally prescribed behavior patterns. There were two main types of relatives: those who centered on the thítakuye (family of birth, "lodge/band relatives") and those who centered on the takúye (family of marriage "relatives").[6] In the Lakȟóta kinship system a man is equated with his brothers and male parallel cousins, while a woman is equated with her sisters and female parallel cousins.[7] Relationships between brothers (including siblings and parallel cousins) were extremely close—the strongest social bond in Lakȟóta society. Relationships between sisters (again, including siblings and parallel cousins) were close, but not as close as those between brothers. Parallel cousins, that is the children of a father's brother and a mother's sister, were treated as siblings. Between same-sex siblings and cousins there should be friendly cooperation and an absence of competition. Historically, relationships between opposite-sex siblings and cousins (hakáta) were characterized by conspicuous respect and partial avoidance, to the degree that by the age of about seven, brothers and sisters did not look at nor speak to one another directly. According to Standing Bear, "The ties of sentiment between brother and sister were strong; nevertheless, no Lakȟóta boy ever spoke directly to his sisters or girl cousins. This rule of conduct a Lakȟóta boy dared not violate, for to do so was showing the utmost disrespect for them. If several boys and girls were playing a game together, and a brother wished to tell his sister something, he would either ask some of the playmates to carry his message for him or else shout it so all could hear."[8]

Even more rigorous avoidance characterized the relationship between a man and his mother-in-law and a woman and her father-in-law. These relatives were strictly prohibited from speaking directly to each other or looking into one another's faces. The relationship between a man and his father-in-law was one of partial avoidance, while a woman and her mother-in-law shared a respect relationship that permitted cooperation and relatively free communication. These stricter relationships were juxtaposed with those between opposite-sex siblings-in-law, which were characterized by obligatory joking, with sexual overtones. This prescribed sexual joking reflected the common practice in traditional Lakȟóta society of the levirate and sororate, in which a man may marry his deceased brother's widow and a woman may marry her deceased sister's widower respectively.[9]

One of the distinguishing features of the Lakȟóta kinship system is bifurcate merging, which means that one's biological parents are merged with their same-sex siblings. Therefore, in addition to one's biological mother and father, there are any number of men and women who are called até (father) and iná (mother), and one would interact with those individuals in the same way as with a biological mother and father. All the men whom one's father refers to as brother or cousin are called father, and all the women whom one's mother refers to as sister or cousin are called mother. Only one's mother's brothers and cousins are called lekší (uncle), and only one's father's sisters and cousins are called tȟuŋwíŋ (aunt).[10] According to Rosebud Sioux elder and educator Albert White Hat Sr., "Our children always have several couples as parents, any of whom would take them in and raise them without question. A child grows up knowing them all and would not feel strange or lonely if raised by someone other than natural parents. A boy has role models in his father, his father's brothers, his cousins, a girl in her mother, her mother's sisters, and cousins."[11]

This bifurcate merging has implications in an individual's own generation. Anyone who is the child of someone referred to as father or mother is called brother or sister. Therefore, Lakȟóta who live by the traditional kinship rules have many people whom they refer to as brother and sister beyond their biological siblings. One would interact with these auxiliary siblings in the same way as with biological siblings. All relatives called by the same term were to be treated in a like manner, whether biological relatives or not. Further, because relatives by marriage are shared, an individual had actual and potential relatives practically everywhere.[12]

There were also various kinds of fictive kin in Lakȟóta society, and these relationships were considered no less real or important than biological ones. The huŋká ceremony could be performed to ritually adopt a member of another thiyóšpaye or even tribe. Two males could formally establish a bond of friendship that was even more binding than that with a sibling. They called one another kȟolá (friend) and exchanged horses and other gifts to mark the occasion.

Possessions were exchanged freely between men in a khólá relationship, and sometimes they even exchanged wives. Similarly, two females might enter a formalized friend relationship, in which they would refer to one another as mitȟáwaše (my female friend), an archaic form of maške (female friend [of a woman]), which is more common today.[13]

The kinship system was complex and exacting. It was central to Lakȟóta etiquette as a means of being courteous, gracious, and kind—of showing goodwill. Kin terms were always the proper form of address and reference because it was considered rude to call someone by a personal name. Therefore, rather than saying "Standing Bear," the more appropriate utterance would be, for example, "my uncle, Standing Bear" or simply "my uncle." Further, it was improper to engage in conversation with anyone without first using the proper kin term, so people were careful to know the right terms for each person. Kin terms were symbols, bundles of meaning obligating individuals to engage with relatives according to the proper attitudes, behaviors, and protocols. For these reasons kinship and kin terms were always a preoccupation among Lakȟóta people, and relationship was the culture's dominant interpretive principle. The better a Lakȟóta individual knew and adhered to kinship rules, the greater his or her prestige and standing in the group.[14] As White Hat explains, "the focus of our philosophy is always on relationship."[15]

Kinship was tied to honor in Lakȟóta culture, and social pressure was a powerful normative force. According to Ella Deloria, "everyone had his part to play and played it for the sake of his honor, all kinship duties, obligations, privileges, and honorings being reciprocal. One got as well as gave . . . kinship had everybody in a fast net of interpersonal responsibility and everybody liked it, because its rewards were pleasant . . . that was practically all the government there was. It was what men lived by."[16]

To ignore or disregard the sacred rules of kinship established by White Buffalo Woman caused one to be classed as witkó (crazy, senseless, foolish, unreasonable, insane, irresponsible), something no reasonable adult would wish for.[17]

The need to first establish proper relationship prevailed in the spiritual domain as well. The term wačhékiya simultaneously means "to pray" and "to address a relative." According to Ella Deloria, "Wačhékiya implies that in every meeting of two minds the kinship approach is imperative; it is the open-sesame to any sincere exchange of sentiment between man and his neighbor or man and his God. Once the channel is clear between the two, a reciprocal trust and confidence are guaranteed. It is tantamount to smoking the peace pipe; in fact, to smoke ceremonially is to waćhékiya."[18]

Culturally significant places and landscapes were also included in the web of kinship. Speaking of the relationship between humankind and the natural world, DeMallie explains, "the Lakhóta thought of the land, the animals, and the people as a single system, no part of which could change without affecting the others. . . . The Indians, the animals, and the land were one."[19] Humans, nonhumans, and land, shared the potential for a common spirit and participated collectively in a personalized, relational universe. Vine Deloria Jr. explored the significance of sacred places in native North America and was deeply concerned by native-nonnative cultural misunderstandings arising from indigenous views about place and landscape. Deloria focuses on the deep and enduring native belief in the sacredness of lands, an integral part of the collective experiences of tribal peoples. For Native Americans, explains Deloria, this belief in the sacredness of lands and the principle of respect for the sacred is "an essential part of their being." "Recognizing the sacredness of lands on which previous generations have lived and died is the foundation of all other sentiment."[20]

According to Deloria, "Every society needs . . . sacred places because they help to instill a sense of social cohesion in the people and remind them of the passage of generations that have brought them to the present."[21] Some sites are places where the sacred or nonhuman mysterious power has appeared in the lives of humans. Connecting sacred places to oral traditions, Deloria explains, "Their sacredness does not depend on human occupancy but on the stories that describe the revelation that enabled human beings to experience the holiness there."[22] Tribal histories are largely land-centered, and all features of landscape are attached to stories.[23] Deloria explains, "Sacred places are the foundation of all other beliefs and practices because they represent the presence of the sacred in our lives."[24]

Strangers were considered suspect, potentially dangerous, and hence not to be trusted. Ella Deloria writes, "The dictates of kinship demanded of relatives that they not harm each other; so it was necessary first to make relatives of erstwhile strangers . . . and then deal with them on that basis."[25] All who were designated lakhóta (friends, allies) were potential relatives, people who could be comprehended and trusted. All who were not lakhóta were thóka (enemies) unless wólakhota (peace) was made with them.[26]

Kinship, symbolized by the sacred pipe, was the major means of settling disputes. When a quarrel broke out between the members of a camp, a chief would thrust the pipe between them and convince them to smoke amicably together to ameliorate the situation.[27] The Oglála holy man George Sword writes, "where bad or foolish men fight within the tribe, he [a chief] will go and appease them, and will carry his pipe and tobacco pouch there; and make them smoke it; and where he can, he will bring forth what of his possessions he deems suitable, and present it to the quarrelling ones, and ask them to leave off their fighting."[28] According to Ella Deloria, "Such an appeal in kinship's name was supreme."[29] Kinship also was used to heal a community after a murder. Rather than instigating a blood feud between families, the family of a murdered person might adopt the murderer in place of his victim.[30]

Ideally, the result of the exacting and relentless kinship system was that the Lakȟóta were a kind, unselfish people who were courteous and generous. Yet, as in any human society, there were enough different types of relatives and varieties of associated expected behaviors and attitudes that the entire spectrum of human emotion and experience could be expressed and enjoyed. Depending on the type of relative present, an individual could be happy and irresponsible, flippant and rude (in jest), excessively respectful and dignified, foolish, or serious and protective, all within a single camp circle. Depending on an individual's mood one could easily find relatives to behave comfortably around. And, because people were enculturated into this way of life from birth, this complicated system was second nature.[31]

Thípi and Thiyóšpaye

The Lakȟóta recognized themselves as an oyáte (a people or nation) united by common language, culture, history, and social organization.[32] The most important kinship unit was the bilateral extended family, called thiyóšpaye (literally, lodge group), and often referred to as band or sub-band in English. All the families of a thiyóšpaye operated as a single unit. Men often hunted together; women did their work, especially fancywork, sitting in circles; families used the same outdoor cooking fire; and the thiyóšpaye horses were kept in a common herd. "It was that informal, harmonious, and natural, since they were all closely related," recalled Ella Deloria.[33]

Although much was shared in the traditional Lakȟóta lifestyle, there was private property, and individuals had the sole right to give or withhold their possessions. The core value of generosity, along with the reciprocal obligations of kinship, meant that one gained honor and prestige for self and band by giving away rather than accumulating or hoarding possessions.[34] Thus, the complex interplay between collectivism and individualism, mediated through kinship, defies simplistic contemporary descriptions of Lakȟóta life as purely communalistic.

A band typically comprised a set of brothers and male cousins with their wives and children, usually numbering fifty to one hundred people. Each band was named, often with a nickname, and membership was by choice, descent being important but residence even more so. Membership in a band was fluid, and there was freedom to move, travel, visit other camp circles, and change one's membership at will. According to the Oglála Bad Bear (Matȟó Šíča), "When a man was not pleased with his camp or his people, he set up his tipi far away from the camp. He was the chief of his own tipi and all who lived in it." A band's prestige was in part determined by its size, itself a reflection of the success of its leader in attracting families and other lodge groups.[35]

Each thiyóšpaye comprised several thiwáhe (families), each living in a thípi (tipi), a conical dwelling made by stretching buffalo hides over a framework of lodgepoles. Each tipi or lodge housed a man with his wife and children and occasionally a widowed grandfather or grandmother. Within each tipi burned a central campfire, an important symbol of both autonomy and unity. More generally, the circle—a key symbol in Lakȟóta culture—symbolized the family group's unity. The tipi was an ingenious and practical dwelling for a nomadic, hunter-gatherer people. It was portable, quickly erected and taken down by the women. By adjusting the ozáŋ (tipi liner or dew curtain), the tipi was warm and cozy in the winter and cool and breezy in the summer. By adjusting the wind flaps, the smoke from the central fire was directed out of the lodge so as not to bother the tenants. The wind flaps could also be closed against the weather. Life inside the tipi was well-organized, and each person had a place. Family members each had their own space where they habitually sat, ate, slept, and worked, and personal belongings were kept in parfleches, rawhide containers handsomely decorated to indicate ownership. There was no need for locks and keys because a good relative would not meddle with another's things. Such foundational lessons were taught to children from an early age, with a grandmother or some other relative admonishing them with, "See, nobody does so."[36]

According to Ella Deloria, "It was this respect for personality that ruled tipi life and made it tolerable for the several, and sometimes many, who dwelt there. . . . The [Sioux] managed to achieve privacy in their own adroit fashion. . . . Harmonious tipi life was easily possible by each person's knowing and playing his role well. He moved cautiously at all times, with a nice regard for the rights of others, according to his relationship to each."[37]

Lakȟóta thiyóšpaye ordinarily stayed together throughout the year and lived in geo-residential units called wičhóthi (camps, or literally, "place where humans dwell"). Formal camps were always circular, while informal camps were linear, with tipis typically erected along a creek bed. Lakȟóta camp circles consisted of each family's tipi, all of them facing inward toward the center of the hóčhoka (camp circle), a common area consisting of open space for socializing and ceremonial activities, the thípi iyókhiheya (council lodge, "tipis joined together") or thiyóthipi ("lodge of lodges"), and the various men's society lodges. Outside of the camp circle stood temporary shelters, sweat lodges, and menstrual lodges.[38]

Lakȟóta life was nomadic. Camps moved frequently, usually following the buffalo herds or generally in search of food, rarely remaining in one location for more than a week or two, aside from the winter camps.[39] The size of a camp varied with the season. Typically, winter camps were small and dispersed along creeks to maximize hunting potential. They tended to be patrilocal, the core of a winter camp consisting of a group of brothers and male cousins, the relatives culturally defined as cooperating most smoothly with one another. In summer the buffalo congregated into large herds and so did the Lakȟóta. Hence, their summer Sun Dance camps were large, tribal affairs, typically followed by a carefully organized communal buffalo hunt.[40]

Sociopolitical Organization

Lakȟóta sociopolitical organization reflected a complex interplay of kin relationships and the personal qualities of individual leaders. Each band had an ithánčhan (leader), usually referred to as "chief" in English, who spoke for his people. He held his position by common consent and had to live up to the ideals of the culture, putting the peoples' welfare ahead of his own, being generous and self-controlled, and speaking and doing no evil. Each camp had a council composed of respected adult men who represented the people of the camp and met to deliberate important events and decisions relating to the common good. As Bad Bear explains, "The councilors were the headmen, usually elderly, and shamans, braves, hunters, and medicine men. These were so by common consent, and anyone could join them and take part in their proceedings but was not looked upon as one of them until he showed his ability in some accepted way." The council discussed camp moves; winter camp plans; relations with other camps, enemies, and whites; and when and where hunting parties should be sent.

The council also approved war parties and arbitrated disputes between camp members. All council decisions had to be by consensus. Ella Deloria writes, "The council-tipi was a lively place. Men came and went, and nobody was barred from it. The men of mature judgement came to deliberate and plan and philosophize." The chief articulated the council's will, the éyapaha (village crier) announced it publicly, and the akíčhita (soldiers, camp marshals) carried it out.[41]

The akíčhita were appointed by the chief in consultation with the council. According to Bad Bear, "The duties of the akíčhita were to see that all the people lived according to the customs of the camp, and to execute any command of the council, and if the chief was sufficiently powerful, to execute his commands also." In a culture that valued individual autonomy, the akíčhita were the closest thing to a police force. As enforcers of the council's dictates, they constantly navigated the fine line between individual autonomy and collective restraint. As the Oglála Thomas Tyon explains, "Everyone in the camp is subordinate to the akíčhita. He is like a policeman and a judge and a jailer and an executioner. All must do as he says, and he can punish anyone, he may even destroy all the property of anyone, or strike anyone, and he may kill anyone."[42]

The akíčhita were typically selected from the men's warrior societies and oversaw specific tasks, like the large summer gatherings and communal buffalo hunts. According to Tyon, "They supervised breaking camp, moving and setting up camp. They supervised a hunting or war party and the distribution of the spoils of the chase or of war." The akíčhita carried whips of ash wood and were said to receive their power from the wakíŋyaŋ, the thunderbeings of the west, whose punishment was swift and severe and a model for the akíčhita themselves.[43]

Generally, the akíčhita enforced only when it was an issue related to the common good. So, if a man went to war or to hunt at a time when the council had forbidden it, the akíčhita could whip the offender and destroy some of his property. Especially in the case of the hunt, the products of the chase were too important to collective survival to allow a single individual to threaten that resource. Therefore, the enforcers could slash a man's wife's tipi cover, break the tipi poles, destroy his buffalo robes or other implements, kill his horses or dogs, or drive the offender out of camp. This punishment was called akíčhita ktépi (soldier killing), and no one was immune to it, not even a chief. Even the great leader Red Cloud (Maȟpíya Lúta) was once whipped into submission by the akíčhita when he refused to obey orders to break camp. If an offender resisted, he might be beaten or even killed, but this was rare, because generally

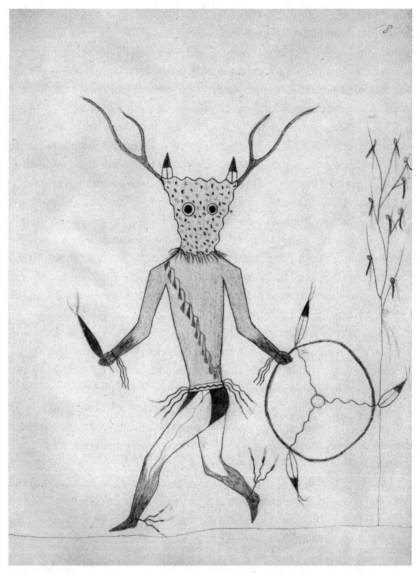

"Elk Society Dreamer" by Walter Bone Shirt (Hohú Ógle), Sičháŋǧu (Brulé), circa 1890, Plate 2. This image depicts a man wearing a horned elk mask with red, blue, and black dots covering it. Courtesy of Walter Bone Shirt Ledger, Archives and Special Collections, Maureen and Mike Mansfield Library, the University of Montana–Missoula.

"Woman in Society Regalia" by Walter Bone Shirt (Hohú Ógle) circa 1890. This is a rare image displaying a woman wearing a red-and-white-striped shawl and a headdress with four feathers. Courtesy of Walter Bone Shirt Ledger, Archives and Special Collections, Maureen and Mike Mansfield Library, the University of Montana–Missoula.

the wishes of the council were recognized as benefitting the individual as well as the group.[44]

Wičháša yatápika (praiseworthy men), called "shirt wearers" in English, were active younger men who had proven themselves to the people through bravery and generosity. They were supposed to be models for the rest of society, and their behavior was under constant scrutiny. The badge of their office was a hair-decorated ceremonial shirt and a pipe.[45] If a shirt wearer failed to live up to the expectations of Lakȟóta culture, if he showed anger or let his emotions overcome his dedication to his people, he was deposed. The most famous example of a deposed shirt wearer is that of Crazy Horse (Tȟašúŋke Witkó), who took a fellow Lakȟóta's wife. According to Crazy Horse's friend He Dog (Šúŋka Bloká), Crazy Horse was still single when he was made a shirt wearer. A few years after this he began to pay attention to the wife of No Water (Mní Waníče). One day Crazy Horse started off on a war expedition and No Water's wife went with him. No Water followed them and when Crazy Horse and the woman were sitting by the fire in a friend's tipi, No Water rushed in saying, "My friend, I have come!" Crazy Horse jumped up and reached for his knife. No Water shot him just below the left nostril. The bullet followed the line of his teeth and fractured his upper jaw. He fell forward into the fire. No Water left the tent at once thinking that he had killed Crazy Horse, and he took his wife back. Because of all this, said He Dog, "Crazy Horse could not be a shirt-wearer any longer. When we were made chiefs, we were bound by very strict rules as to what we should do and what not do, which were very hard for us to follow."[46]

Crazy Horse survived, but he was deposed as a shirt wearer, and the incident led to tension in the community and could have easily led to more bloodshed. Stealing a wife was not uncommon in Lakȟóta culture, but Crazy Horse put his own interests ahead of the people's. This was not appropriate behavior for a shirt wearer. Both George Sword and He Dog said that after Crazy Horse was stripped from his position, everything started to go downhill. The Oglála did not select new shirt wearers and the internal division deepened. Still, Crazy Horse retained his position as the most important blotáhuŋka (war leader).[47]

Okȟólakičhiye (men's societies) were also important. They were primarily social and fraternal organizations, and not governed by an age hierarchy. Membership was by invitation and was based on success in war and raiding and on generosity and living up to the culture's ideals. According to the Oglála Iron Tail, "The idea of belonging to a society and the desire to belong is a matter of social distinction. The ambition of an Indian is principally to be high among his fellow men, to be superior to them in killing enemies, stealing horses, owning a fast horse, belonging to societies, having many wives. And on account of social eminence they belonged to societies. Then, too, the feasts and public gatherings were a great attraction of the societies." Each society had its own distinctive regalia and other ritual objects, such as headdresses, pipes, rattles, whips, swords, and sashes, and they competed with one another for members.[48] Lakȟóta boys looked up to the young men in the warrior's societies and dreamed of one day earning war honors and joining one themselves.

Wakȟáŋyeža: Children and Early Childhood

The life and personality of a child were believed to begin at conception, and a child's character and future could be influenced by its mother's behavior and attitudes. According to Ella Deloria, the Lakȟóta believed that "it was the seed from a man which, when laid in the female's womb, began to grow, the woman's menstrual blood being utilized for the development of the fetus." Vine Deloria Jr. explains that "there was a belief among the Sioux that mothers could, by serious meditation, begin forming the personality of the child before it was born. By thinking, prior to the birth of the child, of the qualities and talents that the new child would need to become a contributing member of Sioux society, the mother sought to lay the groundwork for a healthy personality."[49]

As soon as a baby was born it was washed by an old woman. Then a relative of the same sex as the newborn breathed into the baby's mouth. These relatives had to be of outstanding character because their influence would be formative in the child's character development. Babies were given names shortly after birth, often that of an ancestor whom the parents and grandparents hoped the child would emulate. Children were nursed for at least a year, often as long as three years, and during that time there was a normative abstinence taboo. Once it was established that a woman was pregnant it was considered a religious duty for her husband to abstain from intercourse with her. The ideal was that continence on certain occasions was admirable and manly.[50] For Lakȟóta men, continence was seen as proof of their bravery, and engaging in sexual relations was at odds with the culturally defined warrior ethos.[51]

The Lakȟóta kinship system meant that children were not born into an isolated single nuclear family, but into an entire thiyóšpaye with many mothers, fathers, grandparents, aunts, uncles, brothers, sisters, and cousins beyond their biological relatives. Every child belonged to a certain family, but also to the band, and no matter where it strayed when it was able to walk, it was at home, for everyone in the band claimed relationship, recalled Standing Bear. Paramount to childrearing was teaching children their place in the kinship system. Learning their social duties—which kinship term to use for each person and the proper feelings and behaviors associated with each term—was of utmost importance for children from a very early age. This knowledge was taught explicitly and implicitly, and all adult camp members contributed.[52]

Grandparents frequently cared for young children, providing counsel and indulgent support. The relationship of biological parents to children was more formal, requiring respect. Aunts and uncles taught children about the family and what was considered appropriate for their gender.[53] Normatively, adults did not speak down to children or use baby talk. While children did have a different role and place in Lakȟóta society than adults, they were treated respectfully, in many ways as equals.[54] Children's games and play mimicked adult roles and prepared them with the skills they would need throughout life. Frequently, a public ear-piercing ceremony was performed by a shaman while the child was still an infant, often during a Sun Dance. This ceremony symbolically "opened" the child's ears, meaning the child could now understand and listen and be a true member of Lakȟóta society.[55]

When a boy's voice began to change, he often sought a vision, leading him on the path toward manhood. At the time of their first menstruation, girls were secluded in small huts or išnáthi (menstrual lodges) placed outside the camp circle where they were cared for by their female relatives. At that time, if her family could afford it, a girl might have the buffalo sing performed for her, publicly acknowledging her transition from girlhood to womanhood and marking her as a potential mate. According to Sword, "When a boy's voice is changing he should seek a vision to govern his life. A girl may seek a vision by wrapping her first menstrual flow and placing it in a tree."[56]

Gender Roles

Culturally, gender distinctions were important in Lakȟóta social life. Male and female roles defined behavior. Men were warriors, hunters, and ceremonial practitioners, while women took charge of the tipis, cared for children, processed meat and hides, cooked the food, and gathered wild fruits and vegetables. Tension between male and female roles was expressed in sexual terms, and the Lakȟóta believed that everything relating to sexuality was imbued with wakȟáŋ power and was therefore to be treated cautiously. Young men attempted to seduce young women, analogous to hunting or warfare, but would later publicly humiliate them if their seductions were successful, oftentimes composing tell-all songs about their sexual encounters with specific women. Sexual desires were believed to be stronger in women, but Lakȟóta women were taught to resist the advances of men, as virginity was highly valued and premarital sex was seen as reckless and dishonorable and could make a young woman less desirable as a potential wife. For this reason, after puberty young women were closely supervised by their female relatives.[57]

Until puberty, Lakȟóta children, regardless of gender, spent much of their time together with their mothers and female relatives in the village. After puberty, however, the domains of men and women were quite distinct. Young Lakȟóta men typically became hunters, scouts, warriors, or some combination thereof.[58] They were trained principally by their fathers, in the Lakȟóta sense, which included their paternal uncles and other male relatives. A boy's father taught him practical skills and exhorted him to be respectful and brave. The relationship between fathers and sons was marked by respect and formality. Older brothers also played an important role in disciplining and training their younger brothers, helping to instill bravery in them and teaching them about sex.[59]

Young Lakȟóta women were trained by their mothers and female relatives, who taught them the virtues of generosity and productivity. They were instructed in domestic arts, such as beadwork and quillwork, and practiced by making moccasins, clothing, and other gifts to honor their brothers and male relatives. The relationship between mothers and daughters was less formal than that between fathers and sons.[60] Standing Bear writes, "The girl's training in duties that relate to domestic life began while still a child and continued until she knew how to tan skins, cook, and make sinew thread, garments, tipis, and moccasins. She was then entitled to carry about with her a pretty decorated bag which contained awls, sinew, and other implements of sewing. No young woman who had not rightfully earned it was allowed to possess one. The Lakȟóta girl who did possess one proudly exhibited it as a guarantee of her eligibility to marriage."[61]

There was a marked distribution of labor in traditional Lakȟóta society based on sex and age. Ella Deloria notes, "Both had to work hard, for their life made severe demands. But neither expected the other to come and help outside the customary division of duties; each sex thought the other had enough to do. . . . Outsiders seeing women keep to themselves have frequently expressed a snap judgment that they were regarded as inferior to the noble male. The simple fact is that woman had her place and man his; they were not the same and neither inferior nor superior."[62]Josephine Waggoner, a Húŋkpapȟa, reflected on

"Courting Couple" by Walter Bone Shirt (Hohú Ógle), circa 1890, Plate 8. This image shows a couple wrapped in a blue blanket, the woman's cheeks colored red with vermilion. Courtesy of Walter Bone Shirt Ledger, Archives and Special Collections, Maureen and Mike Mansfield Library, the University of Montana–Missoula.

Lakȟóta women and their roles in society saying that they were mostly "patient and content" and they accepted "cheerfully their share of the labor of keeping their family fed and comfortable. They help in the fields and cook what they have raised and what their husbands kill is taken care of so it will not spoil. The women . . . are no parasites. I don't believe they would rest at home and let their husbands do all the work."[63]

Women typically performed the domestic labor, and in family affairs women had more authority than their husbands. They owned the tipi and all its contents (aside from a man's hunting, warfare, and ritual paraphernalia), they cooked the food, saw to the childrearing duties, gathered wild fruits and vegetables, and processed buffalo hides. The village was the domain of women, symbolically associated with culture, society, kinship, peace, predictability, order, and safety. Lakȟóta men performed the more dangerous and physically taxing labor, including hunting, offensive and defensive warfare, and horse-raiding. Typically, the world outside the village was the domain of men, symbolically associated with nature, war, chaos, and danger.[64] As the Oglála Edward Fire Thunder (Wakíŋyaŋ Pȟéta) explained, "Only within the limits of kinship was there safety; beyond it life was as if spent in a danger zone where the enemy might strike from a hidden source."[65]

A woman's blood was considered very powerful, essential to the creation and maintenance of life. During menstruation, a woman's blood was believed to be harmful to men, not because it was polluting, but because it was a specifically female power that was at odds with male power. For this reason, menstruating women absented themselves from the family tipi and stayed in small dome-shaped menstrual lodges outside the camp circle, where they were attended to by their female relatives. Men zealously guarded their belongings—particularly their hunting, warfare, and religious paraphernalia—against contact with menstruating women. These beliefs, combined with culturally defined notions of traditional masculinity and the fact that sexual relations were considered detrimental to a man's power, explain various abstinence taboos. For instance, sexual activity was prohibited immediately before ceremonial activities and war expeditions because it could potentially render a man's sacred power temporarily impotent.[66]

Marriage was the foundation of social order. Indeed, the sacred pipe, the single most important tangible religious symbol in Lakȟóta culture, represents the union of male and female, the stem and the bowl respectively. A long period of wióyušpa (courtship, "to catch a woman") ideally preceded marriage. A young

man had to prove himself as a good warrior and hunter to be considered desirable as a relative. Standing Bear remembers that "No boy was a full-fledged man
until he had been out with a war-party and not until then was he considered
eligible for marriage." Horses and other gifts were given by the groom to his
bride's family to validate a marriage. This was the most honorable form of marriage, something a woman could boast about for the rest of her life. Typically,
"purchased" women were virgins, as virginity was highly prized.[67]

Standing Bear describes the custom of purchasing a wife: "Sometimes a man,
when courting, feels that the young woman would like a more material demonstration of his sincerity before consenting to marriage with him. That being the
case, the man arranges to present the girl's family with a number of horses. . . .
The family in council, including the girl, will accept the gift. . . . If, however, he
is not accepted, the horses are turned loose to wander home."[68]

Marriage by common consent, with both families approving of the union and
little fanfare, was the more common form. Elopement was the least honorable
form of marriage, as it was risky to the young woman, who could find herself
publicly shamed and dishonored if her mate decided to abandon her after the
initial elopement. Josephine Waggoner reflects on Lakȟóta marriages, writing,
"they fight against love and infatuation as something that is misleading and
untrue. Their marriages are placid and in the old times it was arranged by the
parents mostly. Once in a while there is a romance, a couple would run away to
marry. But without the older people's good judgement and advice, such actions
are disapproved of."[69]

Marriage between related individuals was prohibited, so women typically
married outside the thiyóšpaye into which they had been born. Often, a woman
went to live with her husband's thiyóšpaye after marriage. No kin terms of
address or reference were used between spouses, but other referential terms for
husband and wife were sometime used. Polygynous marriages were common,
particularly sororal polygyny, in which a man married a woman and one or
more of her sisters, but jealousy among theya (cowives) who were not sisters
was common. Female adultery was taken seriously and could result in severe
physical punishment, such as cutting off a woman's hair or even the tip of her
nose or an ear, and divorce was common, particularly among younger men.[70]
Not much has been written about male adultery, causing one to suspect it was
not frowned upon nor punished.

The tipi reflected the distinction between male and female. It was laterally
divided: from the man's point of view at the place of honor opposite the doorway

(čhatkú), the right side of the lodge was the male side and the left the female side. The tipi and most family belongings were owned by the woman, so when divorce occurred, a man simply took his belongings from his wife's tipi and moved into his mother's lodge for the time being. Alternately, a woman might leave her husband's moccasins outside the tipi door, indicating to all that a divorce had occurred.[71]

Hunting provides a good example of the complementary roles of men and women in traditional Lakȟóta society. Typically, men left the village to hunt and brought game back to camp, providing raw materials for the women to process and cook. Women also processed the hides, which were a major form of wealth.[72] White Hawk (Čhetáŋ Ská) and Looking Elk (Heȟáka Wákhita) explain that usually a few women went with a hunting party to help herd the pack horses until the men had the meat ready to load. After the hunting party returned to camp the women finished cutting up the meat in long strips. These were hung in the open air and when thoroughly dried were pounded and mixed with wild cherries, or with the fat of the animal. Meat prepared in this way could be kept indefinitely and constituted a food staple.[73]

In a recent study, historian Pekka Hämäläinen has argued that the fur trade's rise in the 1820s and 1830s caused a major shift in the status of Lakȟóta women. He suggests that since the men were increasingly seeking wealth, they needed more women to work on the buffalo hides, which resulted in an increase in polygyny and a reduction in independence for women who became almost a marginalized workforce.[74] It is true that the fur trade caused changes in Lakȟóta society, but this argument rests on the premise that wealth for the Lakȟóta was measured in the same way as for Euro-Americans. The age-old Lakȟóta custom of purchasing a woman is seen here through Euro-American standards, but in Lakȟóta society the ability to buy a woman demonstrates respect to a woman and her family and should not be viewed as the purchase of a commodity. As Ella Deloria noted, outsiders often misunderstood the role of women, and Waggoner wrote that the "old idea that an Indian [man] was so lazy that he shoved all the work upon the shoulders of the woman and how they had to work half starved most of the time due to their shiftlessness is very false, for I have seen the Indians in their homes unspoiled by white men. To be sure, the women worked hard in the fields and in their homes." She further emphasized the importance of gender roles by praising men. "Lakȟóta husbands, though apparently stolid and indifferent, felt just as responsible for keeping their families fed as any American Father."[75] It is important to remember that, viewed from a twenty-first-century Euro-American perspective, women were not equal to men in Lakȟóta society, but the nuances of a distinctly nineteenth-century Lakȟóta perspective are critical to a fuller understanding.

The expanding fur trade in the early 1830s did, in fact, affect the Lakȟóta in many ways. Bartering with fur and pelts gave the Lakȟóta access to trade goods, but also to whiskey. Alcohol created social problems as drunken men resorted to violence against their wives and children more frequently. Some even sold women in exchange for whiskey. Alcohol has been a constant problem in Lakȟóta communities ever since. Another consequence of the fur trade was the emergence of a new oyáte—Wágluȟe—through marriages between Lakȟóta women and white traders. The Wágluȟe were called Loafers in English, since they lived close to white forts, but for the Lakȟóta they were valuable as interpreters and mediators. Man Afraid of His Horses (Tȟašúŋke Kȟokípȟapi), for example, demanded that whites understand that the white men married to Lakȟóta women and their mixed-blood children were considered kin. Over the years, tensions between "full-bloods" and "mixed-bloods" increased. This tension reverberated well into the reservation period.[76]

Despite some negative consequences of the Lakȟóta involvement in the fur trade, the buffalo-hunting complex was a foundation of Lakȟóta culture in terms of individual and collective identity and economy and subsistence.

Wanásapi (Communal Buffalo Hunt): Subsistence and the Chase

Nineteenth-century Lakȟóta were hunter-gatherers. They depended primarily on hunting for subsistence, and buffalo was the primary game. Each Lakȟóta family or camp circle was on "an eternal quest for bison."[77] According to Bad Bear, the Lakȟóta "were at all times hunters and necessarily became skillful in taking game of all kinds which was found on the plains, but they were especially hunters of the buffalo. The buffalo supplied them with a large part of the necessities of life, their skins being used for clothing, robes and tipis, and their flesh formed a large proportion of their food. Therefore the hunting of buffalo was the principal civil occupation of the Lakȟóta men. [It] was subject to strict laws and customs."[78]

The hunters had to obey the directions of the akíčhita, who directed the approach and attack on the game. "If anyone stampedes the game he must be punished" said Tyon, and "the meat gotten during a hunt must be fairly and equally divided among all members of the party."[79]

Although individuals stalked game and hunted throughout the year, collaborative hunting provided potentially greater returns, so various collective strategies and techniques were used, including the surround and the buffalo jump. But the most common collaborative hunting strategy was the chase, the wanásapi or communal buffalo hunt, held in the late summer or early fall. The communal hunt was essential to the survival of the people as it provided the bulk of the excess hides and dried meat for the lean winter months. A holy man might seek a vision to foretell the success of the hunt and report the results to the council. Scouts would be chosen to locate the herds. Once the buffalo had been located the camp went into a new mode, that of the igláka (moving camp), during which the wakíčhuŋza (deciders) and their specially appointed akíčhita were in control of the camp.[80] Women's labor was essential: They did all the work incidental to moving the camp and making the journey, overhauling clothing, tipis, travois, and harnesses. They made all the preparations for packing and transport. At dawn on the day of the move, all were astir in the camp, the men in groups discussing the plans, the young men and boys rounding up the horses, and the women getting things into shape to pack on the horses, the travois, or on their backs.[81]

They approached the buffalo carefully, so as not to spook and stampede the herd. The akíčhita were responsible for keeping the igláka as compact, silent, and orderly as possible. When the camp was close to the herd, the men left the group at daybreak, approaching from downwind, then separated into two parties to surround the unsuspecting herd. Once the signal was given, the hunters charged simultaneously and tried to keep the herd milling as long as possible to maximize the kill. After the hunt, the buffalo were butchered, and some women, children, and old men joined from the camp to help. The akíčhita ensured that the meat was shared and divided fairly. Much of it was dried and stored for use throughout the winter.[82]

White Hawk discussed the buffalo hunt in the 1910s. He explained that his great-grandfather hunted with arrowheads made from cut flint. His father had used arrowheads made from the outer thickness of rib or marrow bones. White Hawk himself used arrowheads made from steel, cut from the thin frying pans sold by traders or used by white soldiers. White Hawk also discussed Lakȟóta bow- and arrow-making techniques. He said that "a good bow would send an arrow into a buffalo so that the arrow point was imbedded in the flesh, an excellent bow would drive it in almost to the feather, while a fine bow would send the same arrow clear through the animal." Describing his youth, Standing Bear recalls, "I learned that ash was the preferred wood for a warrior's bow. A hunter would use a cherry or cedar bow." Light, flexible woods, such as wípazukȟahu (juneberry) and wičhágnaškahu (wild currant), were preferred for arrow shafts, so that, according to White Hawk, "if a buffalo fell on an arrow, the latter bent without breaking. Thus the arrow could be recovered and used again by its owner."[83] Throughout the nineteenth century the bow and arrow remained the preferred weapon for hunting from horseback, even after the adoption of firearms.[84]

There were spiritual elements central to hunting. Holy men made incantations and medicines and performed ceremonies to ensure success. Many of the hunters took sweat baths to purify themselves and drive away malevolent influences that might hinder their success in the chase.[85] Certain types of dreamers had special kinship relationships with specific animal spirits, established through ceremonies such as the vision quest. In such cases frequently the dreamer had the ability to ritually call that animal, luring it close to the camp, so hunters could easily kill it during times of famine and scarcity. For instance, buffalo dreamers had the ability to call the buffalo close to hunters or to the village. The Ihánkthuŋwaŋna elder Teal Duck (Šiyáka) recorded a medicine man's song to secure buffalo in times of famine and described the accompanying ceremony. First the medicine man painted a buffalo skull with red and blue stripes and laid it beside a filled pipe on a bed of sage. It was believed that the skull transformed into a living buffalo and called other buffalo. The song was sung in the dark, and after the medicine man's ceremony the buffalo came near the camp and the famine was relieved. According to Tyon, the spirit of Tȟatȟáŋka (Buffalo Bull), the patron spirit of the chase and domestic affairs, remains with the skull of the buffalo. The Oglála Bad Wound elaborates on this belief: "The spirit of the buffalo stays with the skull until the horns drop off. If the horns are put on the skull, the spirit returns to it. The earth eats the horns and when they are eaten the spirit goes to the buffalo tipi in the earth."[86]

These rituals are ancient, evoking prehistoric circumpolar traditions dating back thousands of years, well before the adoption of the horse, when the people could accomplish little by way of physical force and instead often resorted to magical processes to procure their food. His Shield (Tȟawáhačhaŋka) provides a vivid description of the practices of a buffalo caller:

> In the tribe, the man who tȟatȟáŋk-iháŋbla 'dreamed the buffalo-spirit' was the one who acted mystically and sang to call the buffalo. . . . who would now draw near in a herd, compelled by the song. During this time, the women and children took their places behind the travois, and each one had a stick in his hand. The rhythm with which they beat on the travois

sticks with their sticks helped to call the buffalo. Now the herd entered
the ring and began to go round and round inside, and to seem not to try
to escape. All the while the holy man continued to sing and the women
and children continued to drum and the buffaloes continued to go round and
round, and the men behind the women and children shot and killed one
here and there.[87]

The men then found a suitable place away from the kill site and laid the finest bull,
cow, and calf from the harvest in a line with their heads facing north. The head-
man then asked the buffalo caller for a piece of buffalo for the people's offering,
and the practitioner proceeded to cut off small pieces of the tips of the tongues
of the three sacrificial animals, tying them up in a piece of skin painted with red
clay. This bundle was offered back to the spirits as a wóphila (thank-offering).[88]

Every part of the buffalo was used for some purpose. Aside from roasting and
eating it fresh, the meat was typically cut into thin strips on the grain and dried
in the sun before being packed in rawhide containers for future use. Buffalo liver
and tongue were especially prized delicacies. Aside from the meat, the hair, bones,
horns, hoofs, and sinews were all used for various purposes. The skull was believed
to retain the spirit of the buffalo; therefore, it was regarded as wakȟáŋ and used
as a portable altar, an intermediary to invoke the aid of Ṫhatȟáŋka, the spirit of
the Buffalo Bull. The skin or hides were used for robes, tipis, clothing, moccasins,
regalia, leather cordage or thongs, and blankets, among other things. Hides also
served as a major form of wealth that fueled inter- and intratribal trade. In the 1850s
Lieutenant L. G. Warren observed how a group of Lakȟóta cared for a buffalo herd
throughout the summer. They did not kill any of the animals and prevented others
from doing so. They wanted to wait until late summer when the hides were thinnest
and better for certain uses. While it is not known how common this practice was,
this demonstrates that the Lakȟóta had intricate knowledge of the environment
in which they lived.[89] The buffalo was a key symbol in Lakȟóta society with great
ecological, economic, social, and cultural significance. The Lakȟóta also hunted
many other species, including but not limited to elk, black- and white-tailed deer,
pronghorn, and bighorn sheep. Porcupines were eaten, their quills plucked and
dyed to use for quillwork embroidery. Domestic dog was both a beast of burden
and a ritual food.[90]

The Lakȟóta gathered various wild fruits and vegetables. Prairie turnips, wild
artichokes, and ground beans were gathered and eaten fresh or dried for future
use. Corn, squash, and melons were obtained through trade with the Lakȟóta's

semisedentary horticulturalist neighbors the Arikara, with whom they enjoyed a complex and tenuous symbiotic relationship. Wild plums, chokecherries, and buffalo berries were gathered in great quantities and eaten fresh or dried for future use. Pemmican, called wasná, was made by mixing grease or buffalo fat with pounded dried meat and cherries.[91]

Hunting and warfare were interrelated. As Standing Bear explains, "most of our troubles were over boundary lines or hunting grounds." Warfare with the Lakȟóta was almost entirely a matter of keeping their hunting territory free from use by rival tribes.[92]

Zuyá (Warfare)

Warfare was an integral part of Lakȟóta life. Being a warrior was a major occupation for men, and success in war was the main way a man earned status and prestige in society, which was subsequently shared by his female relatives. Fighting the enemy was the most honorable duty in a man's life, sanctioned by White Buffalo Woman. War or hostility defined the natural relationship between the Lakȟóta and their tȟókapi (enemies).[93]

At any time, a Lakȟóta individual might go on a war expedition against another tribe for merely personal reasons. Other tribes observed the same attitude toward the Lakȟóta, who were constantly on guard because an enemy might do them some injury, such as killing men or stealing women, children, or horses, or trespassing on their territory or hunting grounds. At all times they were alert, especially when moving camp or on the march.[94]

The ozúye (war party), which was highly structured, provided the principal organization for warfare. According to Bad Bear, "Anyone could get up a war party, but he must do it according to certain forms and customs, and the one getting up a war party was the leader of the party, but subject to certain rules and regulations." The leader, called blotáhuŋka itȟáŋčhaŋ, invited his relatives and friends to participate, and the planned expedition was then presented to the council for approval. Depending on the size of the war party, the leader would appoint as many as eight experienced warriors as subordinate leaders, called simply blotáhuŋka, who would appoint two akíčhita itȟáŋčhaŋ (soldier leaders), who in turn appointed other akíčhita (soldiers). Tuŋwéya (scouts) also played a significant role. War parties could be as small as 8 or 10 men or as large as thousands of men, but the ideal size was between 30 and 60 warriors.[95] Tyon describes the rules of a war party that were recognized by all:

No one shall go on a warpath against friendly Indians. No one shall organize a war party without first getting the consent of the councilors. Anyone may organize a war party if he has the consent of the councilors. If a
councilor is a member of a war party he shall direct the movements and
acts of the party. If a marshal [akíčhita] is a member of a war party he
shall act the same as in camp. If anyone kills an enemy he shall have all
the property the enemy has about his person. If a war party captures a
camp all there is in the camp shall be divided fairly among the party. If
the war party captures women they shall belong to the one who first lays
hands on them. If the war party captures children they shall be given to
any who shall be agreed upon. If a single warrior captures horses or women
or children or dogs, they shall belong to him. The first one who strikes
a dead enemy with something held in his hand is entitled to the scalp of
that enemy. Every member of a war party is obliged to try to prevent the
enemy from taking the scalp of any member of the party.[96]

War parties left camp in the morning, sometimes publicly parading around the
camp circle. If they were successful the warriors returned home with blackened
faces, symbolic of victory, and with much fanfare, holding aloft wičhápȟaha
(enemy scalps) stretched on willow hoops and other trophies of battle. Captured
horses were distributed along kin lines, and men gave the scalps they took to
their sisters and other female relatives, who were honored to carry them in the
iwákčhipi (victory dances), sometimes called "scalp dances" in English, which
followed the return of a successful war party. Much dancing, singing, and feasting
accompanied victory dances.[97] Standing Bear writes, "The victory ceremonies
centered about the young warriors and everyone was very proud of them. This
was because the young hunters and warriors were the protectors of the tribe.
Everyone, young and old, looked to them for protection. Lives, food, and property
were in their keeping and the cost was theirs even to giving up their lives. For
this reason, mothers and sisters joined happily in honoring the braves at these
big celebrations."[98]

The Lakȟóta used the word kté (to kill), meant metaphorically, for war honors or "coups" in English (but derived from French). The coup system was a
complex typology of graded manifestations of bravery that men used to record
their exploits in battle. The public sharing of these records constituted a large
part of a man's identity and autobiography in Lakȟóta society. The primary
sense of "counting coup" referred to touching the body of a fallen enemy, and

four individuals could count coups on a fallen enemy in this way. Scalping was another way in which warriors could accrue honor through the coup system. Killing the enemy in hand-to-hand combat was the highest war honor. Other honors included being wounded in battle, wounding an enemy and bringing him down, having a horse shot out from under you in battle, rescuing the body of a fallen comrade, and serving as a scout against the enemy camp. Each of these categories was subdivided into four grades. A warrior could also earn honors by capturing the enemy's horses or pipe, stealing the enemy's property, and taking wayáka (captives). The coup system demonstrates that the Lakȟóta concept of warfare was largely focused on showcasing individual acts of bravery, rather than any collective battlefield strategy.[99] Bow and arrow, firearms, shields, lances, war clubs, and knives were all utilized by Lakȟóta men in warfare.[100]

In 1864 William Francis Hynes, a soldier in the US army, was a witness to a fight between a Lakȟóta and a Pawnee. In the heat of a battle a Lakȟóta warrior's horse was getting fatigued. The Pawnee immediately seized at the opportunity to get a coup, riding close almost touching the Lakȟóta, and cut him across the face with his riding whip. The Lakȟóta then thrust his knife into his enemy's thigh. The fight continued for some time, both men trying desperately to stay on their horses. At some point the Pawnee tried to grasp his opponent by the throat, but instead "found his finger between the teeth of that savage, who promptly snapped off some of it like a pair of nippers, and spat in his face." In the next few seconds the Lakȟóta lunged toward his enemy, his two knives in his hands, opening a bloody gash in the Pawnee's forehead. The Pawnee then drew his pistol and fired it, but it misfired. The Lakȟóta, realizing he was bleeding and getting weaker, made a final, desperate effort to kill his opponent, but the Pawnee managed to crush the Lakȟóta warrior's skull with the hammer of his pistol. The Pawnee survived the encounter and when asked why he did not just shoot his opponent, he replied: "A papoose [child] can shoot a man in the back. It requires neither courage or skill. A brave man will not resort to an unfair advantage in a challenged personal fight."[101]

This is a classic example of Plains Indian warfare and scenes like these repeated themselves hundreds of times during the intertribal-warfare period on the Northern Plains. Jean-Baptiste Truteau described a different form of fighting in the 1790s when the Lakȟóta attacked the Arikara relentlessly, killing men, women and children mercilessly, eventually forcing the Arikara to flee their villages.[102]

Warfare, like hunting and other aspects of Lakȟóta life, was surrounded by ceremony. Typically, a holy man was consulted before a war party set out, to foresee the success or failure of the endeavor. Wolves were the cultural model for Lakȟóta warriors, and hence wolf dreamers often figured prominently in war parties, acting as scouts and presiding over rituals pertaining to warfare and horse raiding. Red Feather (Wíyaka Lúta) vividly describes the exploits of a wolf dreamer who "acts the wolf," performing various ceremonies while he and his comrades were on the warpath:

> he wears a wolfskin [sic] and a mask (itéha). In his right hand he has a rope which he moves in such a way as to make it look like a snake (zuzéča káǧa [imitates snake]). In his mouth he has the šiyótȟaŋka [flute], which he whistles with: ti-ti-ti. . . . His work is to see the tents . . . or the fires (pȟelwáŋyaŋk lowáŋ [or] pȟéta waŋyáŋk lowáŋ [fire-seeing sing]) of the enemy, i.e., to tell his people where the enemy camps [are]. In the evening the warriors invite him to find it out for them. This is called iwášipi. They bring a pipe (opáǧi) to him. He accepts and holds it towards six directions . . . and then smokes until it is empty [and] held the pipe close to the wolf skin, saying: Blihéič'iya, waúŋšipelo taŋyáŋ slolyé wachíŋ yo [Exert yourself, they asked me, I want to know well!].
>
> Then he goes along the line up and down blowing the whistle: ti ti ti and then again howling like a wolf with the intention to make the wolves howl and then tell him about the enemies what he wants to know (hoúya).
>
> Then he will also sing while walking:
>
> Wakȟáŋyaŋ mawáni ye. I walk in a sacred manner.
>
> Wakȟáŋgli yewáye. I shoot out lightning
>
> The answer which he receives he tells all the warriors: if they will obey, they will kill many; if not, many will be killed.[103]

Other forms of divination were also practiced in relation to warfare. For instance, the congealed blood of animals created a reflective surface, like a mirror, which was used to divine future events. As Tyon explains, "Whoever kills a badger takes out everything from the body cavity (čhuwí mahél), leaving only the blood. And when the blood reflects well, like a mirror, then someone can see himself in it. If the man sees himself in the blood and his entire head is white, then he will become an old man, they believe. And if another looks long inside, and sees himself sick, he will die, they say. If someone sees a red head, then he will kill an enemy." Each warrior would peer into the mirror-like surface created by the coagulated blood. If he saw himself with white hair, he knew he would survive and be successful. If he saw himself bloody or injured, he knew he would be killed, and in this case, he could leave the party and return home without losing face.[104]

Many warriors obtained war bundles or wóthawe (war medicine) from medicine men for protection, swiftness, and other attributes desirable among warriors.[105] Jaw (Čhehúpa; also known as Okíčhize Tȟáwa, "His Battle"), a Northern Lakȟóta of Húŋkpapȟa and Itázipčho ancestry, discussed the basic elements and beliefs associated with war bundles. His war bundle was a hide pouch containing wasé (vermilion or red paint mixed with grease) for painting his face and body when he went to war or to steal enemy horses. Jaw also wore a wolf skin and carried an eagle-bone whistle and a wooden bowl, common paraphernalia in both war and ceremony. To the whistle Jaw fastened his medicine bag, which contained a mixture of four herbs, dried and powdered, which could be used singly or in combination. Jaw's medicine bag was a veritable pharmacopeia of useful herbs used to remedy various ailments potentially faced by a nomadic people.[106]

Intertribal warfare was a chronic state among the Upper Missouri tribes dating back to prehistoric times for many complex reasons. It was a precursor to nineteenth-century warfare with whites. Economic motives were certainly involved, particularly the desire for horses, access to trade routes, and the need to acquire new lands for hunting, trapping, and grazing horses. Revenge for the death of relatives and tribal members at the hands of the enemy also motivated intertribal warfare. Lastly, warfare was essential because Plains Indian cultures embodied a warrior ethos, and success in war was the major means for a male to achieve status and gain prestige in his society.[107]

PART TWO

TRADING AND FIGHTING WITH THE WAŠÍČU

"The Coming of the Good White Man"

By the year 1800, the Lakȟóta had been in contact with the whites for nearly two centuries, but it is only at this point that the whites receive more attention in Lakȟóta winter counts. The winter count kept by the Oglála Long Soldier (Akíčhita Háŋske) records a remarkable event for the year 1799–1800, which he calls the coming of "the first white man ever seen, who used iron" winter. Other winter counts recall the arrival of "the good white man," a trader. Several winter counts also comment on seeing the first horses with shoes on, indicating the presence of white men.[1] Obviously, these were not the first white people seen by the Lakȟóta, but clearly there were still oyáte or thiyóšpaye that had not been in contact with the whites. One winter count even noted the meeting of a white woman with a pictograph showing a woman wearing a typical white woman's dress.[2]

At the turn of the century a new nation entered the colonial power struggles over the interior of North America and the lucrative trade on the Plains and beyond. The United States, little more than a decade old, bought Louisiana from France in 1803 and almost immediately set out to explore and exploit its new domain. The United States sent not only traders, but also military and scientific expeditions to explore the new lands. The Lakȟóta approached these new white men as they had the British, French, and Spanish: as possible trading partners.

The Lakȟóta assumed they could continue to control trading with the whites along the Missouri. They knew they were a formidable power along the river and acted accordingly. Lewis and Clark wrote that the Sioux, or Lakȟóta, were arrogant and treated the traders badly. According to the American Horse winter count, the meeting with this expedition was a significant event where gifts, such as medals and flags, were distributed. For the Lakȟóta, these were a token of friendship and in recognition of Lakȟóta power.[3]

In the years immediately following the meeting with Lewis and Clark, Lakȟóta winter counts largely ignored the presence of the whites, though traders still came to them, providing guns and other goods. Several winter counts note the death of the trader Régis Loisel, who perished when his house burned down. Although this was an isolated event, it shows how significant traders had become for the Lakȟóta.[4] Curiously, after the Lewis and Clark expedition, Lakȟóta winter counts do not take notice of other military expeditions sent by the US government. In 1805, for example, Lt. Zebulon M. Pike led an expedition along the Mississippi and made a treaty with the "The Sioux Nation of Indians."[5] The signers of this treaty were mostly Eastern Sioux or Dakȟóta, but one would have expected the Lakȟóta to take notice of this event, since this was the first time the Sioux ceded land to the United States. However, the Lakȟóta were too busy fighting their traditional enemies to care about events in the east, which was no longer their homeland. They were setting their sights on the lands farther to the west and northwest.

During the first two decades of the nineteenth century, the whites were important for the Lakȟóta as trading partners, while other Indian tribes living along the Missouri and farther west were their main enemies. As the Lakȟóta moved westward, their enemies changed. The winter counts for the late eighteenth century still report the Chippewa (Ȟaȟátȟuŋwaŋ) as the main enemy, but by the early nineteenth century the Mandan (Miwátani) and Arikara living along the Missouri became more prominent in Lakȟóta calendars. Over the course of the century, people living much farther west, the Crow, the Blackfeet, the Flathead (Natóblečha) and in the 1870s even the Métis (Slót'a) living in Canada are mentioned as both trading partners and enemies. While Lakȟóta expansion to the west is well known, these winter counts give a pictographic trail of that expansion from the Lakȟóta perspective.[6]

Lakȟóta calendars depict scenes of minor battles where one or two people were killed, but also major expeditions in which they destroyed entire enemy villages. The Pawnee, Mandan, and Arikara suffered greatly from Lakȟóta aggression,

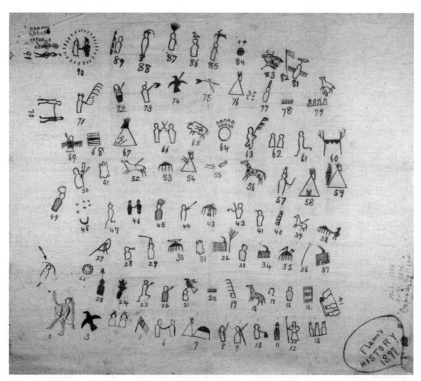

The Flame Itázipčho (Sans Arc) Winter Count. Courtesy of National Anthropological Archives, Smithsonian Institution, NAA MS 2372.

and inch by inch, the Lakȟóta raiding parties pushed farther west. Lone Dog (Šúŋka Waŋžíla) and The Swan (Maǧáska) describe how in the year 1811–12 the Lakȟóta killed as many as twenty Gros Ventre (Ȟewáktokta) in a single raid, and for the following year, Long Soldier noted that fifteen Crow were killed in a battle. A rare peace was attempted with the Kiowa in 1814–15, but it never materialized as one Lakȟóta got frustrated and buried his hatchet into the head of a Kiowa. The event was noted in several winter counts and Battiste Good named the year as "Smashed a Kiowa's head winter."[7]

Cloud Shield (Maȟpíya Waháčhaŋka) reports on another surprising peace effort in the same year when some Lakȟóta struck peace with the Pawnee, and American Horse reports that peace was made with the Crow the year after.[8] How long the peace with these tribes lasted, and how many Lakȟóta oyáte were part of the peace agreement, is not clear. In fact, while American Horse marks 1816–17 as a year of peace with the Crow, Long Soldier names it after a fight with the Crow. The Lakȟóta came home with two scalps on top of poles as trophies. This is a good reminder of how personal these winter counts are, and they should not be read as if they reflected actions and events affecting all Lakȟóta. What was important for some was not worth commemorating for others. Clearly not all Lakȟóta supported the peace efforts in 1816. This and other similar events demonstrate how independent Lakȟóta oyáte and thiyóšpaye were. By 1819 fighting had resumed in its usual fashion.[9]

During the first two decades of the nineteenth century, the winter counts do not report a single Lakȟóta being killed by the whites, or any white man killed by the Lakȟóta. Instead, they describe how more trading posts were established around the Lakȟóta domain and along the rivers crossing their homelands. They continued to enjoy good relations with the white traders. Some Lakȟóta even built log houses for themselves for the first time. These were years of tremendous success for some Lakȟóta bands, while others were struggling. In 1817–18 the Oglála were so successful in their hunt that they had plenty of meat to distribute to their suffering neighbors, the Sičháŋǧu. The Lakȟóta success was hampered by smallpox, whooping cough, and measles that spread among the people almost annually.[10]

Lakȟóta relations with the whites, especially with the United States, were about to change. The Lakȟóta had established themselves as the most powerful people on the Northern Plains, and the United States was inching its way toward the Lakȟóta homelands. From the Lakȟóta perspective, securing trade with the wašíču was of utmost importance, and they had to decide how to do that. Already in 1812, the Lakȟóta and Dakȟóta were faced with a dilemma: whether to look for trading opportunities with the Americans or seek contacts with the British operating from the north. Thus, the Lakȟóta were drawn into the War of 1812 and were caught between the warring colonial powers. The Húŋkpapȟa, living farther north, were more interested in trading with the British, whereas the southern oyáte, the Oglála and Sičháŋǧu, favored the Americans. Since Lakȟóta oyáte were independent, they did not need to find a common ground in their relations with the whites—not just yet. However, following the war, the United States signed a treaty of peace and friendship with groups of Isáŋyathi, Iháŋktȟuŋwaŋ, and Lakȟóta. Even if the treaty had little effect on the Lakȟóta in practical terms, it was the first time the US federal government extended its jurisdiction over them.[11]

In 1825 the United States sent an expedition under Gen. Henry Atkinson and Indian Agent Benjamin O'Fallon to make treaties with the Plains tribes along the Missouri. The US government's aim was to secure its grip on the Plains through formal treaty making. In contrast, for the Lakȟóta, especially the Oglála and Sičháŋǧu, it signified another opportunity to engage in trading and secure future trading prospects with the Americans. Not all Lakȟóta agreed to a treaty. The Húŋkpapȟa of the north favored the Canadian-based traders and viewed the Americans and especially the US Army contemptuously. Lakȟóta winter counts record a surprising event in 1823–24. A group of Lakȟóta allied with American soldiers and fur traders led by Col. Henry Leavenworth and attacked and destroyed an Arikara village. The raid was successful, and the winter was named either the winter when they "fought the Rees [Arikara]" or the winter when they had an "abundance of corn," the latter referencing the corn stolen from the defeated enemies. But the American soldiers' performance did not impress the Lakȟóta. The Northern Lakȟóta felt that the Americans were weak, and it would be beneficial to continue cooperating with the British. Thus, Lakȟóta approaches to the wašíču were mixed as early as 1825, if not before.[12]

The Atkinson-O'Fallon expedition left Fort Leavenworth in mid-May and hoped to meet with the various Lakȟóta oyáte separately. The Sičháŋǧu and Iháŋktȟuŋwaŋ met with them in June and some of the leaders signed the proposed treaty and received gifts and trade goods as a reward. Before meeting with the wašíču the Oglála gathered for their annual Sun Dance and other ceremonies. All Oglála oyáte and thiyóšpaye were present.[13]

The American Horse ledger (a private ledger book kept in the American Horse family) describes how the Oglála erected a thiyóthipi (council lodge), where the chief's council gathered to discuss the upcoming meeting. This ledger provides a previously unseen view of early Oglála societal structures. Even if Lakȟóta society was flexible and ever changing, the same structures, the same actions and behaviors that later came to characterize our understanding of Lakȟóta oyáte structure, leadership, and behavior are present. The chief's council of elder men presided over ceremonies, they chose wakíčhuŋza (deciders) as heralds, akíčhita societies performed "policing" duties, and so on. Thus, these key elements were in place among the Oglála and probably other Lakȟóta oyáte as early as 1825, most likely much earlier.[14]

The Oglála negotiated and quarreled among themselves before agreeing to meet with the Americans. Some oyáte and headmen fiercely opposed any attempts to sign treaties with the wašíču, while others felt the necessity of retaining good relationships with the US government. The Lakȟóta were used to having trade goods, guns, and ammunition. Signing the treaty was the only way to secure continued trade with the Americans. After long discussions between leaders, various men's societies, and forceful pressure from Bull Bear (Mathó Thatháŋka), a major chief, the Oglála decided to meet with O'Fallon and Atkinson. The proceedings of this meeting indicate deep divisions within the Oglála over the question of how to deal with the whites. This divisiveness plagued all Lakhóta oyáte throughout the nineteenth century. But the seeds for this division were sown as early as the 1820s.[15]

During the meeting with the Americans, which began on July 3, the Oglála put on a spectacular display of ceremony and oratory. The Oglála camp was on the north side of Bad River, the entrance facing east, toward the Missouri River. The soldiers camped on the south side of Bad River. The Oglála elected Standing Buffalo as the head akíčhita responsible for monitoring the talks. The following day some Cheyenne and Northern Lakhóta joined the proceedings. Standing Buffalo offered the sacred pipe to the gathered negotiators and after a first day of deliberations the council adjourned, and O'Fallon and Atkinson were given robes and skins as presents. To impress the Lakhóta the soldiers made a display of artillery and "rockets." The actual day of deliberations was July 6. No Lakhóta speeches have survived, but as was their custom, they expressed their demands and hopes through chosen headmen, who were to express the will of the people. The Lakhóta undoubtedly evoked kinship terms referring to the president of the United States as the Great Father as they had done on similar occasions for centuries. The underlying idea for the Lakhóta was to establish a kin relationship, as a father never denies anything to his children. Hence, calling the president Father was a strategic action, not one where the Lakhóta made themselves inferior to the Americans. The US officials referred to the Indians as the "children" of the Great White Father, who through this treaty would extend his protective arm to them, yet the Americans saw this as making them responsible for obeying the wishes of the White Father. The Lakhóta did not need protection but were ready to welcome the benefits of the treaty: amicable relations, continued trade, and gifts to be distributed after the signing of the treaty. After several hours of discussions, leaders of the Northern Lakhóta, Sihásapa, and Itázipčho signed the treaty first, followed by the Oglála and Cheyenne. The treaty did not exactly discuss land sales or territories but noted that each tribe was to respect certain territorial boundaries. For the Lakhóta the major issue, in addition to trade, was allowing the whites to pass through their homelands.[16]

After major Oglála leaders signed the treaty, the expedition continued north presenting it to the Húŋkpapha and Mnikhówožu. The expedition secured several signatures, and they could call the treaty-making a success. The first real treaty with the United States and the Lakȟóta of the Plains had been signed.[17]

Although the American Horse winter count gives great detail about the meeting, other Lakȟóta winter counts do not mention the council or the treaty at all. Most winter counts for 1825–26 focus on a Missouri River flood, remembering it simply as the year when "people drowned."[18] The flood's devastation was a more significant event than signing a treaty with the wašíču.

In many ways, the 1825 treaty changed little for the Lakȟóta; life continued as it had for decades. White encroachment on Lakȟóta lands had not begun in earnest, and the Lakȟóta were expanding their domain westward, fighting their traditional enemies, and trading with the whites.

"The Emigrants Have Been the Cause That Buffaloe Have Left Our Hunting Grounds"

The relationship between the Lakȟóta and the whites remained peaceful until the 1840s. The Lakȟóta had established themselves as the dominant force on the Northern Plains, and the abundance of buffalo gave them more prosperity than ever before. Through their established trade networks, they had more options for access to guns, ammunition, metal goods, and other necessities. The whites were not a problem for the Lakȟóta; some were passing by while others remained to trade, but from a Lakȟóta perspective there was no need to fight against the US government. The wašíču were not even considered enemies (tȟóka). War honors or coups were gained from fighting the real enemies, that is, other Indians. As the whites did not interfere much with the daily life of the Lakȟóta and there was no individual honor to be gained from fighting them, there was no reason to do so. US government officials also noticed this friendly atmosphere. Secretary of War Jefferson Davis noted that Lakȟóta attacks and hostilities against the settlers or soldiers were extremely rare.[19]

The first real problems began in the late 1840s when the United States opened a road from the Missouri River to Oregon and California. The famed Oregon Trail passed through the lands of the Southern Lakȟóta. Suddenly, increasing numbers of wašíču were trespassing through the area the Lakȟóta considered essential hunting grounds. The cattle traveling with the wašíču emigrant trains consumed the grass, upon which buffalo subsisted, and passed on bovine diseases that decimated buffalo herds. Surprisingly quickly, the numbers of buffalo in the Platte River Valley began diminishing, and the annual migration routes changed. In addition, the 1850s and 1860s witnessed severe droughts, an effect

of the end of the Little Ice Age. Before long, the immense buffalo herd would
separate into two, a northern and a southern herd. This development did not go
unnoticed by the Lakȟóta; several winter counts recorded the absence or deple-
tion of the buffalo. Some note that people painted buffalo heads on their tipi
covers seeking assistance from Wakȟáŋ Tȟáŋka to bring back the buffalo. For
the Lakȟóta, the 1825 treaty was one where certain rules were set: although the
whites were allowed to cross their country, the increasing number of travelers
and their impact on the buffalo herds were infringing on that treaty.[20]

Inevitably, tensions arose between the travelers and the Lakȟóta. Joint feasts
could turn into quarrels and escalate into armed conflicts. Trouble was brewing
as the United States pursued its Manifest Destiny ideology and the Lakȟóta
began to see white encroachment on their lands as a growing problem. And,
for the first time ever, the US government sent soldiers into Lakȟóta lands in
1845 to protect white travelers. Soldiers entered the Platte River Valley and
established military bases in the area. The government bought several trading
posts from the American Fur Company, including Fort Laramie, for use by
the army. Situated along Horse Creek in the southeast corner of present-day
Wyoming, it quickly became the most important military base on the southern
edge of Lakȟóta country, and it remained a central trading post until the end
of the 1870s.[21]

The growing tensions were also noticed at the United States Indian Office.
St. Louis District Superintendent Thomas H. Harvey wrote in his report for
1846 that buffalo were becoming scarce and the Lakȟóta were suffering as a
result. He worried that this development would spell trouble. To avoid further
escalation, he suggested that there should be a new treaty with the Lakȟóta.[22]
In response to the ever-increasing flow of travelers, the Oglála and Sičháŋǧu
decided to inform the US government of their discontent and the problems the
Oregon Trail was causing. Sixteen Oglála and Sičháŋǧu leaders wrote a letter to
the President of the United States:

January 14, 1846.

To Our Great Father the President of the United States.

We the undersigned Chiefs and head men of the Ogallallah and Brulé
Bands of Sioux Indians, inhabiting on the borders of Platte River, take
the opportunity through our agent to humbly make you the following
representations.

For several years past the Emigrants going over the Mountains from the United States, have been the Cause that Buffaloe have in a great measure left our hunting grounds, thereby Causing us to go into the Country of our enemies to hunt, exposing our lives daily for the necessary Subsistence of our wives & children and getting killed on several occasions—We have all along treated the Emigrants in the most friendly manner, giving them a free passage through our hunting grounds, and in one and the only instance when our neighbours stole seven of their horses, we went in pursuit Captured the Horses and returned them to the owners gratis—

We are poor and beg you to take our Situation into Consideration, it has been Customary when our white friends made a road through the Red mans' Country, to remunerate them for the injury Caused thereby; and we humbly hope you will not make us an exception to this rule; we do not claim this as a right but respectfully request it of you as a favor; and your Red Children will for ever pray for your happiness & prosperity.[23]

This is the first known letter expressing Lakȟóta points of view on both the treaty signing process and on white encroachment on their lands. The Lakȟóta clearly state that they had nothing against the migrants traveling through their country if they obeyed the treaty signed in 1825. In typical Lakȟóta fashion, they merely asked for compensation for their losses. In Lakȟóta society the right way to compensate damage was to settle the losses with ample provisions, whether in horses or other goods. Here the Lakȟóta asked the US government to do the same. They evoked the old Lakȟóta custom of iglúwašte (reciprocity).[24] The letter provides an explanation for the exacerbation of intertribal warfare on the Plains; because the buffalo was disappearing, the Lakȟóta were forced to travel farther and were thus more likely to clash with other tribes.

Winter counts corroborate what the chiefs were saying. Lakȟóta war parties were engaged in fighting new enemies farther west. For the first time, the winter counts mention fighting against the Arapaho, Shoshone (Susúni), and Flathead living in present-day Wyoming and Montana. For the year 1839–40 Lone Dog reported that the Lakȟóta massacred an entire village of Shoshone. American Horse marked the following year as the one when his father and two others stole two hundred horses from the Flathead.[25] At the same time that Lakȟóta influence was expanding westward, they continued to plague their traditional enemies—the Arikara, Mandan, Pawnee, and Crow. The years following the 1825 treaty up to the late 1840s were a constant cycle of intertribal warfare. The year

1828–29 saw the Lakȟóta kill 200 Hidatsa (Gros Ventre, Ȟewáktokta), and 1836–37 was memorialized by a spectacular battle between the Lakȟóta and the Pawnee across the frozen North Platte River. For the Lakȟóta, the only exemption from the fighting was a peace they made with the Cheyenne in 1840–41. The peace was solidified a couple years later when a Lakȟóta war party captured a Cheyenne sacred arrow during a raid against the Pawnee, and later returned it to the grateful Cheyenne.[26]

This constant turmoil was exactly what worried white travelers and the US government. Intertribal warfare caused unrest and disrupted US commercial interests. In response, the US government began to prepare for a new treaty with the Plains tribes, largely because they needed to secure safe passage for the increasing number of immigrants moving west. When gold was discovered in California—the famous 1849 goldrush—the number of travelers on the Oregon Trail increased dramatically and the possibility of a major confrontation increased correspondingly.[27] For the Lakȟóta, intertribal warfare and the resulting Lakȟóta westward expansion was linked to the buffalo, and through the disappearance of the buffalo, it was linked to the expansion of the United States.

The Lakȟóta found themselves in a new situation when that expansion became impossible to ignore and was affecting their way of life. The chiefs' letter was one way of seeking understanding and mutual, peaceful interaction, but in the end, the Lakȟóta had to make difficult and often divisive choices regarding their attitudes, actions, and policy vis-a-vis the United States. The letter demonstrates that the Lakȟóta were quick to adapt to changing circumstances, embracing a wašíču way of communication—letter-writing. Moreover, it shows that the Lakȟóta were actively trying to influence US policies toward them, not just passively accepting US expansionism. Through this letter, they declared that they were an equal power and negotiating partner.

"Wakpámni Tȟáŋka"—Great Distribution

In 1851 the Plains Indians and the US government signed the first Fort Laramie (Horse Creek) Treaty, marking a significant event for the Lakȟóta. US officials made a genuine effort to reach out to various tribes and tried to entice them to attend the talks. A key figure in this diplomacy was the new Indian Agent Thomas Fitzpatrick. He was actively imposing US authority on the Plains tribes, spending more time at Fort Laramie and Indian camps than his predecessor. Initially he disagreed with former Agent Harvey, who suggested that a council with the Indians should be held every few years; but, over time he became convinced that a major council with the Plains Indians was necessary. Fitzpatrick came to believe that the Indians genuinely wanted to secure peaceful relations while the government's aim was to stop intertribal warfare, promote trade, and secure overland travel for the thousands of immigrants along the Oregon Trail. To succeed they needed to get all the major powers to the same location at the same time. A formidable task, but in September 1851, representatives of the Lakȟóta, Shoshone, Assiniboine, Cheyenne, Arapaho, Arikara, Mandan, Crow, and Hidatsa gathered at Horse Creek.[28]

The need for the council has often been interpreted as a one-way deal: the US government pushing for a treaty and imposing provisions, and the Indians agreeing just for the purpose of receiving presents. As the winter counts demonstrate, presents were important, but to reduce Lakȟóta agency to mere blankets and pots is naive. The Lakȟóta, too, had an agenda. They were eager to have a council with the wašíču. The declining buffalo herds and growing numbers of travelers had not gone unnoticed, and this was not what they had agreed upon in the 1825 treaty. The situation was unacceptable and something had to be done.

The 1840s saw a deepening divide among the various Lakȟóta oyáte in their attitudes toward the whites. Generally, the Northern people, the Húŋkpapȟa, Mnikȟówožu, Itázipčho, and Sihásapa adopted an isolationist policy and did not want to have anything to do with the Americans. However, even within these groups differing opinions led to factionalism and internal division. The Oglála and Sičháŋǧu were more eager to deal with the Americans, and they spearheaded the main diplomatic efforts to persuade all the oyáte to meet and council with the whites.[29] Still, factionalism also plagued the Oglála and Sičháŋǧu. A major event took place among the Oglála in 1841 when two leading chiefs, Smoke (Šóta) and Bull Bear, found themselves at odds. Their feud was not about the whites, but about internal matters, and it climaxed when a young aspiring warrior, Red Cloud, participated in the killing of Bull Bear. This murder led to division in the Oglála oyáte that has lasted into the present. While it was common that bands and thiyóšpaye merged and split, this fractionating happened as the direct result of a feud and political assassination. Alcohol played a crucial role in the affair. Cloud Shield's winter count memorializes 1841–42 as the winter when the "Oglála got drunk on Chug Creek and engaged in a quarrel among themselves," and American Horse notes that the "Oglála engaged in a drunken brawl and the Khiyúksa band separated from the others."[30]

All Lakȟóta oyáte faced the same dilemma of how to deal with the increasing numbers of wašíču in their country. The American Horse ledger describes several important meetings among the Oglála between the years 1845 and 1851 in which the matter was hotly debated. Two main factions emerged out of these talks: the accommodationists and the isolationists.

The men's societies played a crucial role in organizing and determining the proceedings at Lakȟóta councils. The Oglála chose leaders for each faction and shirt wearers were elected so that they could control both factions. During those meetings new leaders emerged who would later become icons of Lakȟóta leadership. Man Afraid of His Horses among the Oglála and Spotted Tail (Siŋté Gleška) and Two Strike (Núm Kapȟá) among the Sičháŋǧu, for example, gained prestige and support. Man Afraid of His Horses rose to prominence as a key orator and mediator. His great vision received at Bear Butte (Matȟó Pahá) inspired his approach: he wanted cooperation, but there had to be compensation for the loss of buffalo and other game. This request was again based on the Lakȟóta concept of iglúwašte. Now that the whites were causing damage, it needed to be remedied.[31]

The picture that emerges in the 1840s is of a Lakȟóta society facing new challenges and actively seeking ways to meet them. Not only that, but they were also drawing from the strengths of their own society with their own "checks and balances" to make sure that the leaders selected to represent the people would ensure the challenges were met on Lakȟóta terms. For that reason, a council with the whites was essential and welcome.

On September 1, 1851, more than 10,000 Indians were present to meet the US representatives at Horse Creek. It took three weeks before the treaty was concluded and the time arrived for the distribution of presents. The actual talks took only eight days; the rest of the time was spent in feasts, games, horse races, and ceremonies, with the Indians and the whites trying to impress each other. The Americans used artillery to demonstrate their power, and the Indians invited the commissioners to feasts and dances. From the Lakȟóta point of view, the most important goal was compensation for the problems caused by the trespassers. For the US commissioners the major aim was to bring the Lakȟóta and other Northern Plains tribes under the authority of the United States. For the first time, the government assigned territories and boundaries for each tribe. While these were not reservations, there was an element that sought to contain Indian movement on the Plains. By assigning territories, the United States also hoped to reduce intertribal conflict.[32]

The Lakȟóta erected a big thiyóthipi (council lodge where meetings were held). This was a symbolic gesture to signify the importance of the event. The US

"Sioux Horse Race during 1865 Treaty Council at Fort Sully." Courtesy of South Dakota State Historical Society, South Dakota Digital Archives (2012-10-22-311).

commissioners offered their own symbol by raising the American flag and firing a cannon every morning. The Lakȟóta further emphasized the importance of the meeting by offering the pipe to all negotiators after each day's proceedings. To the Lakȟóta, this meant that everyone present had spoken the truth and shared common goals. Superintendent D. D. Mitchell, the chief US negotiator, affirmed this. He noted that smoking the pipe was as important as swearing on the Bible for a white man. As a further gesture of friendship and mutual respect, the commissioner finally asked the Lakȟóta to sign, or "touch the pen." For the Lakȟóta that was not necessary, as the offering of the pipe already confirmed everything that had been said during the negotiations.[33]

What puzzled the Lakȟóta was the US government's request that they choose one head chief to represent them all. This, of course, was not a Lakȟóta custom and they refused to do so. "We have decided differently than you Father, about this chief for the Nation," said the Sičháŋǧu chief Blue Earth (Makȟá Tȟósaŋsaŋ). "We want a chief for each band, and if you will make one or two chiefs for each band, it will be much better for you and the whites. . . . But Father, we can't make one chief."[34]

The idea of a head chief was alien to the Lakȟóta, but Mitchell continued to pressure them. Reluctantly, the Lakȟóta yielded and chose the Sičháŋǧu

Scattering Bear (Mathó Wayúhi) to act as their chief. His response to the new office is revealing: "Father, I am a young man and have no experience. I do not want to be the chief. . . . If you Father, and our Great Father, require that I shall be chief, I shall take this office." Never had there been a head chief of all the Lakȟóta oyáte and it would remain unclear what it really meant to the Lakȟóta. Scattering Bear seemed to be concerned that it might lead to problems that a young man without merits for a traditional leadership position was elevated to such a prominent position. He voiced his concerns to Mitchell saying, "Father, I am not afraid to die, but to be chief of all the Dahcotahs, I must be a Big Chief . . . or in a few moons I will be sleeping (dead) on the prairie. . . . If I am not a powerful chief, my opponents will be on my trail all the time. . . . I will try to do right to the whites, and hope they will do so to my people." Addressing the issue of opposing Lakȟóta factions, he reiterated that he did not fear death by assassination. "I know the Great Spirit will protect me, and give many spirits of my enemies to accompany me, if I have to sleep [die] for doing what you and our Great Father asks. The Great Spirit, the sun and moon, and the earth, knows the truth of what I speak." Commissioner Mitchell was delighted. He could claim that he had established a new order among the Lakȟóta and that they now had a person in charge who could decide matters on his own. But that would prove too optimistic. Scattering Bear's influence and tenure as head chief turned out to be both contested and short.[35]

The Lakȟóta were surprised that the US commissioner was not only going to pay the presents as a compensation for the violation of the 1825 treaty, but also wanted them to adhere to some new borders. That did not make sense to the Lakȟóta. They were used to following the buffalo where they wanted. There were areas that could be called borderlands or no-man's lands between tribal territories, but no one had told the Lakȟóta that there would be areas they could not enter. "We claim half of the country; but we don't care for that, for we can hunt anywhere," said Blue Earth. The Oglála Black Hawk further emphasized that drawing borders and lines was not what they wanted. "You have split the country and I do not like it. What we live upon we hunt for, and we hunt from the Platte to the Arkansas, and from here to the Red Butte and the Sweet Water." For him these lands were open to the Lakȟóta, and there was no reason and no way to restrict their right to hunt where they pleased.[36]

While the Lakȟóta never accepted the new borders, the treaty was signed. The council culminated in a magnificent display of presents delivered by the United States to the Indians. The wakpámni tȟáŋka (great distribution) pleased the Lakȟóta and other Indians; many of their demands were met and they got their compensation for the violations of the 1825 treaty. Commissioner Mitchell proudly proclaimed that peace among the tribes was reached, and safe travel along the Oregon Trail secured. Scattering Bear, Blue Earth, Big Partisan (Blotáhuŋka Tȟáŋka), Smutty Bear (Matȟó Sab'íč'iya), and Long Mandan (Miwátaŋni Háŋska) were among the signers of the treaty on behalf of the Lakȟóta. The first four represented the Sičháŋǧu, the last two the Iháŋktȟuŋwaŋ and Oóhenuŋpa respectively. Conspicuously absent were the Húŋkpapȟa, Sihásapa, Mnikȟówožu, Itázipčho, and Oglála.[37]

When the great distribution was over, the tribes dispersed to their hunting grounds or the territories assigned to them. For the Lakȟóta, these lands had tremendous significance. These were lands where they had hunted for decades and where their ancestors were buried. It was a country of great spiritual meaning. It was Lakȟóta tȟamákȟoče, a country with vital resources such as the buffalo that allowed them to maintain a distinctive Lakȟóta way of life, Lakȟól wičhóȟ'aŋ.

"The Soldiers of the Great Father Are the First to Make the Ground Bloody"

In the aftermath of the Treaty of 1851 the Lakȟóta had made peace with the Crow. It was a genuine effort by both sides to end the constant raiding and skirmishing. The peace allowed both tribes to hunt and utilize the game-rich area west of the Black Hills and along the Belle Fourche (Šahíyela Wakpá) and Powder Rivers (Čhaȟlí Wakpá). This area became a "neutral" buffer zone that benefitted both parties: the Lakȟóta got access to the buffalo herds and the Crow had easier access to trading posts as far south as the North Platte River west of Fort Laramie. The northern Mnikȟówožu were most eager to take advantage of the situation. It was Lone Horn (Hewáŋžiča), or One Horn, who was the most vocal advocate for peace, so much so that it has sometimes been referred to as Lone Horn's peace. Other Mnikȟówožu and Oglála bands ventured deep into this neutral area, and as game grew scarcer along the Missouri, they began staying permanently around and west of the Black Hills and the Powder River region.[38]

Several Lakȟóta winter counts memorialized 1851–52, "the great peace," with depictions of the goods distributed during council. The Flame (Boíde), Long Soldier, Major Bush, and Lone Dog remember it as the winter when they made peace with the Crow.[39] Although the Crow were one of the Lakȟóta's main enemies, it is nevertheless interesting that the winter counts specifically mention them. Does it mean that in their minds, peace was only signed with the Crow, not other tribes? Perhaps, since fighting against the Pawnee, who were not present at Fort Laramie, resumed the following year. Despite isolated incidents and Lakȟóta deaths at the hands of the Crow and Blackfeet, the years following the 1851 treaty were relatively peaceful. No major raids for horses or other campaigns were mentioned in winter counts that focused more on hunting, ceremonies, and daily activities than on fighting. Several winter counts depicted new "Spanish blankets" that were distributed among the people.[40]

The US government's push for an end to intertribal warfare seemed to have worked for the moment, although it probably did not end altogether. This was observed by Superintendent of Indian Affairs A. Cummings in his report for the year 1853, in which he wrote that the plains tribes have "maintained friendly relations amongst themselves . . . and manifest an increasing kindliness of disposition toward the whites." He believed that this development would continue when the annual appropriations were again distributed to the tribes as promised in the 1851 treaty. However, the agent of the Upper Platte Agency, Alfred J. Vaughan, was already running into difficulties, especially in relation to the delivery of the promised annuities. These were not distributed on time as planned. In addition, many Húŋkpapȟa did not want to receive the presents in the first place. They preferred to stay independent and make their living by the hunt.[41]

For these Northern Lakȟóta, the Treaty of 1851 did not mean much. Their hunting grounds were far from the Oregon Trail, the main emigrant route. There they were forging stronger alliances with other Lakȟóta oyáte. Especially the Húŋkpapȟa and Sihásapa often stayed together, and were, despite the promise of peace, pushing westward. By the mid-1850s they were hunting as far west as the Powder and Yellowstone Rivers. Húŋkpapȟa chief Bear's Rib (Matȟó Thučhúhu) put the sentiments of the Northern Lakȟóta into words in an 1859 meeting with Capt. William F. Raynolds. Bear's Rib noted that the lands belonged to the Lakȟóta and they did not like it that travelers were still going through their lands. Giving away land would make them poor. "If the white people want my land, and I should give it to them, where would I stay?" he asked. He argued that the country on each side of the Missouri river belonged to them. Evoking a kinship relation, he exclaimed: "If you, my brother, should ask me for it, I would not give it to you, for I like it and I hope you will listen to me." Bear's Rib urged Raynolds to tell the President, what he had said. He was willing to let the whites travel unharmed. "When the Great Father sends white people to this country, I do not strike them, but help them, and act as their friend," he said, but he asked the president to take pity on him and his people and to keep the whites out of their country.[42]

There were, however, divisions growing among the Northern Lakȟóta in their attitude toward the whites. What could be called the isolationist stance was led by the Húŋkpapȟa chief Little Bear (Matȟó Čík'ala), who was backed by the Strong Heart men's society. Running Antelope (Tȟatȟóka Íŋyaŋke), in contrast, was one of the leading men advocating deeper trade relations with the Americans. In 1853 the Lakȟóta were asked to sign an amendment to the 1851 treaty, which they refused to do. One of the main arguments for keeping their distance from the Americans was the fear of being tricked into giving away their lands, a fear not without foundation. Their eastern relatives, the Isáŋyathi, were an example of what could happen when treaties were signed with the Americans. Little Bear was not going to be fooled into signing further agreements. The differing approaches came to a head when Running Antelope saved a few traders from an attack staged by Little Bear's Strong Heart society warriors. Several Indians were killed in the melee, but the traders escaped with their lives.[43]

By 1854, Indian Agent Vaughan was desperate as ever-increasing numbers of Húŋkpapȟa and Sihásapa were in open defiance of the government. He noted that the Indians were constantly violating the treaty and wreaking havoc among the traders and neighboring tribes. A group of Húŋkpapȟa and Sihásapa destroyed government annuities (food, blankets, etc.) and declared they would not accept any goods in the future, demonstrating their intent to remain free of American influence. According to Agent Vaughan, they "talked very hostile" and wanted to do as they pleased. Intertribal peace seemed to have come to an end, as had the peace between the US government and the Lakȟóta. But the Lakȟóta were not the ones who started the spiraling circle of violence. During a meeting with Indian Agent Thomas Fitzpatrick, one Lakȟóta chief observed that "the soldiers of the Great Father are the first to make the ground bloody." [44] The first casualty of the hostilities would be Scattering Bear, the man the whites had elected as the head chief of the Lakȟóta.

While the Northern Lakȟóta were less directly impacted by the effects of the 1851 treaty, the Oglála and Sičháŋǧu bore the consequences of the ever-increasing contacts with the emigrants. Relationships were usually peaceful but there were incidents where joint feasts turned into quarrels, especially when alcohol was involved. Just a couple of years after the treaty, Agent Fitzpatrick noted that there was more turmoil than before, and he was glad that there were more troops readily available at Fort Pierre and Fort Laramie. The emigrants, too, started to complain to the authorities that the Indians asked for more gifts and were increasingly demanding toward the travelers. Military protection was requested. Indeed, the troops at Fort Laramie were itching for a fight with the Indians to prove themselves. They got an excuse to leap into action in the summer of 1854.

Scattering Bear with his Wažáža oyáte of Sičháŋǧu was camped close to the Oregon Trail, peacefully engaging in normal affairs with the traveling whites. Unfortunately, a Mormon ox ventured into the Lakȟóta camp and caused a ruckus. The Lakȟóta were hungry as buffalo were scarce and the annual appropriations had not yet arrived. Eventually, a Mnikȟówožu visiting with the Sičháŋǧu shot it. The owners rushed to Fort Laramie and demanded justice. The post commander, Lieutenant Hugh Fleming, asked the Lakȟóta for compensation. Scattering Bear and other headmen immediately informed Fleming that full compensation would be made, that they did not want trouble. They would pay for the ox with horses, which were far more valuable than the ox. The post commander was initially ready to accept the Lakȟóta offer of compensation, but under pressure from other officers, he changed his mind. He wanted the man who shot the ox. The Lakȟóta knew that Indians had been hanged for lesser offenses. Furthermore, the perpetrator was a visitor in their camp and the Lakȟóta code of ethics called for proper behavior toward a guest. They simply could not give him up to be punished by the wašíču.[45]

While the post commander might have ultimately agreed to Lakȟóta offers for compensation, a young, newly arrived officer, Lt. John L. Grattan, was convinced that the only remedy the Lakȟóta understood was force. He convinced Fleming to let him ride to the Lakȟóta camp and arrest the accused man. The following day he gathered twenty-nine troops and set out on his mission. Meanwhile the Lakȟóta spent an anxious night waiting for possible military action. When Grattan's men arrived, they hoisted a white flag and, waving the flag, Scattering Bear rode toward the soldiers. Without warning Grattan opened fire on the chief and his camp. The chief fell mortally wounded. The stunned Lakȟóta grabbed their arms, and in moments, Grattan and his men lay dead. The whites had spilled the first blood, that of the Lakȟóta whom the whites had chosen to be head chief. Lakȟóta calendars remembered 1854–55 as "Scattering Bear was killed."[46] Lakȟóta-US relations now entered a confrontational stage.

A few days after he was shot, Scattering Bear died. He had been a man of peace who tried to maintain good relationships with the whites. Lakȟóta later remembered that as he was dying, Scattering Bear reminded his people to hold on to the 1851 Treaty. By elevating Scattering Bear to the status of head chief of the Lakȟóta, a position he did not want and one that was not acknowledged by traditional Lakȟóta social structure, the US had inserted an anomaly into Lakȟóta life that conflicted with traditions and created two parallel leadership structures—one composed of traditional chiefs and the other of those appointed by the wašíču. Eventually this arrangement infiltrated Lakȟóta society. A divisive line emerged with those appointed and accepted by the whites becoming more "friendly" toward the whites, while those opposing white encroachment gained prestige and leadership positions in traditional ways. In time, a system developed wherein the whites determined who was considered "friendly" and who was "hostile." This division allowed US authorities to separate the Lakȟóta into progressive and nonprogressive people. While this categorization is artificial and reflects white attitudes more than the realities of Lakȟóta life, it did, especially in the early reservation period, cause tremendous problems for the Lakȟóta. For the United States it proved to be a useful divide and conquer strategy.

Following Scattering Bear's death, the Sičháŋǧu left the area in fear of punishment. Nothing happened, and relative calm continued for a while. The chief's death was only one more event that caused the turmoil reported by Agent Vaughan. He described how, only a few months earlier, he had discussed with Scattering Bear how they could together work to maintain peace and reduce tensions, especially among the northern oyáte. Now he had been killed and those looking to maintain peace with the whites were losing ground. Fur trader Edwin Denig, who lived among the Lakȟóta for many years, noted in his journals rising tensions after 1854. The Northern Lakȟóta intensified their raids against neighboring tribes as far west as the Rocky Mountains. Lakȟóta winter counts, too, describe fighting with the Crow, Assiniboine, and Blackfeet, whose homelands were close to present-day Idaho and western Montana. At the same time, food supplies were becoming critical. Lakȟóta winter counts mention starvation as the buffalo were increasingly scarce and deep snow made hunting for small game difficult. Agent Vaughan and Superintendent Fitzpatrick were concerned about the situation. Hungry Lakȟóta would surely extend their hunting expeditions to the west, which in turn would cause further conflict. They seemed surprised that despite difficult conditions, the Húŋkpapȟa and Sihásapa still refused to accept rations.[47]

Trouble was also brewing among the Southern Lakȟóta. While Scattering Bear had wanted the Sičháŋǧu to stand by the 1851 Treaty, there were younger men, notably his brother Red Leaf (Waȟpé Lúta) and Spotted Tail, who were eager for revenge. In Lakȟóta society that was common practice; revenge had to be effected on those who had killed one's relative. In November 1854, with a small group of men, they attacked an American mail wagon, killing the drivers and taking a lot of money, which they delightedly destroyed. They got their revenge, but there would be a heavy price to pay.[48]

Spotted Tail's raid was too much for the United States. A punitive expedition led by Gen. William S. Harney was sent out in 1855. Harney was instructed not to take prisoners, but to exact revenge for Grattan and the others killed in Spotted Tail's raid. Harney marched through Lakȟóta country as a show of force, and then in September 1855, disaster struck the Sičháŋǧu now led by Little Thunder (Wakíŋyaŋ Čík'ala). Harney's troops attacked the village at Blue Water Creek (Ash Hollow). They killed eighty-six, including many women and children, and took seventy women and children captive. The dead included infants and pregnant women. The Lakȟóta had never faced such a defeat.[49]

Harney, known as Phuthíŋska or "White Whiskers" to the Lakȟóta, continued his march north to Fort Pierre. He ordered all Lakȟóta oyáte to send delegates to the fort. A new peace treaty was to be signed, much on Harney's terms. Harney's march of destruction had impressed the Lakȟóta. It was bold and brutal. It strengthened the resolve of those who opposed the whites, but also affected those who wanted to remain on friendly terms. It seemed that Harney, whom the Lakȟóta also called "The Hornet," had delivered a divisive sting to Lakȟóta society.

In response to Harney's call to come to Fort Pierre, many Lakȟóta gathered there to listen to what Phuthíŋska had to say. Harney pressured and threatened the Lakȟóta leaders, and his efforts bore fruit. Harney demanded the various Lakȟóta oyáte elect chiefs among themselves and camp police to make sure order would be kept. After long deliberations, the Lakȟóta agreed to that arrangement. Among the Húŋkpapȟa, for example, Little Bear led the opposition party, but he and the Strong Heart society had to give in to those working to maintain peace. The chiefs chosen to represent the Lakȟóta oyáte were those of reputation, so Harney's request did not necessarily infringe upon traditional leadership roles. Further, selecting the camp police officers or akíčhita from the existing men's or warrior's societies met traditional sociocultural norms.

By the fall of 1855 a new treaty was established. Lakȟóta winter counts called it the year when "Phuthíŋska captured women and children and made peace." But in fact it had been a massacre so traumatic for the Lakȟóta that most winter counts avoided mentioning it directly; instead, they highlight the women and children Harney took as prisoners and later released.[50]

The atrocities at Blue Water Creek profoundly impacted one young Lakȟóta man. Visiting his Sičháŋǧu relatives, Crazy Horse had been out hunting the day Harney attacked the village. Upon his return he saw the dead and the carnage left behind by Harney's men.

Appalled and enraged, Crazy Horse decided that he would never stop fighting the wašíču.[51]

5

WAŠÍČU TȞAČHÁŊKU ÓTAPI

MANY WHITE MAN'S ROADS

"We Will Give Them Ears"

Thanks to "Lone Horn's peace," the years from 1851 to 1856 saw demonstrably less violence among the Northern Plains tribes. In addition to the Mnikȟówožu, at least the Oglála, Sičháŋǧu, and Oóhenuŋpa were sincere in their attempts to keep the peace.[1] Indian Agents Thomas Twiss and Alfred Vaughan confirmed in their reports that the Lakȟóta were peacefully disposed toward the United States and were even willing to learn to read and write and pursue farming. The real reason for concern, noted Agent Twiss, were white traders and speculators who floated false rumors and lies about the government and its agents. Both Vaughan and Twiss feared that one unscrupulous individual could undo the fragile peace.[2] Despite the peace, Lakȟóta winter counts continued to list annual raids and skirmishes with the Crow and other neighboring tribes. It was the Northern Lakȟóta, the Húŋkpapȟa and Sihásapa, who were not interested in the 1851 Treaty and continued raiding the Crow.[3]

In 1856, following the Harney treaty, the Lakȟóta took action to find common ground against future invasions of their homelands. After all, the election of head chiefs was no business of the wašíču. They sent emissaries to present the sacred pipe to oyáte scattered throughout the vast Lakȟóta tȟamákȟočhe. The pipe was an invitation to attend a council where plans of action would be determined. The Húŋkpapȟa were the most ardent in their opposition to the whites and were looking to strengthen their position through a deeper alliance with the Mnikȟówožu. Four Horns (Ȟé Tópa) a powerful Húŋkpapȟa chief, performed the huŋká ritual of adoption to establish stronger ties with the Mnikȟówožu. He adopted Lame Deer (Tȟáȟča Hušté) and Red Anus,[4] both brothers of Lone Horn and leaders, to be his sons. This maneuver strengthened the northern Lakȟóta position against the southern Oglála and Sičháŋǧu, who were more conciliatory toward the whites. Among the Sičháŋǧu, Spotted Tail was now openly in favor of peace. Similarly, Lone Horn, who had visited Washington, DC, following the Fort Laramie Treaty, was impressed by the power of the whites. He, too, sought peaceful relations. Among the Oglála, Red Cloud, who had established himself as a blotáhuŋka (war leader) was the major force advocating for resistance. Red Cloud, born in 1822, had gained a reputation as a great warrior during raids against the Crow and other native enemies. He was not a hereditary chief of the Oglála like Man Afraid of His Horses, but by the mid-1850s he was a man of power and influence beyond his immediate thiyóšpaye, the Ité Šíča or Bad Face. Red Cloud, like Sitting Bull (Tȟatȟáŋka Íyotake) of the Húŋkpapȟa, was one of the new generation of leaders, who were determined to keep the wašíču out of Lakȟóta territory.[5]

In an atmosphere of divisive tribal politics, a council with representatives from all Lakȟóta oyáte was an unprecedented idea and demonstrates how the Lakȟóta actively sought innovative solutions to the emergent and critical question of how to deal with the wašíču. They were not passive in the face of American imperialism but actively took charge of their own future and destiny.

In the summer of 1857, thousands of Lakȟóta gathered in the vicinity of Bear Butte (Matȟó Pahá). They camped along the Belle Fourche River (Šahíyela Wakpá) just north of the Black Hills to discuss strategies for action. It may have been the largest gathering of Lakȟóta oyáte up to that point, with as many as 10,000 people attending. During the meetings, divisiveness was apparent. Older leaders such as Man Afraid of His Horses and Lone Horn advocated a neutral or friendly approach toward the whites, whereas younger leaders insisted on an aggressive isolationist stance. It is important to remember that in Lakȟóta society no chief alone held supreme power. Even if Harney and other whites elevated some men to more prominent positions, this was not how Lakȟóta society worked. Yellow Hawk (Čhetáŋ Zí), of the Itázipčho, explained this confusion after being appointed as a chief. He said, "[I] was never a chief and did not think of myself as such until I was chosen to visit the Grandfather's home in Washington." That he was chosen by the wašíču put him in an uncomfortable situation. In this position the whites expected him to promote the white man's way of life, which he then chose to do, even if it meant serving the US army as a scout against his own people.[6] When Indian Agent Alexander H. Redfield asked Lakȟóta men why they continued to raid other Indians when there was supposed to be peace, their reply was simple: "How can we ever become chiefs unless we distinguish ourselves by taking many scalps and horses, and by striking our enemies? Without deeds of skill, daring, and bravery we are nothing. Unless we can recount at the war dance many of these deeds or acts, we are no more than women, and can never be fit to be chiefs."[7]

Because they lacked coercive powers, older leaders could not refuse younger men the same route to success that they had taken. Agent Redfield, like other white observers before and after him, lamented this situation. According to Redfield, the old men were wise and peaceful, but they could not control the younger men, and the chiefs appointed by the whites were confused about what was expected of them.[8]

During the 1857 council, younger leaders such as Red Cloud, were in open defiance of older leaders like (Old) Man Afraid of His Horses, the traditional chief of the Oglála.[9] The exact unfolding of events is unclear, but it seems that many Southern Lakȟóta, perhaps following the example of Red Cloud, aligned themselves with the Húŋkpapȟa and Mnikȟówožu, rather than with their own peace-oriented chiefs. Eventually the factions agreed upon a joint resolution: The Lakȟóta would not give the whites additional parts of their homelands or allow whites, except for a few traders, to trespass their country or build new roads. They would not accept annuities if that required them to make peace with the Crow. This decision would cause friction in the future. The Lakȟóta also refused to allow Iháŋktȟuŋwaŋ to enter their country because they had sold part of their lands to the whites. Many Lakȟóta saw that as a betrayal since the lands belonged to all Lakȟóta and Dakȟóta alike.[10]

Although most agreed with the decision, no direct action was taken. To the Lakȟóta, the decision to fight, if necessary, was enough, but the fighting would be done in traditional ways, not in a unified manner. Some scholars have argued that this shows the weakness of Lakȟóta leadership, or a lack of innovation, or that they misunderstood the gravity of the situation. The real reason was that the Lakȟóta had no political or military leadership structure that would have implemented a unanimous plan for defense. In fact, it was not even needed since peace with the whites had just been effected. The whites posed no immediate threat. After declaring they would oppose white encroachment, the Lakȟóta dispersed. Some groups went to hunt, while others resumed raiding their Indian enemies.[11]

Although the Lakȟóta did not build a grand "army" to confront the wašíču threat, they did demonstrate their intention to adhere to the joint "declaration." In small, seemingly independent groups, Lakȟóta warriors patrolled the borderlands of their domain.[12] They raided trading posts, stopped trespassing migrant caravans, and refused to take annuities or sign additional treaties. The first true test of their resolution came in the early fall of 1857 when an army column of topographical engineers led by Lieutenant G. K. Warren approached a Lakȟóta hunting camp near the Inyan Kara (Íŋyaŋ Káǧa) mountain. The Húŋkpapȟa warriors wished to wipe out the wašíču, but after pleas by Mnikȟówožu chiefs, the Húŋkpapȟa let Warren go. The Húŋkpapȟa, led by Bear's Rib, told Warren that they would make an exception this time, but their treaty with Harney specifically stated that no one should be allowed to travel through Lakȟóta lands, except by boat on the Missouri River. Warren wrote in his report that the Indians' justifications were sound: they did not want white people to disturb the buffalo herds that were nearby, and they understood that if Warren were to explore the country, more wašíču would become interested in it. They turned Warren free, but they would never agree to peace with the Crow. The Húŋkpapȟa resolution to defend their lands held.[13]

The Lakȟóta resumed war with the Crow as agreed upon in the "declaration." The Lakȟóta escalated their invasion of Crow country. In 1857–58 the Lakȟóta earned a major victory when they surrounded and killed a group of ten Crow. The fighting raged throughout 1857–59. Both sides attacked each other, suffering considerably. Between 1859 and 1861, the Crow killed several Lakȟóta, and especially the death of Chief Big Crow (Kȟaŋǧí Tȟáŋka) was a notable event. The Crow were occasionally victorious as well. They made daring raids on Lakȟóta camps, and in 1862–63 scalped a young boy while in camp. A year later eight Mnikȟówožu were killed by the Crow. Yet the Lakȟóta were pushing unstoppably into Crow lands. In a two-year period, they drove the Crow out of the Powder River Country and into the Big Horn Mountains (Ȟeyúškiška) and beyond. The early 1860s saw another escalation of warfare with the Assiniboine and Pawnee. While the Lakȟóta expanded their domain westward, winter counts for the late 1850s and early 1860s report both the scarcity of buffalo and the spread of diseases. In the winter of 1858–59 Lone Horn conducted a ceremony wearing a white buffalo robe to secure a successful buffalo hunt. Due to the paucity of buffalo, the Lakȟóta pushed even more vigorously into the Powder River area where game was still plentiful. In fact, winter counts for 1861–62 report an unusual abundance of buffalo there. Several winter counts depict the year with the image of a thípi surrounded by buffalo tracks. These thiyóšpaye were residing in the game-rich western part of the Lakȟóta homelands, recently taken from the Crow.[14]

Despite Lakȟóta successes in the early 1860s, life was not easy for those residing near the Missouri River or along the Oregon Trail. After the 1857 "declaration" the Lakȟóta were clearly divided. Winter counts describe the importance of trade with the white man and the issue of whether to receive annuities. For those living close to the Missouri, the annuities were essential for subsistence, but this violated the "declaration" of 1857. The Lakȟóta understood that accepting the annuities would make them ever more dependent on the whites. While this policy proved to be divisive, it shows that the Lakȟóta were seeking new ways to confront the problem of white encroachment. The stipulations of the "declaration" demonstrate Lakȟóta agency: they were keenly aware of how the United States had pressured other tribes into dependency through land sales and annuities. One Lakȟóta chief told Agent Thomas Twiss how as a young man he had visited the lands of the Potawatomie, Winnebago, and Iháŋkthuŋwaŋ that were infested with white men. "And now our 'Father' tells us the white men will never settle on our lands and kill our game; but see! The whites cover all the lands that I just described," he lamented. "Our country has become very small, and, before our children are grown up, we shall have no more game."[15]

The "declaration" was intended to protect all Lakȟóta from that fate. Yet, in the summer of 1862 this policy led to a fatal fight close to Fort Pierre. After Bear's Rib, the noted Húŋkpapȟa leader, agreed to take annuities for his hungry people, other Lakȟóta brutally killed him for violating the declaration. Following his death, a letter signed by nine Húŋkpapȟa leaders reached Indian Agent Samuel N. Latta. The letter explained the reasons for killing Bear's Rib: "We notified Bear's Rib yearly not to receive your goods; he has no ears, and we gave him ears by killing him. We now say to you, bring us no goods, if any of our people receive any more from you, we will give them ears as we did Bear's Rib." In Lakȟóta culture "having no ears" meant disrespect and immature behavior. By acting against the will of the majority, Bear's Rib had put himself and his people at risk. On the other hand, with hunting getting more difficult each year around Fort Pierre, Bear's Rib needed to provide for his people. The white man's annuities were a welcome addition. The political assassination of a chief of such high standing demonstrates that the divisions within Lakȟóta society in relation to the wašíču were deepening.[16]

Whether the Lakȟóta wanted to or not, by the early 1860s they had become increasingly dependent on the white man's commodities, especially guns, ammunition, and metal tools. As game became scarce, the reality was that the annuities the US government offered were an easy and sometimes necessary means of subsistence. Thus, the Lakȟóta, like so many nations before them, were gradually absorbed into the American imperialistic system. This was exactly what US Indian policy sought to achieve: make the Indians dependent on trade goods, which would lead to gradual assimilation or perhaps extinction. This idea culminated in the reservation policy, which officially began in 1851, the year of the Fort Laramie Treaty. The early reservation policy did not seek to confine tribes to their reservations; rather, each tribe was assigned a specific area and offered annuities in compensation. Thus the 1851 Fort Laramie Treaty was not only designed to secure peace on the Northern Plains, it was also part of a long-term strategy by the US government to control and assimilate native peoples.[17]

The early 1860s saw no major violence between whites and the Lakȟóta. Most US army units had been sent to fight the Civil War, but trouble for the Lakȟóta was brewing in the east. Impoverished Isáŋyathi Dakȟóta took up arms against the whites in Minnesota. Hundreds of settlers, soldiers, and Dakȟóta lost their lives. In the aftermath, surviving Dakȟóta crossed the Missouri River and sought refuge among their Lakȟóta relatives. While many Lakȟóta wanted to avoid conflict with the US Army, they could not refuse help to their relatives in need because that would have violated kinship norms and expectations. Unfortunately, by offering refuge to their relatives, the Lakȟóta were drawn into the conflict. For the US Army and other whites it did not matter whether they fought the Lakȟóta or the Dakȟóta. Conflict was inevitable when the army forces followed the Dakȟóta across the Missouri River.[18]

A separate issue angering the Northern Lakȟóta at the time was a new road crossing their lands to Montana after the discovery of gold there in 1862. That year more than five-hundred gold seekers trespassed on Northern Lakȟóta hunting grounds on their way to the gold fields. The Húŋkpapȟa, especially, did not accept this. In the letter explaining the killing of Bear's Rib, the Húŋkpapȟa chiefs specifically said that they would not tolerate white people traveling by land through their territories or allow boats bringing passengers who would eventually trespass Lakȟóta lands. "If you do not pay any attention to what we now say to you, you may rely on seeing the tracks of our horses on the warpath," they warned. Their warning was not heeded. In response, under Sitting Bull, a leader who was gaining ever-more influence among his people, the Húŋkpapȟa staged several raids against trespassers, precipitating confrontation with US Army forces under Gen. Alfred Sully and Col. Henry H. Sibley.[19]

By this time the Lakȟóta had "forgotten" the devastation that General Harney had caused almost a decade earlier. They were once again ready to wage war against the army. Confident of their power, the Northern Lakȟóta concluded their letter by saying that if the whites would not listen to them, they would give them ears, as they had given ears to Bear's Rib. In defiance they urged the army to bring an army of "real men, not women dressed in soldier's clothes." In Sully and Sibley's forces the Lakȟóta got just what they asked for.[20]

Expanding Lakȟóta Tȟamákȟočhe

During the summer of 1863 Northern Lakȟóta and Isáŋyathi clashed with the US Army forces on several occasions. These military forces were not poorly trained militia groups, but organized and well-equipped army units capable of inflicting stinging defeats. The Lakȟóta lost much of the food and pelts they had collected for the next winter. By fall, Colonel Sibley withdrew back to Minnesota, but Sully's troops remained at Fort Pierre. By spring 1864 they had constructed a new fort, Fort Sully. Throughout the winter the Lakȟóta traded with the whites but sent threatening messages through traders and trappers to Sully. Following the previous summer's losses, the Lakȟóta were now better prepared and promised to destroy Sully's troops. Those sending the threatening messages stayed west in the Powder River Country and the Black Hills area, whereas those engaged in trading mostly remained near the forts, further demonstrating the deepening factionalism within Lakȟóta society. However, there was still a tremendous amount of visiting between various Lakȟóta camps and thiyóšpaye. Those living west were aware of what was going on around the forts and trading posts. There may have been division, but Lakȟóta society was not broken.

By summer 1864, the Lakȟóta were ready to meet Sully's army, and Killdeer Mountain in present-day North Dakota was the scene of battle. Sully's troops, now numbering up to 3,000, ran into a large Lakȟóta camp. The Lakȟóta were so confident that they did not move the camp away from the battle area, and many families gathered to watch the fighting, which lasted most of the day. According to the Húŋkpapȟa White Bull (Tȟatȟáŋka Ská), Sitting Bull's nephew, the Lakȟóta fought in native fashion, dashing daringly in small groups or individually against the troops, before withdrawing rapidly. Lone Dog of the Húŋkpapȟa executed one of the most notable deeds of bravery, taunting the soldiers until they opened fire at him. The battle fluctuated, but toward evening the Lakȟóta were forced to retreat.

The artillery fired at the camp and the Lakȟóta, men, women, and children had to escape into the surrounding hills and Badlands (Makȟóšiča) west of Killdeer Mountain. The soldiers set the entire Lakȟóta camp on fire, and a few people who had remained, including children, were killed. The Lakȟóta, now without provisions, had to seek shelter in other Lakȟóta camps.[21]

Once reinforcements arrived, the Lakȟóta, joined by their Dakȟóta, Cheyenne, and Arapaho allies, decided to counterattack. Several skirmishes took place during August and both sides committed brutal acts. The soldiers placed the heads of three Lakȟóta on poles to demonstrate what would happen to those who opposed the army. In retaliation the Lakȟóta mutilated the bodies of dead soldiers and filled them with arrows. Among the fighting Lakȟóta was Sitting Bull, who according to Lakȟóta testimonies was the most determined to keep up the fighting. He fought day and night the entire summer, said White Bull later. Sitting Bull was severely wounded in the hip after a hand-to-hand fight with a soldier. His companions, including White Bull, came to his rescue and carried him away from the battlefield. By the end of the summer, the Lakȟóta lost interest in the war. They simply disappeared into the Badlands and left Sully without a foe. Having decided enough was enough, they turned their interests toward hunting and raiding their native enemies.[22] Having lost to Sully's army, the Lakȟóta inflicted their revenge on white trespassers: gold miners, settlers, and soldiers were frequently harassed by small groups of Lakȟóta warriors.

The Northern Lakȟóta were responsible for most of the fighting against Sully's forces throughout the summer of 1864, and despite some losses, it was not the most significant event of the year for most Lakȟóta oyáte. Only Lone Dog mentions the fighting in his winter count, noting that this was the year of the "First fight with the white man." For the Northern Lakȟóta this was quite true because the Harney expedition a decade earlier had targeted the Southern Lakȟóta: the Oglála and Sičháŋǧu. The Lakȟóta also decided to make a truce with the Arikara for trading purposes in the late summer of 1864. The Húŋkpapȟa, including Sitting Bull, were invited to an Arikara camp to trade, but things started to go wrong during a friendly horseback race. Both sides took prisoners, and an all-out fight nearly erupted. Sitting Bull and an Arikara chief, however, intervened and deescalated the situation. Trading resumed. This is a good example of the significance of intertribal relations even during a time of war against the whites. Intertribal war was very important, but so was trade. It was an old Plains custom to put warfare aside for trading purposes, sometimes only for a day or two, though sometimes these truces could last longer. It was not uncommon for parties that had fought each other only a few days earlier to find themselves trading peacefully during an intertribal truce. Still, tensions were never too far beneath the surface, as demonstrated by the incident in the Arikara camp.[23]

About this time a significant change took place in Lakȟóta attitudes toward the wašíču. As long as the whites were not considered a real threat to the Lakȟóta homelands and Lakȟóta way of life, they were placed in a different category than Indians. Until now, all Indians who did not speak Lakȟóta were considered thóka (potential enemies), but the whites were simply wašíču, a category outside the indigenous classification. Thus, killing a wašíču did not earn war honors in the same way as killing or wounding an Indian enemy. George Sword, a leading Oglála warrior and shirt wearer in the 1860s and 1870s, recalls that in 1864, just prior to the beginning of the period of major fighting with the whites, the Lakȟóta decided that war honors would also be gained from fighting the wašíču. This change demonstrates Lakȟóta attempts not only to adapt to the increasing threat posed by the expanding United States, but also to actively seek new ways to confront new challenges. Warfare to protect the Lakȟóta homelands from the invading wašíču was more logical and meaningful when personal honor and prestige could be gained in the process. For this to happen, the wašíču needed to be thóka, just like traditional Indian enemies.[24]

The council of chiefs convened and officially announced that the wašíču now belonged to the enemy category. An éyapaha (crier) went around Oglála camp circles announcing: "All young men, hear this! The white men will take our entire land from us and we will no longer comprise a people! Therefore, we will make war on them, so whoever strikes a white man, that shall be a coup against the enemy! Whoever is wounded by a white man, that one shall be wounded by an enemy! And if you take his horses and perform any other deeds, they shall be counted as honors!" With this announcement, the wašíču officially became thóka, incorporated into the coup system of war honors.[25]

While the Northern Lakȟóta fought General Sully, the Oglála and Sičháŋǧu had their own problems. The number of travelers on the western trails leading to the Montana and Colorado goldfields had risen steadily. The Cheyenne and Arapaho were first drawn into conflict, and by 1863 the Oglála and Sičháŋǧu fought beside their allies along the Oregon Trail and the southern Platte River region. Farther south the Kiowa and Comanche also fought the US Army. To secure the travelers' safety, the US government dispatched more troops to the area, some of them voluntary militia units. During the summer of 1864 the fighting spread south where the Lakȟóta inflicted considerable damage to travelers and settlements. They encircled and destroyed the town of Julesburg in present-day Colorado.[26]

The attack on Julesburg was not a minor raid organized by a group of young warriors. Instead, it was a major effort and as well-organized as a communal buffalo hunt. Chiefs, including Roman Nose of the Cheyenne, Spotted Tail of the Sičháŋǧu, and Pawnee Killer (Sčílikté) of the Oglála, led the expedition. Before leaving the main camp, all men dressed in their finest regalia and members of the warrior societies paraded through the camp singing war songs. The Cheyenne first offered the pipe to the Lakȟóta, who accepted, and thus took the lead in organizing the expedition, which consisted of hundreds of men, with their families following. White settlers reported that the Indians were singing and dancing night after night. As the expedition closed in on Julesburg, the akíčhita were ordered to keep the younger men in check so that they would not spoil the carefully planned attack. Against their traditional enemies, the Lakȟóta often sent small decoy parties to lure the enemy into a trap. Eager young men looking for personal glory sometimes could not be kept in check, and so the element of surprise was lost. When the Lakȟóta force approached Julesburg, they decided to use this decoy tactic. Once again, a group of young men disobeyed the directions of the akíčhita, causing the trap to fail. But the Lakȟóta were not discouraged and attacked. The fight lasted several days, and the attackers eventually looted and destroyed the town, carrying away a great number of horses, cattle, and provisions.[27]

After the victory, the camp dispersed and most of the Lakȟóta withdrew northward to the safety of the Powder River country. Even though they had caused considerable destruction, the US Army lacked the capacity to punish them. For the Lakȟóta, the attack on Julesburg was a break with the past, not only because it was so well organized, but because it was conducted in the middle of the winter. Until then, major war parties were only common in the summer, since cold and snow were not ideal for grand undertakings.

After the Lakȟóta camp dispersed into smaller thiyóšpaye in the Powder River country, raids on the wašíču continued on a smaller scale. The Lakȟóta focused their attacks on a trail recently opened between Fort Laramie and the Montana goldfields. This "Bozeman Trail" cut through the richest Lakȟóta hunting grounds, violating the treaties with the whites. Another cause for action during the winter of 1865 was a massacre of nearly 200 Cheyenne at Sand Creek, Colorado Territory, on November 29, 1864. A militia force under Col. John M. Chivington savagely attacked a friendly Cheyenne camp, committing grim atrocities.[28] This massacre

further prompted the Lakȟóta to view the wašíču as tȟóka. Commissioner of
Indian Affairs D. N. Cooley noticed that many Indians had advocated for peace,
but constant violations of treaties, as well as provocations, and atrocities had
turned the situation. He condemned Chivington's actions and directly blamed
him for the escalation of warfare on the Northern Plains. The Sand Creek massacre also brought the Lakȟóta, Cheyenne, and Arapaho closer together as allies
presenting a unified front in the war against a shared enemy.[29]

This alliance earned a series of successes on the battlefield. They launched
raids as they pleased and then withdrew to the safety of the Powder River country. Though army officers reported that they had driven the Lakȟóta off to the
north the Indians had withdrawn there voluntarily. From there they launched
more attacks.

Another success for the Lakȟóta and their allies took place in July 1865. After
their annual Sun Dance and accompanying ceremonies, they staged a well-
organized expedition against a small military fort in western Wyoming, which
has come to be known as the Platte Bridge battle. The fort was built strategically
to protect travelers crossing the Platte River. Although the number of soldiers
in the garrison was small, they could easily control the west bank of the river and
the river valley. The Lakȟóta and their Cheyenne allies gathered a fighting force
of perhaps as many as 3,000 men. Red Cloud, Old Man Afraid of His Horses,
Young Man Afraid of His Horses, and other chiefs employed all the necessary
akíčhita forces to ensure that the young men stuck to the plan of attack. A few
men, including Crazy Horse of the Oglála, were sent to the bridge to lure the
soldiers into the nearby hills where the main force was waiting. Once again,
some eager young men spoiled the plan. The Lakȟóta only succeeded in killing
five and wounding several soldiers. Among the casualties was young Lt. Caspar
Collins, who was known to be sympathetic toward the Indians. Even Crazy
Horse reportedly was fond of the young officer. While the main Lakȟóta force
attempted to capture the bridge, another fight took place a few miles southwest
along the banks of the North Platte River. Here the Indian forces, led by the
Cheyenne, forced a wagon train of five wagons and twenty-five soldiers to
form a defensive circle. After intense fighting, twenty-two soldiers lay dead, and
the Indians emerged victorious, despite losing several men. After the battle, the
Indians dispersed and returned to the Powder River country in time to conduct
their annual buffalo hunts and campaign against the Crow.[30]

In response to Lakȟóta attacks, the US Army dispatched more troops to
the scene. In the summer of 1865, troops approached Lakȟóta country under

Gen. Patrick E. Connor. He divided his force into three columns, which were supposed to surround all Indians they encountered and then build a fort in the Powder River country. Col. James A. Sawyers led a group of civilians to Montana. By mid-August the soldiers inflicted a major blow against the Cheyenne, who lost twenty-four men in a surprise attack spearheaded by Pawnee scouts under command of Capt. Frank J. North. Later, on August 29, General Connor surprised an Arapaho village on the Tongue River (Tȟačhéži Wakpá). The troops were supposed to rendezvous deep in Lakȟóta country, but they lost track of each other's movement in the Black Hills area. The Lakȟóta and their allies constantly harassed the troops. The early days of September saw several major skirmishes on each of the columns trespassing on Lakȟóta lands, and soon the soldiers ran out of supplies.[31]

In the summer of 1865, the Northern and Southern Lakȟóta worked closely together. They may not have organized joint attacks, but readily kept each other informed about troop movements. The Lakȟóta effectively forced the troops into disadvantageous positions and by the end of the summer the troops were starving.[32] Not before late September were the soldiers able to scramble back from Lakȟóta territory. They had been forced to eat their own horses and barely made it back to Fort Connor and then eventually Fort Laramie. Instead of surrounding the Indians and forcing them to surrender, the army had suffered a devastating, embarrassing, and financially disastrous defeat.

The Northern Lakȟóta also threatened military posts and expeditions along the Missouri River. Sitting Bull attacked Fort Rice at the same time Oglála and Sičháŋǧu were engaged at the Platte Bridge.[33] There has been debate as to whether the Lakȟóta and their allies came up with a new strategy in which they united under the leadership of one or two major chiefs. Military defeats like this needed to be explained.

It may be true that the Lakȟóta and their allies were able to fight in a more unified and organized manner than before. The large number of men participating in the raids against the troops was also a new tactic for the Lakȟóta. However, it is incorrect to maintain that there was a unified leadership organizing these warriors in military-style campaigns. Connors's troops entered the Lakȟóta domain and the Lakȟóta were able to exact precise and devastating raids upon the troops in a typical Lakȟóta fashion. Large, well-organized, formal war expeditions were followed and supported by informal and individualistic raiding parties. The Lakȟóta were fighting as they always had, and it proved to be effective. It was still difficult for the whites to accept that this form of warfare could be effective and so challenge the American way.[34]

Although the summer of 1865 had been a military success, Lakȟóta winter counts emphasized fighting traditional enemies and other important events that affected daily life. No Ears called 1864–65 the year when Psáloka Tóp Wičháktepi, "Four Crow were Killed." Other winter counts report that it was the winter when many horses died due to heavy snow falls.[35] Despite whipping the US military, the Lakȟóta were doing what they had always done. The fighting that summer demonstrated that the Lakȟóta were still expanding their domain. As they raided from the Missouri River in the east to western Wyoming, Lakȟóta tȟamákȟočhe was being reinvented.

Protecting the Čhaȟlí Wakpá Makȟóčhe

In the summer of 1865, new and consequential developments were taking place in Washington, DC. A powerful eastern group called the Friends of the Indian gained more influence in the US government after the Civil War. This group was convinced that the best way to solve the "Indian problem" was to demonstrate by kindness and generosity that the white man's way of life was best for the Indians too. Many of these individuals genuinely believed that they were helping the Indians, but their efforts were often paternalistic, and, from native perspectives, not benefitting the Indians at all. President Ulysses S. Grant, however, was willing to listen to the humanitarians. Soon Grant formulated his Peace Policy. Its aim was to reduce Indian warfare, force all Indian tribes onto reservations, Christianize them, and teach them farming, even if lands were completely unsuitable for that purpose. Before the Peace Policy became official policy in 1868, a thorough investigation into the state of Indian affairs needed to be conducted as there were reports of corruption, wrongdoing, and inefficiency. Several commissions were established to investigate various reservations.[36]

The Lakȟóta got a foreshadowing of the new Indian policy three years before it became official. In the summer of 1866, a government commission arrived in Lakȟóta country to discuss peace and future negotiations. The meeting with the Southern Lakȟóta was to be held again at Fort Laramie. The successes of the previous year had established Red Cloud as one of the major leaders of the fighting Lakȟóta. Spotted Tail, the leading chief of the Sičháŋǧu had become the major force speaking against war with the wašíču. Only a few years earlier he had been one of the most active blotáhuŋka, but in the aftermath of the 1854 post wagon attack his opinions began changing. Following the attack, the US

Army pressured the Lakȟóta to turn in the men responsible for the raid. Spotted Tail and other participants voluntarily surrendered, though they were certain they would be hanged. Instead, they were put in jail. Spotted Tail spent a year in prison at Fort Leavenworth, Kansas, where he befriended several of the military personnel. When he came home from prison, he was a changed man. Another important event was the death of Spotted Tail's daughter on the way to Fort Laramie in the winter of 1866. According to the commanding officer of the fort, Col. Henry A. Maynadier, Spotted Tail's daughter wanted to be buried close to the fort. After meeting with the heartbroken Sičháŋǧu chief, Maynadier agreed to this request, and a scaffold was erected not far from the fort. This gesture of friendship deeply affected both men.[37] After shaking hands with the commander Spotted Tail gave an emotional speech, tears running from his eyes: "This must be a dream for me to be in such a fine room and surrounded by such as you. Have I been asleep during the four years of hardship and trial and am dreaming all is to be well again, or is this real! Yes, I see that it is; the beautiful day, the sky blue, without a cloud, the wind calm and still to suit the errand I come on and remind me that you have offered me peace." He pointed out that they were entitled to compensation for the damage caused by the roads that destroyed the buffalo and game. "My heart is very sad, and I cannot talk business; I will wait and see the councilors the Great Father will send."[38]

These experiences convinced Spotted Tail that fighting the wašíču was futile. He became a vocal proponent of peace. This turned other Lakȟóta, even many Sičháŋǧu, against him. Yet his influence remained strong among long-time peace advocates. Divisions that began decades earlier continued to affect Lakȟóta internal politics. Those who decided to live close to the forts were called Wáǧluȟe (Loafers), a name that carried with it a certain amount of contempt from both whites and other Lakȟóta. Still, Colonel Maynadier was convinced that all Lakȟóta were ready for peace by the spring of 1866. The winter had been harsh and many thiyóšpaye were suffering. The American Horse winter count demonstrates Lakȟóta hopes for peace. Perhaps somewhat prematurely his winter count declares that General Maynadier made peace with the Oglála and Sičháŋǧu in the winter of 1865–66.[39]

When government officials came to Fort Laramie in 1866, Spotted Tail and his followers were there to greet them. Red Cloud and many Oglála and Sičháŋǧu remained in the Black Hills. The government officials introduced a draft of a treaty that would, among other things, have allowed the government to establish roads through Lakȟóta country. The roads, of course, needed forts for protection.

In what was already becoming a tradition in treaty making, the treaty proposal included a section noting that the Lakȟóta would need to give up all fighting against the whites and other Indian tribes. As compensation for settling down and taking up farming, the US government would give them appropriations for the next twenty years.[40]

A similar proposition was delivered to the Northern Lakȟóta at Fort Sully. The Húŋkpapȟa, led by Sitting Bull, refused to negotiate. Government officials were able to get signatures from only a few men, whom they described as "progressive chiefs." Red Cloud arrived at Fort Laramie after a week's delay to begin what could be called pre-negotiations. He did not want to begin real talks at all, and soon returned to the Black Hills. Government officials were frustrated with Red Cloud, believing that his signature was crucial as they considered him the head chief of all Lakȟóta.[41] Red Cloud stayed away, playing mind games with the negotiators. Though the commissioners were waiting for him, Red Cloud was in no hurry. Besides, it was the season for ceremonies and hunting. After several weeks, Red Cloud retuned to Fort Laramie, hoping to receive supplies rather than to actually negotiate.

After the customary opening ceremonies, the negotiations finally began. They were cut short when the Lakȟóta learned that there were already soldiers moving along the Bozeman Trail. This was a unit of several hundred soldiers led by Col. Henry B. Carrington tasked with establishing new forts—Fort Reno, Fort Phil Kearny, and Fort C. F. Smith—right in the heart of Lakȟóta country. The Lakȟóta were furious. Man Afraid of His Horses threatened to kill all white men entering Lakȟóta lands, and Red Cloud exclaimed, "The Great Father sends us presents and wants a new road. But the White Chief already goes with soldiers to steal the road before the Indian says yes or no." He continued, shouting, "I will talk with you no more. I will go now, and I will fight you. As long as I live, I will fight you for the last hunting grounds."[42]

Whether this truly happened as reported, is debatable, but Red Cloud, Man Afraid of His Horses, and the majority of the Lakȟóta walked away from the talks. Only a few chiefs deemed "progressive" by the whites remained to sign the treaty. The most notable of these was Spotted Tail. The government officials were jubilant. The chiefs who signed were, of course, not in a position in Lakȟóta society that allowed them to make a deal with the US on behalf of all Lakȟóta, or even all Oglála or Sičháŋǧu. That was not a problem for the government officials. They no longer needed Red Cloud's signature, which only a few weeks earlier had been considered essential to declare success. They informed Washington that the results of their "labor are a treaty entirely conducted with the Oglála and Sičháŋǧu."[43] Their jubilant mood was premature. Without the commissioners realizing it, instead of a permanent peace, the United States was now actually at war with the Lakȟóta.

Red Cloud's War, as it is commonly known, placed Red Cloud at the center of the conflict. While his heritage did not entitle him to the position of chief, he had demonstrated superior abilities and courage on the warpath. He had reportedly accumulated as many as eighty coups.[44] However, during the 1860s the most important chief among the Oglála was Man Afraid of His Horses. Other leading men included Black Twin, also known as Holy Bald Eagle,[45] Red Fox (Šuŋǧílasapa), Pawnee Killer, and Big Mouth (Í Ṫḣáŋka). Among the Sičháŋǧu, Spotted Tail, Swift Bear (Matȟó Lúzahaŋ), and Two Strike were the most prominent leaders.[46] These chiefs along with other leading men were in charge of Southern Lakȟóta decisions, not Red Cloud alone. One Lakȟóta described Red Cloud's position this way: "Red Cloud was not a chief but he was a great chief." Undoubtedly Red Cloud was a key figure in the development of Lakȟóta military tactics throughout the 1866–68 war, but this was together with other Lakȟóta leaders.[47] To keep a large group of Lakȟóta unified in war or anything else required a new way of thinking, and it may be that Red Cloud was the main strategist.

Elsewhere, Sitting Bull was gaining prestige as the main leader of the Northern Lakȟóta. His name appears, perhaps for the first time, in a white man's report written by General Sully in 1864. Even though Sitting Bull, Gall (Phizí), and other Northern Lakȟóta leaders were actively participating in the fighting, the whites were mostly concerned about Red Cloud. At the same time, Commissioner Taylor declared that a permanent peace had been established at Fort Laramie. He now said that Red Cloud was a nobody, and the real Lakȟóta chiefs had signed the new treaty. Taylor believed that it was only some "wild and uncontrollable" young men who might cause trouble but, according to him, major Lakȟóta chiefs had signed the treaty.[48] The whites could not or refused to understand Lakȟóta leadership structures.

After leaving the negotiations, Red Cloud, Man Afraid of His Horses, and their Cheyenne allies conducted a series of raids along the Bozeman Trail. Despite the attacks, Colonel Carrington continued his efforts to build forts along the trail. He was convinced that he could hold off the Indians and complete his job. In July 1866 he began building a new fort along the Little Piney Creek in a strategic location near the foothills of the Big Horn Mountains. The fort was finished without major obstacles and Carrington was able to proudly report that he had accomplished his task. Shortly thereafter Fort C. F. Smith was built farther north. Carrington was so pleased that he told his superiors that if he could get some additional men, he could hold his own against a thousand Indians. However, his men were inexperienced, and Carrington's requests for more experienced troops were denied time and again. Carrington's actions have been heavily criticized since. Although he claimed he could keep the Indians under control, simultaneously he demanded more troops and noted that there was no way to prevent the Indians from attacking anywhere along the Bozeman Trail. He took no real action to stop the raiding.[49]

Carrington witnessed Lakȟóta traditional warfare made more effective by a new strategy. At the start of the war, the Lakȟóta were not even planning to attack the fort. That was inconsistent with Lakȟóta interests; instead, they concentrated their attacks on more vulnerable targets. Standing Bear, who was part of these attacks, said that the white cavalry did not know how to fight. "They stuck together and thus made an easy target for us," and he described how the Lakȟóta fought in circles and "some would go one way and the others would go another way" thus disorganizing the white soldiers. "We would hang on our ponies at times with one leg. This is a real trick to know how to do. Then we would shoot under the horse's neck while the other leg is cramped up on the other side."[50] These rapid attacks caused chaos among the travelers. The Indians attacked almost daily, targeting military units, immigrant wagons, supply trains, parties that were searching for water and firewood; basically, anyone traveling on the hated road or in its vicinity fell prey to the Lakȟóta. By the fall of 1866, travel on the Bozeman Trail had practically ceased.

The Lakȟóta used traditional tactics but in a more unified and disciplined manner than ever before. At the same time, they allowed young men to gain prestige by leading and organizing these raids as they had always done. The white man was now thóka and there were plenty of war honors to be gained for all.

There are still indications that the chiefs had considerable difficulty keeping the forces together and adhering to the larger strategies they were laying out. These differences had become visible already during the summer of 1866. Lakȟóta and their Cheyenne allies moved from the Bozeman Trail farther north and camped along Tongue River for their annual Sun Dance ceremonies. The ceremonies were successful, but major political frictions remained. A Cheyenne peace faction had already discussed with Colonel Carrington the possibility of abandoning the fighting in exchange for goods. They told the colonel that they were afraid of the Lakȟóta, so they wanted to leave and make peace. When the Lakȟóta akíčhita learned about this, they slashed the Cheyenne severely with their own bow strings. The humiliated Cheyenne disappeared from the camp, while the majority of the Cheyenne remained allied with the Lakȟóta.

This was not the only division. Many Lakȟóta leaders were also interested in the goods and gifts the US government was distributing to the Loafers who remained at peace and stayed close to the forts. The warring Lakȟóta maintained contacts with the people living at the forts and made frequent visits there. Even Man Afraid of His Horses was keen to learn more about the possibility of receiving goods in compensation for peace. The Lakȟóta quarreled about the objectives of the war and how long it was to continue. Still, even those Lakȟóta who came to see the whites for gifts and promised to end the war could speak differently when they returned to Powder River. Thus, estimates of the number of Lakȟóta hoping for peace made by whites like Colonel Carrington were too high. Nevertheless, gifts and promises of compensation caused confusion and disagreement among the Lakȟóta.

Red Cloud never wavered in his belief and was determined to carry on the war until the Bozeman Trail and the forts were abandoned. In this tumultuous environment of internal politics and outside influences, he kept his fighting forces united for two long years. This achievement speaks volumes about his leadership qualities. It seems that he was indeed becoming a major chief, a position not traditionally given to anyone in Lakȟóta society.

"Hundred White Men Were Killed"

In December 1866, the Lakȟóta besieged and nearly destroyed a detachment of loggers sent from Fort Phil Kearny. Similar attacks had happened before, but this time it caused real panic among the whites. The Lakȟóta attack showed a new level of effectiveness and potential to cause great damage. Whites now feared that they would attack the fort directly. Instead, the Lakȟóta confined themselves to patrolling the area around the fort, waiting for their opportunity.[51]

Although various attempts to lure soldiers into an ambush near the fort failed because an overzealous warrior sprung the trap prematurely, the Lakȟóta remained in the area, patiently waiting for new opportunities. One presented itself on December 21, 1866.

The Lakȟóta knew in advance that the day would be a success. One of the wičháša wakȟáŋ had completed a ceremony the day before, which promised a positive outcome. In the ceremony he rode back and forth on horseback, gesturing violently. Every time he returned, he fell from his horse, declaring that he was holding a certain number of dead white soldiers in his hand. The fourth time he returned, he reported that there were over a hundred white men in his hand.

The Indians would never go to war if the odds were bad but after this sign the Lakȟóta entered battle with confidence. What unfolded became known to the Lakȟóta as the battle of "Hundred in the Hand."

On December 21, 1866, the Lakȟóta attacked another logging party. Capt. William J. Fetterman was sent from the fort to help and was given strict instructions not to go beyond Lodge Trail Ridge. Once again, the Lakȟóta employed the decoy tactic. A small group of warriors, including Crazy Horse, rode to the vicinity of the fort. Fetterman and his eighty men fell into the trap when they rode out past the ridge.

Fire Thunder (Pȟéta Ilé), age sixteen and one of the participants that day, described what happened in great detail. He recalled Big Road (Čhaŋkú Tȟáŋka) was the chief of their band and that they camped at Tongue River; then they "decided to go on a warpath, several different bands all taking part on horseback. We were out to fight anything, but particularly we were looking after the soldiers."[52]

They decided to go toward the fort at Piney Creek (Fort Phil Kearny) and sent ten men to coax the soldiers out of the fort. They divided into two groups and stood on either side of a hill waiting. Finally, they heard a shot signaling that the soldiers were coming. Fire Thunder waited on the west side of the hill. Some of the decoys got off their horses, pretending that the horses were worn out. Fire Thunder remembers how "the Indians came first downhill and the soldiers followed, firing on the running Indians all the time. . . . I was riding a sorrel horse and just as I was about to get on my horse, the soldiers stopped and began to fight the Indians back up the hill. I hung on to my sorrel. As they charged, I pulled out my six-shooter and began killing them. There were lots of bullets and lots of arrows—like locusts."[53]

The fighting was so thick that soon Indian arrows hit other Indians in the melee. Panicked soldiers charged up the hill, losing men as they went, because there was no place for them to hide. Some of the soldiers let their horses go and a few Indians chased after them. Although Fire Thunder wanted to have a horse for himself, he decided instead that it was a good day to die. He continued fighting. "I wasn't after horses—I was after white men," he recalled later. He scalped one and killed five or six soldiers. By the end of the fight all the soldiers were dead. The only survivor was a dog. "We didn't kill the dog because he looked too sweet," remembered Fire Thunder.[54]

Fire Thunder's story is just one of several Lakȟóta accounts of the battle that were recorded. In No Ear's winter count it was remembered as the year when "Wašíču opáwiŋǧe ktépi" (A Hundred White Men Were Killed). Lakȟóta and Cheyenne accounts mostly agree on the exact unfolding of events.[55] Some discussion has arisen over the role Red Cloud played in the battle and who killed Fetterman. It appears that Red Cloud did not participate in the battle itself but was present to observe and direct the fighting. American Horse, who was in the fight, claimed that he deserved the first coup for killing Fetterman. Although the battle was a great success for the Lakȟóta, it came at a heavy price. There is no accurate tally of the fallen and wounded, but Lakȟóta accounts describe how several wounded died on their way back to camp.[56]

The army immediately labeled the battle a massacre. Stunned by the defeat, it reported that up to 2,000 Indians had been involved in the attack. Colonel Carrington was forced to step down. Furious, Lt. Gen. William T. Sherman, Commander of the Division of Missouri demanded that the Indians be punished harshly. He proposed a punitive expedition that would kill at least ten Indians for every white man lost and expressed a desire to kill the Indians to the point of extinction. Supporters of the Peace Policy were able to prevent him from carrying out the plan. The dispute over Indian policy between the Interior and War Departments flared up again. Almost a year later, General Sherman still lamented that a proper retaliation had not been executed, and this gave the Indians a false impression of the power—or lack thereof—of the army. Of course, Sherman's comments resonated in the press, which published sensational stories about bloodthirsty savages and declared Red Cloud a skillful, if notorious, war chief.[57]

Throughout the spring and summer of 1867, unrest continued on the Bozeman Trail. The Lakȟóta and their allies kept the road practically closed while they besieged the forts. By now, the Indians had attacked Fort Phil Kearny and other travelers on the road fifty-one times. According to War Department records, ninety-one soldiers, five officers, and fifty-eight civilians had been killed. There is no precise information on Indian losses, but they appeared to be negligible. Army reports state that not a day passed without the Indians attacking somewhere in the Powder River country. General Sherman reported that it was virtually impossible to contact the forts in the area. During the winter especially cavalry operations were nearly impossible due to severe frost and snowstorms. Winter also slowed, but did not completely stop, the Indian attacks.[58] Contrary to their usual ways, the Lakȟóta and their allies even attacked Fort Buford in North Dakota in the heart of winter.

Toward a Permanent Peace?

With the war going well for the Lakȟóta, they had no reason to enter negotiations with the whites. They received several messages promising compensation if they abandoned the Powder River area and the besieged Bozeman Trail, but the Lakȟóta did not bother to respond. Surrendering the Powder River country was not negotiable. The Lakȟóta and their allies felt strong, and during the warm season they did not have to worry about food and supplies. A constant stream of spoils of war provided additional goods. The only thing the Indians lacked were weapons and ammunition. The war interfered with trading, and while those living close to the forts provided some trade goods, this supply line was not sufficient.[59]

In the summer of 1867, the Oglála, Sičháŋǧu, and their allies gathered for the Sun Dance. Sitting Bull with some Húŋkpapȟa may have also been present. Sitting Bull had led a successful campaign against Fort Rice, Fort Pierre, and Fort Buford on the northern Plains, but these northern campaigns have often been overshadowed by events along the Bozeman Trail.

Following the Sun Dances, the Indians began to plan attacks for the fall season, but they could not agree on whether to attack the northern forts or the forts along the Bozeman Trail. Eventually they decided to split their forces. One group decided to attack Fort C. F. Smith in present-day Montana and another targeted Fort Phil Kearny a little farther south in Wyoming. At the beginning of August, a joint force of mainly Cheyenne and Arapaho attacked a logging camp near Fort C. F. Smith. However, troops dispatched from the fort armed with new breechloading rifles—the Springfield-Allen Model 1866—forced the Indians to withdraw.[60]

On August 2, Red Cloud led an attack on a woodcutting party near Fort Phil Kearny. Nearly thirty soldiers and a few civilians sought protection behind wagon boxes; the soldiers carried the same new guns that had driven the Indians away the day before. The so-called Wagon Box Fight quickly gained a reputation for displays of great heroism and success among the whites. Shortly after the fight, both soldiers and the press celebrated it as a big victory. Newspapers falsely reported the Indians numbered 3,000 men with losses of more than a thousand. This was the US Army's first major victory in Red Cloud's War and a major morale boost, so its importance could not be overestimated. Public opinion had previously condemned the army's inability to end the war, but now it seemed that the army had finally given the Indians a proper lesson.[61]

Lakȟóta accounts of the battle paint a very different picture. George Sword maintains that no more than 300 men were present. The Lakȟóta fought as they had always done, circling the wagons first on horseback, then attacking on foot. He said the whites were firing rapidly, so they were forced to retreat several times. They made four attempts but lost only three men. One of them, Wasp (Žipála), demonstrated great courage by attacking the wagon "fortress" alone, but the soldiers' bullets dropped him just before he reached the wagons. Of those who survived the fight, the greatest honor went to Fast Thunder (Wakíŋyaŋ Lúzahaŋ) who attacked fiercely and came closer to the enemy than anyone else. Reports from other Lakȟóta corroborate Sword's story. For the Lakȟóta, the fight was by no means a loss, they had managed to steal several horses and mules. In addition, five soldiers were killed. Whether the Lakȟóta losses were as small as Sword suggests is unclear, but they likely were not significant. According to Sword, all major Lakȟóta leaders, such as Red Cloud and Crazy Horse were involved in the fight, though it is unlikely that Sitting Bull was there as Sword claimed.[62]

The Wagon Box Fight assumed legendary proportions among the whites. Even Red Cloud himself fed the legend by telling how he had led several thousand men in that battle, but in 1906 admitted in an interview that he did not remember the affair at all.[63] In fact, the fight that day was not significant to the Lakȟóta or much different from the other battles that year. They were still waging a victorious war.

In late fall 1867, a government commission reached Fort Laramie intent on inducing the Lakȟóta to relinquish their rights to the Powder River area. Red Cloud made his position very clear: there were to be no negotiations. He was hunting in the Black Hills and Powder River area and would not arrive at Fort Laramie until the forts along the Bozeman Trail were abandoned. Only then would he agree to negotiate. At the same time, he expressed the wish that a peace treaty, when finally concluded, would be in force forever.[64]

6

ČHAȞLÍ WAKPÁ
POWDER RIVER

"The Powder River Road Is the Cause of Our Trouble"

During the winter of 1867–68, most Lakȟóta chose to stay away from the agencies except for the most "progressive" ones. The Lakȟóta camps were filled with the spoils of war and the fall hunt was successful. The people were satisfied. The only cause of concern was the shortage of ammunition, but they remained confident in their ability to carry on fighting again in 1868.[1]

War with the Lakȟóta and their allies was costly and complicated for the US government. The army estimated that subduing the Lakȟóta and their allies would require an army of tens of thousands of men. The estimate is interesting, considering that the Indians were almost without ammunition, and the number of fighting men was only a few thousand at any given time. According to some estimates, $1 million had to be spent to kill one Indian. Eastern humanitarians used the government estimates to support demands to end the war. Over time, it would be cheaper to feed them than to forcibly solve the "Indian problem."[2]

Against this backdrop, the US government stepped up its reservation policy, which was inextricably linked to educating and "civilizing" Indians. They were to become Christian farmers within a few years. Because nomadic Indians were just learning the art of agriculture and were not believed to be able to fully support themselves with crops immediately, the US government offered to support them until they made the transition. To this end, Annual Appropriations Acts provided each Indian nation, including the Lakȟóta, with annual compensation in cash and supplies until they became self-sustaining.

This idea was by no means new; the 1851 Treaty had included an article detailing gifts. The Lakȟóta did not give up their own way of life in compensation for the gifts, but believed they were payments for the rights to cross their lands and a compensation for lands they had already given up. The government, however, used the annual appropriations to make the Indians dependent on the United States and thus easier to handle. Indeed, by the end of the 1860s, the Lakȟóta were in many ways dependent on these goods, especially those who lived permanently near white forts and Indian agencies and were no longer able to support themselves by hunting, in part due to the diminishing bison herds. Some tried to take up farming, but the results were meager. One chief complained that he had no tools, and he could not go on digging the land with his nails. Another complained that they were trying to do what the Great White Father asked of them but gained nothing. On the contrary they were poor, and those who prospered were the ones who did not stay close to the agencies trying to farm. Not surprisingly, it was difficult to keep young men from joining those living in the traditional way.[3]

Although the Lakȟóta living farther away were still able to hunt, the goods were welcome. They traveled long distances to the agencies hoping to procure additional supplies. It was quite common for thiyóšpaye and families to visit each other frequently and the visitors were welcome to stay for extended periods. It was not uncommon for guests to spend several years with another thiyóšpaye or oyáte. Despite years of trying to impose a system of government appointed "peace chiefs" and efforts to divide Lakȟóta into progressive and nonprogressive factions, these were still artificial divisions that did not truly reflect the realities of Lakȟóta life. The common perception of the Lakȟóta between 1866 and 1868 as one giant camp—a unified body with unified leadership under Red Cloud—is false. This was not Lakȟóta tradition, and the war did not change these patterns of life. Lakȟóta thiyóšpaye hunted independently and camped independently.[4]

Even the so-called nonprogressive or "free" Oglála and Sičháŋǧu only came close to the agencies when it suited them, and they stayed only as long as it was in their best interest. This constant flow of people back and forth confused the whites. During Red Cloud's War, the government had virtually no knowledge or understanding of who actually received government gifts.[5] To resolve this confusing situation, the government decided in the fall of 1867 to negotiate an agreement with the Lakȟóta. This decision signified the victory of the supporters of the Peace Policy over those who supported war or the extermination of the Indians.

The new Peace Commission was led by Commissioner of Indian Affairs Nathaniel Taylor. Other citizen members were John B. Henderson, Samuel F. Tappan, and John B. Sanborn. William T. Sherman, Alfred H. Terry, and William S. Harney represented the army. Ironically, some of these generals had previously called for the extermination of Indians. Although the Lakȟóta declared that they were not willing to negotiate before the forts along the Bozeman Trail were abandoned, the Peace Commission arrived at Fort Laramie in November 1867. Prior to their arrival, the commission had met with representatives of the Northern Lakȟóta on a steamboat near Fort Sully in August. During negotiations there, mostly with representatives of the progressive parties, the commission was able to get the Indians to choose land near "Fort Sully and the mouth of Big Cheyenne [River], for a permanent settlement."[6]

Government representatives optimistically expected to meet great numbers of enthusiastic Lakȟóta at Fort Laramie. Their hopes were not fulfilled. Despite divisions among the Lakȟóta about their approaches to the wašíču, it was very clear that the Oglála and Sičháŋǧu were unanimous on one issue: the United States had to abandon the roads running through their hunting grounds. During the negotiations every Lakȟóta speaker made this position clear. Even Spotted Tail and others who favored peace insisted that the roads be abandoned. Big Mouth, one of the chiefs representing the Sičháŋǧu, addressed the audience gathered in a thiyóthipi (great council lodge) erected for the occasion. He argued that it was useless to fight the whites, since they were "as thick as the grass," and then he addressed his fellow Lakȟóta: "How many are you? You go to war. Some of you get killed and your people will cry for you. If you kill a white man, who cries for him? Nobody." His implication was that there were so many whites that there was no need to cry over the loss of a few. Then he turned to the commissioners and bluntly told them to tell the Great Father to "quit that road. The Powder River road is the cause of our trouble. It is like setting the prairie on fire."[7] White Crane (Pȟeháŋ Sáŋ) too, strongly opposed white presence on their lands. "You have no business to come and settle on this land. Go off it," he bellowed.[8] Even though Red Cloud was perhaps leading the war effort to oppose white encroachment, he was hardly alone. Perhaps Spotted Tail and others were not willing to join the war, but they supported Red Cloud's efforts. American Horse noted that the commissioners should understand that none of the chiefs present could act alone on behalf of all the Lakȟóta. He personally was for peace but would not sign any treaties before Red Cloud and Man Afraid of His Horses were consulted and all Lakȟóta agreed amongst themselves.[9]

At the end of the talks, the Peace Commission had to admit that it had failed its mission. In its report, the commissioners strongly criticized the government. Among other things, they recommended that the Lakȟóta be assigned a large reservation and that the government increase the amount of annual compensation and make sure it would be distributed by honest men. The commission accused the whites of dishonesty, which was at the root of the current war. Still, the commissioners expected the Indians to gradually accept white civilization. President Grant shaped his Peace Policy, begun in 1869, based on the commission's report.[10]

"I Am Afraid the Whites Will Trouble Us Before We Trouble Them"

Negotiations resumed at Fort Laramie in May 1868. The Lakȟóta insisted on the abandonment of all forts as a condition for peace talks. The US government had no choice but to yield. During the May negotiations it promised to abandon the forts. The Lakȟóta present were delighted but expressed concerns: "I would like to know if the commissioners are earnest in the truth," asked High Wolf (Šuŋkmánitu Waŋkátuya). "I would like to know if the words are strong and binding and truthful. Is it true that the forts will be removed?"[11] Others echoed his sentiments and pointed out that the government had promised to take care of them for fifty years when they signed the 1851 treaty. Swift Bear voiced his misgivings saying "you promised to pay us for this country during [for] fifty years. When you promised us this, I thought it would make us rich and happy . . . when you made us that promise I thought it would be good for us. I hope all you do today will be right. I am afraid the whites will trouble us before we trouble them."[12]

Red Cloud was suspicious: promises were not enough. He would not sign any agreements or treaties before he saw the forts abandoned. Throughout the summer, small parties of Lakȟóta arrived at Fort Laramie, some signed the treaty while others came for provisions before heading back to Powder River country to wait for the government to fulfill its promises. The Oglála and Sičháŋǧu mostly refrained from attacking the forts, but small war parties stole some horses and mules and killed several white men.[13]

At last, US soldiers abandoned Fort C. F. Smith on July 29, 1868. The Indians burned the fort the following day. A month later, soldiers marched out of Fort Phil Kearny, which was also burned to the ground. A few days after that, army troops left Fort Reno. The Lakȟóta had won, but Red Cloud would still not attend the talks. Instead, he went hunting. In the late summer and early fall of 1868, Red Cloud and approximately 100 lodges (400–500 people) camped and hunted along the Rosebud River (Uŋžíŋžiŋtka Wakpá) and Man Afraid of His Horses camped near Bear Butte, where a great council was held after the fall hunt. Some Cheyenne and Arapaho joined the council that evidently was to decide on when Red Cloud would go to Fort Laramie. Finally in November Red Cloud arrived at Fort Laramie to listen to the government's proposals.[14]

While the US government anxiously waited for Red Cloud to sign for the Oglála, it also desired a treaty with the Northern Lakȟóta. They invited the Húŋkpapȟa, Oóhenuŋpa, Itázipčho, Sihásapa, and Mnikȟówožu to Fort Rice for talks, but the Lakȟóta were reluctant to attend. As Red Cloud had done, they let the government officials wait. In late June, Sitting Bull was out with a group of men travelling along Powder River, when they suddenly saw a group of wašíču in the nearby hills. Sitting Bull immediately sent akíčhitas forward to check who these people were and prepared to attack them instantaneously. It turned out to be Father Pierre-Jean De Smet, who was sent to encourage the hesitant Lakȟóta to the talks. A delegation of Lakȟóta, including chiefs Running Antelope and Two Bears (Matȟó Núŋpa) who lived close to the fort and were supportive of peace escorted Father De Smet. Sitting Bull's akíčhitas formed a column and approached the visitors, riding fast toward them and stopping just before reaching De Smet. According to him, the warriors were a most magnificent sight dashing toward them dressed in fine regalia. The warriors determined the visitors came with peaceful intentions, and then returned to Sitting Bull with the news that it was Father De Smet, who was well known and respected by the Lakȟóta. Sitting Bull decided to escort the visitors to the Lakȟóta camp, where he told De Smet that his heart was beating hard in anger and he wanted to send his men against them, but seeing the respected Father, he let his bad feelings pass and welcomed the chance to talk with him.[15]

The large Lakȟóta camp was located on the south side of the Yellowstone River, close to the mouth of Powder River. Most likely it consisted only of Húŋkpapȟa and was led by Four Horns (Hé Tópa), Black Moon (Wisápa), and Red Horn (Héša), all of whom were more disposed to seek peace than the major war leaders Sitting Bull, Gall, and No Neck (Táku Waníča). The visitors were taken to a tipi where a pipe was passed around as a token of friendship. The next morning, June 20, a large thiyóthipi consisting of ten regular tipis was erected. The visitors were seated at the center and opposite them were the major chiefs Four

Horns and Black Moon. Sitting Bull and Gall sat behind them in a semicircle with approximately 500 men. According to De Smet, 4,000 people assembled around them to listen to the talks. Before commencing the proceedings, various thiyóšpaye sang and danced. Finally, Black Moon gave permission to begin the talks.[16]

After remarks by De Smet, Black Moon arose, pointed his pipe toward the heavens and earth, then offered it to De Smet to touch with his lips. After they smoked, they passed the pipe around the circle of men. Black Moon addressed the gathering, reiterating that they did not want war but that "the whites ruin our country" and that he could never sell any part of their territory. He summed up all the wrongs done by the wašíču, but said he was ready to let all that pass and welcomed peace. Then Sitting Bull stood up and expressed his joy at a possible peace. His words were deliberate. He had been "a fool and a warrior" conducting bad deeds he said, but he was forced to do so because his people were "troubled and confused." He was now ready for peace. He sat down but reconsidered. Before anyone else could speak he sprung back up to add that he was never going to sell any of his country and did not want the whites there to cut his timber. He was especially fond of the groves of oak trees at the river bottom, and he wanted to keep them. He concluded by demanding that the whites abandon the forts they had built on Lakȟóta lands. He sat down amidst thundering yells of approval by the audience.[17]

The proceedings of this council provide an important insight into the leadership among these Húŋkpapȟa. While Sitting Bull clearly held much persuasive power among the warriors, it was Black Moon and Four Horns who were the real chiefs. Sitting Bull and Gall were not yet considered chiefs, but merely blotáhuŋka.

The government had in fact agreed to abandon the forts along the Bozeman Trail, but the Northern Lakȟóta wished to close Fort Buford and other northern forts, stop steamboat travel on the Missouri, and end the railroad construction that was threatening their hunting grounds. None of the major chiefs agreed to go to Fort Rice, but they decided to send Gall with several other leading men to listen to what the wašíču had to say.[18]

Discussions at Fort Rice followed past patterns, although several Iháŋktȟuŋwaŋna chiefs spoke excitedly about the possibility of a lasting peace that would determine the future of the entire Sioux nation for years to come. They had chosen to live at peace and now rejoiced over the possibility that the Húŋkpapȟa too were abandoning the war. Húŋkpapȟa representatives demanded that the whites leave their country, made it clear that they desired more powder, but rejected all offers of presents from the government.[19] Gall did not speak, but after the discussions he, along with his companions, put his mark on the treaty. Although government officials were happy, for Gall and other Northern Lakȟóta, the treaty meant little. It did not mention the abandonment of the northern forts or stopping railroad construction, both of which the Lakȟóta chiefs demanded. The treaty merely stipulated that the Lakȟóta would settle on a reservation, which was a moot point for the Northern Lakȟóta. In fact, just two months after Gall signed the treaty, Sitting Bull launched another attack on Fort Buford. It was around this time that the whites became aware of Sitting Bull's rising status as a major Lakȟóta leader.[20]

"This Land Belongs to Me": Fort Laramie, 1868

All through the summer of 1868 the whites were waiting anxiously for Red Cloud. Many local whites believed a war of extermination should have been carried out against the "hostiles." Some hoped that other Lakȟóta chiefs like Man Afraid of His Horses and Spotted Tail would attack Red Cloud's people to force them to surrender.[21] This was, of course, ridiculous. The other Lakȟóta chiefs, although not actively supporting Red Cloud's war effort, would not have been able to muster a force against their own kinsmen, who, after all, were defending their homelands and way of life. Though divisions within Lakȟóta society were tangible, they were not as deep as some whites hoped. In fact, during the negotiations at Fort Laramie in May 1868, Man Afraid of His Horses specifically stated that he wanted the military posts on the Platte to be moved. He also noted that he wanted no more white men coming to Lakȟóta country, and wished that instead of dishonest white agents, mixed-bloods, who were members of his tribe and kin, would "take care of the land" for the Oglála. Man Afraid of His Horses was thus repeating the sentiments already expressed by Spotted Tail, Big Mouth, and others during the September 1867 council.[22]

When Red Cloud finally arrived at Fort Laramie in November, the commissioners were long gone. The treaty document was waiting for him at the fort and the proceedings were left to post commander Maj. William Dyer. Red Cloud, however, was unwilling to talk with Dyer. He was still not ready to shake hands with the wašíču. While other Oglála chiefs shook hands with the officers, Red Cloud, only offered to touch fingertips. When he spoke, he said he was not there to accept a peace, but to gain provisions and ammunition to carry out war against the Crow. When his request was declined, he refused to sign any treaties. The following day he again refused unless he was given ammunition. He emphasized that he was not ready to settle on a reservation in a country he did not know. He would stay on Powder River where game was plentiful. He said that his people knew nothing about farming and did not want to learn. Red Cloud echoed sentiments expressed by Spotted Tail and other chiefs, who, during the May councils, said that while there was buffalo and other game, the Lakȟóta would stick to the old way of life. Where Spotted Tail's vision for the future left the door open for farming and other "civilized" pursuits when game was gone, Red Cloud had no such vision. He wanted to continue hunting and raiding Crow.[23]

After one more day of talks, however, Red Cloud agreed to sign the treaty. He "washed his hands on the dust of the floor," and, together with other chiefs, put his mark on the paper. After a total of 192 days of negotiations and several signing ceremonies at different locations, a final and formal treaty was signed on November 6, 1868. Red Cloud was not the first to sign as one might expect, given his reputation. The first to sign on behalf of the Oglála was Man Afraid of His Horses, which emphasized his position as the hereditary chief among the Oglála. American Horse signed next, and other chiefs followed suit. Red Cloud's signature can be found among the last. Iron Shell was the first Sičháŋǧu to sign, and Spotted Tail's signature appears fourth in the documents signed in April 1868. One Horn was the principal Mnikȟówožu to sign the treaty. Representatives of the Húŋkpapȟa signed a separate version at Fort Rice but Sitting Bull's signature is not on the treaty. Despite signing the treaty, Red Cloud had no intention of settling on the reservation. Instead, he followed up on his promise to go back to Powder River country to hunt bison and fight the Crow.[24]

The 1868 Fort Laramie Treaty established the Great Sioux Reservation. It also designated areas north of Platte River and east of the Big Horn Mountains where whites would have no business going without Lakȟóta permission. This included the sacred Black Hills. In addition, the Lakȟóta were given the right to hunt in the so-called unceded territory. The treaty also stipulated that in the future, no agreement would be valid unless it was signed by at least three-quarters of all adult full-blood male Lakȟóta. This was to protect the Lakȟóta and to safeguard their rights to land. Under the treaty, the Lakȟóta promised to keep the peace, and in return, the government promised to distribute supplies in the form of annual appropriations. The Lakȟóta had gotten a taste of the goods already during the talks, when the government officials distributed supplies worth more than $18,000. After the treaty was signed, supplies were to be distributed at new Indian agencies to be constructed on the banks of the Missouri River far east of the Lakȟóta homelands. The aim was to make the Lakȟóta move east and settle

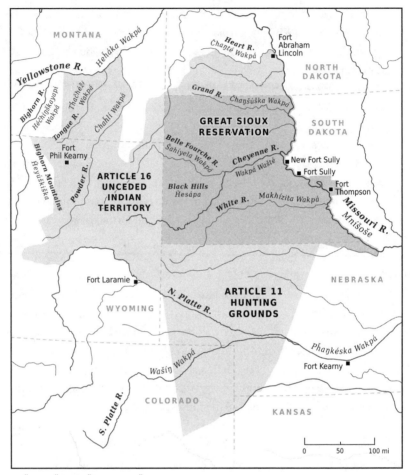

Lakȟóta Tȟamákȟočhe. Lakȟóta homelands circa 1868.

permanently within the confines of the Great Sioux Reservation. This paragraph of the treaty apparently was not explained to the Lakȟóta until much later during a visit Red Cloud and Spotted Tail made to Washington in 1870. The treaty also promised to establish schools for Lakȟóta children and provide allotments of land for those willing to take up farming.[25]

The treaty designated Fort Randall on the Missouri River as an agency for the Lakȟóta. The Lakȟóta, however, were not at all happy with that choice. Eventually, four Indian agencies were established within the Great Sioux Reservation. Red Cloud Agency was established for the Oglála, and Spotted Tail Agency for the Sičháŋǧu. The latter was also known as Whetstone Agency. Indian agencies on Grand River (Pȟaláni Tȟawákpa / Čhaŋšúška Wakpá) and Cheyenne River (Wakpá Wašté) were to cater to the needs of the Northern Lakȟóta.

Without question, Red Cloud's War was a great victory for the Indians. Though several battlefield victories allowed them to make peace on their own terms, the settlement was also possible because of the new Indian humanitarian policy, which culminated in the 1869 Peace Policy. Even if the US military had acted more vigorously and decisively, Lakȟóta success should not be underestimated: they had conducted an effective campaign, contributing to the government's reluctance to continue costly and difficult military operations.[26]

From Lakȟóta perspectives, the 1868 Fort Laramie Treaty was a major success. Winter counts remembered the proceedings as the year when "Much medicine was made," or "Many flags were given them by the Peace Commission." The Swan winter count simply states, "Made peace with General Sherman and others at Fort Laramie."[27] The Lakȟóta and their allies had pressured the United States to abandon the road running through their main hunting grounds. The Great Sioux Reservation guaranteed a huge land base for the Lakȟóta. They were to receive annual appropriations for years to come. Furthermore, they could continue their nomadic traditions in the unceded territory. The treaty gave the Lakȟóta the choices: to settle on the reservation, continue their traditional way of life, or pursue the best of both worlds as it suited them. The Lakȟóta effectively delayed forced acculturation. They would settle on the reservation, but not before all the game was gone. Perhaps they envisioned that would never happen, or that it would occur in the distant future. Perhaps also they remembered a prophecy that said there would be a time when the buffalo would disappear, and together with the buffalo the Lakȟóta people would return into the earth from whence they had emerged.[28] But that day was not yet at hand. Buffalo remained and the Lakȟóta people had just signed a treaty that demonstrated they were still a powerful people.

The Lakȟóta later claimed that not all the details of the treaty were properly explained to them, but their statements during the proceedings clearly demonstrate what they expected from the treaty. They wanted to have their own land base, Lakȟóta tȟamákȟočhe, and keep it intact, with borders as they defined them. In addition to the annual goods from the government they wanted to secure the benefits from continued trading with the whites. For those who were willing to attempt farming and send their children to schools, the treaty also provided that possibility. In practice, this treaty allowed them to make a variety of decisions and retain much of the control of their lands and their own fate, and they had shown exceptional unity in their resolve to meet these objectives. Lakȟóta tȟamákȟočhe was large enough to maintain big herds of buffalo and they had demonstrated that they were strong enough to fight their traditional enemies while simultaneously keeping the wašíču at bay.

"We Are Sitting Bull's Boys": New Leaders and Old Enemies

Thousands of Lakȟóta who did not want to have anything to do with the whites remained outside the newly established Great Sioux Reservation. This group consisted mainly of Northern Lakȟóta: Húŋkpapȟa, Mnikȟówožu, Itázipčho, Oóhenuŋpa, and Sihásapa. Sitting Bull emerged as the most important leader among these oyáte. That is why white contemporaries and scholars have often called this group Sitting Bull's people. It was not a single, cohesive group but consisted of multiple thiyóšpaye with their own leaders. Large numbers of Oglála and Sičháŋǧu decided to join the nonreservation Lakȟóta. One of the rising leaders of the Oglála was Crazy Horse, who, like Sitting Bull, opposed the wašíču way of life. Red Cloud still lived away from the reservation in the Black Hills and Powder River area. Other prominent leaders among the nonreservation Lakȟóta were Black Moon, Four Horns, Gall, Hump (Čhaŋkȟáhu), Man Afraid of His Horses, American Horse, and Big Road. These Lakȟóta continued to live in the traditional manner: hunting buffalo and finding traditional enemies to fight. Reservation boundaries meant little to them.

In the summertime these smaller groups gathered for great religious ceremonies, often followed by war expeditions against neighboring tribes or the wašíču. Then they broke up into smaller camps for winter. During these joint gatherings, it is believed that Sitting Bull and Crazy Horse became friends. Sitting Bull was seven years older than Crazy Horse. His position was more that of a chief, while Crazy Horse was at the height of his military career. At the beginning of the new decade, these two men would lead Lakȟóta resistance, while older leaders like Red Cloud and Spotted Tail would follow a more diplomatic path. This was a common pattern in Lakȟóta culture. Sitting Bull and Crazy Horse refused to compromise. Sitting Bull admitted that the whites might eventually get him—arrest, or even kill him—but until then he would enjoy himself and live like a Lakȟóta.[29]

Crazy Horse was born in the early 1840s to the Húŋkpathila band of the Oglála. His childhood name was Curly Hair (Pȟehíŋ Yuȟáȟa) because of his slightly curly brown hair that some claim suggests he may have had white ancestors. During his childhood, increasing numbers of whites invaded Lakȟóta lands.[30] Young Crazy Horse quickly demonstrated talent as a warrior. He gained fame in battles against the Crow. At age twelve, he rushed into a Crow camp alone and killed his first enemy. Because of his courage in battle, his father gave him his name, Tȟašúŋke Witkó. Crazy Horse's friend, the medicine man Chips (Woptuȟ'a), later said that Crazy Horse was "made for war." Many other Lakȟóta who knew him agreed.[31]

Crazy Horse was appointed a shirt wearer at a young age, together with Sword, American Horse, and Young Man Afraid of His Horses during a large gathering in the late summer of 1868. They were picked to be the new generation of Oglála leaders. Three of the four were sons of former shirt wearers who were now true chiefs. Only Crazy Horse rose to the position through merit. Though the others were renowned warriors as well, their election was to maintain continuity in Lakȟóta leadership. These men were to be the new guardians of the Lakȟóta way of life and Lakȟóta lands.[32] Even though Crazy Horse was later stripped of his status after he stole another man's wife, he retained his position as the preeminent blotáhuŋka (war leader).[33]

As a young man, Sitting Bull of the Húŋkpapȟa was as battle hardened as Crazy Horse. Sitting Bull's interests were in religious meditation, which turned him into a respected wičháša wakȟáŋ. However, at the age of fourteen, he too went on the warpath and earned his first coups. He gained a reputation because of his powerful visions. He was said to have the ability to talk to animals, especially birds. Though he did not directly participate in the Red Cloud War, he led the Northern Lakȟóta against traditional enemies and the whites. While the Oglála and Sičháŋǧu negotiated at Fort Laramie, Sitting Bull organized major expeditions against Fort Buford, Fort Stevenson, and Fort Totten.[34]

For these Northern Lakȟóta, the Bozeman Trail was less significant, but they were angered by the whites' plans to build a railway through their hunting grounds. Sitting Bull, Gall, and other Northern Lakȟóta war chiefs determined to resist. Lakȟóta divisions manifested themselves here as well when several "progressive" chiefs were willing to hand over land to the government. In response, the Northern Lakȟóta decided to do something unheard of. At chief Four Horns' suggestion, they decided to choose one person who alone had the power to decide over war and peace. Almost unanimously, the Húŋkpapȟa, Mnikȟówožu, Itázipčho, Oóhenuŋpa, and Sihásapa elected Sitting Bull. Even some progressives, such as Running Antelope gave their blessing to the plan. During the ceremony installing Sitting Bull as supreme chief, Four Horns proclaimed: "For your bravery on the battlefields and as the greatest warrior of our bands, we have elected you as our war chief, leader of the entire Sioux nation. When you tell us to fight, we shall fight, when you tell us to make peace, we will make peace."[35]

Sitting Bull thus rose to a very remarkable position among the Northern Lakȟóta. In 1872 Assistant Secretary of the Interior Benjamin Cowen met him in his camp and described how the other Lakȟóta men removed the feathers they were wearing to show respect to Sitting Bull. The feathers were a token of their individual coups, and by removing them they acknowledged Sitting Bull's position as their primary chief.[36]

Sitting Bull's appointment signified a break in Lakȟóta ways of thinking and organizing their resistance against the wašíču. The white soldiers were different from traditional enemies, so the Lakȟóta had to change too. Around this time Red Cloud also began to present himself as a kind of "commander-in-chief" among the southern oyáte. According to some Lakȟóta informants, Red Cloud was similarly named the chief who decided about war or peace—specifically in relation to the whites—and acted as the "guardian of Lakȟóta country." These unprecedented appointments would cause friction. In the years to come, Red Cloud's and Sitting Bull's leadership would prove controversial and divisive in both the southern and northern Lakȟóta oyáte.

Despite the Fort Laramie Treaty, the Lakȟóta continued to resist white encroachment. During the 1868 negotiations, Man Afraid of His Horses expressed his misgivings about railroads and navigation of the Missouri River. The Lakȟóta were well aware that white expansion on their lands would continue despite peace treaties.[37] Like steamboats, the railroads were bringing increasing numbers of settlers into the country. Some who passed through enjoyed killing buffalo for sport. The Lakȟóta knew this well, because steamboats traveling along the Missouri had already been, in essence, floating killing machines. For decades, steamboat passengers enjoyed shooting at everything they saw on the banks of the river, and organized hunting excursions upon landing. Even famed naturalist John J. Audubon described in his 1843 journal how he and his companions killed hundreds, if not thousands of animals on their trip up the Missouri.[38] Lakȟóta sentiments about this destruction are captured in the words of Bull Owl (Hiŋháŋ Tatȟáŋka) of the Húŋkpapȟa: "We don't like the white men travelling through our country and bringing steamboats up the river. I hope you will stop this so that the buffalo will come back again."[39] The railroads promised to bring even more destruction. Thus, by the early 1870s, Lakȟóta leaders targeted construction crews of the Northern Pacific Railway.

Continuing problems with the wašíču, growing divisions within the people, and the steady decline of game were constant concerns for both reservation and "free" Lakȟóta. Yet following the Fort Laramie Treaty, life on and off the Great Sioux Reservation was good and people were happy. The winter counts report mundane events such as the eclipse of the sun in the winter of 1869, trading, or incidents like the falling of a tree on a woman who was collecting firewood. They were more preoccupied with battles against the Arikara, Crow, and Pawnee, annual hunting trips, and traditional religious ceremonies. The year 1870 is known, for example, as Chaŋkȟáhu Waŋkátuya Ahí Ktépi, "The Enemies Killed Hump." Hump was on a war expedition with Crazy Horse, and despite bad omens and Crazy Horse's advice, he continued until he was killed.[40] The year 1872 was especially good as it was known as the year Wašíču Kȟolá Waní Tȟípi, "They made a winter camp without a white man"; and 1873 was called Sčíli Opáwiŋǧe Wičháktepi, "A hundred Pawnees were killed." The latter refers to a war party led by Spotted Tail that massacred an entire Pawnee village. Not even Spotted Tail was ready to fully give up old ways and quietly settle on the reservation.[41]

In the winter of 1869–70, a battle took place that reflects the life of these "free" Lakȟóta. Sitting Bull's people were in a winter camp near the Missouri River in present-day Montana and Wyoming, recently appropriated from the Crow Indians. That winter, two Húŋkpapȟa boys returned from a hunting trip when they were surprised by Crow who killed one of them. The other boy escaped to his camp, where Sitting Bull immediately assembled about one hundred warriors to take revenge. Before leaving, Sitting Bull performed a ceremony and promised to sacrifice tobacco, bison, and even his own flesh to Wakȟáŋ Tȟáŋka if Wakȟáŋ Tȟáŋka would look favorably on their expedition.

In the dark of night, the Lakȟóta traced the tracks of their enemies and caught them sheltering behind a rocky slope. The Lakȟóta waited until dawn before attacking. Neither side had many firearms. Each man independently tried to show his bravery and earn as many coups as possible. One by one, they attacked the entrenched enemy, retreated, and tried again from another direction. Sitting Bull, singing war songs, encouraged his men to fight. He too rushed several times against the enemies. He got one first coup after being the first to touch the body of a dead Crow and then earned two second-degree coups after touching the bodies of two other fallen enemies. However, the Crow defended

"Sitting Bull Kills Crow Takes Four Scalps." Drawing by Sitting Bull. After his surrender in 1881, Sitting Bull drew a series of images depicting scenes of war and war deeds. While the writing in the upper part is difficult to read, it is most likely a depiction of his own war deed. Courtesy of the Buffalo Bill Center of the West, Cody, Wyoming, MS 290, Sitting Bull Ledger Drawings Research Collection.

themselves fiercely, and the Lakȟóta lost thirteen men. As the morning turned into day, the Lakȟóta attacked in force, and killed all thirty enemies. Upon their return to camp, the Lakȟóta held a big celebration, but also mourned their fallen comrades. In mourning, Sitting Bull cut his hair, covered his body with mud, and went to camp without moccasins and leggings; he had lost his uncle in the battle. The battle survived in Lakȟóta stories as the "Battle of Thirty Dead Crow."[42]

In the summer of 1870, there was a major battle between the Lakȟóta and the Flathead Indians. The Lakȟóta had gathered in a large camp along the Yellowstone River just below the mouth of the Rosebud River. Two days before the battle, Sitting Bull demonstrated his power as a wičháša wakȟáŋ. He announced he wanted to be left alone so he could seek a vision. He walked through the crowd gathered around him, singing as he walked. As he sang, he saw a fiery ball coming toward him. Just before it hit him, it gave way and disappeared. Upon returning to camp, Sitting Bull once again offered the pipe and announced that he could see in the smoke a battle against enemy forces within two days. In the battle, many enemies would die, but also several Lakȟóta would lose their lives. The next day another medicine man had a vision that confirmed there was an enemy camp to the north. The Lakȟóta gathered a force of more than four hundred men and rode north in search of the enemy camp. In the resulting battle, both sides lost men until both sides had had enough. Most

Lakȟóta retreated and the Flatheads returned to camp. Before long, the Flatheads returned to the battlefield to collect their dead. Only Sitting Bull remained on the battlefield with two of his friends; he and his friends attacked, driving the enemies to flee, but one of them was left behind. Sitting Bull rushed toward him, intending to take his horse, but the man fired his rifle and the bullet penetrated Sitting Bull's left arm. Wounded, Sitting Bull retreated, and his comrades took him to safety.[43]

Although the battle may not have been a great victory for the Lakȟóta, it strengthened Sitting Bull's status as both a wičháša wakȟáŋ and a chief. The battle had taken place within two days as Sitting Bull had prophesized, and several men were killed on both sides. The bullet that wounded Sitting Bull represented the fireball that came toward him in the vision, but he survived the injury.

Such battles against traditional enemies were common in the early 1870s. One Bull (Tȟatȟáŋka Waŋží) explains that in those days they used to scare their enemies by shouting, "Tȟatȟáŋka Íyotake tȟahókšila" or "We are Sitting Bull's boys."[44] It was evidence of how Sitting Bull's power and fame had grown among the Indians, both Lakȟóta and their enemies. Clearly, by the early 1870s the threat represented by the whites was not the most important thing in Lakȟóta minds—life was still enjoyable.

Settling on the Reservation

Life on the Great Sioux Reservation was not yet too restricted. For part of the year, the Lakȟóta hunted far away from the agencies and visited relatives living outside the reservation. Red Cloud continued to live as before, hunting in Powder River country and the Black Hills area. Nor did Spotted Tail immediately move to the agency assigned to him. Indeed, reservation Indian agents complained on several occasions that neither Red Cloud nor Spotted Tail showed any desire to settle. Furthermore, though both chiefs were inclined to maintain peace they did not in any way support "civilizing" efforts such as adopting agriculture and setting up schools. Agents complained that life at the agencies was chaotic, and the threat of war was never far away.[45]

The 1868 treaty had divided the Lakȟóta into Wágluȟe (reservation or agency Indians) and the "wild and untamed" Watȟógla (free or hunting Lakȟóta). Gradually, differences deepened between these groups. Ironically, life on the reservation had become much more difficult for those choosing to live there than for those living off the reservation. The reservation Lakȟóta were constantly forced to move as the government searched for suitable farmlands for them.

Temporary Indian agencies were proposed at times near the Missouri River, at the White (Makhízita Wakpá) and Rosebud Rivers, or on the Platte River near Fort Laramie. The Lakȟóta strongly opposed these. By visiting their relatives at the agencies to pick up government-distributed supplies that did not really belong to them, the free Lakȟóta added to the confusion. Indian agents were often put in difficult situations when supplies had to be made available to the "outsiders," who otherwise threatened to take them by force. One of the military officers, Maj. Gen. David S. Stanley, stationed at Fort Sully, made a detailed report on the chaotic situation in 1869. He wrote that the Grand River Agency supported by Fort Sully and Fort Rice was expected to take care of 2,000 Húŋkpapȟa, 900 Sihásapa, 1,500 Oóhenuŋpa, 1,500 Itázipčho, and 2,000 Mnikȟówožu, of whom approximately 5,000 were, he believed, hostile to the whites. Toward the south, the Whetstone Agency oversaw 2,000 Sičháŋǧu, who were "supposed peaceable," and 2,000 Oglála. Of the Oglála, Stanley said that up to 1,500 were hostile. He pointed out that these numbers fluctuated as people constantly moved around. The large camp along the Yellowstone and Rosebud Rivers was a headquarters for all those whom he referred to as "malcontents." Still, the situation on the Northern Plains had calmed down considerably since the Fort Laramie Treaty. Much of the restless feeling, according to Stanley, could be avoided if the Lakȟóta were allowed agencies in locations they wanted.[46]

Despite frequent requests to move from one place to another, the reservation Lakȟóta were expected to make rapid progress along the "white man's road." In addition to the people becoming farmers, the government required children be sent to schools and churches. The reality was that the lands of the Great Sioux Reservation were not suitable for farming. Many whites also knew this. Year after year, Indian agents reported that agriculture was not the best means of subsistence for the Lakȟóta. The soil of the reservation was largely unsuitable for cultivation. In addition, drought and grasshoppers regularly destroyed even the small crops that the Lakȟóta were able to grow. As late as 1881, Valentine T. McGillycuddy, a longtime Indian agent at Pine Ridge, noted that if 7,000 white people were to start farming in the same area, they would die of starvation within a year if they had to live on their own produce.[47]

The Lakȟóta knew—or cared—nothing about farming. From the start of the reservation period in the late 1860s, the US government stressed the importance of farming, and to that end, farm implements were sent to the reservation and farmers were appointed to advise the Indians on their use. The goods often went unused or were sold by white agency employees at a profit. In 1870, Indian

Agent William H. French described how a group of Khulwíčhaša (Lower Brulé) broke into one of the storage areas to take goods as compensation for a man who drowned hauling supplies across a river. The agent believed that some white men organized the event and probably the goods were sold in exchange for whiskey. Most Lakȟóta simply refused to farm and repeatedly told agents that they did not intend to work under any circumstances, or at least not if there was enough buffalo left to hunt. Regardless of this opposition, some farming attempts were made at all agencies, with meager results. Swift Bear and Grass (Pȟeží) were reported to be the most eager to lead their followers in farming pursuits.[48]

Thus, the situation on the Great Sioux Reservation was rather confused in the early 1870s. Sometimes dishonest agents tried to make as much profit as possible, either for themselves or the groups they represented. At other times, the Lakȟóta took advantage of weak agents and acted as they wished. Red Cloud especially was a skilled politician and manipulator. The whites still regarded him as the main Lakȟóta chief, and he often took advantage of his status by claiming special benefits for himself and his people. He kept whites in uncertainty and under threat of war. However, Red Cloud's position caused a great deal of controversy among his fellow Lakȟóta. The other chiefs, Man Afraid of His Horses, Little Wound, and Spotted Tail, among others, looked jealously at the power and fame bestowed upon Red Cloud by the whites. As a result, disunity among the reservation Lakȟóta grew. Not only did problems arise between Indians and whites, but also between different Lakȟóta oyáte. This situation became apparent in 1870, when Oglála and Sičháŋǧu chiefs visited Washington. Red Cloud received more attention than the others. He had initiated the visit asking for permission to see the president but was angry when other leaders received invitations to meet with the "Great White Father" as well.[49]

Three important developments troubled the chiefs' visit to the east: First, there was an intense struggle for leadership and other problems, specifically between Red Cloud and Spotted Tail. Eventually, Spotted Tail retreated. Ever the diplomat, he allowed Red Cloud to act as the "head" chief, as it was the best solution for the Lakȟóta. Second, negotiations with government representatives revealed that the Lakȟóta were not fully aware of the stipulations of the 1868 treaty. Red Cloud became furious when he heard that he was expected to settle on the reservation permanently and start farming. The Lakȟóta believed that they had entered into an agreement that was about peace and the continuity of trade relations, not relinquishing Lakȟóta land or being forced to farm. As the truth came to light, one of the Lakȟóta present tried to kill himself, saying he could not look into the eyes of his people after being involved in such fraud.

The extent to which the Lakȟóta were truly cheated or if they simply did not understand the content of the 1868 treaty is unclear. As discussed earlier, the Lakȟóta, or at least Lakȟóta chiefs, had a clear idea of what the treaty meant. It may well be that their vision of the treaty was not the same as the vision of white officials. The Lakȟóta understood borders as something that were meant to protect Lakȟóta tȟamákȟočhe and to allow them to control a specific area. They also understood the demand to settle down and farm—it was just not something they were willing to do, and these articles of the treaty were handily forgotten or pushed aside. That said, Lakȟóta reactions in Washington illustrate that many of them did not have a clear grasp of what the treaty required them to do. If this was the case with the chiefs, one wonders what the impression of the treaty requirements and promises was among ordinary Lakȟóta men and women.

The third important occurrence during the trip east was a visit to New York City at the invitation of the Friends of the Indian. There Red Cloud took center stage again, giving a long public speech at the Cooper Institute. With dramatic gestures and powerful words, he portrayed the injustices suffered by his people. He listed the wrongs done since the 1851 treaty, the dishonest traders, and requirements to get their provisions at the Missouri River against their will. "We kept our word. We committed no murders, no depredations, until the troops came. . . . we want to keep peace. Will you help us?" he pleaded to the audience, making them sigh with delight. The audience was dazzled by his performance, applauding and waving white handkerchiefs after every sentence that was translated for them. The newspapers praised him. His performance made an enormous impression on the Friends of the Indian. In his speech Red Cloud portrayed himself as the chief of the entire Sioux Nation: "I am here to represent the whole Sioux Nation and they are bound by what I say." Red Cloud directly attacked Spotted Tail saying: "I am no Spotted Tail to say one thing one day and be bought with a pin the next. Look at me. I am poor and naked, but I am the chief of the Nation."[50] That, of course, was not true and reflects the fierce rivalry emerging between Red Cloud and other chiefs.

The visit to Washington and New York convinced many chiefs that the Lakȟóta had to accommodate, to some degree, the ways and demands of the wašíču. Although Red Cloud did not immediately settle at the agency upon his return, there are signs that he, like many Indian leaders from many different nations before him, finally lost the desire to fight the whites after seeing how powerful they were. While visiting relatives off the reservation, he told them about the wonders he saw in Washington, including huge ships, cannons, and buildings. Understandably, this raised deep suspicions among the free Lakȟóta. Many of them thought that Red Cloud had been bewitched by the "white man's magic"—thus losing the desire to fight. His reports of the white man's power were not believed and the rift between reservation and free Lakȟóta deepened. Spotted Tail even conceded that from now on Lakȟóta men should try their luck in farming. Until now, he said, it was only done by women, but the time for change was now fast approaching. The trip to the east had made a difference; the Oglála and Sičháŋǧu subsequently made fewer attacks on neighboring tribes and even returned stolen horses.[51]

It is true that Red Cloud and other chiefs now understood the power and might of the wašíču differently from other Lakȟóta. Still, it would be unreasonable to say that Red Cloud had surrendered before the white man. On the contrary, he continuously sought to find a balance. He sometimes acted for peace, sometimes for war. Both he and Spotted Tail took on diplomatic roles, with Spotted Tail positioning himself more clearly for peace. They both tried to find ways to help their people in these new circumstances.

"With Him I Will Live and Die": Life at the Agencies

Although there had been government representatives in charge of the Indian agencies before, in 1871 the Bureau of Indian Affairs (BIA), appointed the first "real" Indian agent for the Lakȟóta. They sent John W. Wham, a "decent Christian" from the Episcopal Church, out west. Though not very familiar with Indians, Wham was considered a suitable agent because of his honesty and conscience. The Friends of the Indian had created a system in which Indian agents were selected from Christian denominations. Agents were not required to have prior experience with Native Americans; a Christian background was considered sufficient merit. The idea was to bring the Indians quickly and more efficiently into the Christian church. In addition, the thought was that the Indians could trust them, and that the government would not have to question the agents' conscience. Unfortunately, this logic failed often. Church representatives proved to be as untrustworthy as anyone else.[52]

Although Agent Wham was honest, the Lakȟóta caused him a lot of trouble. Upon arriving at Fort Laramie, Wham convened the leaders of the reservation and proposed to relocate the agency to White River, north of Platte River. Lakȟóta leaders refused. They wanted to keep the agency near Fort Laramie.

Furthermore, Red Cloud stated that he and the other chiefs present could not decide alone. They had to consult with the off-reservation chiefs before making any decisions. This was an unexpected and incomprehensible situation for Wham. How could Red Cloud, supposedly the head chief of all Lakȟóta, not make such a decision? Wham's failure to understand the structure of Lakȟóta society became clear over the coming months. Although Red Cloud's tactic may have been intended to delay decision-making, it was true that many of his own Itéšiča (Bad Faces), led by Big Road, were living off the reservation and wanted to have a say where the agency was located. In the end, they too wanted easy access to supplies and trade.[53]

The first Red Cloud Agency was established on the north shore of the Platte River, about sixty miles from Fort Laramie. As a result, the Lakȟóta began to see the Platte River as a border between themselves and the whites. They adhered strictly to this new principle. As soon as a white man was seen heading north, Lakȟóta warriors followed him to make sure he was not heading to the sacred Black Hills area. Lakȟóta warriors surrounded anyone traveling through their lands to the north. Occasionally, the situation got so bad that Agent Wham and other whites could not leave the agency premises without Lakȟóta threatening them. The agent was sometimes a prisoner in his own office.[54] The situation escalated almost to the point of war when the Oglála blocked supplies to the Spotted Tail Agency (Whetstone), located north of the White River. Supplying Spotted Tail Agency directly from the Missouri River was not feasible, because it was too far away. Therefore, the government proposed that the supplies be transported from Fort Laramie across the Platte River; that is, across the border the Oglála had created. Spotted Tail also strongly opposed this idea. With the threat of war imminent, the government agreed to let Spotted Tail and his people pick up their supplies at Red Cloud Agency. After this concession, the Lakȟóta essentially ran affairs at both agencies as they pleased. Every five days, the government distributed allowances and supplies to the Indians living at the agencies. The goods arrived in abundance: cattle, bacon, flour, blankets, and clothes. The chiefs then distributed the goods to all the people.[55]

Lakȟóta chiefs were expected to be generous. Distributing wealth was an essential part of their office. A Mnikȟówožu chief said simply: "We love the whites and their provisions. That is what draws me with the whites. . . . When I receive the goods, I am not stingy. I hand them to my people and let them do as they please with them. I have a good mind and a heart big enough for all my people if I can help them any."[56] In the absence of clarifying Lakȟóta sources, it is difficult to determine whether it was real chiefs, akíčhitas, or other leading men who were in charge of this distribution. Agents and other whites did not differentiate between Lakȟóta leadership positions.

While it was a way for Lakȟóta leaders to act in a chiefly manner, it was the women who took care of the goods, prepared them for transportation, and handled the butchering of cattle, as they had done after the buffalo chase. This tradition continued well into the 1890s, demonstrating the strong bonds of kinship and traditional gender roles in Lakȟóta society.

In the early 1870s, agencies were chaotic on supply days, at least from the agent's point of view. Lakȟóta released the delivered livestock and chased it as if it were bison. Whites thought it was a most barbaric habit, but for the Lakȟóta it was a celebration and a feast. Meat intended to last for five days was usually consumed at the post-chase feast within a day or two. That was how the Lakȟóta had always acted. When food was available, it was distributed to everyone in need. In the early reservation days, "issue day" provided an opportunity for feasting and visiting with relatives. This was not acceptable to Agent Wham, or his successors.[57]

In the absence of buffalo, the Lakȟóta accepted beef. They did not appreciate other meat products, such as pork or bacon. Likewise, they either threw away the flour they received or sold it to white traders. In return, they often accepted whiskey in payment, after which they continued to sell blankets and other supplies. After they sobered up they often complained to the agent that they had not received enough supplies. Thus, agents were under constant pressure as the Lakȟóta always demanded more food and supplies, even though they had received what they were entitled to according to the 1868 treaty.

For the Lakȟóta the situation was quite good. There was enough food, and no one really forced them to live near the agencies. They could come and go as they pleased. Even Red Cloud and Spotted Tail avoided the agency as much as possible. They often joined their relatives in the Big Horn and Powder River valleys, but even when camping closer to the agencies they opted to keep a thirty- to seventy-mile buffer to avoid interference from the agents. Agents often complained about this, but one agent believed that it was easier for the chiefs to control their younger men when they did not camp in the vicinity of the agency. The Lakȟóta chiefs in fact forced the agent to deliver goods to their camps, rather than having to go to the agency themselves. In short, the chiefs made the rules.[58] In the early 1870s, the Great Sioux Reservation had not yet turned the Lakȟóta into "reservation" Indians. For them, the reservation was simply owákpamni oyáŋke (a place where goods were distributed).

"Would You Want Me to Say I Am the Great Chief?"

In 1872, Agent Wham resigned and was replaced by J. W. Daniels, who was also Episcopalian. The Oglála almost immediately clashed with their new agent, who once again proposed that they move to the White River. The Oglála refused; they were not going to let the wašíču decide where they were to live. In May 1872 Red Cloud, Spotted Tail, and a large delegation of Lakȟóta leaders traveled to Washington to discuss this and other pressing issues. The government also wanted to make sure the reservation Lakȟóta would not join the free oyáte in their opposition to the construction of the Northern Pacific Railway. Several chiefs from Grand River Agency were also invited, but the Commissioner of Indian Affairs acknowledged that neither Sitting Bull nor Black Moon were present. Thus, the results were meager.

Back home the Lakȟóta learned that Agent Daniels planned a census count among the Oglála. Again, the Lakȟóta refused. They did not want the whites to know how many they were. The government wanted to know their number to send the correct number of annuities, but the Lakȟóta were suspicious and believed it was just another way to defraud them.[59]

Taking a census of the reservation Lakȟóta was practically impossible anyway, because the free Lakȟóta, spurred by rumors that there was a tremendous amount of food readily available at the agencies, traveled between agencies regularly. Their presence made any counts inaccurate. They had by no means come to beg for food but demanded what they believed was a fair share of the food and supplies. From the agents' perspectives things were spiraling toward chaos.[60]

In 1873, many Oglála and Sičháŋǧu moved south of the Platte River to hunt bison. According to some sources, Red Cloud and Spotted Tail were with this group at least part of the time. These Lakȟóta stayed in the Republican River area for most of the winter. However, they not only hunted, but also attacked Pawnee hunters, killing nearly seventy people, most of them women and children.[61]

The US government failed to protect the Pawnees, in part because the Friends of the Indian still believed that it was only through Christian kindness that the Lakȟóta would abandon their nomadic lifestyle. No military expedition was sent out to punish the perpetrators. All Agent Daniels did was ask Red Cloud to help stop the raids made by the Sičháŋǧu. Red Cloud's reply was straightforward; he had no authority over the Sičháŋǧu, and he had no desire to intervene. Lakȟóta aggression also caused headlines in the east. The *New York Times* reported on Lakȟóta attacks as attempts to destroy the Pawnee. Their article headline ran briefly as "The Savages."[62] The other Lakȟóta oyáte continued to raid other neighboring tribes. They justified these attacks by saying that it was "no business of the white man what the Indians do among themselves, so long as they do not disturb or kill the whites."[63] The Lakȟóta clearly had no intention of ending bullying of their old enemies.

Red Cloud spent much of his time far from the agency, and during his absence Agent Daniels persuaded other, more white-friendly chiefs to move the agency to the White River. He was able to gain the help of the influential chief Šúŋka Lúta (Red Dog), who was mourning the loss of his son at the time. According to an account, he lay down beside his son's remains, slashed his own body until blood ran to the ground, and prayed. Perhaps he had a vison that gave him a new direction for life. In any event, he declared that the white man's kindness had made an impression on him and "with him I will live and die."[64] After that he worked tirelessly with the agent. Upon returning, Red Cloud learned that there were a considerable number of people now willing to move. Eventually he, too, yielded and informed the agent that moving the agency might be possible if sufficient and additional supplies were distributed as compensation. Above all, he wanted weapons and ammunition.[65] Red Cloud wanted to see where Spotted Tail desired to have his agency before choosing a location of his own. He did not want to move too close to the influential Spotted Tail, a clear indication that the two Lakȟóta chiefs wanted to maintain their power and independence from the agent, while also showing that there was some jealousy and competition between the two men.

Instead of working together, Red Cloud and Spotted Tail quarreled about almost everything. The same applied to other leaders; reservation life brought internal family rivalries to the surface and intensified them. It was therefore difficult for the agents to know what the Lakȟóta were really going to do when one chief promised one thing and others contradicted him almost immediately. The Lakȟóta sometimes took advantage of this to delay important decisions. Nobody it seemed, not even Red Cloud or Spotted Tail, wanted to take responsibility for the decisions. In personal meetings with the agents, they stated that they were on the agents' side, but when they appeared in public, they made demands and excuses to oppose the agents' proposals. In this way, they kept a balance between maintaining a working relationship with the agent and strengthening their position among their people.

When an agent asked Red Cloud why he alone could not decide about the transfer of the agency, he replied, poignantly referring to the fate of Scattering Bear, "I do not want to be the only chief; at the treaty in 1851, we made one great chief and the white men killed him. Would you want me to say I am the great chief?"[66] Agents were still puzzled by the structure of Lakȟóta leadership and internal power struggles resulting from the naming of head chiefs. In fact, Acting Commissioner of Indian Affairs H. C. Clum put this ignorance into words when he reported that some Lakȟóta bands "dissatisfied with Red Cloud, and refusing to recognize him as their leader, have gone to Montana, having for their chief Sitting Bull."[67]

In August 1873, when the Red Cloud Agency was finally relocated to the White River, Agent Daniels left. His place was taken by a new agent, J. J. Saville. Agent Saville's life was as problematic as that of his predecessors. The Oglála in effect ran affairs and the agent did not know how to handle them. Unlike Daniels and Wham, he called on the troops stationed at Fort Laramie to assist him. Eventually, the soldiers established Camp Robinson near the agency and maintained a permanent presence in the area. The camp was renamed Fort Robinson in 1878. The proximity of the soldiers did not shift the power from the Lakȟóta chiefs to the agents. Increasingly, however, Lakȟóta at the Red Cloud, Spotted Tail, Grand River, and Cheyenne River Agencies began to split between those siding with the agent and those who opposed any cooperation. At Crow Creek (Kȟaŋǧí Wakpá Oyáŋke) and Lower Brulé (Khulwíčhaša Oyáŋke) agencies, so-called progressives formed the majority. They were more eager to follow the agents' suggestions on farming and other "civilized" pursuits.[68] Overall, divisions that began decades earlier started to have a real effect on those now living on the reservation. Those willing to work with the agent were often scorned by those rejecting cooperation. Opponents were supported by off-reservation Lakȟóta who often threatened to start a war if their demands were not met. On several occasions the Lakȟóta came close to fighting each other. Small incidents between Lakȟóta factions took place almost every day. As early as 1869, Spotted Tail was in the center of one such incident. One of his rivals, Big Mouth, got drunk and began mocking him for his sympathies toward the whites. To calm the situation, Spotted Tail left the scene. Big Mouth rushed after him, caught him, and suddenly pressed his pistol to Spotted Tail's head and pulled the trigger. Luckily, the weapon did not fire. Spotted Tail took out his own pistol and shot his opponent in the head, killing him on the spot.[69]

POWDER RIVER—ČHAȞLÍ WAKPÁ

DeWitt C. Poole, the Indian agent for Spotted Tail Agency, awoke to a huge commotion. Some Lakȟóta, led by Spotted Tail, had rushed into the agency followed by Big Mouth's furious relatives and friends. Spotted Tail sat down with a rifle in his hand as the relatives began rampaging in the room. Agent Poole was unable to calm the situation until an interpreter suggested the agent state that it would be best for Spotted Tail to donate ten horses as compensation. This eased the tensions, and the men quietly withdrew. In the morning, Big Mouth's grieving brother arrived at the agency threatening to attack Spotted Tail. The same interpreter urged the agent to give him a pair of blankets as a gift. If the interpreter had not intervened each time, the situation could easily have gotten out of hand, and the agent might not have survived the brawl.[70]

One of the most well-known incidents took place in October 1874, when Agent Saville planned to erect a flagpole at Red Cloud Agency. Perhaps he wanted to use the flag as a signaling tool for nearby Camp Robinson. When the Lakȟóta heard about it, they informed Saville that they did not want a flag at their agency. Saville told his men to continue. At that point, Lakȟóta warriors rode up to the yard in full war regalia. They watched silently as the workers continued. Then they rushed to the flagpole and chopped it to pieces. The agent asked Red Cloud to intervene, but he either did not want to or dared not, since many of the warriors were Northern Lakȟóta. The flagpole so irritated the Lakȟóta that American Horse's winter count named the year after the cutting up of the pole.[71]

The agent sent a messenger to Camp Robinson, and a detachment started toward the agency. Hundreds of Lakȟóta warriors soon surrounded the troops and their complete annihilation seemed inevitable. Luckily, Young Man Afraid of His Horses arrived with a few warriors to protect the soldiers and led them to the agency. This incident shocked the Lakȟóta as it was now evident that the people were divided. The event also shocked the army for it barely escaped another disaster.[72]

The incident was also a severe setback for the Friends of the Indian and their cherished peace policy. The agent had called for soldiers, which was considered unnecessary and did not reflect the group's beliefs and wishes or their policy. However, this event could not be swept under the rug as so many others had been when the setbacks and failures of the peace policy were left out of official reports. The press followed events on the Great Sioux Reservation closely and the *New York Times* reported that Lakȟóta did not cooperate and were constantly leaving the reservation to go to war. The newspaper reported that Red Cloud and Spotted Tail had agreed to work against all "civilizing" efforts, yet it also reported that white settlers hated the Indians so deeply that false rumors of Lakȟóta plans to go on the warpath circulated constantly.[73]

At the northern agencies of Cheyenne River and Grand River, the situation was clearer. The Indians living there were mostly "progressive," while the majority of the Húŋkpapȟa, Mnikȟówožu, Itázipčho, Sihásapa, and Oóhenuŋpa resisters were completely beyond the reach of the agency. Although those living close to the agencies were willing to try farming and take other steps along the "white man's road," the actual results were still meager in the early 1870s. At Grand River, Sihásapa chief Grass was one of the few who was willing to try farming and was able to grow good quality corn. By 1873 the agency was moved to Standing Rock where additional areas were made available for cultivation. At Cheyenne River Agency, a few schools had been established and Episcopalian missionaries had built a church nearby. Still, attendance rates at the schools and churches were low. Nor did the Indians seem to be interested in farming. The agents regularly reported that the Lakȟóta refused to work. The agents generally believed that it was unlikely that the Indians would soon be able to support themselves through work. As a possible solution, some agents suggested that instead of farming, the Lakȟóta should be allowed to raise cattle for a living.[74] This idea clashed with the government's goal to turn the Lakȟóta into Christian farmers. More Lakȟóta would have welcomed raising cattle than were interested in farming. It might have been a more productive pursuit.

Despite the turmoil caused by repeated relocations, factionalism, the census, and farming woes, Lakȟóta life on the reservation was quite good. The Friends of the Indian made sure that food and supplies were plentiful. The Lakȟóta spent their days visiting and debating daily matters and making it nearly impossible for the agents to perform the tasks assigned to them. The agents could not control the Lakȟóta. The Fort Laramie Treaty guaranteed that Lakȟóta tȟamákȟočhe remained intact, and Lakȟóta felt they could fight their traditional enemies and resist white encroachment, while also getting the benefits of annuities and trading. The news about railroads, steamboats, and diminishing buffalo herds was disturbing, but they still felt in control of their homeland and destiny. What they did not grasp was the extent to which industrialization, imperialism, and capitalism eyed Lakȟóta lands to exploit and conquer. While the fur trade was waning, the whites discovered a new resource that put those outside forces into motion: gold.

ĦESÁPA

THE BLACK HILLS ARE NOT FOR SALE

Brave Deeds

Between 1872 and 1875, the nonreservation Lakȟóta became increasingly worried about white intrusion on their lands. The railroad inevitably made its way closer to their northern hunting grounds, and settlers in Montana and Wyoming were calling for the opening of Lakȟóta homelands for mining. The Lakȟóta were facing an onslaught of "explorations" organized by civilians searching for gold in the Big Horn Mountains and Black Hills. In addition to civilian trespassers, the US military continued its survey for the railway or entered the area to protect railway construction crews. The Lakȟóta opposed all intrusions. The US government halted one major mining expedition organized by settlers in Wyoming fearing it might lead to a major confrontation with the Lakȟóta. With their Cheyenne and Arapaho allies, the Lakȟóta stepped up attacks on railroad surveyors and military forts in the area.

Once again, the US military shifted attention to the Northern Lakȟóta. Gen. Phillip Sheridan and other military officers were certain that difficulties were unavoidable. To control the Lakȟóta, they proposed in 1873 that a permanent military base should be established in the Black Hills. The problem, of course, was that the 1868 treaty guaranteed the Black Hills to the Lakȟóta.[1]

Sitting Bull, Gall, Crazy Horse, and other Lakȟóta leaders had effectively pushed their land base farther west and north since the treaty. By 1873 they occupied an area extending west to the Big Horn Mountains and north to the Yellowstone River. The Yellowstone, Rosebud, and Powder River valleys contained many buffalo and became essential hunting grounds for the Lakȟóta.[2] While the 1868 treaty stated that the boundary line of the unceded territory extended to the Big Horns, the Lakȟóta now claimed an area that was clearly larger than the whites had envisioned. Sitting Bull, seeking new avenues for trade, was looking even farther north to the Slót'a. He was hoping to get arms and ammunition from them. Unfortunately, the Slót'a brought along plenty of whiskey, which, as so often happened, caused brawls among the Lakȟóta and led to fights with the Slót'a. Those fights were significant events mentioned in the Makȟúla winter count.[3]

The winter of 1871–72 was severe and several Northern Lakȟóta thiyóšpaye spent the season around Fort Peck. Fort Peck was not a traditional post where the Lakȟóta traded or visited, but as the Lakȟóta were expanding their domain, the government tried to find new ways to deal with them. The government lavishly provided goods hoping to make the Lakȟóta dependent on them, and possibly willing to allow the railroad to pass though their lands. In the winter of 1872 this strategy seemed to be working; many Lakȟóta bands would indeed have suffered severely without these supplies. Even Sitting Bull and Black Moon were reported to have drawn rations there. Gall took his people to Grand River. The negotiations at Fort Peck did not yield results. The Lakȟóta were willing to work for peace, but it had to be on their terms, and the railroad pushing through their lands was unacceptable. The Lakȟóta who had pressed the Crow farther west, considered this vast area part of Lakȟóta tȟamákȟočhe, their homeland. They were going to defend it and not let the wašíču take it away.[4]

In April 1872, chief Spotted Eagle (Waŋblí Glešká) arrived with his band at Cheyenne River Agency and informed the whites that they were no longer to enter Lakȟóta lands. All trespassers would be destroyed. Spotted Eagle refused to listen to any objections or accept any gifts. He had come to present an ultimatum, not to negotiate. In August 1872 he made good on his promise. Deep in Lakȟóta country in the Yellowstone River valley, his men attacked a military command led by Maj. Eugene M. Baker. The Lakȟóta numbered as many as 1,000 warriors. According to Old Bull (Tȟatȟáŋkehaŋni), they had been preparing for a major expedition against the Crow when, during a Sun Dance ceremony, they learned of Baker's presence. They now decided to attack the soldiers instead. Lakȟóta leaders hoped to lure the soldiers into a trap, but as so often happened, the young men attacked the enemy prematurely, allowing the soldiers to erect a makeshift fortification. The Lakȟóta individually charged enemy lines to show their bravery, and so the soldiers easily kept them at bay.

One deed of personal valor stood out. After observing the soldiers for a while, Sitting Bull took out his pipe and stepped up toward the soldiers' lines until the bullets could reach him. There he sat down and called on others to come and smoke with him. His friend White Bull and two Cheyenne followed him. The bullets blew dust around the men, but they smoked for a moment, after which Sitting Bull's friends decided to rush for cover. Sitting Bull calmly cleaned the pipe before walking back. Sitting Bull's actions deeply impressed everyone. He had once again proven himself to be the bravest of all, and under the protection of Wakȟáŋ Tȟáŋka. In turn, Crazy Horse also wanted to display his bravery. He rode along the enemy line until his horse was hit and he crashed to the ground, forcing him to run for cover. This time, Crazy Horse's act was overshadowed by the older Sitting Bull. After these brave deeds, the Indians retreated, unable to destroy Baker's column. They had to leave the body of one of their warriors behind. The soldiers took his body from the field and threw it into a fire, shocking the Lakȟóta. A few days later his relatives returned to collect his burned bones.[5]

Over the next few days, small Lakȟóta groups engaged with other military units in the area. The fighting followed the same pattern: the soldiers took shelter and the Lakȟóta attacked them individually. Sitting Bull and Gall threatened to bring in the power of the entire Lakȟóta people to destroy the soldiers, but that never happened. The Lakȟóta were content putting the soldiers on the defensive and stealing their cattle and horses.[6]

Although the Lakȟóta were unable to destroy the military forces, their attacks alarmed white settlers. Washington decision-makers did not know how to proceed. The Northern Pacific Railway was extremely important economically to the United States; General Sherman called it a crucial national venture. At the same time, he realized that the Indians would fight every step of its construction. Indian agents and the Commissioner of Indian Affairs Francis A. Walker agreed. They feared they would have to sacrifice both soldiers and significant amounts of money to complete their railway. It was the money that became the biggest problem. In 1873, a financial panic led to suspension of construction on the Northern Pacific Railway.[7]

The railroad was not the only problem for the Lakȟóta. A new problem emerged in the Black Hills. In the aftermath of the Panic of 1873, rumors of gold were so persistent that in 1874 the army ordered a scientific expedition commanded by Lt. Col. George A. Custer into the area. The goal was to verify the rumors. With nearly a thousand men, Custer entered the hills without encountering any resistance, even though the Lakȟóta certainly knew of his presence, for every evening the regimental band gave quite a concert, making the hills echo with music. Custer also had journalists with him, and thanks to their reports, the rumors of gold grew even bigger, and had many believing there were greater gold deposits than they could have ever imagined. Now that the expedition had confirmed the rumors, the situation was about to get out of hand. Although the US government had promised in the 1868 treaty to prevent any whites, except for those conducting official government business, from entering the Black Hills, it was difficult to keep that promise. The only way to keep the gold prospectors away was to send the army after them. In practice, that did not fix the problem, because the gold seekers returned to the hills as soon as they got out of jail. Army officers regarded the situation as shameful. Although they knew that rumors of gold were exaggerated, they saw no way of keeping prospectors out of the area. The only solution would be for the Lakȟóta to surrender their lands either by reconciliation or by force. After all, the US government was not prepared to take strong measures against its own citizens. Thus, within months, thousands of gold seekers flocked to the Black Hills. Custer had opened the "Thieves' Road."[8]

Until 1874 Lakȟóta winter counts and stories describe a life dominated by following the buffalo herds, attending summer gatherings and ceremonies, and fighting the Crow or other tribal enemies rather than conflicts with wašíču. One memorable event took place in 1870 when a group of Lakȟóta from Standing Rock Agency camped near Sitting Bull's village on the Yellowstone River and entered Sitting Bull's camp fully armed. This made Crow King (Kȟaŋǧí Yátapi), known for his furious nature, mad. Why did these people come armed into his camp in a threatening way? That was not a Lakȟóta custom. Crow King prepared to fight these agency Indians. Sitting Bull, however, welcomed them, and invited them to join in their camp for a Sun Dance. Several days of ceremonies and socializing followed. After the ceremonies the people stayed and hunted in the game-rich Yellowstone Valley. People feasted and enjoyed life, and bonds of kinship were renewed between agency and nonagency Lakȟóta.[9]

Fights with the Crow rather than with the United States preoccupied the Lakȟóta. Old Bull and White Bull recall the late 1860s and early 1870s explicitly for the many skirmishes with the Crow. Highlights were "the battle of 30 Crow killed" in 1869 and a rare event when several Crow came into a Lakȟóta camp and stole all their horses, which was also noted in the Long Soldier winter count. The Rosebud winter count depicts 1872–73 with a ceremony conducted by Bull

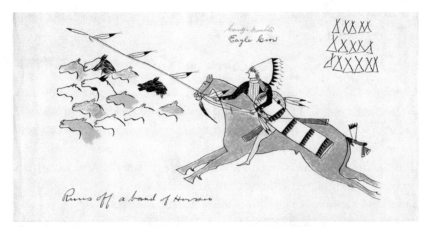

"Kangi Wanbli, Crow Eagle Runs Off a Band of Horses." Drawing by Sitting Bull. Courtesy of the Buffalo Bill Center of the West, Cody, Wyoming, MS 290, Sitting Bull Ledger Drawings Research Collection.

Head (Tȟatȟáŋka Pȟá), and the Húŋkpapȟa remember the years because the Lakȟóta killed a Crow who rode a blue-colored horse. During that time, the Lakȟóta raided deep into enemy country for revenge or plunder. Lakȟóta visited each other, held social dances, formed alliances, and intermarried. In 1872 Sitting Bull remarried, divorcing one of his first wives, after his other wife, Red Woman (Wíŋyaŋ Lúta), died of an illness. Sitting Bull married Four Robes (Tȟašíŋa Tópawiŋ) and Seen By The Nation (Oyáte Wayáŋkapi), a widowed sister of Four Robes, who wanted to live with her sister. This seems to have been a good match as the three remained married until Sitting Bull's death in 1890. Also, during these years, new societies were formed such as the Silent Eaters Society and the White Riders Society, formed by some of Sitting Bull's trusted men.[10]

Life for the nonreservation Lakȟóta seemed to be following essentially traditional patterns, but the presence of the wašíču loomed in the background. During 1874, the Lakȟóta clashed with the army several times, but intertribal warfare with the Crow and others raised the anxieties of white settlers in Montana and Wyoming Territories, who bombarded Washington with messages describing the area as being at the mercy of Sitting Bull. In fact, Lakȟóta warriors seldom approached towns and settlements. They focused their attacks on gold prospectors and other intruders. From the Lakȟóta perspective, they were simply defending Lakȟóta tȟamákȟočhe, their homelands, and they did

not attack whites outside this territory. Yet, they were unable to evict white
invaders from the Black Hills.

"Head Chief of the Land"

By 1874 the Lakȟóta already knew that the government was not going to adhere to
the 1868 Fort Laramie Treaty. A year earlier, a delegation of Oglála and Sičháŋǧu
had been to Washington where they learned that the government was eager to
obtain their lands. After several days of negotiations, they agreed to relinquish
their hunting rights in Nebraska, areas that were guaranteed to them in articles
11 and 16 of the 1868 treaty. The agreement came into effect in 1875. Spotted Tail
and Swift Bear were the most influential Sičháŋǧu leaders to sign, and Little
Wound and Pawnee Killer signed for the Oglála. During the talks the Lakȟóta
also learned about the government's desire to purchase the unceded territory,
including the Powder River country and the Black Hills. The Lakȟóta refused
to discuss the issue: giving up their southern hunting grounds was as far as they
were willing to go.[11]

By 1874, unrest grew to such an extent that war seemed imminent. Apart
from gold, the Black Hills were an excellent agricultural area that was not being
used for that purpose by the Indians. This was another justification to take the
Black Hills from the Lakȟóta. To this end, the government at first searched for
a political solution. The idea was once again to invite Lakȟóta to negotiations
that would result in the Black Hills changing hands. Meanwhile, the US Army
established new military posts around Lakȟóta lands along the banks of the Big
Horn and Tongue Rivers.[12]

The Lakȟóta received invitations for the negotiations in the summer of 1875.
At the Red Cloud and Spotted Tail Agencies, the invitation was looked upon with
suspicion. During August, they sent messages to the nonreservation Lakȟóta,
who were staying in the Powder River and Black Hills areas. The message urged
them all to come to Red Cloud Agency by September. When they learned that the
purpose of that meeting was to discuss the surrender or sale of the Black Hills,
they responded in fury. The free Lakȟóta, Sitting Bull and Crazy Horse in the
forefront, flatly refused to negotiate. Sitting Bull stated that he had never visited
a reservation or an Indian agency, nor did he intend to. He was not a reservation
Indian, and he would never sell his land. The messengers who had come from the
reservation were blamed for delivering the bad news, but Crazy Horse demanded
that everyone show respect to their relatives. By evoking Lakȟóta concepts of
kinship Crazy Horse avoided trouble, and the guests were not molested.[13]

In September 1875, thousands of Lakȟóta gathered near Red Cloud Agency to negotiate with government representatives. The US commission was led by Iowa Senator William B. Allison, who had virtually no knowledge of the Indians. A motley group of representatives from different Christian denominations, political parties, and the military accompanied him. Among them was Gen. Alfred Terry, who was no friend of the Lakȟóta. Another of the members was Pastor Samuel D. Hinman, who had lived with the Dakȟóta for many years and knew their language well. Former merchant G. Beauvais, who was well-known in the West, was also present. Astonishingly, the commission arrived without gifts. The Lakȟóta had come to expect a great quantity of supplies at the meetings to have a proper feast. Hence, the Lakȟóta gathered at Red Cloud Agency were in a bad mood from the start. There was no point to negotiations unless they could enjoy the occasion too. In addition to the reservation Oglála and Sičháŋǧu, about 400 representatives of the Northern Lakȟóta had arrived. Their purpose was to keep a close eye on what was said during the meeting. They claimed that Sitting Bull had sent them to block the sale of the Black Hills. Some men dramatically appeared in their war paint, riding around the meeting place firing their rifles, threatening to kill anyone who signed a treaty with the wašíču.[14]

From the start, it was clear that the Lakȟóta were in no hurry. For several days, they argued with each other about who would represent them in the negotiations and what position should be put forward. The chiefs were jealous of each other. They even quarreled over where the negotiations would be held, and they could not reach an agreement. In the end, the commissioners had to intervene and choose the location. The Lakȟóta did not like this at all. Red Cloud first said he would not move his camp anywhere, but reluctantly agreed to a location along White River chosen by the commission. Representatives of the off-reservation Lakȟóta added to the confusion. Most of the young men living on the reservation sided with their nonreservation relatives. They were ready to defend their land until the end. Government representatives tried to manipulate the chiefs by talking to each chief individually. They tried to convince them to sell the lands but also pleaded for help restraining the younger-generation warriors. A few chiefs tried to find a compromise, but in general, the Lakȟóta were adamantly against selling the Black Hills. There were, in effect, two negotiations taking place: among the Lakȟóta themselves and between the Lakȟóta and the commissioners. Thousands of Indians gathered for the talks, many fully prepared to fight. The situation was tense, and no solution was in sight.[15]

On September 23, government representatives returned to the meeting site backed by a 120-man army unit. The Indians arrived on horseback, riding fast, firing their guns and filling the air with war whoops. They rode toward the commission, veering off at the last minute, leaving—or rather escorting—their leaders to the negotiations. The painted Indians, riding their best ponies, were dressed in their finest regalia and wore their finest headdresses. Indian chiefs placed themselves around the meeting ground calmly talking to each other and smoking. Government representatives waited in wonder. Hundreds of warriors surrounded the meeting ground. Crazy Horse sent Little Big Man (Wičháša Čík'ala), also known as Short Bull (Tȟatȟáŋka Ptéčela), who dressed in full war regalia and threatened to kill all the whites and their sympathizers. The tensions were palpable, but the situation de-escalated without bloodshed. The Lakȟóta did not want to let things get out of hand. It was more a demonstration of power, a tactic to impress the negotiators. After the Lakȟóta show of force, the negotiations continued but proved fruitless. It became clear how differently the Lakȟóta living on the reservation and those off-reservation had begun to think. On the reservation, the Lakȟóta had become somewhat accustomed to the white man's ways. Many of their chiefs had been to Washington and knew how to negotiate with the whites. Obviously, neither Red Cloud nor Spotted Tail wanted to give up the Black Hills any more than Sitting Bull or Crazy Horse did, but they hoped to avoid war and looked for ways to preserve Lakȟóta lands as well as the peace. For them, the idea of renting the hills was a possibility, provided they were sufficiently compensated. Both Red Cloud and Red Dog raised the idea of the government renting the surface of the hills for seven generations. Red Cloud said: "There have been six generations raised, and I am the seventh, and I want seven generations ahead to be fed." Red Dog supported this idea, saying that they would not sell or rent the "whole hills: we will just give where there is gold . . . Not to include the pines. Just the Black Hills."[16] Perhaps they saw an opportunity to reach a compromise, in which the Lakȟóta would own the Black Hills yet receive compensation from the government. Red Cloud's proposal was logical to the Lakȟóta, because in their worldview, seven Lakȟóta generations had passed. Thus, Red Cloud's son represented a new generation from which it was natural to go forward for seven generations. Seven was a sacred number for the Lakȟóta.

Not everyone agreed upon the seven generations solution. Instead of asking for payment for seven generations, Spotted Tail demanded compensation to last forever. "As long as we live on this earth, we expect pay. We want to leave the amount [of money] with the President at interest forever. . . . The amount must be so large that the interest will support us," he said. He then detailed all the items they wanted, including annual delivery of goods in cattle, guns, and ammunition, and concluded: "We want some clothes as long as any Indians live; if only two remain, as long as they live, they will want to be fed, just as they are now. . . . Until the land falls to pieces we want these things; when it does we will give it up."[17]

These leaders expressed the views and ideas of the groups they represented. They were chosen, according to Lakȟóta tradition, as spokesmen expressing what their people had agreed upon jointly. Their task was to express those views regardless of their own opinions. So not only chiefs like Red Cloud or Spotted Tail but less well-known men respected for their skills as orators were elected to speak. One such speaker was Crow Feather (Kȟaŋǧí Wíyaka), who, like many others, emphasized the significance of the Black Hills as the "heart" or "head chief" of their country. Therefore, any compensation for selling or leasing the land should be considerable and last for a long time. The thought of relinquishing the Black Hills forever made Crow Feather feel like the wašíču were "taking the head from my shoulders."[18]

For several days, the Lakȟóta debated whether the Black Hills should be kept, sold, or leased. Each option had its champions. Opponents of the sale were almost invariably younger men ready to defend their country. Older men favored selling or leasing the hills to some extent, but they could not agree on a price. Some wanted compensation in clothing, food, and goods, others asking for tens of millions of dollars. Red Cloud demanded that schools, various buildings, and even a sawmill be built on the reservation. He stated that the whites wanted to make him a white man, so they had to give him all the equipment he needed.

The Lakȟóta demanded up to $70 million, which was too high for government representatives, who promised to pay $6 million for the purchase of the Hills. It was an insufficient amount for such rich lands, especially since gold had just been found there, and the Lakȟóta understood this. They also knew, however, that once the whites came to an area, they would never leave. Knowing the government would not agree to their demands, the Lakȟóta perhaps wanted to buy time.

Lakȟóta demands for compensations in perpetuity from the government were logical. After all, they were giving up their most sacred land base. One could speculate on how well the Lakȟóta in the 1870s understood the difference between selling and leasing, and it is unclear if they grasped the large sums of money that they presented to the commission. Probably the figures of seven million

and seventy million presented during the meeting did not really mean much
to most Lakȟóta. Still, the plans of Red Cloud, Spotted Tail, and others to put
money aside in trust to gain interest, shows that they at least were well informed
and understood what was going on. To dismiss Lakȟóta leaders as ignorant is
inaccurate. They employed a tactic they believed would lead to the best possible
solution. They did receive advice from familiar traders, mixed-bloods, and so-
called squawmen.[19] Many of these men certainly urged Lakȟóta to demand as
much for their land as possible. On the other hand, many traders knew that the
more money the Lakȟóta got, the more likely it would gradually flow into their
pockets. Whatever their agendas, the advisors helped the Lakȟóta determine a
price for the sacred Black Hills.

The negotiations of 1875 eventually failed. Red Cloud and many others did
not even bother to show up on the last day. Spotted Tail was present but said that
the government's conditions were unacceptable. Therefore, the matter was left
open to be decided in the future. The Oglála Black Elk, who was about fourteen
at the time, described the final stages of the talks as tense. After speeches by Red
Cloud and Spotted Tail, One Horn (Hewáŋžiča, also known as Lone Horn) of
the Mnikȟówožu stood up and, pointing to the Indians around him, said: "You
selfish people, we are not the only ones in the Sioux nation. Raise your head up
and look to the north and the west. There are Sioux still out. My people are
out yet. According to that, we should not be selfish. We shall wait and when
this Sioux nation gets together, we shall decide on this." According to Black
Elk, people burst out in loud "Háu, háu" exclamations of agreement. Afterwards,
soldiers walked around the camps offering whiskey, trying to make people sign,
recalled Black Elk.[20]

Shortly after the negotiations, One Horn traveled from one Lakȟóta camp
to another to report on the talks. He told about his experiences at Sitting Bull's
camp. Sitting Bull was pleased and said: "Hau! Brother, it is well that you have
said that; These Hills are a treasure to us Indians. That is the food pack of the
people and when the poor have nothing to eat, we can all go to there and have
something to eat."[21] The message brought by One Horn triggered great concern
among the free Lakȟóta. It seemed that the reservation Lakȟóta could no longer
be trusted. One Horn himself took the matter utterly seriously. He died in the
winter of 1875–76, and according to Lakȟóta stories, he died because of the sad-
ness he felt for the Black Hills.[22]

Whether to sell or lease the land made no difference to the free Lakȟóta. They
viewed it as a complete betrayal. The land could not be sold or rented, and they

saw no reason to let the whites take the Black Hills and give only money and goods in return. They had no use for them either. Indeed, many of the Northern Lakȟóta had for years declined all official annuities anyway. As One Horn had said, the reservation Lakȟóta had no right to decide alone on a matter of this magnitude. For the Northern Lakȟóta and even many Oglála and Sičháŋǧu, the selling of the hunting lands in Nebraska was not a big deal, but it demonstrated that the reservation Lakȟóta would sell land in exchange for money. The Black Hills was their country, and no one could sell it without their consent.

This is perhaps the first time in Lakȟóta history where it was obvious how contacts with the whites had changed their lives. Now it was undeniable that the Lakȟóta traditional way of life and the traditional way of thinking, Lakȟól wičhóȟ'aŋ, was losing ground to reservation realities and the wašíču way of life. The Lakȟóta had to find a way to live in two worlds, and this adaptation would prove difficult.

The Fort Laramie Treaty of 1868 required that three-quarters of adult male Lakȟóta had to approve a new treaty for it to become legal. The commissioners wrote a report stating that the Lakȟóta were opposed to the sale of the area, and in no case would they have been able to obtain sufficient signatures to make the agreement valid. In 1875, so many Lakȟóta lived off the reservation that it was obvious, even to the commissioners, that that number of signatures would be impossible to obtain, and they acknowledged that even reservation Lakȟóta opposed selling the land. The commission suggested that the government come up with another way to get the Black Hills, and that it be presented to the Lakȟóta as a fait accompli.[23]

The commissioners also stated that the Lakȟóta were entirely dependent on government annuities, so the United States could use this as leverage. Thus, the US government, up to the highest political levels, began to devise plans for getting the Lakȟóta out of the Black Hills and to possibly transfer them to the Missouri or Indian Territory. War was one option, but there was no real justification for war. After all, the United States could not attack peaceful Indians. The Friends of the Indian would not let that happen.

The Commissioner of Indian Affairs Edward P. Smith believed that the Lakȟóta posed no threat to white settlers. He wrote that "except under extraordinary provocation, or in circumstances not at all to be apprehended, it is not probable that as many as 500 Indian warriors will ever again be mustered at one point for a fight." Conflicting international interests and the proliferation of white settlements mitigated against any great Indian war ever taking place again on

US territory.²⁴ Secretary of War J. D. Cameron wrote that all Indian wars in the United States would end forever if the Sioux were placed on a reservation. In late 1875, senior government leadership was secretly planning exactly the sort of "extraordinary provocation" Commissioner Smith was worried about. The government had to find an excuse to start military action. The war between the Lakȟóta and the Crow offered a convenient excuse when it caused unrest at the western borders of Lakȟóta country in Montana and Wyoming. The government now determined that the Lakȟóta did not comply with the 1868 treaty in fighting with their neighbors, including white settlers, and an ultimatum was presented to the Lakȟóta. All Lakȟóta had to come to the Indian agencies by January 31, 1876. Those who refused or failed to arrive on time would be classified as hostile and considered to be at war with the United States.²⁵

"I Was Anxious to Perform My Duty on Earth"

In fall 1875, news about the government's ultimatum arrived at Lakȟóta agencies, and was passed on to those living off the reservation. As winter approached, it became obvious that the messengers were unable to deliver the message in time to all the camps, which were scattered throughout Lakȟóta country. Even the camps that received the information had virtually no chance of getting to the agencies by the last day of January, in the dead of winter. The government representatives were well aware of this; the government's ultimatum was in fact an excuse and a declaration of war all in one.

For the Indians, the ultimatum made no sense. They did not wish to go to war with the whites but, getting back to the agencies in the middle of winter was impossible. Moreover, such specific dates meant nothing to the Lakȟóta. Their concept of time was not bound to exact dates. It was enough for the Lakȟóta to agree to arrive at the agencies in the spring; a few months mattered nothing.

The United States now had an excuse to treat the absent Lakȟóta as enemies. The Lakȟóta had not obeyed the orders given to them, so the United States could declare war and open up the coveted Black Hills. The Lakȟóta did not think that they were officially at war with the United States until military units marched into the heart of Lakȟóta country during the winter and spring.

The war arrived in earnest on March 16, 1876. A small group of Lakȟóta and Cheyenne were camped along the Powder River and were surprised by Col. Joseph Reynold's troops early in the morning. The Indians scrambled to organize a defense, but the soldiers destroyed their camp and took almost all their horses. The Indians lost only a few men in the skirmish but had to flee without supplies in the severe cold. A couple of days later they managed to recapture many of the horses they had lost. Nevertheless, the camp was in serious trouble due to the cold weather. Eventually, they straggled into Crazy Horse's camp, where they were welcomed with open arms. Crazy Horse only had a small number of people with him, so it became necessary to seek help from a larger camp. They found safety at Sitting Bull's camp, where the refugees were fed and dressed lavishly.[26]

The whites first thought they had struck Crazy Horse's camp and hailed it as a great victory. Newspapers praised the military's action. Early on the *New York Times* reported that a complete victory over Crazy Horse had been achieved, but it soon became clear that this was not the case. When the Lakȟóta took their horses back, it was obvious the expedition was a failure. On April 23, 1876, the paper admitted that the attack had been a fiasco. The Indians had suffered only minor casualties, and in fact had fought very bravely, inflicting casualties on the army. Soldiers had retreated to Fort Fetterman on the south bank of the North Platte River (present-day Wyoming).[27] The military operation was to be continued with 2,000 men. Gen. Philip H. Sheridan led the military operation from his headquarters in Chicago. He planned a summer campaign with a three-pronged attack. Gen. George Crook was to lead a column from Fort Fetterman, Col. John Gibbon another from Fort Ellis, and Gen. Alfred H. Terry a third from Fort Abraham Lincoln. Terry was assisted by the enthusiastic Lt. Col. George A. Custer.[28]

It was clear to the Lakȟóta that the war to defend Lakȟóta tȟamákȟoče was a reality. Sitting Bull and Crazy Horse had been stressing for some time that they would not attack the whites if they were allowed to live in peace. They would only fight defensive wars. This they had also told to the whites. Now, in the spring of 1876, the time had come for that defensive war, this was not what the younger warriors were looking for. In characteristic Lakȟóta fashion, they defied their chiefs' decisions, and ventured out on raids on their own.

The off-reservation Lakȟóta gathered throughout the early summer of 1876. The Húŋkpapȟa were joined by Itázipčho, Mnikȟówožu, Oglála, Oóhenuŋpa, Sihásapa, and Sičháŋǧu. All Lakȟóta oyáte were represented. In addition, some Iháŋktȟuŋwaŋna and Isáŋyathi, Cheyenne, and Arapaho joined the coalition as well.

In spring 1875, the Lakȟóta conducted a ceremony making some of the northern Cheyenne official members of lakȟólkičhiyapi (Lakȟóta alliance or circle of relatives). Although the Cheyenne had long been friends and allies of the Lakȟóta, especially the Oglála, they were now relatives with all Lakȟóta oyáte. The ceremony was led by Sitting Bull. On this occasion, Sitting Bull wore a breechcloth, moccasins, and an eagle feather headdress. He had painted his body completely yellow. He had painted the lower part of his face black. Black lines stretched all the way to the corners of his eyes and over his forehead. A black stripe was painted around his wrists and ankles, and around his neck was a black plate symbolizing the sun. A black crescent was painted on his right shoulder. Sitting Bull arrived at the sacred tree, the čhaŋwákȟaŋ, erected for the ceremony, riding his horse painted with sacred symbols. After descending, he called one Cheyenne and one Lakȟóta to fill two sacred pipes. By smoking the sacred pipes together, the Cheyenne and Lakȟóta swore allegiance to each other. Then Sitting Bull took both pipes, pointed them toward the sacred tree while dancing to the tree and back. As he danced, he imitated enemy attacks and counterattacks, sometimes announcing loudly that he had received a certain number of enemies in his hands. Eventually, he grabbed the air, and announced that he had captured them all. Wakȟáŋ Tȟáŋka had thus handed over the enemies to the Lakȟóta and the Cheyenne. The ceremony ended with singing and public dancing. The Lakȟóta and Cheyenne had now sworn to oppose together the intrusion of whites into their remaining hunting grounds.[29]

In the spring and early summer of 1876, the off-reservation Lakȟóta camp had perhaps as many as 3,000 to 4,000 people, including about 1,000 fighting-age men. Keeping such a large camp was challenging. The camp had to move every few days when the firewood and grass were used up. Indeed, the Indians were spread out along the Powder, Yellowstone, Rosebud, and Little Big Horn (Pȟežísla Wakpá) Rivers. When camping, the Lakȟóta traditionally formed a large circle. Different oyáte placed their own camp circles in designated places inside the larger circle. The Húŋkpapȟa, who were the largest group, were at the doorway of the camp circle. They always traveled last. The second largest group were the Cheyenne, who traveled first when the camp was on the move. In this way, the Húŋkpapȟa and Cheyenne took the most dangerous places and protected the smaller oyáte.[30]

In the camp, people were happy. The Lakȟóta felt powerful and there were plenty of bison. The biggest question among these free Lakȟóta was how many of the reservation Lakȟóta would join them. Every summer, many people from the agencies arrived north for summer hunting and religious ceremonies. This year the visitors were more eagerly awaited. Black Elk described how his own thiyóšpaye joined Crazy Horse's camp on the upper reaches of the Tongue River after the negotiations of 1875. As they traveled through the Black Hills, where Black Elk had had his great vision a couple of years earlier, he now had another vision that confirmed to him that his duty was to help his people save the Black Hills. "I was anxious to perform my duty on earth," he said later. Crazy Horse's camp along the Tongue River was quite large in the early fall, but as winter came, the crowds dispersed into smaller groups to spend the winter in various familiar locations in the Yellowstone, Powder and Tongue Rivers area. The fall and early winter were spent mainly hunting and fighting the Crow. For Black Elk and other agency thiyóśpaye, the move north was not to join Crazy Horse and others in a campaign against the wašíču, but simply an annual migration that had already become a tradition.[31]

After the Reynolds fight, however, the situation had changed. The annual migration was a great concern for the whites. Estimates of the number of free Lakḣóta ranged as high as tens of thousands, and wild rumors about escaping reservation Lakḣóta circulated among the whites. The military and the press were convinced that a steady stream of Lakḣóta from the agencies led to the Black Hills and beyond to the Powder River. Officials from Red Cloud and Spotted Tail Agencies assured them that nothing like this was going on. They reported that all Indians belonging to the agencies were present. The official census records show that lots of people remained at the agencies, albeit perhaps slightly fewer than in previous years, but Indian Agent H. W. Bingham of Cheyenne River Agency explained that since almost all Lakḣóta were related to each other, it was only natural that some of the Agency Indians visited their relatives living outside the reservation. Commissioner of Indian Affairs J. Q. Smith noted that some of the Lakḣóta had indeed left the reservation during 1875–76 but said this was because they did not have enough food. Government annuities were again completely inadequate and arrived late. The situation was, he lamented, embarrassing, and it was likely to arouse suspicion and opposition among the Indians. The military, in contrast, reported that there were almost no Lakḣóta at the agencies. These discrepancies make it very difficult to determine what the real situation was.[32]

For many Lakḣóta thiyóśpaye and oyáte, seasonal migration transition to the hunting grounds of the north was indeed normal. However, it is obvious that among those heading north there were also warriors preparing for war. Jack Red Cloud, the son of Red Cloud, who joined Sitting Bull and Crazy Horse, was an example of younger generation warriors. His presence sparked considerable debate as to whether Red Cloud gave his consent to him or other Agency Oglála to join the war. If he did, it meant he gave his blessing to war, while trying to convince the whites otherwise. Of course, neither Jack Red Cloud nor anyone else needed Red Cloud's permission. Red Cloud allegedly told General Crook that the Lakȟóta had lots of warriors, guns, and ponies and that they were brave and ready to fight for their country: "They are not afraid of the soldiers or the commander of the soldiers [Crook]. Many warriors are ready to face them. Each Tipi sends his young men, and they say of the Great Father's dogs: Let them come."[33]

After this statement, Red Cloud went back to his familiar rhetoric of peace, once again demonstrating his political ability. He assumed a kind of balancing role between the various Lakȟóta factions and between the Oglála and the whites and continued this role until his death in 1909. Thus, there is no definitive answer to the question about his role in the events of 1876.

Nevertheless, Red Cloud's comments, incited rumors of a great Lakȟóta conspiracy. General Crook, for instance, was convinced that Red Cloud was involved in plotting a great war, and his statements gave impetus to the Army's demands to take over control of Indian agencies on the Great Sioux Reservation. This, in turn, was part of an old struggle within the government over the control of Indian affairs in which the military demanded that the Indians be left entirely to the War Department, while the Friends of the Indian demanded that control should rest with the Interior Department. Because the Interior Department was responsible for the Indians, its agents were either civilians or clergy, but the military believed officers to be more effective and better agents.[34] Before long, the civilian agents for the Lakȟóta had to give way to officers appointed by the army, although this did not take place until the end of July 1876.

In any case, a considerable number of reservation Lakȟóta moved toward the Powder River country after the negotiations of 1875 and in the spring of 1876 where they joined the free Lakȟóta. It is impossible to determine how many, but a specific number was irrelevant to the Lakȟóta; they were many, and they were full of confidence.

"These Men Have No Ears, They Will Die"

In the large Lakȟóta camp, the spring and early summer were cheerful times. The Lakȟóta and their allies prepared for the major religious ceremonies of the summer. In late May Sitting Bull again demonstrated his powers as a wičháša wakȟáŋ. Anticipating future events, he sought a vison and to send a prayer to Wakȟáŋ Tȟáŋka. He climbed on top of a hill near the camp, performed the necessary rituals, and fell into a trance. In a vision he saw a large cloud of dust arriving from the east, accompanied by strong winds. In the opposite direction, a white cloud drifted away. This cloud was an Indian camp next to snowy mountains. A cloud of dust approached the white cloud menacingly and soldiers arrived line after line riding on the ridge of the dust cloud. The clouds collided, thunder rumbled, and lightning flashed. Eventually, the storm passed and there was dust all over, but the white cloud remained untouched.

Sitting Bull returned to the camp and shared his vision with others. His vision was interpreted as a group of soldiers coming to attack the Lakḧóta. However, the victory would fall to the Indians. The vision strengthened Lakḧóta faith in their powers. By the time of the vision, the Lakḧóta were already aware of the military forces moving in the north and west, but Sitting Bull's vision told them that soldiers were also coming from the east. That was General Crook's command, which had left Fort Fetterman. Sitting Bull's vision told the Lakḧóta that a great victory would not be many days away. Sitting Bull promised Wakḧáŋ Tḧáŋka that he would pray in the Sun Dance and sacrifice his own flesh as well as an entire bison if Wakḧáŋ Tḧáŋka spared his people and helped them in difficult times. In the early days of June after the entire large camp settled in the Rose-bud River Valley, as promised, Sitting Bull sacrificed the hide of the bison, then offered the pipe and danced. The Sun Dance was organized by the Húŋkpapḧa, but large crowds from other oyáte gathered to follow the dance, where Sitting Bull sought contact with Wakḧáŋ Tḧáŋka. Standing Bear, a young boy at the time, describes the two days of ceremonies as an event of great importance, but also as a time when all the children played, and boys imitated adults in games of endurance. To him it was a celebration and coming together in festivities. For the adults, it was more serious.[35]

After performing the necessary preparatory rituals, Sitting Bull sat at the foot of the sacred tree; his friend White Bull began to slice tiny pieces of flesh from his arms. Fifty pieces of flesh were cut from each arm to show Sitting Bull's sincerity to Wakḧáŋ Tḧáŋka. After this, Sitting Bull danced, although this time he did not attach himself to the sacred tree with rawhide thongs, as he had often done before. After dancing for a long time, staring at the sun, he finally stopped and sank into a trance. His friends gently lowered him to the ground and waited patiently for him to come to. After opening his eyes, Sitting Bull related an amazing new vision. In the vision, a voice had prompted him to focus his gaze on the point just below the sun. There he saw an image in which soldiers, like a swarm of locusts, rushed toward the Indian camp below. They came with men and horses upside down, legs toward the sky and heads down with hats falling off their heads. Some of the Indians below were also upside down. The voice said to Sitting Bull, "These men have no ears, they will die, but you are not allowed to touch their bodies." This vision was even more powerful than the previous one. The soldiers were coming it said, but victory would surely fall to the Lakȟóta and their allies. In the context of the Sun Dance and in a very religiously charged atmosphere, the power and significance of the vision cannot be overstated. The Lakȟóta knew that the soldiers were coming from three different directions, so the vision pointed to events in the very near future. They could only wait and prepare.

After the Sun Dance, the camp moved along the Rosebud River Valley. Scouts spotted several army units moving toward the same area. According to White Bull, the Lakȟóta chiefs decided not to attack the soldiers: They were still focusing on a defensive mode. Yet, on the night of June 16–17, several hundred young men sneaked out of the camp to attack the soldiers. Thus, the chiefs gave in and on the morning of June 17, both Sitting Bull and Crazy Horse were on the way to engage Crook's army. The Lakȟóta almost succeeded in surprising the soldiers that morning, but vigilant Crow and Shoshone scouts spotted the attackers and raised the alarm. The result was an all-day battle in which fortune sometimes sided with the soldiers and at other times with the Indians.[36] Iron Hawk (Chetáŋ Máza) recalls the confusion: "The fight began with the Crow. Then the soldiers began to advance. We were on one side and when the soldiers attacked, we had to retreat, and they were upon us. Then we headed to join the larger party, but they pursued us and, as we retreated, the Crow began to fight harder, seeing the soldiers coming." Iron Hawk was only fourteen at the time and was scared: "I ran for my life. . . . This was a pitiful long stretched-out battle. Then all at once we began to retreat, and as we were running, we saw ahead about thirty cavalrymen approaching us." Then Iron Hawk heard someone shouting: "Take courage, it is a good day to die. Think of the children and helpless at home." With renewed purpose the Lakȟóta charged on the Crow, but then realized the soldiers were close so they retreated again. "I ran for my dear life," recalled Iron Hawk. In the heat of the battle, he still had time to go back to the camp and sit down to eat. After being scolded by others for not fighting, he reentered the battle only to "run for his dear life" for the third time. During the melee he witnessed a Crow and a Lakȟóta in a close fight, which impressed him greatly. Both were bulletproof and wakȟáŋ.[37]

Despite an all-day battle, both sides suffered minor losses and left the scene convinced that they had won the battle. Army officials said the Lakȟóta eventually escaped and claimed numerous Indians were killed when in reality it had been Crook who was forced to retreat.[38] The Lakȟóta considered themselves be victors, as they stole several horses, and counted many coups on both white and Indian enemies. Lakȟóta scouts saw soldiers withdrawing in a hurry toward their base. Thus, both sides were pleased with the day's achievements, even though the outcome was indecisive. The Lakȟóta victory celebrations were subdued because they had lost several men. Although the Lakȟóta felt they had won, this did not yet correspond to the great victory in Sitting Bull's vision. An even bigger battle was to be expected.

After the battle of the Rosebud, the Indians camped along the Little Big Horn River in present-day Montana in a tree-covered valley. From the nearby hills one could see the snowy peaks of the Big Horn Mountains in the west and open prairie to the east. They settled on a riverside formation, with Húŋkpapȟa guarding the camp edge in the south and Cheyenne at the north end. The other oyáte were organized into a semicircle between them, with the Oglála slightly apart. The camp was so large that it apparently extended for several miles along the river.

"Pȟehíŋ Háŋska Kasótapi" (Wiping Out Long Hair)

Although they were aware that the soldiers might be on their trail, the Lakȟóta and their allies felt safe in their camp in the Little Big Horn River Valley. Soldiers were indeed right on their heels. After the battle of Rosebud, Arikara and Crow scouts enlisted by the US military were convinced that the Lakȟóta and Cheyenne camped somewhere near the Rosebud and Little Big Horn Rivers. The intention of the US military was to attack the Indians from three different directions. Lieutenant Colonel Custer would lead his Seventh Cavalry up the Little Big Horn River and attack the camp. Generals Gibbon and Terry would cut off the route of Indians fleeing north. Custer first led his men to the Rosebud River looking for signs of the Indian camp. No camp was found, but abandoned camp sites and tracks were abundant. On June 24, Custer arrived at the scene of Sitting Bull's Sun Dance vision. Custer's scouts warned him that they were on the trail of an enormous Indian camp. On June 25, the scouts announced they could see the large camp on the horizon. Initially, Custer planned to attack the camp the next morning, but he feared the Indians had been warned about his arrival and would flee. He changed his plans and decided to attack the same day. He ignored his Indian scouts who warned him they would find a large camp. Custer's Seventh Cavalry prepared for the attack in the morning hours of June 25, 1876.[39]

Although the Lakȟóta knew that troops were after them, they had no idea Pȟehíŋ Háŋska (Long Hair / Custer) was so close. They had not placed any kind of guard for their camp. On the morning of June 25, everything was quiet in the big camp. Women prepared food, men cared for their horses, and children played or swam in the river. Black Elk remembers that some men were going hunting and women were collecting turnips. The day was beautiful, but Black Elk felt strange all morning, like something horrible was about to happen. Despite his bad feelings, he decided to go swimming when, suddenly, a cry came from the Húŋkpapȟa village that soldiers were coming. An éyapaha (crier) went from one camp circle to another shouting warnings. Women ran for the hills. Chaos ensued. Iron Hawk described the pandemonium at the start of the battle, saying that they could not see the soldiers, who took shelter among the trees. He could only see the smoke of their guns as firing commenced. This added to the confusion and panic. Then everybody started shouting "Crazy Horse is coming!" He was riding a horse with a white face, recalled Black Elk. Crazy Horse's arrival calmed the people as they trusted him, but still the camp was in disarray.[40]

Crazy Horse and Gall rushed toward the soldiers. Young Black Elk was drawn into the melee and thought of his vision, which gave him courage as he started following the soldiers now rushing up into the woods above him. It was chaos, said Black Elk, soldiers firing and women and children fleeing for their lives. Then, he said, the Indians really became "enraged and it was hard to keep them in check—they were downright crazy."[41]

Soon Black Elk got a chance to earn his first coup on a white man. He saw a soldier kicking on the ground and a man urged him to take his scalp. "I began to take my knife," said Black Elk, "Of course, the soldier had short hair and so I started to cut it off. Probably it hurt him because he began to grind his teeth. After I did this, I took my pistol out and shot him in the forehead."[42]

Both Black Elk and Iron Hawk place the start of the battle as early morning, although the fighting started later in the afternoon. Both descriptions refer to the soldiers' first attack, spearheaded by a force led by Maj. Marcus A. Reno. Reno and his men crossed the Little Big Horn River but then had to retreat to a ridge behind them, now known as Reno Hill. Major Reno later stated in his report that he was forced to withdraw, for suddenly Indians were swarming around him from every direction as if they sprang from the earth. The ferocious counterattack led by Crazy Horse forced the soldiers to dig into positions on the slope where they remained until the following evening. They were of no help to Custer, who had progressed along the ridge northward with the intention of attacking the camp a little lower down the river. Capt. Frederick Benteen had been left in the background as backup. [43]

With Crazy Horse and Gall leading the fighting at Reno Hill, Sitting Bull led the safe retreat of women and children from the camp. He participated in the battle only in its early stages, staying behind as the battle progressed. This led to whites accusing him of cowardice. Even some historians have accepted this as a fact.[44] In 1876, however, Sitting Bull was over forty years old, and his job was to lead the people with advice and wise decisions. His task as chief was to look after the people, whether it was fighting or caring for women and children. Yet, rumors of his cowardice survived among the whites. With an accomplished war record he hardly needed to show his abilities on the battlefield.

White Bull, who was in the thick of things in any fight, was taking care of his horses at the start of the battle but joined Sitting Bull in the initial skirmish against Reno's men. He then continued toward Custer's command. Known for his bravery, White Bull once again showed his abilities fighting Custer's men. Some of the soldiers had already jumped off their horses and settled in defensive positions when White Bull alone rushed at the soldiers and pressed through enemy lines without a scratch. This tremendous feat was a demonstration of the power of his medicine. In the next rush, he counted coup on a fallen enemy. Partly because of his attacks, order among the soldiers began to break down. Volley firing turned into random shooting. Soon other brave men followed White Bull. Crazy Horse appeared on the scene and, along with White Bull, Gall, and others rushed toward the soldiers and broke their organization. White Bull collected seven coups in the battle on the hill. Although his horse died under him, he survived unscathed. Allegedly, it was White Bull who killed Custer, but there have been several candidates for that deed. White Bull himself believed he had killed Custer and made several drawings of the occasion. But there are some inconsistencies in the stories he told at different times. In some versions he killed Custer using his rifle, in others with a pistol. White Bull had several witnesses to the incident, so his story cannot be completely dismissed, nor can it be fully verified. It was a chaotic battle, which White Bull later said was the hardest he ever attended, but it was a grand day: "I collected feathers [coups] from right and left that day," he said afterwards.[45]

A Cheyenne dressed in a magnificent war bonnet and shawl made of hide accomplished another feat that impressed the Lakĥóta. He rode several times in circles in front of the soldiers. He could not be stopped. Iron Hawk watched him with admiration. The Cheyenne then came to Iron Hawk, looking awkward. "Cheyenne friend what is the matter," asked Iron Hawk's friend Little Bear (Matĥó Čík'ala). The man opened the belt holding his shawl and several bullets dropped out. The Cheyenne was wakȟáŋ. He was very "sacred and was thus bulletproof," said Iron Hawk later.[46]

Like Black Elk, Iron Hawk described how angry the Indians were during the battle. As he charged the enemy, he remembered the women and children who were suffering, and fought with renewed determination. As warriors charged, they sang war songs that prepared them for battle and possible death.[47] The Lakȟóta and their allies were fighting to save their families and their people. At Little Big Horn some women also took up arms against the wašíču. Though not common among the Lakȟóta, sometimes women joined men on the warpath. One woman who fought side by side with men was Rocky Butte (Íŋyaŋ Ȟé Wiŋ), also known as Bronco or Cowboy (Pteáwaŋyaŋka). She was a Dakȟóta, origi-nally from Minnesota, but after the war of 1862, she followed her people to live with the Húŋkpapȟa. She was known as a warrior who was always prepared for battle. At Little Big Horn, she was only 28 years old. She rode her horse directly against the soldiers wielding a war club in her hand and killed at least one of the soldiers. She was the only woman known to be present in the final stages of the battle on the hill. In the aftermath of the fighting, she followed Sitting Bull to Canada and after returning lived the rest of her life on Standing Rock.[48] Another woman who fought bravely during the battle was a Húŋkpapȟa, Moving Robe Woman (Tȟašína Máni Wiŋ), who was picking turnips when she heard the soldiers coming. Upon learning her brother had been killed, she painted her face and rode against the soldiers. Her bravery so impressed some of the men that Rain-In the Face (Ité Omáǧažu) urged the men not to hide behind her skirt.[49]

Húŋkpapȟa chief Gall described the final stages of the fight as so intense that the smoke and dust darkened the sky. They hardly saw the soldiers in the dust, but eventually they swept over them with their horses. "After that, the battle was over," concluded Gall. The Sičháŋǧu Short Bull (Tȟatȟáŋka Ptéčela), proudly noted that on that day "they wiped out Custer." Many Lakȟóta winter counts for 1876 recorded, Pȟehíŋ Háŋska kasótapi or Pȟehíŋ Háŋska Ktépi, "the wiping out of Long Hair (Custer)" or "Long Hair (Custer) was killed."[50]

In the end, the Indians' overwhelming numbers gave them the victory. Despite all the chaos and drama, the Indian stories focus on the things they always considered important. During even the hottest fight, some, like Black Elk and White Bull, relied on the powers they received in a vision. Likewise, they focused on showing personal bravery or getting a coup. Lakȟóta stories, like those of Iron Hawk and Black Elk, also demonstrate fear and horror seldom associated with Indian warriors.

In his vision on the Rosebud River, Sitting Bull had seen soldiers fall into the Lakḣóta camp with their heads down. This prophecy had now come true, except for one part. Following the instructions he received in the vision, Sitting Bull forbade the mutilation of the bodies of dead soldiers or the stealing of the soldiers' belongings. Despite this, the clothes and equipment of the fallen soldiers were taken, Custer's ears were pierced, and numerous soldiers were butchered or dismembered. The Lakḣóta had said they would defend their lands. Custer had had no ears, so they were given to him on the battlefield.[51]

All the soldiers with Custer were killed and Major Reno's troops were still under siege on a nearby hill. The Lakḣóta tried several times to dislodge them, but they failed partly because Captain Benteen had brought his detachment to help Reno. Neither of the officers dared to go help Custer. So, they remained in their positions. Fierce fighting claimed casualties on both sides. Eventually, the Indians got tired of the siege and Sitting Bull announced that the victory had already been big enough. The rest of the soldiers would be left where they were. The Lakḣóta stopped the fight for practical reasons as well; the men had to return to the women and children.

Once the battle ceased on the Little Big Horn River, the Lakḣóta and Cheyenne dismantled their camps and moved out of the soldiers' reach. After traveling for four nights, they stopped and set up their camp. They were still in the valley of the Little Big Horn River, but far from the soldiers. Only now did they celebrate their great victory. Celebration of a victorious war expedition had always been an essential part of Lakḣóta culture. The men returning from a successful trip were welcomed in the camp with elaborate ceremonies. This time an enormous number of men, and a few women, had taken part in the battle. The celebrations lasted through the night. Warriors took turns singing about their feats. The Lakḣóta referred to the songs as "kill talk" and this time the kill talks ridiculed Custer. Black Elk, Standing Bear and others recalled a few of them:[52]

> When you came attacking, why did not
> you have more men?
> Why didn't you bring more men so that
> you would be a little stronger
>
> Long Hair, guns I hadn't any.
> You brought me some.
> I thank you.
> You make me laugh!

Long Hair, where he lies nobody knows.
Crying they seek him.
He lies over here.

One of the most powerful kill talks was made by Standing Bear:
A charger he is coming.
I made him come.
When he came, I wiped him out.
He did not like my ways; that is why.[53]

"He did not like my ways," sang Standing Bear, illustrating how the Lakȟóta saw white encroachment on their lands and the attempts to eradicate Lakȟóta culture and ways. The late Wilmer "Stampede" Mesteth, an Oglála spiritual leader, recorded several Little Bighorn victory songs on his album *The Lakota Are Charging*, including these:

I love the ways of war.
I have to face many difficulties, for the love of war.
So said the great chief Crazy Horse.

I had no guns.
Long Knife,
I had no guns, no weapons, when you attacked me.
Thank you for bringing me many weapons and guns.

My friend, Custer,
what is it that you search for when you come charging?
What is it that you search for so you lie in such a way?

Fire on the horizon.
Those of you who stayed behind with the women,
did you not see the fire and smoke on the horizon?
It was I who have done this.
Victory at the Little Bighorn.[54]

Their victory was overshadowed by the fact that they, too, had suffered casualties. According to most reports, including Short Bull's, the Lakȟóta and Cheyenne lost about thirty to fifty men in the battle and at least as many were wounded. Exact figures are impossible to determine, but the most common estimates say hardly many more than thirty dead. Still, in Lakȟóta warfare, this was a considerable loss, and the victory celebration was accompanied by the grief of the relatives of the fallen.[55]

The Lakȟóta and Cheyenne barely had time to perform all the necessary mourning ceremonies. They needed to disperse because there were perhaps as many as 7,000 to 8,000 people in the camp. The Indians did not disperse because the soldiers forced them to do so. Nor did they because they supposedly did not realize they were stronger together. It was simply a matter of supplies. Feeding such a large crowd required a lot of meat, and the horses needed fresh grain. Some therefore headed west toward the Big Horn Mountains, some returned southeast toward the Black Hills, and some even returned to the agencies, where the reception was not warm.[56]

Custer's fate stunned the whites. It did not take long for the press to publish sensational accounts of the "massacre." With every publication the number of Indians taking part in the battle increased from a few hundred to as many as ten thousand. According to some reports the Lakȟóta and Cheyenne camp was believed to have had as many as 40,000 people. Yet, the total population of the Lakȟóta and Cheyenne combined was perhaps a little over 20,000.[57]

Some contemporary whites explained Custer's defeat by claiming that the Indians had developed some superior tactics—how else could it be explained that the military suffered such a total defeat? Others have blamed the defeat purely on Custer's arrogance, which led to a series of costly mistakes. It is true that Custer might have had a good reason to avoid attacking such a large Indian camp, but on the other hand, he may never have fully grasped how large the camp was. In fact, General Terry's instructions to Custer were that he had to prevent the Indians from fleeing. Thus, even the top leadership of the army had underestimated the power of the Indians. No one expected them to make significant resistance, only to make a controlled escape.

Whatever Custer's personal motives were, on that June day in 1876, the US military suffered its greatest defeat in its wars against the Plains Indians. According to General Sherman's report, the US military lost a total of twelve officers, 247 soldiers, and three Arikara scouts. While the Indians were, of course, considered the main culprits of the disaster, the search for others to blame soon began. Custer's fate shook both the US government and policymakers. At the same time, a myth started to emerge about how Sitting Bull and other Native American "generals" defeated the army by brilliant tactics and leadership skills. Some rumors claimed that Sitting Bull had graduated from West Point Military Academy. The myth of the Battle of Little Big Horn began to take on life of its own. Custer was transformed from a scapegoat into a hero and Sitting Bull from a brilliant leader to a coward who fled the scene. This latter image was partly promoted by the Indian Agent James McLaughlin, who in the 1880s took it upon himself to accuse and blame Sitting Bull for things real and unreal.[58]

The victory was sweet but also poisonous for the Lakȟóta and Cheyenne. They had certainly made the wašíču listen. But there was one person who was concerned about the outcome—Sitting Bull. He recalled his vision and its specific orders that were not heeded. Now he prophesied that the Lakȟóta would forever be dependent on the white man because they had not listened. His prophesy was to be proven right.

8

LAKȞÓL WIČHÓȞ'AŊ
DEFENDING LAKȞÓTA WAYS

War and Diplomacy

While thousands of Lakȟóta were fighting the wašíču in the Powder River and Little Big Horn country, thousands of others remained close to the agencies. By the fall of 1876, they were living a very different life from those outside the reservation. The reservation landscape had changed rapidly as the government pushed its "civilization" program. Everywhere new agency buildings were erected: sawmills, administrative buildings, storehouses, stables, farms, schoolhouses, and churches. The agencies became small towns, and the agents proudly hailed the developments in their reports. They were eager to inform their superiors that the Lakȟóta were progressing on the "white man's road." They wrote that the Indians built log houses, and the number of children attending schools grew rapidly.[1]

Despite these developments, most reservation Lakȟóta welcomed the "Wiping out of Custer," but they were concerned about the consequences. They did not need to wait long. The US government once again turned its attention to the reservation Lakȟóta. The previous summer, government representatives had abandoned their idea of buying the Black Hills because they could not collect sufficient Indian signatures. After the Little Big Horn battle, the issue was raised again, and this time the government was going to ignore Lakȟóta wishes and treaty rights.

The opportunity to acquire the Black Hills was made possible by an act of Congress in 1871 that ended treatymaking with native peoples. Tribes were no longer considered separate, independent governments, and were now under the guardianship of the federal government. Agreements replaced treaties. For the Lakȟóta, the form and text of the agreements changed little from treaties, but this technical change paved the way for future laws that enabled the government to exert its power on indigenous people and their lands.[2]

Thus, in the late summer of 1876 a new commission arrived at the Spotted Tail and Red Cloud Agencies. Just after the government reduced food rations for Lakȟóta living on the reservation, threatening to move the Lakȟóta to Indian Territory unless they gave up the coveted areas. The Battle of the Little Bighorn was used as an excuse because the Lakȟóta living on the reservation had supposedly supported the "hostiles," giving the government the right to put pressure on them. For added emphasis, government agents took hundreds of ponies from Red Cloud's people and sold them to whites at discounted prices. The Indians were also required to surrender all weapons. Similar actions occurred at other agencies. Losing the ponies was so devastating that many winter counts record 1876–77 as the year when their ponies were taken away.[3]

Finally, to the Oglálas' surprise, Gen. George Crook informed them that he took the title of chief away from Red Cloud and made Spotted Tail the chief of all Oglála and Sičháŋǧu. All these actions concerned and confused the Lakȟóta who met with the government commission. Red Cloud at first greeted them with open arms, saying their arrival would save them from starvation after the government annuities had not arrived as promised. The reservation Lakȟóta were destitute. The government's pressure was wearing down the resistance. It did not take long for the Lakȟóta under Spotted Tail and Red Cloud to sign a document that handed over the Black Hills to the United States.[4]

The 1871 decision allowed the United States to pretend to have acted lawfully, even though three-quarters of adult male Lakȟóta did not sign the new agreement. The previous year, the unified Lakȟóta front and this technicality had prevented the land seizure, but in the aftermath of the Little Big Horn, the US government did not allow a "technicality" to destroy its operations. The government's actions were both morally and legally questionable and would be at the heart of Lakȟóta attempts to regain the Black Hills in the twentieth century.[5]

The Lakȟóta yielded in the face of government pressure, and yet another cause for suspicion and division was planted in Lakȟóta society. At the same time, the

Lakȟóta and Cheyenne who had wiped out Custer moved in small camps in the Big Horn Mountains, Yellowstone, Tongue, and Powder River area. Victory over the US Army did not hinder them from thinking about traditional enemies. Crazy Horse led a war party against the Crow, bringing home "a lot of scalps," recalled Black Elk.[6] The US military, however, launched new operations in the area. Gen. Philip Sheridan chased the Lakȟóta all winter until they returned to their reservations. Under the pretext of responding to the events of the Little Big Horn, he got almost everything he asked the government for.

Alfred Terry, George Crook, and Nelson A. Miles were Sheridan's field generals. Unfortunately, Miles and Crook envied each other and a few times during the winter of 1876–77, this issue resulted in poor coordination and failed negotiations. General Miles complained that the Indians, who surrendered because of his actions, traveled to Crook's camp to surrender. Crook reaped the credit for work Miles had done. At the same time, the US military established new bases on Lakȟóta lands. Miles established his base at the confluence of the Yellowstone and Tongue Rivers, in present-day Montana, while Crook built his base on the upper reaches of the Powder River near the Big Horn Mountains in Wyoming.[7]

The Lakȟóta were well aware of the army's movements. Several skirmishes took place between the Lakȟóta, Cheyenne, and the army during the fall and winter of 1876–77. The first major confrontation took place on September 9–10, at Slim Buttes (Pahá Zizípela, Žaŋžáŋ Blaská), where the camp of American Horse (the elder) was surprised in the early morning. The Indians took refuge in a nearby ravine. In the fight, American Horse was mortally wounded, and he died refusing care from the US army. The rest of his people fled to other camps. Crazy Horse rallied a force of several hundred men who engaged Crook's main military forces. A running fight ensued that lasted for several days but resulted in few casualties.[8]

In October, Sitting Bull sent a message to the soldiers. He asked a mixed-blood friend John Bruguier to write it in English. Sitting Bull emphasized that the war was brought upon the Lakȟóta by the wašíču. His people were waging a defensive war to protect their lands and way of life. He announced that he had never wanted wars against the whites but only wanted to live in peace and hunt on his own lands. If the whites did not leave, he threatened he would fight them again. The letter was attached to a stick and left for the soldiers to find.[9]

In late October, Sitting Bull and General Miles met for talks. According to White Bull, Sitting Bull did not want to negotiate at all, but had agreed to do so under pressure from other leaders. He let the others speak and only expressed his unwillingness to negotiate. Both parties made demands, but neither was willing to compromise. Sitting Bull refused to talk to Miles directly. The Indians explained to Miles that Sitting Bull was their war chief—it was the task of other chiefs to speak and negotiate. This was a normal practice for the Lakȟóta, but it irritated Miles. His frustrations and anger were answered by the Indians, who likewise grew impatient, and the negotiations ended without results. After the talks, a small skirmish ensued in which both sides lost a few men. Because General Miles had been dressed in a thick bearskin coat, the Lakȟóta named him "Bear Coat."[10]

By November, Crazy Horse was camping along the Little Big Horn River when he learned that General Crook was onto them. The Lakȟóta evaded the soldiers, but the Cheyenne did not. On November 25, disaster struck. Crook, having failed to attack Crazy Horse, turned his attention toward the Cheyenne camping in the Big Horn Mountains. Col. Ranald S. McKenzie led 800 men in an attack on the Cheyenne camp, destroying it. The blow to the Indians was decisive. Cheyenne survivors sought refuge at Crazy Horse's camp more than 150 miles away. They were without tipis, food, or clothing. They were warmly received, but dozens of Cheyenne—men, women, and children—had died during the grueling winter escape. In December, Crazy Horse was ready to sue for peace. He sent a delegation to Miles's cantonment on the Tongue River. The delegation was met by Crow scouts who had suffered in a recent attack led by Crazy Horse. The angry Crow drew their weapons and killed the delegates. Crazy Horse, furious after learning the fate of his men who had gone to see Miles under a flag of truce, went after the Crow. They escaped, swimming over the nearly frozen Missouri. Assuming Miles's soldiers had helped the Crow, the Lakȟóta drove away and killed 250 head of their cattle.[11]

The winter was severe for the non-reservation Lakȟóta. In Crazy Horse's camp on the Tongue River, the Indians decided to continue fighting the wašíču. The Cheyenne performed a sacred arrows ceremony to gain strength and power for the struggling people. A medicine man stood in a circle of warriors who pointed their arrows up in the air. The medicine man then shot an arrow that circled the men and returned to him. This made an impression on the Lakȟóta, and Black Elk thought it might have been the same arrow that he had seen in his own vision. This was an arrow that he believed was going to give them power to meet General Miles in battle.[12]

Several skirmishes took place in freezing temperatures in January 1877.[13] Perhaps the most notable was fought on January 8 at Wolf Mountain along the

Tongue River. Lakȟóta and Cheyenne, led by Crazy Horse and Two Moons, took advantage of high ground positions on the hills overlooking the river valley and nearly surrounded the troops. Miles had two cannons with him and although the cannon balls did not explode, they frightened the Indians. Though not decisive, Wolf Mountain was significant because it demonstrated to the Lakȟóta that the US army was not going to give up, not even during the winter. Winter warfare was problematic for the Lakȟóta, as deep snow prevented them from fully employing their traditional tactics. Additionally, it was hard to both fight and feed the people.[14]

Although numerically and technically superior, the US military was unable to deliver a final blow. Both sides suffered only small losses in a series of skirmishes. However, wild rumors were perpetrated in the press about big battles. According to some, as many as 700 Indians and 300 army soldiers had been killed in a single battle. According to others, Sitting Bull had been killed or at least wounded.[15]

General Sheridan stated that the only way to get the Indians to surrender was to harass them in the winter and prevent them from getting food. A campaign run during the summer would not have produced the same results. Still, the army prepared to continue the campaign in the summer of 1877 with more than 3,000 men.[16]

Lakȟóta unity began to falter when they found out that food rations were regularly distributed to the people at the agencies. Some wanted to surrender and return to the vicinity of the agencies. As a result, divisions in Crazy Horse's camp grew deeper. Crazy Horse had to use akíčhita to prevent anyone from leaving the camp. Despite this, small groups left to surrender at the agencies. There were soldiers everywhere and as one Mnikȟówožu said after returning to Cheyenne River, he was tired of being always on the lookout for danger. He wanted his family to be able to sleep safely without fear of an attack.[17] Sitting Bull also found the situation difficult and after counsel from other leaders, decided to escape to Canada. He wanted to monitor the situation from the safety of Grandmother's land. If those who surrendered were treated well, he might return to the United States, but if disarmed and relocated, he would stay north of the border. Crazy Horse, despite Sitting Bull's attempts to persuade him to join, did not want to leave. He preferred to stay in the Powder River and Black Hills area. Sitting Bull eventually took about 350 people with him and moved to Canada. He remained there until 1881.[18]

While conducting a military operation against Crazy Horse, army officers also used diplomacy to persuade the Lakȟóta to surrender. Red Cloud and Spotted

Tail, among others, were asked to act as intermediaries. Their chances of success were slim because internal conflicts between the Lakȟóta had grown deep. Several delegations from both Red Cloud and Spotted Tail Agencies traveled to Powder River country through winter blizzards, in search of Crazy Horse and other free Lakȟóta. Throughout the winter Sitting Bull and Crazy Horse sent representatives to explore the possibilities of peace. Sitting Bull signaled that he did not want war, but the whites left him no choice. His peace messages were also published in the press.[19] Yet the task of the peace negotiators was daunting. Tensions were high, and on a few occasions the Lakȟóta ended up nearly fighting each other.

The most successful peace effort was made by George Sword, who, along with three companions and at the request of General Crook, had agreed to take a message of peace to Crazy Horse's camp. Since the early 1870s, Sword had become convinced that the whites could not be defeated and decided to live in peace with them. He had even joined the Army as a scout.[20]

Sword and his companions journeyed several days, enduring a snowstorm before finally locating Crazy Horse's camp. Sword was unsure what his reception would be in the camp. He was kindly received, albeit with guns in hand. They soon held a meeting. Sword stood up and first referred to kinship ties: "My friends, you are a people; I consider myself to be from here, so on account of all of you I have gladly come over here. And this day, gladly I join in the big council you have made. And I am filled with happiness." General Crook and the President had sent him, he said, and their hope was that here would be no more fighting. "Throughout the land there will be no fighting, and no matter who, all will be at peace. . . . If my friends return, nothing bad will happen," he promised on Crook's behalf.

Iron Hawk replied:

> Well, Enemy Bait [Sword], sit and listen carefully. This country is mine and in this way the Great Spirit raised me, so this is how I live. But my friend, the white men came from where the sun rises, stealing my land, and now my country is small, so I do not allow him in; yet he comes in and when he sees me, he shoots me, and then I too shoot him and I kill him, and as I stand looking at them, my heart is bad.

Still, Iron Hawk was ready for peace. Moving the camp in the dead of winter would take time, but they would come and make peace, he said. "So, someone acting as Grandfather wishes peace, you say. Well, it shall be a big peace!

As for me, whoever brings good to me will not outdo me," concluded Iron Hawk.[21]

This exchange illustrates Lakȟóta social structure. The meeting followed Lakȟóta ceremonial protocol and symbolism. First, Sword offered the pipe and handed it to the others to demonstrate that he was a relative who wanted good for his kin. In offering the pipe, Sword announced that he had not come as a spy or messenger of the enemy, but as a worried relative who wanted to help. This thought was at the heart of the Lakȟóta worldview; if they had refused the offered pipe, they would have denied kinship obligations. Its consequences, in turn, would have been much greater than just the relationship between Sword and the people present. It would have caused a deep wound among the Lakȟóta, especially within the Oglála. However, the mere offering of the pipe and its approval did not guarantee the outcome of the negotiations. Sword first had to present and justify his case, after which Iron Hawk, as a representative of Crazy Horse, gave a long speech presenting the common position of the entire camp. He, in turn, was carefully observed by an akíčhita, whose task was to make sure that he only presented ideas agreed upon by the entire camp. Sword had to wait a few days for the actual answer.[22]

Eventually, Crazy Horse's representative announced that in the spring they would return to Red Cloud Agency and surrender. They were alone, since most of the Húŋkpapȟa, Mnikȟówožu, and other oyáte had either returned to various Indian agencies already or fled to Canada during the winter. As a condition of their return, they had two wishes: first they wanted to meet Red Cloud, and, more importantly, Crazy Horse wanted a reservation of his own in the Powder River area north of the Black Hills. If this was granted, he would settle in peace with his followers in his own land in the heart of Lakȟóta tȟamákȟočhe.[23]

George Sword appealed to kinship and unity in Lakȟóta society, which despite deep divisions among the people, created powerful obligations that tipped the scale toward final surrender. The credit for Crazy Horse's surrender has often been given exclusively to the US military, usually to Crook or Miles, but the importance of George Sword and other native negotiators has generally been overlooked. In the end, George Sword may have been the person who prevented further bloodshed.

The Surrender

During the late winter and spring of 1877, Gen. George Crook sent several delegations, including Spotted Tail and Red Cloud, to Crazy Horse's camp to make sure that the plans for surrender had not changed. Throughout the spring, small Lakȟóta groups drifted to the agencies. They assured Crook that Crazy Horse was coming. Crook led Crazy Horse to believe that he would have his own reservation in the Powder River area. This was one of his conditions for surrender and Crook had promised to arrange it. The truth was that Crook had no authority in this matter. If Crazy Horse and his people heard that the promises were false, Crook feared it would turn the surrender process on its head. By April, however, it was confirmed that Crazy Horse was indeed on his way and would bring up to 1,500 people with him. Despite Crook's fears, on May 7, 1877, Crazy Horse showed up close to Red Cloud Agency.[24]

Crazy Horse arrived leading a large crowd of warriors, followed by women and children and a large herd of horses. It seemed to be a victory procession rather than a group of refugees arriving to surrender. Crazy Horse greeted Crook's representative, Lt. William B. Clark, and shook hands with him. Allegedly, he had never shaken the hand of a wašíču. Next, he asked the lieutenant to sit down with him and smoke. He Dog, a close friend of Crazy Horse, presented Clark with Crazy Horse's war bonnet, war shirt, and his war horse. Then another war shirt and headdress were given to Red Cloud. Crazy Horse had specifically wanted Red Cloud to be there to receive him. After this, the entire two-mile-long Lakȟóta column continued its journey to Red Cloud Agency, where they arrived singing.[25]

On May 25, the formal surrender took place. At Camp Robinson the Lakȟóta divided into eighteen rows, which advanced in good order past General Crook during a parade review. They then lined up, and the chiefs rode up to Crook, dismounted, and shook hands with the general. Crazy Horse now saw Crook for the first time, shook his hand, and told him that the war was finally over. The *New York Times* reported that Crazy Horse and other chiefs knelt before General Crook, but William Garnett who was present and acting as interpreter, denies this, saying that the men just shook hands and stared firmly at each other until General Crook greeted Crazy Horse, saying, "Háu, kȟolá" (Greetings, friend). The *New York Times* reported that General Crook then led the chiefs inside the fort to the office building. When everyone was inside, silence descended on the room as the Indians settled in place to prepare their speeches. Crazy Horse, not known for speech-making, sat on the floor in front of General Crook and opened the meeting. According to the *New York Times* he spoke in a very low voice:

> You sent tobacco to my camp and invited me here. Once the tobacco had
> arrived at my camp, I began my journey here and continued on the straight

road until I arrived. Ever since then, my face has been turned toward the fortress, and my heart has rejoiced in the journey in that direction. I have chosen a place where I want to live from now on. I hit the ground with a sign in that place. There is a lot of game in that country. All these relatives of mine who are here accept my choice and I would like them to come there with me and we could live together.[26]

After Crazy Horse, the other chiefs spoke. All expressed their desire to live in peace with the whites.

With Crazy Horse surrendering and Sitting Bull a refugee in Canada, the war was over. All that remained now was the question of how Crazy Horse's people would adapt to reservation life, and whether General Crook would really get them a reservation in the Powder River country. Under the new agreement that went into effect in 1877, the US government excluded a huge tract of land from the Great Sioux Reservation, so the Black Hills and the lands north and west of the hills, the so-called Powder River country, no longer belonged to the Lakȟóta at all. Crook's promise of a reservation there was unfounded. The US government did not intend to allow Crazy Horse to take his people back north where it would have been very difficult for the government to control them.

The summer of 1877 was difficult at both Red Cloud and Spotted Tail Agencies. This was partly due to internal power struggles among the Lakȟóta. The chiefs who had been at the agencies for a long time were jealous and did not necessarily appreciate all the respect and attention Crazy Horse and the newcomers received from both whites and Indians. Because they had wiped out Custer the previous summer and fought bravely against the wašíču, the newcomers had influence and prestige, and warriors ready to resume the fight if necessary. According to some reports, Red Cloud was unhappy about the newcomers. This is understandable, since Red Cloud had for several years been the leader of the reservation (or agency) Lakȟóta, especially the Oglála. He had become a link between the whites and the Indians. Red Cloud was known for opposing all white reform efforts but was still adept at advancing his own interests, as well as those of his people. He could keep the white agents and military officers guessing at his true intentions and was constantly at odds with them.[27]

Although General Crook had announced the previous summer that Red Cloud was no longer the chief of the Oglála, it had little practical significance. Red Cloud, along with other so-called non-progressive chiefs, continued to lead and they refused to share power with the agent. Elsewhere, at his own agency,

Spotted Tail was more diplomatic, but the situation at his agency was confusing as well. When Crazy Horse's large and restless group of people was thrown into this already chaotic mix, problems were unavoidable. Two prevailing views address the problems of the summer of 1877. According to the first, Red Cloud was so jealous of Crazy Horse's popularity that he began spreading rumors that Crazy Horse was going to return to the Powder River area and continue the war. This reinforced whites' suspicions of Crazy Horse. In response to these rumors General Crook revoked Crazy Horse's permit to go bison hunting (in August), as a hunting trip might have been too tempting an opportunity to escape from the reservation. The cancellation of the hunting trip was not only an economic blow to the Lakȟóta, but also an indication that Crook could not be trusted.

According to another view, Crazy Horse was completely incapable of living on the reservation and thought only of escape and resuming the war. Both views are problematic. Undoubtedly, Red Cloud was uncertain of his own position after Crazy Horse's arrival, and he had not previously shied away from any means of propping up his own position. Yet there is no actual proof of a conspiracy led by Red Cloud. There is ample evidence of division and power struggle among the Lakȟóta, but that was not new in Lakȟóta society. The problem with the second view is that when he surrendered, Crazy Horse promised both Lieutenant Clark and General Crook that he intended to live in peace for the rest of his life. He gave up both his war bonnet and war shirt. The matter was further sealed by smoking the sacred pipe, making it obvious that Crazy Horse was genuinely going to settle on the reservation.

Admittedly, in return he wanted his own agency in the north. During the summer of 1877 it became clear that obtaining it was unlikely. The Cheyenne, who had also been promised their own reservation in the north, were transported to Indian Territory in late May, which exacerbated Lakȟóta suspicions and fears. During the summer, Crazy Horse was asked to travel to Washington to meet with the president. When he refused, the whites believed that he might not cooperate and might go back on the warpath. Likewise, he refused to sign any papers. For Crazy Horse, however, the point was perfectly clear: He did not want to travel to Washington because he feared what might happen in his absence. Although he refused to go, he announced that his closest men could serve as his representatives in Washington. He Dog later claimed that Crazy Horse was initially willing to leave for Washington, but his friends thought it might have been a trap. Eventually, Crazy Horse came to believe they were right and refused to go. He did not want to sign the papers because he feared he would inadvertently sign a consent to the transfer to Indian Territory or hand over more land. Thus, mutual distrust lasted throughout the summer of 1877. Still, it seems that Crazy Horse really believed that he was going to get an agency in the north and sought to cooperate with the officials.[28]

Suspicions deepened as summer 1877 wore on. The internal conflicts among the Lakȟóta and the disputes between Crazy Horse and the whites became more tense. Over the summer, Crazy Horse and Lt. William Clark had achieved a kind of mutual respect that could even be described as friendship. Clark's superiors, Crook, Sheridan, and Sherman, planned to imprison Crazy Horse. A suitable excuse was found in early September. By this time, Clark had also changed his attitude toward Crazy Horse. When Crazy Horse refused to travel to Washington, Clark informed Crook that only the use of force would get the stubborn chief to listen. Another blow to Clark came when Crazy Horse refused to lead Lakȟóta warriors as part of the US military in the fight against the Nez Percé Indians, who had fled their reservation and inflicted heavy losses on the soldiers who followed them.[29]

Clark had imagined Crazy Horse happily joining the army and going to war against enemy Indians. This did not happen. That Crazy Horse refused to embark on a new expedition, even at the request of the US military, shows that, as promised, he no longer wanted a war against the whites or the Indians. For reasons unknown, Clark informed his superiors of Crazy Horse's intentions to go on a war party of his own. According to one explanation, interpreter Frank Grouard intentionally mistranslated Crazy Horse's words. This has also been interpreted as a sign of an extensive conspiracy by Red Cloud and others against Crazy Horse. However, interpreter, William Garnett, assures that no such translation error occurred. Maybe Clark was simply disappointed at not getting his way. In any case, Clark's report provided a suitable excuse for arresting Crazy Horse.

At the same time, another rumor circulated: Crazy Horse was going to kill General Crook the next time they met. The rumor spread to the newspapers and was used as further excuse to imprison Crazy Horse. Angry about all the rumors surrounding him, Crazy Horse fled to Spotted Tail Agency, where Lt. Jesse Lee assured him that no one was going to harm him. He had to return to Red Cloud Agency to prove his innocence. For some reason, Crazy Horse trusted the young officer, who promised to return with him to Red Cloud Agency.

In early September, Crazy Horse returned to Fort Robinson, where he was to talk with government representatives and officers. Many Indians and soldiers gathered at the scene. When Crazy Horse arrived, a "security force" made up of soldiers and Indians stood around him. Among them were some of Crazy Horse's best friends and most trusted warriors, including Little Big Man. The procession passed through Fort Robinson, but soon it dawned on Crazy Horse that he was being escorted toward a small hut with bars on the windows. He was to be imprisoned. At the door of the house, Crazy Horse tore himself from the grip of his escorts, pulled out his knife, and slashed Little Big Man's arm. Little Big Man grabbed Crazy Horse's arm, and at the same time, one of the soldiers jabbed a bayonet into Crazy Horse's back. He sank to the ground mortally wounded. The wounded chief was taken to the army premises, where doctor Valentine T. McGillycuddy, who would later serve as an Indian agent at Pine Ridge, tried to treat him. McGillycuddy said afterwards that the bayonet had almost passed through Crazy Horse's body right next to the kidneys. No treatment was possible. Crazy Horse died during the night in the presence of his father and a few friends. According to some records, he addressed his father, saying, "It is no use to depend on me. I am going to die." [30]

Several years earlier, the medicine man and friend of Crazy Horse named Chips had prophesied Crazy Horse's death: not from a bullet, but from a knife and only when his hands were shackled by a friend. It is hard to say how accurate the story of Chip's prophecy really was, but it fed the legend that quickly grew around Crazy Horse. Another story that contributed to the myth was that no one knew where Crazy Horse was buried. According to Black Elk, his parents took his body to the Black Hills, while others claim the grave is along Wounded Knee Creek (Čhaŋkpé Ópi) or in the Badlands. According to some rumors, white collectors managed to obtain his skull, which has since been in some secret collection. In any case, in September 1877, one of the most famous Indians of all time was killed. An era in Lakȟóta history had come to a tragic end.[31]

Much has been written about the death of Crazy Horse and the events leading up to it. Whether there was a broad conspiracy will probably never be answered. Immediately after the incident, both military and government representatives claimed that the Lakȟóta were relieved Crazy Horse was dead. According to them, the Indians understood that his presence would only lead to trouble. It is clear from Lakȟóta descriptions, however, that it was a traumatic experience for them because they had lost one of their greatest leaders—a warrior who epitomized Lakȟóta resistance and was a staunch protector of their way of life. Many winter counts named 1877 as the year when Tȟašúŋke Witkó Ktépi, "Crazy Horse was Killed."[32]

While Crazy Horse's death may have benefited Red Cloud and a few others aspiring to become chiefs, it is obvious that his death aided whites more than Indians. In the same way, rumors that Crazy Horse was a victim of Lakȟóta intertribal rivalries and conspiracy benefited those whites who were, in fact, responsible for the decisions that led to his death. They no longer had to consider the possible military threat posed by Crazy Horse, and they no longer had to resolve the question of the location of his future reservation. It was better for them that Crazy Horse was dead so they could continue to work with more pliable chiefs who had lived on the reservations for a long time.

With Crazy Horse's death, the era of Lakȟóta rule of the Northern Plains was over. Only Sitting Bull and his followers were living a "free" life, albeit in exile in Canada. Sitting Bull got along well with the Canadian authorities, who allowed him to live in the area if his people did not cause trouble. They conducted raids on traditional enemies, the Crow and Cree (Maštíŋča Oyáte), and during a buffalo hunt south of the border they skirmished with General Miles's scouts, but they did not harass any white settlements on either side of the border. This is an indication that if the whites did not disturb him, Sitting Bull did not want to fight them, as he had stated on several occasions. To find allies in Canada, Sitting Bull visited both the Assiniboine and the Blackfeet. He assured them that he "came to this country to live in peace; I am not going to make any trouble." He proposed to the Blackfeet that they live in peace forever. "We will be friends to the end of our lives—and my children will be yours and yours will be mine." He even named his son Crow Foot (Sí Kȟaŋǧí) to honor the Blackfeet chief of the same name.[33] Sitting Bull's people were, in fact, trying to extend Lakȟóta homelands, Lakȟóta tȟamákȟočhe, farther west and north. Sitting Bull and his people had come there to stay, and they wanted to make this their new home. Almost 150 years of Lakȟóta transition to the west was now complete. Lakȟóta expansion ended in exile in Canada.[34]

However, the situation in Canada became more difficult year after year as the number of bison decreased and the Canadian authorities grew increasingly bothered by the Lakȟóta presence there. Also, food rations were not available on the Canadian side as they were in the United States, where agreements obliged the government to distribute annuities to reservation Indians. Sitting Bull, however, refused to return to the United States despite assurances from the government. He was certain that the government could not be trusted. Crazy Horse's fate only reinforced his suspicions.[35]

Still, famine and pressure from his closest men led him to return to the United States in 1881, where he surrendered on July 19 at Fort Buford, North Dakota. Col. George S. Young, who was present at the surrender, reported that Sitting Bull said he would never have surrendered if the buffalo had not disappeared. He stated once again that he had never wanted to fight the whites, but that the whites had forced him into war. At Fort Buford Sitting Bull gave his weapon to his son, Crow Foot, who in turn handed it over to Maj. David H. Brotherton. Sitting Bull said that he would give his gun to the major through his young son so that Crow Foot could learn that he was now a friend of the white man. He added that he wished his son to learn white manners and get the same education as white children. Sitting Bull expressed his wish, or rather demanded, that he should continue his traditional way of life by hunting and trading on both sides of the US–Canadian border. Of course, the US government could not agree to that. After Sitting Bull surrendered, he was taken to Fort Randall, where he spent two years as a prisoner of war. While in prison, he made several drawings of his war deeds, made a pictographic autobiography, and acquainted himself with the white man's world. In 1883 Sitting Bull and almost 200 others were taken north via steamboat up the Missouri River, landing at Fort Yates (in present-day North Dakota). Sitting Bull returned to his old homeland. It had changed dramatically. Now the last free Lakȟóta had to find a way to adapt to these changes. It was not going to be easy.[36]

Toward Life on the Reservation

Forcing the Lakȟóta onto the reservation was the first step in the government's plan to control them. However, the reservation period began troubled. As early as 1877, a delegation of Oglála and Sičháŋǧu were invited to Washington to meet with President Rutherford B. Hayes. Red Cloud headed the Oglála delegation and Spotted Tail led the Sičháŋǧu. In the first meeting, the Lakȟóta expressed their dissatisfaction with the previous agreement when they, perhaps unknowingly, had agreed to move to the Missouri, where the government's annuities would henceforth be distributed.[37]

Both Red Cloud and Spotted Tail assured officials in Washington that they had never heard of such a decision. They refused to move to the Missouri. One meeting after another ended in a negative mood, but in the end the Lakȟóta were forced to yield. The government had already taken the necessary steps to transport the goods and annuities to new agencies close to the Missouri River. If the Lakȟóta remained at their current agencies, they would starve to death. The president promised the Oglála and Sičháŋǧu that if they moved to the Missouri for one winter, the following spring they would be able to choose new agencies for themselves on the Great Sioux Reservation.

Reluctantly, the Oglála and Sičháŋǧu began the long trek toward the Missouri. The relocation of several thousand people was a massive task, and many strongly opposed the relocation. Some even decided to go back to the Powder River country. With the help of Indian agents and under the direction of their chiefs, the Lakȟóta journeyed closer to the Missouri River. They were in no hurry and since so many resisted the move, they decided not to travel exactly where the government wanted. Instead, they stayed along the White Earth River, a few days' travel from the planned agency. By this maneuver, they forced the government to transport their supplies the full distance to where they were.

The winter was harsh for the Lakȟóta. Both disease and hunger were their constant problems. By early spring, the Oglála and Sičháŋǧu immediately wanted to move to agencies of their choice. Commissioner of Indian Affairs Ezra A. Hayt led a delegation in July 1878 to discuss the location of the agencies. Spotted Tail gave a speech in which he convinced the commissioner that they could not live close to the Missouri where they suffered from alkaline water and scarcity of wood. Even young people were dying there. Red Cloud gave a similar statement. The Lakȟóta had adopted a friendly stance toward the government officials but were firm in their arguments and demands. The commissioner had to agree with them. The government procrastinated through the summer, and it was not until the fall that the Oglála and Sičháŋǧu were able to settle in locations of their choosing. The Oglála settled along the tributaries of the White River in an area that was eventually named Pine Ridge Agency. The Sičháŋǧu settled east of the Oglála along the Rosebud River.[38]

Thus, the "question of home" had, in a way, ended in victory for the Oglála and Sičháŋǧu, for they were able to remain in the areas of their choice. The government, in turn, renamed the agencies removing the names "Red Cloud" and "Spotted Tail." This was part of a government policy aimed at breaking the influence of the chiefs. Red Cloud and Spotted Tail could no longer call the agencies their own. The Mnikȟówožu, Itázipčo, and Oóhenuŋpa living farther north were settled in the Cheyenne River Agency area. Húŋkpapȟa and Sihásapa settled in the vicinity of Standing Rock Indian Agency, which was also the home of some Iháŋktȟuŋwaŋ and Iháŋktȟuŋwaŋna Dakȟóta.

Reservations in the 1880s became the scene of power struggles between Lakȟóta chiefs and the Indian agents as well as among the Lakȟóta chiefs themselves.

One of the bitterest disputes was between Red Cloud and Agent Valentine T. McGillycuddy at Pine Ridge. This situation lasted seven years and ended in a victory for Red Cloud when McGillycuddy was transferred to another agency. During those seven years, the two men clashed almost daily. Neither wanted to escalate the situation so that military intervention would have been necessary. Indeed, McGillycuddy later stated that he understood from the first moment that he and Red Cloud would be competitors. Yet there was always mutual respect between them. Both understood the situation. Later, Red Cloud praised his former antagonist, saying he was a good agent because he had never called in the military for help. This is an interesting comment, as Red Cloud repeatedly accused McGillycuddy of theft, fraud, and corruption. The Friends of the Indian passed on his accusations to the press and so all the way to the president. Red Cloud complained directly to the president when he visited Washington. So, the relationship between Red Cloud and McGillycuddy was constantly inflamed, but perhaps memories grew sweeter over time for both men.[39]

Another rivalry plagued Standing Rock. Sitting Bull and Agent James McLaughlin disliked each other from their very first meeting in 1881, when Sitting Bull was taken to Fort Randall as a prisoner of war. At the time, McLaughlin described him as a sturdy man who had "a bad face and shifty eyes." According to McLaughlin, Sitting Bull was "a coward and a liar, a man of no skill, and [with] no nobility in nature." He added years later that Sitting Bull had all the faults and wickedness of the Indians, and no character traits that make it easier to forgive the sins committed by some Indians. After Sitting Bull returned to Standing Rock he settled along the Grand River. The conflicts between him and McLaughlin escalated almost immediately. McLaughlin sowed discord among the Lakȟóta, constantly emphasizing the status of "progressive" chiefs, such as John Grass, while downplaying Sitting Bull. Partly due to McLaughlin's pressure, Sitting Bull agreed to embark upon a tour with Buffalo Bill, the stage name of showman William F. Cody.[40]

Buffalo Bill's Wild West show was the first of its kind. As its main attraction, Sitting Bull toured the United States and Europe. Sitting Bull's absence from Standing Rock, however, did not diminish McLaughlin's hostility toward him. Problems resurfaced as soon as Sitting Bull returned home.[41] While it is safe to say that McLaughlin hated Sitting Bull, it is uncertain whether Sitting Bull felt the same way. According to Lakȟóta testimony, he disliked the agent and saw him as an adversary. Sitting Bull tried to accommodate to life on the reservation. He attended the naming ceremony of the reservation with the agent and toward the end of the 1880s tried to do as the agent requested. But he could not yield to McLaughlin's demands to give up his lands and way of life.[42] However, their rivalry was only one part of the confusing situation that the government's Indian policy created among the Lakȟóta.

Maintaining order on the reservation became another controversial issue. As part of the "civilization policy" the government established the Indian police and the Indian court system.[43] At first, the Lakȟóta believed the police undermined traditional warrior societies. Gradually, their attitude toward the police system changed, as they realized that if they did not maintain order themselves, the military would. In this way, the police system took over the tasks of public order previously held by the akíčhita. Over time, the Indian police became paramilitary units loyal to the agents, which caused a great deal of controversy among the Lakȟóta.

The police were ambivalent intermediaries between the agent and members of their own people. They tried to settle issues ranging from minor theft to violent brawls. Sometimes, complained Captain Yellow Breast (Čhešká Zí) at Cheyenne River, they had to resolve the problems of relatives who might even be put in prison. Standing Soldier (Akíčhita Nážiŋ), a police lieutenant at Pine Ridge, noted that the police risked their lives daily while their relatives despised them as defenders of the white man's customs. For all this, they only received $8 a month.[44] Despite the problems, many Lakȟóta men enlisted in the police. In the late 1880s, the strength of the police force at each agency was twenty to fifty men. At Cheyenne River Agency in 1885, there were twenty-two men: one captain led and was assisted by one lieutenant, four sergeants, and sixteen policemen.[45]

An Indian commissioner's report first mentioned the excellent work of the Lakȟóta police as early as 1879, when Capt. George Sword caught a group of Cheyenne who had stolen horses. Sword was among the first to enlist in the police force at Pine Ridge and served until the 1890s. In this first major "police operation," Sword led his men after some Cheyenne horse thieves and surrounded them. After a few rounds of firing, one of the thieves was killed and the others surrendered. In June 1879, during a meeting with the agent and army officers at Pine Ridge, white thieves stealing Indian horses became a major issue. Red Cloud and other chiefs demanded justice. If the agent would not do it, they would send their own men to capture the thieves. That was initially agreed to but then No Flesh (Čhoníčha Waníče) pointed out that if they captured the thieves, punishment would be according to Lakȟóta traditions. "Then the Great Father will feel bad, for I'll kill them," said No Flesh. One of the officers present replied that if so, they should make sure they kill the right men. Becoming cautious, No Flesh decided to drop the whole thing, telling the whites to deal with the issue. He was probably right: Lakȟóta killing white men, even horse thieves, might have ended badly.[46]

The Lakȟóta Indian police force performed well. Almost every agent's report in the 1880s mentioned the excellent service by the police. Agents repeatedly stated that the police were invaluable, though occasionally, there were also problems. At Cheyenne River in 1891 Swift Bird (Ziŋtkála Lúzahaŋ) wrote a letter complaining that the people there were disappointed with the poor performance of a local police lieutenant. They requested a replacement from one of their own people from Moreau River, who knew the people and the area.[47]

The most serious situation between the police and other Lakȟóta came in 1889–1890, when the police received orders to act against their own people in the turmoil that arose around the Ghost Dance religion. As the next chapter details, Sitting Bull was killed by the Indian police. Yet at least some continued to trust the police. In late 1890, people living at Moreau River in fact requested more policemen.[48]

The Indian police system demonstrated that the Lakȟóta were prepared to adapt to a variety of roles if necessary. Some army officers believed that the Lakȟóta should be organized into a separate cavalry unit within the US Army. Although many Lakȟóta served as army scouts in the last conflicts of the late 1880s, no actual cavalry unit was ever established specifically for them.[49]

In addition to the police system, a Court of Indian Offenses was established. The role of these Indian courts was not only to handle crimes committed by Indians on the reservations, but to also try cases of "immoral behavior," such as taking multiple wives, using the services of a wičháša wakȟáŋ, or participating in traditional ceremonies. Judges were selected from among the so-called progressive Indians, but for quite some time the real responsibility for making decisions fell to the Indian agents. In 1883, James G. Wright, the Rosebud agent, complained that the court was not yet functional and that judges could not be elected. The situation was similar at other agencies. This was due in part to lack of funding, but also to the fact that many Lakȟóta were reluctant to serve as judges.[50]

The lack of funding fostered attempts to also make Indian police officers act as judges, albeit with poor success. An Indian policeman, Standing Soldier, for example, said it did not make sense to require police officers to act as judges. In his view, the same person should not be held responsible for both arresting and sentencing. The police were in a difficult position anyway. Instead of the official courts, the Lakȟóta, with the help of the agents, elected a council, a kind of committee to which the leaders of the various oyáte were elected. This semi-formal council took on the task of passing judgments. However, this was only a temporary arrangement to be gradually replaced by more formal courts. The creation of a police and judicial system also required efforts in terms of education, as the selection of illiterate judges did not work. Gradually, during the 1880s, the Lakȟóta courts began to function in a moderately satisfactory manner.[51]

Yet another dimension of the government's attempt to break up Lakȟóta social fabric was trying to diminish the influence of traditional chiefs. This turned out to be difficult to implement. In the late 1880s, Standing Rock Indian Agent James McLaughlin stated that the only way to run affairs smoothly was to turn to the chiefs. The government's goal was to make Lakȟóta think as individuals, like whites did, but they had always followed the example of their leaders. They continued to do so on the reservation. Because chiefs visited Washington and had had more interactions with whites than did "ordinary" people, their advice and experience were often invaluable.

Factional rivalry led to a tragic incident in 1881, when Crow Dog (Kȟaŋǧí Šúŋka) killed his rival Spotted Tail, reportedly over a woman. Factionalism between Spotted Tail and Crow Dog had been intensifying for some time. One day, Crow Dog took matters into his own hands. As Spotted Tail returned home from talks at the agency, Crow Dog surprised him and shot him. Crow Dog fled the scene but was quickly arrested. He was initially sentenced to death in Dakota Territory court, but after an appeal, the US Supreme Court released him, stating that whites had no right to convict Indians of crimes committed on the reservation against other Indians. Following what became known as the Ex Parte Crow Dog decision, in 1885 the US Congress enacted the Major Crimes Act, which allowed Indians to be convicted of serious crimes such as murder.[52]

After Spotted Tail's death, Red Cloud became the key leader among the Southern Lakȟóta, but competition for other leadership positions soon ramped up. The number of men calling themselves chief proliferated during the 1880s. Agents were partially responsible by insisting on calling the head of each family a chief, even though this was not customary in Lakȟóta society. Even among these new ascendants, traditional chiefs held their ground. In this sense the government's desire to downplay the role of chiefs did not materialize. The increase in the number of chiefs and oyáte did not necessarily mean the disappearance of traditional values but was an indication of the ability of Lakȟóta society to change and adapt.

Coping and Adapting

As circumstances changed, the structure of Lakȟóta society changed, just as it had in the past. On the reservations, people settled in various districts. The Lakȟóta moved to areas assigned to them, mainly along creeks and rivers. The traditional thiyóšpaye and tribal system gradually changed so that certain thiyóšpaye lived in certain districts. In these communities, kinship was just as important as it had been in the past. Society was—and still is today—based on these family relationships. They are the unifying force of the community. On Pine Ridge, for example, Little Wound's thiyóšpaye settled along Medicine Root Creek and Red Cloud's occupied the White Clay Creek (Makȟásaŋ Wakpá) area. After his return from Canada, Sitting Bull settled along Grand River on Standing Rock, while Gall made his home in the Wakpála district. On the other reservations, Lakȟóta settlement followed similar patterns. In addition, there was a lot of visiting between settlements, especially during the summer.[53]

Leadership roles also changed. It was no longer possible to rise to prominence through warfare. Yet, generosity had always been one of the central virtues of Lakȟóta chiefs. When the government began to distribute annuities, they initially gave them to the chiefs who then distributed them to their people. Later the goods were given to heads of families, who, of course, were acknowledged according to the US system. The heads of families distributed the supplies to their immediate family as well as other relatives, as good and generous leaders were supposed to do. Everyone who was now in charge of distributing goods was in effect a wičháša itȟáŋčhaŋ (leader). This was yet another indication of the Lakȟóta people adapting and reinventing themselves. Whites did not understand this. Agents were often frustrated when food assigned to one family disappeared into the mouths of dozens of others. They complained that the Lakȟóta were always hungry no matter how much food they were given. This is because traditionally in Lakȟóta communities, food was distributed among everyone, for example, in the form of a big feast. These feasts often occurred on issue days.[54]

Similarly, when someone earned money the salary was often redistributed. Jesuit priest Eugene Buechel complained that the Oglála Black Elk "will always be a beggar, no matter how much money one gives him. . . . I gave him $10 for the extra work done. The next day, he asked for more money, as he had passed it on to guests from Standing Rock. He never has anything and is always asking for something. Poor fellow!"[55] Buechel did not understand that by redistributing money, Black Elk was acting as a leader who put the interests of his people first.

Lakȟóta and whites clearly had different visions of the purpose of the annuities. Whites saw it as aiding the Lakȟóta until they were independent and self-sufficient farmers. Many Lakȟóta, in contrast, felt that the government was indebted to them for the lands they had surrendered and that they were entitled to indefinite payments from the US government. They saw no reason to start cultivating the land. Those who tried faced tremendous obstacles. Lakȟóta lands were not suitable for agriculture—the climate was too harsh and the soil too dry. Almost every summer, droughts, storms, and locusts and other pests destroyed the crops the Lakȟóta did manage to cultivate. As late as 1894, Harry Truly Necklace[56] and Frank High Eagle (Waŋblí Waŋkátuya), living along the Moreau River (Hiŋháŋ Wakpá), complained that the Indians there were frustrated at being expected to learn to do something that was nearly impossible. Their crops simply did not grow.[57] Year after year, the crops failed and the Lakȟóta went hungry and grew increasingly disenchanted.

Indian agents' reports echoed the same frustrations as those from agents of previous decades. Although some progress seemed to take place, there was no way to make the Lakȟóta truly self-sufficient through farming. Their reports also reveal conflicting assessments of the progress of the Lakȟóta "on the white man's road." In 1886, Charles E. McChesney, the agent at Cheyenne River, wrote: "Their crops have been badly damaged. . . . This is very discouraging." He still hoped that the next year they would be able to cultivate a much larger area. The following year, however, he had to conclude that farming in the area was impossible. To be successful, irrigation systems would have to be constructed, which would have drained the agency's financial resources.[58]

Most agents were convinced that cattle raising was a better option than farming. The agents also believed that many Lakȟóta were able to work if they wished to and work was available. Many Lakȟóta preferred working in the transportation and freighting of various goods. Red Cloud and Spotted Tail, among others, suggested that the transportation of annual goods to Indian agencies should be left entirely to the Lakȟóta. In 1885, at Pine Ridge alone, there were 500 wagons available for the Indians to use for this purpose.[59]

By the late 1880s, many Lakȟóta were trying to adapt to reservation life by working odd jobs. In 1889, several Lakȟóta at Cheyenne River wrote to the agent requesting to haul lumber by water, and the following year other agents reported on the large volume of lumber that had been transported. For many, bulk transports were a great way to escape the monotonous life at the agencies.

According to the agents, the Indians proved to be enterprising, hard-working, and reliable.[60]

Another way to escape the monotony of the reservation was to visit friends and relatives off the reservation. While they needed permission from the agent to visit other Lakȟóta agencies or other reservations, they sought this opportunity frequently.[61] Starting in the early 1880s, intertribal visitation became common. During the ten-year period from 1880 to 1890, 768 known trips were made to and from Lakȟóta reservations. Sometimes permission was denied but the Lakȟóta went anyway. In fact, out of those 768 trips as many as 257 were made without permission.[62]

Man Afraid of His Horses was a frequent visitor at other reservations. Sitting Bull even visited former enemies, the Crow. Sometimes small families embarked on friendly visits to other tribes, at times entire thiyóšpaye headed to meetings as far away as Fort Hall, Idaho. Often these visits were for social purposes, dancing and feasting. But there were political reasons as well. Gradually these intertribal meetings became venues for native diplomacy, where strategies to resist government policies were planned and ideas for common native agendas were developed. These visits proved to be important opportunities for sharing experiences, planning, and exchanging news and ideas. This intertribal visitation was the beginning of a pan-Indian movement, which in a way culminated in the spread of the Ghost Dance in the late 1880s. The Ghost Dance religion did not spread into a vacuum, rather its rapid spread from tribe to tribe was based on these existing native networks.[63] The extent of intertribal visitation in the 1880s demonstrates that the Lakȟóta or other plains Indians were not just passively waiting while the wašíču forced them to become copies of an industrious white farmer.

The disappearance of the buffalo caused the greatest disruption of traditional Lakȟóta life. In 1883, a reasonably sized herd of buffalo strayed into the Great Sioux Reservation. The Lakȟóta at Cheyenne River Agency were anxious to go on a hunt and made all the necessary preparations. Agent William A. Swan initially gave permission, but by the order of the Indian Office, later canceled the hunt. The cancellation was a great disappointment to the Lakȟóta, but after some discussion, they told the agent that they "want to do as the Great Father tells us, and we want to obey his instructions." At Standing Rock, Agent James McLaughlin allowed a hunt in 1883 and even joined the chase himself. This would be the last buffalo hunt. It was such a notable event that it was mentioned in most Húŋkpapȟa winter counts.[64] A culture relying so heavily on buffalo hunting and the products derived from it was bound to be negatively impacted by the cessation of the practice. Most supplies now had to be obtained from whites, but perhaps more importantly, the loss of the buffalo affected everyday life. The men had nothing to do. What was the role of the akíčhita or wakíčhuŋza when there were no great hunting expeditions that required scouts or warriors? The slaughter of cattle on issue day was the closest thing to hunting the Lakȟóta had. The whites watched in horror as the Lakȟóta released the cattle given to them, then chased them as if they were buffalo and slaughtered the animals in much the same way as they had done in the past. The women then butchered them and prepared the food. The day often ended with a big feast where the abundance of food, singing, and dancing brought echoes from the past. For the whites, this was a sign of a return to barbaric customs. The "cattle hunt" had to end, they decided.

On the reservation, the traditional male occupations of warfare and hunting were no longer possible. Men's roles began to change. To support their families, they took on various jobs. Of course, women's roles also changed, as there was no longer a need to work on buffalo skins, make clothes, or maintain tipis. Ideas about ownership changed to follow white models. Before, women owned the tipis, but on the reservation the head of each family, usually a male, was the owner of the house or tipi. Increasingly, the materials needed for clothing were cloth instead of hides. Men, especially, began to wear "white man's clothing." This was part of government policy; the Indians were expected to abandon their traditional clothes and wear what was often referred to as civilian clothing or dress. At the same time, they were expected to build log cabins for themselves and abandon tipis. Year after year, as indicators of progress, agents carefully listed how many regularly dressed like a white man or how many log cabins had been built. In the Pine Ridge area in 1883, for example, 500 Indians wore "white man's clothes" regularly, 626 families lived in individual houses, and a hundred new log cabins were completed. In 1889, these numbers had doubled. In practice, Lakȟóta were often forced to give up their tipis when new buffalo hides were no longer available, but canvas tipis stood next to log cabins. Families might stay in tipis, especially during the summer because they were much cooler than musty log cabins.[65]

Although the status and responsibilities of Lakȟóta women also changed, they still took care of the children, household chores, and small garden patches that some tried to cultivate. Men generally refused to do this kind of work. While women kept busy, many men, on the other hand, had nothing to do. Some spent time in societies playing games, conversing, or engaging in social

"White Horse and Swift Horse." Two men on horseback and two women standing in front of a painted canvas thípi, late nineteenth or early twentieth century. Courtesy of South Dakota State Historical Society, South Dakota Digital Archives (2014-12-12-311).

dances, but many also found escape in alcohol. Alcohol abuse increased unrest and violence. The end of buffalo hunting not only affected everyday life, it also had a direct impact on religious life.[66] After all, very many of the religious ceremonies were directly connected to the buffalo. To make matters worse, in 1883, the US government further undermined native ways by banning all traditional religious ceremonies.[67]

Christianity: A New Life?

In 1883, native ceremonies deemed by agents and missionaries to be pagan, were to be replaced by Christian teachings and ceremonies. Christian missionary work among the Lakȟóta and Dakȟóta had begun as early as the late seventeenth century when Catholic missionaries such as Claude Jean Allouez and Louis Hennepin arrived in the wake of the first trading expeditions. Jesuit priest Pierre-Jean De Smet lived with the Dakȟóta in the early nineteenth century. These contacts, however, did not lead to the establishment of permanent missions. The Húŋkpapȟa Mad Bear (Matȟó Gnaškíŋyaŋ) was a young boy in 1851 when he met

Father De Smet. Highly impressed by De Smet's teachings, he became interested in Christianity, and with several friends established a society that promised to hold to the principles taught by Father De Smet. The society was active for many years, and Mad Bear later became one of the most vocal Christian Lakȟóta at Standing Rock Reservation.[68]

Other denominations followed in the footsteps of the Jesuits. By the mid-nineteenth century, Episcopalians, Presbyterians, Congregationalists, and others had established missions among the Dakȟóta. The missionaries translated the Bible and other religious texts into the Dakȟóta language. Many converted Indians served as catechists and some even became priests and ministers. These Christian Indians proved to be vital in conversion work. Both Catholic and Protestant missionaries were convinced that conversion work also required educating the Indians.[69]

While Christianity took root among the Dakȟóta in the east in the early decades of the nineteenth century, the Lakȟóta remained out of reach of the missionaries until the late 1860s. Of course, the Lakȟóta were exposed to basic Christian ideas through visits by "black robes" (Jesuits). When many Dakȟóta moved to the west in the wake of the 1862 war, a growing number of missionaries followed them. The Episcopal Church designated two mission areas west of the Mississippi River as early as 1859. The first permanent missions among the Lakȟóta, however, were not established until the late 1870s. Under its peace policy, the federal government entrusted four Lakȟóta agencies to the Episcopalians. Only Grand River Agency, later renamed Standing Rock, was assigned to the Catholics. In the 1880s, other religious groups also received permission to establish missions among the Lakȟóta. The first permanent Episcopal mission was established in 1879 near Pine Ridge Agency, where a church was built two years later. The Presbyterians established a mission, a church, and a school in the vicinity of Pine Ridge Agency in 1885–86.[70]

One of the influential native Christians on Standing Rock was Phillip J. Deloria, a key figure in establishing the Episcopal mission at Standing Rock. Deloria was the son of an Iháŋktȟuŋwaŋ medicine man. The mission work started slowly, with only nine men involved at first. Within a few years they had established several societies and by 1893 a church had been erected at Little Oak Creek and a larger building at St. Elizabeth.[71] By 1893 Deloria had become a priest and oversaw the St. Elizabeth mission. Pleased with his work, Deloria wrote: "Our hearts are made glad by these things. I myself greatly rejoice in that."[72]

The Indian Church by Mary Sully (Susan Deloria, Dakota, 1896–1963), Mary Sully was the daughter of Rev. Phillip J. Deloria, who was also known as Thípi Sápa, (Black Lodge) on the Standing Rock Reservation. The painting depicts people enter a thípi—people entering Deloria's congregation. The image is full of details and symbolism, combining both native and Christian traditions. At the center is a figure wearing the Niobrara Cross, but in the back is a rainbow and other symbols important for the Lakȟóta. For further analysis, see P. Deloria, *Becoming Mary Sully*, 46–58. Colored pencil on paper, 34.5 × 19 inches. Photo by Scott Soderberg. Courtesy of Phillip J. Deloria.

In the late 1870s, Catholic missionaries arrived at Pine Ridge and Rosebud. Among them was Father Francis M. J. Craft, who formed friendly relations with both the Oglála and Sičháŋǧu, but he did not establish a permanent presence on either reservation.[73]

In 1885, Jesuit priest John Jutz and Brother Ursus Nunlist established the first Catholic mission, St. Francis Mission, at Rosebud, and a year later, Jutz built Holy Rosary Mission at Pine Ridge. The Jesuits also established schools at Pine Ridge and Rosebud. At Standing Rock, Catholic missionary work began under Bishop Martin Marty, and in 1884, Fr. Francis Craft moved to Standing Rock. Cheyenne River's first Catholic mission was not established until 1891. By the late 1880s Catholic and Protestant missions dotted the Great Sioux Reservation, but there was no actual cooperation between them. In fact, competition for Indian souls was fierce among the various denominations.[74]

Among the Lakȟóta, denominational competition caused confusion. Spotted Tail and Red Cloud had specifically asked for Jesuits, but soon there were many denominations, each claiming superiority. In 1890, one Lakȟóta told Jesuit Fr. Florentine Digman that Spotted Tail requested Black Robes as teachers to his people because they always spoke the truth, but instead of Black Robes they got White Robes [Protestants] claiming they were similar. "Now you white men have different prayers," the man complained. "You have the Black Robe Prayers and the White Robe Prayers, and you quarrel with each other saying that the prayers of others are false. We Indians do not want such a controversy. So, leave us alone and let us pray for our own Great Spirit in our own way."[75]

From the beginning, missionaries sought to destroy traditional Lakȟóta ceremonies, customs, and beliefs. The activities of medicine men were of particular concern, as missionaries considered them to be in direct cooperation with the devil. Native ceremonies were considered barbaric. Keeping several wives also shocked missionaries, as did many traditional dances. Attempts to get rid of these was a recurring theme in missionary reports.

Protestant missionaries began publishing newspapers aimed directly at the Indians. Pastor John P. Williamson founded The *Word Carrier* as early as 1871, and it was published at Santee Agency in Nebraska. It reflected not only the opinions of missionaries, but also the thoughts of literate Christian Indians. It originally appeared under the Dakȟóta name *Iapi Oaye*, but from 1873 to 1884 it appeared in both English and Dakȟóta. *Iapi Oaye* differed from the English version in that it was intended for a completely different audience and served specifically as a mouthpiece for missionary work for both the Dakȟóta and Lakȟóta. Another paper published in Dakȟóta was *Anpao Kin* (*The Daybreak*). The newspapers published news, prayers, hymns, various teachings, and biblical phrases, all in Dakȟóta. At times, they issued harsh exhortations to chastity and warned against believing in false prophets or gods. Sam White Bird (Ziŋtkála Sáŋ), for example, said that in the past he had been a wrongdoer, but he "joined the prayers [church]" because "Jesus came on top of the world, so that we would live." He believed that people, who continued to live in the traditional way, were wrongdoers.[76]

The papers also contained articles in which Indians described their experiences in the eastern Indian schools as well as their trips to Europe. In 1888, a Christian Lakȟóta described in *Anpao Kin* how everyone had fallen ill while crossing the ocean, and daily prayers did not seem to bring relief. Still, the author believed that he would survive his journey through his faith. In addition, they had seen a huge grey creature that was as big as a train locomotive. It was a whale, but for the Lakȟóta, it was another sign of the wonders of the white world.[77]

The extent to which these newspapers facilitated the spread of Christianity among the Lakȟóta is impossible to determine, but they document how Christian Indians experienced their new religion. For example, various women's organizations were organized within the protestant churches and their work was often reported in the pages of *Anpao Kin* and *Iapi Oaye*. In the early 1890s there were already several active women's societies on Lakȟóta reservations. Anna Charging Bear, a female leader on Pine Ridge, "formed a women's guild. We were eight women and two girls." They "worked well all the time and finally were able to have a chapel."[78]

She described their meetings: "Well, when we first come together, we sing a hymn and then we pray and then we read part of the Bible, and then some woman exhorts us, after which we sew. Then when we are about to close we sing a hymn.... We always work with reverence towards God, and therefore God has mercy on us and makes us strong."[79] Another letter from the Wounded Knee district describes how in 1893 twenty-two women regularly took part in a women's guild, and, in Crow Creek, up to forty women attended the Boxelder Creek women's guild.[80] In addition to women's societies, there were, for example, young men's Christian societies. At Lower Brulé, St. Andrew's Brotherhood was established with the objective that "Christ's kingdom might grow among the people."[81]

Missionary work in the 1880s was quite extensive. By the end of the decade, the number of churches had increased from six to thirty-one and the number of missionaries from six to fifty-four. Statistics show that the number of Christian Lakȟóta rose from a few hundred at the beginning of the decade to 4,757 by the end of the 1880s. In 1889, the number of Christians who regularly attended church at Pine Ridge was reported to be 2,213, with a total population of 5,611. Two years earlier, the number of churchgoers had been only 1,280. Pastor John Robinson reported that things were in very good shape at Pine Ridge. In 1887, he wrote, "My heart is filled with great joy, and the statistics do not even tell the whole truth." Similar growth was reported at other Lakȟóta agencies.[82]

The last Sun Dance ceremonies in the nineteenth century were held at Pine Ridge and Rosebud in 1882 and 1883.[83] The ban on major religious ceremonies was a heartbreaking loss for the Lakȟóta, a people for whom religion and ceremony had always been an inseparable part of everyday life. Indian agents cheerfully reported that "immoral and barbaric" native ceremonies and dances were gradually coming to an end, though they continued in remote camps and settlements in secret. At Cheyenne River, ceremonies were held on a regular basis in Hump's camp after it became impossible to hold large public religious ceremonies, such as the Sun Dance, in the vicinity of the agencies.

With the ban on traditional ceremonies, one of the pillars of cohesive society disappeared. In this desperate situation, many Lakȟóta converted to Christianity. For many, believing in the Christian God did not mean that they completely abandoned traditional beliefs. Lakȟóta perceptions of forces beyond human comprehension were flexible, so many Christian Lakȟóta combined their own traditional beliefs with those of Christianity. The Christian God became part of the totality of Wakȟáŋ Tȟáŋka. Most missionaries did not accept this syncretism. For them, the only true faith was the Christian one, so what they considered pagan deities and customs had to be destroyed.[84]

In cases of illness, the Lakȟóta often consulted traditional medicine men. Missionaries time and again witnessed supposedly Christian Lakȟóta practicing their traditional ceremonies. Fr. F. M. J. Craft, tried to demonstrate the superiority of Christianity over native healing after hearing a rumor that a local medicine man was trying to cure people suffering from smallpox and tuberculosis by traditional means. Craft approached the patient, ignoring Indian resistance, he listened to his breath and when the sick man vomited, the priest ate his vomit. When he did not fall ill, he told the people it was a great demonstration of the power of Christianity.

Whether the patient got better, Craft does not tell. One can only imagine how the Lakȟóta present reacted to this. After all, Craft's method was not so different from the methods used by traditional wičȟáša wakȟáŋ, who frequently extracted symbolic sickness from a patient and coughed out proof in the form of fingernails, grubs, or blood clots. However, there are no known examples of Lakȟóta healers ingesting vomit as part of their practice. Craft's example is hardly a good description of the methods commonly used by the Jesuits and other clergy, for Craft was in many ways an outsider in this own church. Nevertheless, it reveals the extremes to which some priests were willing to go in their conversion work.[85]

Black Elk, a holy man among the Oglála, relates how Father Joseph Lindebner prevented him from healing when Black Elk was called to help a sick boy. He had just begun his healing ceremony when the priest entered the room. "Satan, get out!" shouted the priest furiously, driving Black Elk out.[86] Although the priests and missionaries at times doubted the faith of the Christian Lakȟóta, the Lakȟóta considered themselves very Christian, while at the same time adhering to their own traditional customs and beliefs. For many Lakȟóta, there was no apparent conflict in embracing a hybridity of religious beliefs.[87]

In this new situation, the churches offered the opportunity to participate in ceremonies and maintain contact with the wakȟáŋ. The Húŋkpapȟa Chief Gall is a good example of this. He opposed everything related to Christianity for a long time, but one day missionaries attracted him to the church. Gall sat on the last bench looking gloomy throughout the ceremony. The following Sunday, however, he returned to church and said it was good to be present at this ceremony. As a religious person, Gall apparently felt good in the church and gradually became an active Christian. The extent to which he abandoned his traditional beliefs is not known.[88]

Red Cloud also converted to Catholicism, but in his old age he stated that when he died one day, he would be happy if his spirit went somewhere other than the white man's heaven. He had had enough of the whites. The life of Black Elk is another excellent example of Lakȟóta religious openness and hybridity, an example of the adaptation and merging of various ways of worship. As late as the 1880s, Black Elk served as a wičháša wakȟáŋ who strongly opposed Christianity. In the 1890s, he converted to Catholicism, began preaching and went from one reservation to another as a catechist. While in Europe with Buffalo Bill's Wild West show, he wanted to travel to Jerusalem to see the place where Christ was crucified. In his old age in the 1930s, he returned to his roots and told John G. Neihardt—and through him the whole world—about the "true and beautiful" religion of the Lakȟóta.[89]

By the end of the 1880s, the Lakȟóta were divided along religious lines. Some sought, where possible, to preserve their traditional religious traditions, others had completely converted to Christianity, while a third group tried to strike a balance between the two religions. Religious divisions exacerbated political divisions. Indeed, political disagreements and controversies had always troubled the Lakȟóta, but confinement on the reservation brought new frictions to the surface. One major factor causing controversy in the 1880s was the US government's effort to gradually shrink and break up the remaining Lakȟóta country. Lakȟóta tȟamákȟočhe was again under attack.

"Father I Have Learnt to Write": Attending the White Man's Schools

In addition to spreading Christianity, missionaries and the US government saw education as essential to eradicate native customs. The establishment of schools had already been included in the Fort Laramie Treaty of 1868, which required the US government to establish enough schools for the Lakȟóta. In practice, the establishment of schools among the Lakȟóta was initially left to the various religious groups. The first schools were mission schools. Often, school buildings also functioned as churches until actual church buildings were completed.

Some natives supported the establishment of schools and the education of children because it would help Lakȟóta to read and write. This, in turn, would give them a better chance of operating in a changing, white-dominated world. Other Lakȟóta fiercely opposed everything related to schools. They sometimes moved to remote corners of their reservations to avoid any contacts with the whites. For many Lakȟóta, schools were horrific places where children's hair was cut, and they were forced to wear white man's clothes. Traditionally among the Lakȟóta hair was cut as a sign of grief and mourning, so it is easy to imagine the feelings forced hair cutting evoked. Lula Red Cloud, the great-great-granddaughter of Red Cloud, reported that as late as the 1950s at boarding school, administrators still insisted on cutting her long hair. Her grandfather objected and came to the school and chased the teachers along the school corridors threatening all who tried to touch his granddaughter's head. Teachers promptly abandoned their plan and Lula was allowed to go to school with her long hair intact.[90]

Despite Lakȟóta opposition, the number of schools increased. In the 1880s, schools, either fully or partially funded by the US government, became more common. There were three main types of schools. Day schools were generally built close to Lakȟóta settlements, allowing children to return home in the evenings. Reservation boarding schools were built in the vicinity of either an Indian agency or a mission. The third type, off-reservation boarding schools were those to which children were usually sent for several years. The first, and probably best known, of these is Carlisle Indian Industrial School in Pennsylvania, founded by a former army officer, Richard Henry Pratt. The first Lakȟóta children from Pine Ridge studied there as early as 1879, and in 1884, for example, 48 children attended Carlisle from Rosebud alone. In 1879–81 both Battiste Good and Rosebud winter counts commented on sending children to school.[91]

Boarding school life was hard. Homesickness, infectious diseases, strict discipline, a punitive system, and a contempt for native customs placed an emotional burden on students. Speaking native languages was forbidden. Indian Commissioner J. D. C. Atkins declared that "English, as taught in the United States, is good enough for all children in the United States, regardless of race."

Most schools applied Atkins's motto literally. Speaking Indian languages always resulted in punishment, as did many other minor offenses.[92]

Josephine Waggoner, who attended the Hampton Institute in Virginia, recalled the English-only policy at school: "no Indian talking was allowed at Hampton, not even whispers. We were compelled to use what English we knew. So there were girls of different tribes [who] had to room together to make sure that the English language would be used." If girls spoke any Indian languages, they were reported to the girls' matron, and forced to acknowledge that they spoke "Indian." Students received "marks" for bad conduct. If they received five "marks" in a week, it meant a zero and those who had a zero were forced to work all Saturday. "If we had two zeros, we had to go to bed after supper instead of joining in the social gathering of games, singing, marching, and other entertainments of different kinds. To miss this fun was surely a hard punishment," Waggoner recalled. Despite this, she felt that "it was wonderful to think how quickly the English was learned: every day we learned to say a dozen different words."[93]

While many Lakȟóta were willing to accept the need for schools and education, sending their children away for years at a time was often heartbreaking, but they often had no other choice. In boarding schools, children were vulnerable to diseases and deaths were common. Tuberculosis, especially, proved to be a killer. Sitting Bull questioned the wisdom of sending children to boarding schools: "We love our children just as much as any white man loves his . . . we don't want you to ask us to send our children to those far off-places." In the treaties, the government had agreed to build schools on the reservations. "Why is this not continued? Why do they want to take our children way out near the ocean where we can't even see them once a year and come home spitting their lungs out?," Sitting Bull asked.[94]

Red Cloud repeatedly said that he wanted schools for children, but in 1886, Indian agent Valentine T. McGillycuddy complained that none of the 400 children belonging to Red Cloud's Ité Šíča band attended school. When the agent asked Red Cloud the reason for this, he received a vague answer: "All Oglála are my children." He thus rejected the claim that he would not allow his children to go to school. After all, children from other oyáte had been sent to schools. In the late 1880s, many Lakȟóta favored such delaying tactics.[95] Lakȟóta attitudes toward education can also be gleaned from the transcripts of the land negotiations in the 1880s. In them, the Lakȟóta repeatedly stated that education was a good thing, but only in the future. The older generation was interested neither in working nor in education. They emphasized that education was a task for distant future generations, their generation did not need education. Josephine Wag-goner remembers this attitude of elders. She wrote: "Most of us studied because we had to, not because we wanted to learn. None of our parents encouraged us to study. Education was a small item to them"[96] Red Cloud described Lakȟóta sentiments when visiting the Hampton Institute, noting that "the Indians love their children, but they send them here, a great ways off, to learn the white man's ways. This shows what we think of it."[97]

Despite Lakȟóta ambivalence, new schools were constantly added. In 1886 there were two boarding schools and six day schools at Cheyenne River, one boarding school and seven day schools at Pine Ridge, two boarding schools and five day schools at Standing Rock, and twelve day schools at Rosebud. The number of children attending school regularly was reported to be close to 5,000. Admittedly, agents may have used somewhat exaggerated figures as their success was tied to demonstrating Lakȟóta progress. Teachers, too, were eager to report success. In the schools, Lakȟóta children learned to read and write along with industrial crafts and practical skills. The boys practiced agriculture, animal husbandry, blacksmithing, printing, shoemaking, masonry, and carpentry. The girls learned chores related to housekeeping and practical skills such as cooking, sewing, ironing, and washing. The intention was to make children disciplined, productive, loyal, and well-integrated citizens. The only problem was that after returning from the boarding schools to the reservation, young people had little use for their new skills. There were hardly any jobs available, and wages were low for those lucky enough to find employment. Returning children often felt alienated from their own people.[98] Some desperately sought to reconnect with their culture. When young Plenty Horses (Tȟašúŋke Óta) shot an army officer in the aftermath of the Wounded Knee massacre, and was asked about the reason for his deed, he replied that he had attended a white man's school, but by his actions hoped to show that he was still Lakȟóta.[99]

Although education caused great anxiety among Lakȟóta elders, many children embraced it. In 1895 Spotted Eagle (Waŋblí Gleška) wrote to the agent asking for a boarding school to be built near Green Grass on Cheyenne River. He said there were many children who were eager to start school. Their closest school, Day School No. 5, was too far and a new school would allow children to attend more regularly. That same year Esther White Head asked the agent for permission to go to Carlisle. Her parents were dead, and she really wanted to go to a boarding school with some of her friends who were already attending.[100]

One of the early successes of schools was an increase in Lakȟóta literacy, as described in a letter by a young Lakȟóta boy in 1876. Written in shaky handwriting, the boy proudly told his father: "I have learnt to write."[101] While many Lakȟóta resisted schools, they understood by the late 1880s that education was essential for Lakȟóta survival. The importance of having people capable of reading and writing would only grow over the years, but learning these skills came at a high cost; families were broken up and Lakȟóta culture, language, and way of life came under more serious attack than the US military ever posed. Education, in many ways, equaled cultural genocide and the trauma it caused runs through generations in Lakȟóta—and other Indigenous—communities today. In the summer of 2021, the remains of several Lakȟóta children who died at the Carlisle Industrial School in Pennsylvania, were brought home to the Rosebud Reservation. They were finally buried with proper ceremonies in their homelands. The trauma lingers on, but some recognition of the atrocities committed in boarding schools is being brought to a wider audience as several recent grim discoveries have been made in Canada as well. Hundreds of unknown graves of Indigenous children have been discovered on boarding school premises, but a variety of groups now seem ready to pursue a more open dialogue that might bring some healing to the many affected Indigenous communities.[102]

Though Indian education could be traumatic, it also had some positive outcomes, including new ways to communicate with other Native American tribes and the US government through letter writing.[103] Until Indian schools, many Lakȟóta would ask mixed-blood and white friends to write for them. Throughout the 1880s literate Lakȟóta were increasingly used for this purpose, allowing Sitting Bull, for example, to communicate widely with white friends as far as Europe. American Horse regularly corresponded with 12-year Edvin Landy from Cincinnati. Others wrote letters to neighboring tribes sharing news and proposing friendly visits. Many Lakȟóta wrote letters to white officials in nearby towns and in Washington, DC. In 1889 several Lakȟóta from Lower Brulé corresponded with an attorney's office to seek legal advice in their efforts to keep their lands. The full extent of letter writing is not known, but in 1890, almost seventy letters were sent by Lakȟóta just to the Commissioner of Indian Affairs. In addition to letters, Lakȟóta were quick to embrace other forms of communication like telegrams and the mail service. Young Man Afraid of His Horses, for example, sent gifts to his friends using US postal services.[104] Several Lakȟóta and Dakȟóta living at the turn of the twentieth century published memoirs defending Indian rights, including Ohíyes'a (Charles Alexander Eastman), Zitkála-Šá (Gertrude Simmons Bonnin), Luther Standing Bear, and others.

Thus, in the 1880s, the Lakȟóta kept their kinship networks central to their lives, but also quickly adapted to changing circumstances. While they were confined on reservations, the Lakȟóta were actively seeking new ways to protect their people. They created expansive networks of native diplomacy through intertribal visitation and regular visits to Washington, DC, as well as writing hundreds of letters to decision makers in the East.[105] Letter writing, together with intertribal visitation, allowed the Lakȟóta and other Native Americans to establish vast communication networks that facilitated native diplomacy and served as an anticolonial tool.[106] Fighting the wašíču was no longer realistic so the Lakȟóta sought new innovative ways to protect their people and Lakȟól wičȟóȟ'aŋ, their way of life.

WANÁǦI WAČHÍPI KIŊ
THE GHOST DANCE

Breaking Up Lakȟóta Tȟamákȟočhe

In 1882, the US government decided to dismantle the Great Sioux Reservation. Using threats and fraud a government commission led by Senator Newton Edmunds tried to force the Lakȟóta to sign a paper that would have surrendered nearly half of their reservation lands. However, the Lakȟóta closed ranks, and eventually the proposal collapsed when the Friends of the Indian also intervened.[1] For the time being the Lakȟóta were able to keep their land. Despite restrictions on movement, there was still plenty of room in the Great Sioux Reservation to avoid contact with whites. As long as this was possible, agents found it difficult to force the Lakȟóta to live permanently in one place to farm. To "tie the Lakȟóta to the land" the government had to come up with a different plan. Reducing "surplus lands" (land not needed for farming or ranching) was a perfect way to control the Lakȟóta by inhibiting their movement. This line of thought culminated in the introduction of the General Allotment Act in 1887, which created the modern reservations.[2]

In 1888, another serious attempt was made to split the reservation and implement allotment. The US government again sent a commission to negotiate the sale of Lakȟóta lands. The Lakȟóta were almost unanimously against the commissioners' proposals. At Standing Rock, the Lakȟóta chose John Grass, Gall, and two others as speakers. They spoke extensively complaining about all the injustices the whites had perpetrated against them. John Grass made the Lakȟóta position clear: "The whole nation that are located on this reservation have come to the conclusion that we will not sign that black paper. . . . We decline."[3] Throughout the proceedings Sitting Bull watched silently in the background to make sure that no mistakes were made. Indeed, his role during the negotiations has been somewhat confusing to whites who were present at the time and scholars ever since. In the minds of the whites, he was the chief whose word weighed the most at Standing Rock, but during the talks, he did not give long speeches, merely urged everyone to speak without bad feelings. Indeed, the Lakȟóta, according to custom, had chosen their representatives to articulate the collective position. Sitting Bull's position and opinions were well known to all, so his presence was limited to that of observer and supporter. Sitting Bull had made his opposition to any land sales clear in 1886 during a visit with the Crow in Montana. There he gave an impassioned speech against Indians selling their lands. It possibly delayed allotment of Crow lands significantly.[4] His views on the issue had not changed; he remained a staunch opponent of selling Lakȟóta lands.

Lakȟóta resistance was strong at other agencies as well. At Lower Brulé, many were frustrated as this proposal caused strife among the people. At Crow Creek the chiefs unanimously declined to sign, saying that the land left to the Lakȟóta would be land that was worthless. "A certain part of your words make my heart bad," said White Ghost (Wanáǧi Ská), and Running Bear (Matȟó Íŋyaŋke) wondered, "What can I have that he [the white man] wants?"[5]

At Pine Ridge, several speakers, including George Sword, were frustrated that the government tried to create a split among the Lakȟóta. He urged the chiefs to stay calm and lead the people. The chiefs, he said, should let every man give his opinion, as was Lakȟóta custom. Sword was chosen as a representative. He patiently listened to the proposal before rejecting it as he had been called to do based on Oglála majority decision.[6] Red Cloud stayed in the background, while American Horse, a great orator, exhausted the commissioners by talking for hours on end, day after day. The Lakȟóta understood the government's terms clearly. They demanded that the government representatives find out what the new borders would be and how much money and how many supplies, schools, shops, or books would be offered to them in return for their land. For the government representatives, it was impossible to comply with these demands. The Lakȟóta were by no means going to give up their lands without proper compensation. After securing only a handful of signatures, the commissioners admitted their failure. The Lakȟóta had won this round, but many knew that the government would not give up. Indian Agent James McLaughlin warned Sitting Bull that the Lakȟóta should accept government offers while the terms were still favorable to the Lakȟóta. The government would take what it wanted eventually, at much less favorable terms. Other agents, mixed-blood interpreters, and most missionaries agreed.[7]

The government had no intention of giving up. Already the following spring, a new commission arrived to negotiate the sale of Lakȟóta lands. This time, former Ohio Governor Charles Foster headed the commission, but its best-known member was Gen. George Crook. Crook was well acquainted with the Indians and soon became the true leader of the commission, which came to be known as the "Crook Commission." Crook employed a different tack from his predecessor. He was in no hurry. At each agency, he invited the Lakȟóta to the meeting and organized fine feasts, with plenty of food and dancing. The intention was to undermine Lakȟóta unity. The negotiations proceeded the same way as the previous year, but behind the scenes Crook sought to influence individual Lakȟóta, talking to those he knew were more favorable to surrendering their lands, threatening some, or promising others whatever they wanted to hear. Gradually, he drove a wedge into what had been a unified Lakȟóta front. Many feared that if they did not now agree to the government's proposals, they would end up without any compensation for their lands.[8]

At Pine Ridge, the people once again elected American Horse as their representative, but after speaking at length against selling the lands, he walked over to the commissioners and signed the paper. His actions have since been seen as inconsistent, but he acted fully in accord with the Lakȟóta system. He had been chosen to represent his people, and in his long speech he faithfully expressed their views. But since he himself believed that the best solution in this situation was to agree to the division of the reservation, he signed the proposed agreement as an autonomous individual. Gradually others followed his example. At Standing Rock, too, resistance slowly crumbled. In the end, only Sitting Bull and his Silent Eaters men's society opposed the surrender of the lands. On the critical day of the negotiations, he was not invited to the meeting. After hearing about the talks, he arrived on the scene furious. "No one told us about the council and we just got here," he exclaimed. But it was too late. In his absence, many had signed the paper that handed more than half of the Great Sioux Reservation over to the whites.[9]

The Crook Commission had succeeded. Sufficient signatures had been obtained at each agency, allowing the Great Sioux Reservation to be divided into six smaller reservations. The Sioux Act of 1889 sealed this final division.[10] Having obtained the required number of signatures, the US government could say it had complied with the law. Yet, whether moral norms were met, is debatable. The Lakȟóta received compensation for the surrender of their lands, but they did not get nearly all that Crook had promised them. It is likely that without Crook's false promises, the signatures obtained would have been insufficient. It is unclear to what extent Crook himself believed he could keep his promises. Later, he tried to persuade decision-makers to follow his promises, but since he had not been authorized to make them, the government was not obliged to fulfill them. In any case, during the negotiations, Lakȟóta resistance was broken. It was another blow to Lakȟóta unity. Tensions immediately erupted between those who signed the agreement and those who opposed it.

The negotiations of 1888 and 1889 led to other, more unpredictable problems. Because the Lakȟóta were away from home for weeks to take part in the negotiations, crops were ruined and cattle died. This resulted in famine, followed by the spread of diseases. Between 1889 and 1890, all Lakȟóta agents reported measles and other deadly diseases wreaking havoc among the Lakȟóta. In 1890, Red Cloud complained that more than 200 people on Pine Ridge alone had died of disease within the last year. He lamented that the past two seasons had been so dry that they could raise little to nothing. Rations were so scant they were obliged to kill their own cattle to keep them "all from starving to death." Still, many of his "people got weak and sick from the want of a proper quantity of food, 217 of them dying since the fall of last year from starvation" he wrote.[11]

Chief Little Wound feared the suffering might lead to trouble. In July 1890, he summarized Lakȟóta sentiments to Agent Hugh Gallagher: "Look at these people around you, see their sunken cheeks and emaciated bodies. Many of these you will notice have drooping heads and an expression of unconcern in their faces that shows plainly [that] the ravages of hunger has reduced them to the verge of idiocy." Many children died from hunger during winter, but still the Great Father refused to provide beef. Desperate, Little Wound sent pleas to the President: "Great Father you promised us plenty to eat. . . . We fear another winter like the past would render our people desperate causing trouble that would give us a bad name."[12]

Little Wound referred to the US government decision to reduce the annual appropriations by almost half, even though one of the conditions for handing over the lands had been to increase them—or so the Lakȟóta believed. The government sought to justify the reduction in annual appropriations by arguing that there

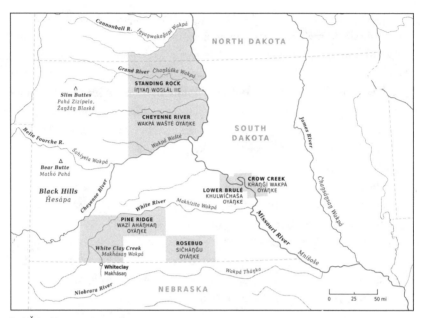

Lakȟóta Reservations after 1889

were no more funds allocated for the purpose. It claimed that the number of Lakȟóta in the census had turned out to be lower than expected. That the figure was lower than expected was likely due to the large number of deaths caused by famine and sickness. In 1890, the government further justified the reduction in appropriations, noting that it was part of the Sioux Act of 1889 accepted by the Lakȟóta. Thus, even though the Lakȟóta surrendered almost half of their lands, their meat rations were reduced by nearly half over the previous year's figure. The gradual reduction in annual goods was also part of the government's conscious policy aimed at forcing the Lakȟóta into working. The logic was as simple as it was devastating: If food rations were reduced, the resulting famine would compel the Indians to work to stay alive. Senator Henry L. Dawes, for example, pointed out that hunger was the only way to get an Indian to work.[13] Thus, despite all the promises, the Lakȟóta found that they had lost their land and received only increased poverty, hunger, and misery as compensation.

When the Sioux Act of 1889 took effect, the lands left over after allotment were sold to white settlers. The Great Sioux Reservation was now reduced to six separate reservations all based on existing administrative divisions. The Húŋkpapȟa and Sihásapa settled on Standing Rocking Reservation (Íŋyaŋ

Wóslal Hé), together with a number of Iháŋkthuŋwaŋ and Iháŋkthuŋwaŋna Dakhóta. The Mnikhówožu and Oóhenuŋpa, as well as Itázipčho, made up the majority on the Cheyenne River Reservation (Wakpá Wašté Oyáŋke); the Pine Ridge Reservation (Wazí Aháŋhaŋ Oyáŋke) became largely home to the Oglála and some Sičháŋǧu, but also housed some Northern Cheyenne, long-time Lakhóta allies. Most of the Sičháŋǧu settled on Rosebud Reservation (Sičháŋǧu Oyáŋke). Two smaller reservations, Crow Creek (Kȟaŋǧí Wakpá Oyáŋke) and Lower Brulé (Khulwíčhaša Oyáŋke), became the home of Iháŋkthuŋwaŋ and Iháŋkthuŋwaŋna, as well as the Lower Brulé. In February 1890, Lakhóta lands were opened to white settlers. The Lakhóta watched in dismay as the whites settled on their former lands. The opening of Lakhóta thamákhočhe was a big news event. Both local and major national newspapers wrote about it. The *Omaha Daily Bee*, published in Nebraska, wrote on its front page that with the opening of the lands, "barbarism and darkness receded as the light of civilization arrived with the settlers."[14]

Although Lakhóta life changed rapidly during the 1870s and 1880s, they did not assimilate into white culture as federal officials had envisioned. Commissioner of Indian Affairs Thomas J. Morgan steadfastly believed in the idea that work and Christianity were the only paths forward for Native Americans. After visiting several reservations in the late 1880s, he noted that despite all evidence to the contrary the Lakhóta had made tremendous progress along the "white man's road." He proclaimed US Indian policies a success. According to Morgan, the Bureau of Indian Affairs had done an "excellent job."[15]

The actual situation among the Lakhóta was dismal. As a result of famine and disease, infant mortality increased sharply. Lakhóta dissatisfaction increased. The fragmentation of the reservation and the reduction in annuity payments made many Lakhóta feel that they had once again been betrayed by the wašíču.

"With This Power the Tree Would Bloom and the People Would Get into the Sacred Hoop"

In 1888 or 1889, a Paiute (Sápa Wičháša) Indian, Wovoka, fell into a trance and had a vision. In his vision he met the Great Spirit, who gave him instructions for a new religion. When Wovoka woke up, he instructed his people in a new dance that would bring about a transformation of the earth. In that new world the white man would not oppress the Indians. There would be buffalo and other game, and dead Indians would be brought back to life. It would be an Indian paradise.

Wovoka's religion appealed to thousands of desperate American Indians from the Great Basin and beyond, including the Great Plains. Soon, Lakȟóta heard rumors of this wonderful new religion. There was a Messiah, somewhere in the west, and he had come upon the earth to help the Indians.

The Lakȟóta, like so many other tribes, wanted to learn more about this new religion. In the spring of 1889, the Lakȟóta held a great council that decided to send a delegation to Nevada to meet the Messiah. The great council chose Short Bull, a Sičháŋǧu holy man, to lead the delegation. He entered the council without knowing what was expected of him but suddenly he was placed at the center of the of the circle and Standing Bear addressed him: "We have a letter from the West saying the Father has come and we want you to go and see him [the Messiah]. You must try and get there, see him, recognize him and tell us what he says, and we will do it. Be there with a big heart. Do not fail."[16]

The Lakȟóta delegation consisted of Short Bull, Kicking Bear (Matȟó Wanáȟtaka), and several others.[17] On their way they met people from other tribes, who also wanted to learn more about the new religion. The Lakȟóta traveled first to Wind River Reservation in Wyoming. There they discussed the religion with the Arapaho and then continued to Fort Washakie. From there, their journey took them by railroad to Fort Hall in Idaho, where they met with Bannock, Northern Arapaho, and Northern Cheyenne, who were also on their way to meet the Messiah. From Fort Hall they boarded a train to Winnemucca, Nevada, and from there another train to Pyramid Lake and then on to the Walker River Agency where they finally met the Messiah. The delegates were shown many strange things and a new world without the wašíču. Kicking Bear and Good Thunder (Wakíŋyaŋ Wašté) were really impressed with the Messiah and his teachings. Good Thunder saw the scars on his hands and feet as testimony that he was indeed the Messiah, or Jesus, whom the whites crucified in the past. Kicking Bear was shown a whole new world with plenty of buffalo. And all this was to come about by dancing and praying.[18]

Upon returning home in the spring of 1890, they informed their people of their experiences in Nevada and so brought new hope to the suffering Lakȟóta.[19] The Spirit Dance (Wanáǧi Wačhípi kiŋ), as the Lakȟóta called the Ghost Dance, promised the return of the buffalo and happier times. The news caused great excitement.[20]

The Lakȟóta of Pine Ridge and Rosebud conducted the first dances soon after the return of the delegates in April 1890. Many Lakȟóta eagerly participated from the beginning. Black Elk remembers how he first learned about this new religion at a meeting at the head of White Clay Creek:

The people gathered together there to hear what these men had to say about it. . . . These people told me that these men had actually seen the Messiah and that he had given them these things. They should put this paint on and have a Ghost Dance, and in doing this they would save themselves, that there is another world coming—a world just for the Indians, that in time the world would come and crush out all the whites. This Ghost Dance would draw them to this other world and that the whites would have no power to get on so that it would crush them. In this other world there was plenty of meat—just like olden times—every dead person was alive again and all the buffalo that had been killed would be over there again roaming around. This world was to come like a cloud. . . . [the] Ghost Dance would make everyone get on the red road again. Everyone was eager to get back to the red road again.[21]

Two early participants, Pretty Eagle (Waŋblí Wašté) and Young Skunk (Maká Čhiŋčála), reported that scores of Lakȟóta came to watch the dances, many were drawn into it and experienced powerful visions. In the visions, the Lakȟóta met their dead relatives and received messages about the return of happier times. Young Skunk met his dead sister, who showed him a large Lakȟóta village, where people lived as in the past. After waking up from their trance, people wept from happiness and many were convinced that a new world was coming.[22]

Young Skunk described his vision during one of these early dances:

We danced a little while and suddenly as I danced with my eyes shut, a light fell on me and my heart beat fast and I felt as though I was going to be affected but regardless I danced. And then I had pain in my liver and could not breathe, I became affected and once was dying of suffocation and my hands too were clenched, so I remember nothing. And then someone went following a path, so I went behind him and he went uphill. And then he said: "Go from here! It is not far from here." So then I went further on and in a little ways there was a hill so I went up it and stood [there]. . . . A horseback rider was coming downhill and beyond the sky was full of smoke. It was a woman who came, and she came to me. And it was my older sister who died long ago.

She came to me and said: "My younger brother you came, so I came to meet you," and she hugged me by the neck and cried so I cried too, and she stopped crying so I stopped too. And then she said: "My younger brother, eat this and then go home from here," and she gave me some pemmican and she said: "My younger brother, you people of the old camp really smell, so even though many come visiting over here they cannot go to the camp! And when you return here, do not wear any metal. So, when you come here again you will go to the camp and you will see your child and your grandmother too," she said.[23]

Soon, more enthusiastic Lakȟóta started to dance, though not all Lakȟóta took part in it. George Sword, for example, said that he did not think "it was the right way to worship," and Dewey Beard (Wasú Máža) said that he never received a vision and could not believe in it. "The spirits would not come to me," he lamented.[24] But many did believe, and the Spirit Dance became a part of reservation life.

Short Bull, Good Thunder, Kicking Bear, and others who had met with Wovoka carried the message from community to community. They drew excited crowds to listen and dance. White officials did not like the new religion. It did not take long before Short Bull was invited to a meeting at Indian Agent J. George Wright's office at Rosebud. To his surprise Short Bull was told that he was to be arrested. The agent told him that his sermons caused the Indians to neglect their farming. Under pressure from the agent, Short Bull promised to stop the Ghost Dance. At Pine Ridge, other Ghost Dance leaders were also arrested. Under threat of arrest, Good Thunder also capitulated to the agent's request to stop dancing. Other Ghost Dance leaders also promised their agents to cease dancing.[25]

On both reservations, however, the meetings continued in secret. At Cheyenne River Reservation Kicking Bear invited all Lakȟóta to a great dance, but after agents cracked down on other reservations, the dance interest waned. Kicking Bear then traveled to the Arapaho, who were already dancing. At Standing Rock, Crow Creek, and Lower Brulé the news about a new religion created little excitement at this stage, because none of the Ghost Dance leaders had yet returned to talk about their experiences. After the initial arrests, the agents were too busy implementing agricultural programs to really pay any attention to the Ghost Dance. They downplayed rumors about a possible Lakȟóta uprising. Newspapers, however, warned about the new Lakȟóta religion, calling it "the Last Powwow" or "the War Dance."[26]

The agents assured officials in Washington that the situation on Lakȟóta reservations was completely peaceful. Only Standing Rock agent James McLaughlin reported that Sitting Bull and some other traditionalists were causing trouble, but this had nothing to with the Ghost Dance. McLaughlin was certain the unrest would quiet down if Sitting Bull were arrested. McLaughlin's actions, in fact, stemmed from years of disputes between himself and Sitting Bull.[27]

In the summer of 1890 crops failed again and severe hunger ensued. White settlers promptly left their farms and moved away, but the Lakȟóta did not have this option. The government's decision to cut Lakȟóta annual rations aggravated the situation. Several chiefs wrote to the Commissioner of Indian Affairs asking for relief. They explained the dire circumstances on the reservations and feared that unrest might follow. The government's response was lackluster. Only in December did Congress propose additional rations for the Lakȟóta, but this effort came too late.[28]

At the end of July, Kicking Bear returned from his visit to the Arapaho and reported that they were openly dancing and practicing their new religion. Desperate Lakȟóta listened attentively when Kicking Bear spoke about the miracles he had witnessed among the Arapaho. They had seen a happy future. Short Bull resumed the Ghost Dances. When the whites were clearly not going to help the Lakȟóta, increasing numbers turned to traditionalist chiefs. Progressive chiefs like Man Afraid of His Horses and American Horse were now much less popular. As signers of the 1889 agreement, they were seen as partially responsible for the Lakȟóta's state of despair.[29]

Soon after Kicking Bear's return, dances were organized on different reservations under the leadership of the Ghost Dance wičháša wakȟáŋ. Despite being nominally Catholic, Red Cloud gave permission for the people to dance, although he never actively participated in the Ghost Dance ceremonies. He said the religion would die on its own if it was false. Little Wound, who was supposedly a "progressive" Christian, called for the rapid organization of a dance, so that the Messiah would not abandon them when the time came. At the beginning of August, three hundred Oglála began organizing dances in his camp. Other dance camps sprung up across Pine Ridge Reservation. In August, 1,200 Oglála, out of 7,000 Pine Ridge residents, were dancing regularly. Many people moved away from their log cabins and erected tipis to camp at the dance sites; the traditional camp circle was revived.[30]

On August 22, several hundred Lakȟóta were dancing at Pine Ridge when they suddenly learned that Agent Hugh D. Gallagher and a group of Indian Police were approaching. About 300 Oglála, some carrying guns, went to meet the agent. Gallagher demanded that they stop dancing. They refused and warned him they would defend their religion. The agent gave in.[31] For the first time, the Ghost Dancers defied the authorities. They had been ready to fight the Indian Police, their own relatives.

News of the Ghost Dancers' defiance spread not only among the Lakȟóta, but among whites as well. White settlers living near the Lakȟóta reservations began fleeing their homes when they heard rumors about Indians gathering arms. Newspapers published exaggerated reports that the greatest Indian war in history was about to begin. Thousands of Indians "crazed by the religion" were reportedly ready to fight.[32] Likewise false reports spread among the Indians. At the end of August, a rumor spread at Rosebud Agency that soldiers had arrived on the reservation and arrested Lakȟóta women and children. This prompted both traditionals and progressives to take up arms, and ride out to meet the soldiers, to free the women and children. The rumor turned out to be false.[33]

During August and September, all agents on Lakȟóta reservations, except for James McLaughlin at Standing Rock, were replaced. The new Republican government rid itself of agents installed by Democrats. Politics determined the selection of new agents. At Pine Ridge, Daniel F. Royer arrived, who was entirely unqualified for the job. He had little experience with Indians and, in many respects, feared them. The Lakȟóta dubbed him Man Afraid of His Lakȟóta. Only a few days after his arrival, Royer called on soldiers for protection. Other agents were not as worried about the Ghost Dance. Rosebud's new agent, Elisha B. Reynolds, was quite indifferent, which Short Bull and his followers quickly used to their advantage. The new Cheyenne River agent, Perain P. Palmer, was also unconcerned as things were quiet near his agency. However, almost 700 Ghost Dancers had gathered along Cherry Creek (Čhaŋpȟá Wakpá) at Hump and Big Foot's (Sitȟáŋka) camp to hear the teachings of Kicking Bear. Although Hump had previously worked as an Indian Police officer, he now openly embraced the Ghost Dance. Big Foot had always carefully navigated the line between traditional and progressive, but despite repeated requests, he had not received more schools on the reservation. Disappointed, he now wanted to hear what the Ghost Dance had to offer.[34]

Moving to the dancing grounds meant the strengthening of the camp circle and hence the unity of the nation. Thus, the white goal of breaking the power of the chiefs and dismantling traditional Lakȟóta society experienced a setback in the fall of 1890. White officials on the reservations and in Washington, DC, became greatly alarmed.

"You Will See Your Relatives"

The Lakȟóta Ghost Dance never followed a single model.[35] It had many variations. The songs might be different, and the number of ceremonial leaders varied. Certain characteristics, however, were shared by all.

The Lakȟóta Ghost Dancers were told in visions that the world was dying and was to be replaced by a new one. Glimpses of this new world were revealed to them in visions, and they were told that the people were now living in the "old camp," referring to life on the reservations. In that world the people smelled bad because of all the terrible things, such as murders, suicides, and other troubles that ravaged the reservations. In Short Bull's vision, the people in the spirit world looked at him strangely because of his smell. In his vision, Short Bull traveled into a big tipi village when "a horseback rider came, galloping fast, and reached me. Then it was my father as a very handsome young man." Short Bull was overcome with emotions but his father said to him: "I see you, my beloved son, but you smell bad, so go back home, and when you get there, wash yourself and come back!"[36]

Young Skunk, Pretty Eagle, and Kicking Bear also describe how the world had become corrupted and filthy and how people "in the old camp" smelled. In their visions the new world was clean and pure, but the time for it was not yet at hand. They had to dance and pray before they could enter the new world of happiness and joy. Many said that after seeing all those wonderful things in visions, they became profoundly sad when they woke up, since everything in the "real" world was grey and the people were poor, and they really smelled. For that reason, purification before the ceremony became particularly important.[37]

Preparing for the dance always began with a cleansing ritual or inípi (sweat lodge ceremony). It was conducted in much the same way as in the past. The lodge was built with the doorway facing east, and a sacred path led to the fire where the stones were heated. To allow as many people as possible to participate, Ghost Dancers built larger sweat lodges that might have two doorways. When a person stepped into the lodge, they carried on their back the burdens of the white man's ways. When people exited through the other door at the end of the ceremony, that burden was lifted. The sweat lodge ceremony thus became a symbol of cultural transformation and rebirth. It symbolized the universe that had been cleansed of strange elements and it was also a symbolic return to the powers of the past. Fasting preceded the dance. Holy men blessed the dance venue. Occasionally they also blessed the dancers by first touching the hallowed ground and then the dancer's forehead. Most traditional Lakȟóta ceremonies started with the smoking of the sacred pipe, but in the Ghost Dance, the ritual was connected to the preparatory sweat lodge ceremony. The sacred pipe was present in the actual Ghost Dance, but in a different way than, for example, in the traditional Sun Dance. In the Ghost Dance, a young woman stood in the center of the dance circle holding the pipe up and pointing it west where the Messiah lived. The person holding the pipe symbolized White Buffalo Woman, who had first brought the pipe to the Lakȟóta.[38]

After purification in the sweat lodge, the Lakȟóta prepared for the dance. Symbols, such as circles, stars, and the crescent moon were painted on the faces of the dancers. Preparations might take the entire morning so that the ceremony usually started in the afternoon. The dancers gathered around the čháŋwákȟaŋ (sacred tree) erected in the center of the dance circle. The tree had been an integral part of the Sun Dance, and it symbolized Lakȟóta unity and the center of the world. Before beginning the ceremony, the dancers shared a bowl of meat, symbolizing the buffalo. In the middle of the dance circle, where the woman holding the pipe stood, another woman shot an arrow in each of the cardinal directions, representing the Lakȟóta, Cheyenne, Arapaho, and Crow nations. The arrows were collected and hung on the sacred tree, along with offerings such as tobacco or stuffed animals.[39]

In the center of the circle stood the ceremonial leaders and a "foresinger," who opened the ceremony with a song. During the song, the dancers raised their arms toward the west because the Messiah lived there, and because the White Buffalo Woman had left the Lakȟóta toward the west. When the song ended, the dancers wept together, took each other's hands, joined in a new song, and started slowly moving from left to right.[40] Gradually the leader of the ceremony increased the speed, alternating between crying and praying toward all directions. As the leader's enthusiasm increased, the other dancers joined him, and all danced faster. They shouted out the names of their deceased relatives, vocally expressing their grief.

Young Skunk recalls:

> And then in the middle of the flats a cottonwood tree was raised, and a red blanket was tied on it, and several men sat there, and then all around them people stood there in a circle. . . . The leader stood by the sacred tree. And that man came along the circle of people and had them hold one another by the hand and he said this as he went along: "From now on whenever you dance you will hold on to one another. . . . and you will hold on firmly to one who is affected . . . you will hold him and take him to the center," he said, "and you will all sing as you dance" . . . "If you love your relatives, cry for them," he said as he went around the circle.
>
> > He comes, he, he, he comes he, he, he comes he he
> > He said this -ye, he said this

He said this ye-ye
The father said this, he said, yo-yo-yo
You will see your relatives, he said
This is why he said, he said ye-ya
The Father said so, he said yo-yo

When he finished the song, the people were crying. . . . In a very large circle and eyes shut we danced.[41]

Seeing dead relatives in the spirit world was of course a highly emotional experience for the dancers. While dancing, they sprinkled soil in their hair to show their anxiety, and gradually fell into trances where receiving visions became possible. As the singing and dancing continued, the excitement grew. Gradually new dancers detached from the circle, screamed and leaped into the air, until they fell on the ground with shaking limbs and finally lay still, as if dead.[42] According to one witness, there may have been as many as a hundred dancers lying on the ground at one time.[43]

The Ghost Dance ceremony ended when enough dancers had fallen into trance. The dancers then sat down in a circle and the holy men leading the dance interpreted their visions. Traditionally, visions were private affairs, only to be discussed with a holy man, but it was an innovation of the Ghost Dance to talk about them publicly. Through these experiences the Ghost Dance evolved, and songs as well as the Ghost Dance shirts were born out of these stories. After a while, the ceremony sometimes resumed. Pretty Eagle remembers:

I danced the dance with my eyes closed and it seemed like those sounds like buffalo hoofs galloping and then again little by little the sound of bird wings were mixed together and it seemed that the buffalo really bellowed and grunted, and it was like a buzzing noise and the dance songs disappeared and were soon gone. And more were really overcome and quickly I looked, but thus they were dancing and they were only ordinary people and my heart was beating fast and I was shaking.[44]

There were sometimes three ceremonies a day and between the ceremonies people played traditional games and feasted. The ceremony always ended with a song at the request of the leaders. Then the dancers would shake the blankets they had worn to remove any evil power from them. Finally, everyone cleansed themselves by bathing.[45]

Many of the songs referred to ancestors and meeting deceased relatives. Also popular was the return from a successful war party or bison hunting. Some of the songs referred to the Messiah or the Father and the eternal life he promised.[46] Kicking Bear, one of the Ghost Dance leaders, used to sing the following two songs:

> He came, he-e, He came, he-e, he came he-e, he came he-e
> Father pity me, many want to see you
> And those they want to see their relatives, have pity on them
> He came bringing this song
> You shall see your relatives
> The Father says so, say it yo yo, say it
> The Father says so, say it yo yo.
>
> My son, hold me by the hand
> You will prosper, ye ye
> Father says this, yo
> My son, hold me by the hand
> You shall prosper ye ye. The Father says this yo!"[47]

Considering the desperation among the Lakȟóta in 1890, it is no wonder that the stories made an impression. In the visions people were happy. They hunted, danced, played games, and did all the things the Lakȟóta used to do. In the new world, there was no illness or suffering. The traditional lifestyle returned. Because it happened in visions, it was clear that it would also happen in the human world. The Lakȟóta had no reason to doubt the message of the visions. Visions had always been integral to the Lakȟóta worldview, and medicine men had always known how to interpret them. Why would it be any different now? The idea of buffalo returning was also completely rational for the Lakȟóta. They had emerged from the earth together with the buffalo. By 1890 the buffalo seemed to have gone back in the earth. The Ghost Dance promised to bring them back. Praying for the prosperity of the Lakȟóta people through the Ghost Dance was uplifting, not strange or scary for them. It was only strange and scary for the whites who could not or refused to understand the new religion.[48]

After receiving powerful visions, Black Elk believed that the Ghost Dance was going to give his people "a place in this earth where they would be happy every day and that their nation might live." It would bring them "back into the hoop." In his youth Black Elk had a vision where he was given the powers to heal and to help his people. In his vision he saw a sacred tree that was in full bloom representing the Lakȟóta people. Now his people were suffering, slowly withering away, like the tree eventually did. Black Elk doubted the Messiah's teachings at first, but then during a Ghost Dance ceremony, he saw this tree in the center of the dance circle and again in a vision: "Under the tree that never bloomed I stood and cried because it faded away. I cried and asked the Great Spirit to help me to [make it] bloom again." After that he wholeheartedly embraced the Ghost Dance as a way to make his people prosper again, and it reminded him of the powers he received in his boyhood vision. His mission was to bring the people back into the sacred hoop through the Ghost Dance.[49]

Countless visions brought new features to the Ghost Dance. The visions inspired new dancing garments that the whites called ghost shirts, or rather Ghost Dance shirts. The Lakȟóta name for the shirts was ógle wakȟáŋ (sacred shirt). These simple fabric shirts were special, because the Lakȟóta believed that they brought protection from the bullets of the whites. There has been much debate over the origins of the shirts, including suggestions that it originated with the Mormons or Wovoka. Regardless of origin, many tribes used special garments while dancing, but their supposed bulletproof nature was a purely Lakȟóta idea.[50]

At first, the shirts were basic garments decorated with traditional images, but in the fall of 1890, when the United States army came to stifle the religious "rebellion," the Ghost Dancers sought protection from the shirts. Kicking Bear believed that the power of the Ghost Dance would protect believers from enemy bullets. "I will take from the whites the secret of making gunpowder, and the powder they now have on hand will not burn when it is directed against the red people, my children, who know the songs and the dances of the ghosts [spirits]," he said. Little Wound was told by the Great Spirit in a vision that if the wičháša wakȟáŋ of the Ghost Dance "would make for the dancers medicine shirts and pray over them, no harm could come to the wearer; that the bullet of any whites that desired to stop the Messiah dance would fall to the ground without doing anyone harm, and the person firing such shots would drop dead."[51]

Pretty Eagle had a vision instructing him how to paint these shirts with protective designs.

The grass was very green and I climbed up and I was standing with someone. Then he said: "Look at this, make shirts in this way and give them to them [the Ghost Dancers]! . . . So when I looked there an eagle was flying off spreading his wings and on both sides there were stars. And a sun was attached to the back of the eagle. And it went flying off. And again it reached there and said this: "Make four in this manner: two for men and two for women."[52]

After the dance a tipi was set up and people gathered to receive shirts painted by Pretty Eagle. Sweet grass was spread out in the tipi and in there Pretty Eagle painted the shirts and the dresses. "On the upper part of the back I painted an eagle; and then on both shoulders I painted stars; and on the chest I painted the moon," described Pretty Eagle. Black Elk too received instructions in a vision, and he claimed to have been the first to make these shirts.[53]

Thus, Ghost Dance shirts functioned the same way as the shields in traditional warfare: their protection arose from their spiritual "power," rather than the material used. The power of the Ghost Dance shirts was based on the symbols that decorated the shirts. Interpreting the Ghost Dance as a sign of warlike intentions or militant tactics is common but incorrect. On October 30, 1890, Short Bull supposedly gave a speech, which has often been interpreted as evidence that ghost shirts were intended for war. In the speech Short Bull discussed sacred shirts that would protect the wearer. He claimed that bullets would not cause any harm and that soldiers and other whites would be dead. In this speech Short Bull makes several references to Lakȟóta traditional beliefs. He discusses the flowering tree that was also present in Black Elk's vision. The *Omaha Daily Bee* and the *Chicago Tribune* published Short Bull's speech and immediately interpreted it as a call to arms. However, no Indian source, not even Short Bull, mentions this speech, and it appears to be a fabrication.[54]

Scholars also interpreted the Ghost Dance shirts as preparatory for war, based on a mistranslation of George Sword's words. Sword wrote in Lakȟóta and according to early translations he said that the shirts were "made for war." A much better translation of that sentence is: "They said that they would wear those [the Ghost Dance shirts and dresses] when they dance and that they would wear them when they fight." The text continues "whenever they shoot bullets at the sacred shirts, sacred dresses, and sacred leggings, the bullets will not pierce them; that is why each man and woman wears them and whoever they have as enemies and point their guns to shoot is not able to do it, and also if they shoot at those, the bullets cannot pierce the shirts."[55]

So, Sword simply noted that the shirts would be worn if there was a fight, not that they were "made for war." It is also crucial to understand that in the traditional Lakȟóta belief system a person could become invulnerable through

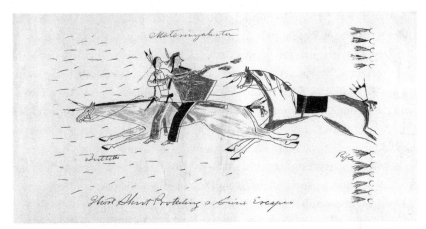

"Ghost Shirt Protecting a Sioux Escape." Drawing by Sitting Bull. The drawing depicts two men wearing bulletproof ghost dance shirts escaping soldiers' fire. Courtesy of the Buffalo Bill Center of the West, Cody, Wyoming, MS 290, Sitting Bull Ledger Drawings Research Collection.

personal sacred experiences and war medicine. His wóthawe (war power / medicine) could protect him. Thus, what Short Bull, Black Elk, Pretty Eagle, and others describe is an innovation derived from Lakȟóta traditions, where invincibility is not strange or uncommon. The shirt gaining protective features reflects growing Lakȟóta concerns; the invulnerability feature appeared only *after* the military invaded Lakȟóta reservations on November 19–20, 1890. A military intervention had seemed likely and many Ghost Dancers were scared. There was a desperate need for these protective garments and the visions of prominent medicine men confirmed that the shirts had the power to protect from the bullets of the wašíču. Short Bull explained it simply, "the ghost shirt is wakȟáŋ."[56]

"Our Dance Is a Religious Dance"

In the fall of 1890, Ghost Dancers were dancing with more regularity. They believed that the more they danced, the faster the new world would come. Wovoka had only told them to dance every six weeks, but the Lakȟóta danced almost daily.[57] This was one of the reasons the whites viewed the dancers with increasing suspicion. Newspapers and settlers in South and North Dakota and Nebraska called for troops to come and put the "uprising" down. Newspapers wrote about fierce fighting between whites and Lakȟóta, only to contradict themselves the next day. Wild rumors about bloodthirsty Indians dancing in their religious orgies spread all the way to Washington, DC. Senator Henry L. Dawes accused the newspapers of sensationalizing and spreading terror, as the agents and soldiers reported that everything was peaceful. Senator Dawes, nevertheless, laid blame on some "malcontents" who refused to work and be educated. They were led by Red Cloud and Sitting Bull, who supposedly fomented the trouble. Dawes believed Sitting Bull commanded as many as 5,000 warriors, while the Lakȟóta did not even have 5,000 warriors willing or able to fight the US Army. Neither Red Cloud nor Sitting Bull were in any way trying to start an uprising.[58]

A common view until recently has been that the Lakȟóta changed both the message and the ceremony of the Ghost Dance because they were militant, hated the whites, and wanted to use the Ghost Dance to start an uprising. Recent scholarship, however, demonstrates that the Lakȟóta Ghost Dance retained its spiritual core until the end, and that external factors caused the ensuing bloodshed. Traditional Lakȟóta spirituality did not have a particular doctrine or unified message. Rather, everyone added his or her experiences to the entire belief system. Although there was a basic structure, the Lakȟóta spiritual world was flexible and revelatory. The changes in the Ghost Dance must be seen as a part of this constantly evolving belief system.[59]

The Lakȟóta Ghost Dance contained elements that could be interpreted as militant, but only after the US Army had been sent to stifle the alleged "rebellion." Even then, Lakȟóta Ghost Dancers did not at any stage approach white settlements or use violence against whites. They did, however, commit depredations on the property of non-Ghost Dancing Lakȟóta, and threatened American Horse, who complained that the dancers had entered his cabin and shot at a picture of himself hanging on the wall. He was afraid he might be killed. "If the Indians should kill me, remember I shall die for a good cause," he lamented. They also stole some of his cattle.[60]

After the arrival of the military, the Ghost Dancers were certainly agitated and worried, but they directed their anger against those Lakȟóta who had signed the 1889 agreement and those who refused to join the Ghost Dance. It was not into a crusade against the wašíču. The Lakȟóta did not forget the Christian teachings of the Ghost Dance, but neither did the Ghost Dance and its Christian characteristics obscure the old beliefs or sacred powers. The Ghost Dance was a syncretic revitalization movement, combining the old religion and Christianity and bringing new dimensions to both. It became part of Lakȟóta spirituality. Throughout the Ghost Dance period the Christian message comes through in the Lakȟóta Ghost Dance and its songs and visions, as well as in speeches by Ghost Dancers.

The Ghost Dance's foundational principle of resurrection is a purely Christian idea, but the traditional Euro-American background can make it challenging to interpret the practice of melding various seemingly disparate practices into "one" religion. Just as with whites at the time, some recent interpretations have rigidly divided the Lakȟóta into Ghost Dancers, or conservatives, and non–Ghost Dancers, or progressives. In practice, this has resulted in a division into Ghost Dancers who opposed the whites and Christian Lakȟóta who sided with the whites. However, the divisions were not that simple.[61]

The religious message of the Ghost Dance was understandable to both "progressive" and "traditional" Lakȟóta. The fact that some progressive Lakȟóta did not turn to the Ghost Dance reflected political divisions rather than religious ones. Many progressives were intrigued by the promise of the Ghost Dance but did not join because they had chosen to live as the whites expected them to. Many feared that disobeying the agents might lead to trouble. Ring Thunder (Čhaŋgléška Wakíŋyaŋ), an elderly Sičháŋǧu, explained his sentiments to former Rosebud agent Lebbeus Foster Spencer: "The Ghost Dancers told me if I would join them, I would never have any more pain or sorrow, but if I followed after the ways of the white man, my path would be hard and full of trouble." Ring Thunder told them that once he was one of their bravest warriors, but now that time was past. "The ways of the white man seem hard at times, but if they will give us back our beef and rations, all will be well with us," he wrote in a hopeful tone.[62]

Good Voice (Hó Wašté) also wrote to Spencer on December 12, 1890, worrying about the Ghost Dance, but also complaining about the dismal situation on the reservation: "I have always been a friend of the whites and try to do as they tell, and I believe the good people of the Church and the good book that tell[s] there is only one God, and that God don't like bad people." He explained that he had always tried to live as white people and sent his children to school since he wanted them to live as white people. "Now in my old days," he wrote, "I am not going to be foolish and join the dance. . . . The Great Father at Washington told us to take our land and I built a house and I ploughed some land and try to raise corn and potatoes, and some years we have some, but last year we had no rain and we had no crop so we have nothing to eat, only what the Great Father at Washington gives us, and we do not get much and we are hungry sometimes."[63]

While Good Voice and Ring Thunder describe practical reasons for not joining the Ghost Dance, some Christian Lakȟóta and Dakȟóta saw the Ghost Dance as a return to heathenism that would lead the Lakȟóta people to destruction. Sam White Bird from Lower Brulé Reservation said that the Messiah was a false prophet and those who believed in him would be deceived and disappointed. He warned: "My friends, I want you to be clear-minded. Many take part in the prayers and they say that they believe in the spirit words. But the sacred book also said this: Messiah lies and false prophets will spring up and they will show big sights and do great deeds, in that way the ones that will choose them will be deceived."[64] Although the Ghost Dance was for some progressive Lakȟóta a way to combine old and new, many opposed it, fearing unrest and suspicion. This practical approach caused an internal conflict amongst the Lakȟóta and exacerbated long-standing factionalism.[65]

On November 20, US Army troops arrived at Pine Ridge and Rosebud, and their arrival early in the morning took the Lakȟóta by complete surprise. Luther Standing Bear at Rosebud describes waking up to loud commands and, to his great surprise, seeing soldiers marching just outside his window. "We were doing nothing which demanded the presence of the troops, but they were coming just the same, and we wondered why."[66]

The army's task was to suppress a rebellion and protect local settlers, and if possible, do it while avoiding bloodshed. That is why the troops wanted to avoid disarming the Indians, a move that was expected to meet resistance.[67] Throughout the reservation years, the Lakȟóta had often argued with their agents, but they had seldom taken matters far enough to warrant the presence of the military. The Lakȟóta knew the power of the US Army all too well, and they feared it. The presence of soldiers at Pine Ridge and Rosebud caused confusion, even panic, among the Lakȟóta. Fearing possible army hostility or violence, hundreds of non-Ghost Dancers moved nearer to the agency buildings on the reservations to show their friendliness. Thomas P. Ashley, a Catholic Lakȟóta, described the fear and confusion he felt in a letter to Agent McLaughlin: "Oh Father help me through this trouble, so that I may live happy in this dark world and work for my Father, who is in heaven."[68] Two Episcopalian girls wrote to Bishop William B. Hare, "But, dear Bishop, do not worry about us, for we are trying very hard not to be led away to believe in false ones. When I hear an Indian talk of this strange story, I tell them of the Saviour who came to save all the world."[69]

The Ghost Dancers were also confused by the arrival of the soldiers. At Pine Ridge, dances continued even more enthusiastically under the leadership of Little Wound, Big Road, and No Water. Warriors under Little Wound's leadership circled around the reservations, urging everyone to join the Ghost Dancers. According to the whites, the Lakȟóta were preparing an attack, but all participating Indians insisted they were keeping guard only to prepare for a possible attack by the soldiers. The Lakȟóta told the whites that they would be dancing throughout the winter. They did not plan to attack, but they would defend themselves if necessary. As Little Wound said: "I understand [heard] that the soldiers have come on the reservation. What have they come for? We have done nothing. Our dance is a religious dance and we are going to dance until spring. If we find then that the Christ does not appear, we will stop dancing; but, in the meantime, troops or no troops, we shall start our dance on this [Medicine Root] creek in the morning." Sadly, his words were interpreted as a declaration of war.[70]

In November, about 40 percent of the Indian population at Pine Ridge and 30 percent at Rosebud were Ghost Dancers. At Cheyenne River, it was 15 percent, and at Standing Rock only 10 percent. At Rosebud more than 1,100 Sičháŋǧu decided to move with Two Strike and Crow Dog toward the western border of the reservation, where they planned to join the Pine Ridge Oglála with Short Bull's people. Along the way, they were joined by 700 Oglála who had lived near the border between the reservations. On Cheyenne River, the news that soldiers had arrived at Pine Ridge and Rosebud caused Ghost Dancers to unite under the leadership of two chiefs. Altogether, 600–700 Mnikȟówožu were dancing almost uninterruptedly in Big Foot and Hump's camp, both of whom at this point were unconditional supporters of the Ghost Dance religion. It is important, however, to understand that these numbers are not exact, as there was much movement back and forth between the Ghost Dance camps and camps close to the agencies. Some people went out of curiosity, while others joined for a time and then went back to the agencies.[71]

On October 9, Kicking Bear had introduced the Ghost Dance at Standing Rock Reservation. By November, dances were held in Sitting Bull's camp on Grand River, but the dancers were closely watched by the Indian Police who were loyal to the agent. Gen. Nelson A. Miles, who was in command of the troops, believed Sitting Bull was responsible for all the unrest and wanted to arrest him. Agent McLaughlin too hoped to arrest Sitting Bull, but he wanted the Indian Police to do it. McLaughlin claimed that he could control the Indians on his reservation and did not need help from the army. He trusted his Indian Police, who had long viewed Sitting Bull as their main rival in the contest for power at Standing Rock.[72]

Many Indians and white visitors at the camp said that Sitting Bull did not truly believe in the Ghost Dance, although he approved of the dancing. They said that Sitting Bull was trying to obtain a vision that would prove that the religion was true. Not having received one, he remained doubtful. Sitting Bull, nevertheless, firmly opposed any violence.[73] He emphasized that if the Ghost Dance was not true the dancing would eventually stop. When accused of taking children out of schools and churches to attend the dances he replied, "I do not want to keep them out of school. I want them to go to school, but they must learn this religion wóčhekiye. As soon as they have learned this religion they shall go back to school." He used the word wóčhekiye (prayer) to describe the Ghost Dance, showing that he understood and was intrigued about its religious message even if he had not received a vision to confirm it.[74]

In fact, Sitting Bull wanted to learn more about the religion firsthand. He even asked Agent McLaughlin for permission to travel west to meet Wovoka. He invited the agent to join him. He promised McLaughlin that if the religion turned out false, upon returning to Standing Rock he would tell his people that it was a lie. The agent declined his offer.[75] Sitting Bull did not give up. In a letter to McLaughlin he tried to explain his position:

> God made you—made all the white race and also made the red race—and gave them both might and hear [sic] to know everything in the world, but gave the whites the advantage over the Indians. But today God, our father, is helping us Indians. So all we Indians believe. Therefore I think this way: I wish no man to come to me in my prayers with gun or knife. Therefore all the Indians pray to God for life, and try to find a good road. . . . This is what we want, and to pray to God. But you did not believe us. You should say nothing against our religion, for we said nothing against yours. You pray to God. So do all of us Indians, as well as the whites. We both pray to only one God, who made us all.[76]

Sitting Bull reflected on his strained relationship with the agent. He wrote: "Therefore, my friend, you don't like me. Well, my friend, I don't like it myself when someone is foolish. You don't like me because you think I am a fool, and you imagine that, if I were not here, all the Indians would become civilized, and that, because I am here, all the Indians are fools." He concluded his letter by writing that he was "obliged to go to Pine Ridge Agency and investigate this Ghost Dance religion."[77]

Sitting Bull was not allowed to go west to meet Wovoka, but he felt the need to go to Pine Ridge to learn more. This ultimately gave McLaughlin an excuse to arrest him. He had been looking for an opportunity for a long time and Sitting Bull's plan to leave the reservation was exactly what he had hoped for. It set in motion a chain of events that dramatically escalated the situation on all Lakȟóta reservations.[78]

A Disaster

On the morning of December 15, 1890, Indian Police knocked on the door of Sitting Bull's cabin. They told him the agent had ordered his arrest. Sitting Bull at first agreed to join the policemen, asking them to let him put on his clothes. Sergeant Bullhead (Tȟatȟáŋka Pȟá), a well-known enemy of Sitting Bull, led the policemen. He had been chosen by McLaughlin, who was well aware of the old disputes between Sitting Bull, Bullhead, and several other policemen in the group. As Sitting Bull came out of the cabin a crowd started to gather. Then Catch the Bear (Matȟó Wáwoyuspa) arrived on the scene and told Sitting Bull not to go. Sergeant Red Tomahawk (Čhaŋȟpí Lúta) held a pistol against Sitting Bull's head. Sitting Bull's young son, Crow Foot, also told him not to go and in reply Sitting Bull changed his mind and said he would not go. There was an exchange of fire, in which Sitting Bull and several other people were killed. Bullhead was mortally wounded, other policemen then entered Sitting Bull's cabin, and policeman John Loneman (Išnála Wičháša) ruthlessly shot Crow Foot, who had been hiding inside the cabin. A US Army unit that was left behind as backup rushed to the scene. In the ensuing fight a few more Indians were killed, but most of Sitting Bull's followers escaped.[79]

Agent McLaughlin had masterfully used existing internal rivalries among the Standing Rock Lakȟóta to set up Sitting Bull. The agent outmaneuvered General Miles, who had also sought to arrest Sitting Bull. One can only surmise that the outcome would have been different if the arrest had been made by the army and not by the Indian police. Rev. Phillip J. Deloria believed that he might have been able to prevent Sitting Bull's death. He had tried to convince the Ghost Dancers to abandon the new religion. Only a day before Sitting Bull was killed, Reverend Deloria was planning to go into his camp and talk to him. McLaughlin forbade him to go, perhaps because it might have interfered with his plan. Many years later Deloria was certain that if he had made the trip, Sitting Bull would not have been killed. In any case, Sitting Bull died at the hands of his own people, just like a bird had told him in a vision a few days earlier.[80]

Ghost Dancers from both Pine Ridge and Rosebud gathered at a safe haven they called Óhaŋzi (place of shelter) in the Badlands. Hundreds of non–Ghost Dancers joined them out of fear of the army. Gen. John R. Brooke, who oversaw the troops in the field, tried to get them to surrender and return to the agencies.

His negotiations bore fruit and some of the Ghost Dancers gradually moved closer
to the agency. Even Little Wound and Big Road now abandoned the religion,
since they feared the possibility of bloodshed. Just then the news of Sitting Bull's
death came, halting the journey to the agency.[81]

Adding to the confusion, chief Big Foot and his people left Cheyenne River
headed toward Pine Ridge. Big Foot had been under tremendous pressure from
the agent to move near the agency and abandon dancing. He assured the agent
that they were not planning to leave the reservation or plotting any violence.
Hump had already abandoned the dancers and was serving as a scout. Big Foot,
too, realized the danger in continuing the dance. He was trying to find a balance between appeasing those who wanted to dance and those who did not.
In addition, Red Cloud, No Water, and Little Wound invited Big Foot to Pine
Ridge where they planned to discuss ways to calm the situation.[82] The news of
Sitting Bull's death was like a spark in a powder keg. Anxiety, uncertainty, fear,
and confusion created an explosive situation. Big Foot's people were told that
the army planned to surround and arrest them. After much hesitation, they
decided to leave for Pine Ridge to seek help from Red Cloud. The escape from
Cheyenne River was hard on the Lakȟóta. The temperature was low and Big
Foot was suffering from pneumonia. Still, they managed to evade the troops
for several days. Eventually, on December 28, Big Foot's party surrendered to
the army unit led by Maj. Samuel Whiteside. One of the warriors approaching
the troops explained later that, as they did not know what the troops were planning, they "agreed not to fight, but to get in line and go toward them abreast
and if the soldiers began firing we would charge and wipe them out."[83] After a
short parley, Big Foot was placed in an ambulance wagon and the refugees were
taken to a camp by Wounded Knee Creek.[84] The next day, the Lakȟóta were to
be taken to Pine Ridge Agency, where they had in fact been headed all along.
Overnight, the army received reinforcements, and Col. James W. Forsyth took
charge. General Miles had been furious when he learned of Big Foot's escape.
He was convinced that Big Foot had left on a war party and ordered his troops
to "find, arrest, disarm, and destroy him" if need be.[85]

At dawn on December 29, the Indians gathered for a meeting. They were
informed that they had to surrender all their weapons. Alice Ghost Horse, who
was only 13 years old at the time, remembered how the soldiers came down to the
tipis and "started to search the wagons for axes, knives, guns, bow and arrows,
and awls. They were really rude about it, they scattered the belongings all over
the ground. The soldiers picked up everything they could find and tied them

up in a blanket and took them."[86] During the talks, the medicine man Yellow
Bird (Ziŋtkála Zí), began to sing Ghost Dance songs and pray for help from
Wakȟáŋ Tȟáŋka. The soldiers thought this was a call to arms. The Lakȟóta men
sat around Big Foot's tent, surrounded by soldiers, and cannons were placed on
a nearby ridge. Chaos ensued when Black Fox (Coyote; Šuŋgmánitu Sápa), who
was deaf and unable to speak, fired his gun. The soldiers panicked and opened
fire on both the men sitting in a semicircle and the women and children in the
camp. Big Foot was immediately killed.[87]

Both Alice Ghost Horse and Dewey Beard remember the chaos. "I heard the
first shot coming from the center followed by rifles going off all over, occasionally a big boom came from the big guns on wheels. The Lakȟóta were all disarmed so all they could do was scatter in all directions. The two cavalry groups
came charging down, shooting at everyone who is running and is a Lakȟóta,"
recalled Alice Ghost Horse. She fled into a ravine amidst heavy gunfire. In the
utter confusion people were calling for their children. "With children crying
everywhere, my dad said he was going to go out to help the others, my mother
objected but he left anyway. Pretty soon, my father came crawling back in and he
was wounded below his left knee and he was bleeding," remembers Ghost Horse.
Her father took her youngest brother who was 6 years old and said he was taking
him farther down the river. Soon, according to Ghost Horse, "he came crawling
back in and said: 'Huŋhuŋhé, michíŋkši kté pelo.' [My son is dead!] He had tears
in his eyes, so we cried a little bit because there was no time to think. My father
said we should crawl further down, but my mother said it's better we die here
together, and she told me to stand up, so I did, but my father pulled me down."
Finally, they were able to crawl to a better hiding place and made their escape.[88]

Dewey Beard was wounded and lost several family members, including his
wife, brother, and father in the massacre. He remembers how the shooting started:
"It appeared to me that all the soldiers began to shoot, and I saw Indians falling all around me. I was not expecting anything like this." Beard recalls how
frightened he was, and he started running through the smoke. He took out his
knife. Suddenly he felt a gun being pointed at him and fired. It was so close that
it burnt his hair. Beard then "grabbed the gun and stabbed at the soldier with
my knife. I stabbed him three times and he let go the gun . . . I saw some soldiers
aiming at me and I felt something hit me in the shoulder and I fell down." The
next thing Beard saw was another soldier aiming at him, but he missed. Beard
soon realized he was seriously wounded: "I began to breathe very hard and every
breath hurt me very much. I got up and tried to run but could not, so I walked.

I was struggling with something warm in my throat and mouth. I spit it out and looked at it, and it was blood, so I knew that I was shot." [89] Dewey Beard survived, but approximately 250 Lakȟóta were killed in the massacre. Most of them were women and children.[90]

Different theories have blamed different people for the massacre, but it is clear that the Indians did not intend to oppose the military. They simply wanted to escape and find refuge in Red Cloud's camp. The army besieged them with Hotchkiss cannons aimed directly at the camp. Clearly the army did not want them to escape a second time. Relevant in this context is General Miles's order to disarm the Indians. The army commander, Gen. John M. Schofield, had repeatedly stated that disarming the Indians was too dangerous. It would only lead to suspicion and probably provoke a fight. Despite this, Miles insisted on disarming the Indians. A massacre resulted.

Wounded Knee devastated the Lakȟóta. Many lives were lost, and chaos ensued at Pine Ridge. Hundreds of people fled to the Badlands, and they forced Red Cloud to join them. In the Badlands they continued Ghost Dancing but there were deep divisions in the camp. The army had demonstrated that it could not be trusted, yet there really was no way to wage war against the wašíču. Man Afraid of His Horses tried to talk in favor of peace. They could not fight in the middle of the winter. The suffering it would cause among their women and children would be enormous. Short Bull, Kicking Bear, and other Ghost Dancers threatened those who wanted to leave the camp. Despite this, in the early days of January small groups slipped away and returned to the agency. Red Cloud was among them.

General Miles arrived at Pine Ridge on December 30 and took charge of the military operations. He sought to negotiate and at the same time tighten the net around the Ghost Dancers. The two-pronged tactic was effective. One of the most successful attempts was made by Standing Bear. Luther Standing Bear later recalled his father's mission: "This was a most dangerous mission to attempt to perform, as the Indians had declared they would kill anyone who came to them, regardless of color. The white man had started the fight, and now he wanted the Indian to act as mediator!" He went to the Ghost Dancers' camp knowing that tensions in the camp were high. He met with the leaders and offered them the pipe. One of the men in the camp shouted to him: "The white people have killed our people without mercy, and we want to fight them. Why have you brought us this pipe of peace?" Standing Bear was afraid he would be killed, but finally the pipe was accepted. Standing Bear had come, like George Sword thirteen years earlier to Crazy Horse's camp, as a concerned relative. Offering the pipe was to evoke kinship rules, and when it was accepted, he knew there would be a chance for peace. Indeed, Standing Bear's effort bore fruit and the remaining Ghost Dancers surrendered on January 15, 1891. Luther Standing Bear later lamented, "Now that peace was finally restored, who was given the credit for it? Did the Indian who had brought the peace pipe receive any honor for the part he played? No, indeed! All the credit went to General Miles, who was proclaimed the great peacemaker."[91]

The Lakȟóta Ghost Dance differed from Ghost Dances as practiced in other tribes. To outside white witnesses it might have looked "wild and barbaric," but the Lakȟóta never militarized it, as has been claimed. It only reflected Lakȟóta religious traditions. The Lakȟóta Ghost Dance also evolved in response to the needs of the Lakȟóta. Traditional Lakȟóta religious ceremonies had been banned in 1883, and the Ghost Dance presented a possibility of practicing their ancestral traditions again. The Ghost Dance was more than an attempt to revitalize a "dying" culture or bring back old ways; it was also an innovation. The Ghost Dance sought to accommodate. It was forward looking.[92] It sought to find a balance between the old way and the new. From the Euro-American perspective, it appeared as a "backward" movement. For the Lakȟóta, the life they were hoping to get back to was better than life on the reservation. The white man's civilization had not yielded prosperity for the Lakȟóta, so perhaps the Ghost Dance can be seen as a progressive religion that sought a path to prosperity for the Lakȟóta as well. The Ghost Dance, Black Elk hoped, would bring the Lakȟóta people back into the sacred hoop. With the Ghost Dance the sacred tree would bloom again and the Lakȟóta people would prosper. That dream died at Wounded Knee.

PART THREE

10

OWÁKPAMNI OYÁŊKE
THE RESERVATION

In the remainder of our book we explore the many ways throughout the twentieth and twenty-first centuries in which the Lakȟóta have continued to adapt to often hostile external forces while maintaining a distinctive Lakȟóta culture and ethos. They survived and even thrived despite disastrous federal policies that often backfired and undermined their cultural and political sovereignty and economic well-being. The Lakȟóta found innovative ways to indigenize their modern experiences, carrying on the warrior tradition by fighting valiantly and honorably in US wars, leading pantribal coalitions of Native American people protecting and preserving their rights, maintaining and revitalizing their traditional culture and spirituality, and playing a fundamental role in the American Indian Movement. All these efforts were part of a broader reclamation and renaissance of Lakȟóta individual and collective identity.

The Spirits No Longer Come to Help

In his July 4, 1903, abdication speech, Red Cloud would reflect on the immense changes that had taken place during his lifetime:

> I was born a Lakȟóta and I have lived a Lakȟóta and I shall die a Lakȟóta. Before the white man came to our country, the Lakȟóta were a free people. They made their own laws and governed themselves as it seemed good to them. Then they were independent and happy. Then they could choose

their own friends and fight their enemies. Then men were brave and to be trusted. The white man came and took our lands from us. They put [us] in bounds and made laws for us. We were not asked what laws would suit us. But the white men made the laws to suit themselves and they compel us to obey them. This is not good for an Indian. . . . The white man has taken our territory and destroyed our game so we must eat the white man's food or die.[1]

Following the 1890 Wounded Knee massacre, several Lakȟóta chiefs traveled to Washington to explain to the authorities what had happened and how they had been misunderstood and mistreated. They complained about life on the reservation and broken promises. The Lakȟóta people were suffering from diseases and always hungry.

The chiefs explained that they tried very hard to do as the white men told them, but there were too many obstacles. Their annual appropriations had been cut, despite promises to the contrary. This, the chiefs said, was the root cause of the trouble. They emphasized that no Lakȟóta, not even the Ghost Dancers, planned any violence, but they were desperate. Little Wound said some people believed the only way to get noticed was to make noise. Good Thunder summarized the events of the previous year, saying, "A whirlwind passed through our country and did much damage, we let that pass." The chiefs indicated they were willing to work with the government for the good of the people, even though it clearly meant they had to find a new way of life.[2]

In 1883, Secretary of the Interior Henry M. Teller established Courts of Indian Offenses and outlawed the Sun Dance, healing ceremonies, spirit keeping, giveaways, traditional dances, and other distinctively indigenous practices. Being confined on reservations robbed the Lakȟóta of their connection to the land and the freedom to roam, a core element of Lakȟól wičhóȟ'aŋ (Lakȟóta traditional ways). Reservation life also impacted gender roles, especially for men, whose traditional pursuits of intertribal warfare and hunting no longer had any place in the reservation context. Further, there were few economic and employment opportunities. Throughout this transitional period, life made little sense, and depression, alcohol abuse, and domestic issues grew alarmingly.[3]

"Nowadays the people live like captives," explained George Bushotter, a Sioux of mixed Iháŋkthuŋwaŋ and Lakȟóta ancestry, in 1887, "and they [the white man] have made women of us," meaning that the traditional ways for men to gain prestige, wealth, and authority had been destroyed when intertribal warfare was prohibited.[4] Luther Standing Bear agreed:

> When I had reached young manhood the warpath for the Lakȟóta was a thing of the past. The hunter had disappeared with the buffalo, the war scout had lost his calling, and the warrior had taken his shield to the mountaintop and given it back to the elements. The victory songs were sung only in the memory of the braves, and even they soon went unsung under a cruel and senseless ban of our overseers. So I could not prove that I was a brave and would fight to protect my home and land. I could only meet the challenge as life's events came to me.[5]

Tuberculosis ravaged an already vulnerable population around the turn of the twentieth century. James R. Walker, the Pine Ridge Agency physician, estimated that nearly half the population was affected by it.[6] Assistant Medical Supervisor Ferdinand Shoemaker at Rosebud Reservation made similar observations in 1914–16. He toured various reservations and proclaimed that the situation at Rosebud was grave. Rosebud lacked a proper hospital, and the nurses, often Lakȟóta women, usually lacked any formal training. Although the Blackpipe District at Rosebud was affected the worst, infant mortality was high throughout the reservation.[7] Anna Charging Bear (Matȟó Watȟákpa) lost her younger son and then witnessed as her older son was sick for eight years before passing away after influenza confined him to bed for the last six months of his life. Before he died the boy consoled his mother: "Mother, I loved my little brother and he has gone from out of my sight, and I want to see him again; and now, mother, father, I shall not follow on with you, but though I go and leave you both, do not be sad."[8]

To make matters worse, many Lakȟóta children were sent away to boarding schools. When they returned to the reservation, it was often as strangers. The language they spoke had changed and the knowledge and skills they learned at school were often impractical in the reservation setting.[9] As George Sword explained, "The young Oglála do not understand a formal talk by an old Lakȟóta, because the white people have changed the Lakȟóta language, and the young people speak it as the white people have written it."[10] In addition to children being taken from their families, the living conditions in the schools were far from healthy. Assistant Medical Supervisor Ferdinand Shoemaker, at one of the boarding schools for Standing Rock children, described the school's sanitary conditions as dismal. Measles and other diseases spread quickly among the

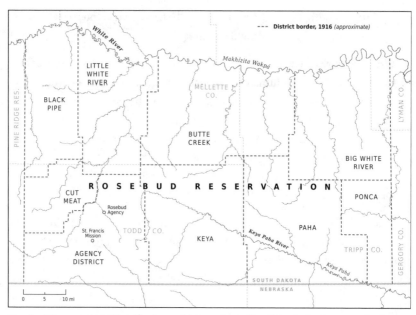

Rosebud Reservation Districts in 1916. Map adapted by Erin Greb Cartography from a drawing in "Report of Assistant Medical Supervisor Ferdinand Shoemaker on the Rosebud Reservation, SD, 1915–1916," MS 681, Buffalo Bill Center of the West, Cody, Wyoming.

students. He reported similar conditions at Rosebud Reservation where day schools were poorly equipped and sanitary conditions abysmal.[11]

There was also a sense of spiritual loss, a fear that the spirits of old had abandoned the Lakȟóta or had retreated before the white man's God. This struck at the heart of Lakȟól wičhóȟ'aŋ and the special relationship between humans and the universe, in which the forces of wakȟáŋ and an appreciation of the mysteries of life were central. According to Little Wound, "In old times everything had its shadow (ghost or spirit). The shaman could invoke the spirit of the Tȟatȟáŋka [Buffalo Bull], or of the Íŋyaŋ [Rock], or any other good and powerful influence (tȟúŋ), and it would come and do his bidding. Now the shamans have lost their power. The spirits no longer come to help men." Echoing these sentiments, the Oglála Afraid of Bear (Matȟó Kȟokípȟapi) explained that "The spirits do not come and help us now. The white men have driven them away. I can bring the spirits sometimes now. But they will not come quickly as they did in former times."[12]

Some Lakȟóta made a conscious decision not to teach their children and grandchildren the Lakȟóta language or traditions. Some felt the only way forward was to assimilate and adopt the ways and religion of the white man. Others, after hearing of native children being punished for speaking their languages at boarding school, decided they did not want to subject their young people to such treatment.[13]

Under the influence of the whites, many young Lakȟóta who went away to boarding schools turned their backs on traditional beliefs and ceremonies. The white man's education taught that the beliefs of their ancestors were primitive superstitions and a barrier to civilization and progress. "When I was a very small boy, I believed in [the sacred things] wholeheartedly, and always thought those things were true which they stated. Now I do not think so," George Bush-otter said.[14] Elaborating on this theme, the Oglála John Thunder Bear (Matȟó Wakíŋyaŋ) said, "The young people laugh at the old Huŋká when they tell of the spirits. Probably some of the old Indians could perform the ceremony in the old way. I think they would not tell the secrets to a white man. These secrets are foolishness. I was told them, but I have put them out of my mind. I do not believe them, though I once did."[15]

The post-Wounded Knee era witnessed the nadir of Lakȟóta culture and vitality. And yet, as they had demonstrated countless times before, the Lakȟóta proved resilient, adaptable people who, instead of shrinking from a challenge and assimilating into the melting pot of mainstream American life, found new ways to thrive and assert their Lakȟótaness in the twentieth century.

From Farming to Fishhooks: Lakȟóta Economy

Today, Pine Ridge, Rosebud, Cheyenne River, and Standing Rock are among the twenty largest reservations in the United States. They are also among the poorest. Sadly, poverty has become a major part of reservation culture. Prejudice resorts to stereotypical answers, claiming that the Lakȟóta will not work and would rather live on welfare and government handouts; that they are unreliable, prone to substance abuse, and lazy. Others blame the inefficiency and corruption of the Bureau of Indian Affairs (BIA), while still others blame the Lakȟóta tribal government and leaders themselves. But the economic problems faced by the Lakȟóta have real historical antecedents, as well as many additional complex intertwined factors.[16]

From the beginning of the reservation period in the late 1800s, US government efforts at economic development focused on ranching and farming. From the 1870s until World War I, cattle raising became the basic economy on Lakȟóta reservations. Beginning in 1871, one animal on the hoof was included in each

Lakȟóta's monthly ration. In those early days the Lakȟóta ran their cattle much as they had their horse herds as part of the bison-hunting lifeway. In any case, an interest in cattle developed among the Lakȟóta, and they enjoyed ranching as it connected with their old nomadic equestrian hunter-gatherer culture. According to official reports, the Lakȟóta had 10,000 head of cattle on the open range by 1885 and 40,000 by 1912.[17]

Although the Lakȟóta enjoyed ranching, most accounts hold that they disdained farming, particularly the men, who saw it as beneath them. They disparaged horticultural tribes that relied on farming for subsistence. In the early 1800s the Lakȟóta treated the neighboring horticulturalist Arikara as semislaves who cultivated corn for them, taking on the role of women. Thus, it was extremely problematic when, in the late 1880s, Lakȟóta men were told to become farmers. It was also unrealistic to expect it to happen overnight.[18]

Some Lakȟóta accounts diverge from this insistence that the Lakȟóta resisted farming. Speaking of the days before the Indian Reorganization Act and the Civilian Conservation Corps (CCC), former Superintendent of Rosebud Reservation Harold Schunk commented that "At that time the Indian . . . had taken on some of the good parts of the white man. They had all learned [to be] excellent gardeners."[19] Dora Shoots Off-Bruguier concurred. Discussing her childhood at Cheyenne River Reservation, she explained that her father "had a garden with a lot of corn and squash and almost everything. And one time something grew up real tall, and we didn't know what it was but my brother and I just tried eating it, and it was good. And you know what it was? It was celery." Dora laughed and continued, "Yeah, and we never knew that before!"[20]

Aside from the shifting pressure to be cattle ranchers one year and farmers the next, the transition to reservation life brought many other changes. In 1901, a new method of issuing beef at Pine Ridge had both symbolic and practical significance. Until that time cattle to be issued were turned loose and killed by men on horseback, reminiscent of traditional buffalo hunts. In 1901 that changed: cattle were to be butchered and the meat issued biweekly. To the frustration of the Lakȟóta, the agent sold the hides and each Lakȟóta received little more than a pittance for them. In prereservation days, hides had been a valuable source of raw material and a measure of wealth for the Lakȟóta.[21]

The Oglála of Pine Ridge Reservation exemplify the Lakȟóta reservations in general. The Pine Ridge economy struggled from the beginning. The BIA's shifting position on farming versus ranching created confusion and frustration. Neither economy had much long-term success for various reasons, a critical one

"Sioux Indian Cowboy, circa 1908." Courtesy of South Dakota State Historical Society, South Dakota Digital Archives (2017-05-25-302).

was federal policies that divided up the reservations, ultimately making any large-scale farming or ranching impossible.

The General Allotment Act of 1887 (also known as the Dawes Act) further retarded development. Though intended to assimilate Lakȟóta, this policy would have far-reaching consequences for Lakȟóta people, culture, and social organization, the implications of which are still evident in Lakȟóta communities today. Reservations would be allotted in severalty to individuals, and those who received allotments would be declared citizens of the United States. It was assumed that once an Indian had his own tract of land, he would rapidly become a "civilized," self-sufficient farmer. Like many assimilation-era policies, allotment had a deleterious impact on the Lakȟóta. Allotment began in earnest on various Lakȟóta reservations in the early 1900s and was recorded in the few winter counts that were still being kept in the early twentieth century. No Ears, for example, noted that people received payments—wagons and other goods—for taking up allotments in 1907.[22] Each individual head of family received 160 acres, each single person or orphan over eighteen received 80 acres, and those under eighteen received 40 acres. The lands were placed in trust for twenty-five years, to prevent the Lakȟóta from selling them to unscrupulous whites.[23] Later, leasing and even selling land was allowed. The savvier mixed-blood families selected the best agricultural lands, further distancing themselves from their full-blood relatives. Initially, the Lakȟóta were encouraged to farm on their allotments, but after recognizing the limitations of reservation soil and the arid climate, the government went back to emphasizing stock raising, which suited the Lakȟóta better than farming.[24]

By the turn of the twentieth century, Lakȟóta men were required to work for rations, and in 1902 young men were hired for summer work and paid in cash instead of rations, a novel situation at the time. In general, mixed-blood families continued to prosper economically and were better able to succeed in the white world, which exacerbated long-standing rifts between mixed-bloods and full-bloods. Despite this, the early years of the twentieth century were relatively prosperous for the Lakȟóta.[25]

Unfortunately, while the outbreak of World War I brought short-lived wealth, it led to a longer-term economic crisis for the Lakȟóta. When livestock prices skyrocketed, the Lakȟóta were encouraged to sell their cattle and horses. By 1916 nearly all the herds had been sold off, and, suddenly flush with cash for the first time, the Lakȟóta purchased cars and other luxury items. They leased their land to nonnative cattlemen, and from 1917 to 1921 all the reservation lands at Pine Ridge were leased to nonnatives. The Lakȟóta lived on money from stock sales and land leases. Keeping their cattle and horses, however, would have been more sustainable. The loss of their cattle herds was a disaster in the long run as it had far-reaching consequences. The cattle market crashed in 1921, and many of the cattlemen defaulted on their leases, leaving the Lakȟóta in a dire situation. In the meantime, the Burke Act of 1906, an amendment to the Dawes Act, had made it possible for Indian people to receive fee simple patents to their allotments and hence be able to sell their lands. The government advertised the availability of reservation lands, and land sales skyrocketed because many Lakȟóta were in desperate financial straits.[26]

After this debacle the government once again encouraged the Lakȟóta to farm, despite periodic droughts and the reality that they lacked the capital and mechanized equipment to compete as farmers with their white neighbors. The financial crash of 1929 ended all hopes of agricultural prosperity on the plains. The resulting depression, along with the Dust Bowl disaster in the 1930s, effectively destroyed the reservation's economy. Once again, the Lakȟóta experienced severe economic distress. Still, the people persevered. Harold Schunk explained their resilience: "I think when times are tough, possibly the Indian fares better than he does when times are good, so to speak. The depression came along, and I believe, for the first time in the history of the Indian, everybody got to work, back in the old CC[C] days." According to Schunk, the CCC gave many an opportunity to work for the first time, and even better, steady jobs in the various new developments initiated though the CCC programs.[27]

Oglala Tribal Council Chairman Frank Wilson explained the crisis differently: "For years we have been having a spell of depression. Formerly the Indians did not know what a depression was but when the white man came here he brought money, and that was his God. He worshipped it. Now he taught the Indians to worship money too and that [is] what causes the depression."[28]

To survive, some Lakȟóta resorted to selling nearly everything they owned. Small amounts of money came from land leases and Indian scout pensions; some families dug potatoes for wages in nearby towns; some earned money by selling hay or working as hired hands for the agency; others became policemen or catechists. The government provided limited rations, and many families supplemented these by gathering chokecherries and other wild foods. Throughout the 1930s the Red Cross and the CCC provided invaluable support with food and other necessities, in addition to income from wage work.[29] The CCC also employed Indians in a variety of conservation-related jobs. Lakȟóta were also recruited to rehabilitate nature reserves, plant forests, restore lakes and streams, and extinguish fires. These projects eventually directed cash flow to Lakȟóta reservations as well.[30]

Prior to World War II, Lakȟóta agriculture was concentrated in small family operations. Arthur Amiotte, an Oglála, describes this new way of life, recalling how his aunt Freda Mesteth Goodsell (Tȟawáčhiŋ Wašté Wiŋ) grew up in a large extended Lakȟóta ranching and farming family, and how she learned many "new" life skills early on. These included industrious self-sustaining activities such as homemaking, methods of modern and traditional food preparation, fine needlework and sewing, and the traditional Native American arts of hide tanning and beading. According to Amiotte, "She was expected to ride horseback, drive a team and wagon, milk cows, and move cows to and from pastures. She also participated in gardening, cultivating, and harvesting of crops for family members and livestock."[31]

Many of the small farms failed during the 1930s. Under the 1934 Indian Reorganization Act (IRA), many tribes bought back land and started tribal ranching ventures. One such project was organized in 1937 by the BIA at Red Shirt Table on Pine Ridge—an agricultural cooperative focusing on livestock and poultry breeding and subsistence gardening. After World War II, farming and ranching became increasingly mechanized. This development, with its increased need for capital and changes in lending policies forced many small individual and tribal operations out of business. For example, the number of Rosebud farmers decreased by more than half from 1940 to 1959.[32]

As small-scale agriculture became increasingly difficult on Lakȟóta reservations, wage labor grew in importance. During the Great Depression the Indian Division of the Civilian Conservation Corp (CCC-ID) was the major employer, employing both married and single men, and concentrating its efforts on reservation development close to home. After the CCC-ID ended in 1942, seasonal agricultural work became the principal employer, with Lakȟóta people working for wages harvesting potatoes, corn, and sugar beets in the fields of white farmers outside the reservations. This was around the time that electricity and running water became more common on the reservations. Some Lakȟóta worked as ranch hands on off-reservation ranches as well. The IRA's Revolving Credit Fund did little to aid the economic situation on the reservations and a government campaign to lure manufacturing jobs to the reservations was largely unsuccessful.[33]

Throughout the 1960s and 1970s, economic development projects were attempted on the reservations but most failed to have long-term impact. For example, at Pine Ridge the Oglála Irrigation Project created the Oglála Dam. Built between 1938 and 1941, it sits just south of the reservation town of Oglála. The BIA built it using CCC and Public Works Administration labor. The Oglála Sioux Tribe owns and operates the dam, but as a development project, it has been a failure for a variety of reasons, most notably shifting BIA emphasis and policies. The project's only positive development was Oglála Lake, the reservoir the dam created. The irrigated area created by the dam was brought under the management of the Oglála Sioux Farm and Ranch Enterprise by the early 1970s. The farm employed several Oglála people who planted row crops, garden crops, and small grains. Over 1,000 acres were used for hay and grazing land. The farm also raised cattle and hogs.[34]

Another example is the Wright and McGill fishhook factories that operated at Pine Ridge from 1961 to 1967. The flagship plant was in Pine Ridge town with others in Wounded Knee, Kyle, and Porcupine. Despite the initial success of the factories—aside from the government, they were the most important economic resource on the reservation—they were never actually profitable for Wright and McGill. In 1968 the minimum wage increased and trade restrictions relaxed with Asia, where the company's main competitors were located. Wright and McGill then transferred all single-snelling operations to Mexico, and by the end of July 1967 all its Pine Ridge operations ceased.[35]

The economy on Lakȟóta reservations has been characterized as a service economy, one largely outside the money economy in most of the United States. Based on treaty promises, it is dependent on the federal government for general welfare and economic support—accepting nonnegotiable goods and services from the government, rather than cash. Lakȟóta individuals receive surplus food, medical care, general assistance money, and educational facilities, with few choices among these or in other economic issues. The Lakȟóta service economy appears to be the major underlying factor for the poverty on most reservations and the general alienation from white society. Despite the massive amounts of money expended annually on government subsidies and social service programs, no noticeable alleviation of poverty has occurred on the reservations, suggesting the general ineffectiveness of a service economy for dealing with real economic problems.[36]

The three major sectors of the economy are: agriculture (including cattle raising), manufacturing and commerce, and government and services. A potential fourth sector is tourism. Major economic concerns include: (1) dependence on the federal government for economic support, resulting in the establishment of a service-oriented economy; (2) lack of tribal unity on economic issues and a general distrust of tribal government; (3) management issues; (4) leadership issues and factionalism; (5) multiple planning agency programs often operating with little or no coordination (tribal, BIA, Economic Development Administration, Office of Economic Opportunity, Departments of Labor and Commerce, etc.); (6) lack of development program continuity tied to the tribal electoral system; and (7) lack of a profit incentive—Lakȟóta culture values expediency over economic profit, and, in general, the reservation economic system is not profit oriented. Finally, the reality of extended kinship ties makes it difficult for individuals to accumulate money; the morality of the kin relationship system demands that an individual share with relatives or else be branded a sellout to the white man's way. This is particularly evident among the more traditional full-blood families, but each of these complex issues has a long history that defies simple explanations or solutions.[37]

Today the main employers on the reservations are the federal government, the BIA, the tribal government, tribal colleges, public and mission schools, and casinos and hotels. There are a few gas stations, convenience stores, and fast-food restaurants, coffeeshops where people meet to socialize, and museums, but these places employ relatively few Lakȟóta people. Some entrepreneurial individuals sell their own artistic creations—beadwork, quillwork, jewelry, artwork, and music—to tourists and through the online marketplace.

Itháščhaŋ Théča—New Leaders

In the early twentieth century each reservation had a tribal council controlled by aging famous nineteenth-century leaders who would make their final journey by about 1910. The few continuing winter counts reported the deaths of old chiefs in the early twentieth century—American Horse in 1908, Red Cloud in 1909, and George Sword in 1910.[38] The councils operated in many ways like the councils of the buffalo-hunting days. Meeting discussions focused on matters of general interest pertaining to the common good. One new function was for them to act as a liaison between US government representatives and the people. However, after a dispute, the superintendent at Pine Ridge dissolved the council during the winter of 1917–18. The chiefs, who by now belonged to a younger generation, then established a Treaty Council to pursue treaty claims against the government. But the superintendent managed to maintain some influence over it. In response to this, another group of young Lakȟóta organized the Council of Twenty-One in 1927. It comprised elected representatives from each of the reservation's districts. The Council of Twenty-One immediately found itself at odds with the Treaty Council.[39]

Initially, mixed-bloods tended to stay out of tribal politics, but this changed with the passage of the Indian Reorganization Act (IRA) (Wheeler-Howard Act or "Indian New Deal") in June 1934. The IRA was the centerpiece of Commissioner of Indian Affairs John Collier's New Deal, which reflected his commitment to strengthening tribal identities and reservation communities by encouraging tribal political organization and cultural preservation. Under the IRA, most Lakȟóta tribes adopted constitutions that called for an elected representative government based on the model of the US government. Many tribal members opposed it because it was alien to Lakȟóta cultural understandings of leadership. Arthur Amiotte summarizes the effects of the IRA, saying that it "created reservation elected leadership in governance modeled after nonnative structures and adopted constitutions which gave rise to policies of registration and enrollment of its members for legitimacy as a Lakȟóta tribal member," resulting in increasing identity politics that are connected to questions of who has the access to "any federal or tribal benefits such as medical-health care, education funding, and employment opportunities."[40]

On Pine Ridge the debate centered on how the various districts would be organized and who would have representatives in the tribal council. For example, the Medicine Root District would not allow mixed-bloods to participate in district policies even though the mixed-bloods were the majority in the area. The

Standing Rock Sioux had accepted the IRA already in 1934, but the new con-stitution and its bylaws were hotly contested as late as 1939 when it came before the people in a referendum. There were allegations that people were misled or promised additional allotments if they voted in favor of the new constitution. Some reportedly were threatened with loss of their jobs if they opposed the proposed constitution.[41]

Thus, Lakȟóta reception of the IRA was mixed and tended to exacerbate exist-ing tensions between full-bloods and mixed-bloods. Many traditionalist "Old Dealers" who rejected the IRA preferred the historical relationship they shared with the United States based on treaties. They considered the IRA governments illegal and therefore did not respect the tribal councils or acknowledge their authority. These bitter divisions continue into the present. Exacerbating this lack of respect for the IRA governments was the fact that they had little power. Decisions ultimately had to be approved by the BIA. In the end some reservations rejected the IRA altogether while others adopted it in whole or in part.[42] Although the IRA's goal was to make the Lakȟóta more autonomous, in the end, the Lakȟóta councils resembled puppet governments. Theoretically, power was theirs, but in practice it was not. Rosebud Tribal Council Chairman Antoine Roubideaux voiced his frustration by asking the Commissioner to clarify how the council was supposed to operate when there was no place for it to meet? How was the council supposed to organize the distribution of rations, or who would determine whether the tribe was allowed to collect revenues from the electricity and water provided by the dam that was located on reservation lands? Indeed, some scholars have called the situation neocolonial dependency or indirect colonialism.[43]

Other Lakȟóta looked at it more favorably. Oglala Tribal Council chairman Frank G. Wilson rejoiced after the passing of the IRA. He compared John Col-lier to Abraham Lincoln, referring to him as the great emancipator of Indian people and told the other councilmen: "We have accepted the Howard Wheeler Act, drafted, and ratified our constitution. We have nominated and elected these representatives and other governing officials [who] have just taken the oath of office. Now you must cooperate one hundred per cent in the governmental machinery."[44] In 1967, Harold Schunk reminisced about the tensions created by the IRA. In particular, he noted the heated disagreements among Lakȟóta people on issues like normalizing peyote and the revitalization of the old thiyóšpaye kinship units.[45] Speaking of attempts to revive those old units, Schunk observed that many spent too much time talking and fighting, and that the IRA could have been a "wonderful opportunity" if used to advantage.[46]

After the disastrous policies of the 1940s and 1950s, namely, termination and relocation, the 1960s brought real and important changes to federal Indian policy. Congress extended eligibility for several existing social programs to include Native Americans. Programs such as the Public Works Administration and Public Housing Authority became directly accessible by tribal members. At the same time, the Office of Economic Opportunity (OEO) began to bypass the BIA and fund tribes directly, which meant that for the first time, tribes had discretionary authority over much of the federal spending on their reservations. These new programs provided job opportunities that drew many educated tribal members back to the reservation and spurred the growth of tribal government. With this development, tribal and federal governments became the most stable employers on the reservations. The OEO organized the Three-University Consortium (TUC), which worked to train reservation leaders in technical and managerial skills in order to access and administer the newly available government programs. The Lakȟóta constructed industrial parks and made other improvements in a continuing effort to make the reservations attractive to outside employers.[47]

Tribal governments gained more flexibility and authority in terms of administration throughout the 1960s and 1970s, although responsibility for the creation and planning of programs remained in Washington. At the same time, the self-determination movement in education led to most reservations having three authorities—tribe, BIA, public-school system—none of which were ultimately responsible. The most important piece of federal Indian legislation of the second half of the twentieth century was the Indian Self-Determination and Educational Assistance Act of 1975, which gave tribes the ability to contract and administer programs previously run by the BIA. The long-term impact of self-determination meant that by the 1990s Lakȟóta tribal governments wielded considerable power over the management of their reservations. The BIA grew into a new cooperative-collaboration role. However, responsibility for the land continued to rest with the federal government, not the tribe, and all decisions relating to this most plentiful and valuable asset were subject to review.[48]

The 1990s saw many Sioux tribes capitalize on their sovereign status by creating new economic opportunities, particularly in gaming. Most Lakȟóta reservations established casinos. Several Sioux tribes enjoyed great success in gaming, including the Shakopee Mdewakanton Sioux Community and the Prairie Island Sioux Community. But among the Lakȟóta farther west, due largely to location and population density, casinos did not become the major economic resource and employer they were among tribes located in more heavily populated areas. On Lakȟóta reservations casinos were often tied to other attractions, such as tourist hotels and recreation facilities.[49]

There have been many political developments at Pine Ridge since the 1990s that have reverberated throughout Sioux Country more generally. Starting in the early 2000s many young leaders banded together to protest alcohol sales and unsolved murders in Whiteclay, Nebraska, a border town south of Pine Ridge town whose economy was based largely on alcohol sales to Pine Ridge residents. The Whiteclay protests culminated in the four liquor stores losing their licenses in 2017. In 2006, tribal president Cecilia Fire Thunder was impeached and removed from office after publicly speculating that abortions could be more readily available at Pine Ridge than elsewhere in the state of South Dakota due to the tribe's sovereign status. In 2007, after years of being housed in a series of trailers, Prairie Wind Casino and Hotel opened on Pine Ridge. In 2008, there was an amendment to the OST Constitution and By-Laws, which established, among other things, a new oath of office for OST Council members.[50]

In 2016, many Lakȟóta from all over the country came together in Cannon Ball, North Dakota, on the Standing Rock Reservation to protest the construction of Energy Transfer Partners' Dakota Access Pipeline. In 2020, the outbreak of the global COVID-19 pandemic led to new tensions and a standoff between Lakȟóta tribal governments and the state of South Dakota over tribal roadblocks and checkpoints on reservation lands.[51]

Lakȟóta Life and Society in the Twentieth Century

The reservation period brought major changes to Lakȟóta social life. As the traditional thiyóšpaye scattered throughout the various reservation districts they gradually disintegrated, and the influence and status of their leaders waned. Numerous communities developed on each Lakȟóta reservation, and churches, dance halls, and day schools were built. The reservation system controlled many aspects of life. The Indian police patrolled the borders, and no tribal member could leave without a pass. Government agents made important economic and political decisions with little input from community members. The paternalism of the reservation system produced dependency rather than self-sufficiency. Male roles were undermined by a lack of economic and employment opportunities and relevant practical skills to pass on to younger generations. Women, whose domestic roles continued much as before, became the economic mainstays of the family, while men had little to do. Over time, this idleness and frustration developed into anomie and apathy, which, combined with poverty, made reservation life extremely difficult.[52]

Sacred ceremonies pertaining to women continued throughout the reservation period and are still observed by some traditional people today. Madonna Swan, who was born on the Cheyenne River in 1928, recalls how the girls' puberty ceremony was conducted as it had been in the previous century. Her parents made a special space for her in the house for her first period. She stayed there for four nights and days doing "something all the time." She was expected to be beading or sewing and not to think any bad thoughts. Her grandmother told her, "Within these days you are not to have bad disposition or think bad thoughts about anyone or anything. Try to be happy and not get angry or else that will also be your way in life." Each day her mother and grandmother would come and pray with her to help her become a good woman, a good worker, and a good wife.[53] Virginia Driving Hawk Sneve remembers how her grandmother had a puberty ceremony conducted in the traditional manner, even if she did not have to stay fully isolated in a separate tipi or building, as previous generations of Lakȟóta women did. Following their first periods a Buffalo ceremony was performed and this song was sung as advice for the girl entering young womanhood:

> The spider is an industrious woman
> She builds a tepee for her children
> and feeds them well.
> The turtle is a wise woman.
> She hears many things and saves them for her children.
> Her skin is a shield.
> An arrow cannot wound her.
> The lark is a cheerful woman.
> She brings pleasant weather to her lodge.
> She does not scold.
> She is always happy.[54]

Madonna Swan went on to live a life of struggle and resilience (wówakiš'ake), as so many other Lakȟóta of her time have. She contracted tuberculosis at age 16, survived seven years at a tuberculosis sanatorium, and afterward received a college degree and worked as a teacher at the Cheyenne River Head Start program.

In 1983 she was acknowledged as the North American Indian Woman of the Year. Virginia Driving Hawk Sneve has written several novels and memoirs about her family living on Rosebud Reservation.[55]

The separation and disintegration of the thiyóšpaye as social units throughout the twentieth century led to further changes in the kinship system. The nuclear family became more independent and surpassed the extended family in importance. Younger Lakȟóta people, educated at mission and boarding schools, spoke English and used English kin terms, so the use of Lakȟóta kin terms declined. Both the Lakȟóta and the English kinship systems were used throughout the twentieth century. Marriage practices, brother-sister avoidance, and the formalities of all kin relationships were relaxed, gradually assimilating into mainstream white models, although the practice of mother-in-law avoidance continued to some degree.[56]

Elaborating on enduring Lakȟóta cultural values despite more than a hundred years of constant change, Arthur Amiotte says that "the traditional ideals are fidelity to kinship; that is, knowing, remembering, and caring not only for one's immediate family, but also for one's extended family of relatives by blood and by marriage and across generations." He explains how traditional virtues still play a key role among twenty-first-century Lakȟóta: "Hospitality, generosity, and charity to all . . . define a good person. Another characteristic is . . . to provide for the basic needs, comfort, and safety of one's family. Courage and fortitude in the face of adversity are considered cultural ideals to be emulated by a mindful Lakȟóta person."[57]

Robert Brave Heart Sr. concurs that being a Lakȟóta is more a question of values than of blood quantum. "It is about a way of life, a way of living. We have certain values, customs, and teachings that we must live by. Wisdom, generosity, courage, respect, fortitude, forgiveness, compassion, mercy, and sobriety." By sobriety he does not mean that all people need to abstain from alcohol, but rather, sobriety referring to refraining from abuse of alcohol, which is still a major problem in the twenty-first century. "Being Lakȟóta is a way of thinking about the world, creation, all living things, and the Creator," continues Brave Heart.

Despite the negative impact of the shift to sedentary reservation life, new opportunities for group interaction emerged. Traditional dances were held in arbors or district dance halls throughout the year. Cowboy and rodeo culture, tied to cattle ranching, became fashionable among the youth, and each spring and fall great roundups were held, which were popular social events. Some Lakȟóta traveled to fairs and rodeos on other reservations or in nearby white communities. Powwow culture also began to develop during this period as

Dance Hall, early twentieth century, Pine Ridge. Courtesy of the Buffalo Bill Center of the West, Cody, Wyoming, MS 239, P.239.587.

the Omaha Dance, developed out of the old war dance, and the Rabbit Dance, the first Sioux couples' dance, gained popularity. The lyrics of typical Rabbit Dance songs dealt with reservation problems and encouraged morality by indirectly referring to sexual misbehavior, in the same way Iktómi or Trickster stories teach lessons by demonstrating what not to do. In the summertime people came together for reservation fairs that included games and horse racing. Fourth of July celebrations were especially popular.[58]

The importance of land as the basis of Lakȟóta life, identity, and culture cannot be overstated. Aside from their economic worth, reservation lands have enormous symbolic value for many Lakȟóta. Even many of those who move away for better job prospects hope to retire to the reservation, and Lakȟóta people have staunchly opposed and resisted attempts by the BIA to appropriate lands divided by inheritance into tiny parcels, a phenomenon often referred to as "checkerboarding." These lands, small though they may be, continue to be intensely meaningful to their owners. Various land exchange programs have been attempted over the years to protect and expand the reservation land base, most notably at Rosebud and Cheyenne River. These programs achieved mixed results, and in some cases corruption played a role in further victimizing many native people.[59]

The farming and ranching economies of the reservations forced most Lakȟóta to lease their land. By the early 1970s more than 80 percent of the Pine Ridge Lakȟóta who owned land leased part or all of it. The percentage was higher among full-bloods. Usually, income from leasing was not enough to support an individual or a family. The BIA supervised the leasing process, and Lakȟóta people often criticized its handling of it. The BIA's system for grazing land gave Lakȟóta ranchers first claim and reduced rates on what they called "grazing units," and this led to tension between Lakȟóta ranchers and landowners, because the latter received significantly less from native lessees than they would from nonnative lessees. Eventually the tribes began setting their own grazing regulations, but perceptions remained that the regulations favored white ranchers over Lakȟóta people.[60] Over the years the issue of leasing lands and grazing rights was discussed during tribal council meetings—often heatedly. The issue was not only about Lakȟóta and non-Lakȟóta ranchers, but also about whether the mixed-bloods were entitled to the same rights as full-bloods.[61]

Housing went through various phases throughout the twentieth century. Until the 1950s most reservation Lakȟóta lived in small log cabins or frame houses dispersed along stream beds. These clusters of dwellings tended to contain related families, members of a common thiyóšpaye, the only social unit from the prereservation era that continued to be important in the reservation context, despite some challenges. This arrangement helped to maintain the traditional kinship system, although it had been under strain since the dawn of the reservation period, due largely to members moving away, white cultural influences, and assimilation. This rural residence pattern survived at most Lakȟóta reservations into the 1960s, especially among full-bloods. On reservations affected by the Pick-Sloan dams (discussed in chapter 11), traditional residence patterns were largely destroyed as many were relocated to newly built tract housing in towns.[62]

Cluster housing projects were constructed in the 1960s under the auspices of the Department of Housing and Urban Development, despite staunch opposition from many Lakȟóta communities that favored homes built on individuals' land. In the end their wishes were ignored, and the housing projects moved forward, plagued by cheap materials, sloppy construction, and many unfinished houses. This further eroded traditional social structure and patterns as Lakȟóta found themselves living close together with people they were not closely related to, leading to tension and conflict. As kinship protocols became burdensome, they were often abandoned, and women in particular struggled to orient themselves in this difficult new social milieu.[63]

In their search for place and identity, one way of expressing a distinct Lakȟóta ethos was the making, practicing, and teaching of traditional tribal artforms of hide tanning and leatherwork; porcupine quillwork and beading; painting and drawing; carving in wood, stone, horn, and bone; feather and hair assemblage for regalia. In time new transitional forms of fabric and fiber arts such as quilting, tailoring, and needlework became increasingly popular and a source of pride and expression of identity.[64]

The 1990s saw a movement among Lakȟóta landowners to move back to their land; they saw rural life as an opportunity to restore the traditional thiyóšpaye social life based on kinship. According to Amiotte this connection to land holds tremendous value to Lakȟóta people. This sense of belonging is "communicated via the oral tradition of wóglaka [storytelling] by elders and succeeding generations of an extended family." This reinforces a sense of place tied to a "mnemonic landscape where elements of the personal family or group history actually took place." Oral tradition also acknowledges sites, landmarks, and regions beyond the reservation, where prereservation ancestors lived, especially the Black Hills. Amiotte provides an example of the importance of place and land when he talks about his aunt Freda. Even though she resided in Custer, she retained contact and communication with her reservation relatives. The family home in Manderson on Pine Ridge continued to be thought of as the "place of origin and the center of tradition—those sacred and secular activities marking rites of passage for generations of her large, extended family." Freda was fluent in the Lakȟóta language, which she spoke with her friends and relatives when they were at the family home. On many occasions, Freda and her husband were substantial, generous contributors to the ceremonial, celebratory, and crisis events as they occurred at her reservation home among her relatives, recalls Amiotte.[65]

This movement to return to the land encountered many obstacles, not the least of which came from Lakȟóta ranchers who held permits to grazing land. This conflict illustrated the difference between Lakȟóta who saw the land as important to identity and culture and those who saw it as valuable property. Throughout the 2000s and 2010s many Lakȟóta received temporary manufactured housing in the form of Federal Emergency Management Agency (FEMA) trailers. These dwellings were distributed by the tribe on a first-come, first-served basis, and were intended to provide intermediate-term shelter, although many Lakȟóta people lived in them permanently.[66]

Education in the Twentieth Century

The goal of Indian education policy throughout most of the twentieth century was the assimilation of Native American children into American society. New Deal-era reforms included closing boarding schools and constructing community day schools that offered community gardens, canning facilities, and vocational training oriented to reservation life. For example, Lakȟóta students managed cattle herds and bilingual curriculum materials were produced. Unfortunately, after World War II, Indian education largely reverted to its assimilationist goals, along with the conflicting aims and attitudes inherent in cross-cultural education, which led to poor results.[67]

The Indian Education Act of 1972 and its successor, the Indian Self-Determination and Educational Assistance Act of 1975, finally put the direction and responsibility for designing education programs in native hands. Many Lakȟóta schools began cultural and language programs. Lakȟóta people lobbied for similar efforts in public schools, including training programs for public school teachers in Lakȟóta culture in areas with large Lakȟóta populations. Lakȟóta influence on local boards of education grew as well, and in the 1990s several tribal councils mandated the teaching of Lakȟóta language in reservation schools. In 2007, Red Cloud Indian School (RCIS), in partnership with Indiana University's American Indian Studies Research Institute, launched the Lakȟóta Language Project (LLP) as a means of promoting and revitalizing Lakȟóta language and culture through curriculum development, faculty training, community engagement, and culturally relevant education. The LLP produced the first comprehensive K–12 Native American language curriculum in the United States, and RCIS now teaches Lakȟóta language each school day in all thirteen grade levels. The LLP also hosts an annual summer language camp, the Maȟpíya Lúta Owáyawa Lakȟól'iya Wičhóthi (Red Cloud Indian School Lakȟóta Language Camp). Philomine Neva Lakȟóta, a respected Lakȟóta elder and Lakȟóta language teacher explains, "We try to do as much of [the camp in] an old-time setting, how our ancestors would teach their children. The first day we made pápa, dried meat from buffalo meat . . . [The camp] helps to empower and strengthen the Lakȟóta language." Also, since the 2010s, language nests, which combine immersion language instruction in Lakȟóta and childcare, have increased in popularity.[68]

Robert Brave Heart Sr., Executive Vice President of Red Cloud Indian School, has dedicated more than twenty-five years to educating Lakȟóta youth. Before becoming an administrator, he served the Pine Ridge community as a teacher, coach, principal, director of spiritual formation, and superintendent. Elaborating on the importance of language, he says: "Language loss is a serious concern. With that the culture would be lost. The next generation may not have a first-language Lakȟóta speaker. We will continue to work to preserve and revitalize the Lakȟóta language. If we don't do that, we will die as a proud people—our culture, and our way of life."[69]

Jace DeCory from Cheyenne River concurs, language and cultural survival go hand in hand. "My two sons are keeping the language alive through singing and praying. It is wonderful to hear them sing and pray in our Lakota language and I am so thankful that they believe our language and Lakota ways of life are important to our survival today."[70]

Tribal colleges and universities have been a major development in Indian education. The idea for their establishment began in the 1950s on Rosebud and interest spread quickly to all the Lakȟóta reservations. Arthur Amiotte reflects on this development: "The history of nonnative educational systems, on and off the reservation have molded and affected native language and acculturation to nonnative perspectives and worldviews, neglecting reference to native identity." Educated Lakȟóta leaders have addressed this adverse effect by creating alternative curriculums for children as well as higher education opportunities. Education programs of self-determination and empowerment for native people have given rise to the tribally controlled colleges and Native Studies programs in white universities. These, he believes, in turn "propel educated Lakȟóta professionals in all fields from medicine to education to administration to further affect the cultural norms and future directions of Lakȟóta society."[71]

In the 1960s several colleges and universities began offering extension courses at satellite education centers in reservation communities. The Lakȟóta tribal colleges emerged from this system. In 1965, Title III of the Strengthening and Developing Higher Education Amendment of the Federal Higher Education Act was passed by Congress, providing the funds needed to convert the satellite centers into tribal colleges. During the late 1970s and the 1980s, Lakȟóta tribal colleges steadily moved toward full accreditation and greater autonomy. In 1992, Sinte Gleska at Rosebud became the first fully accredited Lakȟóta tribal university. By 1998, Sinte Gleska, along with Oglála Lakȟóta College (OLC) at Pine Ridge, were the only tribal colleges in the United States offering master's-level programs. A foundational idea is that Lakȟóta tribal universities are community property and exist to serve their communities; they provide opportunities for tribal members to obtain credentials and skills and they implement community development programs. In 1972, the American Indian Higher Education Consortium (AIHEC) was established. Of the six founders of AIHEC, three were Lakȟóta tribal colleges (OLC, Sinte Gleska, and Standing Rock, now Sitting Bull College), illustrating the pioneering role Lakȟóta leaders and communities have played in the national development of the tribal college and university system. AIHEC played an instrumental role in securing the passage of the Tribally Controlled Community College Act of 1978, which stabilized the tribal college movement by securing a federal funding base for it.[72]

Education has played a key role in economics and employment opportunities on Lakȟóta reservations, and by empowering and preparing Lakȟóta people to pursue careers and leadership positions within and beyond their communities. Education has provided the Lakȟóta with many practical skills that have contributed to the survival of the Lakȟóta people and their traditions.

11

WÓWAKIŠ'AKE

RESILIENCE AND SURVIVAL

Fighting for the Wašíču: Lakȟóta Participation in the
US Military in the Twentieth Century

The Lakȟóta have a long history of fighting alongside the wašíču, not just against them. As early as 1823, they joined forces with Col. Henry Leavenworth in an attack on the Arikara. In the early reservation period men gained prestige and earned income by enlisting as Indian scouts for the army, continuing the warrior tradition of the buffalo-hunting era.[1]

Thousands of American Indians volunteered to fight in World War I, although they had not been drafted because they were not American citizens. Many Lakȟóta people also joined in the war effort, and old chiefs like John Grass urged young men to go and fight the Germans.[2] In recognition of their service, Congress granted citizenship to all American Indians in 1924. But it was America's entry into World War II that marked a real watershed for the Lakȟóta, as thousands registered for the draft or chose to volunteer. Many left the reservations for the first time to join the military, travel overseas, or work in war-related industries around the country. Father Martin Brokenleg explained that "During World War II my parents worked in a defense plant in Hastings, Nebraska. My father was a photographer for the Navy." Leaving the reservation and experiencing the broader world had a profound impact on the Lakȟóta, like the experiences of the Lakȟóta of Black Elk's generation who traveled to Europe with Wild West shows. Sioux men saw action in every branch of the service, from submarines in the Pacific to destroyers in the Atlantic and from the beaches of Normandy to the Battle of the Bulge to the Mariana and Palau Islands. Women served as nurses or in the auxiliary services. There was a unit of Sioux code talkers in the South Pacific, but for the most part the Sioux distinguished themselves in the infantry.[3]

When the Selective Training and Service Act of 1940 reinstated the draft, the army decided to integrate Native American draftees and volunteers rather than establish an all-Indian division. This was transformative. Native servicemembers became immersed in American culture and enjoyed steady jobs, increased wages with a resultant increased standard of living, enhanced status, access to new technologies and goods, and exposure to urban society. Many Native Americans who moved to urban centers to work for the war effort enjoyed similar experiences and benefits.[4]

On the home front, reservation Lakȟóta supported the war effort by conserving resources, organizing giveaways and other ceremonies for those entering and returning home from the service, as well as supporting and consoling those who lost family members, much like they had in the days of intertribal warfare. Ella Deloria writes of a woman whose only son was killed in action: "In her intense grief, she reverted to ancient custom, and demeaned herself by cutting off her hair, wearing her oldest clothes, and wandering over the hills, wailing incessantly. Nor would she be comforted. Did the people do anything? Certainly. In the old-time manner, which they now carry over into their church, they made a feast and invited the bereaved mother." The community members held a memorial service for the woman's son, followed by speeches addressing the mother in the traditional manner of condolence. They washed the tears from her face and dined with her, all in reverent quiet, as is appropriate of ceremony.[5]

Thirty tribal members at Rosebud were designated as official civil defense air raid wardens by the South Dakota National Defense Council. As men left the reservation to fight overseas, women took over much of the workload, driving tractors, repairing agricultural equipment, herding cattle, and harvesting produce. A young Sioux woman at Carleton College in Minnesota edited and published a monthly paper called *Victory News*. Her staff were all Sioux, and the publication was mimeographed at Rosebud Reservation as part of the Victory Club of Rosebud. *Victory News* sent good cheer and news of home to the young men and women fighting all over the world. Service men and women also wrote back to the paper, making for a lively correspondence. Native-operated clubs like the Victory Club of Rosebud existed elsewhere too, preparing army kits and care packages, and writing personal letters to those without parents or whose parents were unable to write.[6]

In early 1942, shortly after the bombing of Pearl Harbor, over 2,000 Sioux left their reservations to work on building depots and air-training centers. This included several Lakȟóta from Pine Ridge and Cheyenne River Reservations, some of whom found permanent employment at military facilities, such as airfields and ammunition depots in Rapid City and other nearby towns. Those Lakȟóta who had received training in handling machinery, laying cement, carpentry, and other practical skills through the reservation CCC projects of the 1930s and early 1940s were well prepared and qualified to enter those fields of work at higher wages. In fact, most Lakȟóta working for the war effort received high incomes and enjoyed luxuries that their reservation counterparts working in the tenuous agricultural economies of the reservations did not. Off-reservation jobs provided real economic opportunities for Lakȟóta people and encouraged others to seek similar employment. Many Lakȟóta women, like Marcella LeBeau (Wígmuŋke Wašté Wiŋ) from Cheyenne River, joined the army as nurses. LeBeau celebrated her 101st birthday in 2021, when she was still involved in historical repatriation projects and has served on the Cheyenne River Sioux Tribal Council.[7]

Code talker Clarence Wolf Guts remembered his time in the service: "We got shot at and we did some shooting ourselves. You know it is not easy shooting at another human being." He often pondered why he was out there fighting, but only later did the true meaning dawn on him: "When I see people laughing and having a good time, I realize why we were over there. . . . We done it for the people and if they are happy, then I am the happiest person alive," he noted proudly more than sixty years later. "I helped win the war, I helped, me and my buddies."[8]

Beyond the death, destruction, and trauma, there was an additional dark side to Lakȟóta participation in the war. Vivian Red Bear, a member of the Crow Creek Sioux Tribe, mentions that many Lakȟóta veterans came back as changed men and women: "The men that went away to service and came back—how shall I say, drunkards? They learned how to drink, but before that, I suppose they did drink; but they weren't as bad. Some of them turned out to be alcoholics after they were away."[9]

The extraordinary contribution of Lakȟóta men and women in World War II was duplicated in Korea, Vietnam, Iraq, Afghanistan, and other American wars in the twentieth and twenty-first centuries. In 2008, US President George W. Bush awarded the Medal of Honor to Sgt. Woodrow Wilson Keeble for his deeds in both World War II and Korea. In 2011, Maj. Stephanie R. Griffith from Crow Creek Reservation was awarded a Bronze Star for her services in the US Marine Corps in Afghanistan. Serving in the military connected with an ancient warrior ethos and was a matter of duty and family tradition for many Lakȟóta. Veterans returning from duty were recognized and honored at powwows and other community gatherings with feasts and giveaways. The "Flag Song" became the "Sioux National Anthem," an essential part of community events, along with the American flag it honors. Intense patriotism is common among the Lakȟóta, particularly among full-bloods and those who have served in the US military, but this trend is fading among the younger generations today who often identify as social justice activists. But a strong sense of loyalty to the US government was a common attribute among many Lakȟóta throughout the twentieth century; a lack of patriotism and suspicion of treasonous beliefs and behavior among members of the American Indian Movement (AIM) made many traditional Lakȟóta oppose AIM and other expressions of the Red Power Movement of the 1970s.[10]

Dams, Termination, and Relocation

In the early 1940s the Army Corps of Engineers and the Bureau of Reclamation separately developed major water projects affecting the Missouri River basin. The Corps' project was called the Pick Plan and the Bureau's project the Sloan Plan. The Pick Plan called for the construction of five dams along the Missouri to control seasonal flooding, while the Sloan Plan focused on developing reservoirs and irrigation projects along the Missouri's tributaries. The two projects were combined and approved by congress as the Flood Control Act of 1944. From the beginning it was known that the Pick-Sloan Project would directly impact Crow Creek, Lower Brulé, Cheyenne River, and Standing Rock reservations, yet these tribes, as well as others, were not informed of the plan until 1947. This three-year delay, whether intentional or not, meant that the tribes had no meaningful input into Pick-Sloan planning or implementation. It also denied them the opportunity to oppose the plan.[11]

The Standing Rock and Cheyenne River people perfectly understood the devastation the dams would cause. Frank Ducheneaux, the Cheyenne River Tribal Council Chairman, summed up their sentiments:

> The construction of this Oahe Dam will affect the lives of every member of the two tribes in one way or another for years to come . . . our greatest concern is to insure to our people the preservation of hunting and fishing

rights and access rights to the reservoir, and the reservation to the tribes of a block of power for their own use from power to be generated by the dam, and reimbursement to the tribes for expenses incurred as a result of the construction of the dam.[12]

While they could not effectively oppose construction of the Oahe dam, they presented the government with a memo entitled "Oahe Contract Agenda" that addressed twenty-two separate issues from the relocation of the agency to the removal of cemeteries, to fishing and hunting rights, breach of the 1868 Fort Laramie Treaty, mineral rights, and reimbursement of expenses incurred by the Cheyenne River Tribe.[13]

Exactly as Chairman Ducheneaux feared, the dams constructed as part of the Pick-Sloan Project had a devastating impact on reservation communities and land holdings. The Big Bend dam flooded 38,000 acres of Crow Creek and Lower Brulé, but the Oahe dam was the most disastrous of all, flooding 104,000 acres at Cheyenne River and 56,000 at Standing Rock. To make matters worse, the areas lost were primarily fertile bottomlands that constituted "90 percent of the reservations' timber land and 75 percent of the wild game and plant supply." The Pick-Sloan Project destroyed tribal lands and displaced approximately 600 Sioux families, more than one-third of the aggregate population of the reservations, yet none were given any opportunity for input or opposition.[14]

The impact of the dams was manifold. The resources of the bottomlands allowed a social and cultural lifeway that was impossible to maintain on the drier uplands. Entire communities had to be relocated, including Cheyenne Agency and the agency headquarters at both Lower Brulé and Crow Creek. Some families at Lower Brulé and Crow Creek displaced by Fort Randall dam were relocated to lands that were later flooded by the Big Bend dam. And because Pick-Sloan coincided with the Voluntary Relocation Program, there was little in the way of government support for reorganizing displaced communities. Further, benefits and compensation from the government were delayed in some cases for fourteen years and were uneven because each tribe had to negotiate independently with Washington. Paradoxically, Cheyenne River lost the most land and received the least compensation, while Lower Brulé and Crow Creek received more, only to see much of it expended on relocation costs. Standing Rock sued the Corps, whose action in taking a portion of their lands by eminent domain was found to be illegal. Unfortunately, the decision came too late to help the other tribes, but Standing Rock received $12 million, the most of the four Lakȟóta tribes.[15]

Although various irrigation projects for the uplands were planned, few were ever completed and none on Lakȟóta land. Congress cut back on the funding of these projects, and attempts to create new sources of income for reservation communities met with limited success. In the 1990s, based on the findings of the Joint Tribal Advisory Committee, Congress enacted legislation to make the original settlements fairer, and tribes began efforts to regain reservation lands taken by the army that remained unflooded.[16] The devastation wrought by the project was poignantly expressed by Vine Deloria Jr., who said that the "Pick-Sloan Plan was, without doubt, the single most destructive act ever perpetrated on any tribe by the United States."[17]

A major concern of the 1934 Indian Reorganization Act had been promoting economic self-sufficiency among Native American tribes and communities. This planted the seed for what would be called "termination," the official policy of the federal government in the 1960s whereby Congress revoked tribes' federally recognized status and by extension their privileges and their access to various support programs. The Bureau of Indian Affairs (BIA) proposed a gradual withdrawal, with programs transferred to other government departments, BIA supervision phased out, the BIA itself abolished, and individual tribes terminated. Rather than the gradual withdrawal proposed by the BIA, in 1953 Congress decided to implement some terminations immediately.[18]

Because most Lakȟóta reservations were categorized as "Predominantly Indian," meaning still adhering to traditional cultural values and practices, the Lakȟóta tribes were never in danger of immediate termination. But the withdrawal of services provided by the BIA negatively impacted them, and they vigorously opposed these and other cost-cutting measures. Plans to consolidate the BIA's operations on Cheyenne River and Standing Rock were shelved after protest from both tribes, and several programs were transferred to other federal departments or to the states, exacerbating tense existing relationships between tribes and states. The transfer of these programs complicated Lakȟóta farming and ranching endeavors and made it harder to get loans. Most disturbing of all was the movement to give states jurisdiction over reservations, something that most Lakȟóta people feared and staunchly opposed.[19]

Lower Brulé was the only tribe in the United States to request termination. This offer was a ploy relating to the Missouri River dams construction and it did not work out for the tribe. The idea was that the tribe would offer to accept termination in exchange for double the compensation they would receive from the land lost to the construction of the Fort Randall Dam. They thought if they

Wilma Straight Head, acting director at Harry V. Johnston Junior Lakota Cultural Center, 2001 Main Street, Eagle Butte, Dewey and Ziebach Counties, South Dakota. From the start of the twentieth century, many Lakȟóta made a living working in the growing tourist industry. Courtesy of South Dakota State Historical Society, South Dakota Digital Archives (2009-07-21-033).

invested the money properly, mainly in land acquisition and cattle operations, they could achieve true economic independence. Then they could be politically independent and sever their relationship with the BIA. The plan appealed to some but was opposed by a majority in Washington. Most tribal members were either opposed to or apathetic about the proposal. In the end, the Lower Brulé withdrew their request to be terminated. Aside from embarrassment, their gambit also delayed disbursement of the dam compensation funds for several years.[20]

The next ill-fated federal Indian policy was relocation to urban areas. Throughout the 1930s and especially the 1940s many Native American people ventured off reservations, experienced the world beyond their home communities, and found work in urban areas. During World War II, many Lakȟóta people worked at military installations. At the end of the war, they located to nearby towns to work and enter the mainstream of American life. Like many others, Freda Goodsell Mesteth moved to Custer in 1949 and joined the household of her two older sisters, recalls Arthur Amiotte. She took care of her own child as well those of her sisters while they worked in the community. Later, Freda worked in the Scheels laundry, as a child caregiver to a private family, and as a housekeeper at Sylvan Lake Resort. She was even employed wielding hammer and nails at the Buckingham munitions box factory east of Custer.[21]

Those who remained in urban areas generally fared better economically, but many who left the reservations returned within six months or a year. The situation was described by the Cheyenne River chairman Frank Ducheneaux: "Unemployment is at an all-time high on the reservation. Jobs in adjacent areas are practically non-existent and in addition people are coming back to the reservation from the coast and other industrial areas where they have been employed for the past few years." These people were unable to find employment locally and were forced to seek relief from the tribe to survive, which caused a terrific burden on the tribal funds. "We must have immediate assistance either in additional funds or in commodities," exclaimed Ducheneaux.[22] Nonetheless, the success that many native people experienced convinced the government that the future for Native Americans lay beyond the reservations. Hence the BIA instituted the Voluntary Relocation Program in 1952 to encourage native people to move to urban areas.[23]

Relocation came at a dire time for many Lakȟóta. Annual income levels were low, and the Pick-Sloan dams had changed the landscape of the reservations, leaving many homeless with no guarantee of government assistance. Each reservation had a relocation officer, and the BIA used high-pressure recruiting tactics. Once relocated to a city, new arrivals received support in the form of counseling services on budgeting, writing checks, keeping time schedules, and other basic skills. Few native people starting out had the kind of skills that were marketable in an urban context, so they often ended up with unskilled, low-paying jobs and housing in low-income neighborhoods. Once housing and a job were secured, assistance ended, leaving native people to fend for themselves in unfamiliar environments far from their relatives and homelands. The United Sioux Tribes South Dakota established employment offices in major cities to help relocated Sioux people. Despite these efforts, the return rate to reservations was high, from 45 percent at Standing Rock to 75 percent at Cheyenne River. Nearly all relocation participants complained of the lack of adequate support in adjusting to city life and the low quality of jobs and housing available to them.[24]

However, there were some success stories. According to Vivian Red Bear, "I have a cousin that went to Cleveland, Ohio . . . on relocation, and he's still gone. He works for the Ford Company, and right now he lives in Salina, Michigan.

But he's never been home. I mean, he comes home for visits. But then he's got his home out there."[25] As Robert Burnette, one-time tribal chairman of the Rosebud Sioux, explained:

> The Indian people of the '30s stayed very close to the reservations and they did through the '40s and except in World War II, which most of them participated in. If they weren't in the service, they went over the border down here in Nebraska in the ordinance business and worked down there. . . . But then in the early '50s . . . a lot of the people, the educated person, and some of the uneducated went out into the cities, Cleveland, Chicago, Los Angeles, and Frisco, . . . and they're there now and making a living.[26]

Burnette believed that about 20 percent of them were doing fairly well. But most of them were "located within the skidrow sections of these cities and are not able to get out. And some of them are in very bad shape."[27]

Federal policies throughout the twentieth century brought native people from all over the country to urban areas. Lakȟóta represented a significant portion of the native populations not only in metropolitan areas near Lakȟóta reservations, but also in Chicago, Los Angeles, San Francisco, and Denver. Lakȟóta in cities faced many of the same problems faced on the reservations, such as discrimination, unemployment, poverty, and poor housing and healthcare. They also tackled several new issues, such as crowded living conditions, noise, pollution, and social isolation. In keeping with kinship protocols, many Lakȟóta in urban centers relied on support networks of relatives and other Lakȟóta to share money, food, other goods, housing, and childcare responsibilities. Typically, Lakȟóta settled into the lower and lower-middle class strata of urban society, creating their own subculture and communities distinct from those of the reservation. Many developed a new awareness of their Indian identity, and the experiences of urban native people brought about a blossoming pan-Indianism or pan-tribalism that was a catalyst for the Red Power Movement.[28]

Vine Deloria Jr., the American Indian Movement, and the Wounded Knee Occupation of 1973

Pan-Indianism or pan-tribalism is an anthropological term used to describe the development of a generic Native American consciousness or feeling of commonality or peoplehood shared by all natives, regardless of tribal affiliation or history. It is the creation of a new essentialized ethnic identity often used for political purposes. Some native people resent the term because it is based on the premise that this new identity would replace tribal identities, while others have argued that it is a useful political tool for Native Americans, where it has paradoxically evolved into a strategy for protecting and strengthening tribalism. Some scholars have pointed out that there is no reason to assume tribalism cannot coexist within pan-tribalism. In any case, pan-tribalism as a state of mind has become widespread, and for many people, the traits, activities, and institutions of the Plains, particularly of the Lakȟóta, have come to symbolize this general pan-tribal Indian identity. Scholars referred to this phenomenon as "pan-Tetonism," referring to Teton, another name for the Lakȟóta. Pan-tribalism is still an important and controversial topic today, as Indian nationalism and political activism developed out of urban mixed native populations where pan-Indianism flourished.[29]

Vine Deloria Jr. (1933–2005) was a member of the Standing Rock Sioux Tribe and the most important Native American intellectual of his generation, possibly ever. His career had an enormous influence on political pan-Indianism and his critique of anthropology was wide-ranging and significant, if often misunderstood. From 1964 to 1967 Deloria served as the executive director of the National Congress of American Indians, the most successful and influential pan-Indian organization. His first book, *Custer Died for Your Sins: An Indian Manifesto*, was published in 1969 and reached a broad popular audience. His writings raised awareness of the continued presence of American Indians in contemporary society and detailed the common experiences of all tribes in their dealings with nonnatives and the government. Deloria's work also called for retribalization, a strengthening of reservation communities and the development of a pantribal Indian nationalism in urban centers, a system of shared attitudes and beliefs toward the land and traditions that fostered a pantribal consciousness. His focus on land and sovereignty through treaties provided the ideological basis for Indian activism and the Red Power Movement, although he was not a member of the American Indian Movement and often disagreed with them and their use of militant tactics. Deloria's focus on land and treaty rights is still vital and relevant today.[30]

One outcome of the growth in urban native populations was the creation of disputes about the role of off-reservation Lakȟóta people in tribal and reservation politics. This issue became central to the controversy surrounding AIM and their occupation of Wounded Knee in 1973, where they were seen by many as urban natives interfering on reservations they did not call home. This issue, similar in some ways to the longstanding tension between full-bloods and mixed-bloods, played out in various ways over the years, including in debates over Pick-Sloan dam project compensation funds and later casino profits and operations.[31]

The American Indian Movement (AIM) was the most visible pantribal activist organization and the most well-known expression of the Red Power Movement. Today one is hard-pressed to learn about other organizations within the Red Power Movement because they are overshadowed by AIM's flashy and dramatic actions that captured and monopolized the spotlight. Founded in Minneapolis, Minnesota, in 1968, its initial goals were to counter police brutality in low-income urban native communities and to achieve real economic independence for Indian people. One of its early leaders was Russell Means, an Oglála of mixed descent who grew up mostly in California. Means was a born showman, a master at staging symbolic, dramatic, publicity-generating protests. Means and other AIM leaders—Dennis Banks and Clyde and Vernon Bellecourt—practiced a distinctively native brand of confrontational politics that made them household names in the 1970s. AIM grew nationwide and soon expanded its base from urban centers to reservations, becoming involved in reservation politics, a move that was controversial in its time and has left AIM with a mixed legacy.[32]

On February 12, 1972, an Oglála ranch hand named Raymond Yellow Thunder was severely beaten by four white men in the town of Gordon, Nebraska. Yellow Thunder died of his wounds the next day. His family felt that justice was not being served in Gordon, and after they were denied assistance by the tribe and the BIA, they asked AIM for help in seeking justice for their relative. Until that point AIM had no real presence on Lakȟóta reservations, but over the next few months they developed a reputation as the protectors of native people, willing to fight for them. AIM came to Gordon and made their presence felt throughout the trial of the men involved in the deadly beating. Emotions during the trial ran high. Two men, Leslie and Melvin Hare, were convicted of manslaughter, but received relatively light sentences. The verdict incensed AIM and led to an increase in membership and the formation of a local chapter at Pine Ridge. Full-blood communities in particular tended to support AIM, although the reception of AIM at Pine Ridge was mixed.[33]

AIM inserted itself in the bitter political dispute raging at that time between some full-bloods at Pine Ridge and mixed-blood tribal president Richard "Dick" Wilson over alleged corruption and intimidation or harassment of political opponents. The federal government also got involved, supporting Wilson against AIM, which it targeted as a subversive militant organization. Wilson saw AIM's involvement at Pine Ridge as an example of urban Indians getting involved in reservation politics that they had no business being involved in. Other Lakȟóta people at the time felt similarly, and AIM became a divisive issue on the reservation and in the greater region. Things came to a head in February 1973 when the Oglála Sioux Civil Rights Organization (OSCRO) raised a petition to impeach Wilson. The government sent eighty federal agents to fortify the Pine Ridge BIA compound, and Wilson began deputizing supporters as tribal police, a quasi-vigilante militia group known as the Guardians of the Oglála Nation or GOON Squad. On February 21, Wilson unprecedentedly presided over his own impeachment trial and acquittal. In response, OSCRO, along with the treaty council and landowners' association, appealed to AIM for aid. At a large gathering in the Calico community, AIM purportedly secured permission from the elders and spiritual leaders of the reservation to intervene. Hence, on February 28, 1973, around 200 armed men and women occupied the community of Wounded Knee, the site of the 1890 massacre.[34]

AIM's popularity and public sympathy for the movement must be understood in the context of the times. The 1960s counter-cultural revolution and push to "go back to the land" and embrace alternative non-Western ideas and philosophies helped the classic *Black Elk Speaks* gain a wide popular audience. Additionally, as part of the Civil Rights Movement, the Red Power Movement gained momentum in mainstream America, and AIM emerged as its most visible and vocal representative. Dee Brown's enormously popular *Bury My Heart at Wounded Knee* (1970) brought the history of Wounded Knee back into public consciousness. The FBI's quasi-military response to the occupation made the parallel between past and present obvious. It was exactly what AIM had hoped for. A siege ensued that lasted seventy-one days. Gunfire was exchanged nearly daily. In late April two Indians, Frank Clearwater and Buddy Lamont, were killed by government fire. Shortly afterward, Chief Frank Fools Crow mediated an end to the standoff. Along with the two killed, twelve natives and two nonnatives were injured, several people went missing under mysterious circumstances, and the trading post, museum, and Catholic church were destroyed. The Wounded Knee community at Pine Ridge has never fully recovered from the 1973 AIM occupation.[35]

After Wounded Knee, the various leaders of AIM became entangled in the US court system causing the movement to lose momentum and direction. In 1975 two FBI agents were shot and killed in a shootout on the Jumping Bull compound at Pine Ridge near the community of Oglála. Leonard Peltier, an active AIM member, was convicted of the killings. Sentenced to two consecutive life terms in prison, he remains a controversial figure today. Due to disagreements among the leadership, AIM split into two major factions in the 1990s, yet it still has a presence on reservations throughout the United States. AIM's legacy is still debated. As more information surfaces, evidence of drug and alcohol abuse, sexism, even rape and murder has piled up against AIM and its leaders. Native opinions of AIM and the Wounded Knee occupation are equally divided. For many Lakȟóta people, the events of 1973 became a symbol of the divisiveness and factionalism that continue to plague them. They see the violence and law-lessness of some AIM leaders as detrimental to Indian people, while generating hostility and fear in mainstream Americans. Others see AIM as usurpers of a peaceful grassroots movement to reclaim and strengthen tribal identities and traditions that was already underway in Lakȟóta communities when AIM came onto the scene in 1972. To others, the events of 1973 represented a rebirth of pride, cultural discovery, and reclamation, a willingness to stand up for native rights and justice. As such it sparked a strong grassroots movement. Often below the public's radar and unmentioned by the mainstream media, ordinary men and women found new ways to help native people in trouble. For example, individuals, invigorated by AIM, took traditional ceremonies to men and women in prison to aid in physical and spiritual healing. Whatever the case, ignoring AIM was impossible and their mastery of symbolic confrontational politics made them a powerful force in the 1970s.[36]

One aspect of AIM that is often seemingly forgotten is the role of women in the movement. In Lakȟóta society women had always played a central role, and within AIM many found ways to engage in political and social activism. Mary Crow Dog was only eighteen when she participated in the Wounded Knee occupation and delivered her first baby during the standoff. Madonna Gilbert Thunder Hawk was one of the key leaders of the organization. Later in life she was one of the cofounders of Women of All Red Nations (WARN). At eighty-one, she is still active in the Women Warriors organization. WARN was actively working to end the forced sterilization of Indian women and pushed for investigations into the causes of leukemia and miscarriages on Lakȟóta reservations. Her work revealed that many health issues were caused by the effects of uranium mining that had contaminated the groundwater at Pine Ridge.[37] For many women, participating in AIM inspired a lifelong commit-ment to improve women's lives and fight for the rights of indigenous people. Despite old controversies and AIM showmanship many twenty-first-century Lakȟóta see that AIM helped to bring about real change. As the historian

David Treuer has pointed out, partly thanks to AIM, "Indian life had become Indian again."[38]

The American Indian Movement and the Revitalization of Lakȟóta Ceremonial Life

Many Lakȟóta have expressed that the most significant and far-reaching changes in Lakȟóta ceremonial life in the twentieth century began with the increased presence of the American Indian Movement at Pine Ridge in the early 1970s.[39]

Quite a few Lakȟóta people claim that the revitalization was already well under way as a grassroots, nonviolent movement—another expression of Red Power—and that AIM came on the scene, usurped the movement, and then took all the credit for it. These Lakȟóta people are understandably critical of AIM and frustrated by the way they are memorialized in history and romanticized in the popular imagination. The cultural and religious revitalization had begun to gain momentum in the late 1960s and was heavily influenced by the works of Vine Deloria Jr. and the emerging Native American intellectual movement he spearheaded; by anthropologist Beatrice Medicine; artist and educator Arthur Amiotte; educator and tribal college president Lionel Bordeaux; and other exemplars of the first generation of college-educated American Indians.[40]

A grassroots movement away from Christianity and membership in Christian churches toward more participation in traditional Lakȟóta ceremonial life was already occurring in Lakȟóta communities before AIM's arrival at Pine Ridge. Arthur Amiotte calls this a process of "reversion," that is, reverse conversion. According to Amiotte, "the turn away from Christianity was something that started in the seventies. . . . People of my generation and people like me were returning back to the reservation as teachers, as professionals, and didn't feel any obligation or social conscience to [be Christian]. I thought there was nothing wrong with rejecting Christianity in favor of tradition. And I even got so adamant at one time that I didn't celebrate Christmas. . . . I proceeded to convert my mother, my auntie, and my grandma."[41] Amiotte further remembers how Freda Mesteth Goodsell and members of her extended family became part of this Lakȟóta revitalization movement in the 1970s and 1980s to recommit to practicing the sacred ceremonies and associated traditions. This included practical elements such as establishing tribal encampments in traditional thípi in natural settings, without any modern amenities. Selected families volunteered to provide feasts for hundreds of participants, families, and guests, recalls Amiotte, continuing "rituals included serving traditional Lakȟóta foods . . . to be used at

Lakȟóta wičháȟpi owíŋža (star quilt) by master quilt maker Freda Mesteth Goodsell (Ťhawáčhiŋ Wašté Wiŋ). Various forms of handcraft, such as beadwork and quillwork, are an important way to continue Lakȟóta traditions. After the buffalo hunting days, star quilts became one of the most honored gifts given during ceremonies. Freda Mesteth Goodsell's uniquely colored quilts are on display in museums from the Vatican to the Smithsonian Institution. Courtesy of the Buffalo Bill Center of the West, Cody, Wyoming.

the annual times of ceremony and renewal of social bonds. An important part of these ceremonies was the giving of gifts and honoria to participants, their families, and guests as acknowledgement of the high regard for others. The gifts demonstrated the Lakȟóta value of lavish generosity." The giveaways, as they are called in English, are known by the Lakȟóta terms of wíȟpeya, otúȟʼaŋ, iglásota, wakíčhaǧapi, and yawániča. The gift giving followed the ceremonial giving of names to children, the sanctification and blessing of young men and women, adoption of others as relatives, and the honoring of achievements by family members. Freda and her relatives all worked diligently a year in advance accumulating and hand crafting the many quilts, decorated garments, moccasins, and jewelry. They also purchased fine Pendleton blankets and other tribally sanctioned goods to be given away, recalls Amiotte.[42]

AIM's role in the revitalization of Lakȟóta culture and spirituality, like AIM's legacy in general, is complex. But before attributing the seeds of the Lakȟóta cultural and spiritual renaissance solely to AIM, caution and further nuanced study are necessary.

12

LAKȞÓL WÓČHEKIYE
LAKȞÓTA SPIRITUALITY

The Historical Roots of Lakȟóta Religious Diversity

Lakȟóta religious expression declined in the early 1900s but resumed in the 1960s. This chapter explores the ways the Lakȟóta have for the past hundred years sought to revitalize their traditional ways—Lakȟól wičhóȟʼaŋ. Lakȟóta culture and religion have always been dynamic, characterized by individuality, adaptation, innovation, and practicality, notwithstanding some vital underlying continuities with the past. Today, religion has superseded kinship as the dominant factor in and central foundation of Lakȟóta culture and identity. Lakȟóta ceremonial life tends to be characterized by an inherent pragmatic openness and tolerance that often leads to interesting hybridities in the religious realm, while still tenaciously maintaining a distinctive Lakȟótaness.[1] These adaptations and hybridities in no way undermine the authenticity or legitimacy of Lakȟóta traditions. The natural state of culture, religion, and tradition is change, and Lakȟóta ceremonial life has always been largely revelatory or vision-inspired, rendering it fluid, idiosyncratic, and antidogmatic at its core.

Some recent developments in Lakȟóta ceremonial life may at first glance seem to challenge the idea of religious continuity. But Lakȟóta ceremonial life has always been a dialectic between past and present, a balancing act between the deep and relatively stable animist relational worldview and the practical

274

realities of modern life.[2] In this way, exploring recent developments in Lakȟóta ceremonial life highlights the deep continuities at its core.

Nineteenth-century Lakȟóta religious organization tended to mirror sociopolitical organization, as well as ecological conditions. Changes in sociopolitical life, along with environmental and ecological adaptations, have been major constraining and determinative forces in the development and evolution of Lakȟóta religion.[3] Historical Lakȟóta religion was diverse and complex. A great diversity of ceremonies brought sacred power into Lakȟóta lives. Many ceremonies expressed individuals' dream experiences. The quest for knowledge of the wakȟáŋ was mostly a personal enterprise and largely the work of men and each formulated a system of belief by and for himself. There was no standard or dogmatic theology or body of belief. Fundamental concepts and symbols were universally shared, but specific knowledge of the wakȟáŋ beings was not shared beyond a small number of religious practitioners. Through individual experience, every man had the opportunity to contribute to and resynthesize the body of knowledge that constituted Lakȟóta spirituality.[4]

The religious foundations and ritual practice of each thiyóšpaye or lodge group reflected its specific sociopolitical organization, reinforcing the individualism and diversity of traditional Lakȟóta belief and ritual. Although the basic underlying elements and symbols were similar, the details and specifics differed from band to band. According to Ella Deloria, Lakȟóta ceremonies "may vary in details, in different bands of the Teton, and they may even mean slightly different things in different times or different bands, but in essence they have remained, and their names have persisted; though there too, there is variation."[5] In essence, each Lakȟóta thiyóšpaye had a distinctive set of religious beliefs and practices that mirrored its social fabric, which reflected the makeup and organization of its specific families and extended families, men's societies, civil and military leaders, and, significantly, religious leaders and ritual specialists.

Despite a common mythology and shared religious symbols with evolving meanings, most or perhaps nearly all practitioners synthesized and developed their own versions of Lakȟóta religious belief based on their own visions and life experiences.[6] According to James R. Walker's Lakȟóta consultants, "Each one believes in the spirits his sect believes in, and laughs at the spirits that another sect believes in. One seeks a vision to learn what sect he must belong to."[7] Lakȟóta individuality allowed each person to define his or her own religious system through vision questing rather than through formalized doctrine.[8] This is true in regard to practitioners as well. Certain individuals had faith in certain waphíye (healers, medicine men, conjurors) while considering others to be frauds.[9]

Diversity and individuality were also fueled by the distinctiveness of a given thiyóšpaye's social fabric, as well as environmental and ecological factors inherent in the nomadic, hunter-gatherer lifestyle of Plains Indians. Based on an idiosyncratic belief system, each practitioner conducted rituals in a characteristic way, again usually based on visionary experiences. Even when two individuals dreamed of the same nonhuman spirit person and shared membership in the same dream society, ritual practice tended toward diversity and individuality. In nineteenth-century Lakȟóta culture, religion and ritual functioned to organize diversity.[10] Today there seems to be a shift in the opposite direction.

Most Lakȟóta people and scholarly sources agree that there were relatively few religious practitioners and ritual specialists in the nineteenth century.[11] In the early 1900s there were only five holy men remaining among the Oglála at Pine Ridge, and only full-bloods had ever achieved that status. In August 1915, Walker lamented that his "most valued informants are all now dead." Later, he says, "The last of the order of holy men among the Oglála has gone before his final judge and the progress of civilization has extinguished the order."[12] Northern Lakȟóta from Standing Rock particularly noted that in the "old days" the treatment of the sick was very specific and done strictly in accordance with visions. Each healer only treated the diseases for which his vision had given him the cures.[13]

In the early 1930s, Luther Standing Bear wrote, "Most young men at some time in their lives tried to become medicine-men. They purified themselves and held the vigil hoping for direct communion with spirit powers, but in this few succeeded."[14] Ella Deloria speaking of religion among the Lakȟóta in the 1930s says that "there is no emphasis on this subject in the Indian's talk anymore. One hears no reference to it, except incidentally, or as in fun, to illustrate some humorous incident. . . . Among the Dakȟóta, not everyone was Wakȟáŋ. Not everyone tried to be. Some were content to be ordinary common men all their lives—kind and generous and hospitable, but not supernatural." In 1937, Deloria intimated that the practitioners were all but extinct. Interestingly, since the 1960s there has been an unprecedented increase in the number of individuals claiming to have wakȟáŋ power, a trend that has been noted by several contemporary Lakȟóta people as a major cultural shift. "I don't understand why everyone wants to be wakȟáŋ nowadays," explained a middle-aged Oglála in disbelief and a little disgust. "When I was growing up, it was considered a burden. That stuff is wókȟokiphe (scary, dangerous, powerful)."[15]

This decline in the number of ritual practitioners parallels the decline in interest and pride in Lakȟóta culture, identity, religion, ritual, and tradition that occurred from roughly 1880 to 1930, until the revitalization of Lakȟóta ceremonial life that gained momentum in the 1960s and 1970s. This decline was the result of the convergence of many interrelated factors, such as settler-colonialism, the decline of the buffalo, missionization, the official ban of Native American spirituality and the subsequent harassment by Indian police, the tragedy at Wounded Knee in 1890, economic hopelessness and dependence, allotment, social fragmentation and deterioration, the boarding-school experience, anger and resentment, assimilation pressures, racism, and relocation. The tribal religion had been founded upon cultural practices, particularly bison hunting and intertribal warfare, that became infeasible to maintain on the reservations.[16]

During the nadir period, the many disruptions left Lakȟóta religion on the verge of becoming moribund. Many Lakȟóta people turned away from traditional religion and embraced Christianity, convinced by missionaries and government agents that it was their only viable option. Some of the old people preferred to take their sacred knowledge to their graves, feeling that it had no relevance or use for the younger generations who needed to make their livelihood in the white man's world.[17] George Sword and others clearly indicate that the younger generations around 1900 had turned their backs on the traditional religious leaders. Further, they document the loss of traditional religious knowledge and the subsequent truncation of many ceremonies.

Speaking of the huŋká (making of relatives) ceremony, Sword writes: "Hardly anyone knows just how to perform the ceremony now. Only old men know how to do so. . . . In former times there were very many huŋká. There are not many huŋká now. . . . The huŋká ceremony is hardly ever performed now. The young people do not care for it now."[18] Elaborating on this theme, the Oglála George Thunder Bear (Matȟó Wakíŋyaŋ) said:

> We now call good men, like the catechists of the church, huŋká. In old times the huŋká were taught what the Indians believed to be good. This would not all be good now. They were taught to be industrious, generous, brave, and to tell the truth. They were also taught to have many wives, to steal horses from an enemy, to kill the enemy, to steal women and children from the enemy, to kill anyone who was the enemy of himself or a huŋká. They were taught to take the scalp, to torture prisoners, to kill little children, to believe in the powers of the medicine men and in the spirits of animals.[19]

In the early 1950s, Robert H. Ruby, a medical doctor at Pine Ridge, reported that there were six practicing medicine men at Pine Ridge, representing perhaps the early beginnings of the resurgence and revitalization of Lakȟóta religion. In the late 1950s, George Flesh explained, "There are more doctors practicing today . . . than in the old days. The old-time doctors had more power than the present-day doctors." In the 1960s and early 1970s, there were relatively few practitioners, many of whom are now famous, such as Frank Fools Crow, Peter Catches Sr., John Fire Lame Deer, and Leonard Crow Dog. With the Red Power movement that gained momentum in the early 1970s came a renewed pride in Lakȟóta culture and identity and a resurgence of interest in and devotion to traditional Lakȟóta religion and tradition. In some sense, many people were born again, (re)discovering their cultural and religious identities through a dynamic process of (re)traditionalization that often took modernized forms.[20] According to Harold Schunk, "There's a few of the old Indians who don't know really what the old beliefs were. You have to get down into the archives to dig out a lot of that material. They have some idea of what it was, and I think fellows like Crow Dog are trying to live in the past. And Crow Dog, in many respects, is a pretty good man, we'll say religiously, so to speak. . . . He has a code of ethics that he goes by."[21]

Waníkiya Wówičala: Lakȟóta Christianity

Christian churches flourished throughout the early 1900s. Roman Catholic, Episcopal, and Congregational were the most common denominations on Lakȟóta reservations, and membership tended to be determined by community. Elements of the old religion merged with Christian symbols. For instance, due to missionization and education many young Lakȟóta began to identify the term Wakȟáŋ Tȟáŋka with the Christian God and older forms of prayer assimilated to Christian ones. The two-pronged influence of education and missionization was widespread, as many young Lakȟóta were educated in the white man's way at mission boarding schools built near the agencies. Community cemeteries were associated with churches, and funerals—along with baptisms and marriages—were among the most vital church functions. Churches also served an important social function, providing a space for Lakȟóta people to gather at a time when most of their traditional social gatherings were outlawed. Denominational summer convocations were especially popular, mirroring in many ways the summer communal Sun Dance gatherings of the past. Communities took turns hosting these convocations, and hundreds of participants came from all over Sioux Country to socialize, feast, reaffirm common bonds, court, and politick.[22]

Famous Oglála holy man Nicholas Black Elk provides an excellent example of the complex realities and hybridities of Lakȟóta religious life. Black Elk was a traditional medicine man and healer as a young man, experiencing a powerful vision of the thunder beings of the west at the age of nine. When the end of tribal freedom came, Black Elk settled on Pine Ridge in the Manderson community. The poverty, inactivity, and disease that plagued the reservations led Black Elk to question his beliefs. In 1886 he traveled to New York and Europe with Buffalo Bill's Wild West show. During this time Black Elk embraced Christian teachings, and he saw the compatibility of Christianity with traditional Lakȟóta religious beliefs. When he returned to Pine Ridge in 1889, he participated in the Ghost Dance, which had Christian connotations. Black Elk continued his traditional healing ceremonies until 1904, when he abandoned them and joined the Roman Catholic Church. He even became a catechist in an attempt to help his people adapt to reservation life and see the connections between Christianity and Lakȟóta spirituality.[23]

In 1930, John G. Neihardt interviewed Black Elk to learn about Lakȟóta religious life. Black Elk and Neihardt became lifelong friends. Two landmark books came from their collaboration: *Black Elk Speaks: Being the Life Story of a Holy Man of the Oglala Sioux* in 1932 and *When the Tree Flowered* in 1951. Another classic work on Lakȟóta spirituality was inspired by *Black Elk Speaks.* Joseph Epes Brown spent the winter of 1947–48 with Black Elk, recording the material that would become *The Sacred Pipe: Black Elk's Account of the Seven Rites of the Oglala Sioux,* originally published in 1953. Scholars have argued about the relationship between Black Elk's traditional Lakȟóta spirituality and Christianity, but clearly he was a complex, if not brilliant, religious thinker.[24]

George Sword provides another important example. Sword adopted the "white people's ways" and religion after visiting Washington, DC, in 1870. Sword's decision to convert to Christianity and adopt another's lifeway was pragmatic, reflecting present realities rather than a crisis of faith. Although he became a staunch Episcopalian, Sword never lost his reverence for Lakȟóta traditions. Sword retained his shaman's medicine bundle, commenting, "I am afraid to offend it. If a shaman offends his ceremonial outfit, it will bring disaster upon him."[25] Sword's decision to become Episcopalian mirrors the decision made by Black Elk to become a Catholic catechist years later.[26]

While many Lakȟóta people were and are Christians, for others the decision to abandon traditional religion and convert to Christianity was more about practical necessity and economic realities than about an actual spiritual break or crisis, and this reflects the adaptability and religious tolerance of the Lakȟóta people. Aaron McGaffey Beede's Lakȟóta consultants maintained that church was a place where people got fed when rations were small. Beede implies that many Lakȟóta were not genuine Christians, and he compares them to "Rice Christians" in China. The yuwípi man George Flesh concurs with Beede saying: "One of the purposes of joining a Christian church is for burial purposes."[27]

Christianity remained a vital force on Lakȟóta reservations throughout the twentieth century. In the mid-1940s virtually all Lakȟóta professed belief in Christianity and at least nominal membership in some church. Most of the communities on the reservations had a church that was the center of social and religious life. The Lakȟóta tolerance for new religious ideas and hybridity helped foster an enjoyment of tent revivals and other worship services outside of their own church affiliations with no real sense of conflict or disconnect.[28]

As the revitalization of traditional belief and ritual gained momentum throughout the 1960s and 1970s, some clergy tried to incorporate Lakȟóta religious elements and symbols, such as the pipe, into their services. One Jesuit priest even prayed with the pipe at the Sun Dance, while several others intentionally blended Christian ideas and personages with traditional Lakȟóta symbols, a practice later referred to as "fulfillment theology." This trend proved to be very controversial and was vehemently opposed by many older church members. Despite this, Christian churches continued to be the customary sites for funerals and many weddings too, even for traditionalists. On Lakȟóta reservations today many denominations and faiths are represented, including Baptist, Pentecostal, and Mormon. Although Christianity flourished among the Lakȟóta, many of whom still identify today as Christians, many continued to practice aspects of their traditional religion. In particular, Pine Ridge and Rosebud emerged as the most conservative reservations in terms of commitment to traditional ceremonial practices.[29]

Pȟetáǧa "Live Coals"

Traditional Lakȟóta religious ceremonies were banned by the federal government in the early 1880s. After the ban, Indian agents and Indian police kept close tabs on ceremonial doings. If a Lakȟóta was caught practicing traditional religion he could be punished in various ways, from having his rations withheld to imprisonment. Jace DeCory, member of the Cheyenne River Sioux Tribe, tells about those days of religious oppression: "Our family has been involved in various Lakota ceremonies over these many years. We even had a relative that had a 'secret' sweat lodge in a root cellar in the late 1800s. He felt it was important to continue the inípi ceremony to purify our family, our relatives, even though if he got caught, he risked punishment, along with those who were praying with him."[30]

Permission for public rituals was occasionally granted in some special cases, such as victory dances for Lakȟóta soldiers returning from World War I. One such victory dance occurred near Fort Yates on Standing Rock Reservation on November 30, 1918, having been postponed due to the influenza pandemic. In the late 1920s mock Sun Dances were held on Pine Ridge and Rosebud at the behest of then-President Calvin Coolidge and the Indian agents. This resumption of public ceremonies was tentative but gained momentum after the influential 1928 Merriam Report and the subsequent passage of the Wheeler-Howard Act, popularly known as the Indian Reorganization Act (IRA) in 1934, which encouraged (the revival of) native cultural practices.[31]

Many Lakȟóta people maintain that ceremonies continued to be practiced throughout this period on an underground basis to avoid interference from Indian agents, Indian police, and other government operatives. DeCory explains: "Many of us remain close to our traditional religious ceremonies and continue to do them today, even though they were once outlawed by the federal government. Our ancestors continued to remember the songs and the protocol associated with our seven sacred rituals, along with others such as the giving of sacred names, marriage, and other ceremonies. They knew that we would be lost if these ways were lost."[32]

Emergent ceremonial forms, particularly nighttime conjuring ceremonies, which were easier to conduct clandestinely, grew in popularity, superseding other older customs. These ritual forms developed from older ones and illustrate the dynamic and antidogmatic nature of Lakȟóta religious belief and practice. The two most common nighttime conjuring ceremonies were yuwípi (wrapped up) and lowáŋpi (sing), ceremonies that focused on practical goals, such as healing the sick, finding lost objects, and foretelling the future. In the yuwípi ceremony the practitioner is wrapped in a quilt and bound head to foot. The lights are extinguished, songs are sung, and prayers are made. Throughout the course of the ceremony the practitioner (yuwípi man) is miraculously released by his spirit helpers. Typically, a yuwípi man was a rock dreamer. According to Thomas Tyon, "if someone loses a horse, they quickly make a feast for the Rock dreamer and they have him look for it. So the rocks tell about whoever stole the horse, even the name and the place; they come to report everything, they say. Therefore they are considered very powerful (wówithuŋpĥeke ló). These Rock dreamers are called the Yuwípi society. Still, even today, they are believed to be wakȟáŋ." Lowáŋpi is similar in form, except the practitioner is not bound.[33]

Anthropologist Gordon Macgregor discusses yuwípi in the context of Rosebud Reservation in the 1940s, writing, "All the religious ceremonies at Rosebud revolve around an attempt to contact supernatural powers to utilize or harness their help. The yuwipi cult is considered by some to be the only continuing cult of the Dakȟóta religion involved in this manipulation."[34] According to anthropologist Stephen Feraca, "Most older Oglálas and Sičháŋǧus declare that matȟó waphíye [bear doctors] were numerous until recent times and that yuwípi men constitute a new type of healer. One reason for this partially erroneous assumption lies in the fact that most of the medicine men on the reservations today are yuwípi men; however, it is quite possible that yuwípi men were relatively rare in pre- and early-reservation days, but they are now often equated with traditional religion."[35]

Frank Fools Crow, one-time ceremonial chief of all the Lakȟóta and the most famous medicine man of his generation, discussed the underground continuity of Lakȟóta religious practice throughout the early twentieth century, particularly the Sun Dance: "at Pine Ridge the dances were held nearly every year in one of two ways: as semipublic Sun Dances without piercing, done quietly with no fanfare and with the occasional knowledge of the agency officials, but no interference from them; or as secret Sun Dances with piercing, performed back in the hills and including audiences."[36] The resurgence of the Sun Dance would play a major role in the revitalization of Lakȟóta ceremonial life.

Piercing in the context of the plains Sun Dance refers to the practice of piercing the pectoral muscles of the dancers as a sacrifice to Wakȟáŋ Tȟáŋka. Wooden skewers are threaded through the pierced chests of any dancer who chooses to pierce, and ropes are used to connect the skewers to the Sun Dance pole (čhaŋwákȟaŋ, sacred tree) in the center of the sacred area. The dancers then attempt to break free from the skewers by tearing through the flesh of the chest. Piercing was vehemently opposed and demonized by pro-ban agents, government officials, and missionaries who, without attempting to understand its cultural, cosmological, and symbolic underpinnings, considered it "savage" and "primitive," a barrier to "civilization" and progress.[37]

Although Lakȟóta religion purportedly remained strong on a more secretive level, the 1928 and 1929 Sun Dances were the first public celebrations of Lakȟóta spirituality since 1883. The dancers at these Sun Dances were mostly elders, none of whom actually pierced. However, some dancers did "mock pierce"—they wore leather harnesses around their upper torsos attached by ropes to the center pole that gave the appearance of being pierced. To some Lakȟóta, the Sun Dances of the late 1920s were reenactments, like the notion of "playing Indian," but to others they were real and meaningful religious experiences that served to reawaken, reestablish, and publicly resume the religious sensibilities of a deeply spiritual people. The 1928 Rosebud Sun Dance in many ways could be viewed as the birth of the revitalization of Lakȟóta religion and ritual that gained momentum throughout the twentieth century, culminating in the 1960s and 1970s.[38]

As the twentieth century progressed, so did the revival of traditional religion, although in many communities there was great hostility toward the annual Sun Dance and other traditional practices, even into the 1960s. Many Lakȟóta had converted to Christianity and saw the old ceremonial ways as backward and counterproductive.[39] In 1917, for instance, Pine Ridge Agency physician James R. Walker wrote, "influenced by education received from white people, the younger generation of the Oglála adopted the modern form of the [Lakȟóta] language, and abandoned the Shamans and their ceremonials, and nearly all the customs of the old Lakȟóta."[40] Luther Standing Bear commented on the condition of spiritual decline among the Lakȟóta in the 1930s, lamenting, "There is but a feeble effort among the Sioux to keep alive their traditional songs and dances."[41] Ella Deloria's consultant "Aunt Eliza" was an elderly Lakȟóta convert to Christianity and antagonistic toward the old beliefs. According to Aunt Eliza, traditional religion was no longer taken seriously in the 1930s and 1940s.[42] John Colhoff, an Oglála, reported that all ceremonial dances at Pine Ridge were largely forgotten by 1949 and that the traditional Pipe Religion was a thing of the past by 1951.[43] George Flesh, a yuwípi man, reported in 1959 that "there are very few full-bloods who will pray with the pipe anymore."[44]

Despite these accounts and tensions between Christian and traditional Lakȟóta people, clearly spiritual knowledge was passed down throughout this period, albeit on an underground basis, and many Lakȟóta continued to practice their ceremonial traditions. According to Robert Burnette, the tribes and the BIA were both involved in outlawing "the Yuwipi Church," which he calls "the original Sioux cultural religion." In 1954, Burnette explained, "three of us younger guys in town rewrote the code [outlawing traditional religion] and we knocked that out and never even argued about it. We just left it out, and so the revival started then. In fact, in 1954, when I took office, it was one day before the tribal fair at Rosebud here, we only had five dancers there in costume all three days. In

1957, we had over 500."[45] By the 1950s and 1960s the Sun Dance was performed publicly on an annual basis but as more of a reenactment for tourists than an actual ritual performance. For instance, the Oglála Sioux Tribe sponsored an annual Sun Dance as part of their summer celebration, which included a pow-wow and rodeo. The tribal council elected a person to handle public relations and news coverage. The tribally sponsored Sun Dance was truncated in various ways and its religious character downplayed. However, piercing was permitted, and the piercing on the last day was the only part of the Sun Dance that really drew a crowd.[46]

The fact that there was a crowd of tourists was part of the problem for many young Lakȟóta who would later be attracted to the American Indian Movement (AIM) in the 1970s. By that time, the attitude of many young Lakȟóta toward traditional religion had begun to change. Men and women grew their hair long, wore it in braids, wore beaded and quilled items on their clothing, and sun dancing and piercing became important symbols of native identity and political commitment. Participation in Sun Dances increased exponentially, as did the number of Sun Dances held.[47]

Other aspects of traditional ceremonial life became more prominent as well. Sweat lodge and yuwípi/lowáŋpi ceremonies became commonplace, while other ceremonies, such as the vision quest, naming, and ghost-keeping became less prominent and often were truncated. These ceremonies, as well as several others, embodied a sense of continuity with the past, bringing it into the present through ritual. The central tangible symbol of that continuity, of Lakȟóta religion and tradition in general, is the Ptehíŋčala Čhaŋnúŋpa, the sacred Buffalo Calf Pipe. As the revitalization of traditional spirituality gained momentum throughout the latter half of the twentieth century, the Calf Pipe resumed its honored position in Lakȟóta ritual life, and pipe carriers once again came to occupy important positions in their communities.[48]

The Buffalo Calf Pipe is the most sacred Lakȟóta ritual object. It was given to the people by Ptesáŋwiŋ (White Buffalo Woman) in a time of famine, along with the sacred teachings of kinship and instructions on how to use the pipe and perform various ceremonies. The pipe is kept in a bundle by a keeper and passed down through the generations. Arvol Looking Horse is the current keeper in 2021. The Calf Pipe bundle is kept at Green Grass on Cheyenne River Reservation and is usually passed down within the Itázipčho tribe.[49]

The only public unwrapping of the pipe occurred in July 1936, during the Dust Bowl droughts that devastated the plains. Martha Bad Warrior was the keeper at the time. She was the first female keeper of the Buffalo Calf Pipe bundle. In an attempt to end the drought, she sat in the sun throughout an entire day, praying and holding the pipe in her lap. The rains eventually came, but the rigors of this impromptu ritual took a toll on Bad Warrior, who died three months later. She was 82.[50]

Reflecting on the importance of these public sacred expositions, Arthur Amiotte notes that they are "continuities based on historical models, modified over time, warranted by the exigencies of modernity." For an individual these public expositions offer an option for expressing identity, depending on one's proclivities. As such they "are Lakota ethnocentric expressions formally declaring and exhibiting the highest ideals, values, and tenants of *Lakȟól wičhóȟ'aŋ.*"[51]

Native American Church

The Native American Church was introduced to the Lakȟóta in the 1910s and 1920s. The Lakȟóta were among the last tribes to embrace it, largely because of their geographic location and the distribution and spread of peyotism throughout the early twentieth century. It spread rapidly throughout the Great Plains, much as the Ghost Dance had decades earlier. Despite vehement opposition from missionaries, Indian agents, and the police, it became popular at Pine Ridge and Rosebud especially, where it is still practiced today. According to John Fire Lame Deer, "The police tried to stamp out this new peyote cult, as they had stamped out the Ghost Dance, not because peyote was a drug—drugs weren't on our mind then—but because it was Indian, a competition to the missionaries."[52]

The Native American Church, by its very name, is a pantribal, syncretic religion, combining elements of traditional Native American belief and practice from various tribes with Christian ideas and symbols. There was a belief that peyote and the traditional pipe religion were antithetical, which led to some prejudice against families who joined the Native American Church. For instance, discussing the Ghost Dance, one of Ella Deloria's consultants said, "For my part, I think it was not so bad as the Peyote cult today that keeps Indians half-doped all the time, making them all the easier prey for the crooked. They stopped the Ghost Dance; they ought to stop the peyote-eating, too!"[53]

Many Lakȟóta people, particularly today, tend to be more syncretic or ecumenical in their spiritual beliefs, seeing things in a pantribal way characterized by the phrase "all roads are good." Other Lakȟóta, however, are more traditional or conservative, less open to hybridity and pantribalism. They tend to be more essentialist, characterized by a belief that "nothing should be added or subtracted" in the ceremonial realm. The traditionalist view is that native cultures are integrated wholes and individuals can and should only fully and properly live within one such system at a time.[54]

Lame Deer summarizes the latter viewpoint, saying, "I was a peyoter for six years. After that I quit it. I found out that it was not my way . . . for us Sioux it is something fairly new, different from our belief in the Great Spirit and the sacred pipe. Slowly I came to realize that I should not mix up these two beliefs, confuse them with each other. I felt that the time had come for me to choose—the pipe or the peyote. I chose the pipe."[55] Elaborating on many of the themes discussed above, Lame Deer said:

> Many of us Sioux go to a church on Sunday, to a peyote meeting on Sat-
> urday and to a yuwipi man any day when we feel sick. At Pine Ridge they
> are building a new Catholic church in the shape of a tipi with a peace pipe
> next to the cross. All this confuses me. I am getting too old for it. I have
> my hands full just clinging to our old Sioux ways—singing the ancient
> songs correctly, conducting a sweat lodge ceremony as it should be, making
> our old beliefs as pure, as clear and true as I possibly can, making them
> stay alive, saving them from extinction. This is a big enough task for an
> old man. So I cannot be a yuwipi, a true Lakȟóta medicine man, and take
> peyote at the same time. It is also that my ideas about drugs have changed.
> Not that peyote is a drug—it is a natural plant. If it were a part of my native
> belief, such as the peace pipe, I would cling to it with all my heart. But as
> I see it now, as I feel it, I want my visions to come out of my own juices, by
> my own effort—the hard, ancient way. I mistrust visions come by in the
> easy way—by swallowing something. The real insight, the great ecstasy
> does not come from this.[56]

Most Lakȟóta members of the Native American Church see their practice and the traditional pipe religion as complementary. Two approaches, styles, or "ways" developed among Lakȟóta peyotists: the Half Moon way, always held in a tipi and consciously native in focus, and the Cross Fire way, which usually holds meetings in church buildings and incorporates the Bible and other Christian symbols and teachings into its services. Historically, the Cross Fire way had a larger Lakȟóta membership.[57]

Mary Brave Bird (Ohítika Woman) describes the role of the Native American Church in her life: "I am a member of the Native American Church, the peyote church, whose symbol is the waterbird. This is the very center of my life. Taking the sacred medicine, singing the ancient songs to the beat of the water drum, sitting in circle with my elders, with people I trust, makes me feel my Indianness, makes me feel as one with the people of all tribes. I was baptized in the peyote religion and I will die in it." She was not initially fond of the mixing of Christian teachings with native traditions, but soon became open to the idea of praying with the pipe and respecting all religions. She also felt strongly about the central role women play in the Native American Church and the connection between the peyote tradition and Lakȟóta traditions of White Buffalo Woman.[58]

Some Lakȟóta were less supportive of peyotism on the reservations. Former Superintendent of Rosebud Harold Schunk insisted that it was the Indian Reorganization Act in 1934 that really normalized peyotism among the Lakȟóta:

> I felt that Mr. Collier, who was then Commissioner of Indian Affairs, should have stayed out of the religious angle of his program [the IRA]. He insisted that the Indian could use peyote, that it was a Native American Church. . . . Well, this to me is a bunch of baloney as far as the Sioux Indian is concerned, because this came in in 1918, this peyote. Anything that came in in 1918, and this was 1934, '35 and you could class that as Native American religion, it's silly.[59]

Clearly, the spread of the Native American Church on Lakȟóta reservations throughout the early twentieth century was complicated and not accepted or welcomed by every part of Lakȟóta society or those closely involved with it.

Lakȟóta Religion as a Force for Cultural Uniformity

In the 1970s, Lakȟóta religious belief and ritual became a force for cultural uniformity, rather than an organizer of diversity, as it had been in the past. Since the 1970s, there has been a significant spike in the number of Lakȟóta ceremonial practitioners. Ritual groups or ritual thiyóšpaye have increased as have the number of Sun Dances occurring throughout Lakȟóta country each summer.[60] These growing numbers are the result of many factors, such as the resurgence of pride in Lakȟóta culture and identity stimulated by the revitalization of the 1960s and 1970s as well as the economic, political, and social benefits of being a practitioner.

From World War II until 1972 there was only one annual communal Sun Dance for both Pine Ridge and Rosebud, sponsored by the Oglála Sioux Tribal Council, and held at the powwow grounds just east of Pine Ridge town. It was directed by Frank Fools Crow. During 1974, there were four Sun Dances held in four separate locations on the reservation. In 1978, there were eight Sun Dances in the entire state of South Dakota. In 1987, there were at least fourteen Sun Dances at Pine Ridge alone. By the summer of 1997 this figure had increased to no less than forty-three. In the summer of 2014, the number of Sun Dances held at Pine Ridge was estimated at over eighty, nearly doubling the figure from 1997.[61] So from 1972 to 2014, just over forty years, Pine Ridge has experienced a staggering increase in the number of annual Sun Dances held on the reservation.

Before the 1970s the Sun Dance was still based on warrior customs and men's societies and was essentially a war ritual featuring militaristic symbolism and led by blotáhuŋkapi (war leaders). Due to the influx of the American Indian Movement and the consequent tension and politics involved, the single, unified Pine Ridge Sun Dance fractionated, and many practitioners began running their own Sun Dances based on Fools Crow's yuwípi-influenced model. Leonard Crow Dog, the famous Sičháŋǧu practitioner, is a prime example. Today most practitioners tend to lead a Sun Dance and are also yuwípi men, apparently an unprecedented development.[62]

Paradoxically, Sun Dances declined in terms of diversity, specificity, individuality, and innovation. There has been a general shift away from idiosyncratic, diverse, vision-influenced, and innovation-driven methods for the treatment of the sick toward generalized conceptions of psychosomatic or mind-body, holistic, spiritual healing, taking place largely through the sweat lodge, Sun Dance, and yuwípi/lowáŋpi ceremonies. The vision quest and other ceremonies still occur on a less-frequent basis, but the sweat lodge, Sun Dance, and yuwípi/lowáŋpi ceremonies are the most popular and visible contemporary ritual practices and expressions of Lakȟóta religious identity today. According to Albert White Hat Sr., in the old days "the spirit would come in and possess the healer. That was the relationship that existed between them. The spirit would enter the healer's body and do the doctoring through them. When that last generation of healers died, however, around the 1940s or so, things went quiet for a while, and when the medicine men came back, they worked in a different way. They practiced in the dark, and the spirits came in and did the doctoring without entering the healer."[63]

During the 1970s many individuals became yuwípi men based largely on Frank Fools Crow's model and those of his acolytes, such as Dawson No Horse.[64] Contemporary ritual practitioners are in many ways jack-of-all-trades specialists, whose repertoire includes curing, counseling, finding missing persons or lost articles, predicting, and conjuring. The habit of practicing without a properly interpreted vision is often blamed for ritual failure, misfortune, disaster, and other obstructions to life movement.[65]

Today ceremonies are seen as a cure for all kinds of social and psychological ills: alcoholism and other forms of substance abuse, PTSD, and historical trauma, all of which may be conceived of generally as spiritual disequilibrium, disharmony, or imbalance. Hence, much contemporary ritual is aimed at (re) centering, (re)generating, (re)orientating, (re)creating, and (re)establishing inter-connectedness and relationship.[66]

There are no practitioners who extract sickness via sucking today, and hence there are no longer any yaǧópa/yapȟá/kiyápȟa practitioners. According to the influential Oglála medicine man Richard Two Dogs, the last of the Bear doctors died out in the Manderson District in the 1960s, there are only a select few herbalists remaining, and the dream societies are all but extinct. Indeed, the major changes occurring in Lakȟóta religion since the dawn of the early reservation period—the shift from specialization to generalization and diversity to uniformity, the decline in religious and ritual innovation, the deterioration of the dream societies, along with the general increase in the number of practitioners and ritual groups (ritual thiyóšpaye, Sun Dance groups or "families," "altars")—all speak to great cultural change over the last century and a half that has not been adequately explored, partly due to a largely presentist, ahistorical taboo against speaking of sacred things. And yet, beneath the surface there remain deep continuities.[67]

Based on method, nearly all contemporary practitioners may be classified as holy men (wičháša wakȟáŋ): they do not administer medicines, nor do they extract illness (via sucking) and produce the physical proof. They treat symbolic illness using largely psychological or mind-body, holistic methods and techniques. The dynamic relationship between the practitioner and the group or collective is still very significant. Being a religious practitioner ultimately means that a person self-ascribes and is ascribed by others as being empowered by or endowed with mysterious powers and abilities, usually through an established and recognized relationship with a spirit being. To put it another way, the content of Lakȟóta social relations changed, while the *form, structure,* and *relation(ship)* between leader and follower persisted.[68]

There is a correlation between the revitalization of Lakȟóta religious belief and ritual and the increase in the number of practitioners. Countless individuals have returned to Lakȟóta religion and ritual since the 1970s, rediscovering their Lakȟóta identities and relearning Lakȟóta traditions. Jace DeCory reflects on her life change: "The best decision of my life occurred in my late teens when I decided to live the čhaŋkú lúta (Red Road) of the čhaŋnúŋpa (Sacred Pipe). Although I did not fully live/practice these ways at first, in my twenties I fully embraced the inípi (sweat lodge), Sun Dance, and the other Lakȟóta rituals. These traditional Lakȟóta ways saved my life and helped me to live a sober, mentally healthy life. We stand with the prayers of our Lakȟóta ancestors."[69]

This return to cultural traditions is driven by various forces, including mere curiosity, a (re)commitment to Lakȟóta identity or Lakȟól wičȟóȟ'aŋ, or sickness. Symbolic or spiritual illness creates a need for the sacred persons and often brings the common people into relationship with the wakȟáŋ.[70]

While this may seem like a dramatic shift at first glance, Lakȟóta religion and ritual have always dealt largely with maintaining spiritual and physical equilibrium, harmony, well-being, and health. The first and most fundamental value is wičȟózani (health). The stem zaní (to be healthy, well, whole) refers to both physical and psychological health and wellbeing. Lakȟóta people value health very highly and pray for it for themselves, their relatives, friends, and tribe. Another important religious value is wičȟóičȟaǧe (the generations, life, growth, and longevity), which captures the idea of continuing health and prosperity for the people into the future and throughout the generations. One of the major functions of Lakȟóta healers is to bring the mind, body, and spirit back into equilibrium or relationship when they have become imbalanced, disrupted, or separated in some way. The common Lakȟóta ritual phrase "That these people may live" captures this focus on sustaining and perpetuating life movement.[71] In the words of Jace DeCory: "Our ceremonies are precious to us. They cannot be bought or sold. Our relatives, human and non-human, all of creation, the animals, the trees, the rocks, the mountains, the water, the air. . . . are all our relations. These are all precious to us. When we say, 'Mitákuye oyás'iŋ,' it means that we are including all of creation in our prayers. Not only our human relatives, but everything in the universe. Mitákuye oyás'iŋ—for all my relations, we are all related."[72]

Ritual Thiyóšpaye and Ceremony Houses: Contemporary Lakȟóta Ceremonial Life

The resurgence of traditional ceremonial life, not just among the Lakȟóta but among other tribes as well, prompted Congress to pass the American Indian Religious Freedom Act (AIRFA) of 1978. Thus, the US government finally officially acknowledged and corrected its hypocritical stance toward free religious expression among the indigenous peoples of North America: "It shall be the policy of the United States to protect and preserve for American Indians their inherent right to believe, express, and exercise [their] traditional religion."[73]

The contemporary Lakȟóta religious landscape consists of ritual groups, which have been referred to as ritual thiyóšpaye. At the center of these groups is a religious practitioner, a symbol of group identity and solidarity. Ritual thiyóšpaye consist of members of families that regularly attend rituals and other corporately sponsored social events. The relationship between a practitioner and his ritual thiyóšpaye is dynamic, characterized by reciprocity, mutual influence, and exchange: the practitioner shapes the beliefs, worldview, and identity of his followers, while simultaneously being shaped by his followers as a representative of their social, psychological, and religious needs, beliefs, and values.[74]

Related to the development of ritual thiyóšpaye is the emergence of ceremony houses, buildings specially constructed for ritual practice. They are often family based and dot the dusty hills, valleys, and roadsides of the reservations. Many families and extended families communally pay for, build, furnish, and maintain ceremony houses. They run the gamut in terms of size, quality, and extravagance and serve as a spiritual home base or center for Lakȟóta ritual activity. Most consist of a room set aside for ritual action and a room for socializing and food preparation. On any given night, rites are conducted, feasts are eaten, and socializing before and after ceremonies takes place. Ceremony houses are the physical symbol of the unity of a given ritual thiyóšpaye or "altar."

Perennially, contemporary Lakȟóta ceremonial life is manifested in two main life-crisis or ad hoc rituals: the sweat lodge and yuwípi/lowáŋpi, which occur on at least a weekly basis among certain ritual groups. The Sun Dance organizes Lakȟóta ceremonial life on a calendrical basis, (re)generating and (re)affirming social ties, spiritual relationships, and individual and collective identities. The Sun Dance has come to be a defining feature of individual identity that binds people to and incorporates them within a ritual group or ritual thiyóšpaye. In many ways a ritual thiyóšpaye may be conceived of as a Sun Dance group or family, as they are often referred to on the reservations. The use of kinship terminology in reference to one's Sun Dance or ritual group is significant and telling and demonstrates continuity with past traditions.[75]

The decline in religious and ritual diversity and specificity may be read inversely as an increase in generalization, orthodoxy, or dogmatism, perhaps even fundamentalism, when combined with some current ideological orientations. There are many reasons and explanations for this trend, one of which is the ascendancy of the yuwípi-man / Sun-Dance leader model based on Fools Crow that has risen to prominence since the early 1970s. Another reason is the increasing rarity of the vision quest. In direct opposition to the past insistence on the determinative role of the vision in relation to ceremonial practice, apparently by the 1950s a vision was no longer a requirement for neophyte practitioners. This is apparently still the case at least at Pine Ridge today. Interestingly, this shift seems to have occurred not just in the religious realm but also in the political and ideological realms, and not just among the Lakȟóta, but also in wider mainstream American culture. In any case, today it seems that belief and ritual have come to function more as replicators of uniformity, rather than organizers of diversity.[76]

The experiences of the Lakȟóta throughout the twentieth century made the ground fertile for the revitalization of Lakȟóta ceremonial life. They were introduced to new spiritual paths, which they were open to, while they also fought to maintain their own traditions. Like the tree that flowered in Black Elk's great boyhood vision, more and more Lakȟóta people today, both young and old, are interested in their culture, learning to speak the language, and participating in traditional ceremonies.

13

MAINTAINING AND RECLAIMING LAKȞÓTA CULTURE AND WAYS
LAKȞÓL WIČHÓȞ'AŊ IN THE TWENTY-FIRST CENTURY

This Is the Seventh Generation

Cutting through the stillness of the mid-afternoon dry summer air, the éyapaha's voice crackles over the loudspeaker. "Attention, all you dancers! Grand Entry in fifteen minutes—start lining up! First call for Grand Entry! Ináȟni po!" Fifteen-minute warnings are offered every twenty minutes for the next hour, and the camp stirs to life. The dust that had settled on tents, on campers, and on cars fills the hot August air as dancers and singers begin to get ready. The sounds of powwow begin echoing throughout the camp—the ringing of ankle bells and jingle dresses being pulled out of suitcases, children yelling as they hurry to get one last bowl of soup, and sewing machines whirring away as aunties rush to finish the hems on those last-minute projects.[1]

Each year at the Oglála Nation Powwow in Pine Ridge, South Dakota, families come together from across Indian Country to share their stories and traditions through song and dance. Not all families powwow, but almost everyone attends

Oglála Nation with its fair and rodeo. It is often said that a good powwow dancer comes from a good powwow family, and there is a role for everyone. There are sewers and beaders, those who make moccasins and roach tiers, feather workers, and jingle rollers. To build a championship dance outfit takes time and it takes skills passed down from generation to generation. There are many families that are famous for their powwow related abilities; some families are recognized as the best roach or bustle makers, others are seen as producing the smoothest Grass Dancers in Indian Country, and there are those who are known for their exquisite bead and quillwork. And for many of these families, it has been that way for well over a hundred years. While strongly rooted in tradition and histories, powwow is a living, breathing, ever-changing expression of culture. Every year new trends are evident, and powwow families work to build new sets of dance clothes in innovative ways that honor and adhere to tradition while embracing modern materials and construction methods.

In Lakȟóta communities, powwows are called wačhípi, and protocols, songs, and dances particular to the Lakȟóta are far more prevalent. This is not to say that the customs, songs, or dances from other tribal communities are excluded, but most dancers, singers, and powwow people are coming from nearby Lakȟóta communities. Wačhípi will feature many songs and dances not often seen at other powwows—Waktégli songs used during the Veterans or Men's Traditional dances, or Ipsíča Wačhí sung for a women's contest, for example. In addition to this, the arena director will be a member of the local community and thus Lakȟóta protocols will be followed inside the arena, such as the directions in which men and women dance, the way dropped feathers are retrieved, or the ways in which individuals are honored.

Dance has always been a part of Lakȟóta culture and communities, and dance and song performance have been at the core of ceremonies, society doings, and social gatherings as long as these institutions have existed. According to Severt Young Bear, long-time lead singer of the Porcupine Singers, Lakȟóta song and dance are inextricably connected: "We never dance without singing and we rarely sing without dancing. The involvement of the whole body is to us part of the balance we look for in our lives. The body and the voice are there along with the mind and the heart. We use our bodies to have fun, to pay respect to others, to pray to the Great Mystery."[2]

Whether dance is happening within a ceremonial or social context, tradition and cultural teachings are maintained, strengthened, and communicated through dance. Each time an individual and his or her family put on their dance clothes, tie on their feathers and bells, and enter the dance arena, they are telling the story of family histories, tribal relationships, native survivance, and personal identity.

The powwow styles of dance familiar today have their roots in men's warrior societies of the Northern and Southern Plains. Much of the organization of the powwow comes from that early society context. The way in which singers and dancers visit one another, enter a camp, and present their songs and dances is based in war dance society protocol and the ways in which tribal nations gift one another and make relatives.[3] While much of how this looks has changed over time, the significance has remained constant. In the early days, dance performance was a key feature of society doings. Men would dance to express themselves, to tell of deeds in battle or hunting, and to publicly display symbols and insignia associated with offices they held in these societies. During the reservation era, most dancing and society performance was outlawed. Dance was allowed within the context of Wild West shows or at times when the Indian agent would organize a dance in a way that either celebrated American holidays or could make a profit from tourists. It was in these contexts that dancing changed so significantly. Society dancing was recontextualized, highlighting a more intertribal aspect. Additionally, the dances and associated dance clothing were shared with more people than they typically had been, as these traveling wild west shows brought together dancers, singers, and actors who had not traditionally interacted. It is also within this context that the idea of contest dancing was introduced.

The Omáha Wačhípi is considered the dance that most strongly influenced modern powwow dance and culture.[4] This dance and its associated cultural context came from the Omaha (Omáha in Lakȟóta) people and was gifted to the Isáŋyathi, Iháŋkthuŋwaŋ, and ultimately Lakȟóta people. During the early reservation days, it was a very popular style of dance and was seen as a dance context that allowed men to express their warrior identities in a way deemed allowable by Indian agents and Wild West show promoters. Many of the styles seen today at powwow—Men's Grass Dance, Northern Traditional, Southern Straight, even Fancy Dancing—have their origins in the Omáha Wačhípi and the associated society complexes.

While dances that exist today have changed over time, for many people, the origins are still known and the dances imbued with meaning—a byproduct of tradition. Although stylistic attributes and the meanings associated with the dances may have changed, personal and tribal motivations behind culturally patterned dance performance remain constant. As modern native people continue to gather at powwows and share in the celebration of contemporary native lifeways, the cultural bonds that transcend tribal boundaries are strengthened. Anya Royce says that dance is "one aspect of human behavior inextricably bound up with all those aspects that make up the unity we call culture," and time and again, Native American dancing has served as a vehicle of cultural unification.[5]

Cultural unification, tradition, and social and symbolic systems—ideas that continually support key aspects of native lifeways and worldview—have remained throughout the history of social dance culture, despite the many forms that dances, dance clothes, or societies have taken over time, and despite countless efforts by the US government to eradicate manifestations of these ideas. Often, oppositional forces help to support native social and symbolic systems: "[Native communities have] experienced pressures of economic, political, or ecclesiastical assimilation into larger organizations. Each has resisted this incorporation in some degree and manner. Each has developed well-defined symbols of identity differentiating it from other peoples, especially from the peoples controlling the state programs that they opposed."[6] This set of symbols is tribal identity, it is tradition, and it is survivance.[7]

Wačhípi is a context where the public performance of identity is integral to maintaining tradition and community identity. As Lakȟóta dancers and singers "perform" culture, the community is supported, and tradition is accessed. When the Lakȟóta flag song is sung at a powwow, people remember the native soldiers who were fighting overseas to support the American war effort in World War I. Every time a Lakȟóta man participates in an annual Sun Dance, it reminds him, his family, and his community of how the pipe and the inspiration for this dance was given to the Lakȟóta people by White Buffalo Woman and from the Creator.[8] Participation in this ceremony continues to connect Lakȟóta people to these symbols and traditions that have existed from the beginning. And as Lakȟóta men and women dance at modern powwows and compete with one another to be recognized as the most knowledgeable, the most successful dancer in the arena, they are still performing Lakȟóta tradition. They are working to embody the values and traditions associated with men's societies going back to the 1800s. These values and traditions have remained constant, as has the job of the men to use the material symbols of dance to express these ideas to the people and other native communities. Contemporary performance of native expressive culture continues to connect the present to the past. It continues to imbue contemporary life and symbols with traditional values and meaning.

Another important cultural force is the resurgence of the buffalo. Despite dramatic social and cultural change throughout the twentieth century, buffalo continue to be icons of Lakȟóta culture. All Lakȟóta tribes are members of the Intertribal Buffalo Council (ITBC), receiving buffalo from Badlands and Yellowstone National Parks. Standing Rock, Cheyenne River, Pine Ridge, Rosebud, and Lower Brulé all maintain herds of varying sizes. The Rosebud and Cheyenne River Sioux Tribes sell hunting licenses for buffalo throughout the year, highlighting the continuing economic role buffalo play in Lakȟóta life. Lower Brulé has two ranges with a combined 2,900 acres and promotes hunts that guarantee a shot at a buffalo. Standing Rock is home to the privately owned Brownotter Ranch that sells twelve "tatanka hunts" a year to hunters and tourists. According to the anthropologist Sebastian Braun, "bison revival has changed into a continuing economic resource for the tribes. I think to speak of 'revival' at this time is no longer accurate. This is a sustained harvest of buffalo as a resource, although people still dispute how to ranch and best manage bison, some arguing for traditional methods. Buffalo herds are beneficial to many tribes in terms of tourism, hunting, and other economic enterprises."[9]

The buffalo is both persistent and pervasive as a core religious symbol and identity marker. Some reservation high schools slaughter a buffalo annually, hauling it to the school grounds for traditional butchering. Before the event, students learn about traditional Lakȟóta buffalo hunting and butchering practices, associated myths and beliefs, and other social and cultural aspects of the Lakȟóta-buffalo relationship. During the butchering process teachers identify various parts of the animal, speaking their Lakȟóta names, along with their use and significance. At Red Cloud Indian School on Pine Ridge students even taste raw liver, which was a delicacy for their ancestors. The week after the butchering the school serves a traditional Lakȟóta lunch, with bison soup as the centerpiece.[10]

Classes on Lakȟóta ecology and foods are offered at tribal colleges on Lakȟóta reservations, and buffalo are central to the curriculum. Buffalo symbolism also remains central to Lakȟóta ceremonial life. Although the last unabridged buffalo-sing ceremony took place in the 1950s, there have been recent efforts to revive the young women's first menstruation ritual. This community-wide effort garnered much support, led by female elders. The buffalo is the foundation for some alcohol, drug, and domestic abuse awareness and prevention programs. Representing powerful continuities with the past, the buffalo remains a model for positive social change and cultural awareness.[11]

In a 2013 exhibit at the Dahl Arts Center in Rapid City, South Dakota, titled Pte Oyate (Buffalo Nation), Lakȟóta artists explored the sacred bond between their people and the bison. "I was taught as a Lakȟóta person that they're our brothers,

they're our family. We come from them, we're related, and they sacrificed themselves for us," curator Mary Bordeaux explains. "Our clothes came from them,
our food, our utensils; they were vital to our survival on the prairie." "Tatanka
is the male buffalo, and pte is the female," explains Lakȟóta artist Roger Broer.
"Our society is a matriarchal society. When you see a herd of buffalo, a female
is in the lead. That's the way it is in our culture, as well: A grandmother or an
aunt is the one in the family who makes the decisions." The sentiments of these
individuals reflect the Lakȟóta past and highlight the enduring significance of
buffalo in their culture.[12]

Buffalo have been central to the Lakȟóta people for generations, not only as
an economic necessity and provider of food, clothing, and shelter, but also as a
powerful spirit being and relative. The buffalo is a model for Lakȟóta society,
teaching individuals how they should act so that the people and generations
might live on. This model has been effective, and there is no evidence that the
foundational role of the bison in Lakȟóta culture is fading away. To the contrary,
it is growing stronger, as a Lakȟóta friend's recent Facebook post illustrates:
"Advice from a Buffalo: Stand your ground, have a tough hide, keep moving on,
cherish wide open spaces, have a strong spirit, roam wild and free, and let the
chips fall where they may!"[13]

"We Have to Stay True to Our Values and Way of Life"

Lakȟóta struggles for their rights continue in the twenty-first century. Although
the standard of living has started to improve, there are still issues with poverty, unemployment, alcoholism, domestic abuse, and drug abuse. Violence,
especially against women, is still a serious concern. Women, young and old,
are murdered or go missing all too frequently. Diseases, such as diabetes, are
still serious problems.

In 2007, several Lakȟóta activists, led by Russell Means, declared the Lakȟóta
completely independent of the United States and the treaties signed with it. Most
Lakȟóta were not supportive of the declaration, but it was a big media event.[14] By
withdrawing from all treaties, they denied US rights to traditional Lakȟóta lands,
including the Black Hills, which, of course, have been an extremely disputed
area since the annexation of 1877. In fact, in 1980, the US Supreme Court ruled
in favor of the Lakȟóta on the hills, affirming that the United States had illegally
seized the Black Hills in violation of the Constitution's Fifth Amendment "just
compensation" clause. This declaration was one more step in the long line of
Lakȟóta resistance and survival. It was a call to action, and, like Little Wound

said a hundred years earlier during the Ghost Dance, they needed to make noise so the government would hear them.

While the Lakȟóta have captured the imaginations of people throughout the twentieth century through books and Hollywood films, it was not often that they received attention from the highest authorities. Only three times in almost a century has the president of the United States visited Lakȟóta reservations. In 1999, President Bill Clinton visited Pine Ridge Reservation, which remains one of the poorest areas in the United States. Clinton's visit received publicity in national and international media. It was a significant symbolic gesture, because not since Franklin D. Roosevelt's visit in the 1930s had a US president visited a Lakȟóta reservation. In a practical sense, however, the results of this visit were meager.

In 2008, Barack Obama was elected president of the United States. High hopes were placed on him from many directions, including Native American communities throughout the country. During Obama's presidency, some influential legislation was passed while others were improved upon, including the Violence Against Women Act, and most notably, the Affordable Care Act (ACA, also known as Obamacare), which directly influenced native communities. In 2014, President Obama visited Standing Rock. Obama was appalled by what he saw, he was especially touched realizing the burdens young people on the reservation had to carry, which were more than young people anywhere should be forced to bear, he noted. Afterwards President Obama called for an overhaul of Indian education and launched other initiatives to improve the lives of native youth. Obama established Generation Indigenous, a network aimed at teaching the next generation of native leaders and removing "the barriers that stand between young people and opportunity."[15] The chairman of the Standing Rock Sioux Tribe, Dave Archambault II, said, "No other president has come close to the honesty and compassion he has shown to our tribal nation."[16] In 2021 much hope is also placed on President Joe Biden, who pledged to make Native American issues one of his top priorities. In a historic move, he named Deb Haaland, a member of the Pueblo of Laguna, as the new Secretary of the Interior.

In recent years, some Lakȟóta experienced increasing discrimination. While racism is not unfamiliar to the Lakȟóta, there have been a growing number of incidents in cities near the reservation such as Rapid City, South Dakota, and Bismarck, North Dakota. Ernie LaPointe, the great-grandson of Sitting Bull and a Vietnam War veteran, has experienced racism firsthand. He notes that racism is often born out of fear. In the past it was perhaps more obvious, but still today fear gives room to racism and greed. LaPointe describes this as an "umbrella of fear." It is easy to unite under the umbrella of fear when you do not understand something or someone, a religion, or ways of life. The fear brings these suspicions together, and under the umbrella of fear, people become its captives, says LaPointe. He also believes that people around the world would benefit from a deeper understanding of native ways of seeing the world. Perhaps he refers to a more spiritual way of being than what is common today.[17]

Claims of discrimination were also voiced during the Covid-19 pandemic. When the Lakȟóta people set up roadblocks to protect and isolate their reservations from the virus, the Governor of South Dakota, Kristi Noem, filed a lawsuit against the Lakȟóta. The question was jurisdictional: whether the Lakȟóta had the right to block public roads going through their reservations or not. The Lakȟóta saw it as a question of protecting their people, whereas the governor viewed it as an infringement of state and federal law. After threats of legal action and negotiations between Cheyenne River Sioux Tribal Chairman Harold Frazier, Oglála Sioux Tribal President Julian Bear Runner, and Governor Noem, a plan to solve the question was introduced. Yet, things escalated quickly. The Bureau of Indian Affairs got involved, as did President Trump. The checkpoints became a major media event and a partisan issue. While the legal actions were running their course, the situation on the ground became difficult for many Lakȟóta. Over the course of the summer, many Lakȟóta experienced racist remarks, for example, on social media platforms.[18]

Several discrimination claims were made during the #NoDAPL movement, when some of the water protectors were thrown in jail, sometimes without cause or explanation. Several protesters claimed they were strip searched in jail and held without charges for several days.[19] Without going too deeply into the political issues of this ongoing, multifaceted topic, it is worth noting that the controversy began with the Energy Transfer Partners plan to build the Dakota Access Pipeline under the Missouri River, just north of Standing Rock Reservation. The project threatened historical and sacred sites and had the potential, if it leaked, to cause serious environmental damage. The Standing Rock Sioux represented, for example, by the Tribal Council Chairman David Archambault II and the Tribal Historic Preservation Officer Wašté Wiŋ Young began a series of consultations with the US Army Corps of Engineers on how to solve the situation.[20] The pipeline construction, however, continued and a group of Lakȟóta began gathering to protest the construction. Soon they began to stay on location and Íŋyaŋ Wakȟáŋağapi Othí (the Sacred Stone Camp) was born. LaDonna Brave

Bull Allard, Wiyaka Eagleman, Joye Braun, Jasilyn Charger, and Joseph White Eyes were among its organizers in April 2016. By fall, there were thousands of people from hundreds of indigenous nations supporting the Water Protectors, as they called themselves. They were not there to protest, but to protect sacred sites and sacred water. Mní wičhóni, water is life, became their rallying cry.[21]

When law enforcement arrived to stop what were considered illegal demonstrations, the situation intensified quickly. Peaceful demonstrations turned violent, largely due to the extreme measures taken by law enforcement, who used water cannons against the demonstrators in the dead of winter. By the time the camp was closed in March 2017 many protestors, or protectors, were charged on various counts and received prison sentences. President Obama stopped the construction of the pipeline as one of his last deeds as president, but Donald Trump immediately allowed it to be finished. By late summer 2021, the pipeline remained open, legal fights continued and some of the water protectors still faced charges raised against them. Yet the opposition to DAPL and other pipelines continued not only in courtrooms but on social platforms, media, and on the ground.[22]

For many Lakȟóta, who participated in #NoDAPL it turned out to be a traumatic, but also a transforming event. Many have continued their fight for environmental issues and for many it was a call to continue or begin a life of fighting for Lakȟóta and indigenous rights, much like AIM had been for many in the 1970s. Experiences in the camp were often life-changing, because living there for several months demonstrated the power of kinship, traditional religion, and faith. In fact, the Sacred Stone Camp was a traditional Lakȟóta camp circle in a very modern, twenty-first-century setting. For many young people it was an education in traditional values and an assurance and strengthening of their Lakȟóta identity. Oglála elder Lula Red Cloud, seventy-six at the time, felt the Lakȟóta traditions come alive in the Sacred Stone Camp. She never believed that in her lifetime she would be able to witness a Lakȟóta camp like that. "It was like the old times alive again," she said, noting also that "the real significance of Standing Rock was not that it happened in Standing Rock particularly, but the event itself because it made people understand who they are. The young people out there learned to respect their way of life, and most importantly they learned about who they are and where they are grounded." Lula Red Cloud believes that the importance and true significance of the event was that it educated and raised awareness around the world.[23]

In recent years, the Lakȟóta on all five reservations have worked toward being less dependent on the federal government. One goal is to become energy self-sufficient. In 2002, Henry Red Cloud began an initiative to bring solar power to homes at Pine Ridge. It soon became evident that there was a call for a larger effort in terms of renewable energies and sustainability. By 2008, the Red Cloud Renewable organization had been formed; its goal "is to help Native Americans and their communities return to sustainability through renewable energy training and projects, alternative building approaches and educating our people about how to grow and preserve nutritious and traditional Lakȟóta foods." Today Red Cloud Renewable is a thriving enterprise that is also engaged in Lakȟóta cultural revitalization while promoting a more sustainable way of life.[24]

On Standing Rock, Anpetu Wi Wind Farm (Morning Light) is developing extensive wind farms to enable efficient and reliable energy sources. This initiative took off after the #NoDAPL protests, as the Standing Rock Sioux "renewed and deepened our commitment to self-determination through institution building and renewable energy development." This initiative was made possible through SAGE Development Authority, which is a federally chartered power authority. The Anpetu Wi Wind Farm seeks to help the reservation "transition from fossil fuel dependence and exploitation to self-determination and sustainability." It aims to be a major revenue source for Standing Rock Reservation.[25] SAGE Development Authority, like the Anpetu Wi Wind Farm, is dedicated to traditional Lakȟóta values, stressing virtues such as generosity, fortitude, bravery, compassion, wisdom, and respect, especially the wisdom to understand the balance of all living things that are connected or related. Respecting Mother Earth and, for example, protecting sacred sites are also at the center of their approach to larger environmental issues. SAGE General Manager Joseph McNeil describes their approach: "This is really how we look at this project, as a prayer to guide our people into the future, into the new day."[26]

Environmental issues are important to many individual Lakȟóta as well. Perhaps the most vocal in recent years has been a young woman from Standing Rock, Tokata Iron Eyes. She is of the same generation as the famous Swedish environmentalist Greta Thunberg. In 2019 these two met and held a rally in Rapid City, South Dakota, and another event at Red Cloud Indian School at Pine Ridge. For a few days that year Lakȟóta environmental concepts were at the center of interest across the globe.[27] Tokata Iron Eyes was an active member of the #NoDAPL movement and visited Finland in 2018 as a representative of her people. Only fifteen at the time, she delivered a powerful speech about her people and the environment. She well matched the great Lakȟóta orators of the nineteenth century.[28] Many Lakȟóta people are developing ways to harness traditional knowledge about plants for use in modern medicine. Food sovereignty, too, has become an increasingly popular issue. The well-known Sioux chef Sean Sherman from Pine Ridge has launched several restaurants and an award-winning cookbook, *The Sioux Chef's Indigenous Kitchen*, which highlights traditional ingredients, dishes, and cooking techniques.[29] These are all important efforts to revitalize and maintain Lakȟól wičȟóȟ'aŋ—Lakȟóta customs and Lakȟóta lifeways.

While Lakȟóta reservations today are often described by outsiders, including the media, as places of utter poverty and hopelessness, there are a lot of positive things happening. More and more Lakȟóta people are engaged in national and international politics. They are also active in various nongovernmental organizations, promoting indigenous rights and cultures. One example of a powerful force in changing the lives of Lakȟóta youth is the Running Strong for American Indian Youth organization. One of its founders was Oglála Billy Mills, the 1968 Olympic Champion in the 10,000 meters. Mills, a modern day Lakȟóta hero, has devoted his life to helping native youth. The young Lakȟóta generation today, the seventh generation, is engaged in actively changing reservation life through the arts. For example, Frank Waln and Nataanii Means reach huge audiences through their music, and the Oglála Keith Brave Heart's art has been very influential. Arthur Amiotte, an Oglála from Pine Ridge who trained with the eminent Iháŋkthuŋwaŋna artist Oscar Howe, is probably the most well-respected and renowned living native artist. His innovative collage style has given birth to the contemporary ledger art style so popular in native art today. Other Lakȟóta people, like the performance artist Suzanne Kite, continue to push the boundaries of indigenous expression in the twenty-first century.[30]

As discussed earlier, the devastating Covid-19 pandemic struck Lakȟóta reservations hard in the fall and early winter of 2020–21. The lack of medical facilities and the prevalence of preexisting medical conditions increased the severity of the pandemic in many communities. Once again, however, the Lakȟóta people acted like good relatives to one another. Those who were able began delivering food and aid to elders, fundraising events were launched on social media platforms, and traditional medicines were delivered to people to make the terrible symptoms easier to bear.[31] Robert Brave Heart Sr. explains that these core Lakȟóta values of "being Lakȟóta and of Lakȟóta life are living in harmony with the Creator, the universe, with mother earth, all mankind, and the powers of the four directions." Equally important, he emphasizes, is to "be a good relative. You must know your relations and address them by relationship, not name. You must help your relatives when asked and support them when needed. This is important to maintaining our identity as Lakȟóta people." Brave Heart continues, tapping into a key issue of identity and belonging: "We must know who we are, where we come from, our ancestors, our history, our culture, and our language. To decolonize, we have to stay true to our values and way of life."[32]

While there really is no cure for Covid-19, the Lakȟóta people, like many native communities in North America, demonstrated what it means to be good relatives, and made the best of a dire situation. Their response to the pandemic was a lesson in kinship and Lakȟól wičȟóȟ'aŋ.

AFTERWORD

A long time ago, during treaty negotiations with the wašíču, Red Cloud and other chiefs demanded that the US government pay compensation for the Black Hills for seven generations. This notion of seven generations has since become an important idea in Lakȟóta thought. Some Lakȟóta prophesized that there would be hardship for seven generations before the Buffalo people would prosper and thrive again. By the end of the 1880s the buffalo were disappearing, retreating back into the earth to preserve themselves for the future. At that time, the Lakȟóta people were also suffering and going back into the earth. Or so it seemed. Today, the buffalo has come back to Lakȟóta reservations and communities, and with the return of the buffalo, Lakȟóta culture, language, and values are being rejuvenated.

This book has demonstrated the continuity of Lakȟól wičhóȟ'aŋ since the earliest available historical sources on the Lakȟóta people—the importance of kinship and relationship, of viewpoint diversity, of perseverance and adaptability. While Lakȟóta culture, like any culture, has changed and evolved over time, there is still a clear foundation rooted in Lakȟóta ways and traditions. They have changed and adapted, while tenaciously maintaining their most sacred cultural precepts. Against unfathomable odds, they are still here and are standing strong.

Perhaps the sacred tree of Black Elk's great vision is finally beginning to bloom, and the people are returning to the sacred hoop. Perhaps now is the time for the seventh generation to take charge and lead the Lakȟóta into a better future for the next seven generations. Mitákuye oyás'iŋ "all my relatives, we are all related."

GLOSSARY OF LAKȞÓTA
TERMS AND PHRASES

akíčhita	soldiers, camp marshals; messenger, representative, lieutenant, scout
Akíčhita Háŋske	Long Soldier
akíčhita ktépi	soldier killing
Akíčhita Nážiŋ	Standing Soldier
Anúŋg Ité	Double Face, Double Woman, Double Women
até	father; father's brothers
Bdewákȟaŋtȟuŋwaŋ	Mdewakanton Dakota, Mdewakanton Sioux
Blé Wakȟáŋ	Sacred Lake
blotáhuŋka	war leader, lieutenant; may also refer to a war prophet or sacred war leader
blotáhuŋka itȟáŋčhaŋ	war leader
Blotáhuŋka Tȟáŋka	Big Partisan
Boíde (Oíle)	The Flame
Čhaȟlí Wakpá	Powder River
čhaŋgléška wakȟáŋ	sacred hoop
Čhaŋgléška Wakíŋyaŋ	Ring Thunder
Čhaŋȟpí Lúta	Red Tomahawk
Čhaŋkȟáhu	Hump

Čhaŋkpé Ópi	Wounded Knee Creek
čhaŋkú lúta	red road
Čhaŋkú Tȟáŋka	Big Road
čhaŋnúŋpa	pipe
Čhaŋpȟá Wakpá	Cherry Creek
Čhaŋté T'íŋza	Strong Heart
čhaŋwákȟaŋ	sacred tree
čhatkú	place of honor opposite the doorway in the tipi or lodge
čhékiya	to beg; to cry, weep, or wail to someone or something; to pray to someone or something, beseech, entreat; to address someone or something using the proper kinship term (chékiyapi is the nominalized form 'prayer')
Čheška Zí	Yellow Breast
Čhetáŋ Máza	Iron Hawk
Čhetáŋ Sápa	Black Hawk
Čhetáŋ Ská	White Hawk
Čhetáŋ Zí	Yellow Hawk
Čhoníčha Waníče	No Flesh
Dakȟóta	Dakȟóta, Eastern Sioux, Santee
eháŋni ohúŋkakaŋ	ancient ones, ancient relatives; mythology, folk traditions, sacred stories
eháŋni wóyakapi	old stories
éyapaha	village crier, herald
há	skin, hide, bark, outer casing or shell of anything; clothes, clothing
hakáta	opposite-sex siblings and cousins
haŋbléčheyapi	vision quest, vision fast, crying for a vision
haŋblóglaka	spirit language, to relate one's vision or spiritual experience
haŋpóšpu hokšíčala	baby doll
Haŋwí	Moon
háu	hello, greetings

Hé Tópa	Four Horns
Hé Wótoka	John Blunt Horn
Heȟáka Sápa	Nicholas Black Elk
Heȟáka Wákhita	Looking Elk
Heȟáka Wakpá	Yellowstone River
Heȟlóǧeȟa Nážiŋ	Standing Hollow Horn
Héša	Red Horn
Ȟesápa	Black Hills
Hewáŋžiča	Lone Horn, One Horn
heyókȟa	contrary, sacred clown
Ȟeyúškiška	Big Horn Mountains
hináphapi	emergence
Hiŋháŋ Tatȟáŋka	Bull Owl
Hiŋháŋ Wakpá	Moreau River
ȟmúŋǧa	to bewitch someone or something
Hó Wašté	Good Voice
hóčȟoka	sacred space, altar; camp circle
Hohú Ógle	Walter Bone Shirt; Never Misses
Hohú Yuhá	Bone Keepers
hoúya	war shaman speaking with wolves
huŋká	hunka, adopted relative; making of relatives ceremony (also refers to an individual who has been honored in this ceremony)
huŋkápi	making of relatives
Húŋkpapȟa	Hunkpapa
Húŋkpathila	Lakȟóta sub-band
hunúŋpa	two legged; ceremonial name for the Bear spirit
hutkȟáŋ	roots
Í Tȟáŋka	Big Mouth
ičáȟpe hú	'rubs against root' or purple coneflower
igláka	moving camp
iglásota	giveaway
iglúwašte	reciprocity
Iháŋktȟuŋwaŋ	Yankton
Iháŋktȟuŋwaŋna	Yanktonai

Iktómi (Iktó)	Spider (the Trickster of Lakȟóta myth and oral tradition)
iná	mother; mother's sisters
iníkaǧapi	life renewal
inípi	sweat lodge, sweat lodge ceremony, purification ceremony
Íŋyaŋ	Rock
Íŋyaŋ Ȟé Wiŋ	Rocky Butte
Íŋyaŋ Wakȟáŋaǧapi Othí	Sacred Stone Camp
Íŋyaŋ Woslál Hé	Standing Rock
Isáŋyathi	Santee
Išnála Wičháša	Lone Man
išnáthi	menstrual lodge
išnáthi awíčhalowaŋpi	preparing a girl for womanhood or the buffalo sing
Itázipčho	Sans Arc
Ité	the Face, the beautiful daughter of the Old Man and the Old Woman
Ité Omáǧažu	Rain In The Face
itéha	mask
Itéšiča	Bad Face
itȟáŋčhaŋ	chief, social or civil leader
itȟáŋčhaŋ théča	young leaders; new leaders
iwákčhipi	victory dance
iwášipi	warrior ceremony for locating enemies and enemy camps
iyé wakȟáŋ	holy language, or the language of the shamans
kasótapi	to wipe something or someone out; to eradicate, exterminate
Káŋka	the Old Woman, the Witch
khiíŋyaŋka očháŋku	racetrack
Khiyúksa	Break One's Own
Kȟaŋǧí Máza	Iron Crow
Kȟaŋǧí Šúŋka	Crow Dog
Kȟaŋǧí Tȟáŋka	Big Crow
Kȟaŋǧí Wakpá Oyáŋke	Crow Creek Reservation

Kȟaŋǧí Wíyaka	Crow Feather
Kȟaŋǧí Yátapi	Crow King
kȟolá	friend, ally
kȟolátakuya	friendship
Khulwíčhaša	Lower Brulé
Khulwíčhaša Oyáŋke	Lower Brulé Reservation
kté	coup, to count coup, to kill
Kuhíŋyaŋ	Sacred Stone Returning
Lakȟól wichóȟ'aŋ	Lakȟóta way of life, Lakȟóta traditions, Lakȟóta customs, Lakȟóta culture
lakȟólkičhiyapi	allies, all people speaking the same language
Lakȟóta	friend, ally; the people; the Sioux; the Lakȟóta (Lakȟótapi is the plural form); Teton
Lakȟóta tȟamákȟočhe	Lakȟóta territory, Lakȟóta homelands
Lakȟól'iya Wičhóthi	Lakȟóta Language Camp
lekší	uncle, my uncle
líla wakȟáŋ	very sacred
lowáŋpi	sing (a type of healing ceremony)
Maǧáska	The Swan
Maȟpíya Lúta	Red Cloud
Maȟpíya Lúta Owáyawa	Red Cloud Indian School
Maȟpíya Waháčhaŋka	Cloud Shield
Maká Čhiŋčála	Young Skunk
Makhízita Wakpá	White River
Makhúla	Breast, also known as Left Heron
makȟá	earth, dirt, country
Makȟá Tȟósaŋsaŋ	Blue Earth
Makȟásaŋ Wakpá	White Clay Creek
Makhízita Wakpá	White River
Makȟóšiča	Badlands
maškέ	female friend (of a woman)
Matȟó Čík'ala	Little Bear
Matȟó Gnaškíŋyaŋ	Mad Bear
Matȟó Íŋyaŋke	Running Bear
Matȟó Kȟokípȟapi	Afraid of Bear

Matȟó Lúzahaŋ	Swift Bear
Matȟó Nážiŋ	Standing Bear
Matȟó Núŋpa	Two Bears
Matȟó Pahá	Bear Butte
Matȟó Sab'íč'iya	Smutty Bear
Matȟó Šíča	Bad Bear
Matȟó Tȟatȟáŋka	Bull Bear
Matȟó Tȟípila	Devils Tower
Matȟó Tȟučȟúhu	Bear's Rib
Matȟó Wakíŋyaŋ	Thunder Bear
Matȟó Wanáȟtaka	Kicking Bear
matȟó waphíye	bear doctors
Matȟó Watȟákpa	Charging Bear
Matȟó Wayúhi	Scattering Bear
Matȟó Wawóyuspa	Catch The Bear
mitákuye oyás'iŋ	all my relatives, we are all related
mitȟáwaše	my female friend
Míwakȟaŋ	George Sword
Miwátaŋni Háŋska	Long Mandan
Mní Waníče	No Water
mní wichóni	water is life
Mnikȟówožu	Minneconjou Lakȟóta, Minneconjou Sioux
Mníšoše	Missouri River
naǧí	spirit, soul, ghost (one aspect of the human soul); may also refer generally to spirits (naǧípi is the plural form); shadow, shade
naǧíla	like-a-spirit, like-a-soul; may also refer to the soul of a nonhuman thing (naǧílapi is the plural form)
naǧípi	souls, spirits
Nakȟóta	Assiniboine, Stoney [not Sioux]
nawíčhašli	measles
niyá	life, breath, life-breath (literally, "that which causes life"); ghost, the animating soul of the body (one aspect of the human soul) (niyápi is the plural form)

Núm Kapȟá	Two Strike
Núŋǧe Waníče	No Ears
Očhéthi Šakówiŋ	Seven Council Fires
Oglála	Oglala Lakȟóta, Oglala Sioux
ógle wakȟáŋ	sacred shirt, ghost shirt
Óhaŋzi	Shade, a safe haven in the Badlands
Ohítika Woman	Mary Brave Bird
okȟólakičhiye	men's societies
Okíčhize Tȟáwa	His Battle, Jaw (a Northern Lakȟóta of Hunk-papa and Sans Arc ancestry who spoke with Frances Densmore in 1913)
Omáha Wačhípi	Omaha Dance
Oóhenuŋpa	Two Kettle Lakȟóta, Two Kettle Sioux
Oóšiča Hokšíla	Bad Wound
opáǧi	ceremonially filled pipe
otúȟʾaŋ	giveaway
owákpamni oyáŋke	reservation
Oyáte Wayáŋkapi	Seen By The Nation
oyáte	people, nation, tribe
ozáŋ	tipi liner, dew curtain
ozúye	war party
ožúha pȟežúta	medicine bag
Pahá Sápa	Black Hills
Pahá Zizípela/Žaŋžáŋ Blaská	Slim Buttes
pápa	jerky, dried, jerked meat
Pȟaláni Tȟawákpa	
/Čhaŋšúška Wakpá	Grand River
Pȟaŋkéska Wakpá	Platte River
Pȟayábya	Pushed to Head
Pȟeháŋ Sáŋ	White Crane
Pȟehíŋ Háŋska	George Custer, "Long Hair"
Pȟehíŋ Yuȟáȟa	Curly Hair (Crazy Horse's boyhood name)
pȟelwáŋyaŋk lowáŋ	
/pȟéta waŋyáŋk lowáŋ	fire-seeing sing
Pȟešlá	Mount Baldy

Pȟéta Ilé	Fire Thunder
pȟetáǧa	live coal
Pȟeží	Grass
pȟežúta	medicine
pȟežúta pȟá	bitter medicine
pȟežúta wičháša	medicine man, medicine men
Phizí	Gall
Phuthíŋska	William S. Harney
póȟpoǧaŋ na pȟešnížala waŋ uŋ woíle	to blow on a little spark to ignite fire with it
Pté Oyáte	Buffalo Nation, Buffalo People, Buffalo Tribe
ptehíŋčala čhaŋnúŋpa	buffalo calf pipe
Ptesáŋwiŋ	White Buffalo (Cow) Woman
Šahíyela Wakpá	Belle Fourche River
Saóne	Northern Lakȟóta
Sčílikté	Pawnee Killer
Sí Kȟaŋǧí	Crow Foot
Sičháŋǧu	Brulé, Rosebud Lakȟóta, Rosebud Sioux
Sičháŋǧu Oyáŋke	Rosebud Reservation
šičúŋ	soul, spirit, imparted nonhuman potency, familiar, spirit guardian, the spirit of a wakȟáŋ (spirit being, nonhuman person) (one aspect of the human soul that is of nonhuman origin; other šičúŋpi [plural form of šičúŋ] can be acquired throughout the life cycle in various ways); the tȟúŋ (potency) of a wakȟáŋ (spirit being, nonhuman person)
Sihásapa	Blackfeet Lakȟóta, Blackfeet Sioux
Siŋté Gleška	Spotted Tail
Sisíthuŋwaŋ	Sisseton Dakota, Sisseton Sioux
Sitȟáŋka	Big Foot
Šiyáka	Teal Duck (a Sioux elder from Standing Rock Reservation interviewed by Frances Densmore in 1912)
šiyótȟáŋka	flute
Škáŋ	Sky, the great spirit of movement

Slót'a	Métis
Šóta	Smoke
Šuŋǧílasapa	Red Fox
Šuŋgmánitu Sápa	Black Fox
Šúŋka Bloká	He Dog
Šúŋka Lúta	Red Dog
Šúŋka Waŋžíla	Lone Dog
Šuŋkmánitu Waŋkátuya	High Wolf
Táku Škaŋškáŋ	Sky, That Which Moves, Moving Spirit (the spirit or aspect of Wakȟáŋ Tȟáŋka that controls all movement and locomotion; sometimes referred to as Škáŋ or Škaŋškáŋ)
Táku Waníča	No Neck
takúye	relative, relatives
Tȟačhéži Wakpá	Tongue River
tȟahúka čhaŋgléška	hoop game
Tȟáȟča Hušté	Lame Deer
tȟaŋčháŋ	body, form
Tȟaópi Čík'ala	Little Wound
tȟápa waŋkáyeyapi	throwing of the ball
Tȟašína Máni Wiŋ	Moving Robe Woman
Tȟašíŋa Tópawiŋ	Four Robes
Tȟašnáheča Yúta	Ground Squirrel Eaters
Tȟašúŋke Kȟokípȟapi	Man Afraid of His Horses
Tȟašúŋke Óta	Plenty Horses
Tȟašúŋke Witkó	Crazy Horse
Tȟaté	Wind
tȟatȟáŋka	buffalo, male or bull buffalo (Tȟatȟáŋka may also refer to buffalo as a spirit being or nonhuman person)
Tȟatȟáŋka Íyotake	Sitting Bull
tȟatȟáŋka lowáŋpi	buffalo sing
Tȟatȟáŋka Pȟá	Bull Head
Tȟatȟáŋka Ptéčela	Short Bull
Tȟatȟáŋka Ská	White Bull
Tȟatȟáŋka Waŋží	One Bull

Tȟatȟáŋkehaŋni	Old Bull
tȟatȟáŋk-iháŋbla	"dreamed the buffalo-spirit"
Tȟatȟóka Íŋyaŋke	Running Antelope
Tȟatúye Tópa	Four Winds, Four Directions, Four Brothers
tȟawáčhiŋ	mind, will, intellect, reason, disposition, understanding
Tȟawáčhiŋ Wašté Wiŋ	Freda Mesteth Goodsell
tȟéya	cowives
thíŋta	plains
thípi	tipi, lodge
thípi iyókhiheya	council lodge, "tipis joined together"
thítakuye	lodge/band relatives
thítȟuŋwaŋ	dwellers on the plains
thiwáhe	family, household
Thiyóčhesli	Defecates in Lodge
thiyóšpaye	lodge group, tipi group, band, extended family
thiyóthipi	council lodge, "lodge of lodges"
thóka	enemy, enemies
Tȟokáhe	First Man
thókakičhiyapi	enemies, those one is related to as enemy
thókapi	enemies
Tȟóyaŋke Wašté-wiŋ	Good Seat
thúŋ	endowed mystical power or quality; power to do miraculous things; essence; potency; potentiality
thuŋwáŋ	potency
thuŋwíŋ	aunt
Tób Kiŋ	The Four Winds
Tóbtob Kiŋ	the four-times-four, the sixteen manifestations of Wakȟáŋ Tȟáŋka
tuŋwéya	scout, scouts
Uŋžíŋžiŋtka Wakpá	Rosebud River
wačhékiya	to pray to or for, to cry to or for; to address someone or something as a relative; to ceremonially smoke the sacred pipe

wačhípi	dance, powwow
Wágluȟe	Loafers
Wagmúŋka ógnaka ičháŋte	Black Hills, the heart of everything that is
Waháčhaŋka Hotȟúŋ	Ringing Shield
waȟmúŋǧa	sorcery, witchcraft
Waȟpé Lúta	Red Leaf
Waȟpétȟuŋwaŋ	Wahpeton Dakota, Wahpeton Sioux
wakȟáŋ	sacred, sacrality, mystery, mysterious, holy, power, powerful, incomprehensible, energy, "medicine"; may also refer to a spirit being or nonhuman person
wakȟáŋ akáŋtula	humans, people, things on top
wakȟáŋ kiŋ	the sacred, the sacred powers of the universe
wakȟáŋ škáŋ wičháša	evil conjuror who causes sickness
Wakȟáŋ Tȟáŋka	Great Mystery, Great Mysterious, Great Spirit, Great Spirits
wakȟáŋ wačhípi	mystery dance, medicine dance, holy dance, sacred dance, medicine lodge ceremony
wakȟáŋpi	spirits, all things that are above humankind
wakȟáŋpila	things like a spirit or exhibiting similar mysterious qualities
wakȟáŋyeža	children
wakíčhaǧapi	giveaway
wakíčhuŋza	deciders
Wakíŋyaŋ	Thunder Being
Wakíŋyaŋ Čík'ala	Little Thunder
Wakíŋyaŋ Lúzahaŋ	Fast Thunder
Wakíŋyaŋ Pȟéta	Edward Fire Thunder
Wakíŋyaŋ Wašté	Good Thunder
Wakíŋyaŋ Watȟákpe	Charging Thunder
Wakpá Wašté	Cheyenne River
Wakpá Wašté Oyáŋke	Cheyenne River Reservation
wakpámni tȟáŋka	great distribution
Wakpášiča	Bad River
Walúta Wápaha	Red Banner

wanáǧi	spirit, ghost, soul separated from the body (refers to unknown people's ghosts, not a particular person's spirit, which is naǧí)
Wanáǧi Ská	White Ghost
Wanáǧi Wačhípi kiŋ	the Ghost Dance
wanáǧi yuhápi	ghost-keeping ceremony, keeping of the ghost
wanásapi	communal buffalo hunt
waníkiya wówičala	Lakȟóta Christianity
waníyetu	winter
waníyetu iyáwapi	winter count
waŋblí gleška	spotted eagle
Waŋblí Waŋkátuya	Frank High Eagle
Waŋblí Wašté	Pretty Eagle
waphíya wičháša	healer, conjuror
waphíye	healers, medicine men, conjurors
Waphȟóštan	Battiste Good
wasé	sacred red earth paint, vermillion
wasná	pemmican
Wasú Máža	Dewey Beard
wašíču	white, white man, Caucasian, Euro-American
Wašíču Thašúŋka	American Horse
wašíčuŋ	spirit, soul; medicine bundle, ceremonial bundle, sacred bundle; indwelling spirit helper (wašíčuŋpi is the plural form)
wašté	good, well
watȟó	herbs
Watȟógla	the hunting bands of Lakȟóta
wayáka	captive, captives
Wazí/Wazíya	Old Man, the Cold, the mythical Wizard of the North
Wazí Aháŋhaŋ Oyáŋke	Pine Ridge Reservation
wazílya	to smudge, incense
Wažáža	a Sičháŋǧu band
Wí	Sun
wičháglata	female singers who sing high harmonies
wičhágnaškahu	wild currant
wičháȟpi owíŋža	star quilt

Wičháȟpi Waŋžíla	Lone Star
wičhápȟaha	human scalp
Wičháša Čík'ala	Little Big Man
wičháša itȟáŋčhaŋ	leader
wičháša wakȟáŋ	holy man, holy men
wičháša yatápika	"praiseworthy men," shirt wearers
wičhóicȟaǧe	the generations; life, growth, longevity
wičhóoyake	oral histories
wičhóthi	camps (literally, "place where humans dwell")
wichózani	health, wellness
Wígmuŋke Wašté Wiŋ	Marcella LeBeau
wíȟpeya	giveaway
wiíčhuwa	love medicine
wíŋyaŋ	woman, female
Wíŋyaŋ Lúta	Red Woman
wíŋyaŋ wakȟáŋ	sacred woman, holy woman
wióyušpa	courtship, "to catch a woman"
wípazukȟahu	juneberry
Wisápa	Black Moon
witkó	crazy, senseless, foolish, unreasonable, insane, irresponsible
wiwáŋyaŋg wačhípi	Sun Dance
wóčhekiye	prayer
wóglaka	telling, storytelling
Wóȟpe	Beautiful Woman (sacred name for White Buffalo [Cow] Woman)
wókȟokipȟe	dangerous, scary, powerful
wólakȟota	related; peace
wóphila	thank-offering, thanksgiving, thanks, gratitude, appreciation, gratefulness; a thanksgiving or appreciation ceremony
wóphiye	medicine bundle, medicine bag, ceremonial bundle, sacred bundle, mystery sack (wóphiyepi is the plural form)
Wóptuȟ'a	Chips
wótakuye	kinship
wótȟawe	war bundle, war medicine

wówakiš'ake	resilience
wówitȟuŋpȟeke ló	very powerful
yaǧópa/yapȟá	healing technique, type of healer who extracts sickness via sucking
yawánič̣a	giveaway
Yumní	Whirlwind
yuwípi	"wrapped up"; doctoring or healing ceremony of binding medicine men (usually performed in the dark and for purposes of finding lost objects and the cause of sickness)
zaní	to be healthy, well, whole
Ziŋtkála Lúzahaŋ	Swift Bird
Ziŋtkála Sáŋ	White Bird
Ziŋtkála Zí	Yellow Bird
Zipála	Wasp
zuyá	warfare
zuzéč̣a káǧa	imitates snakes; snake dreamer

ABBREVIATIONS

AEC	Archives of the Episcopal Church
AHP	American Horse Paper
AISRI	American Indian Studies Research Institute
AIWKSC	Army Investigation of the Battle at Wounded Knee and to the Sioux Campaign of 1890–1891
ARCIA	Annual Report of the Commissioner of Indian Affairs
ARSOW	Annual Report of the Secretary of War
BBMG	Buffalo Bill Museum and Grave
BCIM	Bureau of Catholic Indian Missions
CTCM	Minutes of the Cheyenne River Tribal Council Meetings
EAP	Edward Ashley Papers
EBMC	Eugene Buechel Manuscript Collection
EEAC	Edward E. Ayer Collection
ESRMC	Eli S. Ricker Manuscript Collection
FDP	Father Florentine Digman Papers
HCIAP	House Committee on Indian Affairs Papers
HCSHL	History Colorado, Stephen H. Hart Library and Research Center

HLDP   Henry L. Dawes Papers

HRMSCA   Holy Rosary Mission, Special Collections and Archives

IULL   Indiana University Lilly Library

JMLP   James McLaughlin Papers

JRWC   James R. Walker Collection

JWP   Josephine Waggoner Papers

LC   Library of Congress

LFSP   Lebbeus Foster Spencer Papers

LROIA   Letters Received by the Office of Indian Affairs

LSASPR   Letters Sent to the Office of Indian Affairs by the Agents or
            Superintendents at the Pine Ridge Agency

LTCM   Minutes of the Lower Brulé Tribal Council Meetings

MFT   Museum of the Fur Trade

MHS   Minnesota Historical Society

MUA   Marquette University Archives

NAASI   National Anthropological Archives, The Smithsonian Institution

NARA   National Archives and Records Administration

NCWHMC   Neihardt Collection, Western Historical Manuscript Collection

NDHS   North Dakota Historical Society

NSHS   Nebraska State Historical Society

OAG   Office of the Adjutant General

OTCM   Minutes of the Oglala Tribal Council Meetings

RBIA   Records of the Bureau of Indian Affairs

RG   Record Group

RTCM   Minutes of the Rosebud Tribal Council Meetings

SCIAP   Senate Committee on Indian Affairs Papers

STCM   Minutes of the Standing Rock Tribal Council Meetings

UMA   Upper Missouri Agency

UMC   University of Missouri, Columbia

WDP   Colonel A. B. Welch Dakota Papers

WSCMC   Walter S. Campbell Manuscript Collection

WHC   Western History Collection, Library, University of Oklahoma

WMCC   Walter M. Camp Collection

YCWA   Yale Collection of Western Americana

NOTES

Preface

1. Braun, "Introduction: An Ethnohistory of Listening." See also Meyers, "Native Anthropology," 1–2, 23–33.

2. DeMallie, quoted in J. Walker, *Lakota Society*, 1982, 112.

Prologue

1. Adapted from J. Walker, "The Sun Dance," 164–67; J. Walker, *Lakota Myth*, 2006, 52–57.

2. Adapted from J. Walker, "The Sun Dance," 179–82; J. Walker, *Lakota Myth*, 2006, 157–62. See also Brown, *The Sacred Pipe*, 2012.

Chapter 1

1. The classic sources on Lakȟóta stories are J. Walker, *Lakota Myth*; E. Deloria, *Dakota Texts*. See Buechel, *Lakota Tales and Text*. The original texts written in Lakȟóta are in the Eugene Buechel Manuscript Collection, Holy Rosary Mission Archives. We used the original texts, compared them with those in *Lakota Tales and Texts,* and corrected errors and mistranslations.

2. J. Walker, *Lakota Belief and Ritual*, 68–74; Black Elk, quoted in DeMallie, *The Sixth Grandfather*, 309–11.

3. Black Elk, quoted in Brown, *The Sacred Pipe*, 2012, 3–9.

4. Black Elk, quoted in Brown, 3–9.

5. Black Elk, quoted in Brown, 3–9. See Lone Man, quoted in Densmore, *Teton Sioux Music and Culture*, 2001, 63–68.

6. For a classic but outdated analysis of Lakȟóta society, see Hassrick, *The Sioux*, 2012, 3–30.

7. For use of the term, see DeMallie, "Teton," 799; DeMallie and Parks, "Plains Indian Warfare," 70–73.

8. For a thorough analysis of the structure of Lakȟóta society, see DeMallie, "Sioux Until 1850," 734–48. See also J. Walker, *Lakota Society*, 1992; Price, *The Oglala People*.

9. DeMallie, "Teton," 799–801; DeMallie, "Community in Native America," 190.

10. Schneider, *American Kinship*, 120–24; Sahlins, *What Kinship Is*, ix; Posthumus, "Ritual Thiyóšpaye," 4–21.

11. For excellent summaries of Lakȟóta bands in the historical record by early travelers, see DeMallie, "Sioux Until 1850," 735–48; DeMallie, "Teton," 819–20. For useful descriptions by white observers, see Tabeau, *Tabeau's Narrative*; Denig, *Five Indian Tribes*; Parkman, *Oregon Trail*; Wied, *North American Journals*.

12. The American Horse Ledger is kept by his descendants on the Pine Ridge Reservation. It is not publicly available, but we have used it with the permission of Richard Two Dogs and the American Horse family. See K. Bray, "The Oglala Lakota."

13. K. Bray, The Oglala Lakota," 141–44.

14. This information is based on the American Horse Ledger and conversations between Richard Two Dogs and Kingsley Bray, October–November 2021.

15. See K. Bray, "Teton Sioux Population History"; K. Bray, "Before Sitting Bull."

16. For analysis of Sioux homeland and migration in the seventeenth and early eighteenth centuries, see White, "The Winning of the West," 319–43; Anderson, *Kinsmen of Another Kind*, 1–76; DeMallie, "Sioux Until 1850," 719–25. For early Sioux history see Hämäläinen, *Lakota America*.

17. DeMallie, "Sioux Until 1850," 718–31.

18. See Truteau, *A Fur Trader on The Upper Missouri*, 95–105, 205–14; Anderson, *Kinsmen of Another Kind*, 1–2; DeMallie, "Sioux Until 1850," 719–27; Ostler, *The Plains Sioux*, 13–21; Hämäläinen, *Lakota America*.

19. See Hämäläinen, *Lakota America*, 85–184.

20. John Blunt Horn, quoted in Walker, *Lakota Society*, 1992, 13–14. See Makhúla winter count in Waggoner, *Witness*, 351–52. There are several versions of the Makhúla winter count. One gives the year of the first division of the tribes as 1762, the other gives 1778. The Sacred Lake refers to Mille Lacs in Minnesota.

21. Anderson, "Early Bands of the Saone Group," 87–94.

22. Hassrick, *The Sioux*, 2012, 3–6, 61–75; White, "The Winning of the West," 321–33; DeMallie, "Sioux Until 1850," 731–32.

23. For discussion of the Lakȟóta as riverine people see Hämäläinen, *Lakota America*, 4–5, 168–69; and for a critical commentary see Braun, Review of *Lakota America*, 123–24.

24. For estimates of Lakȟóta population, see DeMallie, "Sioux Until 1850," 748. The US government also vaccinated some Lakȟóta groups in the early 1830s, which aided population growth.

25. Walker, *Lakota Society*, 1992, 128–30; Greene and Thornton, *The Year the Stars Fell*, 138. For Régis Loisel, see Tabeau, *Tabeau's Narrative*; Nasatir, *Before Lewis and Clark*, 113–15.

26. "Lewis and Clarke's Expedition Communicated to Congress," February 19, 1806, American State Papers, 9th Cong., 1st Sess., Indian Affairs, 1:714, https://memory.loc.gov/cgi-bin/ampage, accessed March 18, 2019; Lewis and Clark, *The Definitive Journals of Lewis and Clark*, 3:24. For Lewis and Clark expedition and their comments about the Lakȟóta, see Ostler, *The Plains Sioux*, 18–20; Hämäläinen, *Lakota America*, 127–52. During their trek they had an encounter with the Blackfeet in Montana, and two Indians were killed.

27. Battiste Good and No Ears, quoted in Greene and Thornton, *The Year the Stars Fell*, 81, 101; Walker, *Lakota Society*, 1992, 127. For a classic analysis of winter counts see Mallery, *Picture-Writing of the American Indians*. Excellent collections and analysis on Lakȟóta winter counts are in Cheney, *Sioux Winter Count*; Walker, *Lakota Society*, 1992; Greene and Thornton, *The Year the Stars Fell*; Waggoner, *Witness*. See also DeMallie, "Sioux Until 1850," 732.

28. For the concept of Lakota America as a distinct goal, see Hämäläinen, *Lakota America*.

29. Black Hawk, quoted in the *Missouri Daily Republican*, 1851, in K. Bray, "Lakota Statesmen," 168. Other Indian accounts of hunting and territories are in "Report of Indian Agent Alfred J. Vaughan," ARCIA, 1854, 87–89.

30. Battiste Good, quoted in Greene and Thornton, *The Year the Stars Fell*, 77–83.

31. Van de Logt, "I Was Brought to Life to Save My People," 23–46. Commissioner of Indian Affairs Thomas L. McKenney noted in his 1829 report that the Sioux were constantly fighting with other tribes, and the feuds "were of ancient origin" and would not stop until a weaker tribe was annihilated or absorbed into the other. "Report of the Commissioner of Indian Affairs Thomas L. McKenney, November 7, 1829," ARCIA, 1929, 166. See also, Truteau, *A Fur Trader on The Upper Missouri*.

32. American Horse, quoted in Greene and Thornton, *The Year the Stars Fell*, 97. The exact year the Lakȟóta encountered the Black Hills is debatable. Other winter counts with varying years are the No Ears, Rosebud, Cloud Shield, Red Horse Owner in Walker, *Lakota Society*, 1992, 127; Greene and Thornton, *The Year the Stars Fell*, 96, 99; Makhúla, quoted in Waggoner, *Witness*, 531. Several winter counts state that the Lakȟóta drank cedar tree tea for protection against diseases such as measles. Perhaps Standing Buffalo was searching for medicine from the Black Hills and discovered a conifer, maybe juniper, unfamiliar to the Lakȟóta. Battiste Good gives the date of this event as 1784–85 and claims that it was related to a feast when a sacred man pulled a cedar tree out of the ground, which turned out to be just a trick. Thus, he does not relate this to the discovery of the Black Hills at all. Battiste Good, quoted in Greene and Thornton, *The Year the Stars Fell*, 106–7. See Ostler, *The Lakotas and the Black Hills*, 9–11; Hämäläinen, *Lakota America*.

33. For the names "Heart of Everything that is" and the "Heart of the Hunt" see Bear Eagle, Sina, "Oníya Ošóka." See also Andersson, "Re-Indigenizing National Parks"; Discussion with Corey Yellow Boy, October 16, 2019, Andersson, "Field Notes and Interviews, 2000–2020."

34. Discussions with Robert Brave Heart Sr., August 23, 2019; Corey Yellow Boy, October 16, 2019; and Basil Brave Heart, July 18, 2020, in Andersson, "Field Notes and Interviews, 2000–2020." "Matthew J. Hill, Historicizing the 'Shrine of Democracy': Lakota Perspectives on Mount Rushmore in the Context of the Black Hills." Unpublished manuscript. Used by permission of the author.

Chapter 2

1. Ringing Shield, quoted in J. Walker, *Lakota Belief and Ritual*, 206.
2. No Flesh, quoted in J. Walker, *Lakota Belief and Ritual*, 193.
3. Black Elk, quoted in DeMallie, *The Sixth Grandfather*, 1984, 49–50.
4. V. Deloria, *Spirit and Reason*, 38, 46–53; V. Deloria, *C. G. Jung and the Sioux Traditions*, 80; DeMallie, "*Lakota Belief and Ritual* in the Nineteenth Century," 27–28; DeMallie, "Teton," 806; Posthumus, "All My Relatives," 2017, 383.
5. Thin Elk, quoted in Goodman, *Lakota Star Knowledge*, 40; Posthumus, *All My Relatives*, 2018, 63–64; V. Deloria, *C. G. Jung and the Sioux Traditions*, 84.
6. Posthumus, *All My Relatives*, 2018, 64–72; Amiotte, "Our Other Selves," 27, 29.
7. Finger, quoted in J. Walker, "The Sun Dance," 156; Walker, 87, 156–59; J. Walker, *Lakota Belief and Ritual*, 72–73; Posthumus, *All My Relatives*, 2018, 66–67; Amiotte, "Our Other Selves," 30–32; White Hat, *Life's Journey-Zuya*, 77.
8. J. Walker, *Lakota Belief and Ritual*, 51, 73, 94; Posthumus, *All My Relatives*, 2018, 67–71; Goodman, *Lakota Star Knowledge*, 40–41.
9. Standing Bear, *Land of the Spotted Eagle*, 2006, 193.
10. Standing Bear, 38.
11. Posthumus, "All My Relatives," 2017, 383.
12. See Black Elk, quoted in DeMallie, *The Sixth Grandfather*, 1984; Posthumus, "All My Relatives," 2017, 383–84.
13. DeMallie, *The Sixth Grandfather*, 1984, 80–81; J. Walker, *Lakota Belief and Ritual*, 68–80.
14. Posthumus, "All My Relatives," 2017, 384; Posthumus, *All My Relatives*, 2018, 36–38; DeMallie and Lavenda, "Wakan: Plains Siouan Concepts of Power."
15. Fletcher, "The Elk Mystery or Festival. Ogallala Sioux.," 276, emphasis in original.
16. Good Seat, quoted in J. Walker, *Lakota Belief and Ritual*, 70.
17. Sword, quoted in J. Walker, "The Sun Dance," 152.
18. White Hat, *Life's Journey-Zuya*, 84; Posthumus, *All My Relatives*, 2018, 37.
19. Sword, quoted in J. Walker, *Lakota Belief and Ritual*, 98.
20. Sword, quoted in Walker, 75.
21. Sword, quoted in Walker, 73.
22. V. Deloria, *Spirit and Reason*, 48.
23. V. Deloria, C. G. Jung and the Sioux Traditions, 14.
24. Little Wound, quoted in J. Walker, Lakota Belief and Ritual, 69; DeMallie, The Sixth Grandfather, 1984, 81; Curtis, The North American Indian, 3:60; Densmore, Teton Sioux Music and Culture, 2001, 85n2.
25. See Thomas Tyon, quoted in J. Walker, "The Sun Dance," 159–60.

26. Sword, quoted in J. Walker, "The Sun Dance," 153; Sword, Bad Wound, No Flesh, and Tyon, quoted in J. Walker, *Lakota Belief and Ritual*, 93–95. For a good summary of Lakȟóta concepts of the universe, see Hollabaugh, *The Spirit and the Sky*.

27. Arthur Amiotte, interview by David C. Posthumus, Fieldwork Interviews and Personal Communications; J. Walker, *Lakota Belief and Ritual*, 231, 234; DeMallie and Lavenda, "Wakan: Plains Siouan Concepts of Power," 157.

28. Bushotter, "Lakota Texts by George Bushotter"; Mails and Fools Crow, *Fools Crow*, 50; Powers, *Sacred Language*, 206; Wilson, *Redefining Shamanisms*, 195.

29. E. Deloria, "Gamma. Religion," 2.

30. Posthumus, *All My Relatives*, 2018; Posthumus, "Typology," 239.

31. Posthumus, "Typology," 242; E. Bray and M. Bray, *Joseph N. Nicollet on the Plains and Prairies*, 269; Fletcher, "Complete 1882 Sioux Field Notebook."

32. Posthumus, "Typology," 243–44.

33. Little Wound, American Horse, and Lone Star, quoted in J. Walker, *Lakota Belief and Ritual*, 181–82.

34. J. Walker, "Sun Dance," 58, 62–66, 72; J. Walker, *Lakota Belief and Ritual*, 95, 104; Posthumus, "Typology," 244–45; Hassrick, *The Sioux*, 1964, 288.

35. J. Walker, "The Sun Dance," 90–92, 152–53; J. Walker, *Lakota Belief and Ritual*, 90, 93; Posthumus, "Transmitting," 112; Posthumus, "Typology," 247–48.

36. Sword, Bad Wound, No Flesh, and Tyon, quoted in J. Walker, *Lakota Belief and Ritual*, 95.

37. Sword, quoted in Walker, 93.

38. Fletcher, "Complete 1882 Sioux Field Notebook."

39. Densmore, *Teton Sioux Music and Culture*, 2001, 245; J. Walker, "Sun Dance," 74–75, 79, 90–92, 132–35, 153, 161; J. Walker, *Lakota Belief and Ritual*, 78–79, 85, 94–95, 106, 113, 117, 129, 140; Posthumus, "Typology," 247; Hassrick, *The Sioux*, 1964, 290.

40. Sword, quoted in J. Walker, *Lakota Belief and Ritual*, 79–80.

41. Posthumus, "Typology," 252–53.

42. J. Walker, "Sun Dance," 163; Posthumus, "Typology," 252.

43. J. Walker, *Lakota Belief and Ritual*, 80, 105–6; Posthumus, "Typology," 252–53.

44. Standing Bear, *Land of the Spotted Eagle*, 203, emphasis added.

45. Sword, quoted in J. Walker, *Lakota Belief and Ritual*, 92; J. Walker, "Sun Dance," 163; Posthumus, "Typology," 254.

46. Tyon, William Garnett, Thunder Bear, Sword, and John Blunt Horn, quoted in J. Walker, *Lakota Belief and Ritual*, 105; Posthumus, "Typology," 255–56.

47. Posthumus, "Typology," 257–58.

48. E. Deloria, "Dakota Ceremonies," 65–66.

49. Sword, quoted in J. Walker, *Lakota Belief and Ritual*, 92; J. Walker, "Sun Dance," 161–63; J. Walker, *Lakota Belief and Ritual*, 92, 159, 161–63, 242–43; Fugle, "The Nature and Function of the Lakota Night Cults," 24–25, 27; Posthumus, "Typology," 259–61.

50. Tyon, quoted in J. Walker, *Lakota Belief and Ritual*, 161.

51. J. Walker, *Lakota Belief and Ritual*, 92–93, 161; Posthumus, "Typology," 258–59.

52. See, for instance, Tabeau, *Tabeau's Narrative*, 182; DeMallie, "Male and Female in Nineteenth Century Lakota Culture"; St. Pierre and Long Soldier, *Walking in the Sacred Manner*; Standing Bear, *Land of the Spotted Eagle*, 2006, 146–47.

53. Standing Bear, *Land of the Spotted Eagle*, 2006, 88–89.

54. E. Deloria, "The Dakota Way of Life"; J. Walker, *Lakota Belief and Ritual*, 242; DeMallie, "Male and Female in Nineteenth Century Lakota Culture"; DeMallie, "Kinship and Biology," 134.

55. E. Deloria, "Beta. The Virgin's Fire [and Other Women's Rites]," 32.

56. E. Deloria, "The Dakota Way of Life"; J. Walker, *Lakota Society*, 1982, 107; Wissler, 76–80, 93–94, 98–99; Wissler, "Field Notes on the Dakota Indians," 123; Standing Bear, *Land of the Spotted Eagle*, 2006, 205.

57. Standing Bear, *Land of the Spotted Eagle*, 2006, 150–51.

58. Black Elk, quoted in Brown, *The Sacred Pipe*, 1989, 44, 46.

59. Standing Bear, *Land of the Spotted Eagle*, 2006, 63.

60. Standing Bear, 140–41.

61. Standing Bear, 140–41.

62. Feraca, *Wakinyan*, 71–74; Posthumus, *All My Relatives*, 2018, 173.

63. E. Deloria, *Speaking of Indians*, 28–29; White Hat, *Life's Journey-Zuya*, 75n1; Dorsey, "A Study of Siouan Cults," 435–36; DeMallie, "Teton," 807; Posthumus, *All My Relatives*, 2018, 49–50, 54–55.

64. E. Deloria, *Speaking of Indians*, 1998, 55.

65. Charging Thunder, quoted in Densmore, *Teton Sioux Music and Culture*, 2001, 127; Brown, *The Sacred Pipe*, 1989, 6–7; DeMallie, "Teton," 807.

66. Sword, quoted in J. Walker, *Lakota Belief and Ritual*, 81–83.

67. J. Walker, *Lakota Belief and Ritual*, 69, 75, 99.

68. Little Wound, America Horse, and Lone Star, quoted in Walker, 68.

69. Little Wound, quoted in Walker, 67; DeMallie, "Teton," 807.

70. Sword, quoted in J. Walker, *Lakota Belief and Ritual*, 75.

71. Sword, quoted in Walker, 81.

72. E. Deloria, "Rites and Ceremonies of the Teton," 1; DeMallie, "Deloria, Ella Cara," 2264–65.

73. E. Deloria, "Dakota Ceremonies," 69–70.

74. J. Brown, *The Sacred Pipe*, 1989; Neihardt, *Black Elk Speaks*, 2008; Neihardt, *Black Elk Speaks*, 2014.

75. J. Walker, "Sun Dance," 67–68, 156; J. Walker, *Lakota Belief and Ritual*, 83–84, 100; J. Brown, *The Sacred Pipe*, 1989, 31–43; DeMallie, "Teton," 807; Bucko, *The Lakota Ritual of the Sweat Lodge*.

76. J. Walker, "Sun Dance," 68–69; J. Walker, *Lakota Belief and Ritual*, 83–86, 132–35, 150–53; Densmore, *Teton Sioux Music and Culture*, 2001, 157–94; Curtis, *The North American Indian*, 3:65–70; J. Brown, *The Sacred Pipe*, 1989, 44–66; DeMallie, "*Lakota Belief and Ritual* in the Nineteenth Century," 34–42; DeMallie, "Teton," 807; Posthumus, *All My Relatives*, 2018, 136–67.

77. Fletcher, "The Sun Dance of the Ogallala Sioux"; DeMallie, "Teton," 807; Dorsey, "A Study of Siouan Cults," 450–67; E. Deloria, "The Sun Dance of the Oglala Sioux";

J. Walker, "Sun Dance," 94–121; J. Walker, *Lakota Belief and Ritual*, 176–80; Curtis, *The North American Indian*, 3:87–99; J. Brown, *The Sacred Pipe*, 1989, 67–100; Amiotte, "The Lakota Sun Dance: Historical and Contemporary Perspectives."

78. DeMallie, "Teton," 807; Fletcher, *The Hako*; J. Walker, "Sun Dance," 122–40; J. Walker, *Lakota Belief and Ritual*, 208–40; Densmore, *Teton Sioux Music and Culture*, 2001, 68–77; Curtis, *The North American Indian*, 3:71–87; J. Brown, *The Sacred Pipe*, 1989, 101–15. Andersson, "Field Notes and Interviews, 2000–2020."

79. DeMallie, "Teton," 807; J. Walker, "Sun Dance," 141–51; J. Walker, *Lakota Belief and Ritual*, 241–53; J. Brown, *The Sacred Pipe*, 1989, 116–26.

80. DeMallie, "Teton," 807–8; Fletcher, "The Shadow or Ghost Lodge: A Ceremony of the Ogallala Sioux"; Densmore, *Teton Sioux Music and Culture*, 2001, 77–84; Curtis, *The North American Indian*, 3:99–110; J. Brown, *The Sacred Pipe*, 1989, 10–30.

81. DeMallie, "Teton," 808; J. Brown, *The Sacred Pipe*, 1989, 127–38; Beckwith, "Mythology of the Oglala Dakota," 414.

82. DeMallie, "Teton," 817; Macgregor, *Warriors without Weapons*, 98–99; J. Walker, *Lakota Belief and Ritual*, 153–55; Densmore, *Teton Sioux Music and Culture*, 2001, 204–38; Feraca, *Wakinyan*; Powers, *Yuwipi*; Posthumus, "Ritual Thiyóšpaye."

Chapter 3

1. E. Deloria, *Speaking of Indians*, 1998, 24.

2. E. Deloria, 24; DeMallie, "Teton," 799.

3. E. Deloria, *Speaking of Indians*, 1998, 25. Deloria is talking about the Sioux in general, and particularly the Lakȟóta. At that time "Dakȟóta" was used as an umbrella term to refer to all the Sioux peoples.

4. DeMallie, "Change in American Indian Kinship Systems: The Dakota," 233; DeMallie, "Kinship and Biology," 126, 131.

5. E. Deloria, *Speaking of Indians*, 1998, 25; Standing Bear, *Land of the Spotted Eagle*, 2006, 193, 250; White Hat, *Life's Journey—Zuya*, xx; DeMallie, "Teton," 808.

6. These categories do not designate a clear-cut distinction between consanguineal and affinal relatives. DeMallie, "Kinship," 330–31.

7. DeMallie, 332.

8. Standing Bear, *Land of the Spotted Eagle*, 2006, 37; V. Deloria, *C. G. Jung and the Sioux Traditions*, 143; Mirsky, "The Dakota," 394–400; DeMallie, "Kinship and Biology," 137; DeMallie, "Teton," 809.

9. Mirsky, "The Dakota," 400–403; DeMallie, "Teton," 809; V. Deloria, *C. G. Jung and the Sioux Traditions*, 143–44.

10. E. Deloria, *Speaking of Indians*, 1998, 26; White Hat, *Life's Journey—Zuya*, 88.

11. White Hat, *Life's Journey—Zuya*, 88.

12. E. Deloria, *Speaking of Indians*, 1998, 26; DeMallie, "Kinship and Biology," 135.

13. DeMallie, "Teton Dakota Kinship and Social Organization," 193–94; DeMallie, "Teton," 809; Standing Bear, *Land of the Spotted Eagle*, 2006, 32.

14. Standing Bear, *Land of the Spotted Eagle*, 2006, 148; E. Deloria, *Speaking of Indians*, 1998, 28–30; V. Deloria, Spirit and Reason, 38–39; White Hat, *Life's Journey—Zuya*,

44, 87–88; DeMallie, "Kinship and Biology," 131; Posthumus, *All My Relatives*, 2018, 37, 43, 204.

15. White Hat, *Life's Journey—Zuya*, 44.

16. E. Deloria, *Speaking of Indians*, 1998, 31–32.

17. E. Deloria, *Speaking of Indians*, 37.

18. E. Deloria, *Speaking of Indians*, 28–29; see also White Hat, *Life's Journey—Zuya*, 44; David C. Posthumus, *All My Relatives*, 2018, 49–50.

19. DeMallie, "The Lakota Ghost Dance," 391; Posthumus, "A Lakota View of Pté Oyáte."

20. V. Deloria, *Spirit and Reason*, 326–27, 334.

21. V. Deloria, 328.

22. V. Deloria, 329.

23. V. Deloria, *For This Land*, 252.

24. V. Deloria, *Spirit and Reason*, 337; see also V. Deloria, *For This Land*, 251.

25. E. Deloria, *Speaking of Indians*, 29; see also DeMallie, "Kinship and Biology in Sioux Culture," 131.

26. DeMallie, "Teton," 799; J. Walker, "Oglala Kinship Terms," 97.

27. E. Deloria, *Speaking of Indians*, 1998, 32–33; DeMallie, "Teton," 802.

28. Sword, "Dakota Texts from the Sword Manuscripts," 271.

29. E. Deloria, *Speaking of Indians*, 1998, 33.

30. E. Deloria, 34–37.

31. E. Deloria, 30–31.

32. DeMallie, "Sioux Until 1850," 719.

33. E. Deloria, *Speaking of Indians*, 1998, 40–41.

34. E. Deloria, 41–42.

35. Bad Bear, quoted in J. Walker, *Lakota Society*, 1982, 25; DeMallie, "Kinship," 330–31; DeMallie, "Teton," 801.

36. E. Deloria, *Speaking of Indians*, 1998, 38–40, 44–45; J. Walker, "The Sun Dance," 160; DeMallie, "Teton," 801, 810; Laubin and Laubin, *The Indian Tipi*.

37. E. Deloria, *Speaking of Indians*, 1998, 45. See DeMallie, "Sioux Until 1850," 718.

38. E. Deloria, *Speaking of Indians*, 1998, 38–39; J. Walker, "The Sun Dance," 73–74; DeMallie, "Teton," 801.

39. E. Deloria, *Speaking of Indians*, 1998, 40–41.

40. DeMallie, "Kinship: The Foundation for Native American Society," 334; Posthumus, "A Lakota View of Pté Oyáte (Buffalo Nation)," in Cunfer and Waiser, 278–310.

41. Bad Bear, quoted in J. Walker, *Lakota Society*, 1982, 26–27; E. Deloria, *Speaking of Indians*, 1998, 39; J. Walker, "The Sun Dance," 74–75; J. Walker, *Lakota Society*, 1982, 22–23, 26–30; DeMallie, "Teton," 801–2.

42. Bad Bear, quoted in J. Walker, *Lakota Society*, 1982, 25; Tyon, quoted in Walker, 29; DeMallie, "Teton," 802.

43. Tyon, quoted in J. Walker, *Lakota Society*, 1982, 31; DeMallie, "Teton," 802.

44. J. Walker, *Lakota Society*, 1982, 25, 31, 87; J. Walker, "The Sun Dance," 77; DeMallie, "Teton," 802.

45. DeMallie, "Teton," 802; Standing Bear, *Land of the Spotted Eagle*, 2006, 185.

46. He Dog, quoted in Hinman, "Oglala Sources on the Life of Crazy Horse," 13, 16–17; the best accounts of Crazy Horse's life are Sandoz, *Crazy Horse, the Strange Man of the Oglalas*; K. Bray, *Crazy Horse*.

47. He Dog, quoted in Hinman, "Oglala Sources on the life of Crazy Horse"; Sword, quoted in Jensen, *Voices of the American West*.

48. Iron Tail, quoted in J. Walker, *Lakota Society*, 1982, 34; Wissler; J. Walker, *Lakota Belief and Ritual*, 259–70; DeMallie, "Teton," 803.

49. E. Deloria, "Pregnancy, Birth, and Infancy," 1; V. Deloria, *C. G. Jung and the Sioux Traditions*, 138–39.

50. E. Deloria, "Pregnancy, Birth, and Infancy," 3, 6; V. Deloria, *C. G. Jung and the Sioux Traditions*, 140; DeMallie, "Teton," 808.

51. DeMallie, "Kinship and Biology," 134.

52. Standing Bear, *Land of the Spotted Eagle*, 2006, 5; E. Deloria, *Speaking of Indians*, 1998, 42–43; V. Deloria, *C. G. Jung and the Sioux Traditions*, 138, 142.

53. V. Deloria, *C. G. Jung and the Sioux Traditions*, 142–43; DeMallie, "Teton," 809.

54. Standing Bear, *Land of the Spotted Eagle*, 2006, 7.

55. E. Deloria, *Speaking of Indians*, 1998, 44; DeMallie, "Teton," 808–9; Dorsey, "Games of Teton Dakota Children"; see also DeMallie, "These Have No Ears," October 1, 1993.

56. Sword, quoted in J. Walker, *Lakota Belief and Ritual*, 79; DeMallie, "Teton," 809.

57. Standing Bear, *Land of the Spotted Eagle*, 2006, 98; Standing Bear, *My People the Sioux*, 2006, 196; DeMallie, "Kinship and Biology," 134; DeMallie, "Teton," 808–9.

58. Standing Bear, *Land of the Spotted Eagle*, 2006, 39.

59. J. Walker, *Lakota Society*, 1982, 57; Standing Bear, *Land of the Spotted Eagle*, 2006, 68; DeMallie, "Kinship," 332; DeMallie, "Teton," 809.

60. J. Walker, *Lakota Society*, 1982, 57; DeMallie, "Kinship," 333; DeMallie, "Teton," 809. A wonderful work of ethnographically informed historical fiction that focuses on the lives and roles of Lakȟóta women is Ella Deloria's classic *Waterlily*.

61. Standing Bear, *Land of the Spotted Eagle*, 2006, 105.

62. E. Deloria, *Speaking of Indians*, 1998, 39–40.

63. Waggoner, *Witness*, 165.

64. J. Walker, *Lakota Society*, 1982, 43, 57; Standing Bear, *Land of the Spotted Eagle*, 2006, 90, 126.

65. E. Deloria, "Dakota Commentary on Walker's Legends."

66. J. Walker, *Lakota Society*, 1982, 96; DeMallie, "Kinship and Biology," 134.

67. J. Walker, "Oglala Kinship Terms," 97–98; J. Walker, *Lakota Society*, 1982, 42, 55–56; Standing Bear, *Land of the Spotted Eagle*, 2006, 153–54; DeMallie, "Kinship and Biology," 127–29, 137; DeMallie, "Kinship," 333; DeMallie, "Teton," 801, 808–9.

68. Standing Bear, *Land of the Spotted Eagle*, 2006, 104–5.

69. Waggoner, *Witness*, 165.

70. J. Walker, "Oglala Kinship Terms," 97–98; J. Walker, *Lakota Society*, 1982, 42, 55–56; Standing Bear, *Land of the Spotted Eagle*, 2006, 108–13; DeMallie, "Kinship and Biology," 127–29, 137; DeMallie, "Kinship," 333; DeMallie, "Teton," 801, 808–9.

71. J. Walker, *Lakota Society*, 1982, 41–44, 55–57; DeMallie, "Teton," 801.

72. DeMallie, "Teton," 805.

73. White Hawk, quoted in Densmore, *Teton Sioux Music and Culture*, 2001, 444.

74. Hämäläinen, *Lakota America*, 180–83.

75. Waggoner, *Witness*, 165.

76. Man Afraid of His Horses, Deloria and DeMallie, "Peace Commission," 114–17. See chapters 10–12 this book.

77. E. Deloria, "The Dakota Way of Life," 26.

78. Bad Bear, quoted in J. Walker, *Lakota Society*, 1982, 28; DeMallie, "Teton," 803.

79. Tyon, quoted in J. Walker, *Lakota Society*, 1982, 32.

80. Densmore, *Teton Sioux Music and Culture*, 2001, 437; J. Walker, *Lakota Society*, 1982, 75; DeMallie, "Teton," 805.

81. J. Walker, *Lakota Society*, 1982, 82.

82. Walker, 92–94; Densmore, *Teton Sioux Music and Culture*, 2001, 439–44; Standing Bear, *My People the Sioux*, 2006, 51–52; DeMallie, "Teton," 805.

83. White Hawk, quoted in Densmore, *Teton Sioux Music and Culture*, 2001, 437–38; Standing Bear, *Land of the Spotted Eagle*, 2006, 19.

84. DeMallie, "Teton," 811.

85. J. Walker, *Lakota Society*, 1982, 81.

86. White Hawk, quoted in Densmore, 444; Tyon, quoted in J. Walker, *Lakota Belief and Ritual*, 121; Bad Wound, quoted in Walker, 124; see also Walker, 227–28; J. Walker, *Lakota Society*, 75.

87. His Shield, quoted in E. Deloria, "Alpha First Fox," 40–42.

88. Deloria, 42; see also J. Walker, *Lakota Society*, 94.

89. See "Report of Lieutenant G. K. Warren," ARSOW, 1857, 630–33. The event is discussed also in K. Bray, "Lone Horn's Peace," 43–44.

90. Denig, *Five Indian Tribes of the Upper Missouri*, 13–14; Densmore, *Teton Sioux Music and Culture*, 2001, 437; J. Walker, *Lakota Society*, 1982, 74; DeMallie, *The Sixth Grandfather*, 1984, 147, 209; DeMallie, "Teton," 803–4; Posthumus, "A Lakota View of Pté Oyáte."

91. Denig, *Five Indian Tribes of the Upper Missouri*, 12–13; DeMallie, "Teton," 804–5; Posthumus, "Hereditary Enemies."

92. Standing Bear, *Land of the Spotted Eagle*, 2006, 40–41, 170; Standing Bear, *My People the Sioux*, 2006, 4.

93. Sword, "Dakota Texts from the Sword Manuscripts," texts 5 and 13; DeMallie, "Kinship and Biology," 130; DeMallie, "Teton," 805.

94. J. Walker, *Lakota Society*, 1982, 84.

95. Bad Bear, quoted in Walker, 27; Standing Bear, *Land of the Spotted Eagle*, 2006, 170; DeMallie, "Teton," 806.

96. Tyon, quoted in J. Walker, *Lakota Society*, 1982, 32.

97. Sword, "Dakota Texts from the Sword Manuscripts," text 4; Densmore, *Teton Sioux Music and Culture*, 2001, 375–81; Standing Bear, *Land of the Spotted Eagle*, 2006, 155, 220; DeMallie, "Teton," 806.

98. Standing Bear, *Land of the Spotted Eagle*, 2006, 25.

99. Sword, "Dakota Texts from the Sword Manuscripts," text 3; DeMallie, "Teton," 805.

100. Standing Bear, *Land of the Spotted Eagle*, 2006, 26, 174; DeMallie, "Teton," 812.

101. Quotes from William F. Hynes memoirs, Hynes, William Francis, *Soldiers of the Frontier*, 133–35.

102. Parks, DeMallie, and Vézina, *Truteau*, 243, 355–56. On Sioux-Arikara relations, see Posthumus, "Hereditary Enemies."

103. Red Feather, quoted in Buechel, "Sioux Ethnology Notebook," 26–27.

104. Tyon, quoted in J. Walker, *Lakota Belief and Ritual*, 170; Sword, "Dakota Texts from the Sword Manuscripts," text 4; DeMallie, "Teton," 806.

105. Standing Bear, *Land of the Spotted Eagle*, 2006, 154; Posthumus, *All My Relatives*, 2018, 197–200.

106. Densmore, *Teton Sioux Music and Culture*, 2001, 387–89.

107. DeMallie and Parks, "Plains Indian Warfare," 2003, 66; Ewers, "Intertribal Warfare as the Precursor of Indian-White Warfare on the Northern Great Plains"; White, "The Winning of the West," 1978.

Chapter 4

1. The Long Soldier, American Horse, Battiste Good, and Rosebud winter counts document the coming of the white man in Greene and Thornton, *The Year the Stars Fell*, 126, 128–29, 131. For the horses with shoes, see The Flame, The Swan, and Long Soldier, 131–32.

2. Battiste Good, quoted in Greene and Thornton, *The Year the Stars Fell*, 115.

3. American Horse, quoted in Greene and Thornton, 138. See DeMallie, "Sioux Until 1850," 732–33; Hämäläinen, *Lakota America*, 120–52.

4. Little Beaver's death was noted in the winter counts of American Horse, Lone Dog, The Flame, The Swan, and White Bull. Greene and Thornton, *The Year the Stars Fell*, 144–46; White Bull, *Lakota Warrior*, 14.

5. Kappler, *Indian Affairs: Laws and Treaties*, 2:1031; DeMallie, "Sioux Until 1850," 733.

6. See Makȟúla, Mnikȟówožu, and Lone Dog in Waggoner, *Witness*, 531–36, 548–49, 554–55.

7. Battiste Good, American Horse, No Ears, Rosebud, and Lone Dog, quoted in Greene and Thornton, *The Year the Stars Fell*, 156–57.

8. Cloud Shield and American Horse, quoted in Greene and Thornton, 157–60. For comparison see Makȟúla and Mnikȟówožu in Waggoner, *Witness*, 535, 549.

9. Cloud Shield, quoted in Greene and Thornton, *The Year the Stars Fell*, 167.

10. See Cloud Shield, Lone Dog, The Flame, The Swan, American Horse, Rosebud, Battiste Good, Makȟúla, and Mnikȟówožu in Greene and Thornton, 151–67; Waggoner, *Witness*, 535–36, 549–50. See also K. Bray, "Before Sitting Bull."

11. DeMallie, "Sioux Until 1850," 733; K. Bray, "The Oglala Lakota," 144.

12. The Flame, The Swan, Major Bush, Long Soldier, American Horse, Cloud Shield, and Battiste Good, quoted in Greene and Thornton, *The Year the Stars Fell*, 174–75; K. Bray, "The Oglala Lakota," 144. See Posthumus, "Hereditary Enemies"; Hämäläinen, *Lakota America*, 152–53.

13. For a full account of the meeting and the 1825 structure of the Oglála oyáte, see "K. Bray, "The Oglala Lakota," 142–48. Bray has built his analysis on the American Horse ledger kept by the family. It goes further back in history than most winter counts and contains very specific details about tribal life, including the 1825 council. It differs from the American Horse winter count that is held in the Smithsonian Institution collections and published in Greene and Thornton, *The Year the Stars Fell.*

14. American Horse, quoted in K. Bray, "The Oglala Lakota," 139–46. See also K. Bray, "Before Sitting Bull."

15. K. Bray, "The Oglala Lakota," 144–46. Bray refers also to testimony by Thomas American Horse.

16. The description of the 1825 meeting is largely drawn from the American Horse ledger as presented in Bray, 145–48. For an analysis of the symbolism of evoking kin terms during negotiations see DeMallie, "Touching the Pen."

17. For the treaty proceedings, see Jensen and Hutchins, *Wheel Boats on the Missouri,* 99–106; K. Bray, "The Oglala Lakota," 144–48. The actual treaty with signatures is in Kappler, *Indian Affairs: Laws and Treaties,* 2:230–32.

18. American Horse, quoted in Greene and Thornton, *The Year the Stars Fell,* 178; No Ears and Short Man, quoted in J. Walker, *Lakota Society,* 1992, 135, 136.

19. Davis, "Report of the Secretary of War Jefferson Davis," 4.

20. Lone Dog, The Flame, The Swan, quoted in Greene and Thornton, *The Year the Stars Fell,* 213–14; K. Bray, "Lakota Statesmen," 154–58. See also Posthumus, "A Lakota View of Pté Oyáte"; Isenberg, *Destruction of the Bison*; Cunfer and Waiser, *Bison and People.* See also, Monnett, "Contested Lands."

21. For a summary of the construction of military bases around Lakȟóta country see Lahti, "Forts on the Northern Plains," 130–47. An excellent study of the Sioux and their relationship to Fort Laramie is Nadeau, *Fort Laramie and the Sioux Indians.*

22. K. Bray, "Lakota Statesmen," 156–57.

23. Letter by Lakȟóta leaders quoted in Bray, 158. The original is in "Thomas H. Harvey to Commissioner of Indian Affairs," May 6, 1846.

24. The term iglúwašte is ambiguous. There is no historical record for the term, nor does it appear in any known Lakȟóta dictionary.

25. Lone Dog, The Flame, The Swan, and American Horse, quoted in Greene and Thornton, *The Year the Stars Fell,* 205–8.

26. For the cycles of intertribal warfare 1825–50, see winter counts in Greene and Thornton, 178–225. For the capturing of the Cheyenne sacred arrow, see Van de Logt, "I Was Brought to Life to Save My People," 23.

27. "Treaty of . . . 1851," Kappler, *Indian Affairs: Laws and Treaties,* 2:594–96. See DeMallie, "Teton," 794–95; K. Bray, "Lakota Statesmen," 156.

28. DeMallie, "Touching the Pen"; K. Bray, "Lakota Statesmen."

29. For an early description of Lakȟóta attitudes toward the whites see Denig, *Five Indian Tribes,* 19–31; Ostler, *The Plains Sioux,* 30–35.

30. American Horse and Cloud Shield, quoted in Greene and Thornton, *The Year the Stars Fell*, 210. For a classic description of the feud among the Oglala see Parkman, *Oregon Trail*, 138–39. See also Olson, *Red Cloud and the Sioux Problem*, 19–22; Larson, *Red Cloud*, 58–61.

31. American Horse Ledger, in K. Bray, "Lakota Statesmen," 162–66.

32. For a good analysis of the 1851 Treaty and US Manifest Destiny, see Ostler, *The Plains Sioux*, 37–39.

33. DeMallie, "Touching the Pen," 347–48; K. Bray, "Lakota Statesmen," 160–72.

34. Blue Earth as quoted in DeMallie, "Touching the Pen," 349.

35. Scattering Bear as quoted in DeMallie, 349. See also Scattering Bear as quoted in K. Bray, "Lakota Statesmen," 169. Bray refers to the report in the *Missouri Daily Republican* newspaper.

36. Blue Earth and Black Hawk as quoted in the *Missouri Daily Republican,* published in K. Bray, "Lakota Statesmen," 167–70. See also DeMallie, "Touching the Pen," 349–50.

37. The Treaty of Fort Laramie . . . 1851, reprinted in Kappler, *Indian Affairs: Laws and Treaties*, 2:596. See also K. Bray, "Lakota Statesmen," 165–74.

38. K. Bray, "Lone Horn's Peace," 28–36. There were two major trading posts on the North Platte. The trader John Richard established a trading post farther west and Joseph Bissonnette established a post closer to Fort Laramie.

39. The Flame, Long Soldier, Major Bush, and Lone Dog, quoted in Greene and Thornton, *The Year the Stars Fell*, 229–30. We cannot verify The Flame's Lakȟóta name through censuses. Boíde seems incorrect and it could be Oíle, to burn inside, to catch on fire.

40. See No Ears winter count in Walker, *Lakota Society*, 1992; Makȟúla, Lone Dog, Oglala (Red Horse Owner), quoted in Waggoner, *Witness*, 531–74; Lone Dog, American Horse, Battiste Good, The Swan, The Flame, and Rosebud, quoted in Greene and Thornton, *The Year the Stars Fell*, 230–34.

41. "Report of Superintendent A. Cumming," "Report of Indian Agent Alfred J Vaughan," ARCIA, 1853, 80–82, 112–15.

42. Bear's Rib as quoted in Raynolds, *Journal of Captain W. F. Raynolds*, 22.

43. For Húŋkpapȟa politics in the 1850s, see K. Bray, "Before Sitting Bull."

44. Anonymous Lakȟóta chief, quoted in "Report of Indian Agent Thomas Fitzpatrick," ARCIA, 1853, 126–29. See also "Report of Indian Agent Alfred J. Vaughan," ARCIA, 1854, 87–89.

45. For Lakȟóta accounts see American Horse, Red Cloud, Clarence Three Stars, tablet 16, tablet 25, ESRMC, NSHS. Published also in Jensen, *Voices of the American West*, 277–81, 346–47. Contemporary white accounts relating to the "Grattan massacre" can be found, for example, in "Report of the Secretary of War Jefferson Davis," ARSOW, 1854; "Report of the Secretary of War . . . Respecting the Massacre of Lieutenant Grattan and his Command by Indians," ARSOW, 1856; *Engagement Between United States Troops and Sioux Indians*, H.R. Exec. Doc. No. 63, 33rd Cong., 2nd Sess. (1855) 1–27. The events leading to the battle have been discussed in classic works, such as Hyde, *Red Cloud's Folk*, 72–75; Hyde, *Spotted Tail's Folk*, 55, 61. For more recent accounts, see Larson, *Red*

Cloud, 66–75; DeMallie, "Teton," 795; Ostler, *The Plains Sioux*, 40–41; K. Bray, *Crazy Horse*, 2006, 31–32.

46. Lone Dog, American Horse, The Swan, The Flame, Battiste Good, Long Soldier, No Ears, and Rosebud, quoted in Greene and Thornton, *The Year the Stars Fell*, 237–39. For a recent work that introduces both Indian and white accounts of the Grattan incident and subsequent events, see McDermott, Paul, and Lowry, *All Because of a Mormon Cow*.

47. See Long Soldier, The Flame, The Swan, Lone Dog, and Rosebud in Greene and Thornton, *The Year the Stars Fell*, 87–89. See also Denig, *Five Indian Tribes*, 19–40.

48. For Spotted Tail's raid, see Red Cloud, quoted in Jensen, *Voices of the American West*, 346–47; Hyde, *Spotted Tail's Folk*.

49. For Harney's expedition, see Beck, *The First Sioux War*; Paul, *Blue Water Creek*.

50. See Lone Dog, The Flame, The Swan, Major Bush, Long Soldier, Battiste Good, No Ears, and Rosebud, quoted in Greene and Thornton, *The Year the Stars Fell*, 257–59.

51. For Crazy Horse see K. Bray, *Crazy Horse*, 2006.

Chapter 5

1. K. Bray, "Lone Horn's Peace," 30–36. Agent Alfred J. Vaughan reported that there was peace and quiet on the Plains. In his 1856 report he wrote: "They visit each other, smoke the pipe of peace, go where and when they please, in small parties or alone, and none dare make them afraid." "Report of Alfred J. Vaughan, agent for the Indians within the Upper Missouri agency." ARCIA, 1856, 77–86.

2. Vaughan, ARCIA, 1856, 77–86, and "Report of Thomas S. Twiss, agent for the Indians of the Upper Platte," ARCIA, 1856, 87–103.

3. Lone Dog, Major Bush, American Horse, The Swan, The Flame, Cloud Shield, No Ears, Long Soldier, quoted in Greene and Thornton, *The Year the Stars Fell*, 229–47; K. Bray, "Lone Horn's Peace," 30–36. Edwin Denig also noted that despite some skirmishing, warfare between the Northern Plains tribes had greatly diminished since the 1851 treaty. Denig, *Five Indian Tribes*, 92–94, 195–97.

4. We have not been able to verify his Lakȟóta name.

5. For biographies of Red Cloud see Olson, *Red Cloud and the Sioux Problem*; Larson, *Red Cloud*; Drury and Clavin, *The Heart of Everything That Is*; McDermott, *Red Cloud*.

6. Yellow Hawk quoted in Deloria and DeMallie, "Peace Commission," 35.

7. Lakȟóta men, quoted in ARCIA 1857, 132.

8. "Report of Indian Agent A. H. Redfield," ARCIA 1857, 132.

9. For a brief history of the Man Afraid of His Horses family see Vassenden, *The Lakota Trail*.

10. Other Lakȟóta chiefs expressed their objections to the Yankton land sale during a meeting with Agent Redfield. See "Report of Indian Agent A. H. Redfield," ARCIA 1858, 84–85. See also K. Bray, "Lone Horn's Peace," 42–44.

11. Bray, "Lone Horn's Peace," 44–46.

12. Intertribal fighting became more intense after the Lakȟóta "declaration," which was of great concern to the Indian agents. Agents Redfield and Twiss reported increasing

violence in the northern parts of the Lakȟóta homelands. See, for example, "Redfield,"
ARCIA 1858, 132–36.

13. "Report of Lieutenant G. K. Warren," ARSOW, 630–33; K. Bray, "Lone Horn's
Peace," 43–44; Hämäläinen, *Lakota America*, 234–36.

14. Cloud Shield, Rosebud, Lone Dog, The Flame, The Swan, and No Ears, quoted in
Greene and Thornton, *The Year the Stars Fell*, 242–46. For more on the Lakȟóta-Crow
war of 1857–58 see K. Bray, "Lone Horn's Peace," 44–45.

15. Anonymous Lakȟóta chief, quoted in "Report of Thomas S. Twiss," ARCIA,
1858, 130.

16. Feather Tied to His Hair, Bald, Eagle, Red Hair, The One That Shouts, Little
Bear, The Crow that Looks, Bear Heart, Little Knife, and White at Both Ends to
Indian Agent Samuel N. Latta, ARCIA, 1862, 372–73. For a brief biography of Bear's
Rib and his death see Waggoner, *Witness*, 331–36. The circumstances surrounding
his death were also described by Agent Latta, ARCIA, 1862, 193–94. See also Utley,
The Lance and the Shield, 48–50. On having no ears, see DeMallie, "These Have No
Ears," October 1, 1993.

17. An old but still valuable and comprehensive study of US Indian policy is Prucha,
American Indian Policy in Crisis, 1976.

18. See Anderson, *Kinsmen of Another Kind*; Rieke and Phillips, *Fire in the North*.

19. Feather Tied to His Hair, Bald, Eagle, Red Hair, The One That Shouts, Little Bear,
The Crow that Looks, Bear Heart, Little Knife, and White at Both Ends to Indian Agent
Latta, ARCIA, 1862, 372.

20. Ibid., 372–73. See Utley, *The Lance and the Shield*, 51.

21. The most comprehensive Lakȟóta description of the battle is White Bull in notebook
24, box 105, WSCMC, WHC. For the battle of Killdeer Mountain and other skirmishes,
see Utley, *The Lance and the Shield*, 50–57; K. Bray, *Crazy Horse*, 2006, 83–95; Beck,
Columns of Vengeance, 202–46.

22. White Bull, quoted in notebook 24, box 105, WSCMC, WHC. For a good analysis of the 1864 fighting from Lakȟóta perspectives see Utley, *The Lance and the Shield*,
55–62; Larson, *Gall*, 40–50.

23. White Bull, quoted in notebook 24, box 105, WSCMC, WHC. See also Utley, *The
Lance and the Shield*, 53–54. Interesting descriptions of trading truces are in McGinnis,
Counting Coup and Cutting Horses.

24. DeMallie and Parks, "Plains Indian Warfare," 2003, 72–73. George Sword's later
Lakȟóta-language autobiography and the original Ledgerbook Manuscript 1905–1910 are
deposited in the Colorado State Historical Society Archives in Denver, Colorado, and
in the Division of Anthropology, American Museum of Natural History, New York as
part of the James R. Walker Collection. We have used the copies held at the AISRI and
the partial translations made by Professor Raymond J. DeMallie with his permission.
For more on George Sword and his texts see Red Shirt, *George Sword*.

25. George Sword Autobiography (AISRI). See also Parks and DeMallie, "Plains Indian
Native Literature," 127–28; DeMallie and Parks, "Plains Indian Warfare," 2003, 72–73.

26. For a sense of the situation on the Northern Plains from the perspective of the US officials see, for example, "Report of Superintendent of Indian Affairs Newton Edmunds and Major General John Pope," ARCIA, 1864, 183–99.

27. From the Indian point of view the best source on the battle of Julesburg is George Bent, who was among the Cheyenne. Hyde, *Red Cloud's Folk*, 101–33; Grinnell, *The Fighting Cheyennes*, 182–89.

28. For more on the Sand Creek massacre and its legacy see Kelman, *A Misplaced Massacre*; Greene and Scott, *Finding Sand Creek*.

29. "Report of the Commissioner of Indian Affairs D. N. Cooley," ARCIA, 1865, 24–25.

30. For Indian perspective of the Platte Bridge fight, see Grinnell, *The Fighting Cheyennes*, 216–24. Army reports in ARSOW, 1865. See also Hyde, *Life of George Bent*, 214–22; Drury and Clavin, *The Heart of Everything That Is*, 201–5.

31. Standard interpretations from the military perspective regarding the fighting in the summer of 1865 are McDermott, *The Circle of Fire*; Wagner, *Patrick Connor's War*; Van de Logt, *War Party in Blue*.

32. For Indian accounts, see Grinnell, *The Fighting Cheyennes*.

33. Utley, *The Lance and the Shield*, 67–69.

34. For more on US army difficulties adapting to wars against Native Americans, see Lahti, *Wars for Empire*.

35. Lone Dog, The Flame, The Swan, Major Bush, Short Man, No Ears, quoted in Greene and Thornton, *The Year the Stars Fell*, 255–57; J. Walker, *Lakota Society*, 1992, 144.

36. "Report of the Northwestern Treaty Commission to the Sioux of the Upper Missouri" ARCIA, 1865, 168–76. For the Friends of the Indian and US federal Indian policy see Bannan, *Reformers and the "Indian Problem"*; Hagan, *The Indian Rights Association: The Herbert Welsh Years, 1882–1904*. See also Prucha, *American Indian Policy in Crisis*, 1976; Prucha, *The Great Father*.

37. "Report of Colonel Henry A. Maynadier," ARCIA 1866, 207–8. An old but useful biography on Spotted Tail is Hyde, *Spotted Tail's Folk*. For a newer biography, see Clow, *Spotted Tail*.

38. Spotted Tail, quoted in Maynadier, ARCIA, 1866, 207.

39. Maynadier, ARCIA, 1866, 204–6. See American Horse, quoted in Greene and Thornton, *The Year the Stars Fell*, 257.

40. "Report of the Northwestern Treaty Commission to the Sioux of the Upper Missouri," ARCIA, 1866, 168–76.

41. "Report of the Commissioners Appointed by the President of the United States to Treat with the Indians at Fort Laramie" and "Report of Superintendent E. B. Taylor," ARCIA, 1866, 208–11.

42. Red Cloud, quoted in Carrington, *My Army Life*, 46. Several versions of what Red Cloud actually said exist in the literature. One account comes from Frances Carrington and an enlisted man, William Murphy, both of whom had only recently arrived at Fort Laramie. Carrington's account is often described as an eyewitness account, but she says in her memoirs that she arrived after the incident, so it is not certain this is exactly what was said. Murphy's account is in Carrington, 291–93. For more on the 1866 council,

see Olson, *Red Cloud and the Sioux Problem*, 34–37; Larson, *Red Cloud*, 91–93; Drury and Clavin, *The Heart of Everything That Is*, 242–46. For the military point of view, see McDermott, *Red Cloud's War*.

43. "Report of the Commissioners Appointed by the President of the United States to Treat with the Indians at Fort Laramie," ARCIA, 1866, 208–9. See also "Treaty with the Oglala and Brulé Sioux, June 27, 1866," in Deloria and DeMallie, *Documents of American Indian Diplomacy*, 1368–70.

44. Red Cloud's war deeds were discussed by American Horse, in Jensen, *Voices of the American West*, 281–82. Paul, *Autobiography of Red Cloud* offers interesting work on Red Cloud's early life, including his own stories of his war deeds.

45. We have not been able to find either of his Lakȟóta names.

46. A list of major Oglála and Sičháŋǧu leaders is in "Report of Superintendent H. B. Denman," ARCIA, 1867, 268.

47. The discussion regarding Red Cloud's leadership position has been ongoing for decades, each biography giving a somewhat different interpretation. See, for example, Hyde, *Red Cloud's Folk*, 142–43; Olson, *Red Cloud and the Sioux Problem*, 22–26; Drury and Clavin, *The Heart of Everything That Is*; Larson, *Red Cloud*.

48. "Report of the Commissioner N. B. Taylor and Colonel Henry Maynadier," ARCIA, 1866, 208–9.

49. Colonel Carrington's actions are thoroughly discussed in McDermott, *Red Cloud's War*.

50. Standing Bear, quoted in DeMallie, *The Sixth Grandfather*, 1985, 107.

51. In constructing the narrative of Red Cloud's War and the famous battles fought during the two-year war from a Lakȟóta perspective, we have utilized these Lakȟóta accounts: George Sword, American Horse, Chips, Red Cloud, Clarence Three Stars, tablets 16, 17, 25, ESRMC, NSHS; White Bull, folder 12, box 104, notebooks 25, 53, box 105, WSCMC, WHC; Max Littman, White Bull, folder 12, box 2, envelope 41, folder 1, box 5, WMCC, IULL; Thunder Tail, Singing Bear, EBMC, HRMSCA, MUA; "Notes on Iron Shell, Two Strike, Man Afraid of His Horses, Bear Face, Hollow Horn Bear, He Dog, Red Cloud, Thunder Hawk," JWP, MFT; White Bull Pictographs, AISRI. These sources are scattered in various archival collections, although several have been published in works such as Vestal, *Warpath*; White Bull, *Lakota Warrior*; Jensen, *Voices of the American West*. Most recently, Lakȟóta and Cheyenne accounts have been published in Waggoner, *Witness*; Monnett, *Eyewitness to the Fetterman Fight*.

52. Fire Thunder, quoted in DeMallie, *The Sixth Grandfather*, 1985, 103.

53. Fire Thunder quoted in DeMallie, 103.

54. Fire Thunder quoted in DeMallie, 104.

55. The most comprehensive account of the fight is by White Bull, in Monnet, *Eyewitness to the Fetterman Fight*, 20–33. Monnet offers several Indian accounts of this fight and includes commentary on each. See also No Ears and American Horse, quoted in Greene and Thornton, *The Year the Stars Fell*, 259–60.

56. See American Horse, Red Cloud, tablets 16, 25, ESRMC, NSHS. Published also in Jensen, *Voices of the American West*, 280–81, 341. For a commentary on the role of

Red Cloud and Crazy Horse during the battle see Monnet, *Eyewitness to the Fetterman Fight*, 65–90.

57. For the reactions by the Army and the Eastern press, see "Report of Lieutenant General William T. Sherman," "Report of Major General H. W. Halleck," ARSOW, 1867, 28–29, 31–38, 74 75; *NYT*, December 31, 1866, 5; *NYT*, January 14, 1867, 8; January 19, 1867, 2; *NYT*, February 4, 1867, 5; *NYT*, April 9, 1867, 5; *NYT*, April 17, 1867, 1; *NYT*, April 30, 1867, 1; *NYT*, December 14, 1867, 1.

58. For military accounts of the war, see "Report of Lieutenant General William T. Sherman," ARSOW, 1866, 19–23; "Report of the Secretary of War Ulysses S. Grant," "Report of Lieutenant General William T. Sherman," "Report of Major General Alfred Terry," ARSOW, 1867, 28–29, 31–38, 48–55; "Report of Lieutenant General William T. Sherman," "Report of Major General Phillip T. Sheridan," "Report of Major General C. C. Augur," "Report of Major General Alfred Terry," ARSOW, 1868, 1–8, 10–12, 21–25, 32–37; "List of Murders, Outrages and Depredations Committed by Indians . . . ," ARSOW, 1868, 13–16; "Statement of Campaigns, Expeditions . . . Made in the Department of Platte . . . ," "Report of the Assistant Adjutant General George D. Ruggles," ARSOW, 1868, 25–29, 30–31; "Reports of Military Operations October 15, 1868–March 27, 1869," ARSOW, 1869, 44–53. For an analysis of Native Americans in the press, see Coward, *The Newspaper Indian*.

59. Superintendent H. B. Denman complained about this movement between the "hostiles" and progressive camps. While emphasizing that, for example, Spotted Tail and Swift Bear with their bands remained peaceful, most Indians belonging to the Upper Platte Agency joined the hostile Indians at some point. They were all "mixed up," he said. See "Report of Superintendent of Indian Affairs H. B. Denman," ARCIA, 1867, 268–70.

60. See McDermott, *Red Cloud's War*; Hämäläinen, *Lakota America*.

61. For example, the *New York Times* followed the situation on the Northern Plains closely throughout 1867. See *NYT*, December 31, 1866, 5; *NYT*, February 4, 1867, 5; *NYT*, January 14, 1867, 8; *NYT*, January 19, 1867, 2; *NYT*, April 9, 1867, 5; *NYT*, April 17, 1867, 1; *NYT*, April 30, 1867, 1; *NYT*, August 15, 1867, 1; *NYT*, November 23, 1867, 1; *NYT*, December 1, 1867, 1; *NYT*, December 14, 1867, 1.

62. American Horse, George Sword, Chips, Red Cloud, Clarence Three Stars, tablet 16, tablet 18, tablet 25, ESRMC, NSHS; White Bull, envelope 41, folder 1, box 5, WMCC, IULL; "Notes on He Dog, Yellow Horse, Man Afraid of His Horses," JWP, MFT.

63. Red Cloud, tablet 25, ESRMC, NSHS; Jensen, *Voices of the American West*, 348.

64. Red Cloud, *NYT*, November 23, 1867, 1.

Chapter 6

1. See reports of Agent M. T. Patrick, Special Indian Agent J. P. Cooper, Interpreter Charles Geren, ARCIA, 1868, 249–50.

2. Olson, *Red Cloud and the Sioux Problem*, 70–73; Ostler, *The Plains Sioux*, 46–48.

3. Tow Lance, Long Mandan, Yellow Hawk, Burnt Face, Big Horn, Hare, Long Horn, Bear Like Him, Shield, Red Eagle Plume, Iron Mountain, and Little Pheasant, quoted in Deloria and DeMallie, "Peace Commission," 33–40.

4. For a detailed description of Lakȟóta movements in 1867, see "Report by Superintendent of Indian Affairs H. B. Denman," ARCIA,1867, 268–70. The Iron Crow winter count notes that people camped in a place with plenty of buffalo; cited in J. Walker, *Lakota Society*, 1992, 145.

5. "Report of Superintendent H. B. Denman," ARCIA, 1867, 268–69.

6. For the negotiations, see Deloria and DeMallie, "Peace Commission," 32–49.

7. Big Mouth, quoted in Deloria and DeMallie, 59–60.

8. White Crane, quoted in Deloria and DeMallie, 111.

9. For the speeches made by Lakȟóta chiefs, see Deloria and DeMallie, 57–65, 103–11.

10. See Deloria and DeMallie, "Peace Commission." See Hagan, *The Indian Rights Association*; Prucha, *The Great Father*; Prucha, *American Indian Policy in Crisis*, 1976.

11. High Wolf, quoted in Deloria and DeMallie, "Peace Commission," 117.

12. Swift Bear, quoted in Deloria and DeMallie, 115.

13. For Lakȟóta movements in the summer of 1868, see "Report of Interpreter Charles Geren," ARCIA, 1868, 252–54. Lakȟóta raids were reported by Lt. Col. A. J. Simmer, quoted in Deloria and DeMallie, "Peace Commission," 156–57.

14. The Lakȟóta council plan was reported by Lt. Col A. J. Simmer, quoted in Deloria and DeMallie, "Peace Commission," 156–57. See Olson, *Red Cloud and the Sioux Problem*, 78–80; Larson, *Red Cloud*, 120–24.

15. Sitting Bull's sentiments were reproduced by Father Pierre Jean De Smet, quoted in Deloria and DeMallie, "Peace Commission," 130–31.

16. Report of Father Pierre Jean De Smet, quoted in Deloria and DeMallie, 130–31.

17. Black Moon and Sitting Bull, quoted in Deloria and DeMallie, 132–33.

18. For further discussion of the negotiations, see Utley, *The Lance and the Shield*, 79–81.

19. Man That Goes In The Middle, Bull Owl, Full Heart, Lone Dog, Thunder Bull, Fire Heart, Running Antelope, Long Soldier, Magpie, and Two Bears, quoted in Deloria and DeMallie, "Peace Commission," 137–43.

20. Utley, *The Lance and the Shield*, 79–82.

21. Reilly, *The Frontier Newspapers*, 35.

22. Man Afraid of His Horses quoted in Deloria and DeMallie, "Peace Commission," 114, 115, 117. Other Lakȟóta chiefs expressed similar views. See accounts by Lakȟóta chiefs in Deloria and DeMallie, 103–11.

23. See "Account of Red Cloud signing the Treaty" attached to Deloria and DeMallie, "Peace Commission," 173–76. For accounts by Spotted Tail and other chiefs regarding hunting and possible future farming, see Lakȟóta chiefs quoted in Deloria and DeMallie, 56–67, 103–11.

24. Olson, *Red Cloud and the Sioux Problem*, 80–82; Larson, *Red Cloud*, 123–25.

25. "Fort Laramie Treaty," Indian Treaties, 1789–1869, Record Group 1, General Records of the United States Government, 1778–2006. For a good analysis of treaty significance, see Ostler, *The Plains Sioux*, 46–47, 83–95; Olson, *Red Cloud and the Sioux Problem*, 83–95.

26. Ostler, *The Plains Sioux*, 46–47.

27. Lone Dog, The Flame, and The Swan, quoted in Greene and Thornton, *The Year the Stars Fell*, 260–61.

28. For Lakȟóta understanding of the disappearance of the buffalo, see DeMallie, "These Have No Ears," 1993; Ostler, "They Regard Their Passing as Wakan"; Posthumus, "A Lakota View of Pté Oyáte."

29. For excellent biographies of Sitting Bull see Vestal, *Champion of the Sioux*; Utley, *The Lance and the Shield*; LaPointe, *Sitting Bull*. Crazy Horse's life has been documented in numerous books including Sandoz, *Strange Man of the Oglalas*; Sajna, *Crazy Horse*; Marshall, *The Journey of Crazy Horse*; K. Bray, *Crazy Horse*, 2006. For Lakȟóta accounts about Sitting Bull and his determination to resist the whites, see Old Bull, White Bull, and Robert Higheagle in folders 10–12, 22, box 104, WSCMC, WHC.

30. K. Bray, *Crazy Horse*, 2006, 5–35.

31. For Lakȟóta accounts on Crazy Horse, see Chips, American Horse, and George Sword in Jensen, *Voices of the American West*. See also He Dog and Red Feather, quoted in Hinman, "Oglala Sources on the Life of Crazy Horse," 1976, 9–33. Chips appears in literature and census records with various names, including Chipps and Horn Chipps (Hewóptuȟa). We use "Chips" throughout.

32. For the ceremony inaugurating Crazy Horse as a shirt wearer, see K. Bray, *Crazy Horse*, 2006, 119–22.

33. He Dog, quoted in Hinman, "Oglala Sources on the Life of Crazy Horse," 1976; Jensen, *Voices of the American West*.

34. Utley, *The Lance and the Shield*, 76–80.

35. Four Horns, folder 11, box 104, WSCMC, WHC. Published also in Utley, *The Lance and the Shield*, 87. See also Little Soldier, Robert Higheagle, Old Bull, One Bull, Mrs. One Bull, folder 6, folder 22, box 104; notebook 4, notebook 11, notebook 19, box 105; WSCMC, WHC, Clarence Three Stars, tablet 25, ESRMC, NSHS; Singing Bear, EBMC, HRMSCA.

36. "Report of Hon. B. R. Cowen et. al Commissioners to Visit the Teton Sioux at and near Fort Peck, Montana," ARCIA, 1872, 457. See also Utley, *The Lance and the Shield*, 95–96.

37. Man Afraid of His Horses, quoted in Deloria and DeMallie, "Peace Commission," 117.

38. Audubon, *The Missouri River Journals*, 47–114, 307–426. Similar accounts of the wanton killing of game along the Missouri are in Larsen and Cottrell, *Steamboats West*.

39. Bull Owl, quoted in Deloria and DeMallie, "Peace Commission," 137.

40. American Horse, Battiste Good, Cloud Shield and Mnikȟówožu, quoted in Greene and Thornton, *The Year the Stars Fell*, 268; Waggoner, *Witness*, 551.

41. The Swan, Major Bush, Long Soldier, Cloud Shield, American Horse, Rosebud, Lone Dog, and The Flame, quoted in Greene and Thornton, *The Year the Stars Fell*, 263–73; No Ears, quoted in J. Walker, *Lakota Society*, 144–46. Lakȟóta accounts regarding fighting traditional enemies in the early 1870s are, for example, Little Soldier, Robert Higheagle, Old Bull, and White Bull, in folders 10–12, 22, box 104, WSCMC, WHC; White Bull, *Lakota Warrior*, 44–48, Plate 9–11. See also Bull, "White Bull Pictographs," 1–19; He Dog, Red Feather, quoted in Hinman, "Oglala Sources on the Life of Crazy Horse," 1976, 9–33. See Utley, *The Lance and the Shield*, 97–99; Van de Logt, "I Was Brought to Life to Save My People."

42. Little Soldier, Old Bull, White Bull, Robert Higheagle, and Circling Hawk, folders 6, 10,12, 22, box 104; folders 8, 13, 24, box 105; notebook 50, box 106, WSCMC, WHC; Bull, "White Bull Pictographs," 1–19. See also Lone Dog, The Swan, The Flame, and Cloud Shield, quoted in Greene and Thornton, *The Year the Stars Fell*, 266–67, 272–73.

43. Little Soldier, Old Bull, White Bull, Robert Higheagle, and Circling Hawk, folders 6, 10,12, 22, box 104; folders 8, 13, 24, box 105; notebook 50, box 106, WSCMC, WHC; Bull, "White Bull Pictographs," 1–19. See also Vestal, *Champion of the Sioux*, 113–17; Utley, *The Lance and the Shield*, 97–99.

44. One Bull, folder 11, box 104, WSCMC, WHC.

45. See "Reports of Superintendent of Indian Affairs John A. Burbank and Indian Agents George M. Randall, DeWitt C. Poole, J. N Hearn, Report of Brevet Major General D.S. Stanley," ARCIA, 1869, 301–6, 314–19, 330–31.

46. "Report of Brevet Major General Stanley," ARCIA, 1869, 330–31. For more on the dispute on the location of the agencies, see Hyde, *Spotted Tail's Folk*, 144–69; Olson, *Red Cloud and the Sioux Problem*, 144–48; Jensen, *Voices of the American West*, Appendix B.

47. "Report of Indian Agent Valentine T. McGillycuddy," ARCIA, 1881, 47.

48. Lakȟóta views on farming are included in, for example, "Reports of Indian Agents William H. French, De Witt C. Poole and George M. Randall, and Captain J. A. Hearn," ARCIA, 1870, 218–24. The Indian agents reported annually on Lakȟóta progress in farming and other "civilizing" pursuits. For a thorough study on Oglála farming, see Smedman, "From Warriors and Hunters to Farmers."

49. The visit of the Lakȟóta delegation to Washington and New York is described in "Report of the Commissioner of Indian Affairs Ely S. Parker," ARCIA, 1870, 4–5; *NYT*, June 2, 1870, 4; *NYT*, June 3, 1870, 4; *NYT*, June 4, 1870, 3; *NYT*, June 5, 1870, 1; *NYT*, June 8, 1870, 4; *NYT*, June 15, 1870; *NYT*, July 17, 1870. For a thorough analysis of the visit see Olson, *Red Cloud and the Sioux Problem*, 90–113.

50. Red Cloud, quoted in *NYT*, July 17, 1870, 1–4.

51. Spotted Tail, quoted in "Report of Superintendent of Indian Affairs John A. Burbank," ARCIA, 1870, 206–8. See also "Report of Indian Agent De Witt C. Poole," ARCIA, 1870, 220–22.

52. All prior names for the BIA were eventually subsumed under that name. For history, see https://www.bia.gov/bia. The Commissioners of Indian Affairs reported on the success of the various Christian denominations in their annual reports from the early reservation period onward. For example, *Annual Report of the Commissioner of Indian Affairs*, ARCIA, 1872, 73–74; ARCIA, 1873, 9; ARCIA, 1874, 13–14.

53. See "Report by Indian Agent J. W. Daniels," ARCIA, 1872, 267–69.

54. For more on these early reservation period rivalries, see Olson, *Red Cloud and the Sioux Problem*, 114–43; Larson, *Red Cloud*, 137–46.

55. For the situation on the Great Sioux Reservation from the agents' perspective, see "Reports of Indian Agents, J. C O'Connor, Theodore M. Koues, Edmond Palmer, H. W. Bingham and J. W. Daniels," ARCIA, 1872, 261–62, 267–69; ARCIA, 1873, 230–33, 243–44.

56. Hare, quoted in Deloria and DeMallie, "Peace Commission," 36.

57. The agents complained about his habit throughout the 1880s in the Annual Reports of the Commissioner of Indian Affairs (ARCIA).

58. "Report of Indian Agents William H. French, De Witt C. Poole and George M. Randall, and Captain J. A. Hearn," ARCIA, 1870, 218–24.

59. See "Indian Delegations Visiting Washington during the Year," ARCIA, 1872, 97–98. See Olson, *Red Cloud and the Sioux Problem*.

60. "Report of Indian Agent J. W. Daniels," ARCIA, 1872, 243–44. Interesting summaries of the government's Indian policies, expectations, and achievements are in the ARCIA. See, for example, ARCIA, 1872; ARCIA, 1873.

61. Short Man and Iron Crow, quoted in Walker, *Lakota Society*, 1992, 147.

62. *NYT*, August 13, 1873, 1

63. Anonymous Lakȟóta account in "Report of the Commissioner of Indian Affairs Ely S. Parker," ARCIA, 1870, 9. Indian agents frequently reported devastating Lakȟóta attacks on neighboring tribes. See "Report of the Commission to Negotiate with the Crow Tribe of Indians," "Reports of Indian Agent (for Pawnee) William Burgess, Indian Agent (for Crow) F. D. Pease," ARCIA, 1873, 113–43, 193–94, 248; "Reports of Indian Agent (for Arikara, Mandan and Gros Ventre) L. B. Sperry," Indian Agent Edmond Palmer, ARCIA, 1874, 243–44, 247; ARCIA, 1873, 243–44, 247. See also "Report of Major General George D. Ruggles," ARSOW, 1875, 72.

64. Red Dog, quoted in "Report of Indian Agent J.W. Daniels," ARCIA, 1872, 267–68.

65. "Report of Indian Agent J. W. Daniels," ARCIA, 1872, 267–69. See Olson, *Red Cloud and the Sioux Problem*.

66. Red Cloud, quoted in "Third Annual Report of the Board of Indian Commissioners," ARCIA, 1871, 27.

67. "Annual Report of the Commissioner of Indian Affairs H. C. Clum," ARCIA, 1871, 4.

68. The Agent at the Upper Missouri Agency (Lower Brulé and Crow Creek), Henry F. Livingstone reported that the Indians there had cultivated 350 acres of land and built several log houses, and that two Episcopal missions had been established. Two schools were in operation at the missions as well. For the situation at the Lower Brulé and Crow Creek (Upper Missouri) Agencies, see "Report of Indian Agent Henry F. Livingston," ARCIA, 1873, 233.

69. William Garnett, tablet 1–2, ESRMC, NSHS. Hyde, *Spotted Tail's Folk*, 165–69; Clow, *Spotted Tail*.

70. Hyde, *Spotted Tail's Folk*, 165–69.

71. American Horse, quoted in Greene and Thornton, *The Year the Stars Fell*, 274.

72. For the flagpole incident, see Hämäläinen, *Lakota America*, 344–45.

73. See, for example, *NYT*, April 7, 1872, 1; *NYT*, May 29, 1872, 1; *NYT*, April 29, 1873, 1; *NYT*, April 5, 1874, 1; *NYT*, April 6, 1874, 5; *NYT*, April 13, 1874, 1; *NYT*, April 18, 1874, 2; *NYT*, April 19, 1874, 4.

74. The situation regarding farming and other "civilizing" efforts is carefully detailed in the agents' reports. See "Reports of Indian Agents J. C. O'Connor, Theodore M. Koues, Edmond Palmer and H. W. Bingham," ARCIA, 1871, 525, 528–230; ARCIA, 1872, 261–64; ARCIA, 1873, 230–33.

Chapter 7

1. "Report of Lieutenant General Phillip H. Sheridan," ARSOW, 1871, 28; "Report of Lieutenant General Phillip H. Sheridan," ARSOW, 1873, 39–42; "Report of the Secretary of War W. W. Belknap," ARSOW, 1875, 21–22.

2. For a good description of the nonreservation Lakȟóta movements from 1870 to 1876, see Joseph White Bull, quoted in Vestal, *New Sources of Indian History*, 159–64.

3. Makhúla, quoted in Waggoner, *Witness*, 547.

4. White Bull, quoted in Vestal, *New Sources of Indian History*, 233–34. For more, see Utley, *The Lance and the Shield*, 90–94, 104–5.

5. Little Soldier, Old Bull, White Bull, and Robert Higheagle in folders 6,12, 20–22, box 104; notebook 1–2, 9, box 105; notebook 51, box 106, WSCMC, WHC. Old Bull, quoted in Vestal, *New Sources of Indian History*, 168–70. See Vestal, *Champion of the Sioux*, 125–31; Utley, *The Lance and the Shield*, 106–110.

6. Little Soldier, Old Bull, White Bull, and Robert Higheagle in folders 6, 12, 20–22, box 104; notebooks 1–2, 9, box 105; notebook 51, box 106, WSCMC, WHC. See also Old Bull, quoted in Vestal, *New Sources of Indian History*, 168–70. See Utley, *The Lance and the Shield*, 110–12.

7. For official army and government reports, see "Report of Lieutenant General Phillip H. Sheridan," ARSOW, 1873, 39–42; "Report of the Acting Commissioner of Indian Affairs H. R. Clum," ARCIA, 1873, 4; "Report of the Commissioner of Indian Affairs Francis A. Walker," ARCIA, 1872, 44–45, 75. For more on the fighting and railroads, see Vestal, *Champion of the Sioux*, 125–31; Utley, *The Lance and the Shield*, 106–21; Ostler, *The Plains Sioux*, 52–53.

8. "Report of the Secretary of War William W. Belknap," "Report of Lieutenant General Phillip H. Sheridan," "Report of Major General Alfred Terry," "Report of Brigadier General George Crook," ARSOW, 1875, 21–22, 55–58, 59–65, 69–71; "Report of The Commissioner of Indian Affairs Edward P. Smith," ARCIA, 1874, 6–10; "Report of the Geological Survey of the Black Hills," ARCIA, 1875, 181–83. See also *NYT*, August 28, 1874, 1. Much has been written about Custer's expedition. For more recent works, see Grafe and Horsted, *Exploring with Custer*; Mort, *Thieves' Road*.

9. The story of the 1870 visit and the Sun Dance is in Vestal, *New Sources of Indian History*, 329–33.

10. Húŋkpapȟa, Long Soldier, American Horse, Cloud Shield, Battiste Good, The Flame, No Ears, and Iron Crow winter counts in Vestal, 350; J. Walker, *Lakota Society*, 1992; Greene and Thornton, *The Year the Stars Fell*, 268–75. The Old Bull and White Bull stories are in the Campbell Collection and also in Vestal, *New Sources of Indian History*; Vestal, *Warpath*. On the Silent Eaters, see White Bull, folder 8, box 105, WSCMC, WHC. The White Bull winter count is in folder 27, box 105, WSCMC, WHC. It is not identical to the one called the Húŋkpapȟa winter count in Vestal, *New Sources of Indian History*.

11. "Agreement between the United States and the Sioux for the Relinquishment of Hunting-rights in Nebraska," ARCIA, 1875, 179–80.

12. For the army reports, see "Report of the Secretary of War William W. Belknap," "Report of Lieutenant General Phillip H. Sheridan," "Report of Major General Alfred Terry," "Report of Brigadier General George Crook," ARSOW, 1875, 21–22, 55–58, 59–65, 69–71. See also "Report of the Geological Survey of the Black Hills," ARCIA, 1875, 181–83.

13. Lakȟóta accounts of the events leading to the negotiations include the Little Soldier, Old Bull, White Bull, and Robert Higheagle folders 6, 12–20, 22, box 104, WSCMC, WHC; Henry Twist, Charles Turning Hawk, Red Cloud, American Horse, tablets 18, 25, 35, ESRMC, NSHS; Singing Bear, EBMC, HRMSCA; "Notes on Charger," JWP, MFT; Black Elk, Iron Hawk, Standing Bear, quoted in DeMallie, *The Sixth Grandfather*, 1985, 162–63,168–73.

14. Negotiation proceedings are detailed in "Report of the Commission Appointed to Treat with Sioux Indians for the Relinquishment of the Black Hills," ARCIA, 1875, 184–200. The report includes speeches by the Lakȟóta. The press also followed the talks carefully. See *NYT*, August 13, 1875, 2; *NYT*, August 26, 1876, 4; *NYT*, September 10, 1875, 2; *NYT*, September 22, 1; *NYT*, September 24, 4; *NYT*, September 27, 1. Research literature that discusses the negotiations include Hyde, *Spotted Tail's Folk*, 206–15; Olson, *Red Cloud and the Sioux Problem*, 185–98; Larson, *Red Cloud*, 185–98; Ostler, *The Plains Sioux*; Hämäläinen, *Lakota America*.

15. "Report of the Commission Appointed to Treat with Sioux Indians for the Relinquishment of the Black Hills," ARCIA, 1875, 186–88.

16. Red Cloud and Red Dog, quoted in "Report of the Commission Appointed to Treat with Sioux Indians for the Relinquishment of the Black Hills," ARCIA, 1875, 188.

17. Spotted Tail, quoted in "Report of the Commission Appointed to Treat with Sioux Indians for the Relinquishment of the Black Hills," ARCIA, 1875, 188.

18. Crow Feather, quoted in "Report of the Commission Appointed to Treat with Sioux Indians for the Relinquishment of the Black Hills," ARCIA, 1875, 190. Other Lakȟóta speakers included Flying Bird, Dead Eyes, Stabber, Fast Bear, Spotted Bear and Little Bear. For other Lakȟóta accounts, see Henry Twist, Charles Turning Hawk, tablet 18, ESRMC, NSHS; Singing Bear, EBMC, HRMSCA; Black Elk and Standing Bear, quoted in DeMallie, *The Sixth Grandfather*, 1985, 168–70, 72–73.

19. For Lakȟóta thoughts on mixed-bloods and Squaw-men, see Man Afraid of His Horses, quoted in Deloria and DeMallie, "Peace Commission," 117. See Olson, *Red Cloud and the Sioux Problem*, 274.

20. One Horn and Black Elk, quoted in DeMallie, *The Sixth Grandfather*, 1985, 168–70.

21. Sitting Bull quoted by Iron Hawk in DeMallie, 171–72.

22. Iron Hawk and Standing Bear, quoted in DeMallie, 170–72.

23. "Report of the Commission Appointed to Treat with Sioux Indians for the Relinquishment of the Black Hills," ARCIA, 1875, 184–200.

24. "Report of the Commissioner of Indian Affairs Edward P. Smith," ARCIA, 1874, 4–5. See *Removal of Sioux Indians to the Indian Territory*, S. Exec. Doc. No. 4, 44th Cong., 2nd Sess., 1–3.

25. "Report of the Commissioner of Indian Affairs Edward P. Smith," ARCIA, 1874, 4–5; "Report of the Commissioner of Indian Affairs Edward P. Smith," ARCIA, 1875, 4–9; "Report of the Secretary of War J. D. Cameron," "Report of Lieutenant General William T.

Sherman," ARSOW, 1876, 6, 27–28. See Olson, *Red Cloud and the Sioux Problem*, 199–216; Ostler, *The Plains Sioux*, 60–62; Ostler, *The Lakotas and the Black Hills*.

26. Lakȟóta descriptions of the 1876 fighting are in, for example, the following collections: Short Bull, Kasebier Collection (translated from Lakȟóta by Raymond J. DeMallie, Dennis Christafferson, and Rani-Henrik Andersson), Smithsonian National Museum of American History, 1; Little Soldier, Old Bull, White Bull, Robert Higheagle, folders 6, 20–12, 22, box 104; folder 8, box 105, WSCMC, WHC; Moses Flying Hawk, Standing Bear, Chipps, Iron Hawk, Respects Nothing, Nick Ruleau, Two Moons, tablets 13, 18, 25, 29, A, ESRMC, NSHS; Flying By, One Bull, White Bull etc., folders 6–11, box 2, folder 1, box 3, envelope 41, folder 1, box 5, WSCMC, WHC; "Notes on He Dog, Sitting Bull, Man Afraid of His Horses, Gall, Grey Eagle etc.," JWP, MFT. The Eli S. Ricker interviews are also published in Jensen, *Voices of the American West*; Waggoner, *Witness*. See also Standing Bear, Iron Hawk, Black Elk, quoted in DeMallie, *The Sixth Grandfather*, 1985, 173–95. See White Bull, *Lakota Warrior*, 48–71. See White Bull Pictographs, AISRI. Newspapers published some Indian accounts, especially on the summer 1876 major battles. See, for example, Goose, Eagle Man, The Wreck, Iron Whirlwind, Butcher, Raven, Feeble Bear, Blue Thunder, Tall Timber, *NYT, April 16, 1877*, 5; Low Dog, Crow King, *NYT*, August 10, 1881, 2. Indian accounts are also in Greene, *Indian Views of the Great Sioux War*; Hardorff, *Indian Views of the Custer Fight*.

27. *NYT*, March 1, 1876, 5; *NYT*, April 15, 1876, 2; *NYT*, April 23, 1876, 1; *NYT*, June 7, 1876, 5. For a thorough analysis of summer 1876, see Hämäläinen, *Lakota America*.

28. For official military reports on the 1876 expeditions, see "Report of Lieutenant General William T. Sherman," "Report of Major General Alfred Terry," "Report of Lieutenant General Phillip H. Sheridan, Report (A) of Brigadier General George Crook," ARSOW, 1876, 27–30, 30–32, 440–41, 504; *Military Expedition Against the Sioux Indians*, H. Exec. Doc. No. 184, 44th Cong., 1st Sess., 1–63; "Papers Relating to Military Operations in the Departments of the Platte and Dakota Against the Sioux Indians (Sioux War Papers)," 1876–1896, Microfilm Reels 277, 292, RG 94, OAG, NARA. There is a plethora of research literature on the military side of the 1876 war. See Utley, *Frontier Regulars*; Gray, *Centennial Campaign: The Sioux War of 1876*; Greene, *Slim Buttes*; Overfield, *The Little Big Horn*; Greene, *Battles and Skirmishes*.

29. The description of this ceremony is drawn mainly from Utley, *The Lance and the Shield*, 122–24. Utley attributes this story to White Bull (White Bull or Ice was Cheyenne, not to be confused with the Húŋkpapȟa White Bull) who wrote about it to George Bird Grinnell in a letter in 1906. The letter is in George B. Grinnell Papers, Southwest Museum, Los Angeles. For Lakȟóta-Cheyenne relations, see Wooden Leg, quoted in Marquis, *A Warrior Who Fought Custer*, 177.

30. The camp movements are described by White Bull in Vestal, *New Sources of Indian History*, 159–66.

31. Black Elk, quoted in DeMallie, *The Sixth Grandfather*, 1985, 164–68.

32. "Report of Lieutenant General William T. Sherman," ARSOW, 1876, 27–35, 440–41; "Report of the Commissioner of Indian Affairs Edward P. Smith," "Report of Indian Agents John Burke and J. J. Saville," ARCIA, 1875, 4–5, 244–48, 250–55; "Report of the

Commissioner of Indian Affairs J. Q. Smith," "Report of Indian Agents E. A. Howard and H. W. Bingham," ARCIA, 1876, 4–5, 22–24, 33–35, 38–40; ARCIA, 1876; H. Exec. Doc. No. 1, 44th Cong., 2nd Sess., 382–838, 426–28; *NYT*, June 9, 1876, 5.

33. Red Cloud, quoted in *NYT*, September 18, 1875, 2.

34. For more on the BIA and the feud between the Interior and War Departments, see Henriksson, *The Indian on Capitol Hill*; Wooster, *The Military and the United States Indian Policy*; Fixico, *Bureau of Indian Affairs*.

35. Ceremony details are from Old Bull and White Bull, folder 10, box 104; notebooks 19, 24, folder 10, box 105; notebook 57, box 106; WSCMC, WHC. See Standing Bear, quoted in DeMallie, *The Sixth Grandfather*, 1985, 174–75. Good accounts are in Utley, *The Lance and the Shield*, 133–39. For a thorough analysis on Sitting Bull's vision, see DeMallie, "These Have No Ears," 1993.

36. Lakȟóta and Cheyenne accounts of the Rosebud battle are Iron Hawk, quoted in DeMallie, *The Sixth Grandfather*, 1985, 174–76; White Bull, quoted in Vestal, *Warpath*, 185–90; Bull and Howard, *The Warrior Who Killed Custer*, 48–50. For descriptions focusing on the Indian perspectives, see Powell, *People of the Sacred Mountain*, 954–1002; Utley, *The Lance and the Shield*, 139–42; K. Bray, *Crazy Horse*, 2006, 205–12.

37. Iron Hawk, quoted in DeMallie, *The Sixth Grandfather*, 1985, 174–76.

38. For army accounts, see "Report of Lieutenant General William T. Sherman," "Report of Lieutenant General Phillip H. Sheridan," "Report (B) of Brigadier General George Crook," ARSOW, 1876, 27–30, 442–43, 504–5.

39. Good army sources for the battle are "Report of Lieutenant General William T. Sherman," "Report of Lieutenant General Phillip H. Sheridan," "Report of Major General Alfred Terry," "Report of Brigadier General George Crook," ARSOW, 1876, 27–35, 440–41, 454–71, 498–502. Their correspondence is in "Sioux War Papers," 1876–1896, M 277, 292, RG 94, OAG, NARA. Research literature on the Little Big Horn battle from the army perspective is voluminous and need not be cited here in more detail.

40. For the start of the fight, see Black Elk, Standing Bear, and Iron Hawk, quoted in DeMallie, *The Sixth Grandfather*, 1985, 180–86, 190–93.

41. Black Elk, quoted in DeMallie, 181–83.

42. Black Elk, quoted in DeMallie, 182–83.

43. "Report of Major Marcus A. Reno, Report of Captain Frederick Benteen," ARSOW, 1876, 476–80.

44. For Sitting Bull's actions at Little Big Horn, see Robert P. High Eagle, folder 22, box 104; folder 8, box 105, WSCMC, WHC. Accusations of Sitting Bull's cowardice appeared in the press following the battle and were later promoted by Indian Agent James McLaughlin. For newspapers, see *NYT*, August 2, 1876, 1. McLaughlin, *My Friend the Indian*, 1989, 215–22, 406–11. For an early work on Sitting Bull that promotes the idea of Sitting Bull as a coward, see Johnson, *The Red Record*, 178–79.

45. White Bull, folder 12, box 104, WSCMC, WHC; White Bull Pictographs, AISRI, 6; White Bull, quoted in White Bull, *Lakota Warrior*, 51–56 (Plate 15–21). For more on White Bull and the killing of Custer, see Raymond A. Bucko, preface, *Lakota Warrior*; and Raymond J. DeMallie, preface, Vestal, *Warpath*.

46. Iron Hawk, quoted in DeMallie, *The Sixth Grandfather*, 1985, 190–91. Other Lakȟóta accounts of Little Big Horn include Flying By, folder 1, box 5, WMCC, IULL; Short Bull, Käsebier Collection, 1. Lakȟóta and Cheyenne recollections are also in Greene, *Indian Views of the Great Sioux War*; Hardorff, *Indian Views of the Custer Fight*; Marquis, *A Warrior Who Fought Custer*. For analysis mostly from Lakȟóta perspective see, Hämäläinen, *Lakota America*. See also, Marshall, *The Journey of Crazy Horse*; Marshall, *The Day the World Ended at Little Bighorn*.

47. Lakȟóta war songs by Run the Enemy, Jack Red Cloud, and others, who participated in the Little Big Horn battle were recorded in 1909 and are in *Willard Rhodes Collection of Traditional Music* and *Joseph K. Dixon Collection of North American Indian Music*, Archives of Traditional Music, Indiana University, Bloomington, Indiana.

48. The story of Rocky Butte as told by the Young family, Eugene and Phyllis Young, Tipiziwin Tolman, and Wastewin Young.

49. Moving Robe Woman's story is in Hardorff, *Indian Views of the Custer Fight*, 91–96; Sneve, *Sioux Women*, 19.

50. Short Bull in Käsebier Collection, 1; Cloud Shield and American Horse winter counts in Greene and Thornton, *The Year the Stars Fell*. Many winter counts do focus on other issues. Cloud Shield and American Horse record that several Lakȟóta joined Colonel Ranald McKenzie in fighting the Cheyenne. Indeed, after surrendering, several Oglála acted as scouts for the United States, a very divisive and important issue.

51. The mutilation of the bodies and the battle was discussed in *NYT*. See Goose, Eagle Man, The Wreck, Iron Whirlwind, Butcher, Raven, Feeble Bear, Blue Thunder, Tall Timber, *NYT*, April 16, 1877, 5; Low Dog, Crow King, *NYT*, August 10, 1881, 2. For more on this symbolism, see DeMallie, "These Have No Ears."

52. Kill Talks, quoted in DeMallie, *The Sixth Grandfather*, 1985, 197–98.

53. Standing Bear, quoted in DeMallie, 198.

54. War Eagle, "The Lakota Are Charging, New CD Focuses on Battle of Little Big Horn," *Lakota Country Times*, June 19, 2008.

55. Short Bull in Käsebier Collection, 1.

56. Black Elk gives a detailed account of the dispersal after the battle. See Black Elk, quoted in DeMallie, *The Sixth Grandfather*, 1985, 196–204.

57. For estimates of Lakȟóta and Cheyenne populations, see "Reports of Indian Agents," ARCIA, 1876.

58. See Johnson, *The Red Record*; McLaughlin, *My Friend the Indian*.

Chapter 8

1. For structures built at the agencies, see "Reports of Indian Agents B.W. Bingham, Henry F. Livingston, Tom A. Reily, James S Hastings and E. A Howard," ARCIA, 1876, 23–24, 31–36.

2. *Indian Department Appropriations Act* (Termination of Treaty Making Process), March 3, 1871, AIUSD, 3:2181–85. More on the termination of treaty making in the context of US Indian policies and the Bureau of Indian Affairs in Fixico, *Bureau of Indian Affairs*.

3. The Flame winter count in Greene and Thornton, *The Year the Stars Fell*, 276.

4. The Eastern press was actively following the situation on the Great Sioux Reservation. See *NYT*, August 23, 1876, 5; *NYT*, September 8, 1876, 2; *NYT*, September 10, 1876, 1; *NYT*, September 25, 1876, 5; *NYT*, October 25, 1876, 6; *NYT*, October 27, 1876, 1; *NYT*, December 23, 1876, 3. The question of moving the Lakȟóta to the Indian Territory was also raised by the Commissioner of Indian Affairs J. Q Smith. See ARCIA, 1876, 7–9.

5. For this ongoing controversy, for example, *Petition Regarding Black Hills Settlement 1911*, Welch Dakota Papers WDP; *United States v. Sioux Nation*, 448 US 371, 100 S. Ct. 2716, 65 L. Ed. 2d 844 (1980).

6. Black Elk, quoted in DeMallie, *The Sixth Grandfather*, 1985, 198–99.

7. For more on the career of General Nelson A. Miles, see Wooster, *Nelson A. Miles*.

8. For Slim Buttes, see Greene, *Slim Buttes*.

9. A copy of Sitting Bull's letter can be found in the "Report of Major General Nelson A. Miles, Report of Lieutenant Colonel E. S. Otis," ARSOW, 1876, 482–83 (General Miles's correspondence is also attached, 515–18.)

10. White Bull, folder 12, box 104, WSCMC, WHC.

11. Black Elk, quoted in DeMallie, *The Sixth Grandfather*, 1985, 198–99. See also K. Bray, *Crazy Horse*, 2006, 250–51.

12. Black Elk, quoted in DeMallie, *The Sixth Grandfather*, 1985, 201. For a description of this ceremony, see Little Killer and Standing Elk interviews in Buechel, *Lakota Tales and Text*.

13. For Lakȟóta accounts of the fall and winter of 1876–77 fighting see Flying By, Looking Elk, White Bull, One Bull, envelope 41, folder 1, box 5, WMCC; Little Soldier, One Bull, White Bull, Bob Tail Horse in folders 6, 10–12, box 104; notebooks 11, 21, 37, box 105, WSCMC, WHC. See "Notes on He Dog, Turning Bear, Charger, Grey Eagle", JWP, MFT; He Dog, Red Feather, quoted in Hinman, "Oglala Sources on the Life of Crazy Horse," 1976. See also Red Horse, Charger, Many Shield, Tall Bull, Long Feather, Bear's Face, Spotted Elk, Lazy White Bull, Iron Teeth, Black White Man, Beaver Heart, Eagle Shield, Wooden Leg, White Bull, Hump in Greene, *Indian Views of the Great Sioux War*, 85–148. See also Black Elk, quoted in DeMallie, *The Sixth Grandfather*, 1985, 196–202. Scholarly works describing the fighting from Lakȟóta perspective are Utley, *The Lance and the Shield*, 174–82; K. Bray, *Crazy Horse*, 2006, 241–76.

14. For an analysis of the Battle of Wolf Mountain, see Greene, *Battles and Skirmishes*; Pearson, "Battle of Wolf Mountains"; K. Bray, *Crazy Horse*, 2006, 254–64.

15. See *NYT*, July 15, 1876, 5; *NYT*, July 21, 1876, 5; *NYT*, August 3, 1876, 5; *NYT*, August 15, 1876, 1; *NYT*, August 25, 1876, 4; *NYT*, October 11, 1876, 4; *NYT*, October 22, 1876, 7; *NYT*, November 1, 1876, 5; *NYT*, November 13, 1876, 1; *NYT*, December 5, 1876, 1; *NYT*, December 20, 1876, 1; *NYT*, December 24, 1876, 2; *NYT*, February 7, 1877, 5; *NYT*, February 14, 1876, 5; *NYT*, March 17, 1877, 3.

16. "Report of Lieutenant General Phillip H. Sheridan," ARSOW, 1876, 448.

17. Red Horse, quoted in Utley, *The Lance and the Shield*, 184. Utley refers to Red Horse statement in Col. W. H. Wood to AAG, Dept of Dakota, CRA, February 27, 1877, Frame 714, roll 4, M 1495, RG 393, NARA.

18. Lakȟóta accounts of life after Little Big Horn and the process that led to Sitting Bull's decision to move to Canada and Crazy Horse's surrender are Little Soldier, One Bull, White Bull, Bob Tail Horse, folders 6, 10–12, box 104; notebooks 11, 21, 37, box 105, WSCMC, WHC; Flying By, Looking Elk, White Bull, One Bull, envelope 41, folder 1, box 5, WMCC; DeMallie, *The Sixth Grandfather*, 1985, 197–207. For more see, for example, DeMallie, "These Have No Ears," 1993; Utley, *The Lance and the Shield*, 180–82; McCrady, *Living with Strangers*, 2006.

19. See *NYT*, August 19, 1876, 1; *NYT*, February 15, 1877, 5.

20. For George Sword's life, see Introduction by Raymond J. DeMallie for Walker, *Lakota Society*, 1992. See also Red Shirt, *George Sword*.

21. George Sword autobiography, AISRI (translated by Raymond J. DeMallie, used with his permission); George Sword, Chips, tablets 16, 18, ESRMC, NSHS. Published also in Jensen, *Voices of the American West*, 273–77, 326–30. George Sword's mission has been thoroughly analyzed from an ethnohistorical perspective in DeMallie, "These Have No Ears," 1993, 329–32; Black Elk, quoted in DeMallie, *The Sixth Grandfather*, 1985, 201–2; K. Bray, *Crazy Horse*, 2006, 265–66.

22. DeMallie, "These Have No Ears," 1993, 328–33; K. Bray, *Crazy Horse*, 2006, 261–71.

23. K. Bray, *Crazy Horse*, 2006, 269–85.

24. This description of Crazy Horse's surrender is based on the following: William Garnett, American Horse, Chips, George Sword, tablets 1, 16, 18, ESRMC, NSHS. These are also published in Jensen, *Voices of the American West*, 58–74, 273–77, 326–30. See also George Sword manuscript (translated by Raymond J. DeMallie), AISRI; He Dog and Red Feather, quoted in Hinman, "Oglala Sources on the Life of Crazy Horse," 1976, 10–33; "Notes on He Dog," JWP, MFT (Published also in Waggoner, *Witness*, 481–83); DeMallie, *The Sixth Grandfather*, 1985, 198–207. The events are detailed in ARCIA, 1877. The military accounts are included in ARSOW, 1877. Agent Valentine T. McGillycuddy's statement is in envelope 4, folder 3, box 4, WMCC, IULL.

25. *NYT*, May 8, 1877, 1. For a thorough discussion of the surrender, see Bray, *Crazy Horse*, 2006, 272–305.

26. Crazy Horse, *NYT*, May 8, 1877, 1. The article is interesting because it claims that the most important speech at the meeting was given by Crazy Horse himself. According to the Lakȟóta and William Garnett, others spoke for Crazy Horse. Garnett also claims the venue for the meeting was not the office building at Camp Robinson, but an open field near Red Cloud Agency. The article is an excellent example of how a mythical aura began to develop around Crazy Horse.

27. The situation during summer 1877 and the disputes, intrigues and suspicions surrounding Crazy Horse is well analyzed in Ostler, *The Plains Sioux*, 84–105; K. Bray, *Crazy Horse*, 2006, 314–80. See also, Olson, *Red Cloud and the Sioux Problem*, 243–45; Sandoz, *Strange Man of the Oglalas*, 387–413; Larson, *Red Cloud*, 214–15; Sajna, *Crazy Horse*, 320–24.

28. For an eyewitness description of summer 1877 events, see Louis Bordeaux, tablet 11, ESRMC, NSHS. Published also in Jensen, *Voices of the American West*, 290–302. Louis

Bordeaux was a mixed-blood interpreter at the Spotted Tail Agency in 1877. His mother was a Sičháŋǧu and father a Frenchman.

29. For the Nez Percé, see Sharfstein, *Thunder in the Mountains.*

30. Crazy Horse in Louis Bordeaux, tablet 11, ESRMC, NSHS. Jensen, *Voices of the American West,* 300.

31. Black Elk, quoted in DeMallie, *The Sixth Grandfather,* 1985, 203–4. See also Chips, tablet 18, ESRMC, NSHS. Published in Jensen, *Voices of the American West,* 276–77.

32. No Ears winter count in J. Walker, *Lakota Society,* 1992, 148; White Bull winter count White Bull, *Lakota Warrior,* 22; American Horse and Battiste Good winter counts in Greene and Thornton, *The Year the Stars Fell,* 278–79.

33. Sitting Bull, quoted in Vestal, *New Sources of Indian History,* 237–38.

34. For Lakȟóta place naming and the making of Lakȟóta Tȟamákȟočhe in Canada, see Thomson, "Lakota Place Names."

35. Lakȟóta accounts of the years in Canada include Old Bull, White Bull, Bob Tail Bull, Two Bull, Iron Dog, folders 10–12, box 104; notebooks 8, 11–12, 16, 19, 35, box 105; notebook 52, box 106, WSCMC, WHC. "Notes on Sitting Bull, Grey Eagle, Gall, Big Foot", JWP, MFT; Black Elk, quoted in DeMallie, *The Sixth Grandfather,* 1985, 204–13. See also Vestal, *New Sources of Indian History,* 236–45. Sitting Bull's years in Canada are described in Utley, *The Lance and the Shield,* 183–210; McCrady, *Living with Strangers,* 2009; Papandrea, *They Never Surrendered.* For a recent study see, Utley, *The Last Sovereigns.*

36. Sitting Bull's views are in George S. Young, envelope 64, folder 11, box 5, WMCC, IULL; *Report of the Commission appointed to . . . Meet the Sioux Chief, Sitting Bull . . . to Avoid Hostile Incursions . . . from the Dominion of Canada,* H. Exec. Doc. No. 1, 45th Cong., 2nd Sess., 1–10; *Sioux War Papers,* 1876–1896, M 283, RG 94, OAG, NARA. Lakȟóta views of the surrender are in Vestal, *New Sources of Indian History,* 246–60. The original Lakȟóta accounts are in WSCMC, WHC. See also Utley, *The Lance and the Shield,* 199–224.

37. For the relocation of the Lakȟóta, see "Report of the Commissioner of Indian Affairs J. Q. Smith," "Report of Agent James S. Hastings," "Report of Agent E. A. Howard," ARCIA, 1876, 15, 33–35; "Report of the Commissioner of Indian Affairs Ezra A. Hayt," ARCIA, 1877, 17–18; "Report of the Commissioner of Indian Affairs Ezra A. Hayt," "Report of Agent James Irwin," "Report of Agent William J. Pollock," ARCIA, 1878, 28–32, 36–40.

38. "Report of the Commissioner of Indian Affairs Ezra A. Hayt," "Report of the Sioux Commission," ARCIA, 1878, 28–32, 156–61.

39. Valentine T. McGillycuddy, envelope 41, folder 4, box 5, WMCC, IULL; Red Cloud, quoted in Hyde, *A Sioux Chronicle,* 164. For more on Red Cloud and McGillycuddy, see Olson, *Red Cloud and the Sioux Problem,* 264–85; Larson, *Red Cloud,* 217–48. For more on Agent McGillycuddy, see McGillycuddy, *Blood on the Moon.*

40. For more on Lakȟóta performers with Buffalo Bill, see Friesen, Littlemoon, and Chladiuk, *Lakota Performers in Europe*; Burns, *Transnational Frontiers.*

41. Agent McLaughlin's hatred toward Sitting Bull is revealed in his personal correspondence. See James McLaughlin to the Commissioner of Indian Affairs Thomas J. Morgan, June 18, 1890, 8, reel 1, M 4728, Special Case (SC) 188, RG 75, NARA; McLaughlin

to Morgan, October 17, 1890, 31–43, reel 1, M 4728, SC 188, RG 75, NARA; McLaughlin to Herbert Welsh, January 12, 1891, 47–64, roll 22, M230, JMLP, MHS; McLaughlin to Mary Collins, December 26, 1890, 27–30, roll 22, M 230, JMLP, MHS; McLaughlin to Winfield Jennings, January 4, 1891, 33, roll 22, M 230, JMLP, MHS. See also McLaughlin, *My Friend the Indian*, 1989.

42. Lakȟóta accounts of the relationship between Sitting Bull and McLaughlin include Lone Man, envelope 41, folder 1, box 5, WMCC, LL; One Bull, Mrs. One Bull, Four Blanket Woman, envelope 41, folder 1, box 5, WMCC, LL; Robert P. Higheagle, folder 22, box 104, WSCMC, WHC; Old Bull, notebook 11, box 105, WSCMC, WHC; One Bull, folders 10–11, box 104, WSCMC, WHC.

43. For the establishment of the Indian police, see Hagan, William T., *Indian Police and Judges*.

44. Captain of Indian Police Yellow Breast (also known as Straight Head) to Agent Perain P. Palmer, March 26, (year unreadable), box 249, Cheyenne River, RG 75, NARA, Kansas City, MO; Standing Soldier, quoted in "Report of Indian Agent Valentine T. McGillycuddy," ARCIA, 1884, 41.

45. "Report of Indian Agent William A. Swan," ARCIA, 1885, 16–17.

46. No Flesh, quoted in "Proceedings held at Sun Dance, (Pine Ridge) June 9, 1879," box 52, Miscellaneous Letters Sent by the Agent, Pine Ridge, 1876–1914, RG 75, NARA. Stealing horses became a major issue at all Lakȟóta agencies, and of course, the Lakȟóta themselves went on raids to other reservations as late as the 1890s. For more on Lakȟóta raids in the 1880s and 1890s, see McGinnis, *Counting Coup and Cutting Horses*.

47. Swift Bird to Agent Perain P. Palmer, November 20, 1891, box 570, Cheyenne River, RG 75, NARA. The agents reported on the conduct of the police in their reports throughout the 1880s. These can be found in the Annual Reports of the Commissioner of Indian Affairs.

48. Noheart to Agent Perain P. Palmer, November 5, 1890, NARA, RG 75, Cheyenne River, box 570.

49. This idea was also floated in the press. See, for example, *Harper's Weekly* 34, no. 1 (1875): 1002, 1004–6.

50. "Report of Indian Agent James G. Wright," ARCIA, 1883, 42.

51. Standing Bear, quoted in "Report of Indian Agent Valentine T. McGillycuddy," ARCIA, 1884, 41.

52. See Henriksson, *The Indian on Capitol Hill*, 79–81; Harring and Harring, *Crow Dog's Case*.

53. For the districts and areas of settlement in 1889, see "Reports of Agents Charles E. McChesney, L. F. Spencer, James McLaughlin," ARCIA, 1889, 130, 137, 165–66, For Lakȟóta political structure, see Hassrick, *The Sioux*, 2012, 31, Price, *The Oglala People*, 172–73; DeMallie, "Teton," 812.

54. Report of Agent James McLaughlin, ARCIA, 1887, 57.

55. Father Eugene Buechel, quoted in DeMallie, *The Sixth Grandfather*, 1985, Introduction 22–23.

56. We have not been able to verify his Lakȟóta name and cannot find him in the census records.

57. Harry Truly Necklace and Frank High Eagle letter to the agent, September 9, 1894, box 569, Cheyenne River, RG 75, NARA, Kansas City, MO.

58. "Reports of Agent Charles McChesney," ARCIA, 1886, 51; ARCIA, 1887, 17. These themes recurred in almost all reports by Lakȟóta agents throughout the 1880s.

59. "Report of Indian Agent Valentine T. McGillycuddy," ARCIA, 1885, 38.

60. Four Bear et al. in James Ramsey to Agent, May 23, 1889, box 570, Cheyenne River, RG 75, NARA; No Heart to Agent Perain P. Palmer, November 5, 1890, box 570, Cheyenne River, RG 75, NARA; Frank High Eagle et al. to Agent Perain P. Palmer, September 9, 1894, box 569, Cheyenne River, RG 75, NARA.

61. See requests by several families from the Crow Creek agency to visit other Lakȟóta agencies, box 1, Crow Creek Transfers and Passes 1887, RG 75, NARA.

62. The numbers regarding Lakȟóta visits are from Gage, *We Do Not Want the Gates Closed between Us*, 84–85. As examples of requests to visit other reservations, see Letter of Request quoted in Indian Agent James McLaughlin to Indian Agent Charles E. McChesney, May 27, 1890, box 251, Cheyenne River, RG 75, NARA; Letter of Request quoted in A. G. Hennisee to Indian Agent Charles E. McChesney, August 25, 1890, box 251, Cheyenne River, RG 75, NARA.

63. For a thorough study on Native networks in the early reservation context, see Gage, *We Do Not Want the Gates Closed between Us*.

64. For the 1883 hunt and Lakȟóta response to the cancellation, see "Report of Agent William A Swan," ARCIA, 1883, 21–22. See Long Soldier winter count in Greene and Thornton, *The Year the Stars Fell*, 282.

65. The agents' reports include lists and tables on these external markers of assimilation, and they can be found in the Annual Reports of the Commissioner of Indian Affairs. See Smedman, "From Warriors and Hunters to Farmers."

66. For change and continuity in womens' lives, see Sneve, *Sioux Women*.

67. For the ban of religious ceremonies, see Prucha, *Documents of United States Indian Policy*, 160–62.

68. For Mad Bear, see JWP, MFT and Waggoner, *Witness*, 305–6.

69. For the establishment of Christianity among the Lakȟóta, see Woodruff, *The Episcopal Mission*; Enochs, *The Jesuit Mission*; Markowitz, "The Catholic Mission and the Sioux"; Deloria, "The Establishment of Christianity."

70. Hein, "Episcopalianism among the Lakota/Dakota."

71. For more on the St. Elisabeth in Wakpála, see Waggoner, *Witness*, 205–6.

72. Phillip J. Deloria to *Anpao Kin*, October 1893, Letter written in Dakȟóta, Translated and compiled by Reverend William J. Cleveland. Published in Cleveland, *Sioux Letters*, 14–16. For more on Philip J. Deloria and his work, see Deloria, *Becoming Mary Sully*, 50–55.

73. See, Foley, *Father Francis M. Craft*.

74. Good descriptions of the missionary work are in diaries and reports by the missionaries Father Emil Perrig; Father Florentine Digman S.J.; Aaron Beede; Edward. Missionaries' reports were also included in the Annual Reports of the Commissioners

of Indian Affairs. For a thorough study on the St. Francis Mission, see Markowitz, *Converting the Rosebud.*

75. Anonymous man in FDP, September 30, 1890; Digman to Father Stephan, October 2, 1890, reel 20, Series 1-1, BCIM, MUA.

76. Sam White Bird, *Iapi Oaye* 19, no. 11 (November 1890), 38 (translated by Rani-Henrik Andersson). Published also in Andersson, *Whirlwind*, 343–45. See also, Louis Mazawakiyanna, Samuel Spaniard, *Iapi Oaye* 19, no. 11 (November 1890), 39; *Word Carrier* 20, no. 11 (November 1890), 29; *Word Carrier* 19, no. 12 (December 1890), 35; Louis Mazawakiyanna, Samuel Spaniard, *Iapi Oaye* 19, no. 11 (November 1890), 39; *Word Carrier* 20, no. 11 (November 1890), 29; *Word Carrier* 19, no. 12 (December 1890), 35

77. *Anpao Kin* 6, no. 7 (July 1887), 1–5 (translated by Rani-Henrik Andersson, Raymond DeMallie, and Dennis Christafferson).

78. Anna Charging Bear to *Anpao Kin,* May 26, 1893, in Cleveland, *Sioux Letters*, 19–23.

79. Anna Charging Bear to *Anpao Kin,* May 26, 1893, in Cleveland, 19–23.

80. Luisa B. Scares Hawk to Anpao Kin, October 27, 1893, in Cleveland, 23–25; Julia Tackett to Anpao Kin, June 1893, in Cleveland, 30–31; Joseph Crows-in-the-Morning to Anpao Kin, April 20, 1894, in Cleveland, 28–30.

81. C. J. Spotted Bull to *Anpao Kin*, March 3, 1893, published in Cleveland, *Sioux Letters*, 26–28.

82. See "Reports of the Missionaries," ARCIA, 1887; "Reports of the Missionaries," ARCIA, 1889.

83. For a description of the last Sun Dance held at Little Wound's camp on Pine Ridge see H. G. Webb, NAASI, MS 1394-A.

84. For the discussion on how the Lakȟóta not only merged their beliefs with Christianity but also shaped the way Christianity was taught on the reservations, see Markowitz, *Converting the Rosebud.*

85. Foley, *Father Francis M. Craft*, 11–30. Jesuit attitudes toward Lakȟóta religion are in Perrig Diary; Digman Papers; Foley, 11–30.

86. Black Elk, quoted in DeMallie, *The Sixth Grandfather*, 1985, 14.

87. See Posthumus, "Transmitting."

88. For Gall, see Deloria, *Speaking of Indians*, 1998, 100–101. See also "Notes on Gall," JWP, MFT; and Waggoner, *Witness.*

89. DeMallie, *The Sixth Grandfather*, 1985. For Black Elk's life, see Steltenkamp, *Black Elk*; DeMallie, *The Sixth Grandfather*, 1985. DeMallie.

90. Discussions with Lula Red Cloud, May 2018, Andersson, "Field Notes and Interviews, 2000–2020."

91. Battiste Good and Rosebud winter counts in Greene and Thornton, *The Year the Stars Fell*, 281. For Lakȟóta accounts of life in a boarding school see, for example, Standing Bear, *My People the Sioux*, 1975, 133–60; Standing Bear, *Land of the Spotted Eagle*, 1978, 226–46.

92. For US Indian policies and genocide, see Fenelon, *Culturicide*; Ostler, *Surviving Genocide.*

93. Waggoner, *Witness*, 201.

94. Sitting Bull, quoted in Waggoner, 204.

95. Red Cloud in Report of Agent Valentine T. McGillycuddy, ARCIA, 1885, 34.

96. Waggoner, *Witness*, 187–88.

97. Red Cloud, quoted in Gage, *We Do Not Want the Gates Closed between Us*, 35. Gage refers to *Southern Workman*, August 5, 1885, 85. Several Lakȟóta accounts about education are in S. Exec. Doc. No. 17, 50th Cong., 2nd Sess., 1–283; S. Exec. Doc. No. 51, 51st Cong., 1st Sess., 1–215.

98. The agents diligently reported Lakȟóta school attendance in their annual reports throughout the 1880s. For example, "Reports of Agent William A. Swan, John G. Gassman, Valentine T. McGillycuddy, James G. Wright, Agent James McLaughlin," ARCIA, 1884, 20–23, 36–48, 52–57; ARCIA, 1885, 16–18, 33–47, 51–56. Letter of William Holmes, teacher at Moreau River Day School, November 15, 1890, box 580, Cheyenne River, RG 75, NARA. For Lakȟóta, especially Oglála, school attendance, see Smedman, "From Warriors and Hunters to Farmers."

99. See "Report of the Commissioner of Indian Affairs Thomas J. Morgan," ARCIA, 1891, 132–35.

100. Spotted Eagle to the Agent, Date unclear, 1895, box 580, Cheyenne River, RG 75, NARA; Ester White Head to the Agent, April 22, 1895, box 580, Cheyenne River, RG 75, NARA.

101. James Auger to his father in Postmaster A. Ausguth to the Commissioner of Indian Affairs, M 234/258, DSI, RG 75, NARA.

102. Vi Waln, "Special to Indian Country," https://indiancountrytoday.com/news/now-theyre-home. In recent years several books have been published on boarding school experiences. See, for example, Childs, *Boarding School Seasons*; Fear-Segal and Rose, *Carlisle Indian Industrial School*; Adams, *Education for Extinction*.

103. For letter-writing as way to bring forth Native agency, see Gage, *We Do Not Want the Gates Closed between Us*. See also, Ostler, *The Plains Sioux*, 159.

104. For more, see Gage, *We Do Not Want the Gates Closed between Us*, 17–44. American Horse correspondence with Edvin and James Landy is in YCWA, AHP.

105. See Request by Lakȟóta of Standing Rock to visit Washington DC, in James Mclaughlin correspondence with the Commissioner of Indian Affairs J. D. C Atkins, April 18, 1888, box 249, Cheyenne River, RG 75, NARA; White Swan to the President in Acting Commissioner (name unclear) to Indian Agent Charles E. McChesney, July 13, 1886, box 570, Cheyenne River, RG 75, NARA.

106. For letter writing and intertribal visitation as anticolonial tools, see Gage, *We Do Not Want the Gates Closed between Us*.

Chapter 9

1. For the report by the Edmunds Commission, see S. Exec. Doc. No. 70, 49th Cong., 1st Sess.

2. *An Act to Provide for the Allotment of Lands in Severalty to Indians on the Various Reservations* (General Allotment Act or Dawes Act), US Statutes at Large, 24 Stat, 388–91, in Prucha, *Documents of United States Indian Policy*, document 104.

3. John Grass in S. Exec. Doc. No. 17, 50th Cong., 2nd Sess., vol. 1, serial, 2610, 1–283, 79.

4. The 1888 proceedings with full speeches by the Lakȟóta chiefs are in S. Exec. Doc. No. 17, 50th Cong., 2nd Sess., vol. 1, serial, 2610, 1–283. For Sitting Bull and the Crow reservation, see Ostler, *The Plains Sioux*, 221–22.

5. White Ghost, Running Bear and chiefs at Lower Brulé in S. Exec. Doc. No. 17, 50th Cong., 2nd Sess., vol. 1, serial, 2610, 150,157, 178–96.

6. George Sword and American Horse in S. Exec. Doc. No. 17, 50th Cong., 2nd Sess., vol. 1, serial, 2610, 212–13, 219. American Horse expressed his views on the proposed reduction of the reservation later in 51st Cong., 1st Sess., House of Representatives Committee on Indian Affairs, Unpublished Hearing, April 15, 1890, 1–3, Card 1, Microfiche, IULL.

7. The full Lakȟóta speeches are in S. Exec. Doc. No. 17, 50th Cong., 2nd Sess., vol. 1, serial, 2610, 1–283. For the agents' point of view, see *Report of Agent James McLaughlin*, ARCIA, 1890.

8. Full Lakȟóta speeches are included in S. Exec. Doc. No. 51, 51st Cong., 1st Sess., vol. 5, serial 2682, 1–215. For more on the 1888 and 1889 land negotiations, see Greene, "The Sioux Commission," 41–72; Utley, *Last Days*, 3:268–80; Utley, *The Lance and the Shield*, 269–80; Ostler, *The Plains Sioux*, 221–41.

9. Sitting Bull in S. Exec. Doc. No. 51, 51st Cong., 1st Sess., vol. 5, serial 2682, 213. See, Utley, *The Lance and the Shield*, 275–80; Ostler, *The Plains Sioux*, 221–41.

10. See, US Statutes at Large, 25 Stat., Act of 1889, Section 1–7, 888–90.

11. Red Cloud to T. A. Bland, December 10, 1890, in Bland, *A Brief History*, 19–21. Read in the House of Representatives, December 19, 1890, Cong. Rec., 51st Cong. 1st Sess., vol. 21, part 14, December 19, 1890, 702–3. Published in full in Andersson, *Whirlwind*, 167–69.

12. Little Wound in Hugh D. Gallagher to the Commissioner of Indian Affairs Thomas J. Morgan, July 23, 1890, 335–36, roll 10, M 1282, LSASPR, RG 75, NARA. Published also in Andersson, *Whirlwind*, 149–50. For additional comments by Lakȟóta chiefs, see Little Wound, Young Man Afraid of His Horse, Fast Thunder in Gallagher to Morgan, July 23, 1890, 335–38, roll 10, M 1282, LSASPR, RG 75, NARA; American Horse in Report of Major General Nelson A. Miles, September 24, 1891, ARSOW, 1891, 136; American Horse, H. Exec. Doc. No. 36, 51st Cong., 2nd Sess., 6; *Council Held with a Delegation of Sioux Indians*, 51st Cong., 1st Sess., United States Congress House of Representatives, House Committee on Indian Affairs., April 15, 1890, Unpublished Hearing, IULL, Microfiche, Card 1, 1–9.

13. For the Sioux Commission recommendations, see S. Exec. Doc. No 51, 51st Cong., 1st Sess., vol. 4, serial 2682, 23–31. For more on Dawes' opinions on the Lakȟóta, see Andersson, *Lakota Ghost Dance*, 250–70.

14. *ODB*, February 11, 1890, 1, 4; *ODB*, February 13, 1890, 1; *ODB*, February 17, 1890, 2.

15. Thomas J. Morgan's views on Indian policy, ARCIA, 1891, 1–144.

16. Short Bull in "As Narrated by Short Bull," recorded by George C. Crager, MS [1891], BBMG. Published in Andersson, *Whirlwind*, 40–56.

17. There has been extensive discussion on the number of Lakȟóta delegations, although there most likely was only one. The names of the delegates vary depending on the story.

Even Short Bull gave different names. For comparison, see Mooney, *The Ghost-Dance Religion*, 816–24; Utley, *Last Days*, 3:60–63; Coleman, *Voices of Wounded Knee*, 10; Maddra, *Hostiles?*, 22–23; Andersson, *Lakota Ghost Dance*, 31–48; Greene, *American Carnage*, 69; Warren, *God's Red Son*, 182–86; Gage, *We Do Not Want the Gates Closed between Us*, 153–68.

18. Lakȟóta accounts of the journey are included in, for example, Short Bull in "As Narrated by Short Bull," recorded by George C. Crager, 1891, Buffalo Bill Museum and Grave, Golden, Colorado (MS [1891]); Short Bull in EBMC, HRMSCA, MUA; Short Bull in Wolfgang Haberland, "Die Oglala Sammlung Weygold im Hamburischen Museum fur Völkerkunde" [Weygold's Oglala Collection in the Hamburg Museum of Ethnology], Mitteilungen aus die Museum für Völkerkunde, 1977, 37–38; Kicking Bear in McLaughlin, *My Friend the Indian*, 1910, 185–89; Good Thunder in Eastman, *Sister to the Sioux*, 143–44. A shorter version is in Eastman, "The Ghost Dance War and Wounded Knee Massacre of 1890–1891," 26–42. These accounts are in full in Andersson, *Whirlwind*. For the route of the journey, see Mooney, *The Ghost-Dance Religion*, 820; Utley, *Last Days*, 3:61–64; Andersson, *Lakota Ghost Dance*, 32–38; Gage, "Intertribal Communication," 234–36; Warren, *God's Red Son*, 182–86; Gage, *We Do Not Want the Gates Closed between Us*, 150–62.

19. The delegation left sometime in the fall of 1889 and returned in early 1890. See Mooney, *The Ghost-Dance Religion*, 816–24; Andersson, *Lakota Ghost Dance*, 31–48; Warren, *God's Red Son*.

20. A better translation for the Ghost Dance would be Spirit Dance. The Lakȟóta word *wanáǧi* refers to the spirits of the departed and the name for the Ghost Dance in Lakȟóta is *wanáǧi wachípi kiŋ*, the spirit dance. See Andersson, *Lakota Ghost Dance*, 29, 46–54. For the effect of the early rumors, see Mooney, *The Ghost-Dance Religion*, 816–24; Utley, *Last Days*, 3:66–86; Ostler, *The Plains Sioux*, 243–56; Andersson, *Lakota Ghost Dance*, 31–48.

21. Black Elk in DeMallie, *The Sixth Grandfather*, 1985, 258–82. Published also in Andersson, *Whirlwind*, 116–41. For the original manuscripts see NCWHMC, UMC.

22. For first dances, see Short Bull, Young Skunk, Pretty Eagle in EBMC, HRMSCA. See also Buechel, *Lakota Tales and Text*. Rani-Henrik Andersson retranslated these texts from the original in the *Buechel Collection* with Raymond J. DeMallie and Timo Oksanen in 2015–2016. Another description from a different perspective is in Indian Agent Hugh D. Gallagher's letter to the SPM 1282, roll 10, 315.

23. Young Skunk in EBMC, HRMSCA, story 1. Published in Andersson, *Whirlwind*, 99–101.

24. George Sword to the Commissioner of Indian Affairs Thomas J. Morgan, undated, received November 22, 1890, Letters Received, Letter 36111, box 680, RBIA, RG 75.4, NARA; Beard in MSS 653, JRWC, HCSHL. See Walker, *Lakota Society*, 1992, 157–68; Andersson, *Whirlwind*, 258–59, 275–86.

25. Short Bull in "As Narrated by Short Bull;" Sword, "Wanagi Wacipi Toranpi owicakiyakapi kin lee," Manuscript 936, NAASI. Translated by Rani-Henrik Andersson. For the agents' point of view, see Andersson, *Lakota Ghost Dance*, 104–5.

26. Andersson, 40–44, 100–111. For early newspaper reporting on the Lakȟóta Ghost Dance, see *ODB*, April 6, 1890, 1; *WP*, April 6, 1890, 1; *WP*, April 16, 1890, 2; *CT*, April 7, 1890, 9; *NYT*, April 6, 1890, 1.

27. For Sitting Bull's life and his struggles with Agent James McLaughlin, see Vestal, *Champion of the Sioux*; Utley, *The Lance and the Shield*.

28. Little Wound, Young Man Afraid of His Horses, Fast Thunder, in Indian Agent Gallagher's letter to Commissioner of Indian Affairs, July 23, 1890, 335–38, roll 10, M 1282, LSASPR, RG 76, NARA; American Horse, 51st Cong., 1st Sess., House of Representatives Committee on Indian Affairs, *Council Held with a Delegation of Sioux Indians*, Unpublished Hearing, April 15, 1890, IULL, Microfiche, Card 1, 1–9 (See Part 2). For more about additional rations to the Lakȟóta, see *Sioux Indian Appropriation*, H. Exec. Doc. No. 36, 51st Cong., 2nd Sess.; *Additional Provisions for Sioux*, H. Exec. Doc.,no. 37, 51st Cong., 2nd Sess. For more on congressional politics and the Ghost Dance, see Richardson, *Wounded Knee*.

29. These emerging divisions are described in American Horse to J. Landy, December 22, 1890, AHP, MSS S 903, YCWA; Short Bull Document, BBMG, 3; American Horse in *Report of Major General Nelson A. Miles*, ARSOW, 1891, 136; American Horse, 51st Cong., 1st Sess., House of Representatives Committee on Indian Affairs, Unpublished Hearing, April 15, 1890, IULL, Microfiche, Card 1, 1–3; Little Soldier, Shoots Walking, One Bull, 21, folder 5–6, box 104, WSCMC, WHC.

30. Young Skunk, story 1–3, EBMC, HRMSCA; Pretty Eagle, story 1–2, EBMC, HRMSCA; Red Cloud's letter to T. A. Bland, December 10, 1890, read in the US Congress, Cong. Rec., 51st Cong., 2nd Sess., December 19, 1890, 702–3; Red Cloud, in Charles A. Eastman's letter to Frank Wood, November 11, 1890, 1/98–100, reel 1, M 4728, SC 188, RG 75, NARA; Indian Agent Daniel F. Royer's letter to Commissioner of Indian Affairs Thomas J. Morgan, November 8, 1890,, 62–65, vol. 1, roll 1, M 983, AIWKSC, RG 94, NARA; Little Wound, *NYT*, November 23, 1890, 5; *CT*, November 23, 1890, 1; *ODB*, November 23, 1890, 1; Little Wound in Eastman E. G. 1945, 30. See Phillip Wells, Table 5, box 4, ESRMC, NSHS. See also Eastman, *From the Deep Woods to Civilization*, 100; Coleman, *Voices of Wounded Knee*, 48–49; Boyd, *Recent Indian Wars*, 183; Miller, *Ghost Dance*, 56. On the life of Elaine Goodale Eastman, see Eastman, *Sister to the Sioux*.

31. Phillip Wells, tablet 1–5, box 4, ESRMC, NSHS; Agent Gallagher's letter to Commissioner of Indian Affairs, August 28, 1890, 387–88, roll 10, M 1982, LSASPR, RG 75, NARA; ARCIA, 1891, *Report of the Commissioner of Indian Affairs T. J. Morgan*, October 1, 1891, H. Exec. Doc. No. 1, 52nd Cong., 1st Sess., 274–75; Cong. Rec., 51st Cong., 2nd Sess., vol. 22, part 1, December 12, 1890, 47–48. See Utley, *Last Days*, 3:91–94; Ostler, *The Plains Sioux*, 274–76; Andersson, *Lakota Ghost Dance*, 104.

32. See, for example, *CT*, July 12, 1890, 1; *CT*, September 26, 1890, 1; *CT*, October 28, 1890, 1; *ODB*, July 7, 1890, 6; *ODB*, October 28, 1890, 1; *WP*, September 27, 1890, 1, *WP*, October 28, 1890, 1; *NYT*, October 28, 1890, 3. On the newspaper reporting, see Andersson, *Lakota Ghost Dance*, 193–200.

33. Standing Bear, *My People the Sioux*, 1975, 221; Miller, *Ghost Dance*, 91–93; Mooney, *The Ghost-Dance Religion*, 92.

34. For comments on Big Foot, see Joseph Horn Cloud, Dewey Beard, tablet 12, box 4, tablet 30, box 5, ESRMC, NSHS. See Seymour, *Sitanka*, 53; Andersson, *Lakota Ghost Dance*, 46.

35. Andersson, *Lakota Ghost Dance*, 54–73.

36. Short Bull in EBMC, HRMSCA. See also Manhart, *Lakota Tales and Texts*, 519–32. Retranslated from the original in the *Buechel Collection* by Rani-Henrik Andersson and Raymond J. DeMallie.

37. Pretty Eagle, story 1–2, EBMC, HRMSCA; Short Bull in tablet, 1, ESRMC, NSHS. Published also in Jensen, *Voices of the American West*, 189–90; Short Bull in EBMC, HRMSCA. Retranslated and published in full in Andersson, *Whirlwind*, 56–63, 70–71, 92–97. For a slightly different translation, see Buechel, *Lakota Tales and Text*, 509–18. See also Little Horse in Moorehead, "Ghost Dances in the West," 332.

38. This description is drawn from Andersson, *Lakota Ghost Dance*, 48–67.

39. Several Lakȟóta accounts of the ceremony are published in Andersson, *Whirlwind*. A good description of the Lakȟóta Ghost Dance comes from Special Agent E. B. Reynolds, who witnessed it in September 1890. See Indian Agent Elisha B. Reynolds's letter to the Commissioner of Indian Affairs Thomas J. Morgan, September 25, 1890, 1/22–26, reel 1, M 4728, SC 188, RG 75, NARA. Another description is in Eastman, *Sister to the Sioux*, 32–33. For standard descriptions, see Mooney, *The Ghost-Dance Religion*, 823, 915–16, 1063–64; Miller, *Ghost Dance*, 60–61; Andersson, *Lakota Ghost Dance*, 56–66. About symbols used in the Ghost Dance, see Thomas, "Crisis and Creativity."

40. Reynolds's letter to the Commissioner of Indian Affairs Morgan, September 25, 1890, 24–26, reel 1, M 4728, SC 188, RG 75, NARA; Mooney, *The Ghost-Dance Religion*, 823, 920–21, 1061. For more about traditional Lakȟóta dances, see Densmore, *Teton Sioux Music and Culture*, 1992, 84–151, 468–84.

41. Young Skunk in story 1, EBMC, HRMSCA.

42. Young Skunk in story 1, EBMC, HRMSCA.

43. Reynolds's letter to the Commissioner of Indian Affairs Morgan, September 25, 1890, 24–26, reel 1, M 4728, SC 188, RG 75, NARA; *The Illustrated American*, 17 January 1891, 329; Mooney, *The Ghost-Dance Religion*, 915–22.

44. Pretty Eagle, story 2, EBMC, HRMSCA, retranslated from the original EBMC by Rani-Henrik Andersson in Andersson, *Whirlwind*, 93–97.

45. See Reynolds's letter to the Commissioner of Indian Affairs Morgan, September 25, 1890, 1/25–26, reel 1, M 4728, SC 188, RG 75, NARA; Mooney, *The Ghost-Dance Religion*, 915–21. For traditional games, see Densmore, *Teton Sioux Music and Culture*, 1992, 485–91.

46. Lakȟóta Ghost Dance songs can be found in Sickels, "The story of The Ghost Dance. Written in the Indian Tongue by Major George Sword, an Ogallala Sioux, Major of Indian Police"; Powers, *Voices from the Spirit World*, 27–45; Mooney, *The Ghost-Dance Religion*, 1061, 1064–70; Andersson, *Lakota Ghost Dance*, 56, 59–60, 71; Wildhage, *Geistertants-Lieder Der Lakota*, 9–40.

47. Kicking Bear as quoted by Young Skunk in story 3, EBMC, HRMSCA. For Young Skunk story 3, see Andersson, *Whirlwind*, 102–7.

48. For more on this discussion, see DeMallie, "The Lakota Ghost Dance: An Ethnohistorical Account"; Andersson, *Lakota Ghost Dance*; Posthumus, "A Lakota View of Pté Oyáte."

49. Black Elk's account in DeMallie, *The Sixth Grandfather*, 1985, 256–82. We have used Raymond J. DeMallie's edited notes with his permission. For the original manuscripts, see NCWHMC, UMC. Published in Andersson, *Whirlwind*, 117–41. See also Andersson, *Lakota Ghost Dance*, 48–73.

50. For the origin, development, and significance of the Ghost Dance shirts, see Ostler, *The Plains Sioux*, 279–87; Andersson, *Lakota Ghost Dance*, 69–73; Warren, *God's Red Son*, 13–18, 105–7. For protective designs, see Wissler, *Some Protective Designs of the Dakota*.

51. Little Wound in Warren K. Moorehead, "Ghost Dances in the West," *Illustrated American*, January 17, 1891, 330–31; Kicking Bear in McLaughlin, *My Friend the Indian*, 1910, 185–89. Both accounts are published in Andersson, *Whirlwind*, 83–87, 108–9.

52. Pretty Eagle, story 2, EBMC, HRMSCA.

53. Pretty Eagle, story 2, EBMC, HRMSCA; Black Elk in DeMallie, *The Sixth Grandfather*, 1985, 256–82. Both accounts in Andersson, *Whirlwind*, 95–96, 122–24.

54. Short Bull's speech was published in *ODB*, November 22, 1890, 1; *CT*, November 22, 1890, 2; ARSW 1891, H. Exec. Doc. No. 1, 52nd Cong., 1st Sess., 142–43. For a thorough analysis of Short Bull's speeches, see Andersson, *Whirlwind*, 37–87. For Black Elk's vision and the flowering tree, see Andersson, 116–47.

55. Sword, "Wanagi Wacipi Toranpi owicakiyakapi kin lee," Manuscript 936, NAASI. Translated by Rani-Henrik Andersson, Andersson, *Whirlwind*, 250–58. George Sword's account was first published in English in Sickels, "The Story of The Ghost Dance. Written in the Indian Tongue by Major George Sword, an Ogallala Sioux, Major of Indian Police," 28–36. This translation was adopted by James Mooney in his 1891 book, Mooney, *The Ghost-Dance Religion*, 798. Many scholars have followed Mooney's interpretation ever since. For more on this discussion, see Raymond J. DeMallie, Introduction to Mooney, xxii; Maddra, *Hostiles?*, 31–32; Andersson, *Lakota Ghost Dance*, 33–40; Warren, *God's Red Son*, 349–51.

56. Short Bull in JRWC, HCSHL. We have used transcripts made by Raymond J. DeMallie, American Indian Studies Research Institute, Indiana University. Short Bull's account is published also in Walker, DeMallie, and Jahner, *Lakota Belief and Ritual*, 143; Andersson, *Whirlwind*, 71–72. See Andersson, *Lakota Ghost Dance*, 67–73, 288–90.

57. Lakȟóta accounts of the frequency of dancing can be found in Andersson, *Whirlwind*. For the dancing from the agents', missionaries', and military's perspectives, see Andersson, *Lakota Ghost Dance*, 100–191.

58. For the opinions of settlers, see New England City, ND, residents' letter to Minister of War Redfield Proctor, November 26, 1890, 246–47, vol. 1, roll 1, M 983, AIWKSC, RG 94, NARA; Chardon, NE, residents' letter (no recipient), November 26, 1890, 252–54, vol. 1, roll 1, M 983, AIWKSC, RG 94, NARA; Petition of Citizens of Chadron, Nebraska, November 26, 1890, box 117, RG 46, SCIAP, NARA, and box 106, RG 233, HCIAP, NARA. For Senator Dawes's comment, see, for example, Cong. Rec., 51st Cong., 1st Sess., vol. 21, Part 14, December 4, 1890, 69; Henry L. Dawes's letter to Electa Dawes, December 2,

1890, folder–August–December 1890, box 15, LC, HLDP; Henry L. Dawes's letter to Electa Dawes, December 3, 1890, folder August–December 1890, box 15, LC, HLDP. Newspapers reported on the situation almost daily in the end of November. For example, *NYT*, November 27, 1890, 1; *NYT*, November 28, 1890, 5; *WP*, November 27, 1890, 1; *WP*, November 28, 1890, 1; *ODB*, November 26, 1890, 1; *ODB*, November 27, 1890, 1; *CT*, November 27, 1890, 1; *CT*, November 28, 1890, 2. A good sample of photographs taken during the Ghost Dance are in Carter, "Making Pictures for a News-Hungry Nation." A thorough analysis on the discussion in Congress is in Andersson, *Lakota Ghost Dance*, 251–70; Richardson, *Wounded Knee*.

59. For Ghost Dance as a continuation of Lakȟóta traditions and as an innovation, see DeMallie, "The Lakota Ghost Dance: An Ethnohistorical Account"; DeMallie, *"Lakota Belief and Ritual,"* 34; Andersson, *Lakota Ghost Dance*; Warren, *God's Red Son*; Andersson, *Whirlwind*.

60. American Horse to John Landy, December 1, 1890, MSS S 903, AHP, YCWA; Andersson, *Whirlwind*, 209–10; Gage, *We Do Not Want the Gates Closed between Us*, 202–5.

61. Traditionally scholars have divided the Lakȟóta into progressives and non-progressives, and interpreted the Ghost Dance as simply the latter group's means to cause unrest or even an uprising. Recent scholarship has clearly proven this argument inaccurate. See Mooney, *The Ghost-Dance Religion*; Utley, *Last Days*; DeMallie, "The Lakota Ghost Dance: An Ethnohistorical Account," 385–405; Ostler, *The Plains Sioux*, 205, 212; Andersson, *Lakota Ghost Dance*; Maddra, *Hostiles?*, 6, 19–26; Warren, *God's Red Son*.

62. Ring Thunder to Spencer, December 5, 1890, MSS 596, LFSP, HCSHL. Published in Andersson, *Whirlwind*, 328–29.

63. Good Voice to Spencer, December 12, 1890, MSS 596, LFSP, HCSHL. Several Lakȟóta letters discussing their concerns about the Ghost Dance can be found in Andersson, 327–43. See also Gage, *We Do Not Want the Gates Closed between Us*.

64. Sam White Bird *Iapi Oaye*, November 1890, 38. Translated and published in Andersson, *Whirlwind*, 343–45.

65. Andersson, *Lakota Ghost Dance*, 20–23. See also DeMallie, "The Lakota Ghost Dance: An Ethnohistorical Account," 56; Warren, *God's Red Son*. See also Indian Agent Perain P. Palmer's letter to Commissioner of Indian Affairs Thomas J. Morgan, November 10, 1890, 30–32, vol.1, roll 1, M 983, AIWKSC, RG 94, NARA.

66. Standing Bear, *My People the Sioux*, 1975, 216–30. Standing Bear's story is also published in Andersson, *Whirlwind*, 374–84.

67. For the army view, see Miles's telegram to AG, November 24, 1890, 219, vol. 1, roll 1, M 983, AIWKSC, RG 94, NARA; Miles's telegram to AG, November 25, 1890, 235, vol. 1, roll 1, M 983, AIWKSC, RG 94, NARA; General Thomas H. Ruger's telegram to AG, November 23, 1890, 195, vol. 1, roll 1, M 983, AIWKSC, RG 94, NARA; Miles's telegram to AG, November 26, 1890, 263, vol. 1, roll 1, M 983, AIWKSC, RG 94, NARA; Miles's telegram to AG, November 27, 1890, 268, vol. 1, roll 1, M 983, AIWKSC, RG 94, NARA.

68. Thomas P. Ashley to James McLaughlin, November 11, 1890, James McLaughlin Papers, roll 2. See Andersson, *Whirlwind*, 327.

69. Anonymous Lakȟóta girls to Bishop William H. Hare as quoted in a statement by Bishop Hare in 18–19, folder 2, box 110, WSCMC, WHC. Published also in Andersson, 342–43.

70. Little Wound in John M. Sweeney to Agent R. F. Royer, November 22, 1890, MS 3176, EEAC; Little Wound as quoted in *NYT*, November 23, 1890, 5; *CT*, November 23, 1890, 1; *ODB*, November 23, 1890, 1; Weasel in Boyd, *Recent Indian Wars*, 194–95. See, Ostler, *The Plains Sioux*; Andersson, *Lakota Ghost Dance*, 78–81.

71. See Andersson, *Lakota Ghost Dance*, 76–77.

72. For a discussion on McLaughlin and his motives, see Utley, *The Lance and the Shield*; Andersson, *Lakota Ghost Dance*, 113–18.

73. See Reverend G. W. Reed, envelope 41, folder 1, box 5, WMCC, IULL; Missionary Mary C. Collins, envelope 78, folder 3, box 6, WMCC, IULL; Aaron Beede Diary, North Dakota Historical Society, Bismarck, ND, vol. 2, 242, vol. 5, 50–53; Bishop Martin Mary in Berghold, *The Indians' Revenge*, 225–27.

74. Sitting Bull in Aaron Beede Diary, NDHS, vol. 2, 242.

75. Sitting Bull in McLaughlin to the Commissioner of Indian Affairs Thomas J. Morgan, November 19, 1890, ARCIA, 1891, 330–31. See Andersson, *Whirlwind*, 174–75.

76. Sitting Bull as dictated to Andrew Fox, November 1890, folder 5, box 105, folder 6, box 114, WSCMC, WHC. For a discussion of this letter and the different versions of it, see Andersson, *Whirlwind*, 175–76.

77. Sitting Bull as dictated to Andrew Fox, November 1890, folder 5, box 105, folder 6, box 114, WSCMC, WHC.

78. For more on McLaughlin and Sitting Bull, see Vestal, *Champion of the Sioux*; Utley, *The Lance and the Shield*; Andersson, *Lakota Ghost Dance*.

79. Lakȟóta accounts by Grey Eagle, Old Bull, Robert P. Higheagle and John Loneman describing Sitting Bull's death are in Andersson, *Whirlwind*, 186–200, 272–74. The originals are in the WSCMC and WMCC. Red Tomahawk's account of the killing of Sitting Bull can be found in WDP, Red Tomahwk interview 1931. See also Vestal, *Champion of the Sioux*, 280–307; Utley, *The Lance and the Shield*, 291–307; Andersson, *Lakota Ghost Dance*, 84–88; Waggoner, *Witness*, 175–76, 218–24; Greene, *American Carnage*, 185–86.

80. Sitting Bull's vision is described by One Bull in folder 21, box 104, WSCMC, WHC. The Deloria family tradition has long held the belief that Reverend Deloria actually met with Sitting Bull the night before his death, but according to his own testimony he did not. Discussion with Phillip Deloria, October 4, 2007. For Deloria's planned visit to Sitting Bull's camp see Phillip J. Deloria, envelope 65, folder 12, box 55, WMCC, IULL. See also Andersson, *Lakota Ghost Dance*, 177–78.

81. For a discussion of these events, see Andersson, *Lakota Ghost Dance*, 88–91; Greene, *American Carnage*, 191–201.

82. Red Cloud, No Water and Big Road to Big Foot quoted by Dewey Beard in tablet 30, box 5, ESRMC, NSHS. Also in Jensen, *Voices of the American West*, vol.1, 209.

83. Andrew Good Thunder, envelope 90, folder 14, box 6, WMCC, IULL.

84. For a very detailed description of the escape and eventual surrender, see Alice Ghost Horse in *Hearing Before the Select Committee on Indian Affairs*, United States Senate, 102nd Cong., 1st Sess., April 30, 1991 (Washington, DC: Government Printing Office, 1991), 58–69. Other Lakȟóta accounts include Andrew Good Thunder, envelope 90, folder 14, box 6, WMCC, IULL; Statement of the Survivors, envelope 5, folder 4, box 4, WMCC, IULL; James Pipe On Head, 75th Cong., 1st Sess., *House Committee on Indian Affairs, Published Hearing*, March 7, May 12, 1938, 18–19, Card 4, Group 3, Microfiche, IULL; Beard in Walker, *Lakota Society*, 165; Dewey Beard, James Pipe On Head, Rough Feather, White Lance, John Little Finger, Donald Blue Hair, Afraid Of The Enemy, Richard Afraid Of Hawk, Dog Chief, Charlie Blue Arm in McGregor, *The Wounded Knee Massacre*.

85. Army views on these events are in Miles's telegram to AG, December 28, 1890, 626, vol. 1, roll 1, M 983, AIWKSC, RG 94, NARA; Lieutenant Fayette W. Roe's letter to Colonel James W. Forsyth, December 26, 1890, 751,vol. 2, roll 1, M 983, AIWKSC, RG 94, NARA; General John R. Brooke's letter to Major Samuel M. Whiteside, December 27, 1890, 752,vol. 2, roll 1, M 983, AIWKSC, RG 94, NARA; Roe's letter to Whiteside, December 217, 1890, 753,vol. 2, roll 1, M 983, AIWKSC, RG 94, NARA; Testimony of Brigadier General J. R. Brooke, January 18, 1890, 740–747,vol. 2, roll 1, M 983, AIWKSC, RG 94, NARA.

86. Alice Ghost Horse in *Hearing Before the Select Committee on Indian Affairs*, 58–69, in Andersson, *Whirlwind*, 287–96.

87. For recent reconstructions of events at Wounded Knee, see Ostler, *The Plains Sioux*; Andersson, *Lakota Ghost Dance*, 90–98; Greene, *American Carnage*, 215–46. For a classic account of the massacre, see Utley, *The Last Days of the Sioux Nation*, 201–30.

88. Alice Ghost Horse in *Hearing Before the Select Committee on Indian Affairs*, 58–69, in Andersson, *Whirlwind*, 287–96.

89. Beard in MSS 653, HCSHL, JRWC. Also in Walker, *Lakota Society*, 1992, 157–68; Andersson, *Whirlwind*, 275–86.

90. For Lakȟóta casualties, see Greene, *American Carnage*, 287–88, Appendices E and F.

91. Standing Bear, *My People the Sioux*, 1975, 216–30. For more on Luther Standing Bear's thoughts on the Ghost Dance and his father's mission, see Andersson, *Lakota Ghost Dance*, 97–98; Andersson, *Whirlwind*, 374–84.

92. Warren, *God's Red Son*.

Chapter 10

1. Red Cloud, quoted in J. Walker, *Lakota Belief and Ritual*, 137–38.

2. Lakȟóta Chiefs, quoted in Bland, *A Brief History*, 12–14; Turning Hawk, George Sword, American Horse, Spotted Horse, ARCIA, 1891, 180–81. The speeches are published in full in Andersson, *Whirlwind*, 232–42.

3. Prucha, *Documents of United States Indian Policy*, 160–62; DeMallie, "Lakota Traditionalism," 5; DeMallie, "Teton," 812, 814–15.

4. Bushotter, "Lakota Texts," text 118; DeMallie, "Lakota Traditionalism," 5.

5. Standing Bear, *Land of the Spotted Eagle*, 2006, 68.

6. Walker, *Lakota Belief and Ritual*, 8–9; DeMallie, "Teton," 814.

7. "Report of Assistant Medical Supervisor Ferdinand Shoemaker on the Rosebud Reservation, SD, 1915–1916," MS 681, McCracken Research Library, Buffalo Bill Center of the West.

8. Anna Charging Bear to *Anpao Kin,* May 26, 1893, published in Cleveland, *Sioux Letters,* 19–23.

9. Walker, *Lakota Belief and Ritual,* 21, 29–30; DeMallie, "Teton," 814–15.

10. Sword in Walker, *Lakota Belief and Ritual,* 75.

11. "Report of Assistant Medical Supervisor Ferdinand Shoemaker on Medical and Sanitary Conditions, Bismarck School, ND," January 28, 1914, "Report on Rosebud SD 1915–16," MS 681, McCracken Research Library, Buffalo Bill Center of the West.

12. Little Wound in Walker, *Lakota Belief and Ritual,* 196; Afraid of Bear in Walker, *Lakota Belief and Ritual,* 201–2; DeMallie, "Lakota Traditionalism: History and Symbol," 5.

13. DeMallie, "The Lakota Ghost Dance," 402–3; DeMallie, "Teton," 817; Swan, "Early Osage Peyotism," 63–64; Jackson, "Recontextualizing Revitalization," 193.

14. Bushotter, "Lakota Texts," text 228.

15. Thunder Bear in Walker, *Lakota Belief and Ritual,* 211–12.

16. DeMallie, "Pine Ridge Economy," 237–39.

17. Macgregor, *Warriors without Weapons,* 37–38.

18. ARCIA, 1901, 363; Tabeau, *Tabeau's Narrative,* 130; Parks, DeMallie, and Vézina, *Truteau,* 199–201, 311–15; Macgregor, *Warriors without Weapons,* 38; DeMallie, "Pine Ridge Economy," 241; DeMallie, "Teton," 815; Posthumus, "Hereditary Enemies."

19. Harold Schunk, interview by Joseph H. Cash.

20. Dora Shoots Off-Bruguier, interview by Greg C. Huff and Beverly Barkosky.

21. ARCIA, 1901, 363; Macgregor, *Warriors without Weapons,* 38; DeMallie, "Teton," 815.

22. No Ears in J. Walker, *Lakota Society,* 136.

23. See The General Allotment Act in Prucha, *Documents of United States Indian Policy,* document 104.

24. Prucha, *Documents of United States Indian Policy,* 171–74; Macgregor, *Warriors without Weapons,* 38–39; DeMallie, "Teton," 816.

25. ARCIA, 1902, 337; DeMallie, "Teton," 814–16; DeMallie, "Pine Ridge Economy."

26. Macgregor, *Warriors without Weapons,* 39; Prucha, *Documents of United States Indian Policy,* 207–9; DeMallie, "Teton," 816.

27. Schunk, interview.

28. Chairman Frank G. Wilson, OTCM, July 20, 1938, Pine Ridge, RG 75, BIA, NARA.

29. Macgregor, *Warriors without Weapons,* 40–41; Mekeel, "The Economy of a Modern Teton Dakota Community," 9–10; DeMallie, "Pine Ridge Economy," 258–59; DeMallie, "Teton," 816.

30. OTCM, June 16, 1938, Pine Ridge, RG 75, BIA, NARA. See Broemert, "The Sioux and the Indian-CCC."

31. Amiotte, "Freda Goodsell Mesteth Obituary"; personal communication with authors, fall 2020.

32. Macgregor, *Warriors without Weapons,* 67, 212–13; DeMallie, "Pine Ridge Economy," 280–83; Christafferson, "Sioux, 1920–2000," 825.

33. Macgregor, *Warriors without Weapons*, 40, 45–46; DeMallie, "Pine Ridge Economy," 259–60; Christafferson, "Sioux, 1920–2000," 825; Schunk interview.

34. DeMallie, "Pine Ridge Economy," 281–83.

35. DeMallie, 283–86.

36. DeMallie, 286–87.

37. DeMallie, 287–99.

38. See, for example, No Ears and Short Man in Walker, *Lakota Society*, 156–157.

39. DeMallie, 260–61; DeMallie, "Sioux in Dakota," 257–58; DeMallie, "Teton," 816; Christafferson, "Sioux, 1920–2000," 821.

40. The issue of intermarriage between natives and nonnatives, which occurred even in prereservation times, is embedded in the tribal enrollment process of quantifying hybridity by mathematical degrees called blood quantum. This issue remains a topic of Lakota identity for some. Amiotte, personal communication with authors, fall 2020.

41. OTCM, November 25, 1935, Pine Ridge, RG 75, NARA; Eugene Younghawk, Joe Red Bear, James Weasel Bear and Clarence Greyeagle to Senator Lynn Frasier, September 21, 1939, Standing Rock, RG 75, BIA, NARA.

42. Cash and Hoover, *To Be an Indian*, 121–34, 142–50; Biolsi, *Organizing the Lakota*, 68–84, 151–81; Burnette, *The Tortured Americans*, 18, 86–87; Deloria Jr. and Lytle, *The Nations Within*, 140–53, 266–70; Prucha, *Documents of United States Indian Policy*, 222–28; Young Bear, *Standing in the Light*, 142–45; DeMallie, "Pine Ridge Economy," 260–61, 274–76; Christafferson, "Sioux, 1920–2000," 821, 829; Reinhardt, *Ruling Pine Ridge*.

43. Rosebud Tribal Council Chairman Antoine Roubideaux to John Collier, June 16, 1935, Office File of John Collier, file 3207, Rosebud 1936, RG 75, BIA, NARA. See Reinhardt, "A Crude Replacement."

44. Speech by Oglala Tribal Council President Frank G. Wilson, April 15–16, 1936, Pine Ridge, RG 75, BIA, NARA. Harold Schunk, using Cheyenne River as an example, said, "had the Cheyenne River people with two million acres of land taken just half the advantages that the old IRA gave them, they could have had paths beaten all over the reservation to their door to get their business. If they'd just worked half as hard as they were capable of working, and taken advantage of these opportunities, it would have really been something." Schunk interview.

45. Schunk interview.

46. Schunk interview.

47. P. Deloria, "Era of Indian Self-Determination," 194–97; DeMallie, "Pine Ridge Economy," 285–86; Grobsmith, *Lakota of the Rosebud*, 33, 110–11; Philp, *Indian Self-Rule*, 221; Christafferson, "Sioux, 1920–2000," 825.

48. Deloria Jr. and Lytle, *The Nations Within*, 197, 222; Kurkiala, *Building the Nation Back Up*, 104–8; Christafferson, "Sioux, 1920–2000," 829.

49. Christafferson, "Sioux, 1920–2000," 826.

50. Reinhardt, *Welcome to the Oglala Nation*, 195–213.

51. Reinhardt, 214–16; Braun, "Culture, Resource"; Romo, "Checkpoint Clash"; Boyette and Hanna, "South Dakota's Governor Will Allow Checkpoints on Tribal Roads, but Not State Highways in a Possible Compromise."

52. Macgregor, *Warriors without Weapons*, 66–77; Grobsmith, *Lakota of the Rosebud*, 20; DeMallie, "Pine Ridge Economy," 283–84; DeMallie, "Teton," 817–18.

53. Pierre, *Madonna Swan*, 40–42.

54. Sneve, *Completing the Circle*, 100–102; Sneve, *Sioux Women*, 15.

55. For Madonna Swan's life see, Pierre, *Madonna Swan*, 40–42. For Virginia Driving Hawk Sneve and her family histories see, Sneve, *Completing the Circle*; Sneve, *Sioux Women*; Sneve, *Grandpa Was a Cowboy*.

56. E. Deloria, *Speaking of Indians*, 1998, 43, 90–95; Macgregor, *Warriors without Weapons*, 55–63; DeMallie, "Teton," 818.

57. Amiotte, personal correspondence with authors, fall 2020.

58. Bad Heart Bull and Blish, *A Pictographic History of the Oglala Sioux*, 423–46; Macgregor, *Warriors without Weapons*, 38; Mekeel, "A Discussion of Culture Change as Illustrated by Material from a Teton-Dakota Community"; DeMallie, "Teton," 818–19; Sneve, *Grandpa Was a Cowboy*.

59. See, for example, Minutes of Robertson, *The Power of the Land*, 230–31; Burnette, *The Tortured Americans*, 35–37, 120–21; Biolsi, *Organizing the Lakota*, 118–19; Lawson, *Dammed Indians*, 142; Christafferson, "Sioux, 1920–2000," 827.

60. Maynard and Twiss, *That These People*, 70–74; Robertson, *The Power of the Land*, 218, 221; Grobsmith, *Lakota of the Rosebud*, 30–33; Burnette, *The Tortured Americans*, 37, 55–57; Christafferson, "Sioux, 1920–2000," 828.

61. See, for example, Sam LaPointe to John Collier, January 28, 1935, Office File of John Collier, RG 75, BIA, NARA; OTCM, November 25, 1935, and April 15–16, 1936, Pine Ridge, RG 75, BIA, NARA; OTCM, July 26–28, 1943, and 10–16, 1944, Pine Ridge, RG 75, BIA, NARA.

62. Macgregor, *Warriors without Weapons*, 52–73; Malan, "The Dakota Indian Family," 34–59; Maynard and Twiss, *That These People*, 114, 129–32; Lawson, *Dammed Indians*, 145–59; Christafferson, "Sioux, 1920–2000," 828–29.

63. Robertson, *The Power of the Land*, 219–20; Grobsmith, *Lakota of the Rosebud*, 23–26; Burnette, *The Tortured Americans*, 145; Kurkiala, *Building the Nation Back Up*, 93–96; Medicine, *The Native American Woman: A Perspective*, 93–96; Christafferson, "Sioux, 1920–2000," 829.

64. Amiotte, personal communication with authors, 2020–2021.

65. Amiotte, Freda Mesteth Goodsell Obituary; personal communication with the authors, fall 2020.

66. Robertson, *The Power of the Land*, 221; Christafferson, "Sioux, 1920–2000," 829.

67. Wax, Wax, and Dumont, Jr., "Formal Education in an American Indian Community," 4–8; Szasz, *Education and the American Indian*, 60–88; Szasz, "Thirty Years Too Soon," 3–9; Christafferson, "Sioux, 1920–2000," 826–27.

68. Cash and Hoover, *To Be an Indian*, 190–91, 221–23; Medicine, "Self-Direction in Sioux Education"; Christafferson, "Sioux, 1920–2000," 827; "Red Cloud Indian School Rolls Out Nation's First Comprehensive K-12 Lakota Language Curriculum—Red Cloud Indian School"; "About the Lakota Language Program—Red Cloud Indian School."

69. Robert Brave Heart Sr., personal correspondence and discussion with the authors, 2019, 2020.

70. Jace Cuny DeCory, personal communication with the authors, spring 2020.

71. Amiotte, personal correspondence with the authors, fall 2020.

72. Stein, *Tribally Controlled Colleges*, 41–43, 46, 57–58, 61, 102, 109–17, 119–41; Medicine, "Self-Direction in Sioux Education," 17; Grobsmith, *Lakota of the Rosebud*, 103; Christafferson, "Sioux, 1920–2000," 827.

Chapter 11

1. "Correspondence Relative to Hostilities of the Arickaree Indians"; Posthumus, "Hereditary Enemies"; Parks, "Arikara," 367; White, "The Winning of the West," 1978, 332; DeMallie, "Teton," 812.

2. See John Grass interview, WDP.

3. Britten, *American Indians in World War I*; Martin Brokenleg, interview by Freda Hosen.; Krouse, *North American Indians in the Great War*; Bernstein, *American Indians and World War II*, 22, 35, 40, 51, 61; Christafferson, "Sioux, 1920–2000," 821.

4. Bernstein, *American Indians and World War II*, 22–23, 58–73; Christafferson, "Sioux, 1920–2000," 821–22.

5. E. Deloria, *Speaking of Indians*, 1998, 139–41; Bernstein, *American Indians and World War II*, 67, 73; Christafferson, "Sioux, 1920–2000," 821.

6. E. Deloria, *Speaking of Indians*, 1998, 141–42; Christafferson, "Sioux, 1920–2000," 821.

7. Macgregor, *Warriors without Weapons*, 46; Bernstein, *American Indians and World War II*, 68–73; Christafferson, "Sioux, 1920–2000," 821. For Marcella LaBeau, see, Sneve, *Sioux Women*, 66–68. For more on Marcella LaBeau see, Library of Congress, "Marcella Ryan Le Beau Collection." Discussion with Gerri Labeau, February 12, 2021.

8. Clarence Wolf Guts quoted in Greg Flakus, "Last of Sioux Code Talkers." For more on the Lakȟóta code talkers, see Page, *Sioux Code Talkers*.

9. Vivian Red Bear, interview by M. P. Cuney.

10. Daniels, "Cultural Identities among the Oglala Sioux," 235–42; Maynard and Twiss, *That These People*, 36; Christafferson, "Sioux, 1920–2000," 829; Sneve, *Sioux Women*, 66. For Stepahanie Griffith and her service, see Eagle, "Native Sun News."

11. Lawson, *Dammed Indians*, 18–21, 45–47; Lawson, "Federal Water Projects," 24, 27; Christafferson, "Sioux, 1920–2000," 822–23.

12. Chairman Frank Ducheneaux, January 2, 1950, CTCM, RG 75, BIA, NARA.

13. March 6–9 and June 5–9, "Oahe Contract Agenda," May 28, 1951, CTCM, RG 75, BIA, NARA.

14. Lawson, "Federal Water Projects," 25; Lawson, *Dammed Indians*, 47–52; Christafferson, "Sioux, 1920–2000," 823.

15. Lawson, "Federal Water Projects," 25–30; Lawson, *Dammed Indians*, 116–19, 134, 146–55; Christafferson, "Sioux, 1920–2000," 823.

16. Christafferson, "Sioux, 1920–2000," 823.

17. Vine Deloria, "Foreword," in Lawson, *Dammed Indians*, xiv.

18. Cowger, "'The Crossroads of Destiny,'" 122–28; Philp, *Termination Revisited*, 68–78; Schusky, *The Forgotten Sioux*, 206; Christafferson, "Sioux, 1920–2000," 823.

19. Philp, *Termination Revisited*, 75; Grobsmith, *Lakota of the Rosebud*, 33; Lawson, *Dammed Indians*, 72–73; Maynard and Twiss, *That These People*, 36; Christafferson, "Sioux, 1920–2000," 823–24.

20. Schusky, *The Forgotten Sioux*, 226; Lawson, *Dammed Indians*, 126; Christafferson, "Sioux, 1920–2000," 824.

21. Arthur Amiotte, Freda Goodsell Mesteth, "Obituary," and personal communication with the authors, fall 2020.

22. Frank Ducheneaux to Congressman Francis Case, in CTCM, February 7–10, 1950, Cheyenne River, RG 75, BIA, NARA.

23. Bernstein, *American Indians and World War II*, 148–49; Christafferson, "Sioux, 1920–2000," 824.

24. Cash and Hoover, *To Be an Indian*, 138–39, 203–4; Philp, "Stride toward Freedom," 182–85, 189; Christafferson, "Sioux, 1920–2000," 824. For more on Indian relocation programs, see Fixico, *Termination and Relocation*; Fixico, *The Urban Indian Experience in America*; Treuer, *The Heartbeat of Wounded Knee*, 233–80.

25. Red Bear interview.

26. Robert Burnette, interview by Joseph H. Cash.

27. Burnette interview.

28. Ablon, "Relocated American Indians in the San Francisco Bay Area," 297–98, 302–4; Cash and Hoover, *To Be an Indian*, 214; Philp, "Stride toward Freedom," 184, 189; Christafferson, "Sioux, 1920–2000," 824.

29. Hertzberg, *The Search for an American Indian Identity*, viii; Thomas, "Pan-Indianism," 77, 79–81; Powers, "Contemporary Oglala Music and Dance: Pan-Indianism versus Pan-Tetonism"; Jackson and Levine, "Singing for Garfish," 301–3; Ewers, *Indian Life on the Upper Missouri*, 187–203; Christafferson, "Sioux, 1920–2000," 824, 834–35.

30. V. Deloria, *Custer Died for Your Sins*; V. Deloria, *God Is Red*; DeMallie, "Vine Deloria Jr. (1933–2005)," 932–33; Christafferson, "Sioux, 1920–2000," 835.

31. Shoemaker, "Urban Indians and Ethnic Choices," 434; Schusky, *The Forgotten Sioux*, 205; Braun, *Transforming Ethnohistories*, 215; Christafferson, "Sioux, 1920–2000," 824.

32. Sherman, "The News: A History of AIM"; Hagan, *Russell Means*; Christafferson, "Sioux, 1920–2000," 835.

33. Sherman, "The News: A History of AIM," 4; Burnette, *The Road to Wounded Knee*, 193; Magnuson, *The Death of Raymond Yellow Thunder*; Reinhardt, *Ruling Pine Ridge*; Christafferson, "Sioux, 1920–2000," 835.

34. Burnette, *The Road to Wounded Knee*, 220–25; DeMallie, "Pine Ridge Economy," 306–7; Dewing, "SD Newspaper Coverage"; Dewing, *Wounded Knee*; Dewing, *Wounded Knee II*; Reinhardt, "Spontaneous Combustion"; Trimbach and Trimbach, *American Indian Mafia*; Christafferson, "Sioux, 1920–2000," 835–36.

35. Neihardt, *Black Elk Speaks*, 2008; Brown, *Bury My Heart at Wounded Knee*; Burnette, *The Road to Wounded Knee*, 226–50; Matthiessen, *In the Spirit of Crazy Horse*, 59–83; Riegert, *Quest for the Pipe of the Sioux*; Christafferson, "Sioux, 1920–2000," 836.

36. Magnuson, *Wounded Knee 1973*; Hendricks, *The Unquiet Grave*; Donnelly, "Killing Anna Mae Aquash, Smearing John Trudell"; Frosch, "The Truth About Leonard"; Posthumus, Fieldwork Interviews and Personal Communications; Andersson, Fieldwork and Interviews, 2000–2020.; Christafferson, "Sioux, 1920–2000," 836.

37. Oswald and Ragan, "Radiation." For more on Women of All Red Nations, see "Women of All Red Nations", and for the Warrior Women organization, see "Warrior Women Project." For Mary Crow Dog's life, see Crow Dog and Erdoes, *Lakota Woman*. For Madonna Thunder Hawk, see Castle, "The Original Gangster."

38. Treuer, *The Heartbeat of Wounded Knee*, 357; Andersson, Fieldnotes and Interviews, 2000–2020.

39. Posthumus, Fieldwork Interviews and Personal Communications; Dewing, *Wounded Knee*; Dewing, *Wounded Knee II*; Magnuson, *Wounded Knee 1973*; Roos et al., "Impact of AIM," 96–99; Smith and Warrior, *Like a Hurricane*; Trimbach and Trimbach, *American Indian Mafia*.

40. Posthumus, Fieldwork Interviews and Personal Communications.

41. Posthumus, Fieldwork Interviews and Personal Communications.

42. Amiotte, Freda Goodsell Mesteth, "Obituary," and personal communication with the authors, fall 2020.

Chapter 12

1. See Posthumus, "Transmitting," 448–68; Feraca, *Wakinyan*, 31, 42, 81; Ruby, "Yuwipi Ancient Rite of the Sioux," 74; Ruby, *The Oglala Sioux*, 16; Grobsmith, *Lakota of the Rosebud*, 61; Lynd, *The Religion of the Dakotas*, 2:168.

2. Bucko, *The Lakota Ritual of the Sweat Lodge*.

3. Klass, *Ordered Universes*, 5.

4. DeMallie, *The Sixth Grandfather*, 1984, 82–83.

5. E. Deloria, "Dakota Ceremonies," 1.

6. Turner, *The Ritual Process*, 52.

7. J. Walker, *Lakota Belief and Ritual*, 105.

8. DeMallie, "Lakota Traditionalism," 11.

9. Fugle, "The Nature and Function of the Lakota Night Cults," 10.

10. See Wallace, "Individual Differences and Cultural Uniformities"; Wallace, "Epilogue."

11. Bad Heart Bull and Blish, *A Pictographic History of the Oglala Sioux*, 201; Hassrick, *The Sioux*, 1964, 277; Posthumus, Fieldwork Interviews and Personal Communications.

12. J. Walker, *Lakota Belief and Ritual*, 36, 47, 50.

13. Densmore, *Teton Sioux Music and Culture*, 2001, 244–45.

14. Standing Bear, *Land of the Spotted Eagle*, 2006, 39.

15. E. Deloria, "Gamma. Religion," 1; J. Walker, *Lakota Belief and Ritual*, 44; Posthumus, Fieldwork Interviews and Personal Communications.

16. DeMallie, "Pine Ridge Economy," 296–97; DeMallie, "Teton," 814–15; Posthumus, "A Lakota View of Pté Oyáte"; Prucha, *Documents of United States Indian*

Policy, 157–60; Jackson, "Recontextualizing Revitalization," 193; Swan, "Early Osage Peyotism," 51–71.

17. DeMallie, "Lakota Traditionalism," 14.

18. Sword in Walker, *Lakota Belief and Ritual*, 198, 200.

19. Thunder Bear in Walker, 211–12.

20. Ruby, "Yuwipi Ancient Rite of the Sioux," 75–76; Fugle, "The Nature and Function of the Lakota Night Cults," 25; Posthumus, Fieldwork Interviews and Personal Communications.

21. Schunk interview.

22. Macgregor, *Warriors without Weapons*, 91–96; DeMallie, "Teton," 814, 817.

23. DeMallie, "Black Elk 1863–1950"; DeMallie, *The Sixth Grandfather*, 1984.

24. DeMallie, "Black Elk 1863–1950"; Neihardt, *Black Elk Speaks*, 2008; Neihardt, *When the Tree Flowered*; Neihardt, *Eagle Voice Remembers: An Authentic Tale of the Old Sioux World*; Brown, *The Sacred Pipe*, 1989.

25. Sword in J. Walker, *Lakota Belief and Ritual*, 75; DeMallie, "Lakota Traditionalism: History and Symbol," 6.

26. DeMallie, *The Sixth Grandfather*, 1984, 16–27, 46–47, 58–63; DeMallie, "Lakota Traditionalism," 6–7.

27. Beede, Journals and Letters; Flesh in Fugle, "The Nature and Function of the Lakota Night Cults," 26.

28. Macgregor, *Warriors without Weapons*, 93; Feraca, *Wakinyan*, 7; Posthumus, "Transmitting," 460–68; Christafferson, "Sioux, 1920–2000," 833–34.

29. Grobsmith, *Lakota of the Rosebud*, 84; Feraca, *Wakinyan*, 86; Steinmetz, *Pipe, Bible, and Peyote*; DeMallie and Parks, *Sioux Indian Religion*, 13; Garner, *To Come to a Better Understanding*; Christafferson, "Sioux, 1920–2000," 834.

30. Jace Cuny DeCory, personal correspondence with the authors, spring 2021.

31. Prucha, *Documents of United States Indian Policy*, 157, 160, 219–25; DeMallie, "Lakota Traditionalism," 14; Feraca, *Wakinyan*, 10–11; Mails, *Sundancing*, 6; Posthumus, "Transmitting," 437–38; Christafferson, "Sioux, 1920–2000," 831.

32. Jace Cuny DeCory, personal correspondence with the authors, spring 2021.

33. J. Walker, *Lakota Belief and Ritual*, 154; Macgregor, *Warriors without Weapons*, 98–99; J. Walker, *Lakota Belief and Ritual*, 153–55; Densmore, *Teton Sioux Music and Culture*, 2001, 204–38; DeMallie, "Lakota Traditionalism," 14; DeMallie, "Teton," 817; Posthumus, "Transmitting," 438–42; Powers, *Yuwipi*; Christafferson, "Sioux, 1920–2000," 831.

34. Macgregor, *Warriors without Weapons*, 98.

35. Feraca, *Wakinyan*, 53.

36. Fools Crow in Mails, *Sundancing*, 6.

37. See Mails and Fools Crow, *Fools Crow*; Walker, *Lakota Belief and Ritual*; Posthumus, "Transmitting," 438n310.

38. Feraca, *Wakinyan*, 11–15; Posthumus, "Transmitting," 438–39. See P. Deloria, *Playing Indian*.

39. Feraca, *Wakinyan*, 11, 22; Christafferson, "Sioux, 1920–2000," 831.

40. J. Walker, "The Sun Dance," 57.

41. Standing Bear, *Land of the Spotted Eagle*, 2006, 255.

42. E. Deloria, "Correspondence with Franz Boas" (Philadelphia, 1934 1927), MS 31, Boas Collection, American Philosophical Library, "The modern medicine-man."

43. John Colhoff, "Letters to Joseph Balmer" (1948–1953), Letters 13, 41.

44. Fugle, "The Nature and Function of the Lakota Night Cults," 26.

45. Burnette interview.

46. "Minutes of the Oglala Sioux Tribal Council Meetings, July 14–16, 1964," RG 75, BIA, NARA. folder 002125-003-1024. See Feraca, *Wakinyan*, 11–22; Lewis, *The Medicine Men*, 22–23, 53–65; Christafferson, "Sioux, 1920–2000," 831.

47. DeMallie, "Lakota Traditionalism," 4; Medicine, "Native American Resistance to Integration," 281, 283; Medicine, "Indian Women and the Renaissance of Traditional Religion"; Young Bear, *Standing in the Light*, 157.

48. Bucko, *The Lakota Ritual of the Sweat Lodge*, 15; Lewis, *The Medicine Men*, 71–105; Crow Dog and Erdoes, *Crow Dog*; Looking Horse, "The Sacred Pipe in Modern Life"; DeMallie and Parks, *Sioux Indian Religion*, 4–5; Roos et al., "Impact of AIM"; Christafferson, "Sioux, 1920–2000," 831.

49. Curtis, *The North American Indian*, 3:55–56; Thomas, "A Sioux Medicine Bundle"; Smith, "A Short History of the Sacred Calf Pipe of the Teton Dakota"; Riegert, *Quest for the Pipe of the Sioux*; Looking Horse, "The Sacred Pipe in Modern Life"; DeMallie, "Teton," 817.

50. Smith, "A Short History of the Sacred Calf Pipe of the Teton Dakota," 8–10; Thomas, "A Sioux Medicine Bundle"; DeMallie, "Teton," 817.

51. Arthur Amiotte, personal communication with the authors, 2020–2021.

52. Lame Deer and Erdoes, *Lame Deer, Seeker of Visions*, 63; Feraca, *Wakinyan*, 59–60, 63; DeMallie, "Teton," 817; Stewart, *Peyote Religion*; Maroukis, *The Peyote Road: Religious Freedom and the Native American Church*.

53. Feraca, *Wakinyan*, 59–60; E. Deloria, *Speaking of Indians*, 1998, 83; DeMallie, "Teton," 817.

54. Amiotte and Först, interview with Arthur Amiotte; Posthumus, "Transmitting," 478–80; DeMallie, "Teton," 817; Jackson, "Recontextualizing Revitalization," 192.

55. Lame Deer and Erdoes, *Lame Deer, Seeker of Visions*, 64.

56. Lame Deer and Erdoes, 216–17.

57. Macgregor, *Warriors without Weapons*, 100–102; Ruby, *The Oglala Sioux*, 53–60; Feraca, *Wakinyan*, 59–70; DeMallie, "Teton," 817.

58. Mary Brave Bird quoted in Brave Bird and Erdoes, *Ohitika Woman*, 70–73.

59. Schunk interview.

60. Posthumus, "Ritual Thiyóšpaye."

61. Medicine, "Native American Resistance to Integration," 283; Mails, *Sundancing*, 6; Porterfield, "The Selling of the Sun Dance"; Powers, *Oglala Religion*, 95–100, 141; Roos et al., "Impact of AIM," 96–97; Steinmetz, *Pipe, Bible, and Peyote*, 32–35; Posthumus, Fieldwork Interviews and Personal Communications; Christafferson, "Sioux, 1920–2000," 831; DeMallie, "Pine Ridge Economy," 253; Powers, *Oglala Religion*, 202–3.

62. Posthumus, Fieldwork Interviews and Personal Communications; Crow Dog and Erdoes, *Crow Dog*; Roos et al., "Impact of AIM," 96–98.

63. White Hat, *Life's Journey—Zuya*, 140.

64. Powers, *Oglala Religion*, 207; Feraca, *Wakinyan*, 53; Steinmetz, *Pipe, Bible, and Peyote*.

65. Feraca, *Wakinyan*, 26, 43.

66. Boyd and Thin Elk, "Indigenous Perspectives on Healing"; Kapferer, "Beyond Symbolic Representation: Victor Turner and Variations on the Themes of Ritual Process and Liminality," 6; Rice, *Before the Great Spirit*, 19–24; Posthumus, Fieldwork Interviews and Personal Communications.

67. Posthumus, Fieldwork Interviews and Personal Communications; Posthumus, "Ritual Thiyóšpaye."

68. Powers, *Oglala Religion*, 203.

69. Jace Cuny DeCory, personal communication with the authors, spring 2021.

70. Powers, 205–6; Posthumus, Fieldwork Interviews and Personal Communications.

71. DeMallie and Parks, *Sioux Indian Religion*, 211; DeMallie, *The Sixth Grandfather*, 1984, 102n3; Posthumus, "Ritual Thiyóšpaye."

72. Jace Cuny DeCory, Personal Correspondence with the authors, spring 2020.

73. Prucha, *Documents of United States Indian Policy*, 288–89; Christafferson, "Sioux, 1920–2000," 831–33. O'Brien, "A Legal Analysis of the American Indian Religious Freedom Act," 38–39.

74. For a more detailed discussion of contemporary Lakhóta ritual groups, see Posthumus, "Ritual Thiyóšpaye."

75. Posthumus, Fieldwork Interviews and Personal Communications; Posthumus, "Ritual Thiyóšpaye."

76. Densmore, *Teton Sioux Music and Culture*, 2001, 244–45; Hurt and Howard, "A Dakota Conjuring Ceremony," 293; Geertz, "Shifting Aims, Moving Targets," 10.

Chapter 13

1. Nicky Belle has studied and participated in powwow for over twenty-five years. He graciously provided this account of the role of powwow in Lakhóta culture.

2. Young Bear, *Standing in the Light*, 38.

3. Young Bear, 54.

4. Browner, "A Reexamination of the Peji Waci," 73–75; Young Bear, *Standing in the Light*, 55.

5. Royce, *The Anthropology of Dance*, 17–18.

6. Spicer, "Persistent Cultural Systems," 797.

7. On survivance see Vizenor, *Manifest Manners*; *Fugitive Poses*; *Survivance*.

8. Powers, *War Dance*, 68; Brown, *The Sacred Pipe*, 1989, 67.

9. Posthumus, "A Lakota View of Pté Oyáte"; Braun, *Buffalo Inc.*

10. Posthumus, "A Lakota View of Pté Oyáte."

11. Posthumus.

12. Posthumus.

13. Posthumus.

14. For more on the Republic of Lakotah, see "Republic of Lakotah."

15. See, Landry, "Barack Obama"; "Highlights." For Generation Indigenous see, "Generation Indigenous."

16. David Archambault II, quoted in "Standing Rock Sioux Tribe."

17. Discussion with Ernie and Sonia LaPointe, September 26, 2019, Andersson, Field Notes and Interviews, 2000–2020. About living in the Lakota way, see Marshall, *The Lakota Way*; Marshall, *Crazy Horse Weeps*.

18. Walker, "South Dakota Checkpoints." For media coverage, see Walker and Cochrane, "Tribe in South Dakota Seeks Court Ruling"; Sidner et al., "South Dakota Sioux Tribe." Lakȟóta sentiments are gathered from social media outlets and several discussions over summer 2020, Andersson, Field Notes and Interviews, 2000–2020.

19. Discussion with Lakota participants, May 2018, Andersson, Field Notes and Interviews, 2000–2020.

20. For the consultations and the ensuing legal case, see *Standing Rock Sioux Tribe v. US Army Corps of Engineers*, 2016 WL 4033936 (D.D.C.) 69; *Standing Rock Sioux Tribe v. US Army Corps of Engineers*, 239 F. Supp. 3d 77, 81 (D.D.C. 2017); *Standing Rock Sioux Tribe v. US Army Corps of Engineers*, 205 F. Supp. 3d 4 (D.D.C. 2016), WL 4734356. See also, Pajunen, "Sacred Water"; Discussion with Lakota participants, May 2018, Andersson, Field Notes and Interviews, 2000–2020.

21. Estes and Dhillon, *Standing with Standing Rock*, 48–52; Andersson, Field Notes and Interviews, 2000–2020. A good summary of the events and media coverage is in Pajunen, "Sacred Water."

22. An important collection of Lakȟóta accounts on #NoDAPL is published in Estes and Dhillon, *Standing with Standing Rock*.

23. Discussions with Lula Red Cloud, May 2018, Andersson, Field Notes and Interviews, 2000–2020. For further discussion, see Braun, "Culture, Resource"; Estes, *Our History Is the Future*.

24. "Red Cloud Renewable."

25. "Help Us Leave a Legacy."

26. Joseph McNeil in "About SAGE."

27. Rausch, "Who Is Tokata Iron Eyes." See, Thomas, "Tokata Iron Eyes."

28. Tokata Iron Eyes, Wašté Wiŋ Young, Lula Red Cloud, Gemma Lockhart, LaDonna Brave Bull Allard, Pearl Means, and Sky Roosevelt-Morris spent three days in Finland in May 2018 discussing #NoDAPL and an upcoming movie Kring, *End of the Line: The Women of Standing Rock*.

29. Andersson, Fieldnotes and Interviews, 2000–2020. See "The Sioux Chef."

30. See Billy Mills, *Lessons of a Lakota*, and https://indianyouth.org/. For recent discovery of the artwork of Mary Sully from Standing Rock, see P. Deloria, *Becoming Mary Sully*.

31. Discussions with Lakȟóta people involved in charitable work during the pandemic, Andersson, Field Notes and Interviews, 2000–2020.

32. Robert Brave Heart Sr., personal correspondence with the authors, 2019–2021.

BIBLIOGRAPHY

Primary Sources

Archival and Manuscript Sources

American Horse Papers, MSS S 903. Yale Collection of Western Americana, Beinecke Rare Book and Manuscript Library, Yale University.

American Indian Research Project, 1967–1994. Archives of the South Dakota Oral History Center, Vermillion, SD.

Amiotte, Arthur, and Dietmar Först. Interview with Arthur Amiotte, July 18, 1994.

Andersson, Rani-Henrik. "Field Notes and Interviews, 2000–2020."

"As Narrated by Short Bull," recorded by George C. Crager, MS [1891]. Buffalo Bill Museum and Grave, Golden, CO.

Ashley, Edward, Papers, 1883–1931. Archives of the Episcopal Church, Episcopal Diocese of South Dakota, Center for Western Studies, Sioux Falls, SD.

Ayer, Edward E., Collection, MS 3176. Newberry Library, Chicago, IL.

Beede, Aaron McGaffey, "Journals and Letters." 1920, 1912. Orin G. Libby Manuscript Collection, University of North Dakota, Grand Forks, ND.

Beede, Aaron, Diary, volume 2. North Dakota Historical Society, Bismarck, ND.

Boas Collection, MS 30–31, 271. American Philosophical Library, Philadelphia, PA.

Brokenleg, Martin. 1975. Interview by Freda Hosen. American Indian Research Project AIRP 42. South Dakota Oral History Center. Research data obtained through the archives of the South Dakota Oral History Center, on behalf of the University of South Dakota, Vermillion, SD.

Buechel, Eugene, Manuscript Collection. Holy Rosary Mission, Special Collections and Archives, Marquette University Archives, Milwaukee, WI.

————. "Sioux Ethnology Notebook," n.d. Special Collections and University Archives, Raynor Memorial Libraries, Marquette University, Milwaukee, WI.

Bureau of Catholic Indian Missions, Series 1-1, Correspondence, Pine Ridge Agency, Holy Rosary Mission, Rosebud Agency, St. Frances Mission, Standing Rock Agency, Fort Yates. Microfilm, Reels 19–20, Special Collections and Archives, Marquette University Archives, Milwaukee, WI.

Burnette, Robert. 1967. Interview by Joseph H. Cash. American Indian Research Project AIRP 18. South Dakota Oral History Center. Research data obtained through the archives of the South Dakota Oral History Center, on behalf of the University of South Dakota, Vermillion, SD.

Bushotter, George. "Lakota Texts by George Bushotter; Interlinear translations by James Owen Dorsey, aided by George Bushotter and John Bruyier." Washington, DC, 1888 1887. Manuscript No. 4800/103(1–3). Dorsey Papers, National Anthropological Archives, Smithsonian Institution.

Camp, Walter M., Collection. Lily Library, Indiana University, Bloomington, Indiana.

Campbell, Walter S., Manuscript Collection. Western History Collection, University of Oklahoma, Norman, OK.

Colhoff, John. "Letters to Joseph Balmer," 1948–1954.

Dawes, Henry L., Papers, Library of Congress, Washington, DC.

Deloria, Ella Cara. "Alpha First Fox." Bloomington, Indiana, n.d. Dakota Indian Foundation.

————. "Beta. The Virgin's Fire [and Other Women's Rites]." Chamberlain, SD, n.d. Dakota Indian Foundation.

————. "Correspondence with Franz Boas." Philadelphia, 1934 1927. MS 31, Boas Collection. American Philosophical Library.

————. "Dakota Ceremonies." Chamberlain, SD, n.d. Dakota Indian Foundation.

————. "Dakota Commentary on Walker's Legends." Philadelphia, 1938 1937. MS 30 (X8a.5), Boas Collection. American Philosophical Library.

————. "The Dakota Way of Life." Bloomington, IN, 1995.

————. "Gamma. Religion." Chamberlain, SD, n.d. Dakota Indian Foundation.

————. "Pregnancy, Birth, and Infancy." Chamberlain, SD, n.d. Dakota Indian Foundation.

————. "Rites and Ceremonies of the Teton." Chamberlain, SD, n.d. Dakota Indian Foundation.

Digman, Father Florentine S. J., Papers. History of St. Francis Mission 1886–1922, St. Francis Mission Collection, Marquette University Archives, Milwaukee, WI.

Dixon, Joseph K., Collection of North American Indian Music. Archives of Traditional Music, Indiana University, Bloomington, IN.

Fletcher, Alice C. "Complete 1882 Sioux Field Notebook," 1882.

————. "The Elk Mystery or Festival. Ogallala Sioux." In *16th Report of the Peabody Museum of American Archaeology and Ethnology, Harvard University, [for] 1882*, 3 [1880–1886]:276–88. Cambridge, MA, 1887.

————. "The Shadow or Ghost Lodge: A Ceremony of the Ogallala Sioux." In *16th Report of the Peabody Museum of American Archaeology and Ethnology, Harvard University, [for] 1882*, 3 [1880–1886]:296–307. Cambridge, MA, 1887.

———. "The Sun Dance of the Ogalalla Sioux." *Proceedings of the American Association for the Advancement of Science, 31st Meeting, Held at Montreal, Canada* 30 (1883): 580–84.

Harvey, Thomas H., to Commissioner of Indian Affairs, May 6, 1846, LROIA, UMA, RG 75, NARA, Washington, DC.

Käsebier, Gertrude, Collection. Smithsonian National Museum of American History, Washington, DC.

"Marcella Ryan Le Beau Collection." Experiencing War: Stories from the Veterans History Project, October 26, 2011. Library of Congress. https://memory.loc.gov/diglib/vhp-stories/loc.natlib.afc2001001.24202/.

McLaughlin, James, Papers. Minnesota Historical Society, St. Paul, MN.

Letters Received by the Office of Indian Affairs, Upper Missouri Agency, RG 75, NARA, Washington, DC.

Letters Sent to the Office of Indian Affairs by the Agents or Superintendents at the Pine Ridge Agency, 1875–1914, M 1282, vol. 9, roll 10. RBIA, RG 75, NARA, 1985.

Major Council Meetings of American Indian Tribes, Part 1, Section 2: Chippewa, Klamath, and Sioux (Standing Rock, Rosebud, Pine Ridge, and Cheyenne River), 1911–1956, RG 75, Bureau of Indian Affairs, Central Classified Files, Decimal 054, NARA, Washington, DC.

Major Council Meetings of American Indian Tribes, Part 2, Section 2: Sioux (Standing Rock, Rosebud, Pine Ridge, and Cheyenne River), Chippewa, and Klamath, 1957–1971, RG 75, Bureau of Indian Affairs, Central Classified Files, Decimal 054, NARA, Washington, DC.

Native Americans and the New Deal: The Office Files of John Collier, 1933–1945. Records of the Office of the Commissioner of Indian Affairs, Entry 178: Office File of Commissioner John Collier, RBIA, RG 75, NARA, Washington, DC.

Neihardt Collection, Western Historical Manuscript Collection, University of Missouri, Columbia, MO.

Papers Relating to Military Operations in the Departments of the Platte and Dakota Against the Sioux Indians (Sioux War Papers), 1876–1896. Microfilm Reels 277, 283, 292, Records of the Office of the Adjutant General, RG 94, NARA, Washington, DC.

Perrig, Father Emil, Diary. Bureau of Catholic Indian Missions, Holy Rosary Mission Collection Marquette University Archives, Milwaukee, WI.

Posthumus, David C. "Fieldwork Interviews and Personal Communications, 2008–2020."

Records of the Bureau of Indian Affairs (RBIA). Cheyenne River, Crow Creek, Lower Brulé, Pine Ridge, Standing Rock. RG 75, NARA, Kansas City, MO.

Records of the Bureau of Indian Affairs (RBIA). Letters Received. RG 75.4, NARA, Washington, DC.

Red Bear, Vivian. 1980. Interview by M. P. Cuney. American Indian Research Project AIRP 1098. South Dakota Oral History Center. Research data obtained through the archives of the South Dakota Oral History Center, on behalf of the University of South Dakota, Vermillion, SD

Report of Assistant Medical Supervisor Ferdinand Shoemaker on the Rosebud Reservation, SD, 1915–1916, MS 681. McCracken Research Library, Buffalo Bill Center of the West, Cody, WY.

Rhodes, Willard, Collection of Traditional Music. Archives of Traditional Music, Indiana University, Bloomington, IN.

Ricker, Eli S., Manuscript Collection, Nebraska Historical Society, Lincoln, NE.

Schunk, Harold. 1967. Interview by Joseph H. Cash. American Indian Research Project AIRP 17. South Dakota Oral History Center. Research data obtained through the archives of the South Dakota Oral History Center, on behalf of the University of South Dakota, Vermillion, SD

Shoots Off-Bruguier, Dora. 1994. Interview by Greg C. Huff and Beverly Barkosky. American Indian Research Project AIRP 1396. South Dakota Oral History Center. Research data obtained through the archives of the South Dakota Oral History Center, on behalf of the University of South Dakota, Vermillion, SD

Special Case 188–The Ghost Dance, 1890–1898, M4728–29. Microfilm publication, 1973. Reels 1–2, RBIA, RG 75, NARA, Washington DC.

Spencer, Lebbeus Foster, Papers, MSS 596. History Colorado, Stephen H. Hart Library and Research Center, Denver, CO.

Sword, George, Autobiography. American Indian Studies Research Institute, Indiana University, Bloomington, IN.

———. "Dakota Texts from the Sword Manuscripts." Translated by Ella Cara Deloria. Philadelphia, 1938. X8a.18, Boas Collection, American Philosophical Library.

Waggoner, Josephine, Papers. Museum of the Fur Trade, Chadron, NE.

Walker, James R. Collection, MSS 653, History Colorado, Stephen H. Hart Library and Research Center, Denver, CO.

Webb, H. G. Description of Oglala Sun Dance 1883, MS 1394-A. National Anthropological Archives, Smithsonian Institution.

Welch, Colonel A. B., Dakota Papers. https://www.welchdakotapapers.com/.

White Bull Pictographs. Copies at American Indian Studies Research Institute, Indiana University, Bloomington, IN.

Wissler, Clark. "Field Notes on the Dakota Indians," 1902. Department of Anthropology, American Museum of Natural History, New York.

———. Some Protective Designs of the Dakota. Anthropological Papers of the American Museum of Natural History, vol. 1, pt. 2. New York: Order of the Trustees [of S. the American Museum of Natural History], 1907.

———. Societies and Ceremonial Associations in the Oglala Division of the Teton-Dakota, Anthropological Papers of the American Museum of Natural History, 11, no. 1 (1912): 1–99.

Government Documents

Davis, Jefferson, "Report of the Secretary of War Jefferson Davis," S. Exec. Doc. No. 1, 33rd Cong., 2nd Sess. Washington, DC: Government Printing Office, 1854.

General Records of the United States Government, 1778–2006, Series: Indian Treaties, 1789–1869 (Fort Laramie Treaty). RG 1, NARA, Washington, DC.

"Lewis and Clarke's Expedition Communicated to Congress," February 19, 1806. American State Papers, 9th Cong., 1st Sess., Indian Affairs, 1:714. https://memory.loc.gov

/cgi-bin/ampage?collId=llsp&fileName=007/llsp007.db&recNum=715, accessed March 18, 2019.

Report of Investigations into the Battle at Wounded Knee Creek, South Dakota, Fought December 29, 1890. Reports and Correspondence Relating to the Army Investigation of the Battle at Wounded Knee and to the Sioux Campaign of 1890–1891. Rolls 1–2, Vol. 1, M 983, RG 94, Records of the Adjutant General's Office, 1780–1917, NARA, Washington, DC, 1974.

"Report of Lieutenant G. K. Warren," *Annual Report of the Secretary of War,* 1857.

US Congress House

Correspondence Relative to Hostilities of the Arickaree Indians. Documents Accompanying the Message of the President of the United States to Both Houses, at the Commencement of the First Session of the Eighteenth Congress. H. Doc. No. 2., 18th Cong., 1st Sess. Serial No. 89. Washington, DC, 1823.

Council Held with a Delegation of Sioux Indians. Unpublished Hearing, April 15, 1890, 51st Cong., 1st Sess., House of Representatives Committee on Indian Affairs. Card 1, Microfiche. IULL.

Documents of the United States Indian Policy. H.R. Exec. Doc. No. 1, 48th Cong., 1st Sess. (1883). Serial 2190, 10–12. https://digitalcommons.law.ou.edu/indianserialset /5739/.

Additional provisions for Sioux Indians. H.R. Exec. Doc. No. 36., 51st Cong., 2nd Sess. (1890). https://digitalcommons.law.ou.edu/indianserialset/8221/.

House Committee on Indian Affairs. Published Hearing, March 7, May 12, 1938, 75th Cong., 1st Sess. Card 4, group 3, microfiche, Law Library, Indiana University, Bloomington, IN.

House Committee on Indian Affairs Papers. Records of the United States Congress, House of Representatives, RG 233, NARA, Washington, DC.

Military Expedition Against the Sioux Indians. H.R. Exec. Doc. No. 184, 44th Cong., 1st Sess. (1876). https://digitalcommons.law.ou.edu/indianserialset/2358/.

US Congress Senate

Congressional Record: Containing the Proceedings and Debates of the 51st Congress, 1st Session. Vol. 22, Part 14. Washington, DC: Government Printing Office, 1891.

Congressional Record: Containing the Proceedings and Debates of the 51st Congress, 2nd Session. Vol. 22, Parts 1–2. Washington, DC: Government Printing Office, 1891.

Alice Ghost Horse, *Hearing Before the Select Committee on Indian Affairs,* United States Senate. 102nd Cong., 1st Sess., Washington, DC: Government Printing Office, 1991.

Senate Committee on Indian Affairs Papers. Records of the United States Congress, Senate, RG 46, NARA, Washington, DC.

S. Exec. Doc. No. 70, 49th Cong., 1st Sess. (1886). Serial Set Washington DC: Government Printing Office. https://digitalcommons.law.ou.edu/cgi/viewcontent.cgi?article =5081&context=indianserialset.

S. Exec. Doc. No. 17, 50th Cong., 2nd Sess. Vol. I, Serial 2610. Washington, DC: Government Printing Office, 1890.

S. Exec. Doc. No. 51, 51st Cong., 1st Sess. (1890). Vol. 4, Serial 2682. Washington DC: Government Printing Office, 1891. https://digitalcommons.law.ou.edu/indianserialset/7729/.

Published Primary Sources

Annual Report of the Commissioner of Indian Affairs 1824–1902. (ARCIA.) Washington, DC: Government Printing Office, 1824–1902. Individual years accessible here: https://digicoll.library.wisc.edu/cgi-bin/History/History-idx?type=browse&scope=History.IndianTreatiesMicro.

Annual Report of the Secretary of War 1854–1891. (ARSOW.) Washington, DC: Government Printing Office 1854–1891.

Dorsey, J. Owen. "A Study of Siouan Cults." In *11th Annual Report of the Bureau of [American] Ethnology [for] 1889–90,* 351–544. Washington, DC: Smithsonian Institution, 1894.

Raynolds, W. F. *Journal of Captain W. F. Raynolds, United States Army Corps of Engineers.* Washington, DC: Government Printing Office, 1868.

Walker, James R. "The Sun Dance and Other Ceremonies of the Oglala Division of the Teton Dakota." In *American Museum of Natural History Anthropological Papers* 16, no. 2 (1917): 51–221.

Periodicals Cited

Anpao Kin (Dakota language newspaper)
Chicago Tribune (CT)
Iapi Oaye (Dakota language newspaper)
Illustrated American
Indian Helper
New York Times (NYT)
Omaha Daily Bee (ODB)
Washington Post (WP)
Word Carrier

Secondary Sources

Ablon, Joan. "Relocated American Indians in the San Francisco Bay Area: Social Interaction and Indian Identity." *Human Organization* 23, no. 4 (1964): 296–304.

Adams, David Wallace. *Education for Extinction: American Indians and the Boarding School Experience, 1875–1928.* Lawrence: University Press of Kansas, 2020.

Amiotte, Arthur. "The Lakota Sun Dance: Historical and Contemporary Perspectives." In *Sioux Indian Religion,* edited by Raymond J. DeMallie and Douglas R. Parks, 75–89. Norman: University of Oklahoma Press, 1987.

———. "Our Other Selves: The Lakota Dream Experience." *Parabola: Myth and the Quest for Meaning* 7, no. 2 (1982): 26–32.

Anderson, Gary C. *Kinsmen of Another Kind: Dakota-White Relations in the Upper Mississippi Valley, 1650–1862.* Minneapolis: Minnesota Historical Society Press, 1997.

Anderson, Harry. "An Investigation of the Early Bands of the Saone Group of Teton Sioux." *Journal of the Washington Academy of Sciences* 46, no. 3 (1956): 87–94.

Anderson, Jeffrey D. *The Four Hills of Life: Northern Arapaho Knowledge and Life Movement*. Studies in the Anthropology of North American Indians. Lincoln: University of Nebraska Press, 2001.

Andersson, Rani-Henrik. *The Lakota Ghost Dance of 1890*. Lincoln: University of Nebraska Press, 2008.

———. "Re-Indigenizing National Parks: Toward a Theoretical Model of Re-Indigenization." *Dutkansearvi* 3, no. 2 (2019): 65–83. Accessed January 16, 2021. https://www.dutkansearvi.fi/rani-henrik-andersson-re-indigenizing-national-parks-toward-a-theoretical-model-of-re-indigenization/.

——— *A Whirlwind Passed Through Our Country: Lakota Voices of the Ghost Dance*. Norman: University of Oklahoma Press, 2019.

Anpetu Wi Wind Farm. "Help Us Leave a Legacy on Our Native Land," 2021. https://anpetuwi.com/.

Audubon, John J. *The Missouri River Journals of John James Audubon*. Edited by Daniel Patterson. Lincoln: University of Nebraska Press, 2016.

Bad Heart Bull, Amos, and Helen H. Blish. *A Pictographic History of the Oglala Sioux*. Lincoln: University of Nebraska Press, 1967.

Bannan, Helen M. *Reformers and the "Indian Problem": 1878–1887 and 1922–1934*. Syracuse, NY: Syracuse University, 1976.

Bear Eagle, Sina. "Oníya Ošóka: The Interpretation of Oglála Lakȟóta Continuing and Historical Relational Connections at Wind Cave National Park." MA thesis, University of California, Los Angeles, 2018.

Beck, Paul N. *Columns of Vengeance: Soldiers, Sioux, and the Punitive Expeditions, 1863–1864*. Norman: University of Oklahoma Press, 2014.

———. *The First Sioux War: The Grattan Fight and Blue Water Creek, 1854–1856*. Lanham, MD: University Press of America, 2004.

Beckwith, Martha Warren. "Mythology of the Oglala Dakota." *Journal of American Folklore* 43, no. 170 (1930): 339–442. https://doi.org/10.2307/535138.

Berghold, Alexander. *The Indians' Revenge; or Days of Horror. Some Appalling Events in the History of the Sioux*. San Francisco: P. J. Thomas Printer, 1891.

Bernstein, Alison R. *American Indians and World War II: Toward a New Era in Indian Affairs*. Norman: University of Oklahoma Press, 1991.

Biolsi, Thomas. *Organizing the Lakota: The Political Economy of the New Deal on the Pine Ridge and Rosebud Reservations*. Tucson: University of Arizona Press, 1992.

Biolsi, Thomas, and Larry J. Zimmerman, eds. *Indians and Anthropologists: Vine Deloria Jr. and the Critique of Anthropology*. Tucson: University of Arizona Press, 1997.

Bland, Thomas A. *A Brief History of the Late Military Invasion of the Home of the Sioux*. Part 2. Washington, DC: Indian Defence Association, 1891.

Boyd, Beth, and Gene D. Thin Elk. "Indigenous Perspectives on Healing." *Communiqué*, Special Section: Psychology and Racism, Ten Years After the Miniconvention August 2008. (American Psychological Association, Office of Ethnic Minority Affairs, Public Interest Directorate), 44–46.

Boyd, James P. *Recent Indian Wars: Under the Lead of Sitting Bull, and Other Chiefs: With a Full Account of the Messiah Craze, and Ghost Dances.* 1891. Facsimile edition. Scituate, MA: Digital Scanning Inc., 2000.

Boyette, Chris, and Jason Hanna. "South Dakota's Governor Will Allow Checkpoints on Tribal Roads, but Not State Highways in a Possible Compromise." CNN, May 13, 2020. https://www.cnn.com/2020/05/13/us/south-dakota-sioux-tribes-checkpoints/index.html.

Braun, Sebastian Felix. *Buffalo Inc.: American Indians and Economic Development.* Norman: University of Oklahoma Press, 2008.

———. "Culture, Resource, Management, and Anthropology: Pipelines and the Wakan at the Standing Rock Sioux Reservation." *Plains Anthropologist* 65, no. 253 (January 2, 2020): 7–24. https://doi.org/10.1080/00320447.2018.1554550.

———. "Imagining Un-Imagined Communities: The Politics of Indigenous Nationalism." In *Tribal Worlds: Critical Studies in American Indian Nation Building*, edited by Brian Hosmer and Larry Nesper, 141–60. Albany: State University of New York Press, 2013.

———. "Introduction: An Ethnohistory of Listening." In *Transforming Ethnohistories: Narrative, Meaning, and Community*, edited by Sebastian Felix Braun, 3–22. Norman: University of Oklahoma Press, 2013.

———. Review of *Lakota America: A New History of Indigenous Power*, by Pekka Hämäläinen. *Journal of American Ethnic History* 40, no. 4 (Summer 2021): 123–24.

———, ed. *Transforming Ethnohistories: Narrative, Meaning, and Community.* Norman: University of Oklahoma Press, 2013.

Brave Bird, Mary, and Richard Erdoes. *Ohitika Woman.* Illustrated edition. New York: Grove Press, 2009.

Bray, Edmund C., and Martha Coleman Bray, eds. *Joseph N. Nicollet on the Plains and Prairies: The Expeditions of 1838–39, with Journals, Letters, and Notes on the Dakota Indians.* Publications of the Minnesota Historical Society. St. Paul: Minnesota Historical Society Press, 1976.

Bray, Kingsley M. "Before Sitting Bull: Interpreting Hunkpapa Political History, 1750–1867." *South Dakota History* 40, no. 2 (2010).

———. *Crazy Horse: A Lakota Life.* Norman: University of Oklahoma Press, 2006.

———. "Lakota Statesmen and the Horse Creek Treaty of 1851." *Nebraska History* 98 (2017): 153–76.

———. "Lone Horn's Peace: A New View of Sioux-Crow Relations, 1851–1858." *Nebraska History* 66 (1985): 28–47.

———. "The Oglala Lakota and the Atkinson-O'Fallon Treaty of 1825." *Nebraska History* 98 (2017): 137–52.

———. "Teton Sioux Population History, 1655–1881." *Nebraska History* 75 (1994): 165–88.

Britten, Thomas A. *American Indians in World War I: At Home and at War.* Albuquerque: University of New Mexico Press, 1997.

Broemert, Roger. "The Sioux and the Indian-CCC." *South Dakota History*, no. 8 (1978).

Brown, Dee. *Bury My Heart at Wounded Knee: An Indian History of the American West.* New York: Holt, Rinehart and Winston, 1970.

Brown, Joseph Epes, ed. *The Sacred Pipe: Black Elk's Account of the Seven Rites of the Oglala Sioux*. Norman: University of Oklahoma Press, 1989. 2012 edition ePub and Kindle.

Browner, Tara. "A Reexamination of the Peji Waci." *American Music Center Research Journal* 5 (1995): 71–81.

Bucko, Raymond A. *The Lakota Ritual of the Sweat Lodge: History and Contemporary Practice*. Studies in the Anthropology of North American Indians. Lincoln: University of Nebraska Press, 1998.

Buechel, Eugene. *Lakota Tales and Text: In Translation*. Edited by Paul Manhardt. Chamberlain, SD: Tipi Press, 1998.

Bull, W., J. W. Bull, and J. H. Howard. *The Warrior Who Killed Custer: The Personal Narrative of Chief Joseph White Bull*. Lincoln: University of Nebraska Press, 1969.

Burnette, Robert. *The Road to Wounded Knee*. New York: Bantam Books, 1974.

———. *The Tortured Americans*. Englewood Cliffs, NJ: Prentice-Hall, 1971.

Burns, Emily C. *Transnational Frontiers: The American West in France*. Norman: University of Oklahoma Press, 2018.

Carrington, Frances C. *My Army Life and the Fort Phil Kearny Massacre: With an Account of the Celebration of "Wyoming Opened."* Philadelphia: Lippincott, 1910.

Carter, John E. "Making Pictures for a News-Hungry Nation." In *Eyewitness at Wounded Knee*, edited by Richard E. Jensen, Eli R. Paul, and John E. Carter. Lincoln: University of Nebraska Press, 1991.

Cash, Joseph H., and Herbert T. Hoover, eds. *To Be an Indian: An Oral History*. New York: Holt, Rinehart, and Winston, 1971.

Castle, Elisabeth. "'The Original Gangster': The Life and Times of Red Power Activist Madonna Thunder Hawk." In *The Hidden 1970s: Histories of Radicalism*, edited by Dan Berger, 267–84. New Brunswick, NJ: Rutgers University Press, 2010.

Cheney, Roberta C. *Sioux Winter Count: A 131-Year Calendar of Events*. Translated by Kills Two. Illustrated reprint. Happy Camp, CA: Naturegraph, 1979.

Childs, Brenda J. *Boarding School Seasons: American Indian Families, 1900–1940*. Lincoln: University of Nebraska Press, 2000.

Christafferson, Dennis M. "Sioux, 1920–2000." In *Plains*, edited by Raymond J. DeMallie, 821–39. Vol. 13 of *Handbook of North American Indians*. Washington, DC: Smithsonian Institution, 2001.

Cleveland, William J., ed. *Sioux Letters with English Translations*. Scholar Select, n.d.

Clow, Richmond L. *Spotted Tail: Warrior and Statesman*. Pierre: South Dakota Historical Society Press, 2019.

Coleman, William S. E. *Voices of Wounded Knee*. Lincoln: University of Nebraska Press, 2000.

Coward, John M. *The Newspaper Indian: Native American Identity in the Press, 1820–90*. Champaign: University of Illinois Press, 1999.

Cowger, Thomas W. "'The Crossroads of Destiny': The NCAI's Landmark Struggle to Thwart Coercive Termination." *American Indian Culture and Research Journal* 20, no. 4 (1996): 121–44. https://doi.org/10.17953/aicr.20.4.gro3lo2667m65235.

Crow Dog, Leonard, and Richard Erdoes. *Crow Dog: Four Generations of Sioux Medicine Men.* New York: Harper Collins Publishers, 1995.

Crow Dog, Mary, and Richard Erdoes. *Lakota Woman.* Reprint edition. Grove Press, 2014.

Cunfer, Geoff, and Bill Waiser, eds. *Bison and People on the North American Great Plains: A Deep Environmental History.* Connecting the Greater West. College Station: Texas A&M University Press, 2016.

Curtis, Edward S. *The North American Indian.* Vol. 3. 1908. New York: Johnson Reprint Corporation, 1970.

Daniels, Robert E. "Cultural Identities among the Oglala Sioux." In *The Modern Sioux: Social Systems and Reservation Culture,* edited by Ethel Nurge, 198–245. Lincoln: University of Nebraska Press, 1970.

Deloria, Ella Cara. *Dakota Texts.* Bison Books ed. Lincoln: University of Nebraska Press, 2006.

———. *Speaking of Indians.* Lincoln: University of Nebraska Press, 1998.

———. "The Sun Dance of the Oglala Sioux." *Journal of American Folklore* 42, no. 166 (October 1, 1929): 354–413. https://doi.org/10.2307/535232.

Deloria, Philip J. *Becoming Mary Sully: Toward an American Indian Abstract.* Seattle: University of Washington Press, 2019.

———. "The Era of Indian Self-Determination: An Overview." In *Indian Self-Rule: First-Hand Accounts of Indian-White Relations from Roosevelt to Reagan,* edited by Kenneth R. Philp, 191–207. Logan: Utah State University Press, 1995.

———. *Playing Indian.* New Haven: Yale University Press, 1998.

Deloria, Vine. *C. G. Jung and the Sioux Traditions: Dreams, Visions, Nature and the Primitive.* Edited by Philip J. Deloria and Jerome S. Bernstein. New Orleans: Spring Journal Books, 2009.

———. *Custer Died for Your Sins: An Indian Manifesto.* New York: Macmillan Company, 1969.

———. "The Establishment of Christianity among the Sioux." In *Sioux Indian Religion: Tradition and Innovation,* edited by Raymond J. DeMallie and Douglas R. Parks. Norman: University of Oklahoma Press, 1987.

———. *For This Land: Writings on Religion in America.* Edited by James Treat. New York: Routledge, 1998.

———. *God Is Red.* New York: Grosset & Dunlap, 1973.

———. "Schlesier, Other Anthropologists, and Wounded Knee." *American Anthropologist* 82, no. 3 (1980): 560–61.

———. *Spirit and Reason: The Vine Deloria, Jr., Reader.* Edited by Barbara Deloria, Kristen Foehner, and Samuel Scinta. Golden, CO: Fulcrum Publishing, 1999.

Deloria, Vine, and Clifford M. Lytle. *The Nations Within: The Past and Future of American Indian Sovereignty.* New York: Pantheon Books, 1984.

Deloria, Vine, Jr., and Raymond J. DeMallie. *Documents of American Indian Diplomacy: Treaties, Agreements, and Conventions, 1775–1979.* 2 vols. Norman: University of Oklahoma Press, 1999.

———, eds. "Proceedings of the Great Peace Commission of 1867–1868: With an Introduction." Institute for the Development of Indian Law, 1975.

DeMallie, Raymond J. "Black Elk 1863–1950." In *Encyclopedia of Environmental Ethics and Philosophy*, edited by J. Callicott and Robert Frodeman, 1:114–15. Detroit: Macmillan Reference USA, 2009.

———. "Change in American Indian Kinship Systems: The Dakota." In *Currents in Anthropology: Essays in Honor of Sol Tax*, edited by Robert Hinshaw, 221–41. The Hague: Mouton Publishers, 1979.

———. "Community in Native America: Continuity and Change among the Sioux." *Journal de La Sociétés de Américanistes* 95, no. 1 (2009): 185–205.

———. "Deloria, Ella Cara." In *Encyclopedia of Religion*, edited by Lindsay Jones, 2nd ed., 4:2264–65. Detroit: Macmillan Reference USA, 2005.

———. "Kinship and Biology in Sioux Culture." In *North American Indian Anthropology: Essays on Society and Culture*, edited by Raymond J. DeMallie and Alfonso Ortiz, 125–46. Norman: University of Oklahoma Press, 1994.

———. "Kinship: The Foundation for Native American Society." In *Studying Native America: Problems and Prospects*, edited by Russell Thornton, 306–56. Madison: University of Wisconsin Press, 1998.

———. "Lakota Belief and Ritual in the Nineteenth Century." In *Sioux Indian Religion: Tradition and Innovation*, edited by Raymond J. DeMallie and Douglas R. Parks, 25–43. Norman: University of Oklahoma Press, 1987.

———. "The Lakota Ghost Dance: An Ethnohistorical Account." *Pacific Historical Review* 51, no. 4 (November 1, 1982): 385–405.

———. "Lakota Traditionalism: History and Symbol." In *Native North American Interaction Patterns*, edited by Regna Darnell and Michael K. Foster, 2–21. Ottawa, ONT: Canadian Museum of Civilization, 1991.

———. "Male and Female in Nineteenth Century Lakota Culture." In *The Hidden Half: Studies of Native Plains Women*, edited by Patricia Albers and Beatrice Medicine, 237–65. Washington, DC: University Press of America, 1982.

———. "Pine Ridge Economy: Cultural and Historical Perspectives." In *American Indian Economic Development*, edited by Sam Stanley, 237–312. The Hague: Mouton Publishers, 1978.

———. "The Sioux in Dakota and Montana Territories: Cultural and Historical Background of the Ogden B. Read Collection." In *Vestiges of a Proud Nation: The Ogden B. Read Northern Plains Indian Collection*, edited by Glenn E. Markoe, 19–69. Burlington: Robert Hull Fleming Museum, University of Vermont, 1986.

———. "Sioux Until 1850." In *Handbook of North American Indians, Volume 13: Plains*, edited by Raymond J. DeMallie, 2:718–60. Washington DC: Smithsonian Institution, 2001.

———, ed. *The Sixth Grandfather: Black Elk's Teachings Given to John G. Neihardt*. Lincoln: University of Nebraska Press, 1985.

———. "Teton." In *Plains*, edited by Raymond J. DeMallie, 2:794–820. Vol. 13 of *Handbook of North American Indians*. Washington, DC: Smithsonian Institution, 2001.

———. "Teton Dakota Kinship and Social Organization." PhD diss., University of Chicago, 1971.

———. "'These Have No Ears': Narrative and the Ethnohistorical Method." *Ethnohistory* 40, no. 4 (1993): 515–38.

———. "Touching the Pen: Plains Indian Treaty Councils in Ethnohistorical Perspective." In *Major Problems in American Indian History: Documents and Essays*, edited by Albert L. Hurtado and Peter Iverson, 344–55. Lexington, MA: D. C. Heath and Company, 1994.

———. "Vine Deloria Jr. (1933–2005)." *American Anthropologist*, New Series, 108, no. 4 (December 1, 2006): 932–35.

DeMallie, Raymond J., and Robert H. Lavenda. "Wakan: Plains Siouan Concepts of Power." In *The Anthropology of Power: Ethnographic Studies from Asia, Oceania, and the New World*, edited by Raymond D. Fogelson and Richard N. Adams, 153–65. Studies in Anthropology. New York: Academic Press, 1977.

DeMallie, Raymond J., and Douglas R. Parks. "Plains Indian Warfare." In *The People of the Buffalo: The Plains Indians of North America: Essays in Honor of John C. Ewers*, edited by Colin F. Taylor, Hugh A. Dempsey, and John C. Ewers. Wyk Auf Foer, Germany: Tatanka Press, 2003.

———, eds. *Sioux Indian Religion: Tradition and Innovation*. Norman: University of Oklahoma Press, 1987.

Denig, Edwin T. *Five Indian Tribes of the Upper Missouri: Sioux, Arickaras, Assiniboines, Crees, Crows*. Norman: University of Oklahoma Press, 1961.

Densmore, Frances. *Teton Sioux Music and Culture*. Lincoln: University of Nebraska Press, 1992, 2001.

Dewing, Rolland. "South Dakota Newspaper Coverage of the 1973 Occupation of Wounded Knee." *South Dakota History* 12, no. 1 (1982): 48–64.

———. *Wounded Knee: The Meaning and Significance of the Second Incident*. New York: Irvington Publishers, 1985.

———. *Wounded Knee II*. Chadron, NE: Great Plains Network, 1995.

Donnelly, Michael. "Killing Anna Mae Aquash, Smearing John Trudell." CounterPunch .org, January 17, 2006. https://www.counterpunch.org/2006/01/17/killing-anna-mae -aquash-smearing-john-trudell/.

Dorsey, J. Owen. "Games of Teton Dakota Children." *American Anthropologist* 4, no. 4 (1891): 329–46.

Drury, Bob, and Tom Clavin. *The Heart of Everything That Is: The Untold Story of Red Cloud, An American Legend*. New York: Simon & Schuster, 2013.

Eagle, Karin. "Native Sun News: Crow Creek Sioux Woman Earns Bronze Star." Indianz .com, December 1, 2011. https://www.indianz.com/News/2011/003922.asp.

Eastman, Charles A. *From the Deep Woods to Civilization*. Mineola, NY: Dover Publications, 2012.

Eastman, Elaine Goodale. "The Ghost Dance War and Wounded Knee Massacre of 1890–1891." *Nebraska History* 26, no. 1 (1945): 26–42.

———. *Sister to the Sioux: The Memoirs of Elaine Goodale Eastman, 1885–91*. Edited by Kay Graber. Lincoln: University of Nebraska Press, 1986.

Eggan, Fred, and Joseph A. Maxwell. "Kinship and Social Organization." In *Plains*, edited by Raymond J. DeMallie, 2:974–82. Vol. 13 of *Handbook of North American Indians*. Washington, DC: Smithsonian Institution, 2001.

Enochs, Ross A. *The Jesuit Mission to the Lakota Sioux: Pastoral Theology and Ministry, 1886–1945*. Reference, Information and Interdisciplinary Subjects Series. Lanham, MD: Rowman & Littlefield, 1996.

Estes, Nick. *Our History Is the Future: Standing Rock Versus the Dakota Access Pipeline, and the Long Tradition of Indigenous Resistance*. Illustrated edition. New York: Verso, 2019.

Estes, Nick, and Jaskiran Dhillon, eds. *Standing with Standing Rock: Voices from the #NoDAPL Movement*. Minneapolis: University of Minnesota Press, 2019.

Ewers, John C. *Indian Life on the Upper Missouri*. Civilization of the American Indian Series 89. Norman: University of Oklahoma Press, 1968.

———. "Intertribal Warfare as the Precursor of Indian-White Warfare on the Northern Great Plains." *Western Historical Quarterly* 6, no. 4 (October 1, 1975): 397–410.

Fear-Segal, Jacqueline, and Susan D. Rose, eds. *Carlisle Indian Industrial School: Indigenous Histories, Memories, and Reclamations*. Lincoln: University of Nebraska Press, 2018.

Fenelon, James V. *Culturicide, Resistance, and Survival of the Lakota*. New York: Routledge, 2014.

Feraca, Stephen E. *Wakinyan: Lakota Religion in the Twentieth Century*. Lincoln: University of Nebraska Press, 1998.

Fixico, Donald L. *Bureau of Indian Affairs*. Santa Barbara: Greenwood, 2012.

———. *Termination and Relocation: Federal Indian Policy, 1945–1960*. Albuquerque: University of New Mexico Press, 1986.

———. *The Urban Indian Experience in America*. Illustrated edition. Albuquerque: University of New Mexico Press, 2000.

Flakus, Greg. "Last of Lakota Sioux Code Talkers Recalls WWII Service." *Voanews*, November 1, 2009. https://www.voanews.com/a/a-13-2007-09-27-voa58/402780.html.

Fletcher, Alice C. *The Hako: Song, Pipe, and Unity in a Pawnee Calumet Ceremony*. Lincoln: University of Nebraska Press, 1996.

Foley, Thomas W. *Father Francis M. Craft, Missionary to the Sioux*. Lincoln: University of Nebraska Press, 2002.

Forbes-Boyt, Kari. "Litigation, Mitigation, and the American Indian Religious Freedom Act: The Bear Butte Example." *Great Plains Quarterly* 19, no. 1 (1999): 23–34.

Friesen, Steve, Walter Littlemoon, and François Chladiuk. *Lakota Performers in Europe: Their Culture and the Artifacts They Left Behind*. Norman: University of Oklahoma Press, 2017.

Frosch, Dan. "The Truth About Leonard." *In These Times*, March 18, 2004. http://inthesetimes.com/article/715/the_truth_about_leonard.

Fugle, Eugene. "The Nature and Function of the Lakota Night Cults." *W. H. Over Museum, University of South Dakota, Museum News* 27, no. 3–4 (1966): 1–38.

Gage, Justin. "Intertribal Communication, Literacy, and the Spread of the Ghost Dance." PhD diss., University of Arkansas, 2015.

———. *We Do Not Want the Gates Closed between Us: Native Networks and the Spread of the Ghost Dance*. Illustrated edition. Norman: University of Oklahoma Press, 2020.

Garner, Sandra L. *To Come to a Better Understanding: Medicine Men and Clergy Meetings on the Rosebud Reservation, 1973–1978*. Lincoln: University of Nebraska Press, 2016.

Geertz, Clifford. "Shifting Aims, Moving Targets: On the Anthropology of Religion." *Journal of the Royal Anthropological Institute* 11, no. 1 (March 1, 2005): 1–15.

Goodman, Ronald. *Lakota Star Knowledge: Studies in Lakota Stellar Theology*. Edited by Alan Seeger. Mission, SD: SGU Publishing, 2017.

Grafe, Ernest, and Paul Horsted. *Exploring with Custer: The 1874 Black Hills Expedition*. Custer, SD: Golden Valley Press, 2002.

Gray, John S. *Centennial Campaign: The Sioux War of 1876*. Norman: University of Oklahoma Press, 1988.

Greene, Candace S., and Russell Thornton. *The Year the Stars Fell: Lakota Winter Counts at the Smithsonian*. Lincoln: University of Nebraska Press, 2007.

Greene, Jerome A. *American Carnage: Wounded Knee, 1890*. Illustrated edition. Norman, Oklahoma: University of Oklahoma Press, 2014.

———. *Battles and Skirmishes of the Great Sioux War, 1876–1877: The Military View*. Norman: University of Oklahoma Press, 1996.

———. *Lakota and Cheyenne: Indian Views of the Great Sioux War, 1876–1877*. Norman: University of Oklahoma Press, 1994.

———. "The Sioux Land Commission of 1889: Prelude to Wounded Knee." *South Dakota History* 1, no. 1 (1970).

———. *Slim Buttes, 1876: An Episode of the Great Sioux War*. Norman: University of Oklahoma Press, 1982.

Greene, Jerome A., and Douglas D. Scott. *Finding Sand Creek: History, Archeology, and the 1864 Massacre Site*. Norman: University of Oklahoma Press, 2013.

Grinnell, George Bird. *The Fighting Cheyennes*. Norman: University of Oklahoma Press, 1983.

Grobsmith, Elizabeth S. *Lakota of the Rosebud: A Contemporary Ethnography*. Case Studies in Cultural Anthropology. New York: Holt, Rinehart and Winston, 1981.

Hagan, Helene E. *Russell Means: The European Ancestry of a Militant Indian*. Xlibris Corp, 2018.

Hagan, William T. *Indian Police and Judges: Experiments in Acculturation and Control*. Lincoln: University of Nebraska Press, 1980.

———. *The Indian Rights Association: The Herbert Welsh Years, 1882–1904*. Tucson: University of Arizona Press, 1985.

Hämäläinen, Pekka. *Lakota America: A New History of Indigenous Power*. New Haven: Yale University Press, 2019.

Hardorff, Richard G. *Indian Views of the Custer Fight: A Source Book*. Norman: University of Oklahoma Press, 2005.

Harring, Naih, and Sidney L. Harring. *Crow Dog's Case: American Indian Sovereignty, Tribal Law, and United States Law in the Nineteenth Century*. Edited by Frederick Hoxie. Cambridge: Cambridge University Press, 1994.

Hassrick, Royal B. *The Sioux: Life and Customs of a Warrior Society*. The Civilization of the American Indian Series, 72. Norman: University of Oklahoma Press, 1964, 2012.

Hein, David. "Episcopalianism among the Lakota/Dakota Indians of South Dakota." *Historiographer* 40 (2000): 14–16.

Hendricks, Steve. *The Unquiet Grave: The FBI and the Struggle for the Soul of Indian Country*. New York: Thunder's Mouth Press, 2006.

Henriksson, Markku. *The Indian on Capitol Hill: Indian Legislation and the United States Congress, 1862–1907*. Jyväskylä: SHS, 1988.

Hertzberg, Hazel W. *The Search for an American Indian Identity: Modern Pan-Indian Movements*. Syracuse, NY: Syracuse University Press, 1971.

Hill, Matthew J. "Historicizing the "Shrine of Democracy": Lakota Perspectives on Mount Rushmore in the Context of the Black Hills." Unpublished manuscript.

Hinman, Eleanor H. "Oglala Sources on the Life of Crazy Horse." *Nebraska History* 57, no. 1 (1976): 1–51.

Hollabaugh, Mark. *The Spirit and the Sky: Lakota Visions of the Cosmos*. Lincoln: University of Nebraska Press, 2018.

Hurt, Wesley R., and James H. Howard. "A Dakota Conjuring Ceremony." *Southwestern Journal of Anthropology* 8, no. 3 (October 1, 1952): 286–96.

Hyde, George E. *Life of George Bent: Written from His Letters*. Norman: University of Oklahoma Press, 2015.

——. *Red Cloud's Folk: A History of the Oglala Sioux Indians*. Norman: University of Oklahoma Press, 1937.

——. *A Sioux Chronicle*. Civilization of the American Indian. Norman: University of Oklahoma Press, 1956.

——. *Spotted Tail's Folk: A History of the Brulé Sioux*. Norman: University of Oklahoma Press, 1961.

Hynes, William Francis. *Soldiers of the Frontier*. Denver, 1943.

Isenberg, Andrew C. *The Destruction of the Bison: An Environmental History, 1750–1920*. Studies in Environment and History. Cambridge: Cambridge University Press, 2000.

Jackson, Jason Baird. "Recontextualizing Revitalization: Cosmology and Cultural Stability in the Adoption of Peyotism among the Yuchi." In *Reassessing Revitalization Movements: Perspectives from North America and the Pacific Islands*, edited by Michael E. Harkin, 183–205. Lincoln: University of Nebraska Press, 2004.

Jackson, Jason Baird, and Victoria Lindsay Levine. "Singing for Garfish: Music and Woodland Communities in Eastern Oklahoma." *Ethnomusicology* 46, no. 2 (April 1, 2002): 284–306. https://doi.org/10.2307/852783.

Jensen, Richard E., ed. *Voices of the American West*. Vol 1, *The Indian Interviews of Eli S. Ricker, 1903–1919*. Lincoln: University of Nebraska Press, 2006.

Jensen, Richard E., and James S. Hutchins, eds. *Wheel Boats on the Missouri: The Journals and Documents of the Atkinson-O'Fallon Expedition, 1824–26*. Helena: Montana Historical Society Press, 2001.

Johnson, Willis F. *The Red Record of the Sioux: Life of Sitting Bull and History of the Indian War of 1890–91*. Philadelphia: Edgewood, 1891.

Kapferer, Bruce. "Beyond Symbolic Representation: Victor Turner and Variations on the Themes of Ritual Process and Liminality." *Suomen Antropologi: Journal of the Finnish Anthropological Society* 33, no. 4 (2008): 5–25.

Kappler, Charles J. *Indian Affairs: Laws and Treaties*. Vol. 2, *Treaties*. Washington, DC: Government Printing Office, 1904.

Kelman, A. *A Misplaced Massacre: Struggling Over the Memory of Sand Creek*. Cambridge, MA: Harvard University Press, 2013.

Klass, Morton. *Ordered Universes: Approaches to the Anthropology of Religion*. Boulder, CO: Westview Press, 1995.

Kring, Shannon. *End of the Line: The Women of Standing Rock*. Los Angeles: Red Queen Media, 2020.

Krouse, Susan Applegate. *North American Indians in the Great War*. Studies in War, Society, and the Military. Lincoln: University of Nebraska Press, 2007.

Kurkiala, Mikael. *"Building the Nation Back Up": The Politics of Identity on the Pine Ridge Indian Reservation*. Acta Universitatis Upsaliensis. Uppsala Studies in Cultural Anthropology 22. Uppsala, Sweden: Uppsala University, 1997.

Lahti, Janne. "Forts on the Northern Plains." In *A Companion to Custer and the Little Big Horn Campaign*, edited by Brad D. Lookingbill, 130–47. West Sussex, UK: Wiley Blackwell & Sons, 2015.

———. *Wars for Empire: Apaches, the United States, and the Southwest Borderlands*. Norman: University of Oklahoma Press, 2017.

Lakota Language Project Maȟpíya Lúta Lakȟól'iyapi Wóuŋspewičhakhiyapi. "About the Lakota Language Program-Red Cloud Indian School." Accessed December 30, 2020. http://www.lakotalanguageproject.org/.

Lame Deer, John (Fire), and Richard Erdoes. *Lame Deer, Seeker of Visions*. New York: Simon and Schuster, 1972.

Landry, Alisa. "Barack Obama: 'Emotionally and Intellectually Committed to Indian Country.'" IndianCountryToday.com, November 1, 2016. https://indiancountrytoday.com/archive/barack-obama-emotionally-and-intellectually-committed-to-indian-country-tiTULWItlkuFWojXZcorcQ.

LaPointe, Ernie. *Sitting Bull: His Life and Legacy*. Layton, UT: Gibbs Smith, 2009.

Larsen, Lawrence H., and Barbara J. Cottrell. *Steamboats West: The 1859 American Fur Company Missouri River Expedition*. Norman: University of Oklahoma Press, 2010.

Larson, Robert W. *Gall: Lakota War Chief*. Norman: University of Oklahoma Press, 2012.

———. *Red Cloud: Warrior-Statesman of the Lakota Sioux*. Norman: University of Oklahoma Press, 1999.

Laubin, Reginald, and Gladys Laubin. *The Indian Tipi: Its History, Construction, and Use*. Norman: University of Oklahoma Press, 1989.

Lawson, Michael L. *Dammed Indians: The Pick-Sloan Plan and the Missouri River Sioux, 1944–1980*. Norman: University of Oklahoma Press, 1982.

———. "Federal Water Projects and Indian Lands: The Pick-Sloan Plan, A Case Study." *American Indian Culture and Research Journal* 7, no. 1 (1982): 23–40.

Lewis, Meriwether, and William Clark. *The Definitive Journals of Lewis and Clark, Vol 3: Up the Missouri to Fort Mandan*. Edited by Gary E. Moulton. New edition. Lincoln: Bison Books, 2002.

Lewis, Thomas H. *The Medicine Men: Oglala Sioux Ceremony and Healing*. Lincoln: University of Nebraska Press, 1990.

Looking Horse, Arvol. "The Sacred Pipe in Modern Life." In *Sioux Indian Religion: Tradition and Innovation*, edited by Raymond J. DeMallie and Douglas R. Parks, 67–73. Norman: University of Oklahoma Press, 1987.

Lynd, James W. *The Religion of the Dakotas*. Vol. 2. Collections of the Minnesota Historical Society. St. Paul: Minnesota Historical Society, 1889.

Macgregor, Gordon. *Warriors without Weapons; a Study of the Society and Personality Development of the Pine Ridge Sioux*. Chicago: University of Chicago Press, 1946.

Maddra, Sam. *Hostiles?: The Lakota Ghost Dance and Buffalo Bill's Wild West*. Norman: University of Oklahoma Press, 2006.

Magnuson, Stew. *The Death of Raymond Yellow Thunder: And Other True Stories from the Nebraska–Pine Ridge Border Towns*. Lubbock: Texas Tech University Press, 2008.

———. *Wounded Knee 1973: Still Bleeding: The American Indian Movement, the FBI, and Their Fight to Bury the Sins of the Past*. Chicago: Now & Then Reader, 2013.

Mails, Thomas E. *Sundancing: The Great Sioux Piercing Ritual*. Tulsa, OK: Council Oak Books, 1998.

Mails, Thomas E., and Frank Fools Crow. *Fools Crow*. Garden City, NY: Doubleday, 1979.

Malan, Vernon D. "The Dakota Indian Family, Community Studies on the Pine Ridge Reservation (1958)." *Research Bulletins of the South Dakota Agricultural Experiment Station (1887–2011)*. 470. https://openprairie.sdstate.edu/agexperimentsta_bulletins/470.

Mallery, Garrick. *Picture-Writing of the American Indians*. Mineola, NY: Dover Publications, 1972.

Markowitz, Harvey. "The Catholic Mission and the Sioux: A Crisis in the Early Paradigm." In *Sioux Indian Religion: Tradition and Innovation*, edited by Raymond J. DeMallie and Douglas R. Parks. Norman: University of Oklahoma Press, 1987.

———. *Converting the Rosebud: Catholic Mission and the Lakotas, 1886–1916*. Norman: University of Oklahoma Press, 2018.

Maroukis, Thomas Constantine. *The Peyote Road: Religious Freedom and the Native American Church*. Civilization of the American Indian Series 265. Norman: University of Oklahoma Press, 2010.

Marquis, Thomas B. *A Warrior Who Fought Custer*. Lincoln: University of Nebraska Press, 1971.

Marshall, Joseph M. III. *Crazy Horse Weeps: The Challenge of Being Lakota in White America*. Golden, CO: Fulcrum Publishing, 2019.

———. *The Day the World Ended at Little Bighorn: A Lakota History*. Illustrated edition. New York: Penguin Books, 2008.

———. *The Journey of Crazy Horse*. Reprint edition. New York: Penguin Books, 2005.

————. *The Lakota Way: Stories and Lessons for Living*. Reprint edition. New York: Penguin Books, 2002.

Matthiessen, Peter. *In the Spirit of Crazy Horse*. New York: Viking Press, 1980.

Maynard, Eileen, and Gayla Twiss. *That These People May Live: Conditions among the Oglala Sioux of the Pine Ridge Reservation*. Pine Ridge, SD: US Public Health Service, 1969.

McCrady, David G. *Living with Strangers: The Nineteenth-Century Sioux and the Canadian-American Borderlands*. Lincoln: University of Nebraska Press, 2006.

————. *Living with Strangers: The Nineteenth-Century Sioux and the Canadian-American Borderlands*. Toronto, ONT: University of Toronto Press, 2009.

McDermott, John D. *Circle of Fire: The Indian War of 1865*. Mechanicsburg, PA: Stackpole Books, 2003.

————. *Red Cloud: Oglala Legend*. Pierre: South Dakota Historical Society Press, 2015.

————. *Red Cloud's War: The Bozeman Trail, 1866–1868*. Norman: University of Oklahoma Press, 2010.

McDermott, John D., R. Eli Paul, and Sandra J. Lowry, eds. *All Because of a Mormon Cow: Historical Accounts of the Grattan Massacre, 1854–1855*. Norman: University of Oklahoma Press, 2018.

McGillycuddy, Julia B. *Blood on the Moon: Valentine McGillycuddy and the Sioux*. Lincoln: University of Nebraska Press, 1969.

McGinnis, Anthony. *Counting Coup and Cutting Horses: Intertribal Warfare on the Northern Plains, 1738–1889*. Lincoln: University of Nebraska Press, 2010.

McGregor, James H. *The Wounded Knee Massacre: From the Viewpoint of the Sioux*. Rapid City, SD: Fenske Printing, Inc., 1997.

McLaughlin, James. *My Friend the Indian*. Boston: Houghton Mifflin, 1910, 1989.

Medicine, Beatrice. "Indian Women and the Renaissance of Traditional Religion." In *Sioux Indian Religion: Tradition and Innovation*, edited by Raymond J. DeMallie and Douglas R. Parks, 159–71. Norman: University of Oklahoma Press, 1987.

————. "Native American Resistance to Integration: Contemporary Confrontations and Religious Revitalization." *Plains Anthropologist* 26, no. 94 (1981): 277–86.

————. *The Native American Woman: A Perspective*. Austin, TX: National Educational Laboratory Publishers, 1978.

————. "Self-Direction in Sioux Education." *Integrated Education* 13, no. 6 (1975): 15–17.

Mekeel, H. Scudder. "A Discussion of Culture Change as Illustrated by Material from a Teton-Dakota Community." *American Anthropologist*, New Series, 34, no. 2 (April 1, 1932): 274–85.

————. "The Economy of a Modern Teton Dakota Community." *Yale University Publications in Anthropology* 3, no. 6 (1936): 3–14.

Meyers, Richard, "Native Anthropology, to be a Native Scholar, or a Scholar that is Native: Reviving Ethnography in Indian Country." *Anthropology Now* 11 (2019):1–2, 23–33.

Miller, David H. *Ghost Dance*. Lincoln: University of Nebraska Press, 1985.

Mills, Billy. *Lessons of a Lakota: A Young Man's Journey to Happiness and Self-Understanding*. Carlsbad: Hay House, 2005.

Mirsky, Jeannette. "The Dakota." In *Cooperation and Competition among Primitive Peoples*, edited by Margaret Mead, 382–427. Boston: Beacon Press, 1937.

Monnett, John H. "Contested Lands: Climate Change and the Struggle for the Powder River Country, 1856–1866." *Journal of the West* 59, no. 2 (Spring 2020): 3–11.

———. *Eyewitness to the Fetterman Fight: Indian Views*. Norman: University of Oklahoma Press, 2017.

Mooney, James. *The Ghost-Dance Religion and the Sioux Outbreak of 1890*. Lincoln: University of Nebraska Press, 1991.

Mort, Terry A. *Thieves' Road: The Black Hills Betrayal and Custer's Path to Little Bighorn*. Amherst, NY: Prometheus Books, 2015.

Nadeau, Remi A. *Fort Laramie and the Sioux Indians*. American Forts Series. Englewood Cliffs, NJ: Prentice-Hall, 1967.

Nasatir, Abraham P. *Before Lewis and Clark: Documents Illustrating the History of the Missouri, 1785–1804*. Norman: University of Oklahoma Press, 2002.

Neihardt, John G. *Black Elk Speaks*. Complete edition. Lincoln: University of Nebraska Press, 2014.

———. *Black Elk Speaks: Being the Life Story of a Holy Man of the Oglala Sioux*. Excelsior Editions. Albany, NY: State University Press of New York, 2008.

———. *Eagle Voice Remembers: An Authentic Tale of the Old Sioux World*. Annotated. A Bison Classic Edition. Lincoln: University of Nebraska Press, 2021.

———. *When the Tree Flowered: The Story of Eagle Voice, a Sioux Indian*. Lincoln: University of Nebraska Press, 1991.

O'Brien, Sharon. "A Legal Analysis of the American Indian Religious Freedom Act." In *Handbook of American Indian Religious Freedom*, edited by Christopher Vecsey, 27–43. New York: Crossroads Publishing, 1991.

Olson, James C. *Red Cloud and the Sioux Problem*. Lincoln: University of Nebraska Press, 1965.

Ostler, Jeffrey. *The Lakotas and the Black Hills: The Struggle for Sacred Ground*. New York: Penguin, 2010.

———. *The Plains Sioux and U.S. Colonialism from Lewis and Clark to Wounded Knee*. Cambridge: Cambridge University Press, 2004.

———. *Surviving Genocide: Native Nations and the United States from the American Revolution to Bleeding Kansas*. New Haven: Yale University Press, 2020.

———. "'They Regard Their Passing as Wakan': Interpreting Western Sioux Explanations for the Bison's Decline." *Western Historical Quarterly* 30, no. 4 (1999): 475–97.

Oswald, Sherry, and Colleen Ragan. "Radiation: 'Dangerous to Pine Ridge Women,' W.A.R.N. Study Says." *Akwesasne Notes*, Spring 1980. http://www.oocities.org/lakotastudentalliance/warnstudy_radiation.pdf.

Overfield, Loyd J. *The Little Big Horn, 1876: The Official Communications, Documents, and Reports, with Rosters of the Officers and Troops of the Campaign*. Lincoln: University of Nebraska Press, 1990.

Page, Andrea. *Sioux Code Talkers of World War II*. Gretna, LA: Pelican, 2017.

Pajunen, Minna. "Sacred Water: Standing Rock, Power and Environmental Discourses in North American Indigenous People's Media Texts." MA thesis, University of Helsinki, 2020.

Papandrea, Ronald J. *They Never Surrendered, The Lakota Sioux Band That Stayed in Canada.* 4th ed. rev. La Vergne, TN: Ronald J. Papandrea, 2012.

Parkman, Francis. *The Oregon Trail: Sketches of Prairie and Rocky-Mountain Life.* New York: Library of America, 1991.

Parks, Douglas R. "Arikara." In *Handbook of North American Indians.* Vol. 13. *Plains,* edited by Raymond J. DeMallie, 1:365–90. Washington, DC: Smithsonian Institution, 2001.

Parks, Douglas R., and Raymond J. DeMallie. "Plains Indian Native Literatures." *boundary 2* 19, no. 3 (Autumn, 1992): 105–47. https://doi.org/10.2307/303551.

Parks, Douglas R., Raymond J. DeMallie, and Robert Vézina, eds. *A Fur Trader on the Upper Missouri: The Journals and Description of Jean-Baptiste Truteau, 1794–96.* 2 vols. Lincoln: University of Nebraska Press, 2018.

Paul, R. Eli. *Autobiography of Red Cloud: War Leader of the Oglalas.* Helena: Montana Historical Society Press, 1997.

——. *Blue Water Creek and the First Sioux War, 1854–1856.* Norman: University of Oklahoma Press, 2012.

Pearson, Jeffrey V. "Nelson A. Miles, Crazy Horse, and the Battle of Wolf Mountains." *Montana: The Magazine of Western History* 51 (Winter 2001): 53–67.

Philp, Kenneth R., ed. *Indian Self-Rule: First-Hand Accounts of Indian-White Relations from Roosevelt to Reagan.* Logan: Utah State University Press, 1995.

——. "Stride toward Freedom: The Relocation of Indians to Cities, 1952–1960." *Western Historical Quarterly* 16, no. 2 (1985): 175–90.

——. *Termination Revisited : American Indians on the Trail to Self-Determination, 1933–1953.* Lincoln: University of Nebraska Press, 1999.

Porterfield, K. Marie. "The Selling of the Sun Dance: Spiritual Exploitation at Heart of Pine Ridge Controversy." *Indian Country Today.* August 4, 1997.

Posthumus, David C. *All My Relatives: Exploring Lakota Ontology, Belief, and Ritual.* New Visions in Native American and Indigenous Studies. Lincoln: University of Nebraska Press, 2018.

——. "All My Relatives: Exploring Nineteenth-Century Lakota Ontology and Belief." *Ethnohistory* 64, no. 3 (July 1, 2017): 379–400.

——. "Hereditary Enemies? An Examination of Sioux-Arikara Relations Prior to 1830." *Plains Anthropologist* 61, no. 240 (November 2016): 361–82.

——. "A Lakota View of Pté Oyáte (Buffalo Nation)." In *Bison and People on the North American Great Plains: A Deep Environmental History,* edited by Geoff Cunfer and Bill Waiser, 278–310. Connecting the Greater West. College Station: Texas A&M University Press, 2016.

——. "The Ritual Thiyóšpaye and the Social Organization of Contemporary Lakota Ceremonial Life." *Journal for the Anthropology of North America* 22, no. 1 (2019): 4–21.

———. "Toward a Typology of Nineteenth-Century Lakota Magico-Medico-Ritual Specialists." In *Healers and Empires in Global History: Healing as Hybrid and Contested Knowledge*, edited by Markku Hokkanen and Kalle Kananoja, 239–71. London: Palgrave Macmillan, 2019.

———. "Transmitting Sacred Knowledge: Aspects of Historical and Contemporary Oglala Lakota Belief and Ritual." PhD diss., Indiana University, 2015.

Powell, Peter .J. *People of the Sacred Mountain: A History of the Northern Cheyenne Chiefs and Warrior Societies, 1830–1879 : With an Epilogue, 1969–1974*. Vols. 1–2. San Francisco: Harper & Row, 1981.

Powers, William K. "Contemporary Oglala Music and Dance: Pan-Indianism versus Pan-Tetonism." In *The Modern Sioux: Social Systems and Reservation Culture*, edited by Ethel Nurge, 268–90. Lincoln: University of Nebraska Press, 1970.

———. *Oglala Religion*. Lincoln: University of Nebraska Press, 1982.

———. *Sacred Language: The Nature of Supernatural Discourse in Lakota*. Civilization of the American Indian Series 179. Norman: University of Oklahoma Press, 1986.

———. *Voices from the Spirit World: Lakota Ghost Dance Songs*. Kendall Park, NJ: Lakota Books, 1990.

———. *War Dance: Plains Indian Musical Performance*. Tucson: University of Arizona Press, 1990.

———. *Yuwipi: Vision and Experience in Oglala Ritual*. Lincoln: University of Nebraska Press, 1982.

Price, Catherine. *The Oglala People, 1841–1879: A Political History*. Lincoln: University of Nebraska Press, 1996.

Prucha, Francis Paul. *American Indian Policy in Crisis: Christian Reformers and the Indian, 1865–1900*. Norman: University of Oklahoma Press, 1976.

———. *Documents of United States Indian Policy*. Lincoln: University of Nebraska Press, 1990.

———. *The Great Father: The United States Government and the American Indians*. Lincoln: University of Nebraska Press, 1986.

Rausch, Natasha. "Who Is Tokata Iron Eyes and Why Did Greta Thunberg Come to the Dakotas to See Her?" *Grand Forks Herald*, October 7, 2019. https://www .grandforksherald.com/news/government-and-politics/4710375-Who-is-Tokata-Iron -Eyes-and-why-did-Greta-Thunberg-come-to-the-Dakotas-to-see-her.

Raynolds, W. F. *Journal of Captain W. F. Raynolds*. United States Army Corps of Engineers. Washington, DC: Government Printing Office, 1868.

"Red Cloud Indian School Rolls Out Nation's First Comprehensive K–12 Lakota Language Curriculum-Red Cloud Indian School." Accessed June 30, 2020. https://www .redcloudschool.org/news/2013/1030/red-cloud-indian-school-rolls-out-nations-first -comprehensive-k-12-lakota-language-curriculum.

Red Cloud Renewable. "Red Cloud Renewable, Pine Ridge." Accessed January 17, 2021. https://www.redcloudrenewable.org.

Red Shirt, Delphine. *George Sword's Warrior Narratives: Compositional Processes in Lakota Oral Tradition*. Lincoln: University of Nebraska Press, 2016.

Reilly, Hugh J. *The Frontier Newspapers and the Coverage of the Plains Indian Wars.* Santa Barbara, CA: Praeger, 2010.

Reinhardt, Akim D. "A Crude Replacement: The Indian New Deal, Indirect Colonialism, and Pine Ridge Reservation." *Journal of Colonialism and Colonial History* 6, no. 1 (2005).

———. *Ruling Pine Ridge: Oglala Lakota Politics from the IRA to Wounded Knee.* Plains Histories. Lubbock: Texas Tech University Press, 2007.

———. "Spontaneous Combustion: Prelude to Wounded Knee 1973." *South Dakota History* 29, no. 3 (1999): 229–44.

———, ed. *Welcome to the Oglala Nation: A Documentary Reader in Oglala Lakota Political History.* Lincoln: University of Nebraska Press, 2015.

"Republic of Lakotah–Mitakuye Oyasin," 2021. http://www.republicoflakotah.com/.

Rice, Julian. *Before the Great Spirit: The Many Faces of Sioux Spirituality.* Albuquerque: University of New Mexico Press, 1998.

Richardson, Heather Cox. *Wounded Knee: Party Politics and the Road to an American Massacre.* Illustrated edition. New York: Basic Books, 2011.

Riegert, Wilbur A. *Quest for the Pipe of the Sioux: As Viewed from Wounded Knee.* Rapid City, SD: J. M. Fritze, 1975.

Rieke, Reuben D., and Thomas D. Phillips. *Fire in the North: The Minnesota Uprising and the Sioux War in Dakota Territory.* Ashland, OR: Hellgate Press, 2018.

Robertson, Paul M. *The Power of the Land: Identity, Ethnicity, and Class Among the Oglala Lakota.* New York: Routledge, 2002.

Romo, Vanessa. "Checkpoint Clash Escalates Between South Dakota Governor, Tribal Leaders." NPR.org, May 12, 2020. https://www.npr.org/sections/coronavirus-live -updates/2020/05/12/854333737/checkpoint-clash-escalates-between-south-dakota -governor-tribal-leaders.

Roos, Philip D., Dowell H. Smith, Stephen Langley, and James McDonald. "The Impact of the American Indian Movement on the Pine Ridge Indian Reservation." *Phylon* 41, no. 1 (1980): 89–99.

Royce, Anya Peterson. *The Anthropology of Dance.* Bloomington: Indiana University Press, 1977.

Ruby, Robert H. *The Oglala Sioux: Warriors in Transition.* Lincoln: University of Nebraska Press, 2010.

———. "Yuwipi Ancient Rite of the Sioux." *Montana: The Magazine of Western History* 16, no. 4 (1966): 74–79. https://doi.org/10.2307/4517096.

SAGE Development Authority. "About SAGE." Accessed January 17, 2021. https://www .sagesrst.com/about-sage.

Sahlins, Marshall. *What Kinship Is-And Is Not.* Chicago: University of Chicago Press, 2013.

St. Pierre, Mark *Madonna Swan: A Lakota Woman's Story.* Norman: University of Oklahoma Press, 1994.

St. Pierre, Mark, and Tilda Long Soldier. *Walking in the Sacred Manner: Healers, Dreamers, and Pipe Carriers–Medicine Women of the Plains Indians.* New York: Simon & Schuster, 1995.

Sajna, Mike. *Crazy Horse: The Life Behind the Legend.* New York: Wiley, 2000.

Sandoz, Mari. *Crazy Horse, the Strange Man of the Oglalas: A Biography.* 50th anniversary ed. Lincoln: University of Nebraska Press, 1992.

Schneider, David M. *American Kinship: A Cultural Account.* Chicago: University of Chicago Press, 1980.

Schusky, Ernest L. *The Forgotten Sioux: An Ethnohistory of the Lower Brule Reservation.* Chicago: Nelson-Hall, 1975.

Seymour, Forrest W. *Sitanka: The Full Story of Wounded Knee.* W. Hanover, MA: Christopher Pub House, 1981.

Sharfstein, Daniel J. *Thunder in the Mountains: Chief Joseph, Oliver Otis Howard, and the Nez Perce War.* New York: W. W. Norton, 2017.

Sherman, Bob. "The News: A History of AIM." *American Indian Journal* 6, no. 1 (1980): 3–9.

Shoemaker, Nancy. "Urban Indians and Ethnic Choices: American Indian Organizations in Minneapolis, 1920–1950." *Western Historical Quarterly* 19, no. 4 (1988): 431–447.

Sickels, Emma. "The Story of The Ghost Dance. Written in the Indian Tongue by Major George Sword, an Ogallala Sioux, Major of Indian Police." *The Folk-Lorist* 1, no. 1 (1892): 32–36.

Sidner, Sara, Leslie Perrot, Artemis Moshtagian, and Susannah Cullinane. "South Dakota Sioux Tribe Refuses to Take down Checkpoints That Governor Says Are Illegal." CNN, May 13, 2020. https://www.cnn.com/2020/05/10/us/south-dakota-sioux-checkpoints -coronavirus/index.html.

Smedman, Rainer. "Sotureista ja Metsästäjistä Maanviljelijöitä: Oglalat Valkoisen Miehen Tiellä 1868–1888 (From Warriors and Hunters to Farmers: Oglalas on the White Man's Road 1868–1888.)" PhD diss., University of Tampere, 2000.

Smith, John L. "A Short History of the Sacred Calf Pipe of the Teton Dakota." *W. H. Over Museum, University of South Dakota, Museum News* 28, no. 7–8 (1967).

Smith, Paul Chaat, and Robert Allen Warrior. *Like a Hurricane: The Indian Movement from Alcatraz to Wounded Knee.* New York: New Press, 1996.

Sneve, Virginia Driving Hawk. *Completing the Circle.* Lincoln: University of Nebraska Press, 1998.

———. *Grandpa Was a Cowboy and an Indian and Other Stories.* Lincoln: University of Nebraska Press, 2003.

———. *Sioux Women: Traditionally Sacred.* Pierre: South Dakota Historical Society Press, 2016.

Spicer, Edward H. "Persistent Cultural Systems." *Science* 174, no. 4011 (1971): 795–800.

Standing Bear, Luther. *Land of the Spotted Eagle.* Lincoln: University of Nebraska Press, 1978, 2006.

———. *My People the Sioux.* Lincoln: University of Nebraska Press, 1975, 2006.

"Standing Rock Sioux Tribe Welcomes Obama for Historic Visit." Indianz.com. June 16, 2014. https://www.indianz.com/News/2014/06/16/standing-rock-sioux-tribe-welc-2 .asp.

Stein, Wayne J. *Tribally Controlled Colleges: Making Good Medicine.* New York: Peter Lang, 1992.

Steinmetz, Paul B. *Pipe, Bible, and Peyote among the Oglala Lakota: A Study in Religious Identity*. Knoxville: University of Tennessee Press, 1990.

Steltenkamp, Michael F. *Black Elk: Holy Man of the Oglala*. Norman: University of Oklahoma Press, 1993.

Stewart, Omer Call. *Peyote Religion: A History*. Civilization of the American Indian Series 181. Norman: University of Oklahoma Press, 1987.

Swan, Daniel C. "Early Osage Peyotism." *Plains Anthropologist* 43, no. 163 (1998): 51–71.

Szasz, Margaret. *Education and the American Indian: The Road to Self-Determination Since 1928*. Albuquerque: University of New Mexico Press, 1974.

———. "Thirty Years Too Soon: Indian Education Under the Indian New Deal." *Integrated Education* 13, no. 4 (1975): 3–9.

Tabeau, Pierre Antoine. *Tabeau's Narrative of Loisel's Expedition to the Upper Missouri*. American Exploration and Travel Series, vol. 3. Norman: University of Oklahoma Press, 1939.

"The Sioux Chef—Revitalizing Native American Cuisine / Re-Identifying North American Cuisine." Accessed January 17, 2021. https://sioux-chef.com/.

Thomas, Robert K. "Pan-Indianism." In *The American Indian Today*, edited by Stuart Levine and Nancy O. Lurie, 77–86. Deland, FL: Everett Edwards, Inc., 1968.

Thomas, Sidney J. "A Sioux Medicine Bundle." *American Anthropologist*, New Series, 43, no. 4 (1941): 605–9.

Thomas, Tess. "Tokata Iron Eyes on Why the Climate Movement Needs to Listen to Indigenous Voices." Malala Fund, November 18, 2020. https://assembly.malala.org/stories /tokata-iron-eyes-on-why-the-climate-movement-needs-to-listen-to-indigenous -voices.

Thomas, Trudy Carter. "Crisis and Creativity: Visual Symbolism of the Ghost Dance Tradition." PhD diss., Columbia University, 1988.

Thomson, Claire. "Lakota Place Names in Southern Saskatchewan," May 13, 2020. https:// turbot-indigo-jg98.squarespace.com/blog/lakota-place-names-in-southwestern -saskatchewan.

Treuer, David. *The Heartbeat of Wounded Knee: Native America from 1890 to the Present*. New York: Riverhead Books, 2019.

Trimbach, Joseph H., and John M. Trimbach. *American Indian Mafia*. Denver: Outskirts Press, 2007.

Truteau, Jean-Babtiste. *A Fur Trader on the Upper Missouri: The Journal and Description of Jean-Baptiste Truteau, 1794–1796*. Edited by Raymond J. DeMallie. Lincoln: University of Nebraska Press, 2017.

Turner, Victor W. *The Ritual Process: Structure and Anti-Structure*. Chicago: Aldine Publishing Company, 1969.

Utley, Robert M. *Frontier Regulars: The United States Army and the Indian, 1866–1891*. Lincoln: University of Nebraska Press, 1984.

———. *The Lance and the Shield: The Life and Times of Sitting Bull*. New York: Ballantine Books, 1994.

———. *The Last Days of the Sioux Nation*. Vol. 3. New Haven: Yale University Press, 1963.

———. *The Last Sovereigns: Sitting Bull and the Resistance of the Free Lakotas.* Illustrated edition. Lincoln: Bison Books, 2020.

Van de Logt, Mark. "'I Was Brought to Life to Save My People from Starvation and from Their Enemies': Pahukatawa and the Pawnee Trauma of Genocide." *American Indian Culture and Research Journal* 40, no. 3 (2016): 23–46.

———. *War Party in Blue: Pawnee Scouts in the U.S. Army.* Norman: University of Oklahoma Press, 2010.

Vassenden, Kaare. *The Lakota Trail on Man Afraid of His Horses.* Bergen, Norway: John Grieg AS, 2000.

Vestal, Stanley. *New Sources of Indian History, 1850–1891.* Norman: University of Oklahoma Press, 1934.

———. *Sitting Bull: Champion of the Sioux: A Biography.* Norman: University of Oklahoma Press, 1989.

———. *Warpath: The True Story of the Fighting Sioux Told in a Biography of Chief White Bull.* Lincoln: University of Nebraska Press, 1984.

Vizenor, Gerald, ed.. *Survivance: Narratives of Native Presence.* Lincoln: University of Nebraska Press, 2008.

Vizenor, Gerald Robert. *Fugitive Poses: Native American Indian Scenes of Absence and Presence.* Lincoln: University of Nebraska Press, 1998.

———. *Manifest Manners: Narratives on Postindian Survivance.* Lincoln: University of Nebraska Press, 1994.

Waggoner, Josephine. *Witness: A Hunkpapha Historian's Strong-Heart Song of the Lakotas.* Edited by Emily Levine. Lincoln: University of Nebraska Press, 2013.

Wagner, David E. *Patrick Connor's War: The 1865 Powder River Indian Expedition.* Norman, OK: Arthur H. Clark Company, 2010.

Walker, Dalton. "South Dakota Checkpoints: Timeline of Events." IndianCountryToday.com, June 25, 2020. https://indiancountrytoday.com/news/south-dakota-checkpoints-timeline-of-events-RosKQp-sdkq5JdR6HjszuQ.

Walker, James R. *Lakota Belief and Ritual.* Edited by Raymond J. DeMallie and Elaine A. Jahner. Lincoln: University of Nebraska Press, 1980, 1991.

———. *Lakota Myth.* Edited by Elaine A. Jahner. Lincoln: University of Nebraska Press, 2006.

———. *Lakota Society.* Edited by Raymond J. DeMallie. Lincoln: University of Nebraska Press, 1982, 1992.

———. "Oglala Kinship Terms." *American Anthropologist,* New Series, 16, no. 1 (January 1, 1914): 96–109.

Walker, Mark, and Emily Cochrane. "Tribe in South Dakota Seeks Court Ruling Over Standoff on Blocking Virus." *New York Times,* June 24, 2020. https://www.nytimes.com/2020/06/24/us/politics/coronavirus-south-dakota-tribe-standoff.html.

Wallace, Anthony F. C. "Epilogue: On the Organization of Diversity." *Ethos* 37, no. 2 (2009): 251–255.

———. "Individual Differences and Cultural Uniformities." *American Sociological Review* 17, no. 6 (December 1, 1952): 747–50.

War Eagle, Nicole. "The Lakota Are Charging, New CD Focuses on Battle of Little Big Horn." *Lakota Country Times*, June 19, 2008. https://www.lakotatimes.com/articles /the-lakota-are-charging-new-cd-focuses-on-battle-of-little-big-horn/.

Warren, Louis S. *God's Red Son: The Ghost Dance Religion and the Making of Modern America*. New York: Basic Books, 2017.

Warrior Women Project. "Warrior Women Project," 2020. https://www.warriorwomen .org.

Wax, Murray Lionel, Rosalie H. Wax, and Robert V. Dumont Jr. "Formal Education in an American Indian Community." *Social Problems* 11, no. 4 (1964).

White Bull, Joseph. *Lakota Warrior*. Edited by James H. Howard. Lincoln: University of Nebraska Press, 1998.

White Hat, Albert, Sr. *Life's Journey—Zuya: Oral Teachings from Rosebud*. Edited by John Cunningham. Salt Lake City: University of Utah Press, 2012.

The White House. "Generation Indigenous." Accessed January 17, 2021. https:// obamawhitehouse.archives.gov/node/334361.

White, Richard. "The Winning of the West: The Expansion of the Western Sioux in the Eighteenth and Nineteenth Centuries." *Journal of American History* 65, no. 2 (1978): 319–43.

whitehouse.gov. "Highlights: President Obama Visits Standing Rock Reservation, North Dakota, June 13, 2014," June 14, 2014. https://obamawhitehouse.archives.gov /featured-videos/video/2014/06/14/highlights-president-obama-visits-standing-rock -reservation-north.

Wied, A. P. Maximilian. *The North American Journals of Prince Maximilian of Wied: April–September 1833*. Edited by Marsha V. Gallagher. Norman: University of Oklahoma Press, 2014.

Wildhage, Wilhelm. *Geistertants-Lieder Der Lakota: Eine Quellen Samlung*. Wück auf Foehr: Verlag für Amerikanistik, 1991.

Wilson, David Gordon. *Redefining Shamanisms: Spiritualist Mediums and Other Traditional Shamans as Apprenticeship Outcomes*. Bloomsbury Advances in Religious Studies. New York: Continuum, 2013.

"Women of All Red Nations." Equality Archive. Accessed January 17, 2021. https:// equalityarchive.com/issues/women-of-all-red-nations/.

Woodruff, K. Brent. *The Episcopal Mission to the Dakotas, 1860–1898*. South Dakota Historical Collections, vol. 17, 1934.

Wooster, Robert. *Nelson A. Miles and the Twilight of the Frontier Army*. Lincoln: University of Nebraska Press, 1996.

———. *The Military and United States Indian Policy 1865–1903*. Lincoln: University of Nebraska Press, 1995.

Young Bear, Severt. *Standing in the Light: A Lakota Way of Seeing*. American Indian Lives. Lincoln: University of Nebraska Press, 1994.

INDEX